THE GREAT WAR
AT SEA

THE GREAT

A NAVAL ATLAS 1914–1919

MARCUS FAULKNER

Introduction by
ANDREW LAMBERT

Cartography by
PETER WILKINSON

WAR AT SEA

Seaforth
PUBLISHING

TITLE PAGE: Merchant ships in dazzle camouflage schemes during the First World War, painted in 1918 by Herbert Everett.
(© National Maritime Museum, Greenwich, London, BHC0668)

Text copyright © Marcus Faulkner 2015
Maps copyright © Seaforth Publishing 2015

First published in Great Britain in 2015 by
Seaforth Publishing,
Pen & Sword Books Ltd,
47 Church Street,
Barnsley S70 2AS

www.seaforthpublishing.com

British Library Cataloguing in Publication Data
A catalogue record for this book is available from the British Library

ISBN 978 1 84832 183 0

All rights reserved. No part of this publication may be reproduced or transmitted in any form or by any means, electronic or mechanical, including photocopying, recording, or any information storage and retrieval system, without prior permission in writing of both the copyright owner and the above publisher.

The right of Marcus Faulkner to be identified as the author of this work has been asserted by him in accordance with the Copyright, Designs and Patents Act 1988.

Cartography, design and layouts by Peter Wilkinson, Charlbury, Oxford
Printed and bound in China by Imago

Preface

THE GREAT WAR was a genuinely global conflict from the outset. By the time Britain declared war on Germany on 4 August 1915, thus becoming the last European great power to enter the conflict, naval operations were underway in all of the major oceans. Although the assassination of Archduke Franz Ferdinand of Austria and his wife in Sarajevo on 28 June was the catalyst for war, some of the root causes may be traced back to maritime concerns. A naval arms race, economic competition and overseas colonial possessions were all contributory factors and ones in which the control and use of the world's oceans was central.

Naval events certainly form part of the conflict's core narrative; the battles of Jutland and Heligoland Bight, along with the U-boat campaign, are key events and feature along with Verdun or the Somme in any overviews of the war. Those familiar with the war will be aware of *Vizeadmiral* von Spee's exploits in the Pacific and his ultimate defeat at the Battle of the Falklands in December 1914. The Dardanelles campaign in 1915 also offers another example many will be familiar with, principally because of the failure to force the strait by naval means alone led to the campaign itself. Beyond these, however, knowledge of the events at sea and evolution of naval operations recedes significantly. Secondary theatres like the Baltic or Black Sea receive almost no attention and even the U-boat campaign is often portrayed through the lens of the Battle of the Atlantic in the Second World War rather than the more complex and destructive campaign that was waged between 1914 and 1918.

In a war of unprecedented scale, fought by vast armies inflicting horrendous casualties upon each other, the seeming lack of visible naval action has affected how the war at sea is remembered and portrayed. When battle and destruction are the measure the naval war compares poorly with that on land. The outcome of the Battle of Jutland did not fulfil wider expectations even if its impact was crucial to the eventual allied victory. The focus on naval battles misunderstands the nature of the naval war and its role in the conflict. Decisive naval battles are rare throughout history while blockades, trade defence, minelaying operations, coastal bombardments and landings are overlooked. All these were features of the Great War.

A comprehensive atlas offers an ideal way of understanding not only the evolution of naval operations, but also the interaction between theatres of war and the strategic impact the sea had on the wider conflict. The war took place at a time of great change with many new technologies in their infancy. Mines, torpedoes, long-range gunnery, submarines, diesel engines, wireless communication, oil-fired capital ships, aviation and more were reaching a degree of maturity or coming into service. All affected naval operations and together fundamentally altered the way in which fleets operated. In addition, the absence of major conflict in the previous decades meant that commanders lacked the experience of war, the skills in handling fleets and a full understanding of the implications of the new developments.

Admirals had to learn how to adapt to the new conditions as much as generals had to learn to wage a new type of industrial war. The North Sea theatre demonstrates this well and the sequence of maps shows clearly and concisely how British and German operations evolved. The result was an increasingly complex and constrained battle space. Many of the operations and engagements during the war are simply too complex to understand without a visual aid. The same may be said of the mechanics of the U-boat campaign.

In a conflict full of complexity this book is designed to bring clarity while not compromising important details and developments. All major events are covered along with a representative overview of types of naval operations and events in the secondary theatres. It is organised in a chronological manner but certain theatre and campaign overviews break the pattern. Each map is designed to be as self-contained as possible.

A general convention underpins the composition of the atlas although on occasion this is adapted for ease of reference. The use of ship symbols has been streamlined to show general ship types as sheer range of types at the time and different national designations would make a more specific system unwieldy. Time has been harmonised to the British account apart from a few cases where there was no British involvement and local time has been adopted. The names of the senior most commanders are given in full while those of subordinates are cut down. Royal and noble ranks are largely omitted. Naval affiliations are omitted unless a commander was neither British nor German or his origin cannot be inferred from the context. Most terms are translated into English for ease although the key German ones are given at the outset for completion. German ranks are retained.

Acknowledgements

In the aftermath of the publication of *War at Sea* a number of people, to long to list, got in touch to offer critique, provide suggestions or simply inspiration to carry on with this endeavour. Nonetheless, I must thank a few people specifically who have provided support during the course of compiling *The Great War at Sea*. My colleagues Alessio Patalano and Jeffrey Michaels always provide encouragement and perspective. Richard Dunley has been the source of many interesting conversations over the past years. Len Barnett not only answered many specific questions, but also came to assistance with source materials I was unable to obtain. Andrew Lambert provides sage guidance and particularly so in the case of this project. He also allowed me to raid his library on numerous occasions and borrow certain materials on very long-term loan. At Seaforth Publishing Julian Mannering has continued to provide direction and shown remarkable patience in the face of what was another substantial project. Once again, though, special thanks must go to Peter Wilkinson without whom this book simply would not have been possible.

Marcus Faulkner
London, June 2015

Contents

Preface	v
Contents	vi
The Great War At Sea by Andrew Lambert	viii
General Key and Abbreviations	xiv

The Maps

Sea Power on the Eve of War, 1914	2
Naval Operations 1914	**4**
Dispositions of the British and German Fleets in Home Waters 1914	6
The Escape of SMS *Goeben* and *Breslau*, 3–10 August 1914	8
The Escape of SMS *Karlsruhe* and *Dresden*, July – August 1914	10
Operations by SMS *Königsberg*, August – September, 1914	11
The North Sea Overview, 1914–mid 1915	12
The Approach for the Heligoland Bight Operation, 27 August 1914	13
The Battle of Heligoland Bight, 28 August 1914	14
The Movement of the British Expeditionary Force, August – September 1914	16
Atlantic Operations, 1914	18
The Pacific Theatre, 1914	20
The Naval Blockade of Germany, 1914–17	22
The Loss of HMSs *Aboukir*, *Hogue* and *Cressy*, 22 September 1914	23
North Sea Operations, Autumn 1914	24
The Baltic Theatre, 1914–15	26
The Adriatic Theatre, 1914	28
The Siege of Tsingtao, October–November 1914	29
Battle of Coronel, 1 November 1914	30
Battle of the Falklands, 8 December 1914	31
The Yarmouth Raid, 3 November 1914	32
Bombardment of the Dardanelles Forts, 3 November 1914	34
The Voyage of SMS *Emden*, September – November 1914	35
The Black Sea Theatre, 1914–15	36
The German Raids on Scarborough, Hartlepool and Whitby, 16 December 1914	38
The Cuxhaven Raid, 25 December 1914	40
Naval Operations 1915	**42**
The Sinking of HMS *Formidable*, 1 January 1915	44
Dogger Bank, Opening Movements, 23–24 January 1915	45
Battle of the Dogger Bank, 24 January 1915	46
The Hunt for SMS *Dresden*, December 1914 – March 1915	48
The Red Sea Theatre, 1914–15	50
The Dardanelles Campaign, Overview	51
The Dardanelles Bombardments, February 1915	52
The Dardanelles: The Attack on the Narrows, 18 March 1915	54
High Sea Fleet Minelaying Operation, 17–18 April 1915	56
The Dardanelles: Landing Operations	58
The German U-boat Campaign, 1915–18	60
The Adriatic Theatre, 1915–16	62
Strategic Communications	64
The Auxiliary Patrol, 1914–15	66
The Voyage of SMS *Meteor*, May–June 1915	67
The Dardanelles: Allied Supply Routes	68
Battle of the Åland Islands, 2 July 1915	70
Destruction of SMS *Königsberg*, July 1915	71
The Loss of SMS *Meteor*, 6–9 August 1915	72
Gulf of Riga Operations, August 1915	74
Naval Bombardments of the Belgian Coast, 1914–17	76
The Amrum Bank Minefield Operation, 10–12 September 1915	78
British Submarine Operations in the Baltic, 1915	80
Naval Losses in the Dardanelles, 1915	81
The Mesopotamian Campaign, 1914–16	82
The German Sweep of the Skagerrak, 16–18 December 1915	83
Action off Durazzo, 29 December 1915	84
Naval Operations 1916	**86**
The Bosphorus Approaches, 1914–17	88
The Voyage of SMS *Möwe*, December 1915 – March 1916	90

The Lowestoft Raid, 24–25 April 1916	92
Operation XX, 2–5 May 1916	94
The Battle of Jutland, 31 May–1 June 1916	96
Jutland – Phases 1 and 2	98
Jutland – Phases 3 and 4	100
Jutland – The Withdrawal	102
Mine Operations, German Bight 1915–16	103
Kapitänleutnant de la Perière's Patrol, July – August 1916	104
Minesweeping in the Dover Area, 1916–17	105
The Disposition of the North Sea Blockade, 1916	106
19th August 1916	108
The High Sea Fleet Sortie, 19 October 1916	110
Allied Merchant Shipping Losses, September 1916 – January 1917	111
The German Raid on the Dover Strait, 26–27 October 1916	112
The Voyage of SMS *Möwe*, November 1916 – March 1917	114
Naval Operations 1917	**116**
The Voyage of SMS *Seeadler*, 1916–17	118
The Black Sea Theatre, 1916–18	119
The Voyage of SMS *Wolf*, December 1916 – February 1918	120
Allied Merchant Shipping Losses, February – April 1917	121
The German Raid on the Dover Strait, 25 February 1917	122
Allied Shipping Losses in the Mediterranean, February – June 1917	124
The German Raid on the Dover Strait, 20–21 April 1917	126
Battle of the Strait of Otranto, 14–15 May 1917	128
Allied Merchant Shipping Losses, May – July 1917	130
The Allied Convoy System 1917–18	131
Allied Shipping Losses in the Mediterranean, July – December 1917	132
Operation Albion, 10–20 October 1917	134
Allied Merchant Shipping Losses, August – October 1917	136
Action off Lerwick/Norwegian Convoy Attack, 17 October 1917	137
The Second Battle of Heligoland Bight, 17 November 1917	138
Allied Merchant Shipping Losses, November 1917 – January 1918	140
Norwegian Convoy Attack, 12 December 1917	141
Naval Operations 1918	**142**
The United States Navy in Europe, 1917–18	143
The Dover Patrol Area, 1918	144
The Dardanelles, 1917–18/Battle of Imbros, 20 January, 1918	146
Allied Merchant Shipping Losses, February – April 1918	148
The Deployment for the Zebrugge and Ostend Operations, 22 April 1918	149
The Zeebrugge Raid, 22–23 April 1918	150
The Last Sortie of the High Sea Fleet, 23–25 April 1918	152
Allied Merchant Shipping Losses, May – July 1918	154
The Otranto Barrage	155
U-boat Operations in American Waters, late June – September 1918	156
The Northern Barrage, 1918	158
Allied Merchant Shipping Losses, August – October 1918	159
The Adriatic Theatre, 1917–18	160
Operation Plan 19, October 1918	161
The Surrender of the High Sea Fleet, 21 November 1918	162
Naval Operations, 1919	**163**
Operations in Northern Russia, 1917–19	164
The Scuttling of the High Sea Fleet, 21 June 1919	165
Bibliography (and Note on Sources)	166
Index	169

The Great War at Sea

Navies, sea power and great power politics

THE NAVAL BALANCE IN AUGUST 1914 suggested that the possession of a great fleet of costly warships would secure important strategic goals, goals appropriate to the proud names they carried. Around 1890 a fleet of capital ships, cruisers and torpedo craft had been an essential symbol of great power in an unstable world, propelled by imperialism and Social Darwinism towards ever larger empires. Having run out of distant territory to seize, the major powers began appropriating the portfolios of waning imperial states. In the Spanish-American War of 1898 a rising nation used naval might to seize the empire of a weak, moribund rival, with barely a scrap of justification. The equally ambitious Germans arrived too late. The argument that a big battlefleet was the key to world power had been made by American strategist Captain Alfred Thayer Mahan USN in his 1890 bestseller, *The Influence of Sea Power upon History, 1660-1783*. Mahan's eloquent proposition of the connection between sea power and world status persuaded his continentally-minded countrymen to pay for a costly fleet rather than renew the old American naval model of cruiser warfare and coast defences. Translated into the languages of empire, past, present and future, Mahan failed to warn his readers that sea power was unique and indivisible; only one state, or coalition could secure the benefits, and they tended to be a long time coming.

Among Mahan's readers were President Theodore Roosevelt and Kaiser Wilhelm II who imagined that possessing and parading the tools of sea power equated to securing the main prize. They were not alone. By 1900 Russia and France were rebuilding, while Germany, Japan and the United States were creating battlefleets from scratch. The naval build-up relied on standardised designs: battleships with four heavy guns, a dozen or so 6in pieces, and rapid firing anti-torpedo boat cannon; large armoured cruisers traded heavy guns for speed, for fleet operations or commerce destroying, while smaller cruisers scouted for the fleet. Propelled by coal-hungry, maintenance-intensive triple-expansion machinery and equipped to fight at short range, at only one or two miles, these vessels were far more impressive on the eye and ear than in battle. In the arena of international imperial rivalry they were worth more as measures of power than tools for combat. Their names emphasised the point: national, imperial, royal and military bombast was the norm; very few had anything to do with the sea, or sea power.

The investment in these ships was immense; they were the most costly, complex machines yet built, but that was as nothing to the investment of national pride in totems of imperial might and modernity. The public display of naval power, at fleet reviews, national jamborees and battleship launches, became a commonplace, cementing the ship as icon into the national consciousness.[1] For most states possessing these ships was more important than any use that might be made of them in war. Many misunderstood these symbols for sea power, and imagined that keeping the ships would secure some political benefit. Most forgot that successful navies are composed of skilled men, not inert symbols of power. Few followed the successful British recruitment model of professional seamen with long service, preferring cheaper conscripts.

The classic example of this approach was the Imperial German battlefleet created in 1897, to serve the vanity of an unstable emperor, and the more specific ambitions of his State Secretary of the Navy, Admiral Alfred von Tirpitz. Tirpitz melded Mahan's battlefleet sea power with Heinrich von Trietschke's rabidly anti-British nationalism to create the 'Risk Fleet Theory', in which a German battlefleet, approximately one third smaller than the Royal Navy, but concentrated in the North Sea, would exert diplomatic influence on Britain, whose fleet would necessarily be spread across the globe. However, the political alignment that supported the fleet, an alliance between landed agriculture and heavy industry, shattered relations with Russia and Britain, while the cost of the fleet exposed Germany's fragile fiscal sinews. Finally, the fleet plan, enshrined in public Navy Laws, assumed that shipbuilding costs would remain stable.

The British response was predictable. A major naval arms race was launched with the emergence of the first modern capital ship, HMS *Dreadnought*, an all-big gun design, capable of long-range gunnery, and driven by turbine machinery for higher speed and greater reliability. This costly ship obliged Germany to follow suit or admit defeat. It struck at the fiscal weaknesses of the Imperial State, both by radically increasing the unit cost of battleships, and by obliging Germany to rebuild the strategic Kaiser Wilhelm Canal between the Baltic and the North Sea. The First World War could not begin until the canal was completed, in August 1914. After 1905 Britain kept up the pressure on tight German budgets by steadily increasing the size, firepower and cost of battleships. By constructing nine dreadnoughts in 1909 Britain effectively ended the arms race, and when these units were completed in 1912 Germany admitted defeat. In 1914 the Anglo-German numbers gap was widening. The *Dreadnought* also cut the number of navies with a modern

---

[1] Rüger, J. *The Great Naval Game: Britain and Germany in the Age of Empire*. Cambridge 2007.

battlefleet; only Britain, Germany and the United States acquired ten dreadnoughts before 1914. Other great powers had so few that they became too precious to risk.

British global maritime strategy

While Mahan focussed on securing sea power in battle, his British contemporary Sir Julian Corbett stressed that the key issue was the control of sea communications. In *Some Principles of Maritime Strategy* of 1911 Corbett explained that while this might require a big battle, the historical record suggested it was far more likely to be unchallenged. He recognised that Britain, a small, weak state, lacking the military manpower of the other Great Powers, was restricted to a limited, maritime strategy. It would be the height of folly to engage in a total military effort.

While continental powers built battle fleets and dealt in symbolism, the Royal Navy remained the cutting edge of a national strategy based on global sea control. This was no accident. The British state depended on global commerce for food, raw materials, trading revenue and investment income; the Navy's mission was to ensure that the oceans were safe for a trade largely carried in British-built and -owned merchant ships, insured in London. Shipbuilding was also a major export activity, in the military and commercial sectors. The interests of the City of London, the centre of international finance, prevailed over every other sector of the economy, and the City ensured that successive governments maintained a dominant Navy, as the insurance policy on the entire global system. Consequently, sea power was the basis, and the purpose of, everything that Britain did in the war, and it remained the highest national priority, despite the human and economic cost of the principal land front.

Long before 1914 the British had developed a system of global control based on submarine telegraph cables, wireless, subsidised mail steamships, secure bases, merchant shipping and credit. Britain alone had the command systems in place to direct a global war effort, and it was ready to wage that global war on the first day. The first British gun to be fired in August 1914 was at Port Philip Head, outside Melbourne, where the shot stopped a German merchant ship. Economic war began early, and so did the attack on German signals – the ship's code books were seized, and used.

This distant maritime commencement of the war was entirely consistent with pre-war planning. Maurice Hankey, Secretary to the Committee of Imperial Defence, the unique civil/military co-ordinating body, observed, 'when the war came upon us our policy was quite clear – economic pressure plus a small expeditionary force which, if the French and Russians had been efficient, ought to have prevented a disaster.' Not only did Prime Minister Asquith hesitate before sending the British Expeditionary Force to France, but he made sure it remained a limited commitment. Yet, by a curious combination of political events, Field Marshal Lord Kitchener became Secretary of State for War, and mobilised a mass volunteer army for continental service, without consulting the Cabinet or the Committee: 'thus partly by the play of circumstance ... and partly by the failure of our Allies our main effort became a military one.'[2]

Military mobilisation greatly increased the human and economic costs of war, wrenched British manpower and industrial resources out of their normal maritime context, damaged key export industries and suspended battleship construction for the duration. It made British policy more continental and less maritime/imperial when the purpose of pre-war diplomacy had been to keep Europe quiet and stable, to enable Britain to concentrate on her economic interests in the wider world. The danger came from the United States and Japan, which continued to build battleships, and attacked British export markets in South America and Asia where they aggressively replaced the goods that British industry, having been mobilised for war, could no longer provide.

Sea control established

Winning the arms race was decisive. In 1914 Britain, France, Russia and Japan outnumbered the Central Powers by three to one in all categories of naval power, so they had won the war at sea before the conflict opened. There was very little the world's second fleet could do, trapped in the strategic *cul de sac* of the southern North Sea, other than lose a big battle. Haunted by the nightmare of a Trafalgar, the German Navy, and their Austro-Hungarian allies, preferred to secure their ships as political assets. While the Central Powers waited and wasted in harbour, the Allies exercised sea control without a fight. Nor could Germany challenge British sea control beyond the North Sea because, as Mahan observed, the British Isles lay like a vast breakwater between Germany and the great oceans. The handful of detached cruisers and armed merchant ships outside Europe could not break the British global system. Nearer home, the High Sea Fleet adopted defensive positions, to secure the Baltic and the Heligoland Bight. It had no role in the national war plan, merely a mandate to ensure that naval coal trains travelling north from the Ruhr did not interfere with the westward movement of troop trains for the invasion of Belgium and France. This gave Britain the luxury of imposing sea control around Europe without a challenge, moving the Grand Fleet to Scapa Flow, to secure the Scotland–Norway gap, with a Channel Fleet at Dover to hold the southern barrier.

---

[2] Hankey to Captain G Blake, 3.9.1928: Roskill, S. W. *Hankey: Man of Secrets: Vol. 1 1877-1918*. London, Collins, 1970 pp.134-5.

German telegraph cables off Britain's Western Approaches were picked up, cut and re-deployed for British traffic on the first day of war, while German radio masts in the Cameroons and Yap were early targets for British naval forces. While Germany lost direct contact with the outside world, Britain and France could exploit the global market for food, fuel, raw materials and industrial production, and draw on Imperial manpower for the land war. Germany had to access such resources indirectly, through neutrals. By 1916 the impact was so severe that large commercial submarines were built to obtain nickel, manganese, rubber and other essentials from the United States. These submarines exemplified Germany's strategy: a clever engineering response to the self-inflicted disaster of waging war against Britain. They were soon converted into warships.

Behind the great fleets Britain's economic war was conducted by obsolete cruisers, armed merchant cruisers and armed boarding vessels that intercepted, inspected and, when necessary, detained ships attempting to enter the North Sea. The 10th Cruiser Squadron, operating to the North of Scotland, conducted the naval element of a strategy that exploited economic and diplomatic activity to reduce the possibility of illegal shipments even attempting to break the blockade. In 1914 the cruisers also picked up German reservists travelling home to fight.

Predictably, legal disputes with interested neutrals, Denmark, Holland, Norway, Sweden, and especially the United States, complicated the British position. Neutrals were anxious to make money, and Germany needed their food and raw materials. President Woodrow Wilson was anxious to remain neutral, secure the votes of meat and cotton exporters, and avoid getting dragged into a major war against Britain caused by maritime belligerent rights, because he detested German militarism. Consequently, while the United States protested against British actions it did so with words, not war, because the blockade did not kill any Americans, unlike the U-boat counter-blockade. Anglo-American diplomacy steadily reduced the flow of supplies to Germany, and when the United States joined the war the physical blockade was replaced by Anglo-American global shipping control.

Outside Europe the German cruiser war produced some spectacular highlights such as the cruise of the *Emden*, and victory at the battle of Coronel, but they were fleeting and futile. They had negligible impact because British resources and communications dominance simply overwhelmed German efforts. British power was demonstrated in the strategic moves that led to the battle of the Falkland Islands. Two battlecruisers were sent to the South Atlantic, another went to the Caribbean terminus of the Panama Canal, a fourth had already driven German cruisers from the South Pacific to Chile, and a fifth, a pasteboard replica built on a merchant ship, deterred German liners from leaving New York for war operations.

In the North Sea battlecruiser engagements in the Heligoland Bight, and on the Dogger Bank maintained British dominance, without inflicting crushing losses on the Germans. British losses to German submarines and mines were greater, part of the price to be paid for sea control. The war at sea would be grindingly dull and essentially attritional, as naval wars have invariably been.

The western front at sea
In 1914 population density, rail communications and the short distances involved ensured that sea power could have little direct impact in Western Europe. In September 1914 the German advance into Northern Belgium became a strategic threat to British control of the Channel. Winston Churchill, First Lord of the Admiralty, pressed for military action, but the allied armies were too focussed on operational problems to see the strategic picture. So he created the Royal Naval Division from untrained naval reservists and recruits and veteran Royal Marine officers and NCOs. Churchill's bold attempt to hold the great fortress at Antwerp and the ports of Ostend and Zeebrugge failed, but naval firepower stopped the German Army occupying the entire country and annihilating the Belgian army. The Belgian ports proved to be a major strategic problem throughout the war, used by U-boats and destroyers raiding British commerce and communications. Counter-measures at sea proved costly, and relatively ineffective, so the British tried direct action, beginning with long-range naval bombardment, using heavy armed monitors, sustained strategic air attack, a method of war pioneered by the Royal Naval Air Service, a grand military offensive that ended in the mud of Passchendale, also known as the Third Battle of Ypres and, finally, amphibious raids to block the harbours. While none were effective, improved minefields and patrols limited the effect of the German campaign.

Strategic options
By the end of 1914 the British and their allies had secured control of the broad oceans and the northern end of the Western Front, albeit leaving Germany in possession of the Belgian ports, instigated economic warfare, and concentrated imperial resources towards Europe. British strategists now had the luxury of choice. While Kitchener's armies were mobilising they could attempt a maritime strategic offensive to open the enclosed seas that flanked the Central Powers: the Baltic and the Black Sea.

Churchill's original offensive concept for seizing the German North Sea Islands was impractical. While this might have brought on a major battle, Britain had no need to fight in the southern North Sea, where Germany would have the advantage, being able to deploy many more short-range torpedo boats. In late October 1914 Lord Fisher returned as First Sea Lord, and immediately developed plans to threaten German control of the Baltic. Aware that the German war economy depended on Swedish iron, finished steel products, and copper, along with increasing quantities of food, he saw a threat to the Baltic as the only way to bring the High Sea Fleet to battle. To render the threat plausible Fisher ordered a large force of specialist craft, light draught battlecruisers, monitors, minesweepers, and armoured landing craft to be built. It is unlikely that he had any intention of sending surface ships into the Baltic before the High Sea Fleet had been defeated, expecting instead a battle outside the Danish Narrows. German anxiety about the Baltic was emphasised in the *E13* episode.

Unfortunately, while Churchill accepted the strategy, he was not prepared to wait. Desperate for a career boosting victory Winston decided that reserve-manned naval forces, backed by the Greek Army promised by Prime Minister Venizelos, could open the Dardanelles, defeat Ottoman Turkey, destroy the fugitive German battlecruiser *Goeben*, and secure Russian grain. The concept was grand, and attractive, but both the planning and resource base were inadequate. Fisher objected, and the Greeks dropped out, but Admiral Carden began a low tempo operation against the outer defences. The failure of the big naval offensive, and the amphibious follow-on, were predictable. When Churchill began dragging his Baltic armada into the failed campaign Fisher brought down the Admiralty Board and Churchill lost his job. Then Fisher overplayed his hand. Seeking the same level of dictatorial power over strategy exercised by Kitchener, Prime Minister Asquith and the King became convinced that he had lost his senses. Without his direction the Baltic concept faded, but the logic endured.

A year later Admiral Sir John Jellicoe planned a major sweep into the Kattegatt but it was aborted by the German sortie that led to the battle of Jutland. In truth, any British attempt to enter the Baltic would have prompted a German invasion of Denmark, and on balance British interests were better served by the fragile neutrality of the Scandinavian states.

By contrast, naval operations inside the two enclosed seas, although on a relatively large scale, were essentially irrelevant. Although the Russian fleets did well they were unable to cut German or Turkish strategic communications, and were eventually defeated by the Communist Revolution. This enabled Finland and the Baltic States to escape Russian rule, while the Ukraine and Georgia enjoyed brief periods of independence. By 1919 the Royal Navy dominated the Baltic and the Black Sea, and had a presence on the landlocked Caspian, perhaps the high water mark of British global power.

Peripheral campaigns and strategic supplies
Sea power proved highly effective in supporting peripheral campaigns in regions where land communications were less advanced than in Western Europe, and force to space ratios far lower. The opening moves in the South Pacific and sub-Saharan Africa were entirely maritime, cutting German wireless links, and securing positions of strategic significance. Using obsolescent warships and specially-built river craft the Royal Navy sustained a major offensive in Mesopotamia, supported the Arab revolt from the Red Sea, and the offensive into Palestine in 1917–18. In contrast to the high-risk frontal assault at the Dardanelles these operations exploited the mobility and ubiquity of naval power to avoid fixed defences. Another vital function of sea control was to supply allies. France relied on British coal and hardware, and increasingly British-funded American supplies. Britain also supplied the Tsarist armies with hardware and consumables, from domestic and American production. Supplies went to the new Arctic port of Murmansk, and Archangel on the White Sea, for rail transport to Petrograd and beyond. By 1915 the Royal Navy had a considerable presence in the region, and the supplies began to pile up faster than the trains could carry them away. In 1918 the Arctic supply dumps prompted British intervention, to keep them out of the hands of a Bolshevik Government that had pulled out of the war and reneged on Russia's massive financial obligations. Naval operations against the new enemy of British imperial power continued long after the Armistice.

Jutland
For two years the main battlefleets had been waiting, the Germans more fearful of losing control of the Baltic than they were keen to risk battle, while the British, as Fisher observed, having everything they needed, had no reason to head south for a showdown. Stasis served the British. In large measure the problem was technical. The High Sea Fleet could not force battle off Scapa Flow as German destroyers lacked the range; while the longer-legged British flotillas were restricted to a single day in the Heligoland Bight.

Finally, both fleets accepted the need to be more ambitious; the British planned to enter the Kattegatt, the Germans to raid north in search of a detached British force they could annihilate. Forewarned by radio intelligence, Jellicoe's Grand Fleet set off before Admiral Reinhard Scheer had even left harbour. The partial engagements on the afternoon of 31 May 1916 exposed major failures in signals procedure and ammunition handling in Sir

David Beatty's Battle Cruiser Fleet, but Jellicoe's superb positional awareness put the more powerful Grand Fleet right across the bows of the advancing Germans, inflicting heavy damage on the leading German battleships and battlecruisers. Although Scheer escaped disaster by executing a complex reverse course manoeuvre under fire, he had to do this twice and remained cut off from his base by Jellicoe's fleet. Uncertain where the enemy were, and unable to comprehend the totality of the battle, Scheer set a course for home after nightfall, and then gave it away by radioing for Zeppelin reconnaissance the next morning. The Admiralty read the signal, but failed to inform Jellicoe, who was left to guess which of the three German routes through the minefields to cover. He made the wrong choice, and Scheer escaped destruction at daybreak. While the Grand Fleet suffered heavier losses, six big ships to two, the German fleet fled the field of battle, twice, and arrived home with many powerful units heavily damaged. Britain retained command of the sea. Expectations of a 'decisive' battle proved to be wholly unfounded, as Julian Corbett had predicted. Churchill later observed that Jellicoe could have lost the war in an afternoon: little wonder that he was risk averse. Jutland highlighted the failure of the Tirpitz plan; an inferior fleet had not prevented Britain joining the war, and it could not defeat the British in battle.

Unrestricted U-boat war
After Jutland the German naval high command recognised the hopelessness of their position, and proposed shifting the basis of naval warfare to an unrestricted attack on all merchant shipping entering a 'war zone', one which they would define. This would restore the relevance of the navy to the German war effort, and save it from becoming irrelevant to a post-war German state. The decision also marked a fundamental change of culture. Tirpitz, a student of Mahan and Clausewitz, had considered commerce destroying a minor, indecisive form of warfare, and a waste of resources. Yet, like Louis XIV and Napoleon before them, the German leadership had no choice, adopting the classic anti sea power strategy of commerce destroying, the default mode for a continental state facing a dominant sea power, because the battlefleet vision had failed.

Germany had violated pre-war international agreements, restricting the use of mines and requiring the passengers and crew of any captured vessels to be placed in safety before the ship was sunk, from the first day of the war. These violations allowed the British to take the moral high ground, despite their unscrupulous approach to the legalities of the blockade, because German actions cost neutral lives, while British actions only caused economic losses. The German use of mines and U-boats were national war crimes, not individual, or specific actions, being expressly sanctioned by the naval High Command and military Government. They violated laws that Germany had freely signed. Individual U-boat commanders were tried for war crimes after 1918, but German courts managed to pardon them. In 1945 the victorious powers, duly forewarned, were less obliging.

The German decision reflected their experience of unrestricted submarine warfare in 1915 and 1916, ended by the diplomatic fall-out from the sinking of the *Lusitania* and *Arabic*, which suggested submarines could sink ships faster than Britain could replace them. Such losses would force Britain to seek peace, and without British money and munitions France and Russia would surrender before the United States could act. However, the evidence used in the 'Holtzendorff Memorandum' was little more than wishful thinking. If the opening phase of unrestricted U-boat operations equalled tonnage expectations, it also prompted President Wilson to declare war, and forced the Royal Navy to change commerce protection. Furthermore, these levels of success were unsustainable; defences became more effective, and U-boat casualties mounted. Escorted convoys, often with air cover, slowly reduced merchant losses to manageable levels. The convoy system created in 1917 was primarily a matter of organisation, inter-agency co-operation, statistical analysis, and improving internal transport links in order to hasten the movement of cargoes out of overcrowded ports. Working with shipping and insurance industries the Royal Navy maintained imports, and provided strategic shipping to continue the war. New escort vessels were built and destroyers released from the Grand Fleet, which only went to sea in full force once after January 1917, while intelligence analysis of German radio traffic helped target individual submarines.

The U-boat campaign seriously damaged the German Navy as mounting losses drained the High Sea Fleet of its best junior officers, engineers and NCOs. Even heavier losses were suffered by the minesweepers clearing the channels through the Heligoland Bight for U-boats. It was no coincidence that these minesweepers were central to the last major surface action of the war. Although mines were the most successful method of destroying U-boats, convoys were far more effective in restricting their impact on the allied war effort. The Royal Navy had the wisdom to pursue both strategies, along with attack at source and net barriers in the Channel, because there was no easy answer to the submarine. Any lingering German hopes for victory were ended by the prospect of a million American troops arriving in France, over an Atlantic ocean that Germany simply could not control. Ironically, many would travel on German ships, interned in the United States since 1914.

Death or Glory?
The failure of the U-boat campaign and the 1918 spring military offensive forced the hand of the German

Government facing the prospect of defeat. The naval High Command, more concerned with the survival of the service than waging the current conflict, planned a Wagnerian death-ride to create an heroic legacy by sending the entire High Sea Fleet into the Thames Estuary, the outermost point of Tirptiz's strategic ambition in 1897. The U-boats were recalled from the war on commerce to join the operation. The High Command hoped that a glorious defeat would enshrine the memory of the battleship fleet for future generations; but bored, hungry, demoralised sailors had other ideas. Discipline collapsed into mutiny, and the Kaiser's fleet, built to secure a 'place in the sun', brought down his empire. Sailors hoisted the Red flag at Kiel and Wilhelmshaven, prompting an Imperial retreat to neutral Holland. The new Government, left to pick up the pieces, had to hand over the Fleet as guarantee of good behaviour during the Armistice. David Beatty, now Commander-in-Chief of the Grand Fleet, treated the event as the surrender of a beaten foe. Beatty knew that economic warfare had been a key element in the defeat of the German state, and the inability of the German navy to interrupt that strategy defined its failure.

The end

Sea power shaped the conflict, restricting the Central Powers to a European war, while securing key resource flows for Britain and her allies. In addition it had defeated an old threat, commerce destroying, in its dramatic and illegal new form. The tools of modern sea power were still evolving in 1918, notably carrier aviation and submarine detection systems, while existing ships, systems and skills had been greatly enhanced. Every other navy was anxious to learn as much as possible from the Royal Navy, not least the rapidly growing United States Navy. The United States entered the war in 1917 with a top-heavy deterrent battlefleet, lacking the cruisers and flotilla craft to fight effectively. The 1916 programme had reinforced this weakness, because it had been designed to coerce Britain, rather than fight Germany. The 1918 programme carried this agenda into the post-war world, and so alarmed Congress that it ultimately resulted in the major naval arms limitation treaty signed in Washington as a means of bringing the Royal Navy down to America's level, and definitely not that of bringing the USN up to the level of the RN.

While the Royal Navy had, with a little help from its allies, won the war at sea, and delivered overwhelming military resources to decide the conflict, the economic cost of the land war and the expansion of the empire in Africa and the Middle East meant Britain was no longer a sea power. For the first time in its history Britain accepted international restrictions on the size and quality of the Navy and its warships. In the Washington Treaty of 1922 it accepted parity with the United States, abandoning the unique strength that had built and secured the last great sea empire: naval superiority, sustained by arms races or, very occasionally, battle.

This reflected a loss of faith in sea power. The war at sea had not lived up to unrealistic expectations; the Royal Navy had not won a 'decisive' battle, at either the Dardanelles or Jutland, and it had struggled to master the U-boat campaign. While this was entirely consistent with the experience of previous wars, public perceptions were dominated by the horrific business of trenches, gas, machine-guns, high explosive, and death on an unprecedented scale. Sea power and dreadnoughts seemed irrelevant, outdated symbols of imperial bombast. When Churchill began his memoirs in 1922 he considered two titles; 'The Great Amphibian', and 'Sea Power and the World Crisis', his American publishers rejected both.[3] The book became *The World Crisis*, because Americans did not see the sea in the allied victory.

Perhaps the last word belongs to a young German naval officer, Lieutenant Commander Ernst von Weisäcker, writing on 5 November, 1918:

> The Navy! It sprung forth from the hubris of world power, and for 20 years it has been ruining our foreign relations. It never kept its promises in wartime. Now it sparks the revolution![4]

Weisäcker's words could equally well be applied to the navies of Austria-Hungary and Imperial Russia, navies that, for all the professional skill displayed by their personnel, were essentially irrelevant to the outcome of the conflict. All three fleets mutinied, the first and last playing prominent parts in the downfall of the Imperial orders that created them, as symbols of prestige and power, too precious to use. Their leaders did not understand that the success of a navy is decided by people, not ships.

ANDREW LAMBERT

---

[3] Churchill to his wife 30.1.1922: Gilbert, M. *Winston S. Churchill. Vol. V. 1922-1939*. London Heinemann 1976. p.4

[4] Quoted in Seligmann, M.S., Nägler, F. & Epkenhans, M. eds. *The Naval Route to the Abyss: The Anglo-German Naval Race, 1895-1914*. Aldershot, Navy Records Society 2015 p.xxxv

General Key and Abbreviations

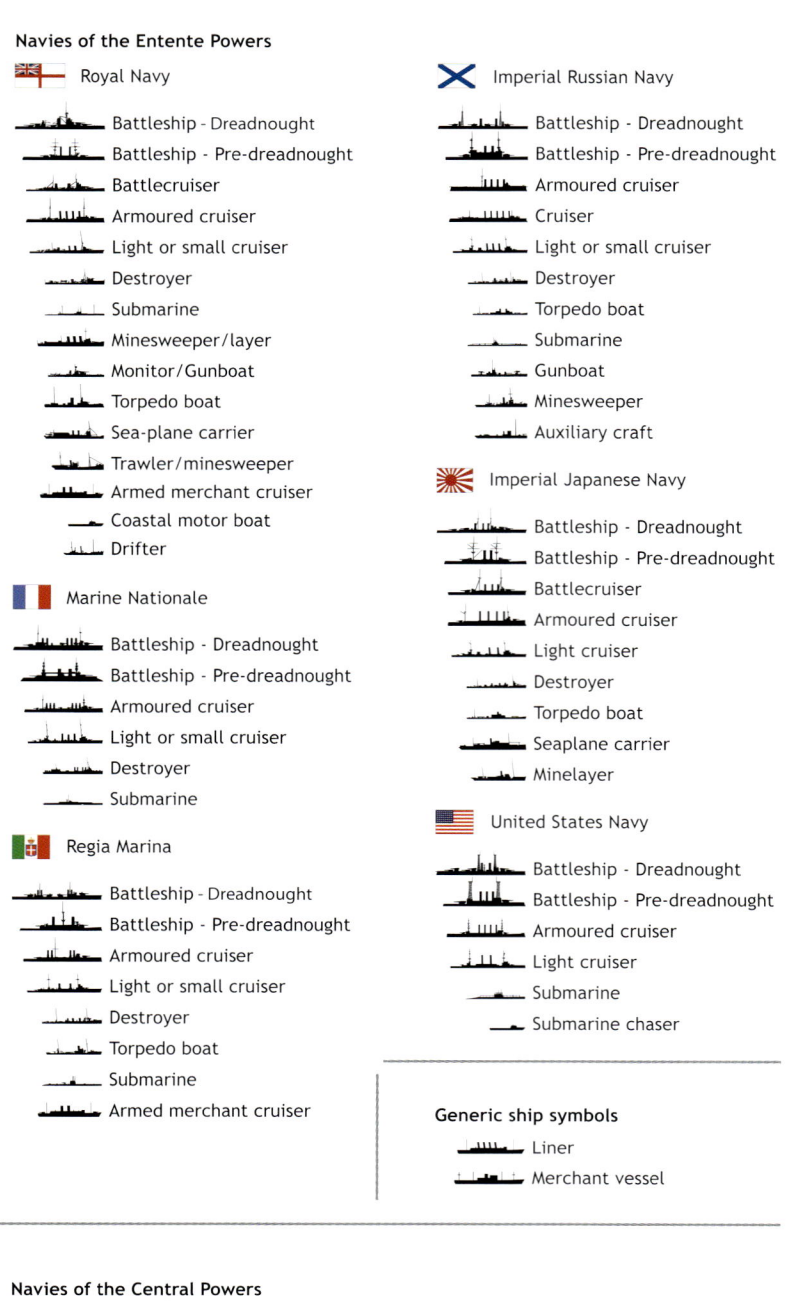

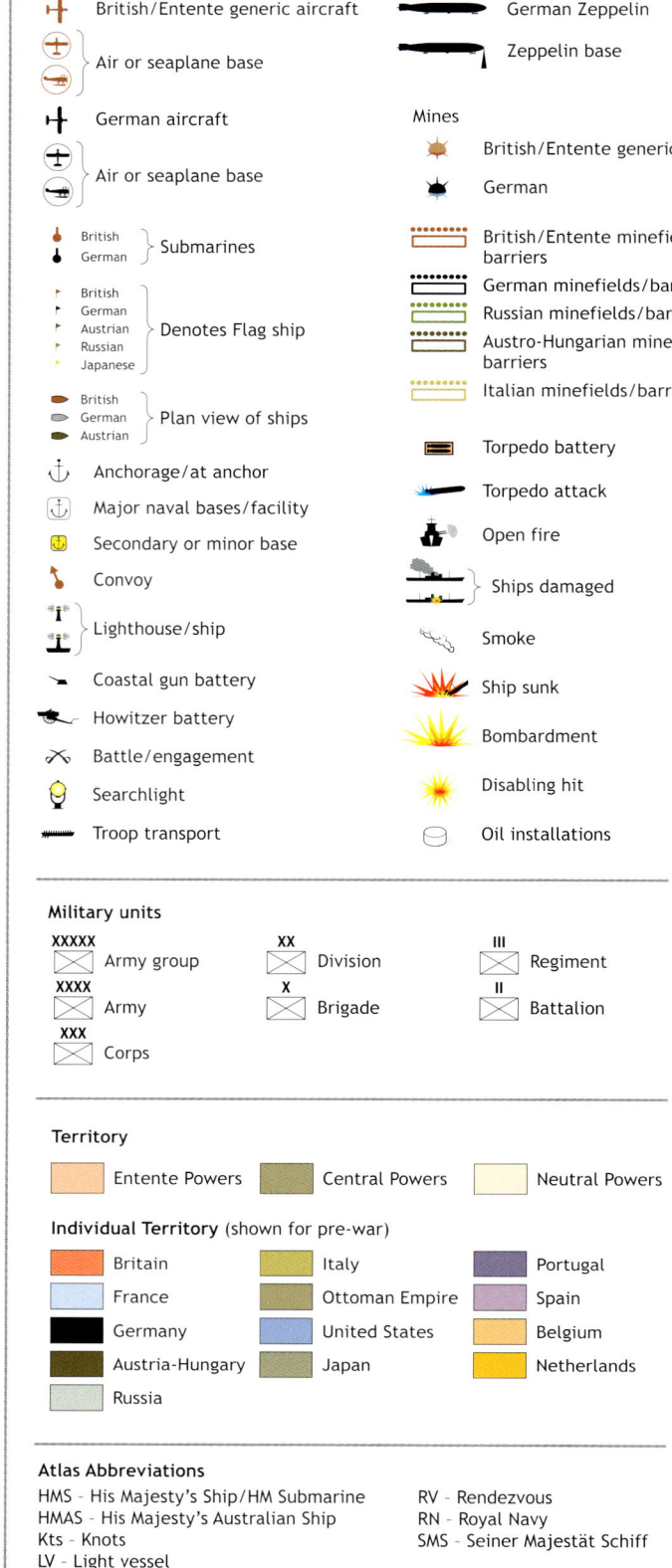

Atlas Abbreviations

HMS – His Majesty's Ship/HM Submarine
HMAS – His Majesty's Australian Ship
Kts – Knots
LV – Light vessel
RV – Rendezvous
RN – Royal Navy
SMS – Seiner Majestät Schiff

Note: Ship prefixes are not employed throughout the atlas. Some of the early war maps do employ them in an illustrative manner and exceptionally they are used on an individual basis on subsequent maps where it adds to clarifying events.

THE GREAT WAR AT SEA

A Naval Atlas

Sea Power on the Eve of War, 1914

The reasons why the confrontation between the Austro-Hungarian empire and Serbia developed rapidly into a global war may be traced back to myriad of regional conflicts and wider tensions in the international system. A significant factor was European imperialism that, over the previous decades, had driven the expansion of colonial possessions and informal empires across the globe. Linked to this development was a general increase in naval expenditure as navies became prerequisites for any overseas presence. Population growth, industrialisation and colonial expansion led to a more integrated global economy that, in turn, depended on the movement of goods and people across the oceans. The Atlantic Ocean was the global hub that linked Europe to the Americas and carried all European trade with India and the Far East.

Anglo-German rivalry generated the main naval competition. Both countries were leading industrial nations and, for Britain, naval power was of fundamental importance for its own defence and for that of its empire. For Germany the acquisition of a first-class navy was seen as a symbol of greatness and a guarantor of a place in the sun. Beginning with the 1898 Naval Law that was followed by another in 1900 together with further amendments

Key

- Britain
- France
- Germany
- Austria-Hungary
- Russia
- Italy
- Ottoman Empire
- United States
- Japan
- Portugal
- Spain
- Belgium
- Netherlands
- Trade routes

THE GREAT WAR AT SEA 1914

Navies of the Great Powers, 1914

	Britain		Germany		France		Italy		Russia		Austria-Hungary		United States		Japan	
	In Service	Under Construction	In Service	Under Construction	In Service	Under Construction	In Service	Under Construction	In Service	Under Construction	In Service	Under Construction	In Service	Under Construction	In Service	Under Construction
Battleship - Dreadnought-type	22	13	15	5	2	10	3	3	10	7	3	1	10	4	2	2
Battleship - Pre- or Semi-dreadnought	40	–	22	–	17	–	8	–	10	–	9	–	23	–	11	–
Battlecruiser	9	1	5	3	–	–	–	–	–	–	–	–	–	–	6	2
Coastal defence ship	–	–	8	–	2	–	5	–	1	–	3	–	–	–	3	–
Armoured Cruiser	34	–	9	–	22	–	10	–	6	–	3	–	12	–	12	–
Light, Protected or Scout Cruiser	87	–	34	–	14	–	18	–	6	–	6	–	22	–	21	–
Destroyers or large torpedo boat	250+	–	130+	–	150+	–	100+	–	90+	–	40+	–	50	–	80+	–
Submarine	73	–	31	–	50+	–	20	–	22	–	5	–	18	–	12	–
Merchant shipping (GRT)	19,849,200		4,743,100		1,793,300		1,274,100		–		–		4,302,300		1,500,000	

Note: Comparing the fleet numbers on the eve of the First World War poses numerous problems and any simple tabular comparison is merely a reflection of the relative strengths of the navies. With the dawn of the Dreadnought era entire ship types rapidly became obsolete. This not only concerned the pre-dreadnought battleships but also numerous categories of protected and scout cruisers that were increasingly being replaced by light cruisers. The old generations of warships were generally inferior to the new designs. The various navies used different terminology to describe the same types of vessels and the same terms to describe very different types. For example the actual shape and size of warships considered to be light cruisers varied considerably. The Japanese classified four large cruisers as battlecruisers, but these were not comparable to British or German battlecruisers. The terms destroyer and torpedo boats were often used interchangeably. The Germans possessed torpedo boats that were larger and more capable than destroyers in other navies. Again the differences between large and small, new and old torpedo boats were significant. Numbers also provide no indication of the actual state of readiness, training of the crews and quality of the weapons or communications equipment. The Russians had a large submarine force, but it never left the Gulf of Finland.

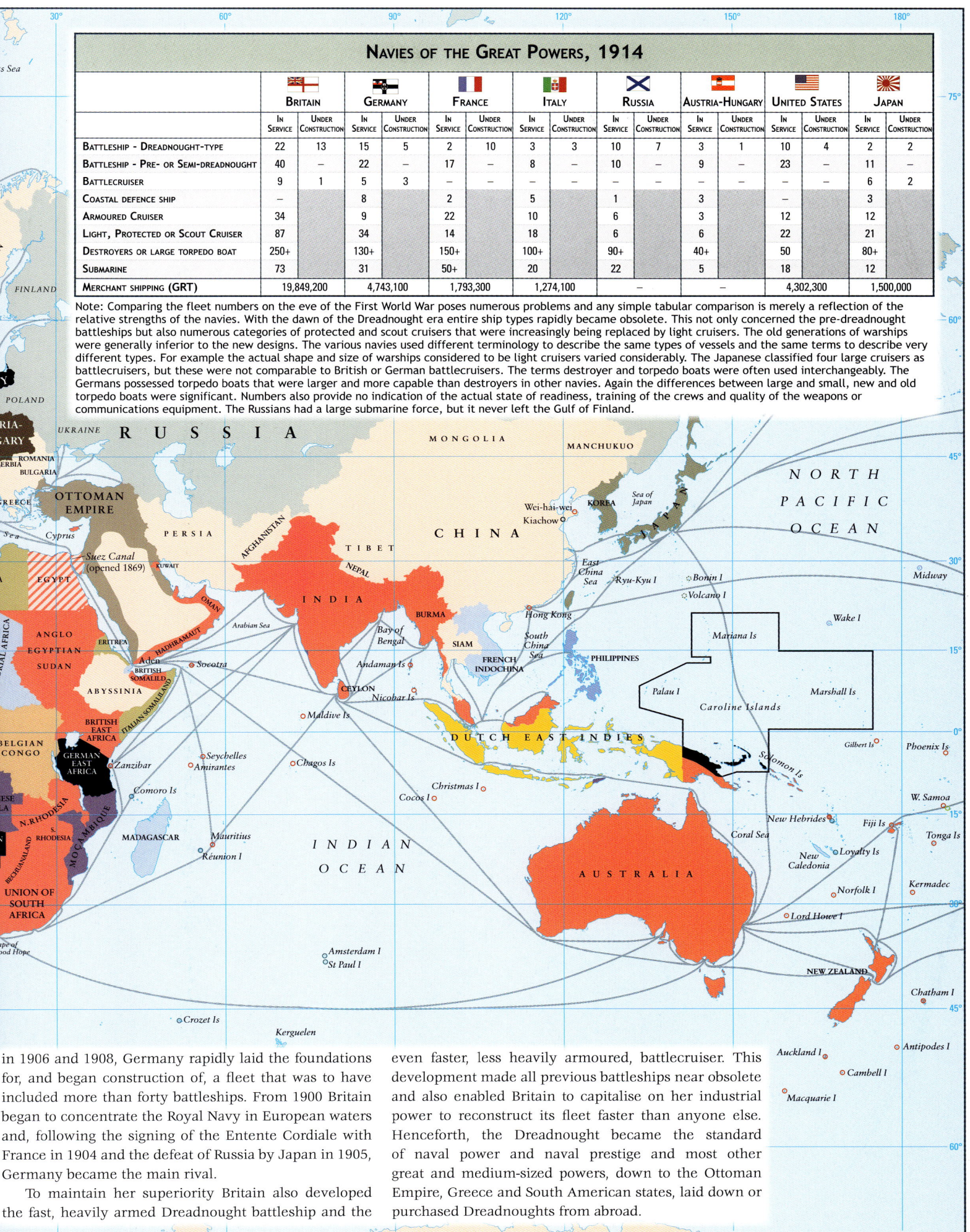

in 1906 and 1908, Germany rapidly laid the foundations for, and began construction of, a fleet that was to have included more than forty battleships. From 1900 Britain began to concentrate the Royal Navy in European waters and, following the signing of the Entente Cordiale with France in 1904 and the defeat of Russia by Japan in 1905, Germany became the main rival.

To maintain her superiority Britain also developed the fast, heavily armed Dreadnought battleship and the even faster, less heavily armoured, battlecruiser. This development made all previous battleships near obsolete and also enabled Britain to capitalise on her industrial power to reconstruct its fleet faster than anyone else. Henceforth, the Dreadnought became the standard of naval power and naval prestige and most other great and medium-sized powers, down to the Ottoman Empire, Greece and South American states, laid down or purchased Dreadnoughts from abroad.

Naval Operations 1914

Preparations for the oncoming conflict accelerated throughout the July Crisis as all the major navies mobilised and began to concentrate their battlefleets for war. In the final days of peace British warships were deployed to find, or shadow, German warships on overseas stations and capture or blockade merchant vessels in neutral ports. The Germans, in anticipation of this, had already begun to send the cruisers deployed in the Caribbean and the Pacific and Indian Oceans out to sea where they would constitute a threat to allied maritime communications. The German merchant fleet was another matter and many of the ships that were in foreign ports when war broke out would not make it back to Germany.

From a naval perspective the first five months of the war were dominated by two campaigns. In the North Sea, the principal naval theatre throughout the war, the anticipated clash between the British and German battlefleets did not take place. Geography and numerical inferiority prevented the Germans from challenging the British for control the sea. Nonetheless, both sides attempted to erode the strength of the other and create favourable conditions for a major engagement. The impact of submarines, torpedoes and mines on fleet operations was immdediate.

The second campaign involved the struggle for global maritime communications. Both the British and French relied on the resources of their empires to wage war in Europe. One of the core missions of the

The North Sea The p12

The Naval Blockade of Germany p22

North Sea Operations Autumn p24

German Mining in British Waters p25

First Canadian troop convoy bound for Europe October

The Yarmouth Raid 3 November p32-33

Naval Bombardments on the Belgian Coast 1914–17 p76-77

The Movement of the British Expeditionary Force August – September p16-17

Atlantic Operations p18-19

Movement for colonial troops Metropolitan F August

The Escape of SMS Karlsruhe and Dresden July – August p10

Destruction of the SMS Kaiser Wilhelm der Große 26 August p19

The Pacific Theatre Admiral von Spee's Squadron September – November p20-21

Expeditions to secure German African Colonies in Africa

Battle of Coronel 1 November p30

Battle of the Falklands 8 December p31

Key

- Entente Powers
- Central Powers
- Major offensives and campaigns
- Neutral Powers

THE GREAT WAR AT SEA 1914

allied navies was to secure the passage of troops and other military *materiel* between theatres. The presence of German raiders on the world's oceans not only constituted a threat to military movements, but also to allied trade. Although the number of German cruisers operating on foreign stations was limited they tended to be of modern design, were supplemented by some auxiliary cruisers and were able to hide in the vastness of the oceans. Until they could be hunted down they tied down considerable allied resources.

As well as neutralising these raiders the Allies sent out expeditions to capture Germany's colonial possessions in Africa and the Pacific. As these were defended by only limited forces, with no chance of any reinforcements being sent out, they stood little chance of holding out against the allied expeditions. In German East Africa the local German forces did though manage to resist British attempts at taking the colony and went on to tie down considerable numbers of allied men and material for the duration of the war.

The Mediterranean remained a relatively quiet theatre after the escape of the German squadron to refuge in the Ottoman Empire. The Austro-Hungarian navy did not attempt to interfere with Anglo-French control of the sea. The Turkish entry into the war towards the end of the year saw some limited naval activity at the eastern end of the Mediterranean. The Russians remained largely on the defensive in the Baltic and Black Seas, but in both witnessed some limited naval engagements predominately between light forces.

Dispositions of the British and German Fleets in Home Waters 1914

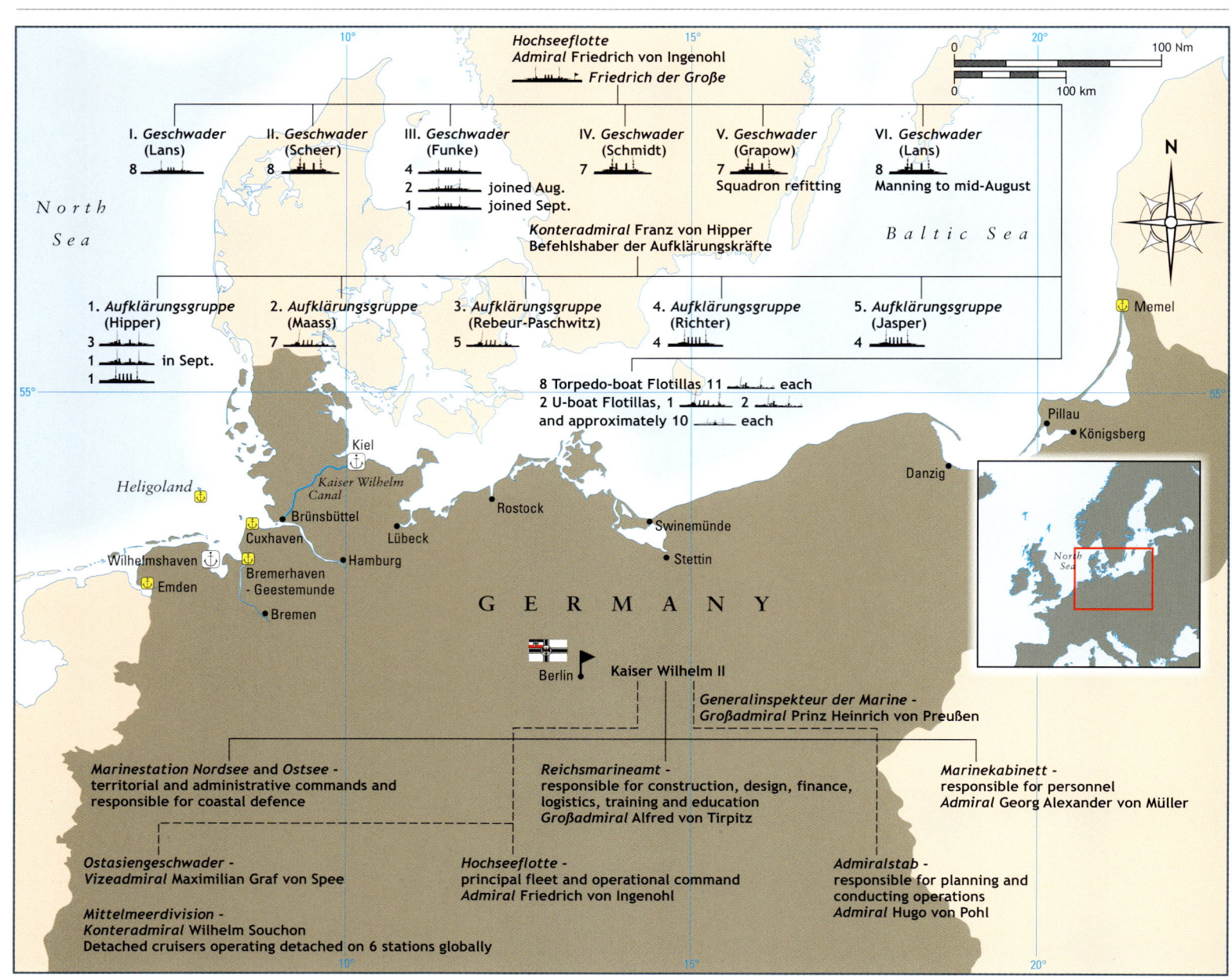

Key

- Major Naval Base
- Secondary or Minor Base

Reichsmarineamt – Imperial Naval Office
Marinekabinett – Naval Cabinet
Generalinspekteur der Marine – General Inspector of the Navy
Admiralstab – Admiralty Staff
Marinestation Nordsee and Ostsee – Naval Stations
Hochseeflotte – High Sea Fleet
Ostasiengeschwader – East Asia Squadron
The commanders of these offices had direct access to the Kaiser
Mittelmeerdivision – Mediterranean Squadron
Geschwader – Squadron
Aufklärungsgruppe – Scouting Group

The Royal Navy was controlled by the Board of Admiralty which, in turn, was headed by the First Lord, a political appointee, and a position held by Winston Churchill since 1911. The senior naval officer was the First Sea Lord who was responsible for operations, while Lords looked after personnel, construction and logistics. A naval war staff had recently been established to run naval operations but it was to take some time for it to become an effective body. The incumbent First Sea Lord, Admiral Prince Louis of Battenberg was an able officer, but owing to his German heritage he was soon replaced by the illustrious Admiral Jackie Fisher who had previously held the position.

By the summer of 1914 only a small portion of its capital ship strength, battlecruisers and old pre-dreadnought battleships, served overseas. The wartime organisation of the navy focused on the Grand Fleet that was composed of active frontline units of the First Fleet and some of the newer pre-dreadnoughts from the Second Fleet. Its task was to counter the High Sea Fleet and maintain the blockade of Germany. The remaining ships of the Second and Third Fleets, kept at various states of readiness, formed the more loosely organised Channel Fleet and provided some of the cruisers used to patrol southern waters. A significant portion of the navy's light forces were organised into what became the Harwich Force, which defended the southeast coast and operated in the German Bight.

The Imperial German Navy suffered from a convoluted command structure and did not have a single commander or body overseeing its administration. The admiralty staff, fleet and station commanders, the naval ministry and cabinet all had direct access to the Kaiser. The single most important officer was the navy's pre-war architect and head of the ministry, *Admiral* Tirpitz. He, though, had no operational control of the fleet and his power declined as the war progressed. The commander of the High Sea Fleet was also limited in what he could do as he was required to seek approval from the Kaiser for major operations.

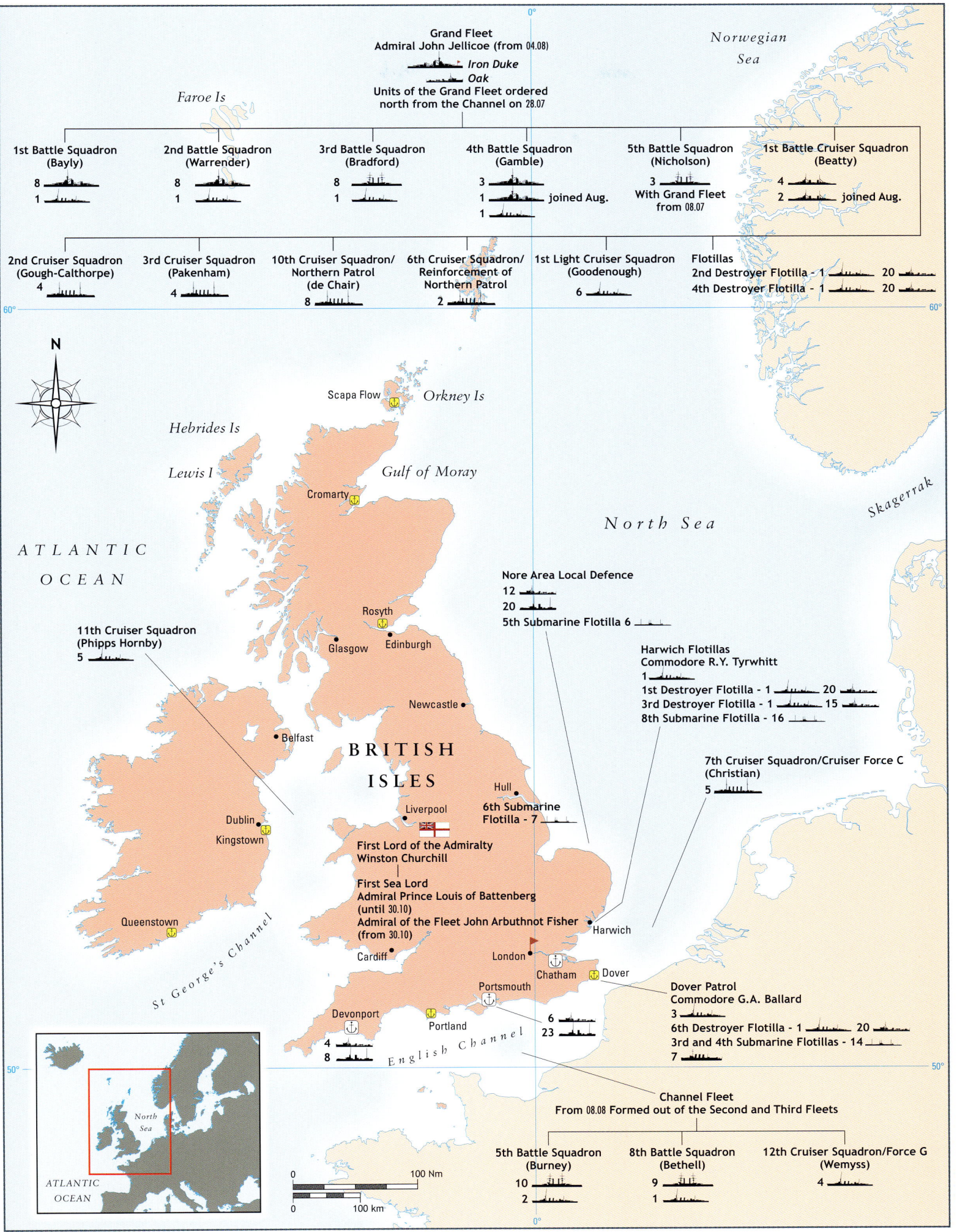

The Escape of SMS Goeben and Breslau, 3–10 August 1914

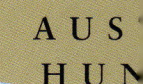

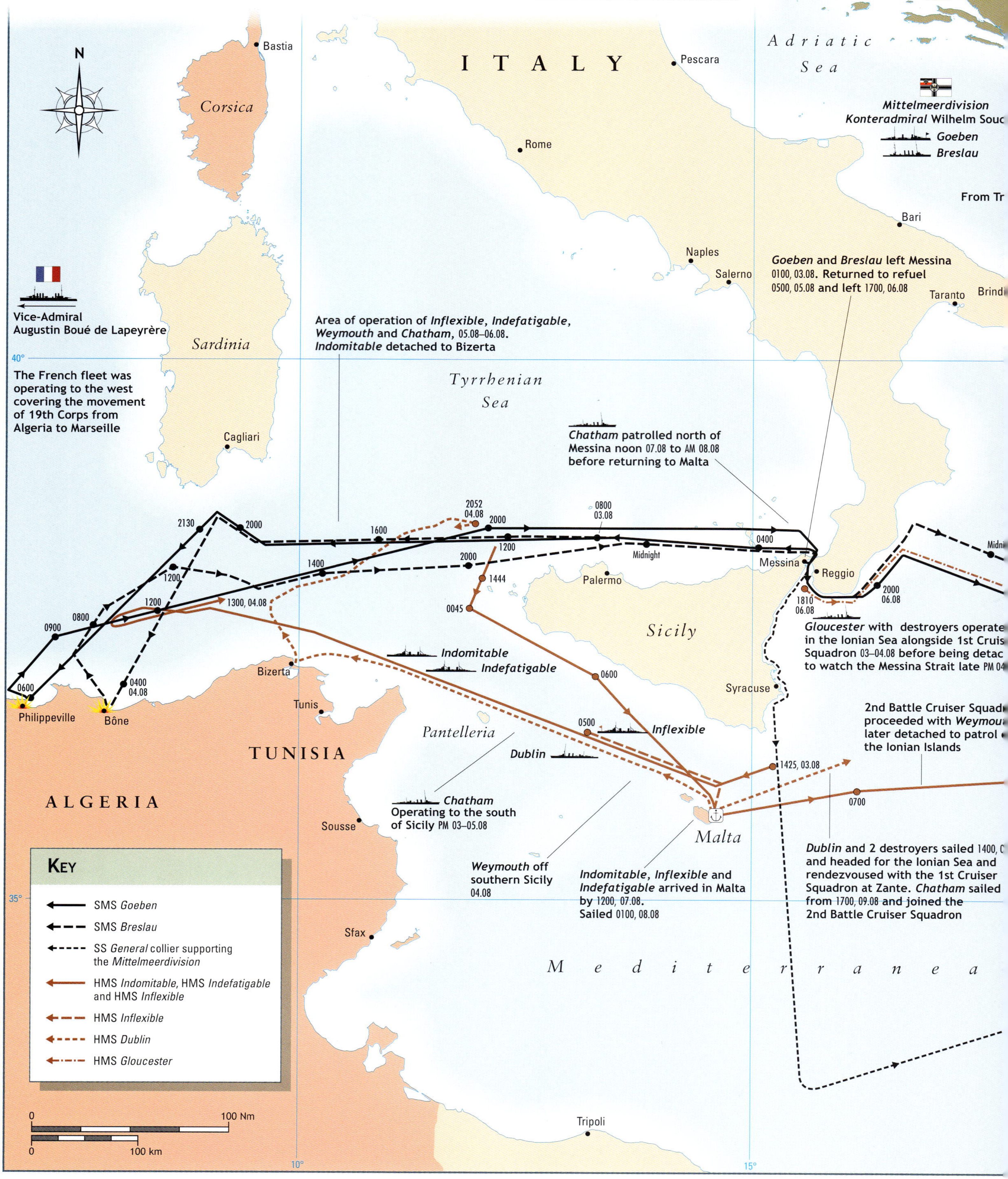

THE GREAT WAR AT SEA 1914

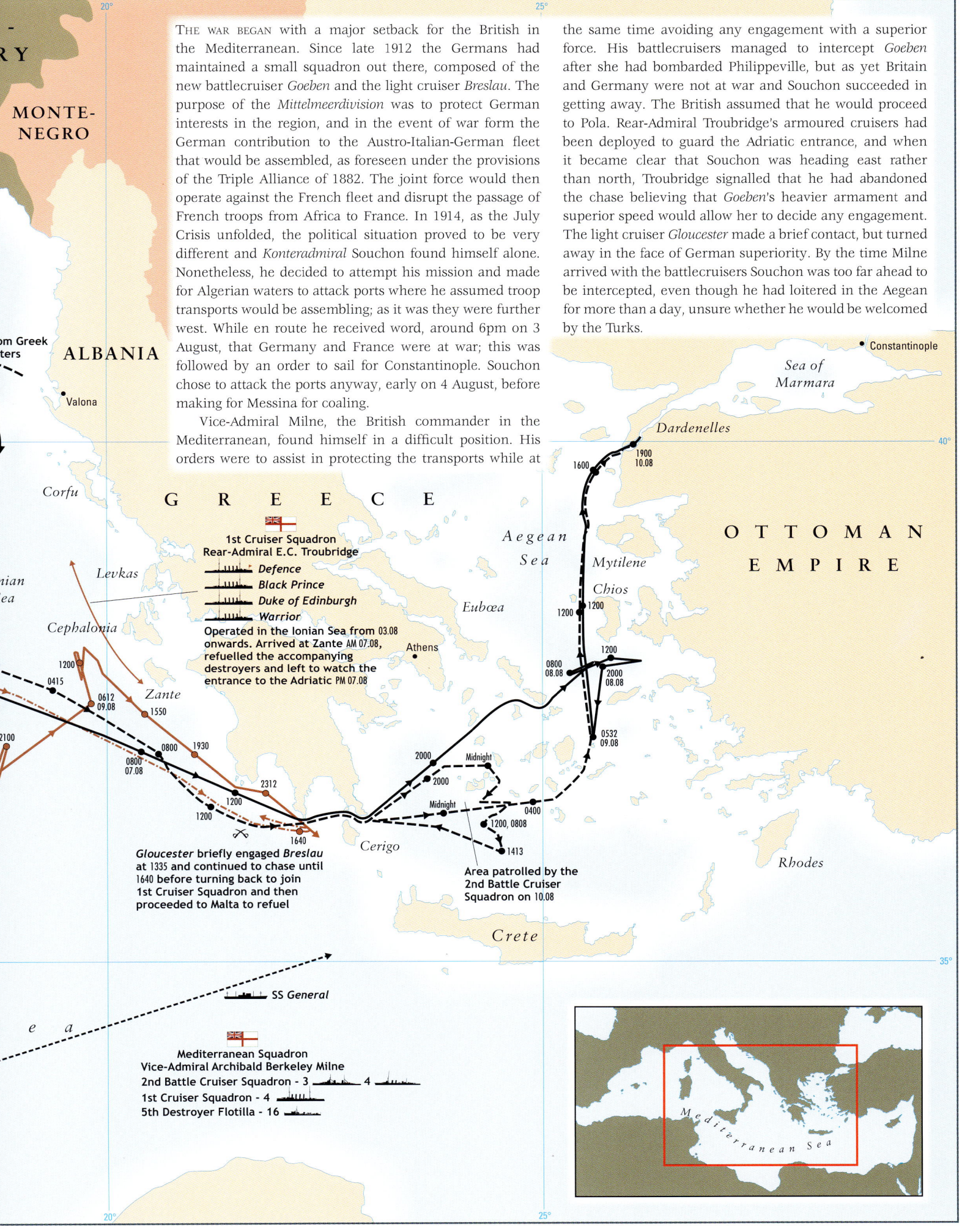

THE WAR BEGAN with a major setback for the British in the Mediterranean. Since late 1912 the Germans had maintained a small squadron out there, composed of the new battlecruiser *Goeben* and the light cruiser *Breslau*. The purpose of the *Mittelmeerdivision* was to protect German interests in the region, and in the event of war form the German contribution to the Austro-Italian-German fleet that would be assembled, as foreseen under the provisions of the Triple Alliance of 1882. The joint force would then operate against the French fleet and disrupt the passage of French troops from Africa to France. In 1914, as the July Crisis unfolded, the political situation proved to be very different and *Konteradmiral* Souchon found himself alone. Nonetheless, he decided to attempt his mission and made for Algerian waters to attack ports where he assumed troop transports would be assembling; as it was they were further west. While en route he received word, around 6pm on 3 August, that Germany and France were at war; this was followed by an order to sail for Constantinople. Souchon chose to attack the ports anyway, early on 4 August, before making for Messina for coaling.

Vice-Admiral Milne, the British commander in the Mediterranean, found himself in a difficult position. His orders were to assist in protecting the transports while at the same time avoiding any engagement with a superior force. His battlecruisers managed to intercept *Goeben* after she had bombarded Philippeville, but as yet Britain and Germany were not at war and Souchon succeeded in getting away. The British assumed that he would proceed to Pola. Rear-Admiral Troubridge's armoured cruisers had been deployed to guard the Adriatic entrance, and when it became clear that Souchon was heading east rather than north, Troubridge signalled that he had abandoned the chase believing that *Goeben*'s heavier armament and superior speed would allow her to decide any engagement. The light cruiser *Gloucester* made a brief contact, but turned away in the face of German superiority. By the time Milne arrived with the battlecruisers Souchon was too far ahead to be intercepted, even though he had loitered in the Aegean for more than a day, unsure whether he would be welcomed by the Turks.

The Escape of SMS Karlsruhe and Dresden, July–August 1914

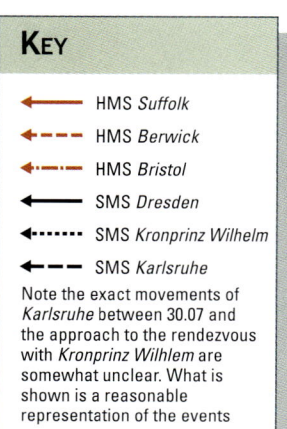

KEY

- HMS *Suffolk*
- HMS *Berwick*
- HMS *Bristol*
- SMS *Dresden*
- SMS *Kronprinz Wilhelm*
- SMS *Karlsruhe*

Note the exact movements of *Karlsruhe* between 30.07 and the approach to the rendezvous with *Kronprinz Wilhelm* are somewhat unclear. What is shown is a reasonable representation of the events

As the crisis in Europe deepened the situation in the Caribbean resembled that in the Mediterranean with the Royal Navy attempting to find, shadow and chase German forces. The Imperial Navy normally kept a single light cruiser on station to protect German interests, but that summer had two as the new *Karlsruhe* was sent out to replace *Dresden* that was in need of repair. With war seemingly imminent the *Admiralstab* ordered *Dresden* into the South Atlantic while *Karlsruhe* proceeded first to Havana and then to an isolated anchorage in anticipation of attacking British shipping.

The main British concern was the safety of the North Atlantic routes and the threat posed by the larger number of fast German liners in American ports. With *Dresden* leaving the region, Rear-Admiral Cradock concentrated on *Karlsruhe*, known to have been in Havana on 29 July but gone by the time *Berwick* arrived. *Berwick* proceeded to search the Florida Straits and through the Bahamas picking up *Karlsruhe*'s radio communications on 5 August. Meanwhile, *Dresden* had wrongly been reported off New York on 4 August causing the Admiralty to order *Essex* and *Bristol* north. Cradock made for Bermuda and at 11am on 6 August made contact with *Karlsruhe* and *Kronprinz Wilhelm*. Upon the outbreak of hostilities *Karlsruhe* made arrangements to rendezvous with the liner to equip her with armaments for her commerce warfare role. *Karlsruhe*'s superior speed allowed her to escape from *Suffolk* and, later that evening, from *Bristol*, ordered back to intercept her.

Operations by SMS Königsberg, August–September, 1914

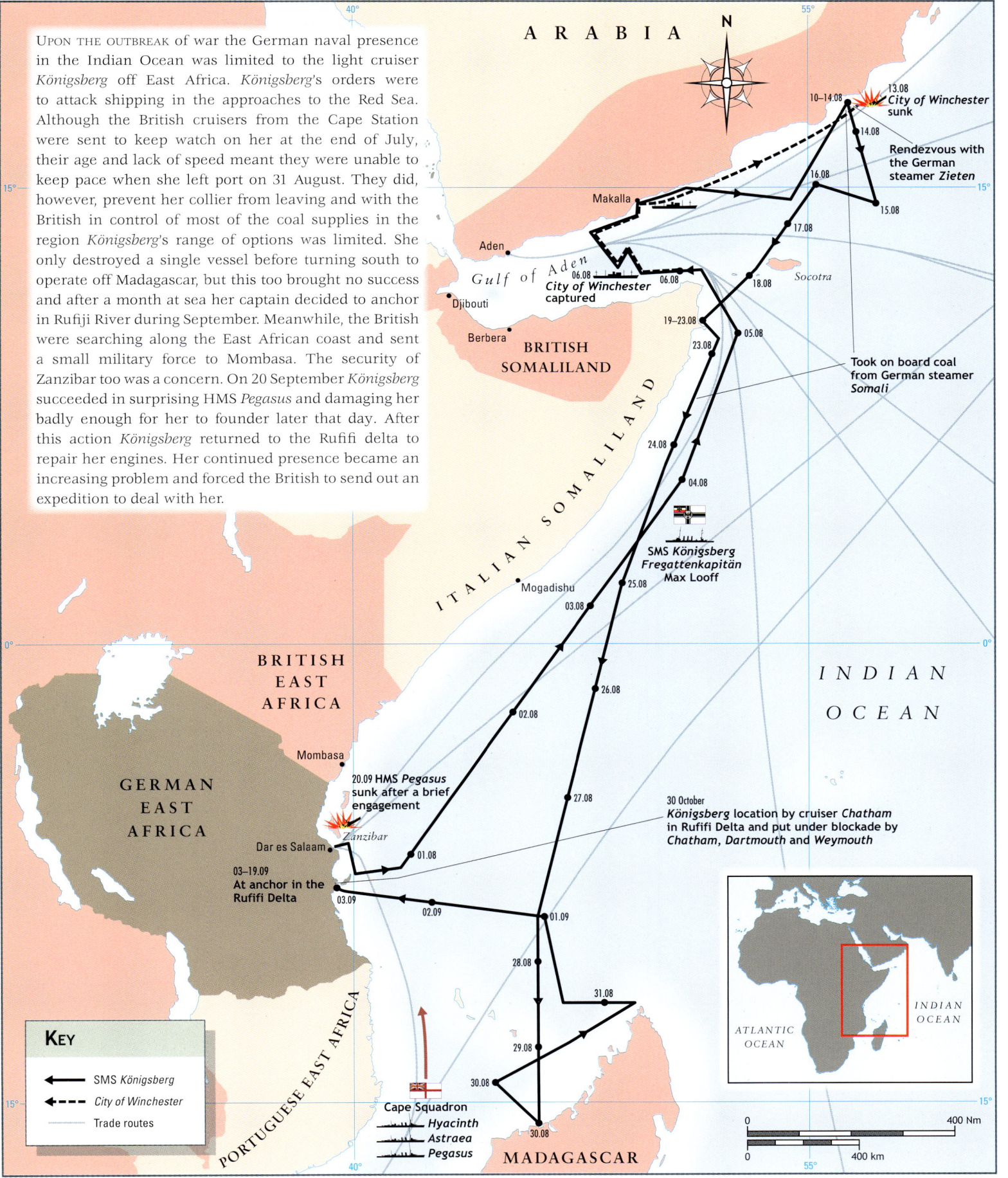

Upon the outbreak of war the German naval presence in the Indian Ocean was limited to the light cruiser *Königsberg* off East Africa. *Königsberg*'s orders were to attack shipping in the approaches to the Red Sea. Although the British cruisers from the Cape Station were sent to keep watch on her at the end of July, their age and lack of speed meant they were unable to keep pace when she left port on 31 August. They did, however, prevent her collier from leaving and with the British in control of most of the coal supplies in the region *Königsberg*'s range of options was limited. She only destroyed a single vessel before turning south to operate off Madagascar, but this too brought no success and after a month at sea her captain decided to anchor in Rufiji River during September. Meanwhile, the British were searching along the East African coast and sent a small military force to Mombasa. The security of Zanzibar too was a concern. On 20 September *Königsberg* succeeded in surprising HMS *Pegasus* and damaging her badly enough for her to founder later that day. After this action *Königsberg* returned to the Rufifi delta to repair her engines. Her continued presence became an increasing problem and forced the British to send out an expedition to deal with her.

THE NORTH SEA OVERVIEW, 1914–MID 1915

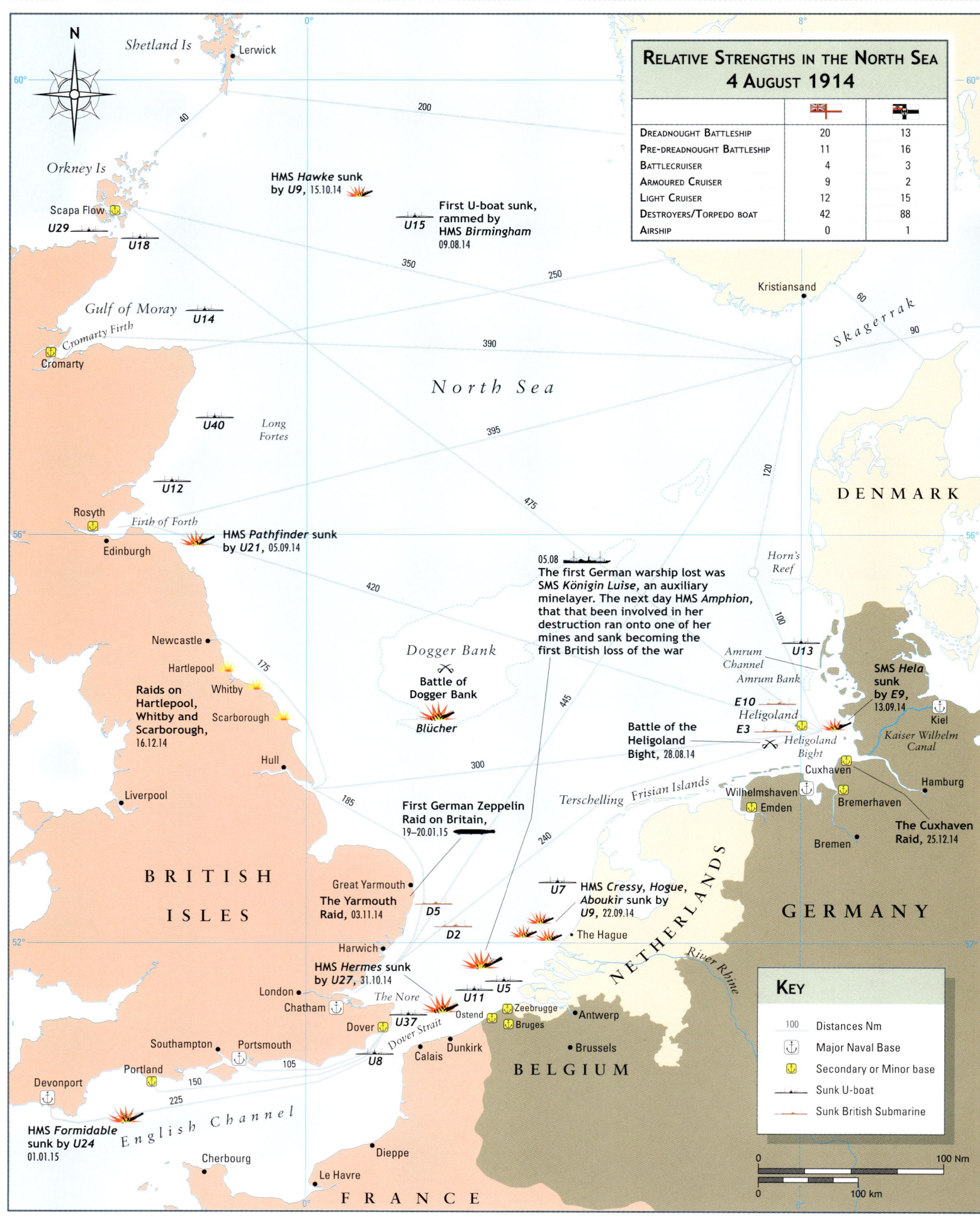

The Great War at Sea 1914

The Approach for the Heligoland Bight Operation, 27 August 1914

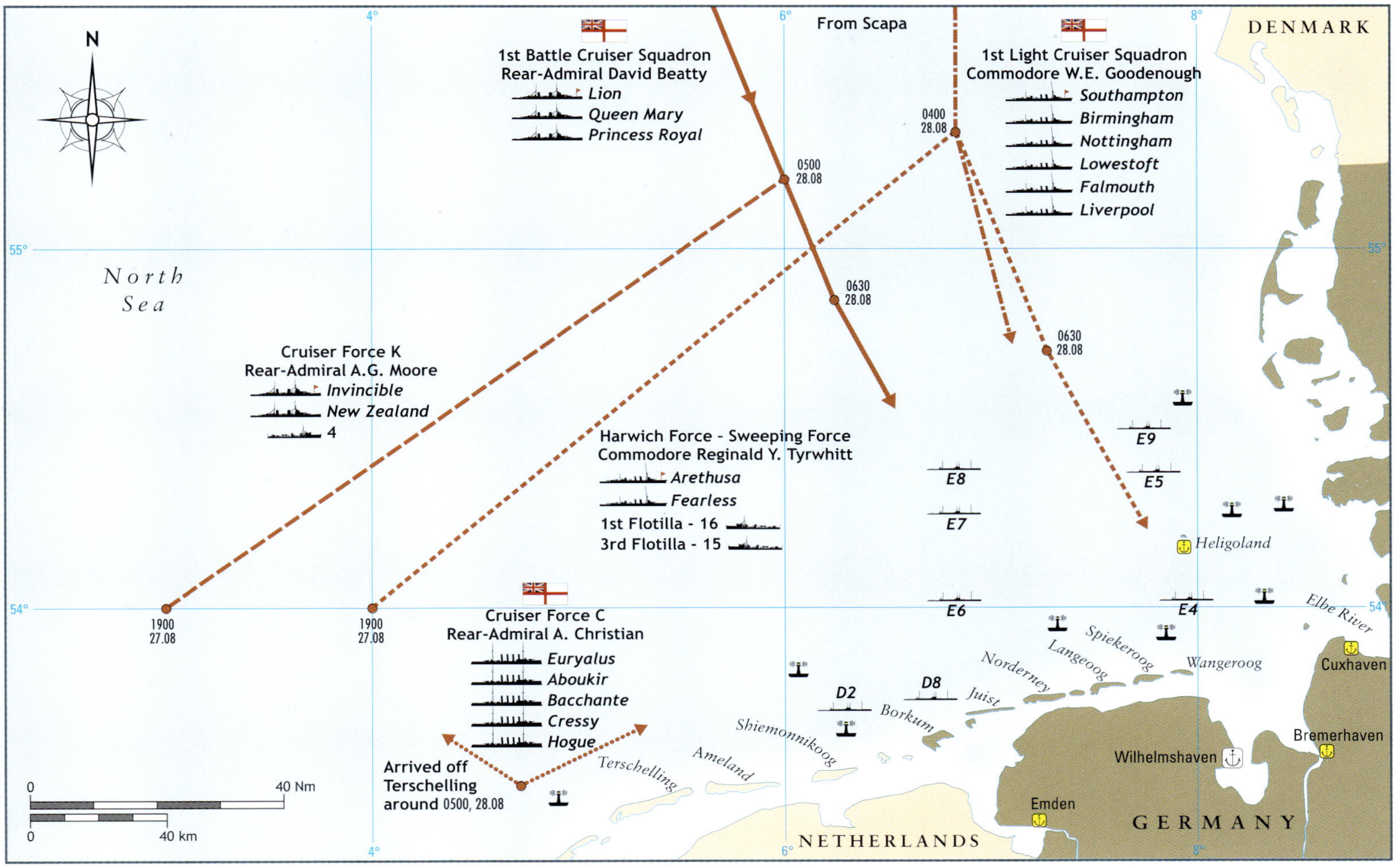

The scheme for a sweep of the Heligoland Bight originated with Commodore Roger Keyes, commander of the 6th and 8th Submarine Flotillas. Keyes, with the support of Commodore Reginald Tyrwhitt, commander of the Harwich Flotillas, proposed it as a way of breaking the deadlock that was emerging in the North Sea. With enemy forces remaining within the German Bight, the British had little chance to engage them. Submarine reconnaissance revealed that the Germans deployed torpedo boats as the outer defence of the Bight, but their high speed made it difficult for the slower submarines to conduct attacks.

To address this problem Harwich Force was to sweep from east to west using the submarines as bait to keep the German pickets out at sea. Additional submarines would be stationed off the Jade to engage any larger warships that came out to assist. With a rapidly expanding global war to contend with, the Admiralty initially devoted little attention to the plan and it was only after Keyes went directly to the First Lord, Winston Churchill, that the plan was set in motion on 24 August. Keyes had hoped that the Grand Fleet might be deployed as cover for the operation, but Admiral Sturdee, Chief of the War Staff, only attached some armoured cruisers and battlecruisers.

The plan relied on a rapid sweep so that more, and importantly heavier, German warships could not deploy from the Jade. It also depended on a high degree of coordination between the various British forces. Admiral Jellicoe, not originally informed of the operation, was sufficiently concerned by the risks involved that he sent the 1st Battle and 1st Light Cruiser Squadrons as reinforcement. In turn, neither Tyrwhitt nor Keyes was informed of these reinforcements.

The sweep initially unfolded as planned, but the presence of the *Stettin* and *Frauenlob*, and the damage that *Arethusa* sustained in an engagement with the latter, meant that by mid-morning Tyrwhitt found himself in trouble as more German light cruisers joined the engagement. Commodore Goodenough's light cruisers, having failed to find Tyrwhitt, were unable to offer support, and the danger that a British submarine might torpedo one of his cruisers led Goodenough to briefly withdraw to the north.

Meanwhile, Beatty, picking up Tyrwhitt's wireless transmissions, was aware of the unfolding situation. He faced the dilemma of having either to take his battlecruisers into mined waters and risk an engagement with superior elements of the High Sea Fleet or witness British losses. First, he sent Goodenough's light cruisers back east before committing his ships at 11.35am; the balance turned in favour of the British and their superior firepower decimated the German forces. By the early afternoon the battle had been decided. The British sustained one light cruiser and three destroyers damaged, while the Germans lost three cruisers and a destroyer and three further light cruisers were heavily damaged.

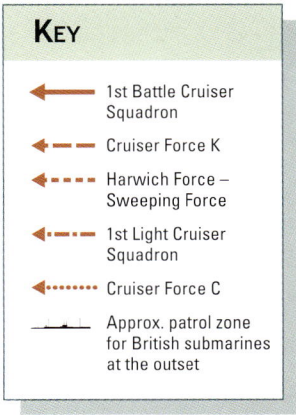

The Battle of Heligoland Bight, 28 August 1914

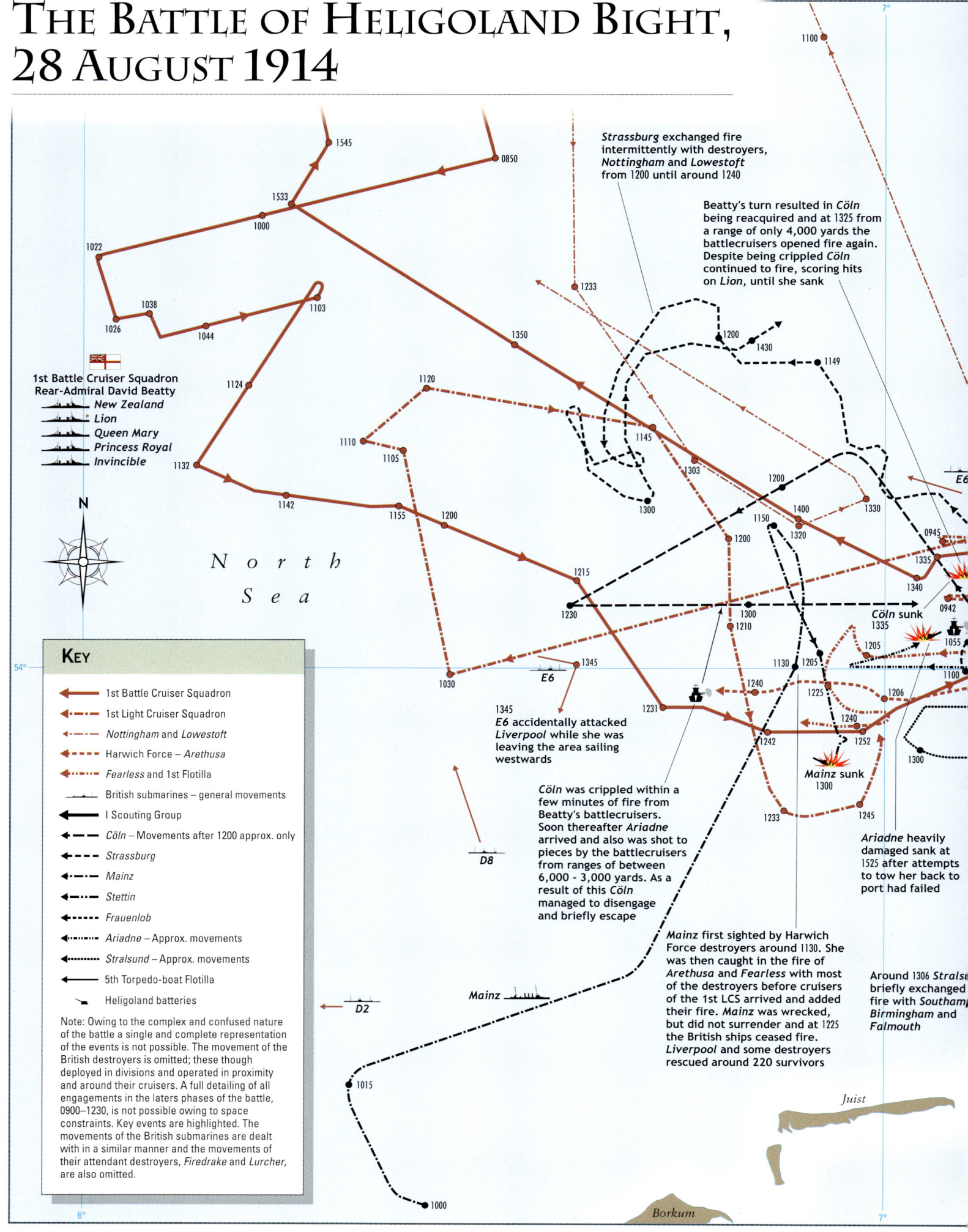

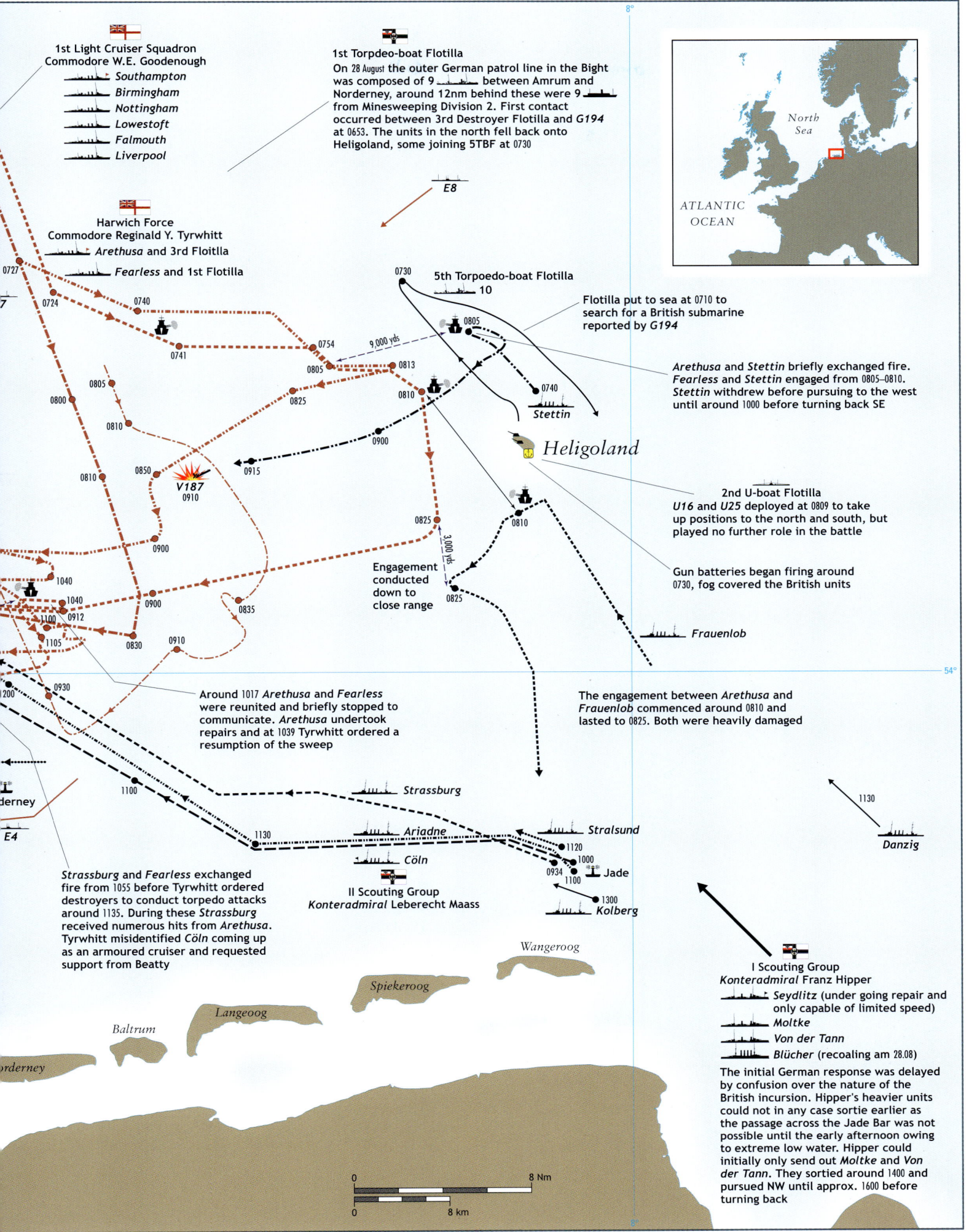

The Movement of the British Expeditionary Force, August – September 1914

As well as guarding the British Isles from invasion, a principal task of the Royal Navy at the outset of the war was the transportation of the British army to France and ensuring its supply. The despatch of a British Expeditionary Force across the Channel in the event of a war with Germany had been a possibility for some time, and during the previous three years the Admiralty and War Office had been working on the details. The BEF encompassed the majority of the active peacetime strength of the army, six infantry and a cavalry division, amounting to some 132,000 men.

On 4 August the War Council made the decision to send the BEF to France, but two divisions were removed from the initial deployment. Worries about a possible German invasion caused the 4th Division to be retained for home defence and the 6th Division brought back from Ireland. The transportation of the BEF across the Channel to its assembly points in northeastern France proceeded as planned, albeit with a two-day delay due to problems moving the troops and their supplies by rail to the embarkation ports. By 23 August 358 shipments, or around 24 a day, had been conveyed, and even the 4th Division was sent to France as, with the Royal Navy firmly in control of the North Sea, the invasion threat was considered negligible.

Having completed this huge transportation feat, the British immediately found themselves having to organise the evacuation of the bulk of the BEF's supplies and service organisation to western France as the German sweep through Belgium and northeastern France during August placed the Channel ports in a vulnerable position. The German advance, however, was checked on the Marne at the beginning of September and a static frontline developed. The remaining British land forces – marines, naval troops and army territorials – were sent across to Flanders throughout September and October.

The Germans made no attempt to prevent the movement of the BEF or attack its supply lines; the army and navy had failed to coordinate their war plans and the former considered the British a minimal threat. This view changed in the second half of August and the navy began to send U-boats down to the Flanders coast, but these achieved little against the supply lines. The first coordinated effort against troop movements occurred in October when a number of boats were sent to the Channel to intercept the first shipments of Canadian troops which, it was believed, were headed for Boulogne; in fact, they were destined for Britain.

Key

- ← German offensive, August – early September
- ---- Maximum extent of German advance
- ▬▬ Western Front, autumn 1914 onwards
- →← Race to the Sea, 17.09–19.10
- — Transport routes for the BEF, 09–23.08
- --- Routes used during the relocation to western France
- ······ Movement of 6th Division from Ireland to British mainland 14–16.08
- Main naval forces involved in the securing of the shipping routes to France shown

16

Atlantic Operations, 1914

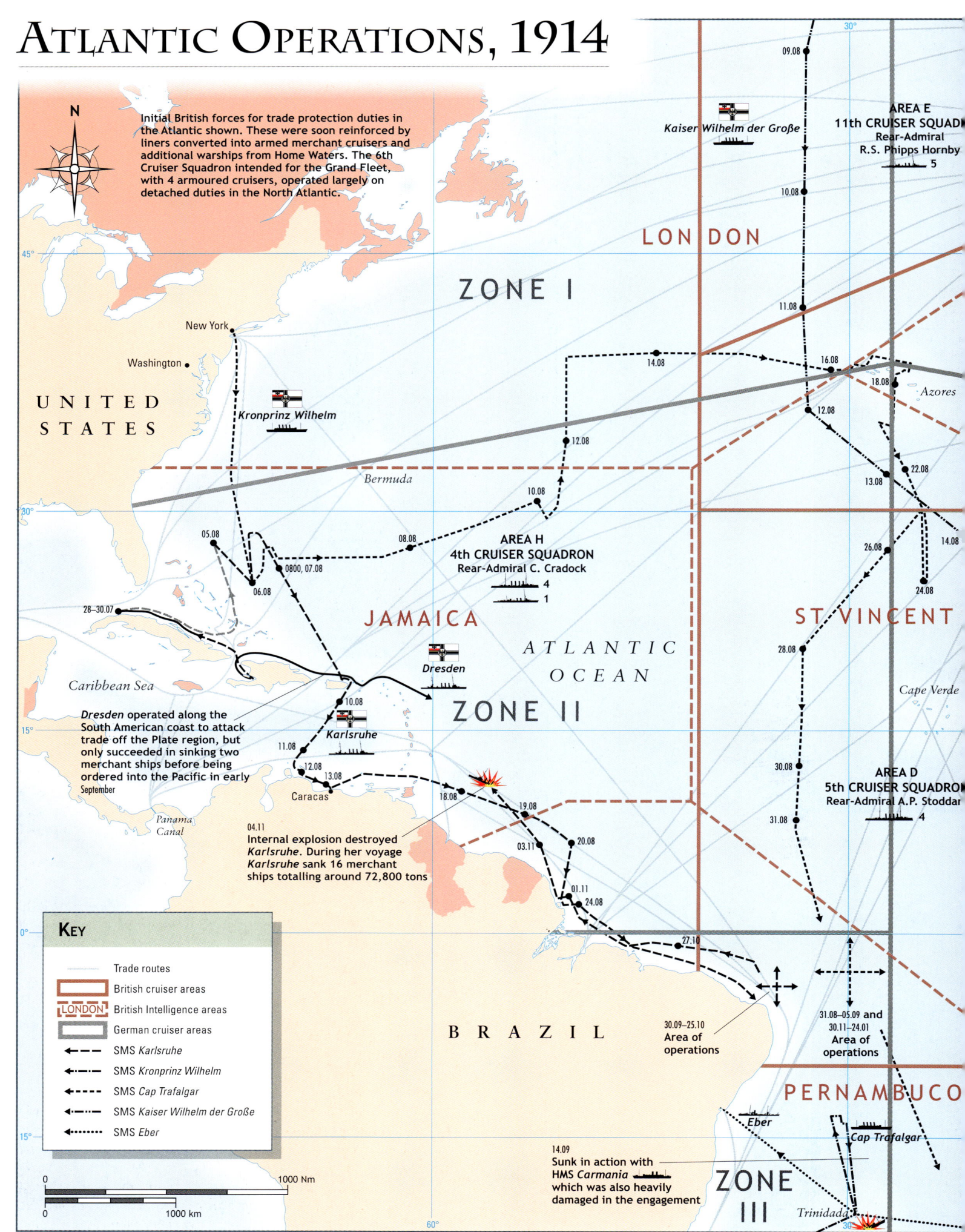

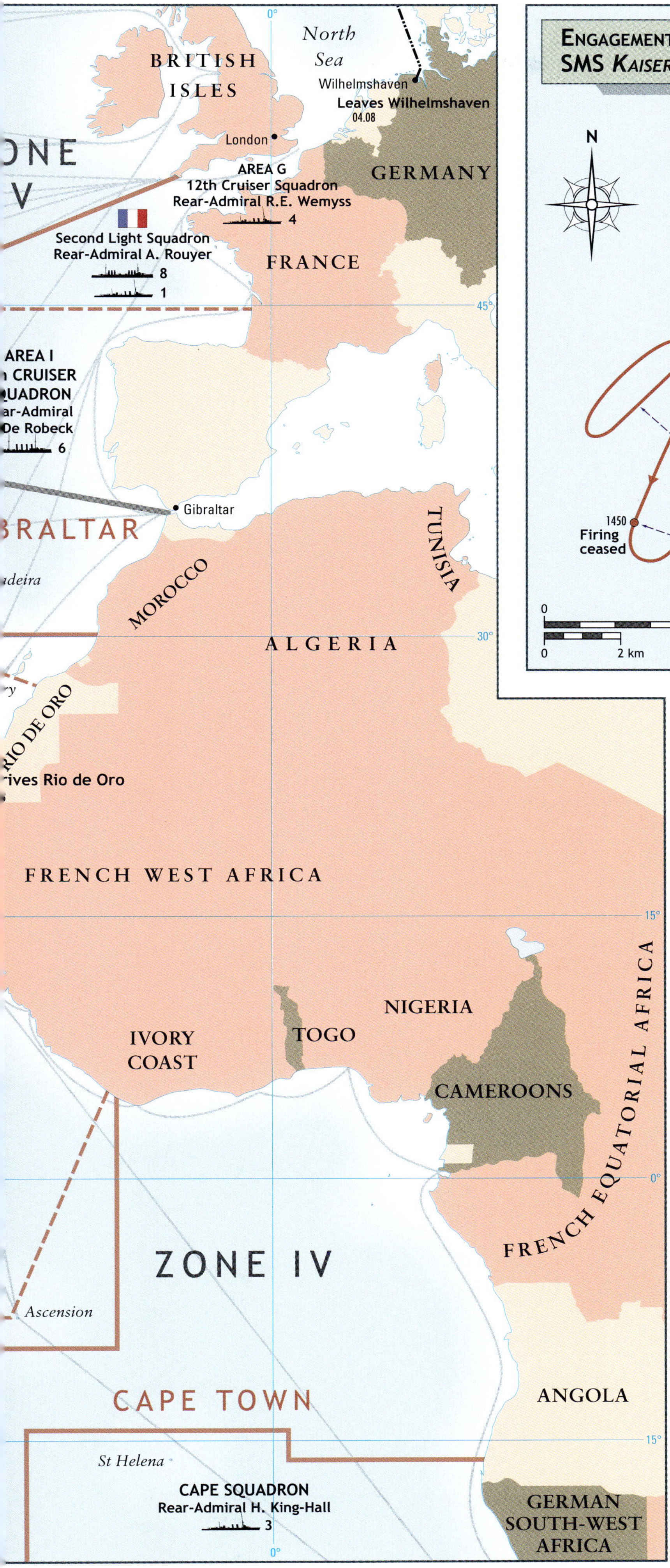

THE GREAT WAR AT SEA 1914

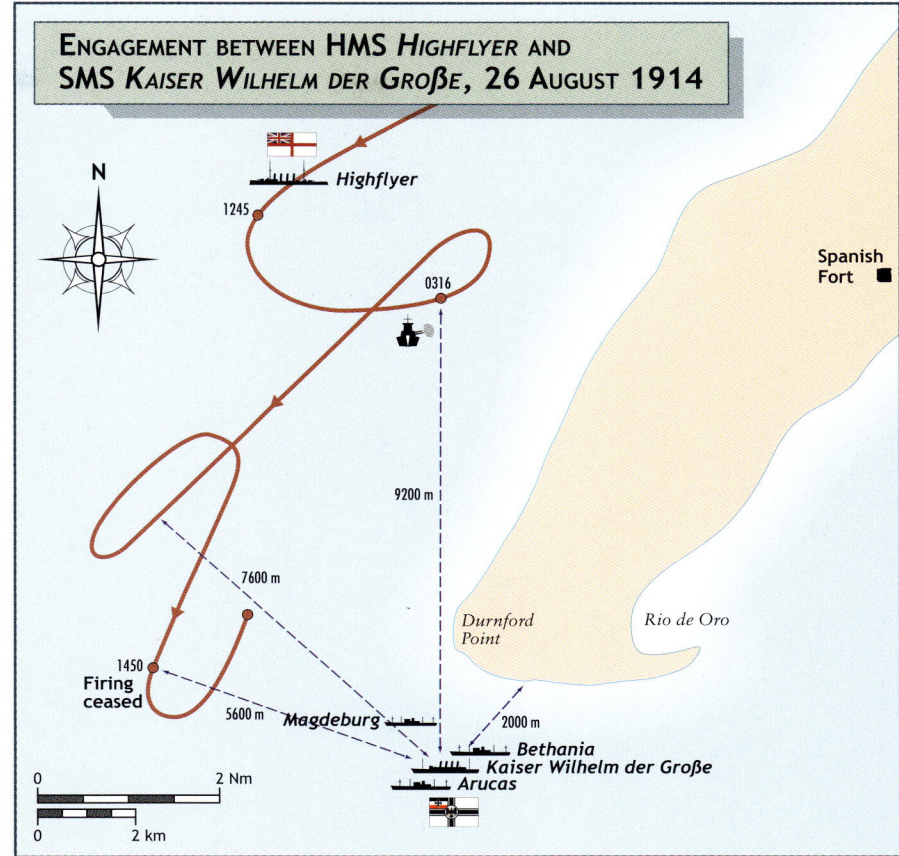

ENGAGEMENT BETWEEN HMS *HIGHFLYER* AND SMS *KAISER WILHELM DER GROßE*, 26 AUGUST 1914

THE SECURITY OF the Atlantic trade routes featured prominently in both British and German pre-war planning. For Britain and its empire, the Atlantic was of central importance for trade and for the movement of military forces. The British Isles were dependent on food imports from North and South America while the latter was also the source for key raw materials like nitrates from Chile, vital for both agriculture and the production of explosives. This dependence on trade made Britain vulnerable, but equally it afforded her great economic strength underpinned by a large merchant fleet and global communications. As one of the most industrialised nations, with the second largest merchant fleet in the world, Germany too profited from Atlantic trade, but in the face of British naval supremacy would forfeit this in the event of a great power war. In addition, Germany would most likely lose much of her shipping fleet in foreign ports.

Although some German naval forces were stationed overseas, British concern focused on the large, fast German transatlantic liners being armed at the outset of any conflict and operating against North Atlantic traffic. While it took time to bring the individual station forces up to strength, by 14 August the Admiralty felt the northern trade routes were safe. The scale of the German operations was more modest than expected. Only one auxiliary cruiser was despatched from Germany and the *Kaiser Wilhelm der Große* proved very inefficient and was sunk in action with the *Highflyer* on 26 August. The light cruisers *Dresden* and *Karlsruhe* operated against the southern routes. The latter had a reasonably successful voyage, but it did not dislocate Atlantic trade flows, and on 4 November she sank after an internal explosion. The loss was kept secret and it was not until the spring of 1915 that the British were sure she was no longer a threat. *Cap Trafalgar*, armed from the gunboat *Eber*, achieved little before being sunk in action. *Kronprinz Wilhelm* stayed out for eight months before returning to the United States in April 1915 in need of repair. During her voyage she accounted for fifteen merchant ships of 60,500 tons.

19

The Pacific Theatre, 1914

THE GREAT WAR AT SEA 1914

In the Pacific the allied strategy rotated around neutralising the threat posed by the German East Asiatic Squadron and securing German imperial possessions in Micronesia and Tsingtao. Since the 1890s Germany had maintained a permanent naval presence in the Far East, and since 1911 two modern armoured cruisers had formed its core. In comparison to the British and Japanese forces, the German squadron was small, but it was composed of modern vessels and the vastness of the ocean offered ample opportunity to hide. However, the position in which Vizeadmiral von Spee found himself was daunting. If he stayed in the Far East he would be destroyed, but equally his chances of reaching Germany were slim. He chose to evade the Allies by crossing the Pacific and, to increase the chances of survival, concentrate all available warships, including those in American waters, and supply vessels into a single group. To spread uncertainty about his whereabouts and intentions he sent the cruiser *Emden* to the Indian Ocean and had *Nürnberg* cruise off Hawaii.

For the Allies this posed a problem. The German territories were quickly occupied by New Zealand, Australian and Japanese expeditions and Tsingtao blockaded. With the battlecruiser *Australia* covering these operations there was a powerful unit in the Central Pacific, but there was no indication where von Spee had sailed. Concern for the safety of the first troop convoy from Australia and New Zealand heading for the Middle East led to a concentration of allied naval forces in this region. After the British defeat at Coronel Australian and Anglo-Japanese forces in the western Pacific were sent to cut off any attempt by von Spee to head back into the Pacific.

KEY

- **→** Vizeadmiral von Spee with SMS *Scharnhorst* and SMS *Gneisenau*
- **←· ·** SMS *Emden*   **←− −** SMS *Nürnberg*
- **· · ·** SMS *Leipzig*   **←·−·** SMS *Dresden*
- **· · · ·** SMS *Geier* 20.08 it meets with *Emden* at sea. Arrives in Honolulu 15.10, interned on 02.11
- **↕** Area of operations for SMS *Prinz Eitel Friedrich* and SMS *Cormoran* 09–10.14. Left Tsingtao on 06 and 08.08
- **→** Australian and NZ Expeditionary Forces
- **- - ->** HMAS *Australia* movements after covering the expeditions
- **→** Australian–New Zealand Troop Convoy
- **- - ->** Rear-Admiral Cradock's squadron
- **·····** Vice-Admiral Sturdee's squadron – see page 31
- **→** Japanese operations against German Micronesia

Note: Only the general movements of key formations and warships shown. For *Emden*'s cruise see page 35.

THE NAVAL BLOCKADE OF GERMANY, 1914–17

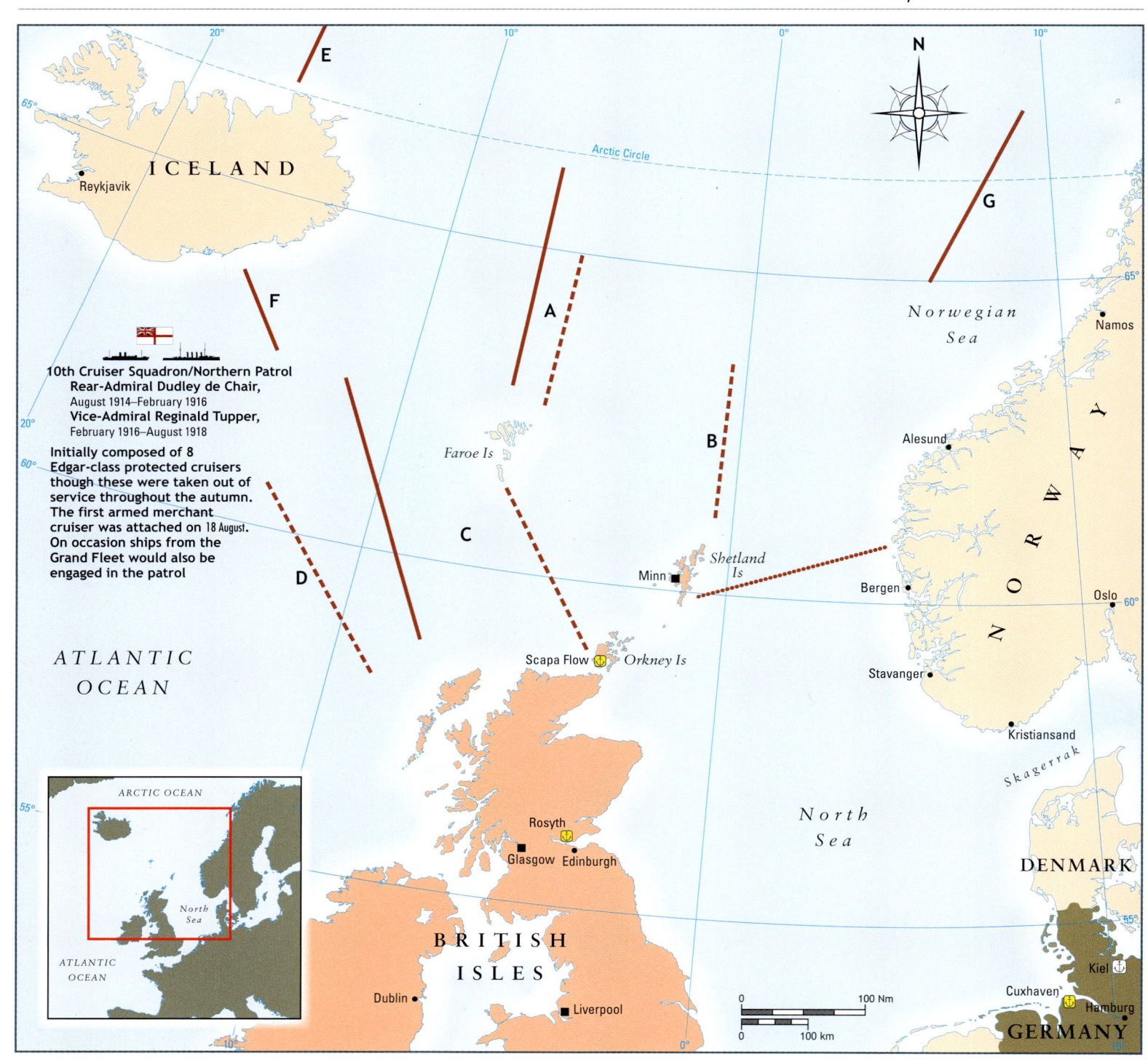

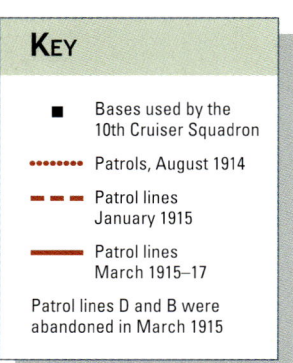

10th Cruiser Squadron/Northern Patrol
Rear-Admiral Dudley de Chair, August 1914–February 1916
Vice-Admiral Reginald Tupper, February 1916–August 1918

Initially composed of 8 Edgar-class protected cruisers though these were taken out of service throughout the autumn. The first armed merchant cruiser was attached on 18 August. On occasion ships from the Grand Fleet would also be engaged in the patrol

Key

- Bases used by the 10th Cruiser Squadron
- Patrols, August 1914
- Patrol lines January 1915
- Patrol lines March 1915–17

Patrol lines D and B were abandoned in March 1915

The blockade was Britain's traditional tool for use in great power conflicts. Its long-term effects upon an enemy could be devastating, bringing about the collapse of economies. However, it was a slow instrument, the effect of which was difficult to anticipate. British economic power, underpinned by her commercial activity and safeguarded by the Royal Navy, enabled this strategic choice; however, it depended on more than just ships at sea. British dominance of the global financial system and control of worldwide communications was also a prerequisite for a successful blockade.

Innovations such as mines and torpedoes made the implementation of a close blockade of an enemy coastline no longer such an easy option. In Germany's case geography overcame this problem and provided the British with a crucial advantage. The British Isles acted as a barrier and channelled German seaborne trade into relatively constrained pathways. The English Channel was easy to control and thus impassable for German traffic.

Implementing the blockade proved to be a far more complex task than originally envisaged as, in anticipation of a short war, little practical thought had been given to many aspects. The small force of obsolete cruisers assigned to the 10th Cruiser Squadron proved totally inadequate and suffered badly with the onset of the harsher autumn weather. They were replaced by armed merchant cruisers. The original patrol area between the Shetlands and Norway was abandoned owing to the growing threat from U-boats and mines, the loss of HMS *Hawke* to *U9* on 15 October clearly demonstrating this vulnerability. In response, patrol lines further out in the Atlantic were adopted in 1915.

The Loss of HMSs Aboukir, Hogue and Cressy, 22 September 1914

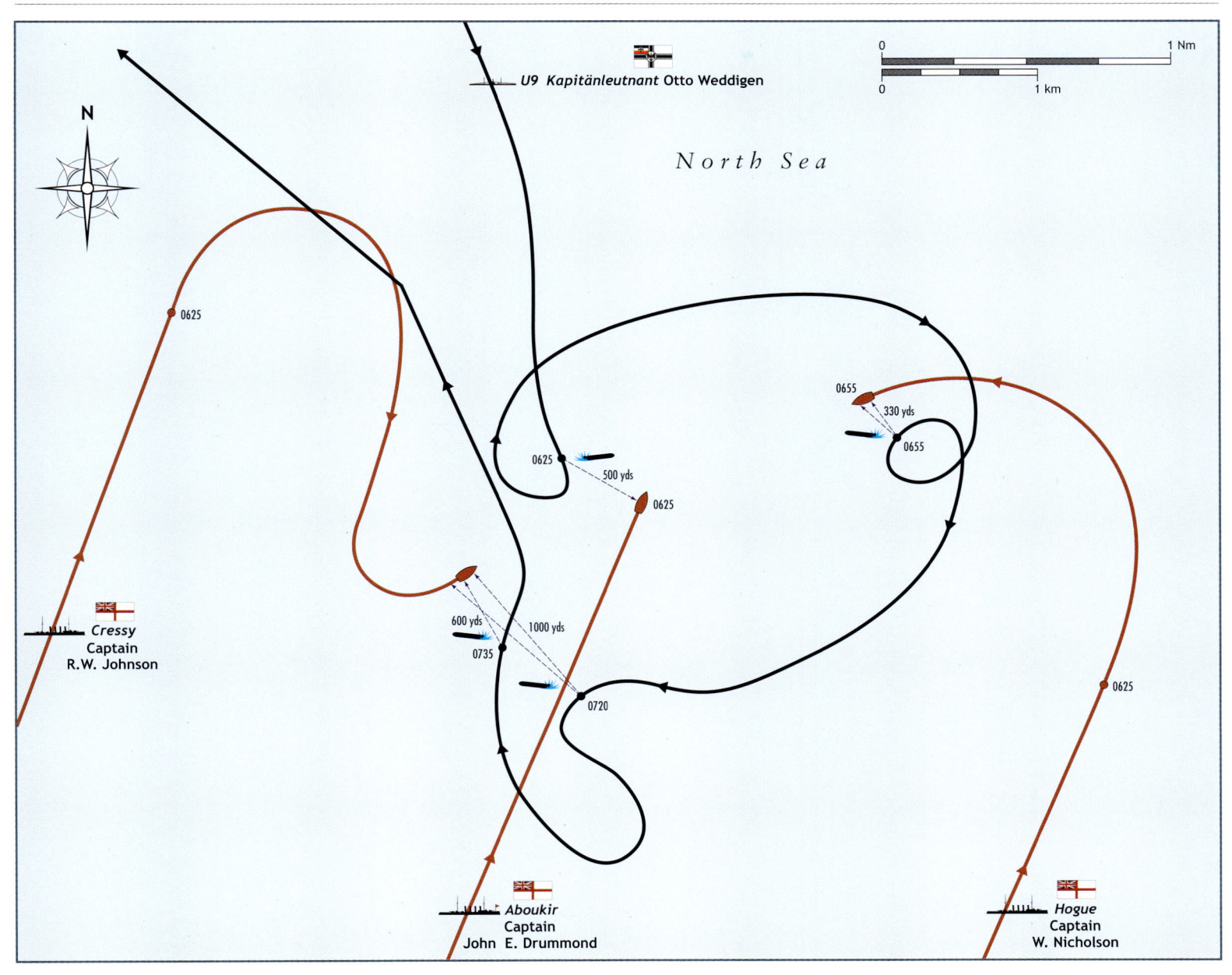

Across the conflict the submarine had a significant impact on the character of naval warfare and affected fleet operations and trade defence in equal measure. Yet at the beginning of the war they remained something of an unknown quantity and the events of 22 September profoundly shocked the British and provided a boost to German morale. The Germans employed U-boats for coastal defence and scouts for the High Sea Fleet and it was in this capacity that their area of operations was slowly extended across the North Sea in August and September 1914. The sinking of the British scout cruiser *Pathfinder* in the Firth of Forth by *U21* on 5 September indicated that the U-boat had offensive potential.

When, in mid-September, increased troop movements across the Channel were detected, the *Generalstab* asked the *Admiralstab* to consider interdicting the flow of British reinforcements. The naval reaction was muted, influenced also by bad weather, and only a single boat, *U9*, was sent out on 20 September. However, *U9*'s captain, *Kapitänleutnant* Otto Weddigen, was one of the most experienced German submariners. It was also the only German boat to have practised reloading its torpedo tubes while submerged.

The British were concerned that the Germans intended to block the Scheldt estuary and had deployed the 7th Cruiser Squadron in the Broad Fourteens, an area of deep water off the Dutch coast. Bad weather forced accompanying destroyers to remain in port. At daylight on 22 September, Weddigen spotted three British armoured cruisers approaching in a line abreast formation. From close range *U9* fired a single torpedo at *Aboukir* and then made its way around to attack *Hogue*, momentarily stopped. *Cressy* was hit an hour after the first attack whilst rescuing *Aboukir*'s crew, and fatally hit in a second attack ten minutes later. In just over an hour three warships had been sunk and around 1,460 sailors lost.

NORTH SEA OPERATIONS, AUTUMN 1914

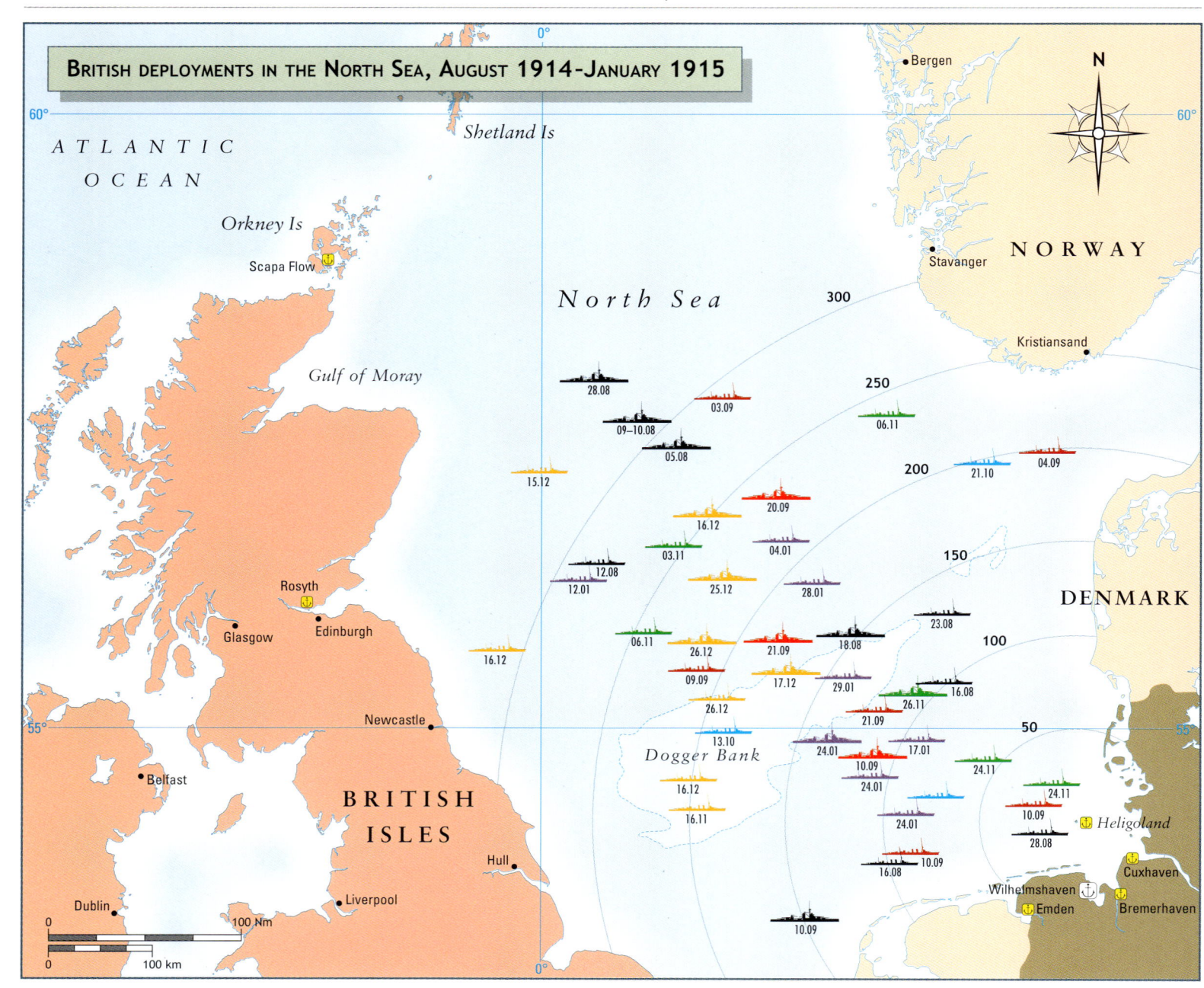

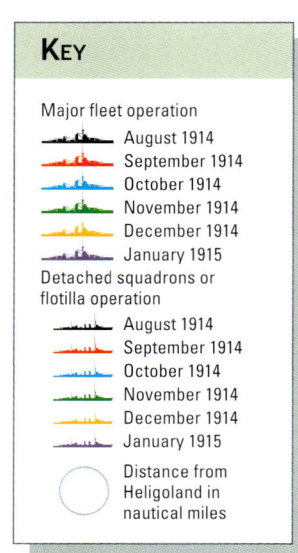

BRITISH DEPLOYMENTS IN THE NORTH SEA, AUGUST 1914-JANUARY 1915

Key

Major fleet operation
- August 1914
- September 1914
- October 1914
- November 1914
- December 1914
- January 1915

Detached squadrons or flotilla operation
- August 1914
- September 1914
- October 1914
- November 1914
- December 1914
- January 1915

Distance from Heligoland in nautical miles

Contrary to the widely held view that the war would begin with a major fleet engagement, the German naval leadership acted very cautiously in its use of the High Sea Fleet. From the outset, conversely, and in an attempt to dominate the North Sea and force the Germans into an engagement, the British acted much more assertively with far more sweeps through the central and lower North Sea by the Grand Fleet or detached elements than were undertaken later in the war. The Heligoland Bight action in August had come as a surprise to the Germans and thereafter they ceased to use the North Sea for training or trials and began to lay extensive defensive minefields.

The British had now to counter the German U-boats and mines, and these new threats progressively limited the way in which the Grand Fleet could operate and how shipping could pass safely up and down the east coast. The appearance of U-boats off Scotland and the Orkney Islands soon after hostilities began led Admiral Jellicoe to move the Grand Fleet to bases further west while Scapa Flow's defences were upgraded. U-boats also influenced fleet operations as it was never felt that there were sufficient destroyers to protect the battle squadrons at sea.

Offensive minelaying had been a key feature of pre-war German strategy and, indeed, the first operation in the North Sea was a minelaying operation during which the auxiliary minelayer *Königin Luise* was lost. The Germans informed neutral powers that the access routes to British ports would be regularly mined, but when three weeks later German minelayers laid large fields off the Tyne and Humber no statement was issued. The Humber was, as a result of the mining, abandoned as a forward base for battlecruisers. A further problem for the British that autumn was that it was often hard to tell whether ships were lost to mines or U-boat action and this confusion and uncertainty had a major impact. While in 1914 the Germans relied on a small number of substantial minefields, in 1915 they increasingly used U-boats to lay larger numbers of small fields thereby increasing the sea areas affected by mines.

THE GREAT WAR AT SEA 1914

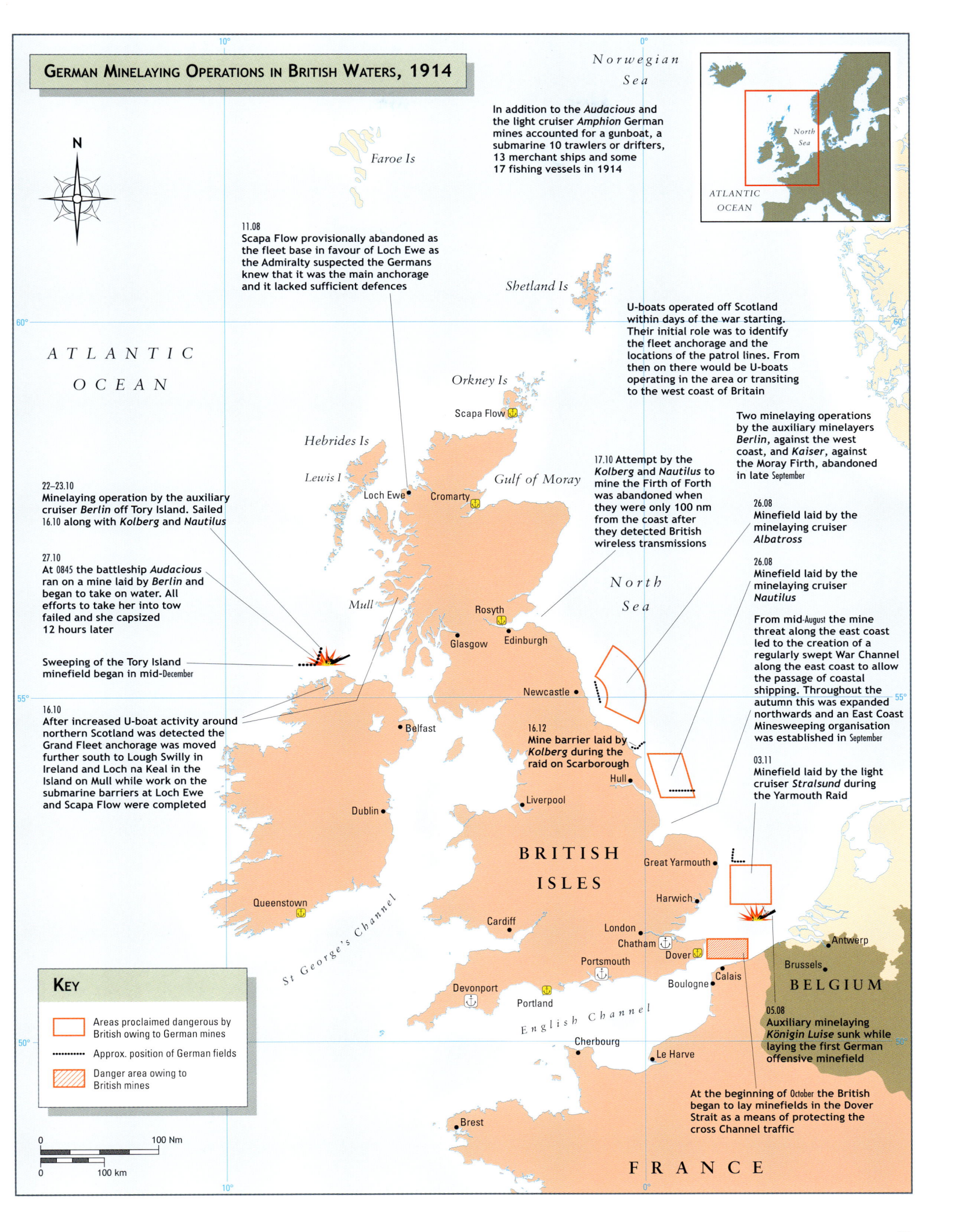

GERMAN MINELAYING OPERATIONS IN BRITISH WATERS, 1914

In addition to the *Audacious* and the light cruiser *Amphion* German mines accounted for a gunboat, a submarine 10 trawlers or drifters, 13 merchant ships and some 17 fishing vessels in 1914

11.08 Scapa Flow provisionally abandoned as the fleet base in favour of Loch Ewe as the Admiralty suspected the Germans knew that it was the main anchorage and it lacked sufficient defences

U-boats operated off Scotland within days of the war starting. Their initial role was to identify the fleet anchorage and the locations of the patrol lines. From then on there would be U-boats operating in the area or transiting to the west coast of Britain

Two minelaying operations by the auxiliary minelayers *Berlin*, against the west coast, and *Kaiser*, against the Moray Firth, abandoned in late September

22–23.10 Minelaying operation by the auxiliary cruiser *Berlin* off Tory Island. Sailed 16.10 along with *Kolberg* and *Nautilus*

17.10 Attempt by the *Kolberg* and *Nautilus* to mine the Firth of Forth was abandoned when they were only 100 nm from the coast after they detected British wireless transmissions

26.08 Minefield laid by the minelaying cruiser *Albatross*

26.08 Minefield laid by the minelaying cruiser *Nautilus*

27.10 At 0845 the battleship *Audacious* ran on a mine laid by *Berlin* and began to take on water. All efforts to take her into tow failed and she capsized 12 hours later

From mid-August the mine threat along the east coast led to the creation of a regularly swept War Channel along the east coast to allow the passage of coastal shipping. Throughout the autumn this was expanded northwards and an East Coast Minesweeping organisation was established in September

Sweeping of the Tory Island minefield began in mid-December

16.10 After increased U-boat activity around northern Scotland was detected the Grand Fleet anchorage was moved further south to Lough Swilly in Ireland and Loch na Keal in the Island on Mull while work on the submarine barriers at Loch Ewe and Scapa Flow were completed

16.12 Mine barrier laid by *Kolberg* during the raid on Scarborough

03.11 Minefield laid by the light cruiser *Stralsund* during the Yarmouth Raid

05.08 Auxiliary minelaying *Königin Luise* sunk while laying the first German offensive minefield

At the beginning of October the British began to lay minefields in the Dover Strait as a means of protecting the cross Channel traffic

KEY
- ▭ Areas proclaimed dangerous by British owing to German mines
- ⋯ Approx. position of German fields
- ▨ Danger area owing to British mines

The Baltic Theatre, 1914–15

Key

- Minefields
- ——— Russian
- ••••••• German
- ••••••• Danish
- ▭ German cleared channels
- ⬅--- Shipping route for German imports of Swedish iron ore
- Zeppelin base
- ⊕ German airbase
- ⊕ Russian airbase

Major warships lost and damaged shown

The Great War at Sea 1914

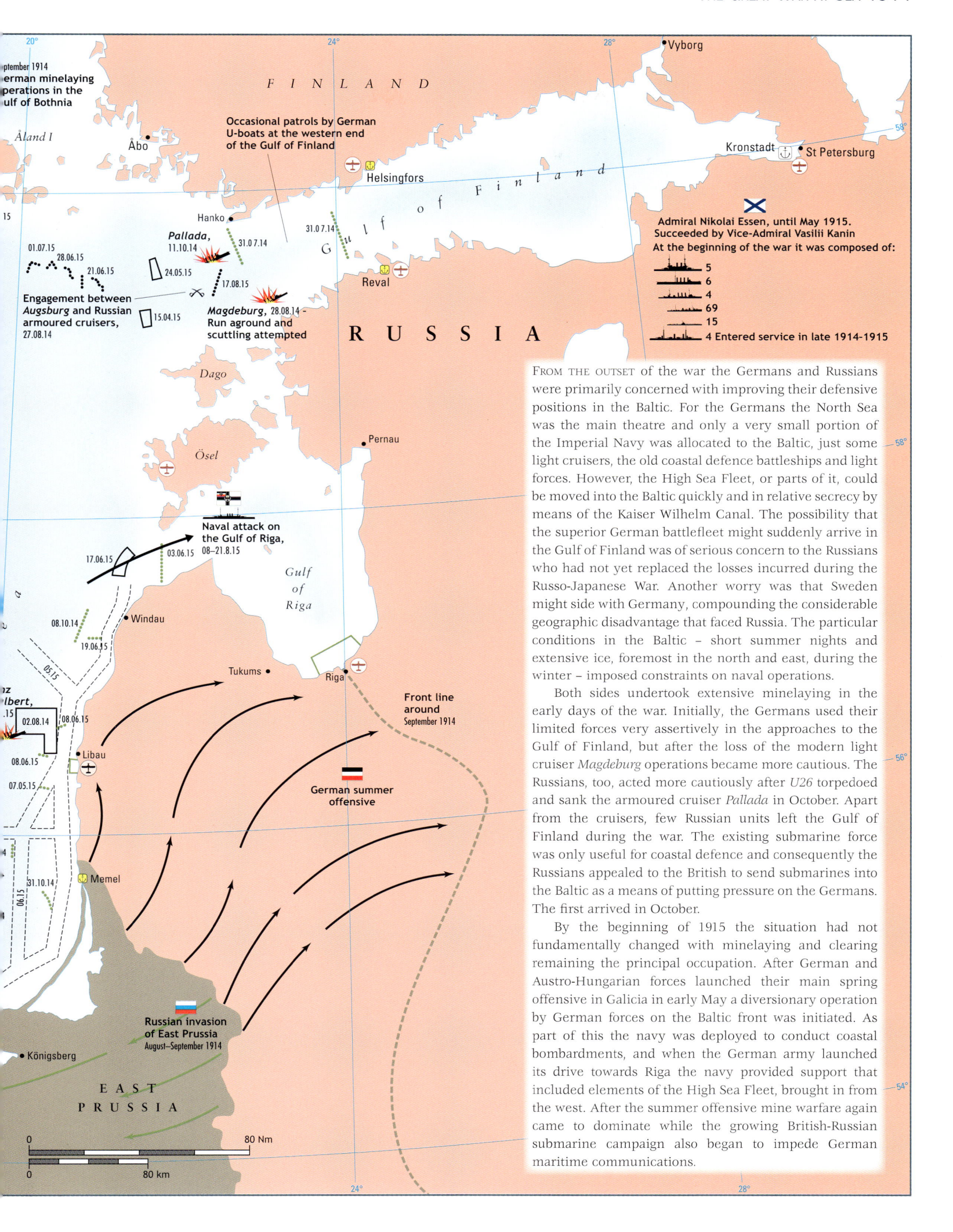

Occasional patrols by German U-boats at the western end of the Gulf of Finland

September 1914 German minelaying operations in the Gulf of Bothnia

Pallada, 11.10.14

Magdeburg, 28.08.14 – Run aground and scuttling attempted

Engagement between *Augsburg* and Russian armoured cruisers, 27.08.14

Admiral Nikolai Essen, until May 1915. Succeeded by Vice-Admiral Vasilii Kanin
At the beginning of the war it was composed of:
- 5
- 6
- 4
- 69
- 15
- 4 Entered service in late 1914–1915

Naval attack on the Gulf of Riga, 08–21.8.15

Front line around September 1914

German summer offensive

Russian invasion of East Prussia August–September 1914

From the outset of the war the Germans and Russians were primarily concerned with improving their defensive positions in the Baltic. For the Germans the North Sea was the main theatre and only a very small portion of the Imperial Navy was allocated to the Baltic, just some light cruisers, the old coastal defence battleships and light forces. However, the High Sea Fleet, or parts of it, could be moved into the Baltic quickly and in relative secrecy by means of the Kaiser Wilhelm Canal. The possibility that the superior German battlefleet might suddenly arrive in the Gulf of Finland was of serious concern to the Russians who had not yet replaced the losses incurred during the Russo-Japanese War. Another worry was that Sweden might side with Germany, compounding the considerable geographic disadvantage that faced Russia. The particular conditions in the Baltic – short summer nights and extensive ice, foremost in the north and east, during the winter – imposed constraints on naval operations.

Both sides undertook extensive minelaying in the early days of the war. Initially, the Germans used their limited forces very assertively in the approaches to the Gulf of Finland, but after the loss of the modern light cruiser *Magdeburg* operations became more cautious. The Russians, too, acted more cautiously after *U26* torpedoed and sank the armoured cruiser *Pallada* in October. Apart from the cruisers, few Russian units left the Gulf of Finland during the war. The existing submarine force was only useful for coastal defence and consequently the Russians appealed to the British to send submarines into the Baltic as a means of putting pressure on the Germans. The first arrived in October.

By the beginning of 1915 the situation had not fundamentally changed with minelaying and clearing remaining the principal occupation. After German and Austro-Hungarian forces launched their main spring offensive in Galicia in early May a diversionary operation by German forces on the Baltic front was initiated. As part of this the navy was deployed to conduct coastal bombardments, and when the German army launched its drive towards Riga the navy provided support that included elements of the High Sea Fleet, brought in from the west. After the summer offensive mine warfare again came to dominate while the growing British-Russian submarine campaign also began to impede German maritime communications.

THE ADRIATIC THEATRE, 1914

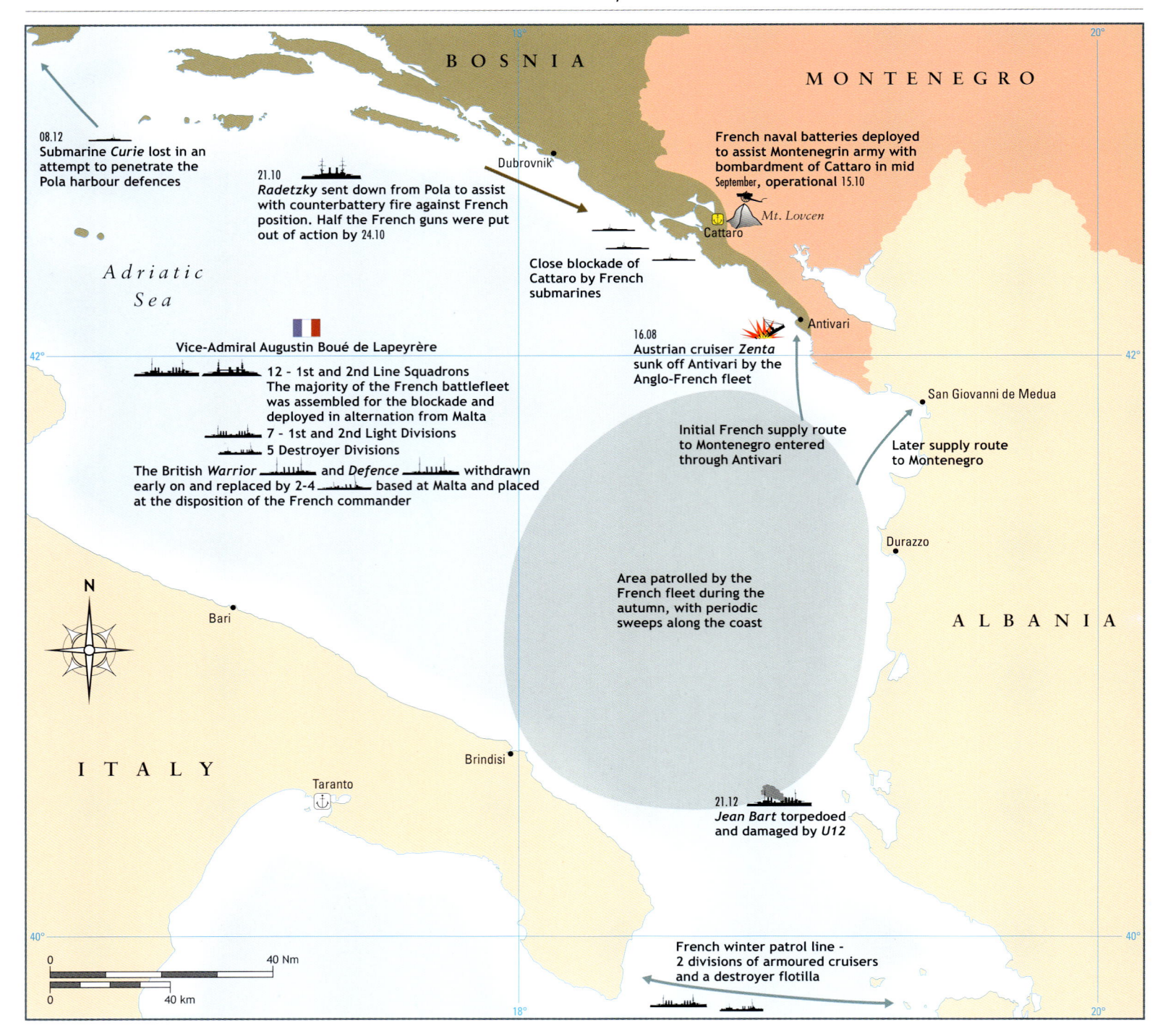

Map annotations

- **08.12** Submarine *Curie* lost in an attempt to penetrate the Pola harbour defences
- **21.10** *Radetzky* sent down from Pola to assist with counterbattery fire against French position. Half the French guns were put out of action by 24.10
- French naval batteries deployed to assist Montenegrin army with bombardment of Cattaro in mid September, operational 15.10
- Close blockade of Cattaro by French submarines
- **16.08** Austrian cruiser *Zenta* sunk off Antivari by the Anglo-French fleet
- Initial French supply route to Montenegro entered through Antivari
- Later supply route to Montenegro
- **21.12** *Jean Bart* torpedoed and damaged by *U12*
- Area patrolled by the French fleet during the autumn, with periodic sweeps along the coast
- French winter patrol line - 2 divisions of armoured cruisers and a destroyer flotilla

Vice-Admiral Augustin Boué de Lapeyrère
- 12 – 1st and 2nd Line Squadrons. The majority of the French battlefleet was assembled for the blockade and deployed in alternation from Malta
- 7 – 1st and 2nd Light Divisions
- 5 Destroyer Divisions

The British *Warrior* and *Defence* withdrawn early on and replaced by 2-4 based at Malta and placed at the disposition of the French commander

Locations: Bosnia, Montenegro, Dubrovnik, Cattaro, Mt. Lovcen, Antivari, San Giovanni de Medua, Durazzo, Albania, Adriatic Sea, Bari, Brindisi, Taranto, Italy

---

THE PRACTICALITES OF the Anglo-French division of wartime responsibilities in the Mediterranean were settled on 6 August. The French would take over the general direction of operations in the Mediterranean while the British kept their force of three battlecruisers and three armoured cruisers in the sea until the fate of the *Goeben* and *Breslau* had been sealed. In the event, their escape up the Dardanelles meant that the British ships had to be kept in the Mediterranean and in effect the sea became divided into French and British areas. As Italy remained neutral the Austrians constituted the largest naval threat to the allies and the French fleet would be responsible for securing the Adriatic exit and engaging with the Austrian fleet. The French fleet would be based at Malta.

France declared war on Austria-Hungary on 12 August and a day later Vice-Admiral Lapeyrère took the French fleet into the Adriatic. Although the French had a clear numerical superiority this could not easily be translated into success at sea. While the Austrian fleet was unable to leave the Adriatic it could not be forced into battle either. Its main base at Pola was out of reach and the idea of a naval attack on the base at Cattaro was also dismissed. The hope that the Austrians might come south receded quickly. Within days maintaining a large fleet in the lower Adriatic became a huge logistical challenge for the French and soon ships were rotated between the Adriatic and Malta for replenishment and repair. The torpedoing of *Jean Bart* demonstrated the vulnerability of a battlefleet used as a patrol force and by the end of the year a more distant blockade had been adopted.

The Siege of Tsingtao, October–November 1914

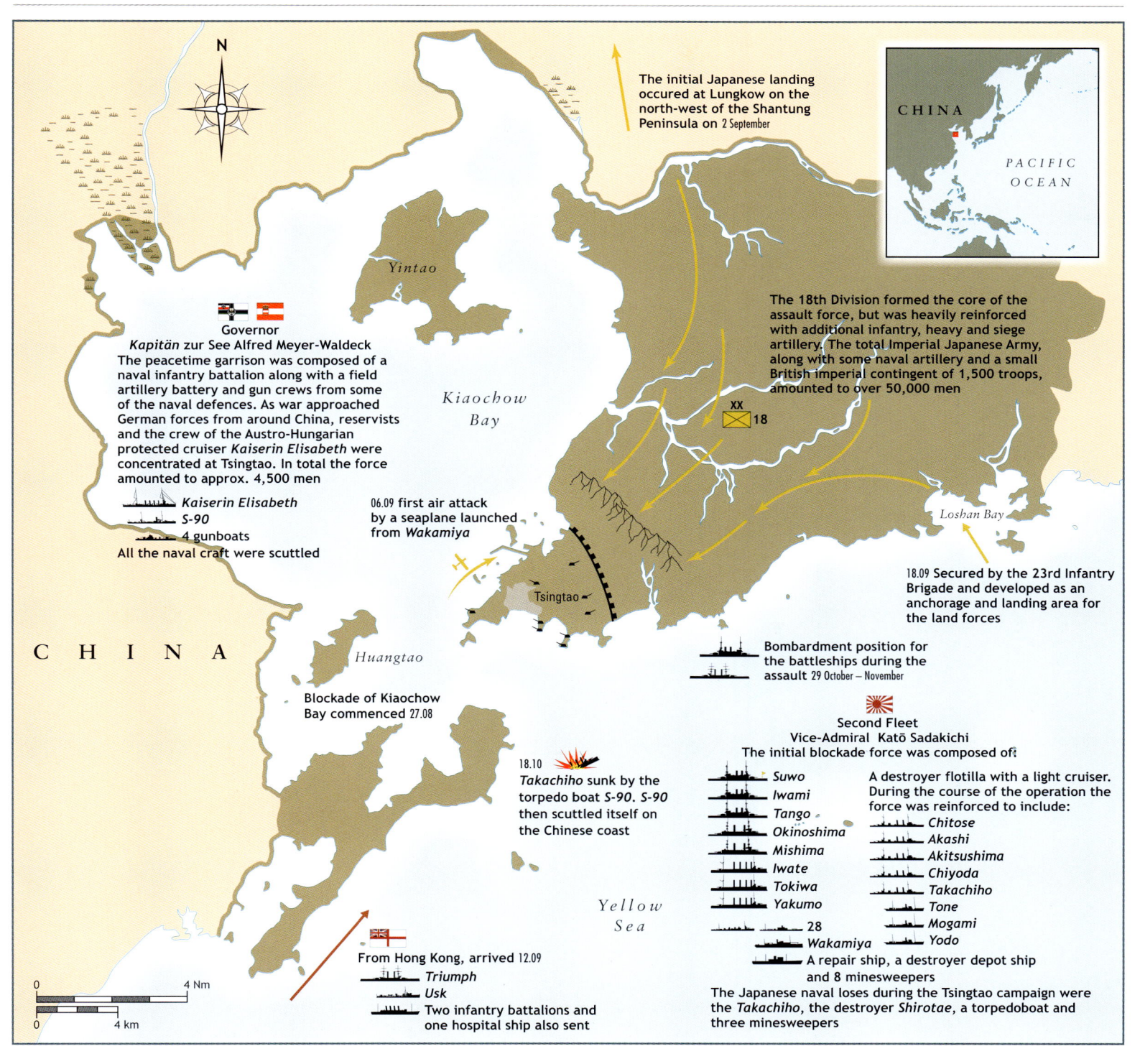

Map annotations

Governor — *Kapitän zur See* Alfred Meyer-Waldeck
The peacetime garrison was composed of a naval infantry battalion along with a field artillery battery and gun crews from some of the naval defences. As war approached German forces from around China, reservists and the crew of the Austro-Hungarian protected cruiser *Kaiserin Elisabeth* were concentrated at Tsingtao. In total the force amounted to approx. 4,500 men.

- *Kaiserin Elisabeth*
- *S-90*
- 4 gunboats

All the naval craft were scuttled.

The initial Japanese landing occured at Lungkow on the north-west of the Shantung Peninsula on 2 September.

06.09 first air attack by a seaplane launched from *Wakamiya*.

The 18th Division formed the core of the assault force, but was heavily reinforced with additional infantry, heavy and siege artillery. The total Imperial Japanese Army, along with some naval artillery and a small British imperial contingent of 1,500 troops, amounted to over 50,000 men.

18.09 Secured by the 23rd Infantry Brigade and developed as an anchorage and landing area for the land forces.

Bombardment position for the battleships during the assault 29 October – November.

Blockade of Kiaochow Bay commenced 27.08.

18.10 *Takachiho* sunk by the torpedo boat *S-90*. *S-90* then scuttled itself on the Chinese coast.

Second Fleet — Vice-Admiral Katō Sadakichi
The initial blockade force was composed of:
- *Suwo*
- *Iwami*
- *Tango*
- *Okinoshima*
- *Mishima*
- *Iwate*
- *Tokiwa*
- *Yakumo*
- 28
- *Wakamiya*

A destroyer flotilla with a light cruiser. During the course of the operation the force was reinforced to include:
- *Chitose*
- *Akashi*
- *Akitsushima*
- *Chiyoda*
- *Takachiho*
- *Tone*
- *Mogami*
- *Yodo*

A repair ship, a destroyer depot ship and 8 minesweepers.

The Japanese naval loses during the Tsingtao campaign were the *Takachiho*, the destroyer *Shirotae*, a torpedoboat and three minesweepers.

From Hong Kong, arrived 12.09:
- *Triumph*
- *Usk*
- Two infantry battalions and one hospital ship also sent.

Key
- Defensive line
- Heavy gun batteries, over 100mm

N.B. Approx. 30 battery positions with lighter guns ranging from 37–90mm. In total there were around 90 guns.

Holding on to the colony of Tsingtao, in view of the vastly superior British and Japanese forces in the Far East, was never a possibility for the Germans. All that *Kapitän zur See* Meyer-Waldeck, its governor, could do was to assist *Vizeadmiral* von Spee's operations in the Pacific. The remaining German forces in China were concentrated at Tsingtao and a torpedo boat and two gunboats still managed to reach the port. By redistributing the shipboard artillery two liners – *Prinz Eitel Friedrich* and a captured Russian liner renamed *Cormoran* – were fitted out as auxiliary cruisers. A number of merchant ships, carrying valuable coal, were sent out to join von Spee.

On 15 August the Japanese demanded a disarming or withdrawing of German naval vessels in the region and this was followed with a blockade on 27 August. It was conducted by the Second Fleet, composed of largely obsolete warships which were more than adequate to undertake the task and provide fire support for the army. In the event, Tsingtao held out longer than expected as neither were the Japanese in a rush to assault the defended port nor did the early autumn weather permit it. An assault was prepared throughout late September and October and Tsingtao fell in early November after a week long naval and land bombardment.

BATTLE OF CORONEL, 1 NOVEMBER 1914

ANTICIPATING THAT VIZEADMIRAL von Spee might be making for South America, the Admiralty instructed Rear-Admiral Cradock to assemble a squadron in the South Atlantic in mid-September. At the beginning of October intercepted German signals confirmed that that this was the German intention. Cradock's forces had been searching for the cruiser *Dresden*, now ordered by von Spee to meet him off Easter Island. By mid-October the German squadron, with all its support ships, had assembled and was heading for South America. Cradock meanwhile spent much of October around the Falklands awaiting the arrival of the pre-dreadnought *Canopus* sent out from the Channel Fleet as reinforcement. However, the old battleship was too slow to be of any value beyond protecting colliers.

On 22 October Cradock left the Falklands bound for Coronel after a radio intercept placed the *Leipzig* in the vicinity. He erroneously believed that von Spee was far out in the Pacific, but in fact all German communication was being routed through *Leipzig*. Shortly after rendezvousing with *Glasgow* on 1 November contact with the Germans was made and, expecting only the *Glasgow*, they were equally surprised to find a British squadron. The German ships soon closed the distance and their superior armament enabled them to open fire first in what became a one-sided engagement. The British lost 1,569 men and two armoured cruisers.

Battle of the Falklands, 8 December 1914

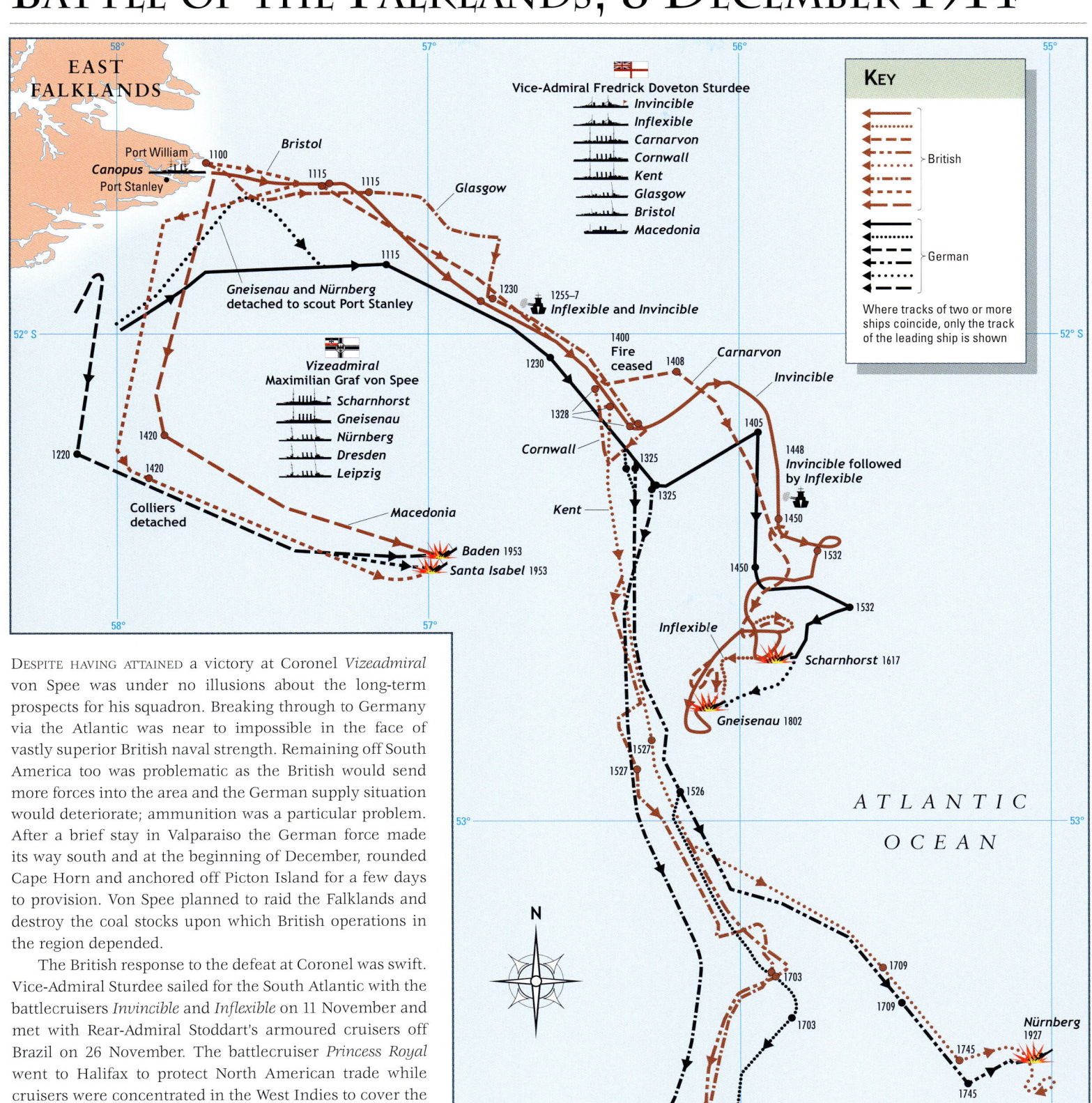

Despite having attained a victory at Coronel *Vizeadmiral* von Spee was under no illusions about the long-term prospects for his squadron. Breaking through to Germany via the Atlantic was near to impossible in the face of vastly superior British naval strength. Remaining off South America too was problematic as the British would send more forces into the area and the German supply situation would deteriorate; ammunition was a particular problem. After a brief stay in Valparaiso the German force made its way south and at the beginning of December, rounded Cape Horn and anchored off Picton Island for a few days to provision. Von Spee planned to raid the Falklands and destroy the coal stocks upon which British operations in the region depended.

The British response to the defeat at Coronel was swift. Vice-Admiral Sturdee sailed for the South Atlantic with the battlecruisers *Invincible* and *Inflexible* on 11 November and met with Rear-Admiral Stoddart's armoured cruisers off Brazil on 26 November. The battlecruiser *Princess Royal* went to Halifax to protect North American trade while cruisers were concentrated in the West Indies to cover the Panama Canal.

Sturdee arrived in the Falklands on 7 December and began coaling. Von Spee arrived the next day and sent two ships to land forces at Port Stanley. When the British battlecruisers were detected he immediately turned his squadron away. His intention was to sacrifice the armoured cruisers to enable the light cruisers to escape and continue commerce warfare. Although the British ships only left harbour singly, they were in far better trim and throughout the afternoon hunted down four German cruisers. Only the *Dresden* escaped and around 2,000 German sailors were killed, including von Spee and his two sons.

THE YARMOUTH RAID, 3 NOVEMBER 1914

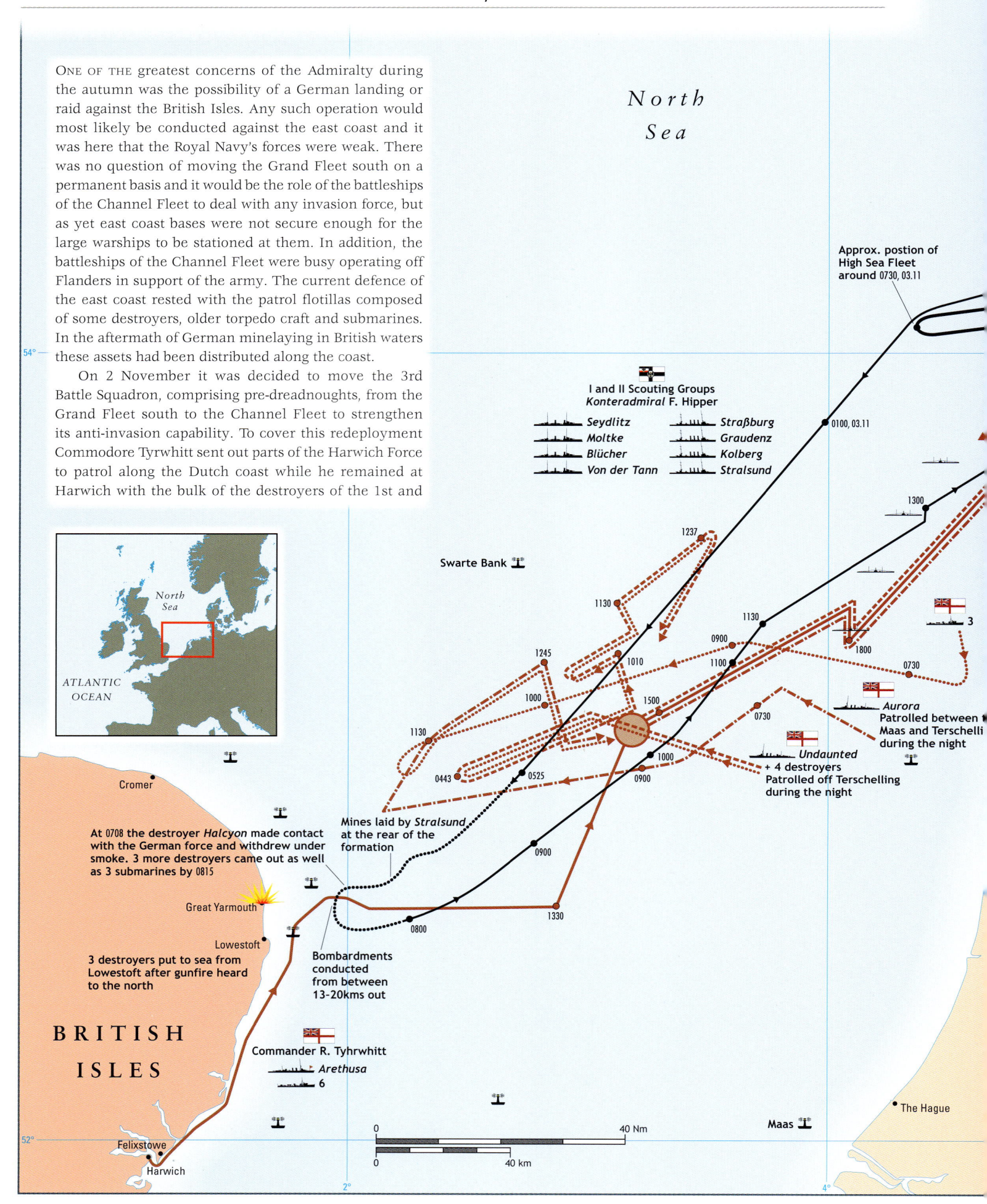

One of the greatest concerns of the Admiralty during the autumn was the possibility of a German landing or raid against the British Isles. Any such operation would most likely be conducted against the east coast and it was here that the Royal Navy's forces were weak. There was no question of moving the Grand Fleet south on a permanent basis and it would be the role of the battleships of the Channel Fleet to deal with any invasion force, but as yet east coast bases were not secure enough for the large warships to be stationed at them. In addition, the battleships of the Channel Fleet were busy operating off Flanders in support of the army. The current defence of the east coast rested with the patrol flotillas composed of some destroyers, older torpedo craft and submarines. In the aftermath of German minelaying in British waters these assets had been distributed along the coast.

On 2 November it was decided to move the 3rd Battle Squadron, comprising pre-dreadnoughts, from the Grand Fleet south to the Channel Fleet to strengthen its anti-invasion capability. To cover this redeployment Commodore Tyrwhitt sent out parts of the Harwich Force to patrol along the Dutch coast while he remained at Harwich with the bulk of the destroyers of the 1st and

THE GREAT WAR AT SEA 1914

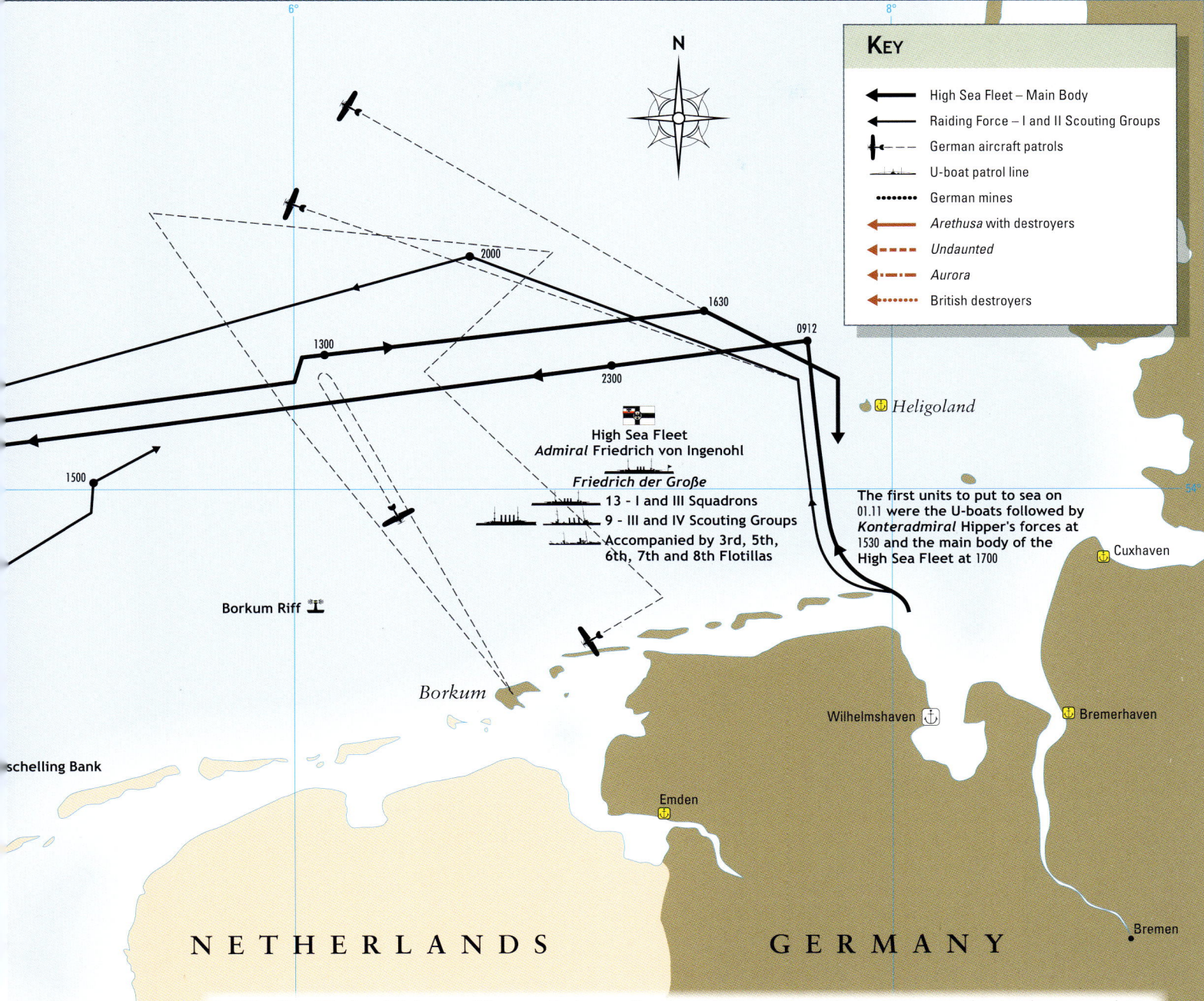

KEY
- High Sea Fleet – Main Body
- Raiding Force – I and II Scouting Groups
- German aircraft patrols
- U-boat patrol line
- German mines
- *Arethusa* with destroyers
- *Undaunted*
- *Aurora*
- British destroyers

High Sea Fleet
Admiral Friedrich von Ingenohl
Friedrich der Große
13 – I and III Squadrons
9 – III and IV Scouting Groups
Accompanied by 3rd, 5th, 6th, 7th and 8th Flotillas

The first units to put to sea on 01.11 were the U-boats followed by *Konteradmiral* Hipper's forces at 1530 and the main body of the High Sea Fleet at 1700

Heligoland
Cuxhaven
Borkum Riff
Borkum
Wilhelmshaven
Bremerhaven
Emden
Bremen
schelling Bank

NETHERLANDS   **GERMANY**

3rd Flotillas. The local defence of the coast between Great Yarmouth and Harwich rested with the 7th Flotilla spread between those ports. A major reorganisation of naval forces in the area was due later in November as more destroyers and auxiliary craft were brought into service.

The night of 2–3 November would witness the first major German operation against the English coast. However, counter to the British fear, the bombardment was not a precursor to an invasion attempt but rather part of a minelaying operation. As minelaying in the Firth of Forth area had been abandoned in mid-October, *Admiral* von Ingenohl planned to strike coastal shipping off the Norfolk and Suffolk coasts. Rather than relying on surprise and single minelayers, a force of battlecruisers and cruisers would be employed, covered from a distance by the remainder of the High Sea Fleet.

The operation unfolded as planned and *Konteradmiral* Hipper's forces reached British waters undetected and took the local defences by surprise, although the minefield was laid somewhat further out than envisaged. After a brief bombardment of Great Yarmouth the Germans withdrew, the principal objective having been to achieve a moral victory.

News of the attack reached Tyrwhitt at Harwich immediately and while the forces in port raised steam he ordered *Undaunted* and *Aurora* to attempt to cut off the withdrawing Germans. It took some time for accurate reports to reach the Admiralty and by the time Rear Admiral Beatty's battlecruisers at Rosyth had raised steam the Germans were well out of range. Around 10am *Undaunted* briefly made contact with Hipper's force, but in view of their superiority Tyrwhitt chose to concentrate his forces into a more powerful unit. By the time this had been achieved, at around 3pm, the High Sea Fleet was half way home.

The raid demonstrated that the Germans held the initiative when it came to such attacks, but the operation was not a resounding success as on 4 November the armoured cruiser *Yorck* ran into a German minefield off Wilhelmshaven and sank with the loss of over 300 men. The British also lost a submarine to a mine when it attempted to attack Hipper's force off Yarmouth.

Bombardment of the Dardanelles Forts, 3 November 1914

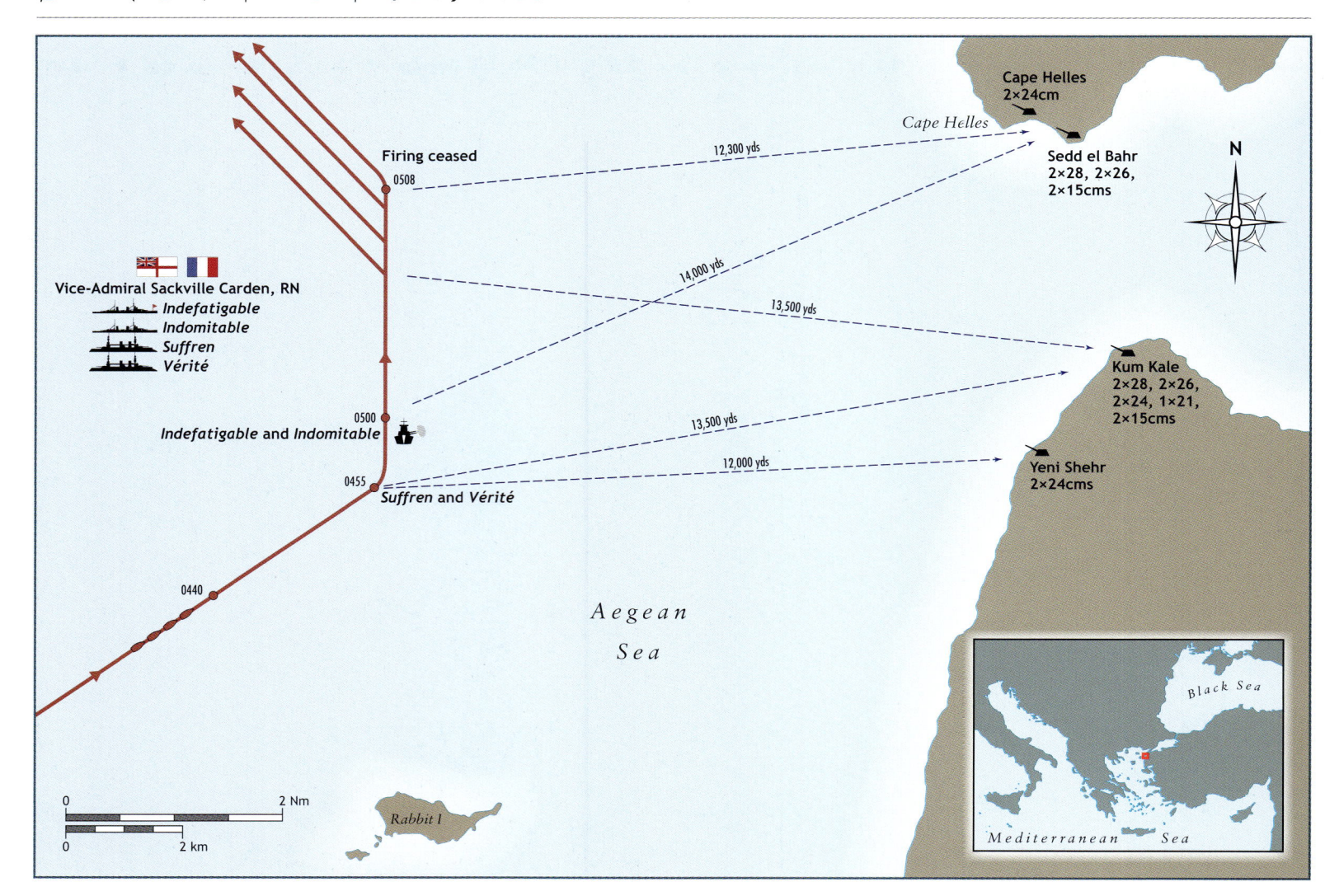

After the *Goeben* and *Breslau* passed through the Dardanelles, the British assembled a sizeable naval force in the Aegean and the Admiralty ordered that the two ships be considered hostile regardless of which flag they flew. The Turks began to mine the Straits in August, and at the end of September largely closed them to maritime traffic. While the German ships had been sold to the Turks, and their crews now served in the Turkish navy, it was not until mid-October that the Ottoman government entered the war on the side of the Central Powers. On 29 October the Turkish navy bombarded Russian Black Sea ports without a formal declaration of war. This made hostilities between Britain and France and the Ottoman Empire inevitable.

On 1 November two British destroyers searched the Gulf of Smyrna and sank a Turkish vessel, and the next day the Admiralty ordered Vice-Admiral Carden, in charge of British naval forces in the Eastern Mediterranean, to conduct a bombardment of the forts at the entrance of the Dardanelles. The main objective of the operation was to ascertain the effective range of the guns of the forts in addition to any potential moral value such a demonstration might have on the Turks. Scheduled for dawn of 3 November the bombardment force comprised two British and two French ships. They would close to within 12–14,000 yards and fire four salvos from each primary turret before turning away.

The operation itself was conducted as planned, although smoke quickly obscured the target areas. A large explosion over the Sedd el Bahr was seen five minutes into the bombardment. After a few minutes the Turkish guns returned fire, but by then the ships had turned away. Considering that during peacetime there was no practice of shore bombardment, that the duration of fire was short, and that light conditions were poor and there was no means of observing the shoot, the outcome was a success; some days later a merchant ship coming out of the Dardanelles reported that Sedd el Bahr fort lay in ruins. On the Asiatic side the damage was far less extensive.

The allied force patrolling the entrance to the Dardanelles and the Gulf of Smyrna was progressively strengthened throughout the winter, with the French more than doubling the number of their ships. The Turks too improved and reinforced the defences in the Dardanelles, but they only made a single naval sortie as far west as the entrance. On 5 November four small boats retired back up the straits after an engagement with British destroyers. On 12 December the British submarine *B11* entered the Dardanelles and sank the old Turkish battleship *Mesudiye* off Chanak the next day.

The Great War at Sea 1914

The Voyage of SMS Emden, September–November 1914

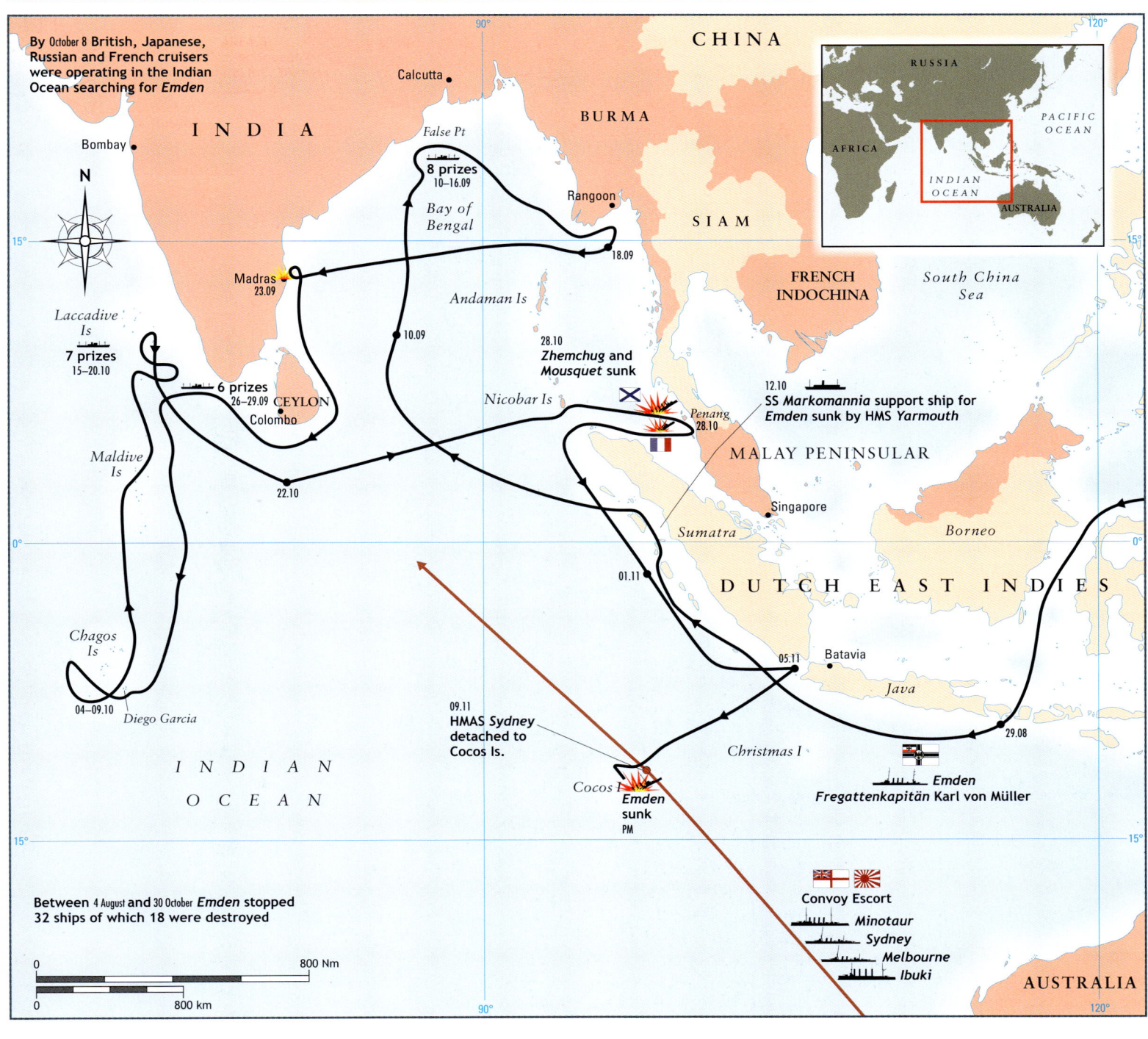

In mid-August, *Emden* left Admiral von Spee's squadron and headed for the Indian Ocean to raid the shipping routes. As his first area of operations *Fregattenkapitän* Müller chose the Bay of Bengal and there, on the route to Calcutta, *Emden* achieved her first successes in mid-September. The British were taken completely by surprise at the presence of a German raider, believing that *Emden* was with von Spee. Having received information that allied warships were off Burma and Malaya, Müller headed west and decided to attack the port of Madras. The bombardment, late on 22 September, prompted the British to stop all shipping in the Bay and the short-term economic impact of *Emden*'s voyage was considerable. Admiral Jerram, the British commander, split his forces between searching for *Emden* on key trade routes, and patrolling areas useful for coaling; in the vastness of the Indian Ocean the Allies were always a step behind.

In order to keep *Emden* replenished Müller relied on a network of captured and neutral steamers. In October she spent a week at Diego Garcia to rest and undertake maintenance. After some success to the west of India Müller again headed for Malaya and in a raid on Penang sank two allied warships. This latest surprise caused the British concern for the safety of the large imperial troop convoy about to cross the ocean from Australia to Egypt and Europe. *Emden* was sunk by one of the convoy's escorts, the cruiser *Sydney*, after the British coaling station in the Cocos Islands sent out a distress signal that it was under attack by the German raider.

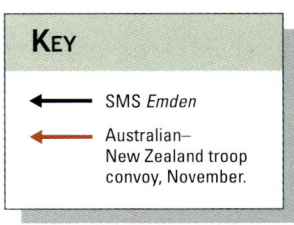

Key

→ SMS *Emden*

→ Australian–New Zealand troop convoy, November.

THE BLACK SEA THEATRE, 1914–15

MAJOR OPERATIONS AND EVENTS

The new battleship *Imperatritsa Mariya* entered service in late summer followed by the *Imperatritsa Ekaterina Velikaya* in December. Each together with cruisers formed a division with the older pre-dreadnoughts making up the third division of the fleet

29.10.14 — Odessa

Mecidiye mined in raid on Odessa, 03.04.15

03.04.15 Raid on Russian shipping routes by *Goeben* and *Breslau*, encountered Russian battlefleet. Fire exchanged, but Russians could not pursue owing to slower speed

25.12 Skirmish between *Breslau* and torpedo boats along with the Russian battlefleet. Another similar encounter occurred 06.01.14

Battle Cape S 18.11.14

First patrol by a German Uboat, *UB7* occurred 05–07.07.15. Followed by *UB8* and then *UB14* and *UC13*

ROMANIA

BULGARIA
Bulgaria concluded treaties with each of the Central Powers on 6 September and declared war on Serbia on 14 October

28.03.15 Major Russian demonstration and minelaying operation off the Bosporus - force then split into smaller groups to attack Anatolian coast.
25.04 A similar operation and bombardment of the coastal defences to coincide with allied landings at Gallipoli

06.11.14 Bombardment by Russian battle fleet
23–24.12 Attempted Russian raid to sink blockships in Zonguldak harbour thwarted by weather conditions and contact with *Breslau*.
07.03.15 Russian battlefleet shell coal facilities at Eregli and Zonguldak. The frequency of attacks on this part of the coastline increased to around two a month in the late spring

5.11.14 First Russian minelaying operation covered by battlefleet

For details of Russian minelaying in the Bosporus approaches see pp.88-89

Vice-Admiral Wilhelm Souchon Commander of the Ottoman Fleet
- *Goeben* - *Yavuz Sultan Selim* in Turkish service
- *Breslau* - *Midilli* in Turkish service
- *Barbaros Hayreddin*
- *Turgut Reis*
- *Mesudiye*
- *Hamidiye*
- *Mecidiye*
- 8

29.11.15 *UC13* ran aground off Kefken Island. Two Turkish gunboats sunk by Russian destroyers when trying to salvage the wreck on 10.12

THE GREAT WAR AT SEA 1914

In the years leading up the war the Russians possessed the dominant navy in the Black Sea. Although that theatre played second fiddle to the Baltic, and the Black Sea Fleet received far fewer resources than its Baltic counterpart, Turkish naval strength was markedly inferior in qualitative and quantitative terms. However, given the old age of their existing battleships, the Russians did not feel confident enough to mount any sustained naval campaign against the Ottoman Empire, particularly if it was in alliance with another power. When the Turkish navy ordered two modern battleships from British shipyards in 1911 the Russians ordered four for service in the Black Sea, but the first would not be ready for service until 1915. Thus the arrival of the German *Goeben* and *Breslau* at Constantinople in August had profound short- and medium-term implications for the situation in the Black Sea.

Under the guise of being purchased by the Turks, the German warships were incorporated into the Turkish navy; *Konteradmiral* Souchon became its commander and German officers took other key posts. Throughout the autumn the Turkish Minister of War, Enver Pasha, steered the empire towards the Central Powers and on 22 October instructed Souchon to attack the Russian fleet if encountered at sea. Souchon chose instead to launch a surprise attack on key Russian ports thus bringing about war.

With *Goeben* the single most powerful warship in the theatre, the Russians acted cautiously and in the first year tended to deploy the battlefleet as a single unit. Souchon could raid Russian targets at will, but he too needed to be cautious as there was no way of repairing any major damage to his ships and no possibility of receiving more. At the only significant engagement off Cape Sarych he used his superior speed to withdraw after sustaining a hit. From the outset *Goeben* and *Breslau* were used to cover the shipment of supplies for the Caucasus front and as the Russian army's advance continued in 1915 this only became more important. By mid-1915 newly commissioned Russian warships were shifting the balance in Russia's favour as its forces grew while Turkish ones declined. Turkish coastal trade suffered increasingly from attacks, while the arrival of a small number of U-boats did not have a significant impact on Russian traffic, although the threat did lead the Russians to expend resources in protecting their shipping routes.

Periodic sweeps of the Anatolian coastline by the Russian battlefleet. Skirmishes between it and *Breslau* and *Hamidiye* occurred 27.1.14. In 1915 the Russians increased the frequency of the raids and tended to rely on cruisers and newly commissioned large destroyers. By the autumn of 1915 only *Goeben* could deal with Russian incursions and she increasingly was used to convoy troop movements and coal shipments

07.11 First Russian bombardment, repeated throughout the war

November 14 Ottoman counteroffensive

Area occupied by Russia 1914–15

Main supply route for the Caucasus Front, shipping often escort by cruisers and destroyers as part of sorties to bombard or lay mines along the Russian coast

The German Raids on Scarborough, Hartlepool and Whitby, 16 December 1914

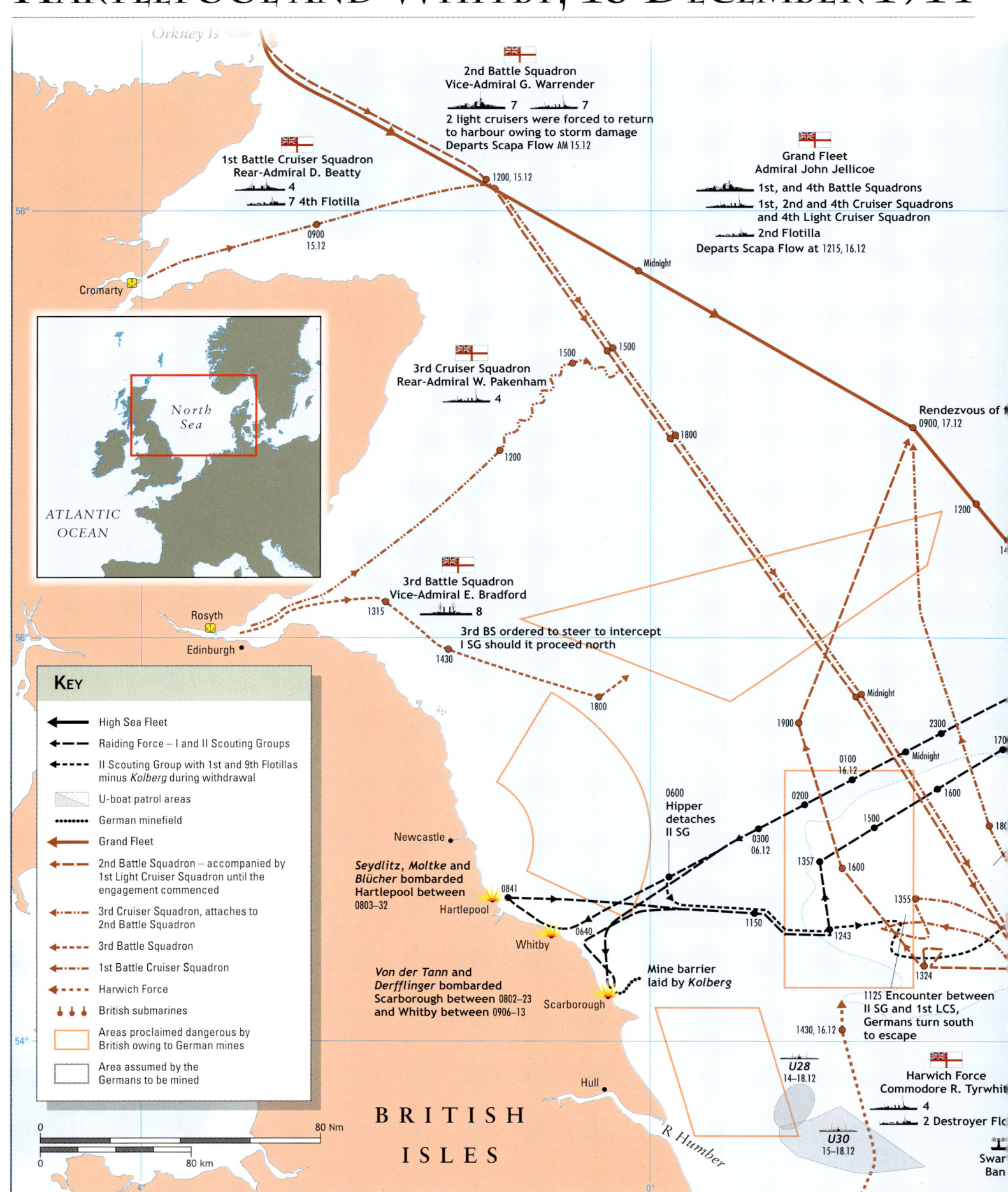

The Great War at Sea 1914

Encouraged by the Yarmouth raid, *Admiral* von Ingenohl was bent upon another bombardment of the English coastline as soon as possible. Despite some German success during the autumn, the British dominance of the North Sea seemed unbroken and morale was ebbing in the German fleet. The temporary detachment of two British battlecruisers to the South Atlantic also narrowed the margin of strength between main British and German fleets. The plan was for the I Scouting Group battlecruisers to bombard Hartlepool and Scarborough while a light cruiser from II Scouting Group laid a mine barrier. It was hoped that any British forces coming south to intercept the Germans would run over the newly laid mines and sustain losses. To support *Konteradmiral* Hipper's force, Ingenohl planned to take the High Sea Fleet out and as far west as Dogger Bank, contrary to the Kaiser's order that risky actions should be avoided.

The implementation of the plan was delayed from late November until mid-December as the battlecruiser *Von der Tann* needed repair and poor weather delayed preliminary U-boat reconnaissance. Early on 15 December the operation commenced, but the British were forewarned and for the first time in the war signals intelligence collected by Room 40 indicated an imminent German sortie. The radio traffic concerned movements of the Scouting Groups and so Admiral Jellicoe ordered the deployment of a force consisting of a battle squadron, the remaining battlecruisers and two cruiser squadrons to be waiting west of Dogger Bank. To prevent a rerun of the Yarmouth raid the Harwich Force would also be at sea.

Poor conditions on 16 December affected both sides and during the course of the day each, unbeknownst at the time, had the opportunity to corner a smaller force of the other. Early in the morning British destroyers made contact with the High Sea Fleet's screen and intermittent skirmishing took place but neither side knew which forces they were opposing. Ingenohl chose to withdraw and having been informed that contact had been made Hipper sent back his light forces in support. Around 7.30am Rear-Admiral Beatty started to search for a German armoured cruiser that had been spotted and soon the whole British force turned east.

From 8.41am onwards reports that German battlecruisers had attacked Scarborough reached Beatty and Vice-Admiral Warrender. This completely altered the tactical situation and prompted both to turn back for the coast although Warrender was well aware his forces might have to enter a designated danger zone. Hipper's attack only encountered minor resistance and as a result of the encounter between II Scouting Group and the British forces he turned north and escaped. By noon further German signals indicated that the fleet was at sea and this prompted Admiral Jellicoe to bring out the Grand Fleet while the Harwich Force was moved north. During the early afternoon Beatty turned south in an attempt to intercept Hipper, but as the latter had chosen a northerly retreat this proved futile and was abandoned. Harwich Force submarines were sent into the Heligoland Bight but also to no avail.

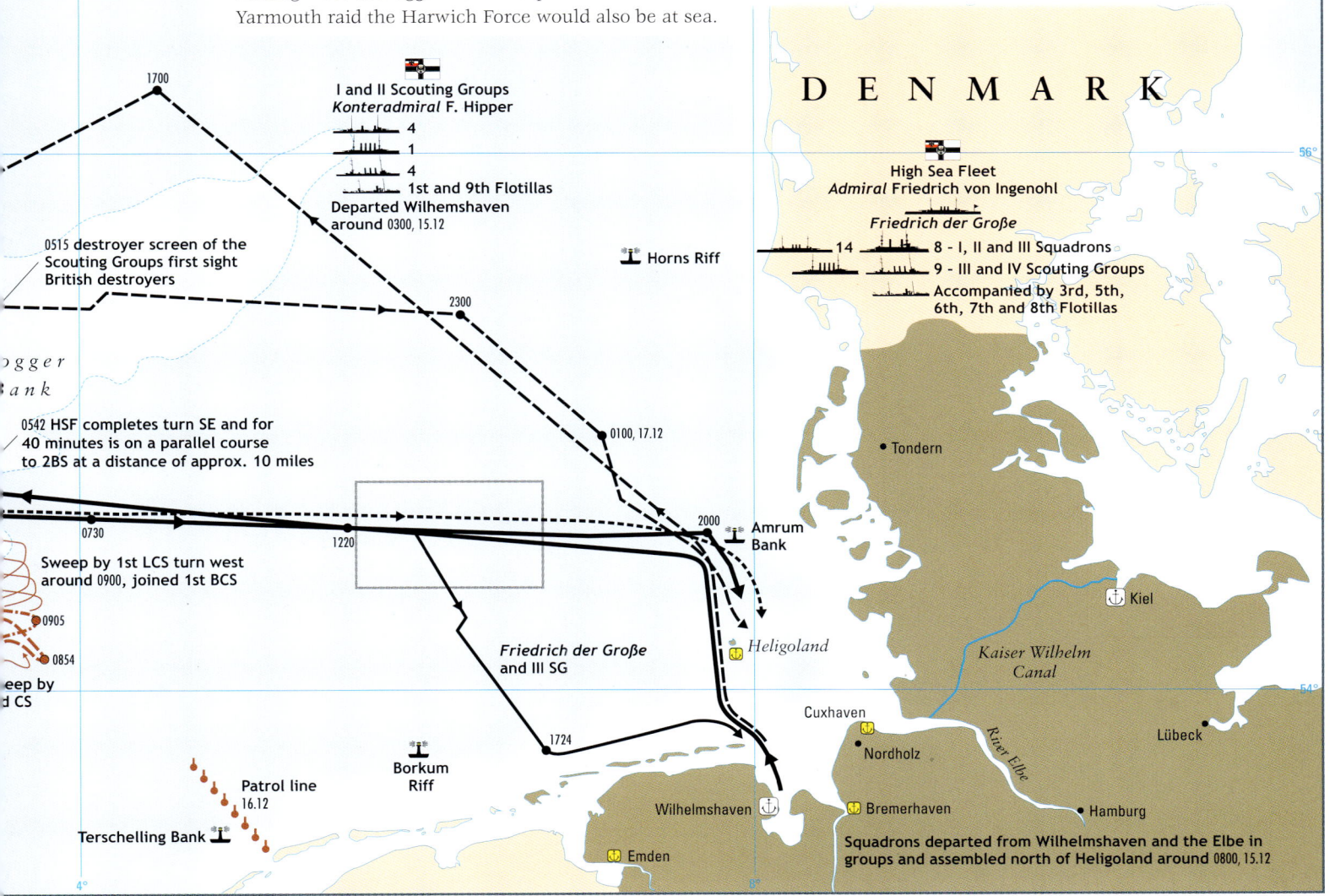

The Cuxhaven Raid, 25 December 1914

THE GREAT WAR AT SEA 1914

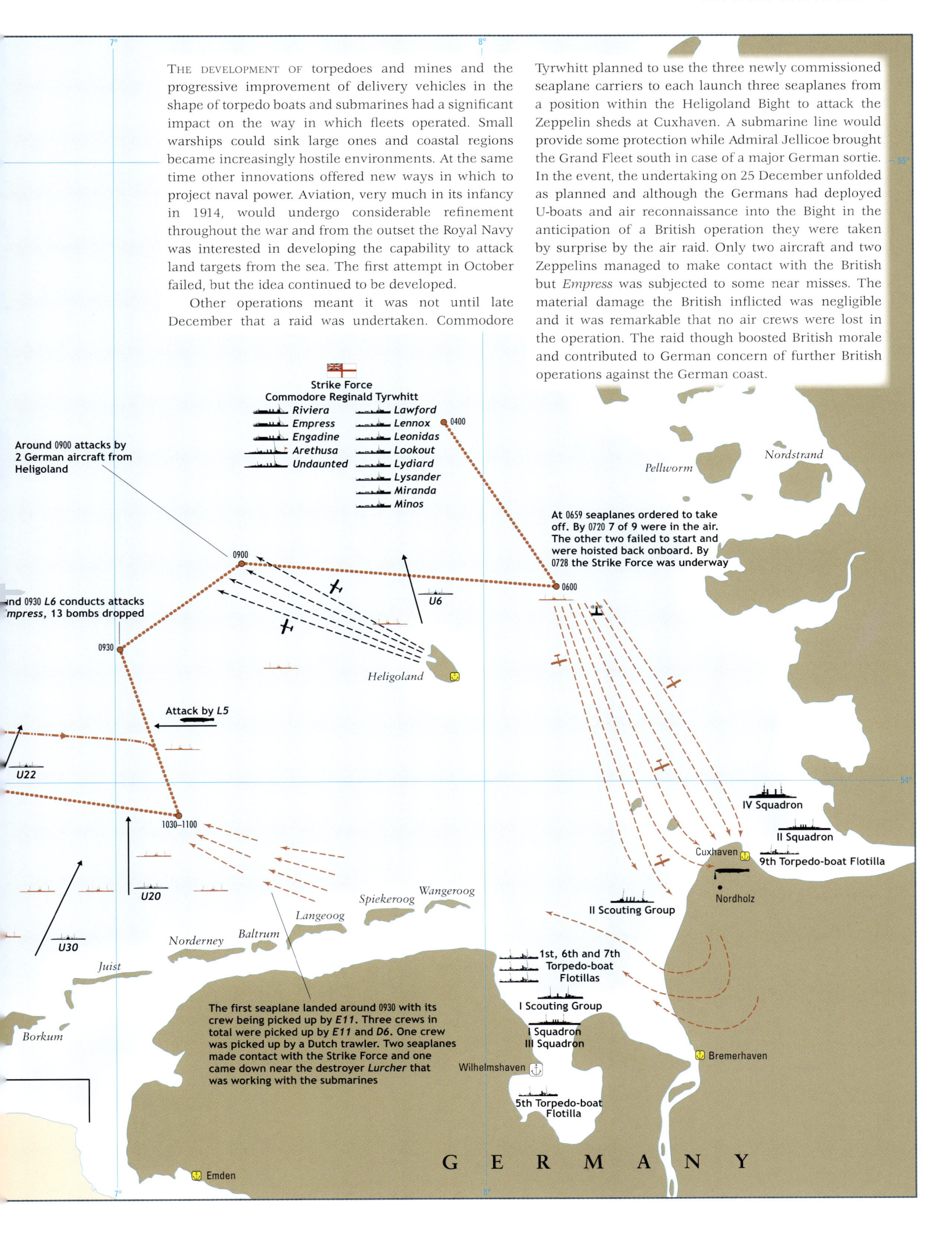

The development of torpedoes and mines and the progressive improvement of delivery vehicles in the shape of torpedo boats and submarines had a significant impact on the way in which fleets operated. Small warships could sink large ones and coastal regions became increasingly hostile environments. At the same time other innovations offered new ways in which to project naval power. Aviation, very much in its infancy in 1914, would undergo considerable refinement throughout the war and from the outset the Royal Navy was interested in developing the capability to attack land targets from the sea. The first attempt in October failed, but the idea continued to be developed.

Other operations meant it was not until late December that a raid was undertaken. Commodore Tyrwhitt planned to use the three newly commissioned seaplane carriers to each launch three seaplanes from a position within the Heligoland Bight to attack the Zeppelin sheds at Cuxhaven. A submarine line would provide some protection while Admiral Jellicoe brought the Grand Fleet south in case of a major German sortie. In the event, the undertaking on 25 December unfolded as planned and although the Germans had deployed U-boats and air reconnaissance into the Bight in the anticipation of a British operation they were taken by surprise by the air raid. Only two aircraft and two Zeppelins managed to make contact with the British but *Empress* was subjected to some near misses. The material damage the British inflicted was negligible and it was remarkable that no air crews were lost in the operation. The raid though boosted British morale and contributed to German concern of further British operations against the German coast.

Strike Force
Commodore Reginald Tyrwhitt
- Riviera
- Empress
- Engadine
- Arethusa
- Undaunted
- Lawford
- Lennox
- Leonidas
- Lookout
- Lydiard
- Lysander
- Miranda
- Minos

Around 0900 attacks by 2 German aircraft from Heligoland

[an]d 0930 *L6* conducts attacks [E]mpress, 13 bombs dropped

At 0659 seaplanes ordered to take off. By 0720 7 of 9 were in the air. The other two failed to start and were hoisted back onboard. By 0728 the Strike Force was underway

Attack by *L5*

The first seaplane landed around 0930 with its crew being picked up by *E11*. Three crews in total were picked up by *E11* and *D6*. One crew was picked up by a Dutch trawler. Two seaplanes made contact with the Strike Force and one came down near the destroyer *Lurcher* that was working with the submarines

IV Squadron
II Squadron
9th Torpedo-boat Flotilla
Cuxhaven
Nordholz
II Scouting Group
1st, 6th and 7th Torpedo-boat Flotillas
I Scouting Group
I Squadron
III Squadron
Wilhelmshaven
Bremerhaven
5th Torpedo-boat Flotilla

Nordstrand
Pellworm
Heligoland
Wangeroog
Spiekeroog
Langeoog
Baltrum
Norderney
Juist
Borkum
Emden

GERMANY

Naval Operations 1915

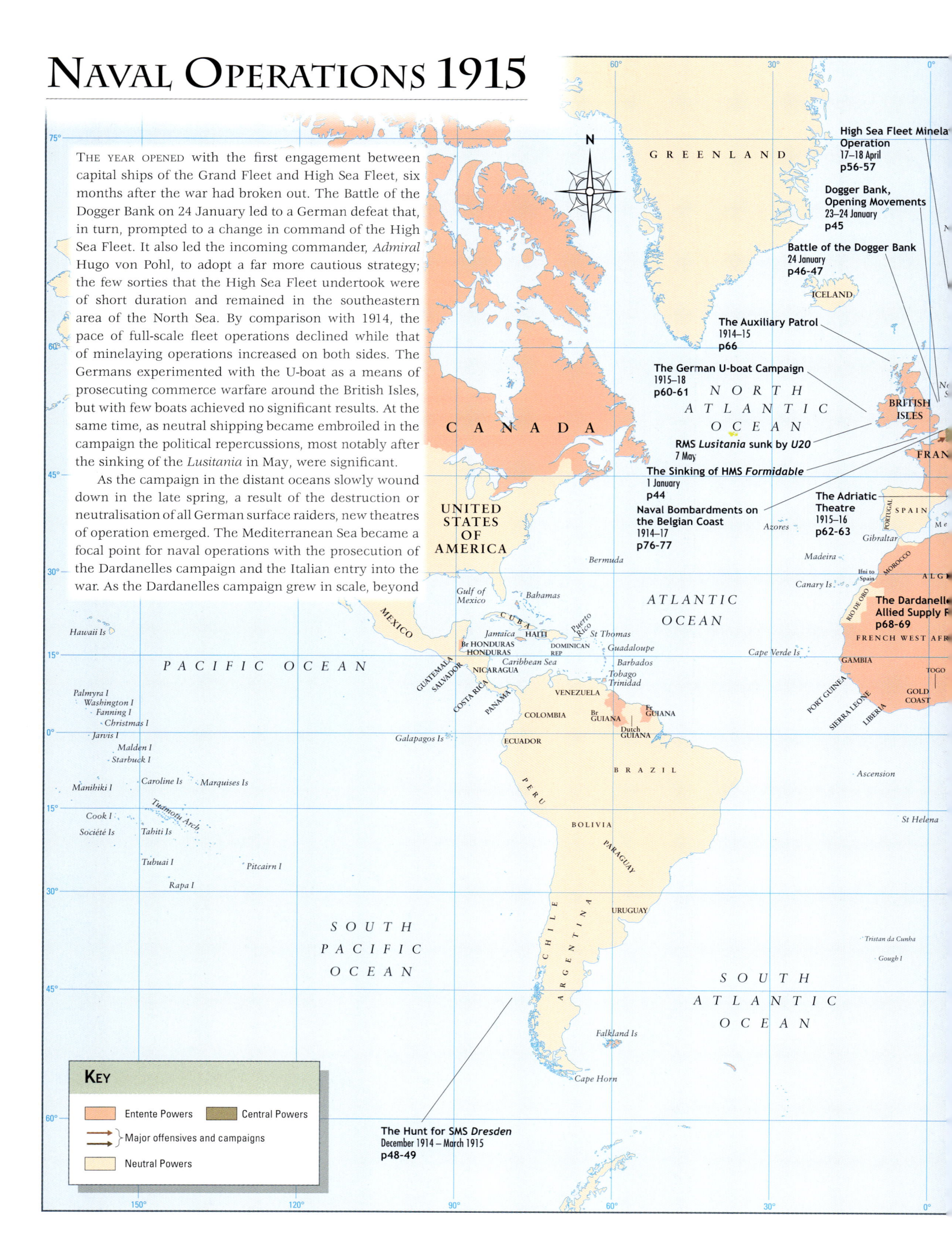

The year opened with the first engagement between capital ships of the Grand Fleet and High Sea Fleet, six months after the war had broken out. The Battle of the Dogger Bank on 24 January led to a German defeat that, in turn, prompted to a change in command of the High Sea Fleet. It also led the incoming commander, *Admiral* Hugo von Pohl, to adopt a far more cautious strategy; the few sorties that the High Sea Fleet undertook were of short duration and remained in the southeastern area of the North Sea. By comparison with 1914, the pace of full-scale fleet operations declined while that of minelaying operations increased on both sides. The Germans experimented with the U-boat as a means of prosecuting commerce warfare around the British Isles, but with few boats achieved no significant results. At the same time, as neutral shipping became embroiled in the campaign the political repercussions, most notably after the sinking of the *Lusitania* in May, were significant.

As the campaign in the distant oceans slowly wound down in the late spring, a result of the destruction or neutralisation of all German surface raiders, new theatres of operation emerged. The Mediterranean Sea became a focal point for naval operations with the prosecution of the Dardanelles campaign and the Italian entry into the war. As the Dardanelles campaign grew in scale, beyond

High Sea Fleet Minela Operation
17–18 April
p56-57

Dogger Bank, Opening Movements
23–24 January
p45

Battle of the Dogger Bank
24 January
p46-47

The Auxiliary Patrol
1914–15
p66

The German U-boat Campaign
1915–18
p60-61

RMS *Lusitania* sunk by *U20*
7 May

The Sinking of HMS *Formidable*
1 January
p44

Naval Bombardments on the Belgian Coast
1914–17
p76-77

The Adriatic Theatre
1915–16
p62-63

The Dardanelle Allied Supply
p68-69

The Hunt for SMS *Dresden*
December 1914 – March 1915
p48-49

Key
- Entente Powers
- Central Powers
- Major offensives and campaigns
- Neutral Powers

THE GREAT WAR AT SEA 1915

anything envisioned at its inception, ever increasing numbers of merchant ships and warships of all types were sent to the Aegean to support allied forces. The Germans saw an opportunity and dispatched U-boats to attack allied supply lines and provide some relief to their Turkish allies. In the Adriatic Italian and Austro-Hungarian forces became involved in a campaign that very much mirrored the experience in the North Sea, albeit on a smaller scale.

The Baltic Sea witnessed some of the most intense naval activity throughout the war following the German offensive into the Russian Baltic provinces. The Germans attempted to use their naval superiority to assist with land operations in and around the Gulf of Riga throughout the summer but the Russians adopted very strong defensive positions and little headway was made. The introduction of a small number of British submarines into the Baltic to attack German warships and the iron ore shipments from Sweden ensured that the Germans failed to acquire uncontested control of the Baltic Sea itself. In the Black Sea the Russian and Ottoman-German forces conducted raids and minelaying operations against each other's coastlines as well as supporting military forces ashore, principally on the Caucasus front.

The German Sweep of the Skagerrak
18 December

The Voyage of SMS Meteor
May–June
p67

Battle of the Åland Islands
2 July
p70

Gulf of Riga Operations
August
p74

The Loss of SMS Meteor
6–9 August
p72–73

British Submarine Operations in the Baltic
p80

The Amrum Bank Minefield Operation
10–12 September
p78–79

The Dardanelles Campaign, Overview
p51

The Dardanelles Bombardments
February
p52–53

The Dardanelles: The Attack on the Narrows
18 March
p54–55

The Dardanelles: Landing Operations
p58–59

Naval Losses in the Dardanelles
p81

The Mesopotamian Campaign
1914–16
p.82

The Red Sea Theatre
1914–15
p50

Destruction of SMS Königsberg
July
p71

Action off Durazzo

Strategic Communications
p64–65

The Sinking of HMS Formidable, 1 January 1915

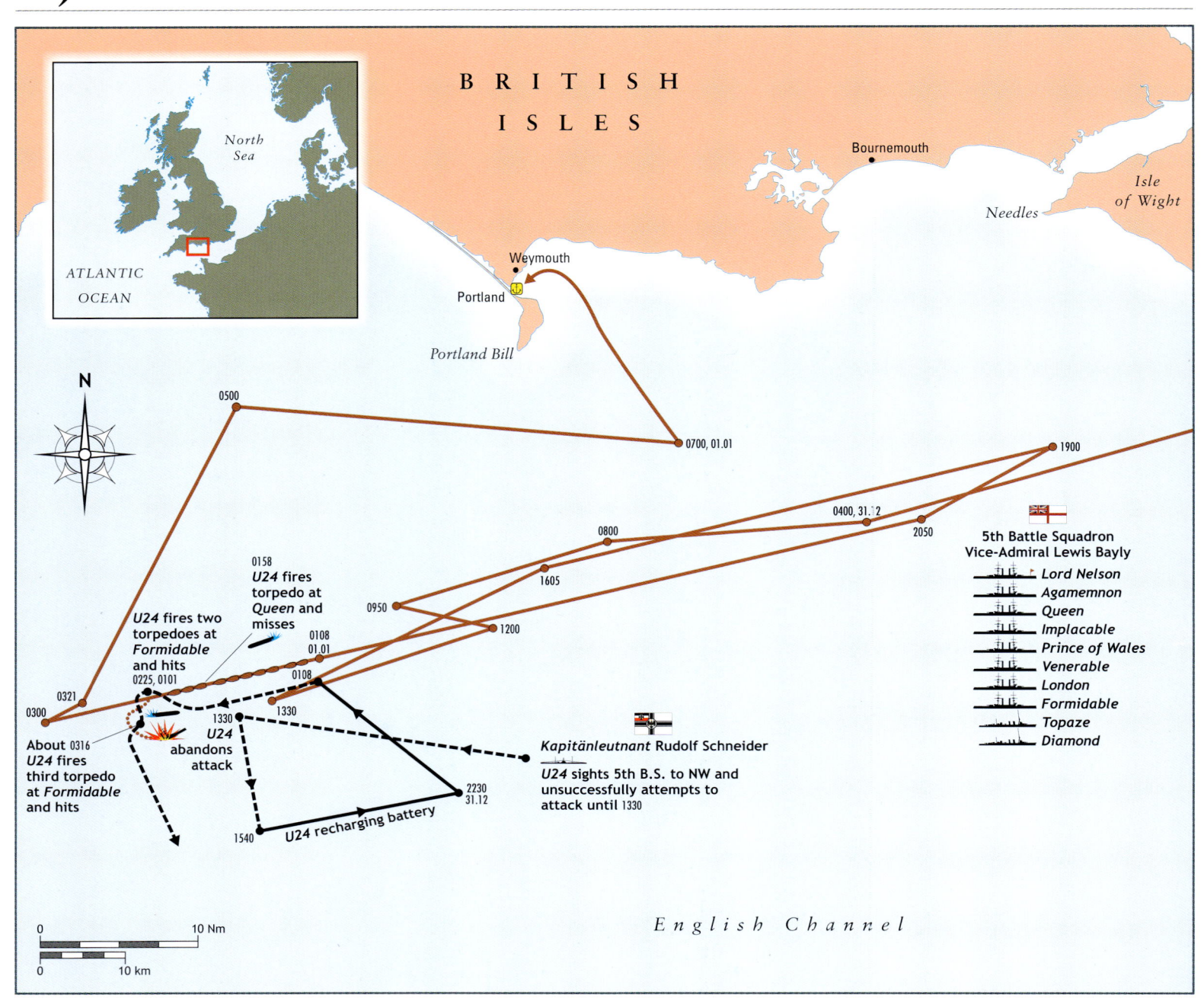

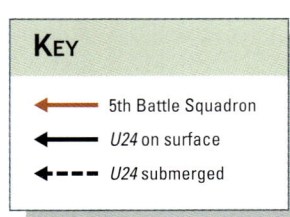

Although the threat of U-boats changed the way in which the Royal Navy operated in the autumn and winter of 1914, thus far no battleship had been sunk by a submarine. In December the 6th Battle Squadron was sent south to reinforce the Channel Fleet in the aftermath of the German attacks on the British Isles and to support the BEF (British Expeditionary Force) on the Belgian coast. Vice-Admiral Bayly was appointed to take command of this sizeable force, comprising fifteen pre-dreadnoughts based at Sheerness. As the Thames estuary was unsuited for gunnery practice ships normally exercised off the south coast. This development coincided with an increase in U-boat activity in the Channel and minelaying in response to British operations along the Flanders coast.

On 30 December Bayly took the 5th Battle Squadron around to the south coast accompanied by six Harwich Force destroyers as far as Folkstone. During the day the squadron exercised off Portland and as there was no sign of U-boat activity Bayly remained at sea. *U24* had left the Ems on 22 December for Zeebrugge, and after a brief stopover set out to operate off Plymouth. Around mid-morning on 31 December *Kapitänleutnant* Schneider spotted smoke, dived and attempted to close with the squadron. Because this had turned east in the afternoon he gave up and surfaced to recharge *U24*'s batteries. At 10.30pm he turned westward and shortly after midnight spotted the battleships. Undetected, *U24* closed in, missed one attack on *Queen*, but conducted two on *Formidable*. The attack took the British by surprise, and in the ensuing confusion the battleships were ordered to Weymouth while the cruisers picked up survivors. *Formidable* sank at 0439 and *U24* escaped. Following the incident Bayly was relieved of his command.

The Great War at Sea 1915

Dogger Bank, Opening Movements 23–24 January 1915

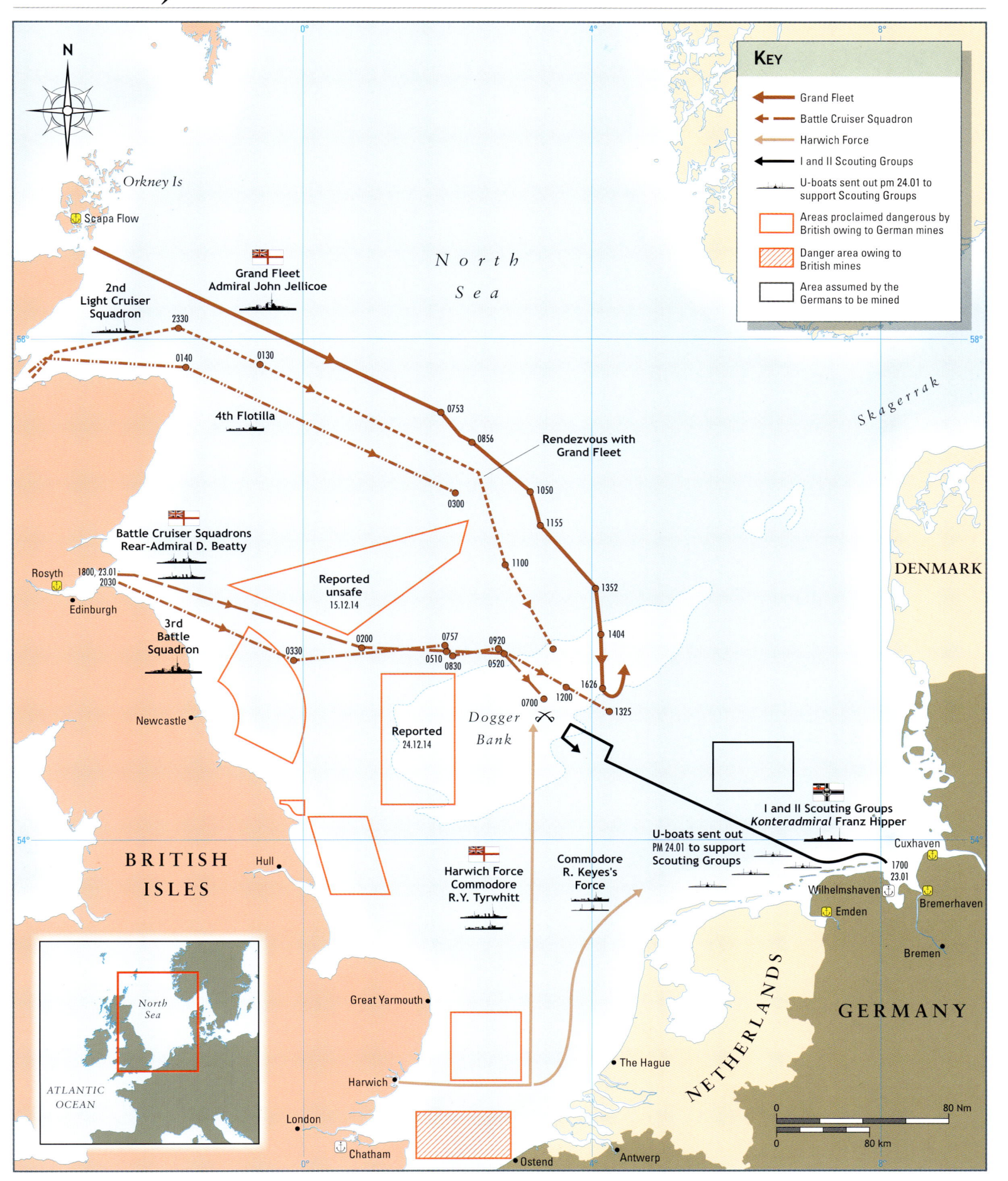

Battle of the Dogger Bank, 24 January 1915

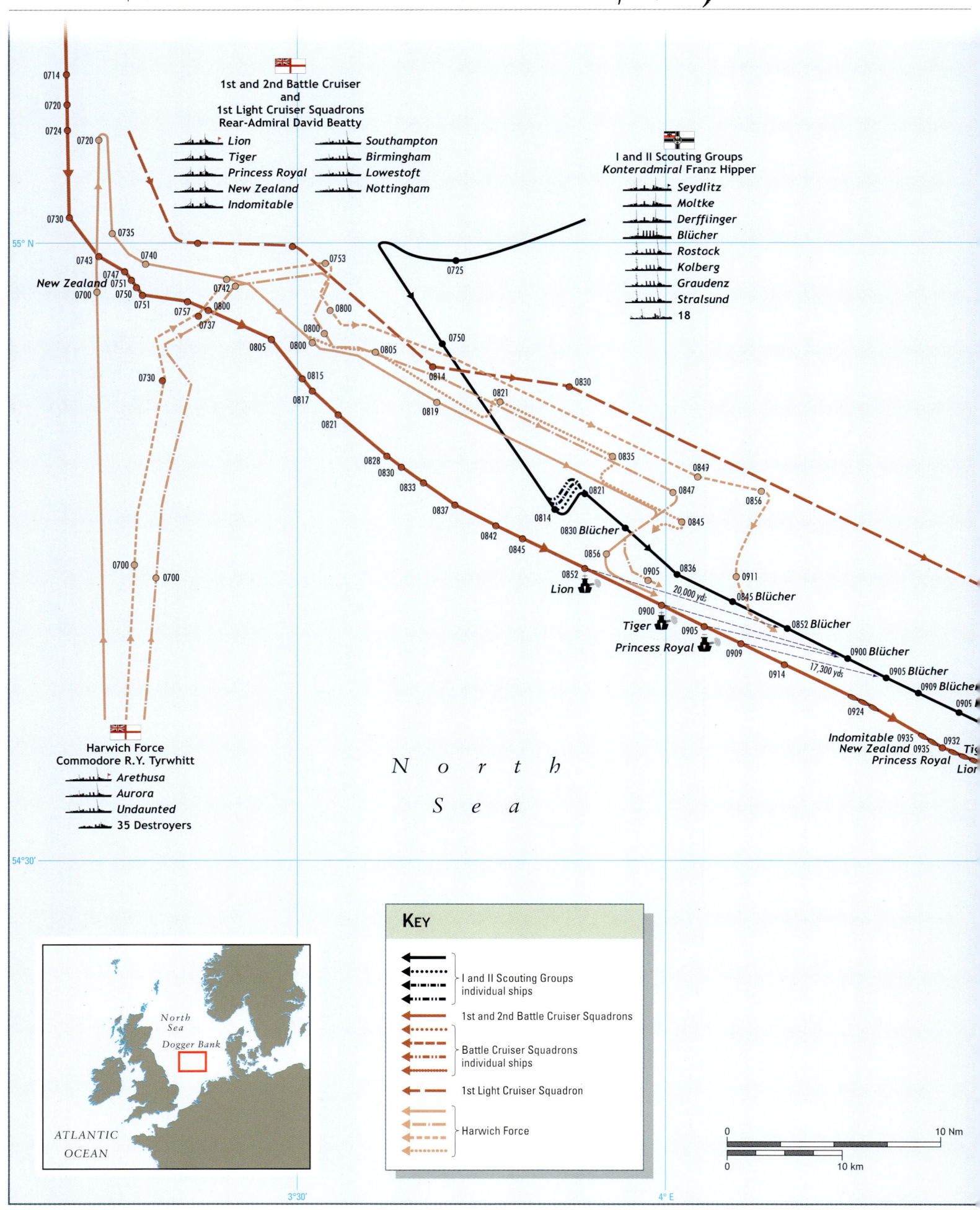

THE GREAT WAR AT SEA 1915

Although the German raids on the English coast in late 1914 had a considerable effect on the morale of the British public, their material impact was modest and they had not led to a general engagement on terms favourable to the Germans. What concerned senior High Sea Fleet officers was the seeming British ability to detect German movements and deploy forces accordingly, severely limiting any possibility of destroying Royal Navy detachments in piecemeal fashion. The root cause of this was suspected to be wireless-equipped fishing vessels that relayed German movements back to the Admiralty; these craft might also be operating under neutral flags. The fact that German warships always encountered such craft when sortieing made it a reasonable assumption. In fact, the British were not using small craft in this way, but were slowly beginning to make use of intercepted German wireless communications.

Within the High Sea Fleet a plan emerged to sweep the Dogger Bank with the Scouting Forces – where most fishing vessels operated – because it dominated the exits of the German Bight. The objective was to destroy any small craft encountered and draw British battlecruisers coming to their aid eastwards onto the High Sea Fleet. The winter weather caused delays but on 22 January it cleared and *Konteradmiral* Hipper believed the conditions to be favourable. The High Sea Fleet, though, was not at full strength with the Third Battle Squadron working up in the Baltic, and the battlecruiser *Von der Tann* in refit, so that she was replaced in the I Scouting Group by the large armoured cruiser *Blücher*. Light forces too were understrength.

Crucially, the British picked up a signal on the morning of 23 January outlining the German intention and sent out numerous forces that evening. The plan was for the German Scouting Groups to be caught between Rear-Admiral Beatty's battlecruisers and the Harwich Force, while the Grand Fleet provided cover from the north. Just as Hipper finished his sweep he encountered Beatty's light cruiser screen. Turning southeast he made for home and radioed *Admiral* von Ingenohl to bring up the High Sea Fleet, but as it had yet to assemble it was too far away to have an impact. The four-hour battle developed into a high-speed chase in which initial fire was opened and hits attained at hitherto unprecedented ranges.

Both flagships took hits around 11am, and Beatty's *Lion* had to fall out of line. A German torpedo boat attack caused the British to briefly slow their pursuit, but then fire focused on the trailing *Blücher* which was finally sunk after noon. It was only after 1pm that Beatty was able to take command again, now in *Princess Royal*, and by then the Germans were out of sight and so the British withdrew.

Neither side could be content with the outcome. In the fast paced battle huge quantities of ammunition had been expended with limited results, and confusion also took its toll. Ultimately, German losses were far greater and the destruction of *Blücher* would in due course make the Kaiser even less willing to risk his capital ships. *Admiral* von Ingenohl's failure to deploy the High Sea Fleet early enough to support Hipper and potentially destroy Beatty's battlecruisers cost him his command. After six months of activity the High Sea Fleet had achieved little.

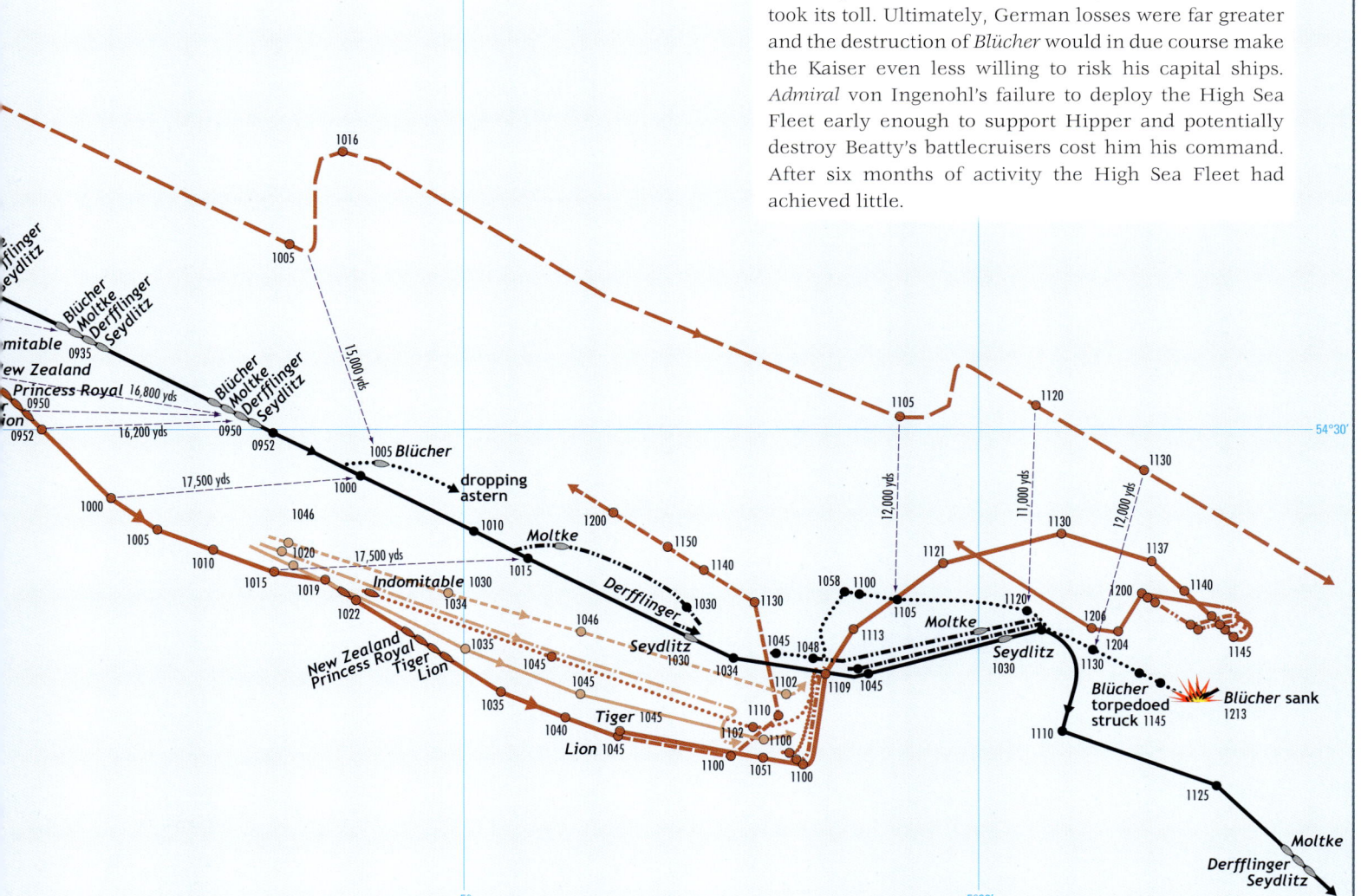

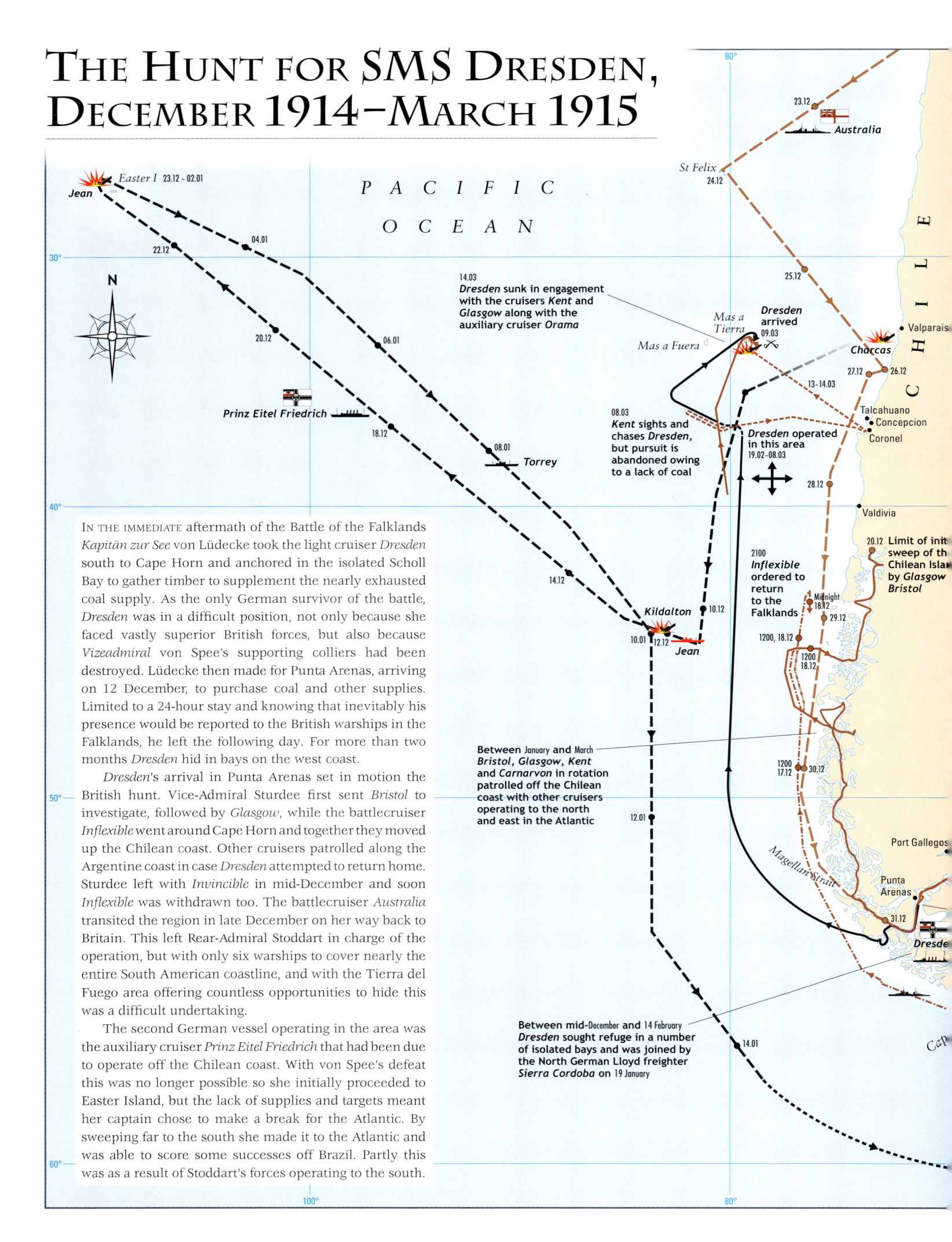

The Hunt for SMS Dresden, December 1914 – March 1915

14.03 Dresden sunk in engagement with the cruisers *Kent* and *Glasgow* along with the auxiliary cruiser *Orama*

08.03 *Kent* sights and chases *Dresden*, but pursuit is abandoned owing to a lack of coal

Dresden operated in this area 19.02–08.03

2100 Inflexible ordered to return to the Falklands

20.12 Limit of initial sweep of the Chilean Islands by *Glasgow* *Bristol*

Between **January** and **March** *Bristol*, *Glasgow*, *Kent* and *Carnarvon* in rotation patrolled off the Chilean coast with other cruisers operating to the north and east in the Atlantic

Between **mid-December** and **14 February** *Dresden* sought refuge in a number of isolated bays and was joined by the North German Lloyd freighter *Sierra Cordoba* on **19 January**

IN THE IMMEDIATE aftermath of the Battle of the Falklands *Kapitän zur See* von Lüdecke took the light cruiser *Dresden* south to Cape Horn and anchored in the isolated Scholl Bay to gather timber to supplement the nearly exhausted coal supply. As the only German survivor of the battle, *Dresden* was in a difficult position, not only because she faced vastly superior British forces, but also because *Vizeadmiral* von Spee's supporting colliers had been destroyed. Lüdecke then made for Punta Arenas, arriving on 12 December, to purchase coal and other supplies. Limited to a 24-hour stay and knowing that inevitably his presence would be reported to the British warships in the Falklands, he left the following day. For more than two months *Dresden* hid in bays on the west coast.

Dresden's arrival in Punta Arenas set in motion the British hunt. Vice-Admiral Sturdee first sent *Bristol* to investigate, followed by *Glasgow*, while the battlecruiser *Inflexible* went around Cape Horn and together they moved up the Chilean coast. Other cruisers patrolled along the Argentine coast in case *Dresden* attempted to return home. Sturdee left with *Invincible* in mid-December and soon *Inflexible* was withdrawn too. The battlecruiser *Australia* transited the region in late December on her way back to Britain. This left Rear-Admiral Stoddart in charge of the operation, but with only six warships to cover nearly the entire South American coastline, and with the Tierra del Fuego area offering countless opportunities to hide this was a difficult undertaking.

The second German vessel operating in the area was the auxiliary cruiser *Prinz Eitel Friedrich* that had been due to operate off the Chilean coast. With von Spee's defeat this was no longer possible so she initially proceeded to Easter Island, but the lack of supplies and targets meant her captain chose to make a break for the Atlantic. By sweeping far to the south she made it to the Atlantic and was able to score some successes off Brazil. Partly this was as a result of Stoddart's forces operating to the south.

The Great War at Sea 1915

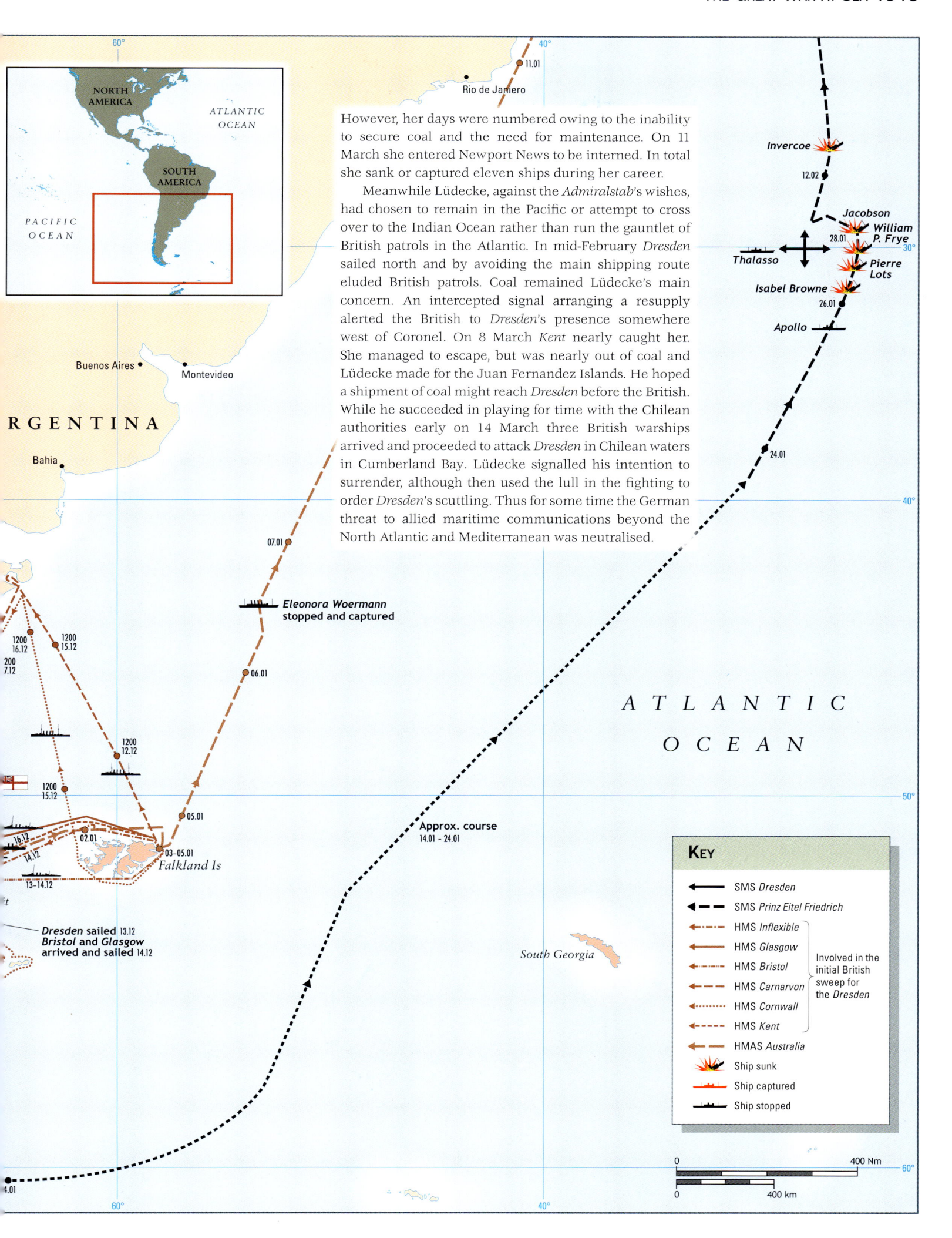

However, her days were numbered owing to the inability to secure coal and the need for maintenance. On 11 March she entered Newport News to be interned. In total she sank or captured eleven ships during her career.

Meanwhile Lüdecke, against the *Admiralstab*'s wishes, had chosen to remain in the Pacific or attempt to cross over to the Indian Ocean rather than run the gauntlet of British patrols in the Atlantic. In mid-February *Dresden* sailed north and by avoiding the main shipping route eluded British patrols. Coal remained Lüdecke's main concern. An intercepted signal arranging a resupply alerted the British to *Dresden*'s presence somewhere west of Coronel. On 8 March *Kent* nearly caught her. She managed to escape, but was nearly out of coal and Lüdecke made for the Juan Fernandez Islands. He hoped a shipment of coal might reach *Dresden* before the British. While he succeeded in playing for time with the Chilean authorities early on 14 March three British warships arrived and proceeded to attack *Dresden* in Chilean waters in Cumberland Bay. Lüdecke signalled his intention to surrender, although then used the lull in the fighting to order *Dresden*'s scuttling. Thus for some time the German threat to allied maritime communications beyond the North Atlantic and Mediterranean was neutralised.

Key

- SMS *Dresden*
- SMS *Prinz Eitel Friedrich*
- HMS *Inflexible*
- HMS *Glasgow*
- HMS *Bristol*
- HMS *Carnarvon*
- HMS *Cornwall*
- HMS *Kent*
- HMAS *Australia*
- Ship sunk
- Ship captured
- Ship stopped

Involved in the initial British sweep for the Dresden

THE RED SEA THEATRE, 1914–15

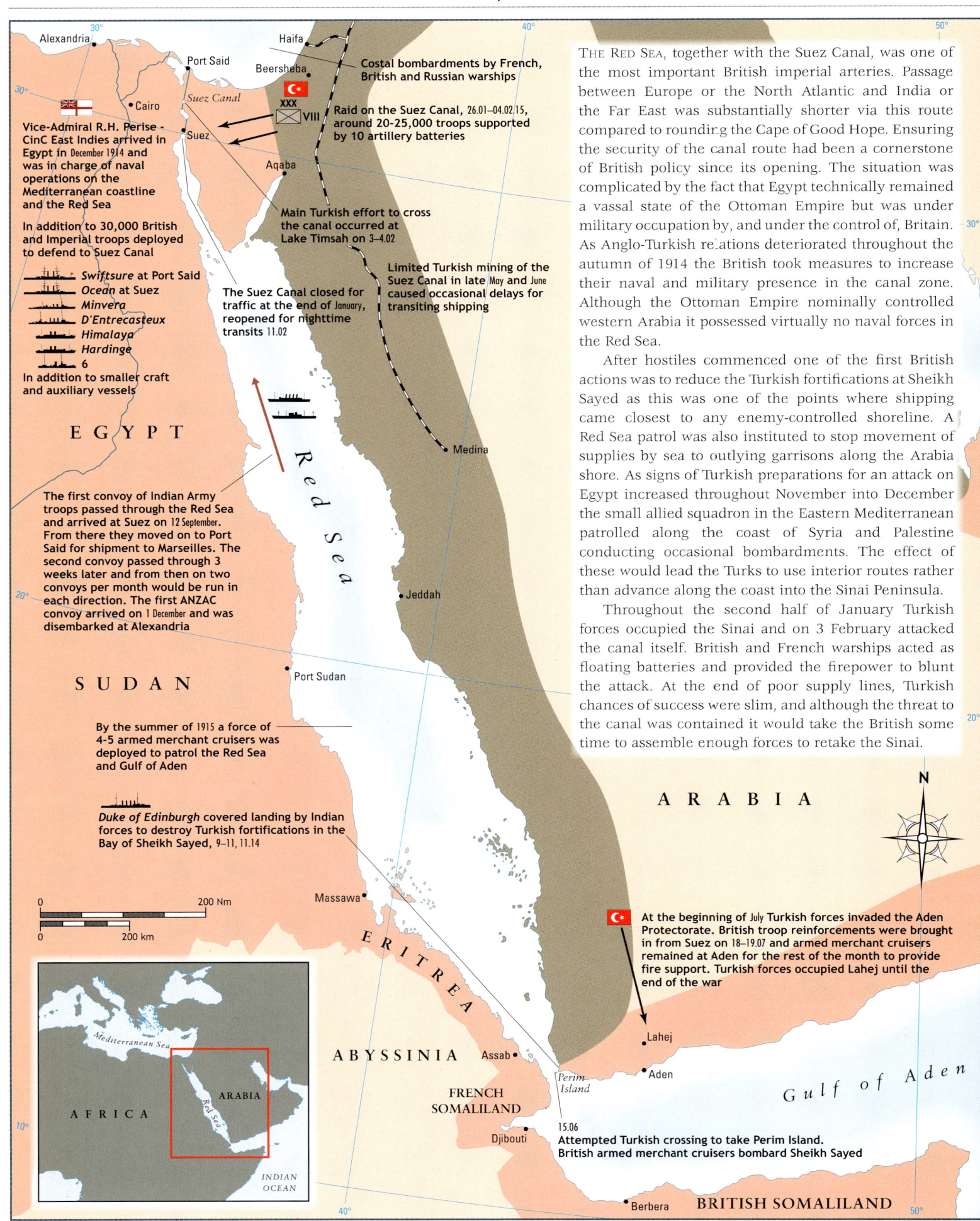

Costal bombardments by French, British and Russian warships

Raid on the Suez Canal, 26.01–04.02.15, around 20–25,000 troops supported by 10 artillery batteries

Vice-Admiral R.H. Perise - CinC East Indies arrived in Egypt in December 1914 and was in charge of naval operations on the Mediterranean coastline and the Red Sea

In addition to 30,000 British and Imperial troops deployed to defend to Suez Canal
- *Swiftsure* at Port Said
- *Ocean* at Suez
- *Minvera*
- *D'Entrecasteux*
- *Himalaya*
- *Hardinge*
- 6

In addition to smaller craft and auxiliary vessels

Main Turkish effort to cross the canal occurred at Lake Timsah on 3–4.02

Limited Turkish mining of the Suez Canal in late May and June caused occasional delays for transiting shipping

The Suez Canal closed for traffic at the end of January, reopened for nighttime transits 11.02

The first convoy of Indian Army troops passed through the Red Sea and arrived at Suez on 12 September. From there they moved on to Port Said for shipment to Marseilles. The second convoy passed through 3 weeks later and from then on two convoys per month would be run in each direction. The first ANZAC convoy arrived on 1 December and was disembarked at Alexandria

By the summer of 1915 a force of 4–5 armed merchant cruisers was deployed to patrol the Red Sea and Gulf of Aden

***Duke of Edinburgh* covered landing by Indian forces to destroy Turkish fortifications in the Bay of Sheikh Sayed, 9–11, 11.14**

At the beginning of July Turkish forces invaded the Aden Protectorate. British troop reinforcements were brought in from Suez on 18–19.07 and armed merchant cruisers remained at Aden for the rest of the month to provide fire support. Turkish forces occupied Lahej until the end of the war

15.06 Attempted Turkish crossing to take Perim Island. British armed merchant cruisers bombard Sheikh Sayed

---

THE RED SEA, together with the Suez Canal, was one of the most important British imperial arteries. Passage between Europe or the North Atlantic and India or the Far East was substantially shorter via this route compared to rounding the Cape of Good Hope. Ensuring the security of the canal route had been a cornerstone of British policy since its opening. The situation was complicated by the fact that Egypt technically remained a vassal state of the Ottoman Empire but was under military occupation by, and under the control of, Britain. As Anglo-Turkish relations deteriorated throughout the autumn of 1914 the British took measures to increase their naval and military presence in the canal zone. Although the Ottoman Empire nominally controlled western Arabia it possessed virtually no naval forces in the Red Sea.

After hostiles commenced one of the first British actions was to reduce the Turkish fortifications at Sheikh Sayed as this was one of the points where shipping came closest to any enemy-controlled shoreline. A Red Sea patrol was also instituted to stop movement of supplies by sea to outlying garrisons along the Arabia shore. As signs of Turkish preparations for an attack on Egypt increased throughout November into December the small allied squadron in the Eastern Mediterranean patrolled along the coast of Syria and Palestine conducting occasional bombardments. The effect of these would lead the Turks to use interior routes rather than advance along the coast into the Sinai Peninsula.

Throughout the second half of January Turkish forces occupied the Sinai and on 3 February attacked the canal itself. British and French warships acted as floating batteries and provided the firepower to blunt the attack. At the end of poor supply lines, Turkish chances of success were slim, and although the threat to the canal was contained it would take the British some time to assemble enough forces to retake the Sinai.

THE DARDANELLES CAMPAIGN, OVERVIEW

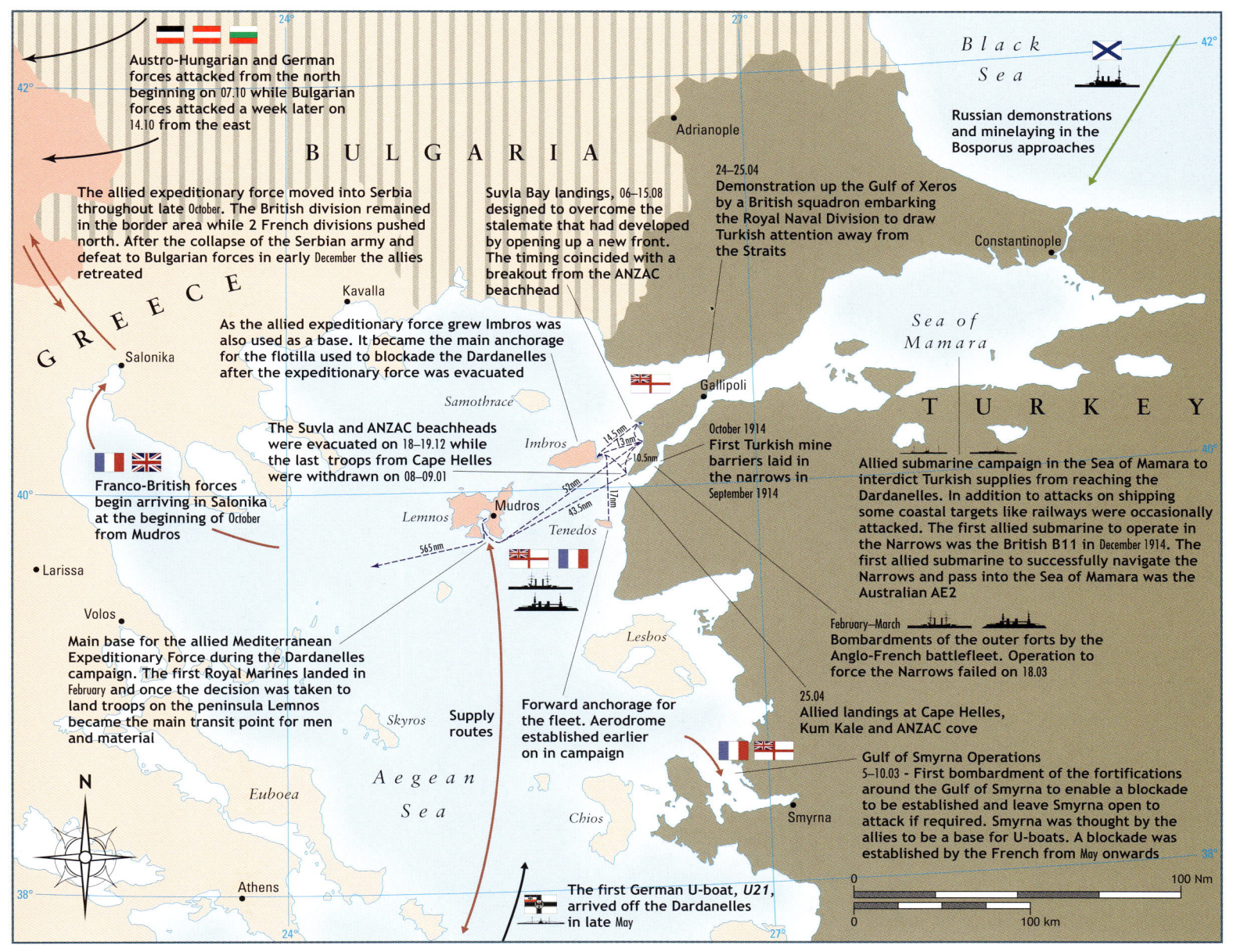

THE GREAT WAR AT SEA 1915

Map annotations

- **Austro-Hungarian and German forces attacked from the north beginning on 07.10 while Bulgarian forces attacked a week later on 14.10 from the east**
- **The allied expeditionary force moved into Serbia throughout late October. The British division remained in the border area while 2 French divisions pushed north. After the collapse of the Serbian army and defeat to Bulgarian forces in early December the allies retreated**
- **Suvla Bay landings, 06–15.08** designed to overcome the stalemate that had developed by opening up a new front. The timing coincided with a breakout from the ANZAC beachhead
- **24–25.04** Demonstration up the Gulf of Xeros by a British squadron embarking the Royal Naval Division to draw Turkish attention away from the Straits
- **Russian demonstrations and minelaying in the Bosporus approaches**
- As the allied expeditionary force grew Imbros was also used as a base. It became the main anchorage for the flotilla used to blockade the Dardanelles after the expeditionary force was evacuated
- The Suvla and ANZAC beachheads were evacuated on 18–19.12 while the last troops from Cape Helles were withdrawn on 08–09.01
- **Franco-British forces begin arriving in Salonika at the beginning of October from Mudros**
- **October 1914** First Turkish mine barriers laid in the narrows in September 1914
- Allied submarine campaign in the Sea of Mamara to interdict Turkish supplies from reaching the Dardanelles. In addition to attacks on shipping some coastal targets like railways were occasionally attacked. The first allied submarine to operate in the Narrows was the British B11 in December 1914. The first allied submarine to successfully navigate the Narrows and pass into the Sea of Mamara was the Australian AE2
- **February–March** Bombardments of the outer forts by the Anglo-French battlefleet. Operation to force the Narrows failed on 18.03
- **Main base for the allied Mediterranean Expeditionary Force during the Dardanelles campaign.** The first Royal Marines landed in February and once the decision was taken to land troops on the peninsula Lemnos became the main transit point for men and material
- **Forward anchorage for the fleet. Aerodrome established earlier on in campaign**
- **25.04** Allied landings at Cape Helles, Kum Kale and ANZAC cove
- **Gulf of Smyrna Operations** 5–10.03 - First bombardment of the fortifications around the Gulf of Smyrna to enable a blockade to be established and leave Smyrna open to attack if required. Smyrna was thought by the allies to be a base for U-boats. A blockade was established by the French from May onwards
- The first German U-boat, *U21*, arrived off the Dardanelles in late May

---

THE OTTOMAN EMPIRE'S entry into the war in the autumn of 1914 did not immediately make the Dardanelles a target for any major allied operation. The bombardment of the outer forts defending the straits on 3 November was little more than a demonstration; the main British concern was to prevent the *Goeben* and *Breslau* from breaking out into the Mediterranean. An assault on the Dardanelles to counter-attack the Ottoman threat to Egypt was dismissed due to lack of troops needed for any operation. Throughout the winter the situation changed and a number of factors slowly set in motion a campaign that would expand to a magnitude that no one anticipated.

At the Admiralty Winston Churchill was not only generally keen to undertake some offensive action, but also to make use of the navy's inventory of older warships and the new monitors then under construction. These had been earmarked for offensive action against Germany, either in the North Sea or the Baltic, but Admiral Jackie Fisher was willing to consider applying more pressure on the Turks. Within the British government there were divisions between those who sought to use Britain's growing military strength in France and those who believed that the existing stalemate could be overcome by operations elsewhere.

On 2 January 1915 Grand Duke Nicholas, the Russian commander-in-chief, appealed to the French and British to undertake some action against the Turks to relieve the pressure they were applying against the Russians in the Caucasus. Churchill proposed a naval operation to force the Dardanelles with the ultimate objective of reaching Constantinople and knocking the Turks out of the war. Quite how this might be achieved remained unclear, but it was thought to be an attractive option that offered the bonus of opening up a supply line to Russia. Throughout February and March British and French warships bombarded the outer forts, but made little headway given that they were neither trained nor equipped for the task. Thus it was decided to undertake a landing operation, and by the spring sufficient troops were available. From the outset the landings encountered heavy resistance and the campaign became bogged down in the inhospitable terrain.

The Dardanelles Bombardments, February 1915

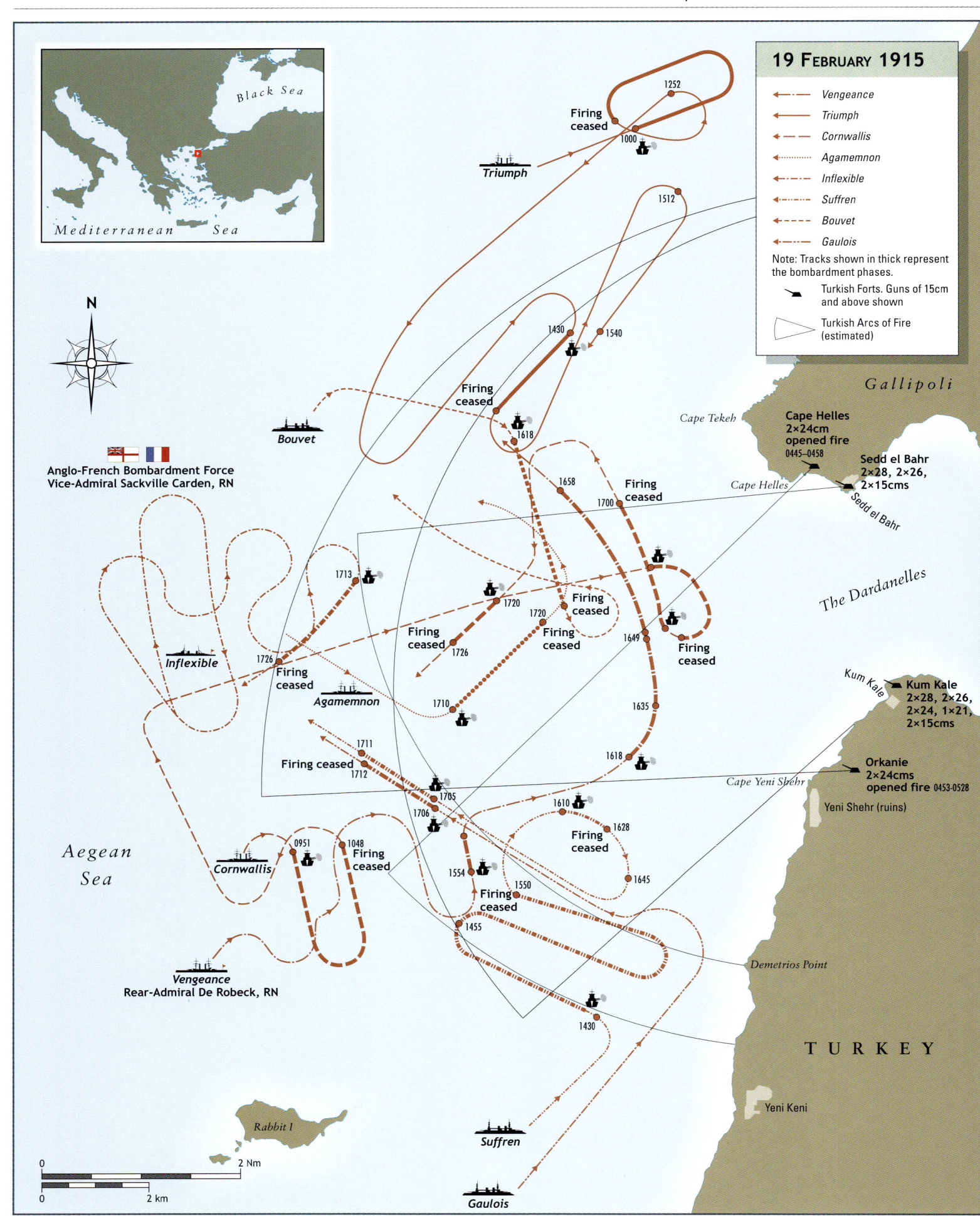

THE GREAT WAR AT SEA 1915

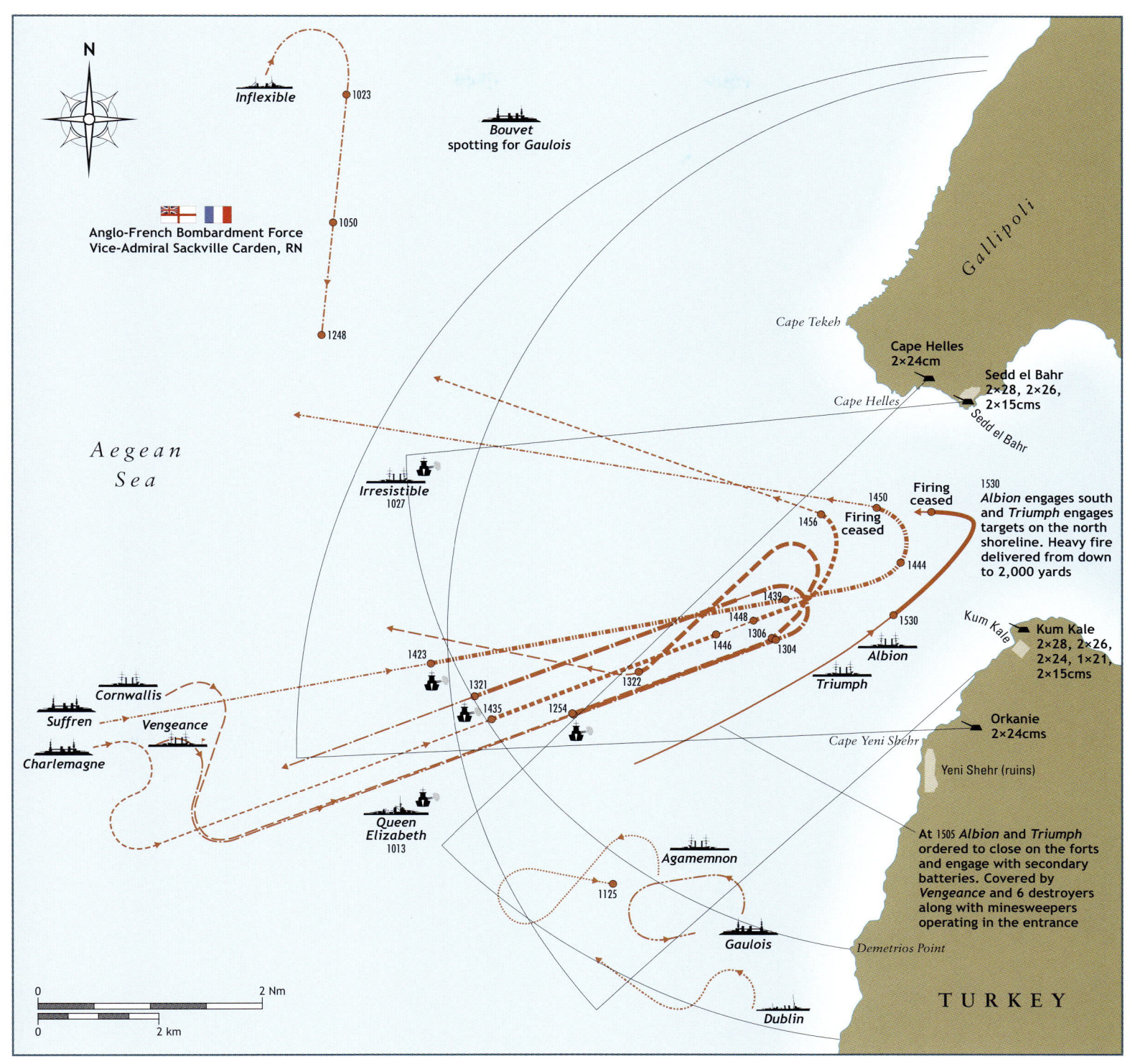

VICE-ADMIRAL CARDEN in his reply, at the beginning of January, to Winston Churchill's questioning as to whether the Dardanelles might be forced by ships alone was adamant that such an operation could be undertaken only as a protracted and methodical one. A large number of ships would be required. The orders Carden received in early February tasked him to put the Turkish defences from the outer forts to the Narrows out of action, sweep the minefields from the Straits to the Narrows and silence the forts above the Narrows to enable the passage of a fleet into the Sea of Marmara.

A task like this had never been undertaken before and bombardments were not practiced in peacetime. Carden was put under pressure to start the operation before all the reinforcements had arrived. Ammunition expenditure was strictly limited in anticipation of operations after the breakthrough. In particular, the new dreadnought *Queen Elizabeth* was to conserve her supply. Aerial reconnaissance was only available from mid-February and then only in a very limited form, and spotting for naval gunfire was only in its infancy.

The approach used on both 19 and 25 February was a two-stage attack. Initially, long-range fire was used to silence the guns from outside their areas of fire. Ships fired while at rest or at very slow speed. Then some battleships closed in and engaged the targets with overwhelming fire from their secondary batteries. For each bombarding ship another would spot the shells' impacts to enable the fire to be corrected, but smoke and haze made this difficult in practice. The results on 19 February were very limited and only marginally better on 25 February. It was near impossible to take out individual guns in unsurveyed positions with single shots, and without saturating a target with fire it could not be neutralised.

The Dardanelles: The Attack on the Narrows, 18 March 1915

As a result of allied operations in February and early March the Turkish coastal defence batteries at the entrance of the straits had been neutralised through a combination of bombardments and demolition parties that were sent ashore. Against the more numerous and longer-ranged guns of the allied fleet the outer defences could not be held and the Turks withdrew some of the remaining intact equipment to strengthen the inner defences. As March progressed allied efforts came to a standstill as operations within the straits themselves proved to be far more challenging than expected. The constricted nature of the waters favoured the defenders and, in addition, the Dardanelles boasted one of the most extensive systems of forts and artillery emplacements. Though by contemporary standards a number of the gun batteries within the confines of the area were obsolete, they still posed a threat against lightly-protected vessels.

Since the first allied bombardment in November the Turks had augmented the number of batteries on both sides of the straits and created a layered defensive system. The principal defence rested in a relatively small number of batteries equipped with modern artillery around the Narrows. These were, however, out-ranged by battleship guns and any slow, methodical, allied operation might have neutralised them, and to prevent the allied battleships from taking up positions within the straits, the Turks deployed a number of howitzer batteries on each side. Though these could not sink battleships, their barrage fire would be sufficiently dangerous to keep warships on the move and so reduce their accuracy. The howitzer fire was, however, lethal to destroyers and minesweepers as were the quick-firing light and medium emplacements and field artillery batteries that were positioned to defend the Kephez minefields. The mines in turn posed a great

Anglo-French Bombardment Force
Rear-Admiral John de Robeck, RN
First elements of the bombardment force entered the Straits at 1030

First Division

1st Sub-Division
- Queen Elizabeth
- Inflexible

2nd Sub-Division
- Agamemnon
- Lord Nelson

Second Division

3rd Sub-Division
- Ocean
- Irresistible
- Albion
- Vengeance

4th Sub-Division
- Swiftsure
- Majestic

5th Sub-Division
- Canopus
- Cornwallis

Third Division

6th Sub-Division
- Suffren
- Bouvet
- Gaulois
- Charlemagne

7th Sub-Division
- Triumph
- Prince George

Note: The deployment of the Anglo-French force is shown in a simplified manner to provide a clearer account. Lines A and B were the planned bombardment positions; throughout the day the British ships on Line A moved further to the south. The French ships were deployed in two pairs acting together rather than a neat line. They also moved to avoid Turkish fire.

The French division passed through Line A around 1220 to take up position on Line B. Under heavy fire from the outset. Began to retire around 1345

Distributed among the mobile battery positions on the European shore were 12×15cm and 4×12cm howitzers, 10×21cm and 6×15cm mortars

The relief force was ordered up to replace the French force around 1345 and passed through Line A at 1430

Distributed among the mobile battery positions on the Asiatic shore were 20×15cm howitzers and 8×21cm mortars

Rumili Medjidie 2×28 and 4×24

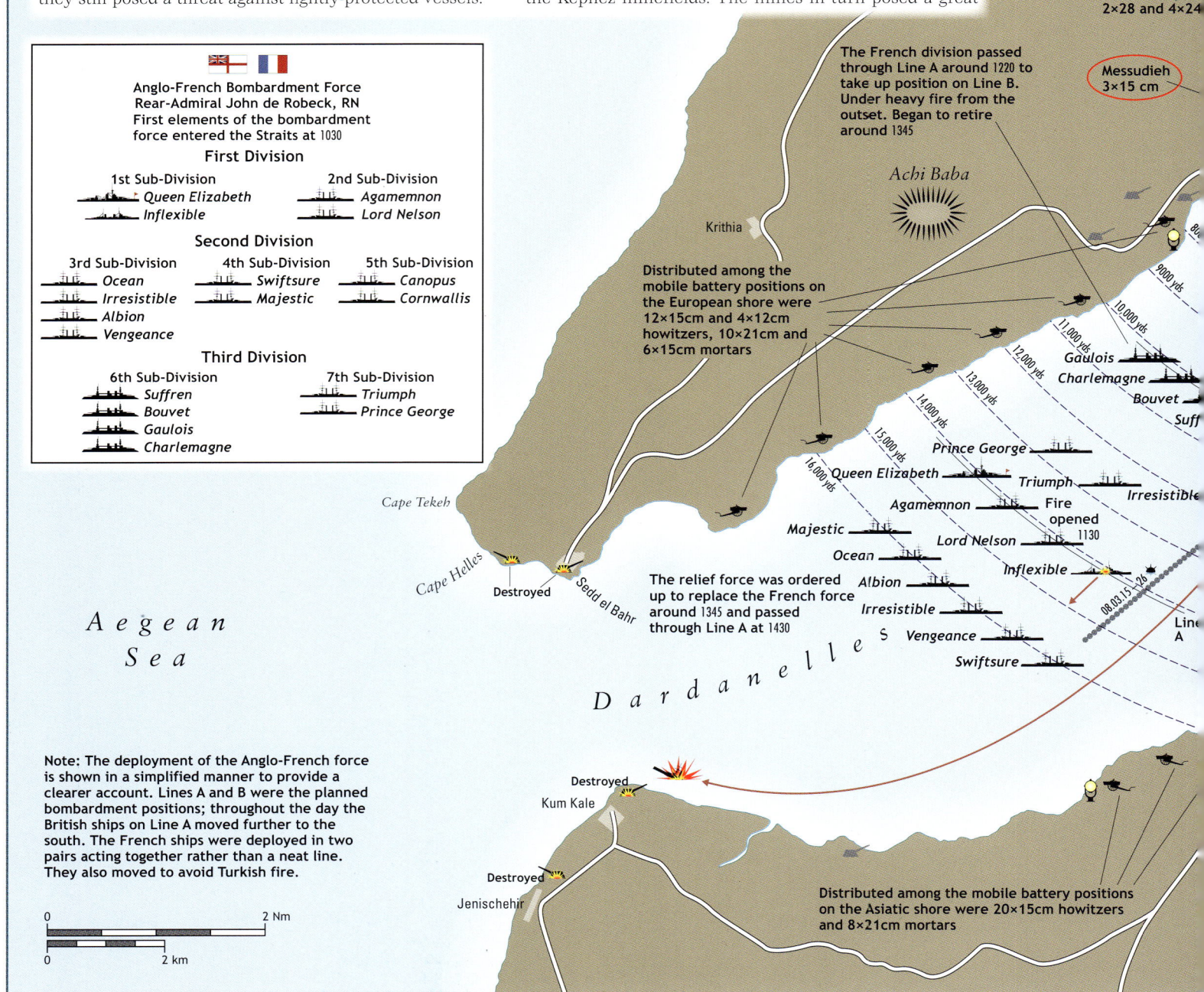

Messudieh 3×15 cm

THE GREAT WAR AT SEA 1915

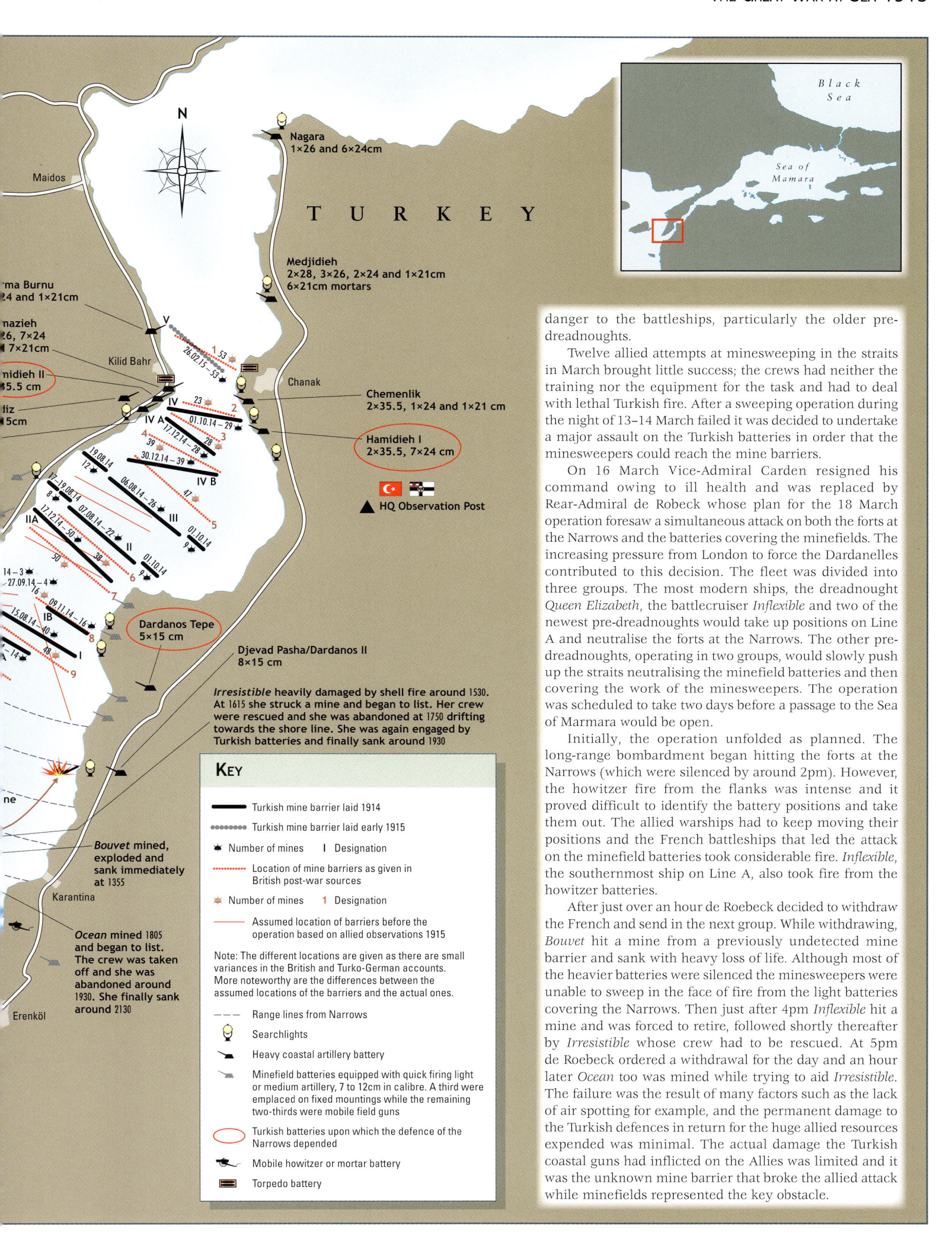

danger to the battleships, particularly the older pre-dreadnoughts.

Twelve allied attempts at minesweeping in the straits in March brought little success; the crews had neither the training nor the equipment for the task and had to deal with lethal Turkish fire. After a sweeping operation during the night of 13–14 March failed it was decided to undertake a major assault on the Turkish batteries in order that the minesweepers could reach the mine barriers.

On 16 March Vice-Admiral Carden resigned his command owing to ill health and was replaced by Rear-Admiral de Robeck whose plan for the 18 March operation foresaw a simultaneous attack on both the forts at the Narrows and the batteries covering the minefields. The increasing pressure from London to force the Dardanelles contributed to this decision. The fleet was divided into three groups. The most modern ships, the dreadnought *Queen Elizabeth*, the battlecruiser *Inflexible* and two of the newest pre-dreadnoughts would take up positions on Line A and neutralise the forts at the Narrows. The other pre-dreadnoughts, operating in two groups, would slowly push up the straits neutralising the minefield batteries and then covering the work of the minesweepers. The operation was scheduled to take two days before a passage to the Sea of Marmara would be open.

Initially, the operation unfolded as planned. The long-range bombardment began hitting the forts at the Narrows (which were silenced by around 2pm). However, the howitzer fire from the flanks was intense and it proved difficult to identify the battery positions and take them out. The allied warships had to keep moving their positions and the French battleships that led the attack on the minefield batteries took considerable fire. *Inflexible*, the southernmost ship on Line A, also took fire from the howitzer batteries.

After just over an hour de Roebeck decided to withdraw the French and send in the next group. While withdrawing, *Bouvet* hit a mine from a previously undetected mine barrier and sank with heavy loss of life. Although most of the heavier batteries were silenced the minesweepers were unable to sweep in the face of fire from the light batteries covering the Narrows. Then just after 4pm *Inflexible* hit a mine and was forced to retire, followed shortly thereafter by *Irresistible* whose crew had to be rescued. At 5pm de Roebeck ordered a withdrawal for the day and an hour later *Ocean* too was mined while trying to aid *Irresistible*. The failure was the result of many factors such as the lack of air spotting for example, and the permanent damage to the Turkish defences in return for the huge allied resources expended was minimal. The actual damage the Turkish coastal guns had inflicted on the Allies was limited and it was the unknown mine barrier that broke the allied attack while minefields represented the key obstacle.

55

High Sea Fleet Minelaying Operation, 17–18 April 1915

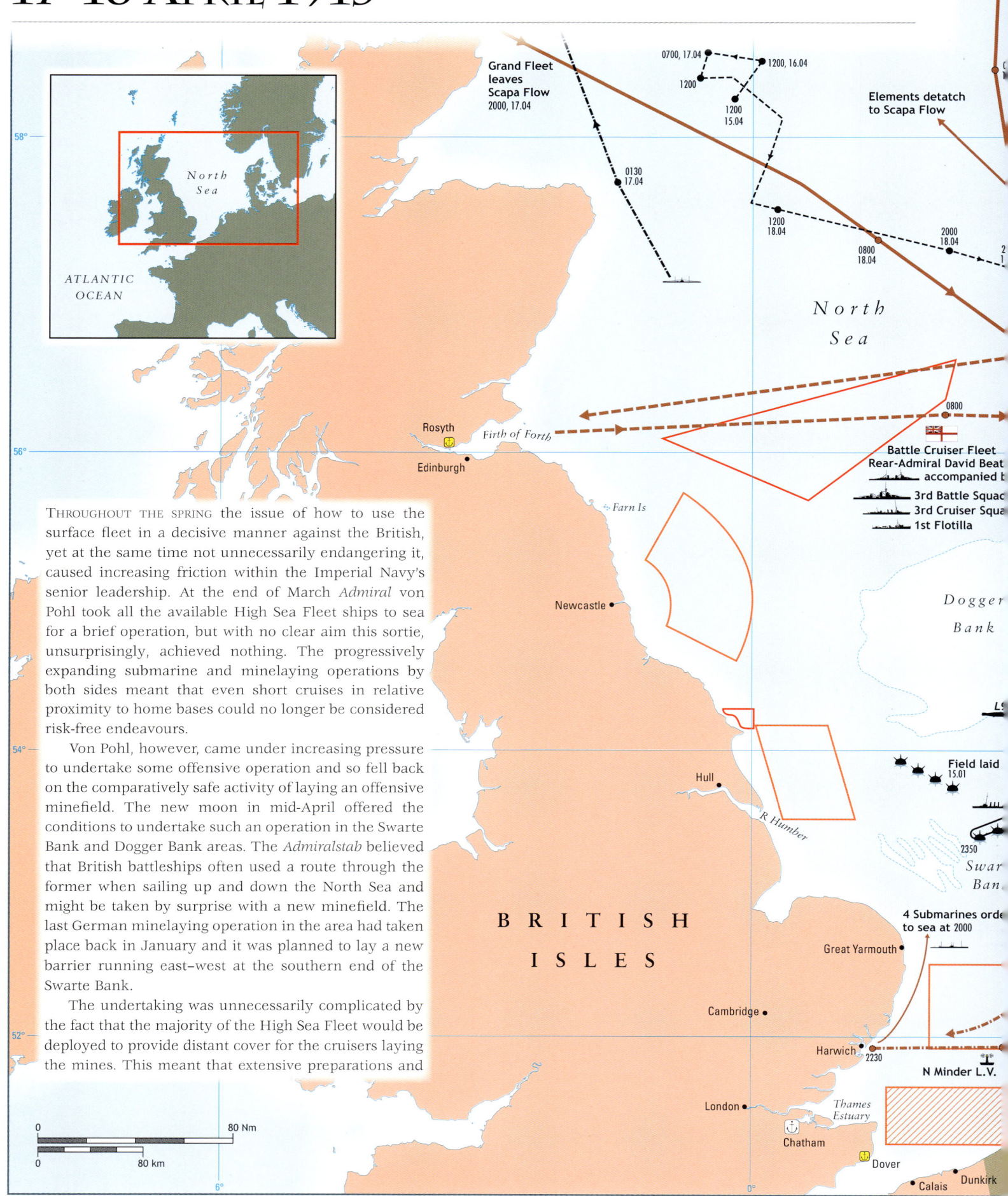

Throughout the spring the issue of how to use the surface fleet in a decisive manner against the British, yet at the same time not unnecessarily endangering it, caused increasing friction within the Imperial Navy's senior leadership. At the end of March *Admiral* von Pohl took all the available High Sea Fleet ships to sea for a brief operation, but with no clear aim this sortie, unsurprisingly, achieved nothing. The progressively expanding submarine and minelaying operations by both sides meant that even short cruises in relative proximity to home bases could no longer be considered risk-free endeavours.

Von Pohl, however, came under increasing pressure to undertake some offensive operation and so fell back on the comparatively safe activity of laying an offensive minefield. The new moon in mid-April offered the conditions to undertake such an operation in the Swarte Bank and Dogger Bank areas. The *Admiralstab* believed that British battleships often used a route through the former when sailing up and down the North Sea and might be taken by surprise with a new minefield. The last German minelaying operation in the area had taken place back in January and it was planned to lay a new barrier running east–west at the southern end of the Swarte Bank.

The undertaking was unnecessarily complicated by the fact that the majority of the High Sea Fleet would be deployed to provide distant cover for the cruisers laying the mines. This meant that extensive preparations and

THE GREAT WAR AT SEA 1915

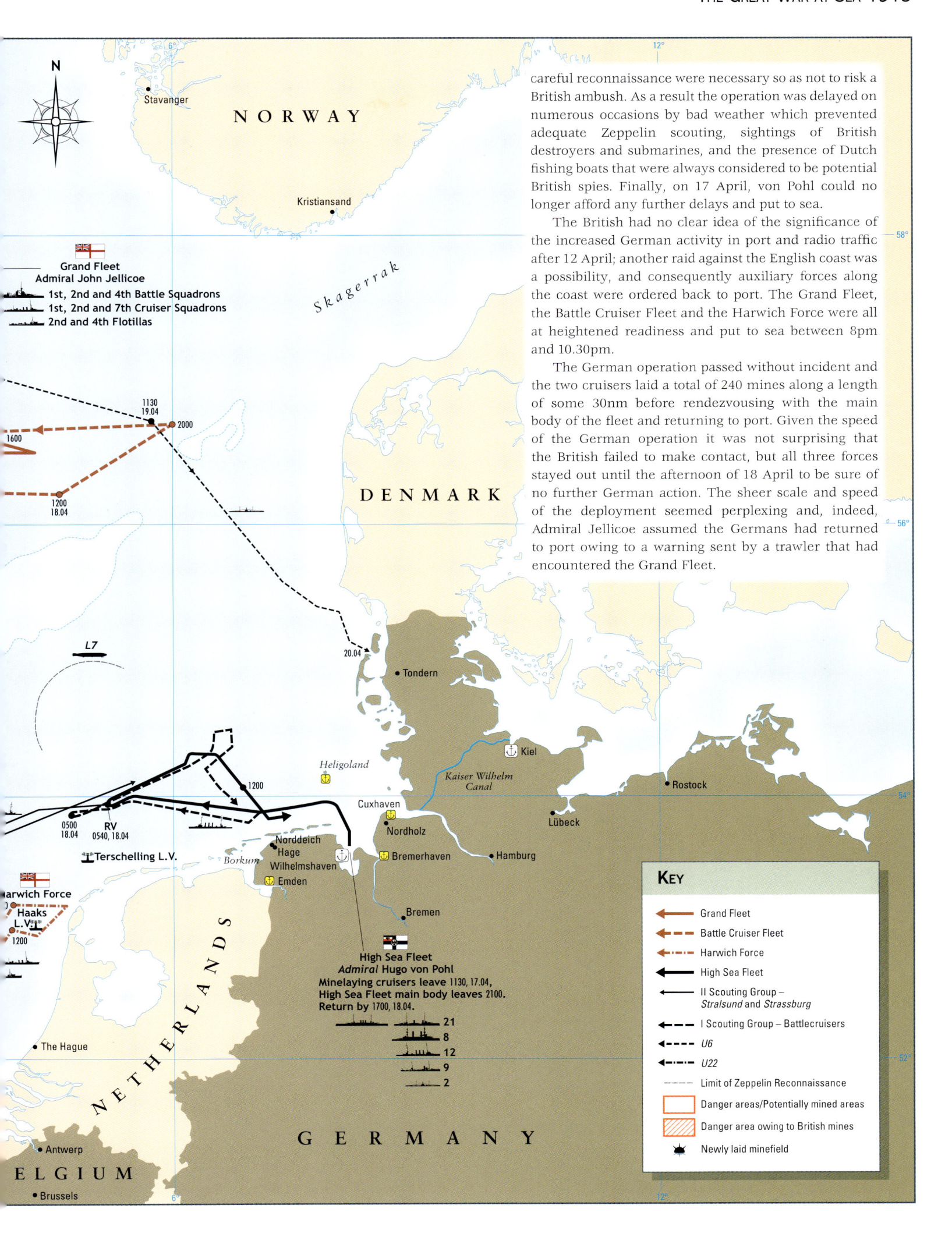

careful reconnaissance were necessary so as not to risk a British ambush. As a result the operation was delayed on numerous occasions by bad weather which prevented adequate Zeppelin scouting, sightings of British destroyers and submarines, and the presence of Dutch fishing boats that were always considered to be potential British spies. Finally, on 17 April, von Pohl could no longer afford any further delays and put to sea.

The British had no clear idea of the significance of the increased German activity in port and radio traffic after 12 April; another raid against the English coast was a possibility, and consequently auxiliary forces along the coast were ordered back to port. The Grand Fleet, the Battle Cruiser Fleet and the Harwich Force were all at heightened readiness and put to sea between 8pm and 10.30pm.

The German operation passed without incident and the two cruisers laid a total of 240 mines along a length of some 30nm before rendezvousing with the main body of the fleet and returning to port. Given the speed of the German operation it was not surprising that the British failed to make contact, but all three forces stayed out until the afternoon of 18 April to be sure of no further German action. The sheer scale and speed of the deployment seemed perplexing and, indeed, Admiral Jellicoe assumed the Germans had returned to port owing to a warning sent by a trawler that had encountered the Grand Fleet.

THE DARDANELLES: LANDING OPERATIONS

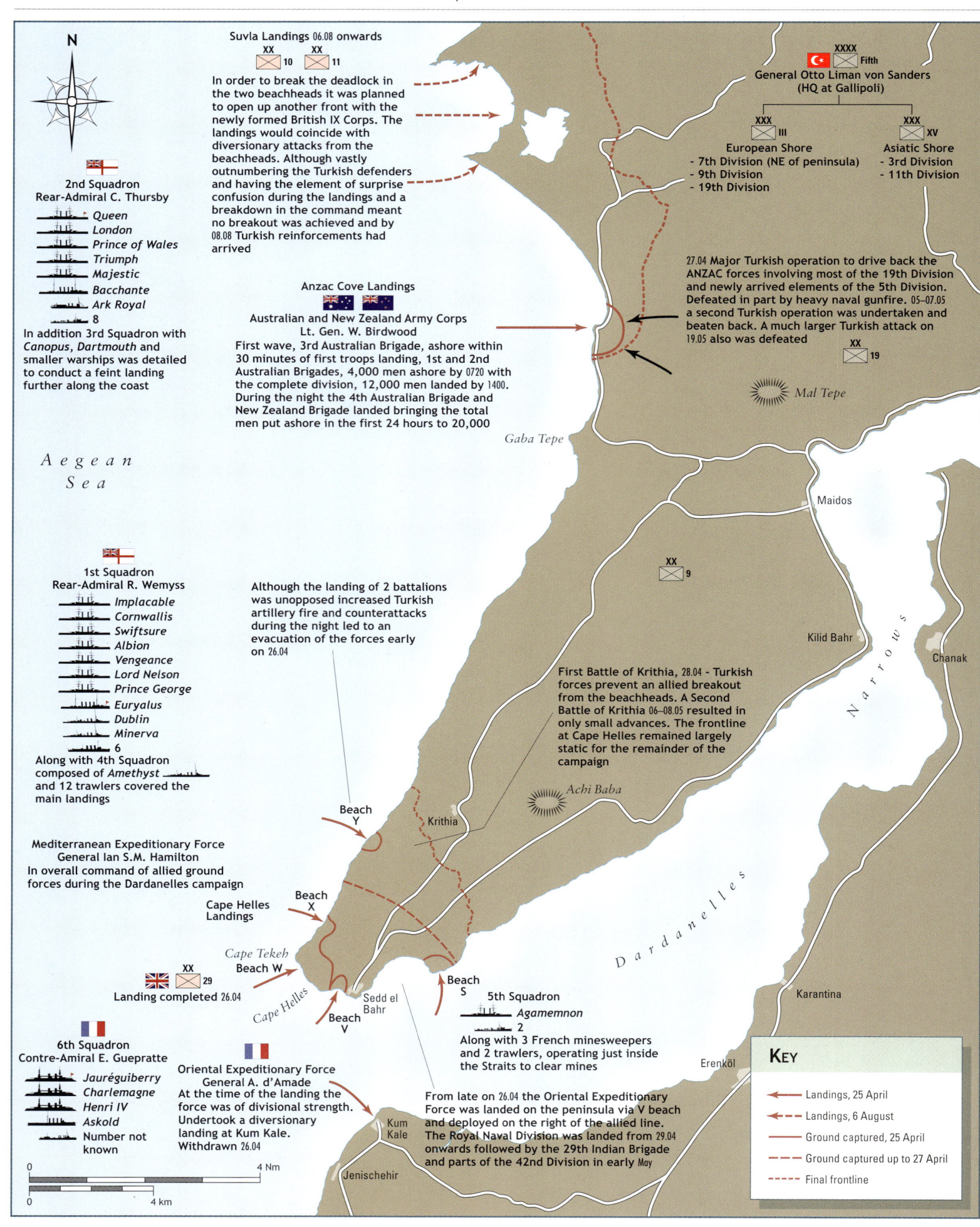

2nd Squadron
Rear-Admiral C. Thursby
- Queen
- London
- Prince of Wales
- Triumph
- Majestic
- Bacchante
- Ark Royal
- 8

In addition 3rd Squadron with *Canopus, Dartmouth* and smaller warships was detailed to conduct a feint landing further along the coast

Suvla Landings 06.08 onwards
XX 10 XX 11
In order to break the deadlock in the two beachheads it was planned to open up another front with the newly formed British IX Corps. The landings would coincide with diversionary attacks from the beachheads. Although vastly outnumbering the Turkish defenders and having the element of surprise confusion during the landings and a breakdown in the command meant no breakout was achieved and by 08.08 Turkish reinforcements had arrived

Anzac Cove Landings
Australian and New Zealand Army Corps
Lt. Gen. W. Birdwood
First wave, 3rd Australian Brigade, ashore within 30 minutes of first troops landing, 1st and 2nd Australian Brigades, 4,000 men ashore by 0720 with the complete division, 12,000 men landed by 1400. During the night the 4th Australian Brigade and New Zealand Brigade landed bringing the total men put ashore in the first 24 hours to 20,000

XXXX Fifth
General Otto Liman von Sanders (HQ at Gallipoli)

XXX III — European Shore
- 7th Division (NE of peninsula)
- 9th Division
- 19th Division

XXX XV — Asiatic Shore
- 3rd Division
- 11th Division

27.04 Major Turkish operation to drive back the ANZAC forces involving most of the 19th Division and newly arrived elements of the 5th Division. Defeated in part by heavy naval gunfire. 05–07.05 a second Turkish operation was undertaken and beaten back. A much larger Turkish attack on 19.05 also was defeated

XX 19
Mal Tepe

Aegean Sea

Gaba Tepe

Maidos

1st Squadron
Rear-Admiral R. Wemyss
- Implacable
- Cornwallis
- Swiftsure
- Albion
- Vengeance
- Lord Nelson
- Prince George
- Euryalus
- Dublin
- Minerva
- 6

Along with 4th Squadron composed of *Amethyst* and 12 trawlers covered the main landings

Although the landing of 2 battalions was unopposed increased Turkish artillery fire and counterattacks during the night led to an evacuation of the forces early on 26.04

XX 9

Kilid Bahr

First Battle of Krithia, 28.04 - Turkish forces prevent an allied breakout from the beachheads. A Second Battle of Krithia 06–08.05 resulted in only small advances. The frontline at Cape Helles remained largely static for the remainder of the campaign

Achi Baba

Mediterranean Expeditionary Force
General Ian S.M. Hamilton
In overall command of allied ground forces during the Dardanelles campaign

Beach Y

Krithia

Chanak

Narrows

Beach X
Cape Helles Landings

Cape Tekeh
Beach W

XX 29 — Landing completed 26.04

Cape Helles
Beach V
Sedd el Bahr

Beach S

5th Squadron
- Agamemnon
- 2

Along with 3 French minesweepers and 2 trawlers, operating just inside the Straits to clear mines

Dardanelles

Karantina

6th Squadron
Contre-Amiral E. Guepratte
- Jauréguiberry
- Charlemagne
- Henri IV
- Askold
- Number not known

Oriental Expeditionary Force
General A. d'Amade
At the time of the landing the force was of divisional strength. Undertook a diversionary landing at Kum Kale. Withdrawn 26.04

Kum Kale

Jenischehir

From late on 26.04 the Oriental Expeditionary Force was landed on the peninsula via V beach and deployed on the right of the allied line. The Royal Naval Division was landed from 29.04 onwards followed by the 29th Indian Brigade and parts of the 42nd Division in early May

Erenköl

0 — 4 Nm
0 — 4 km

KEY
- Landings, 25 April
- Landings, 6 August
- Ground captured, 25 April
- Ground captured up to 27 April
- Final frontline

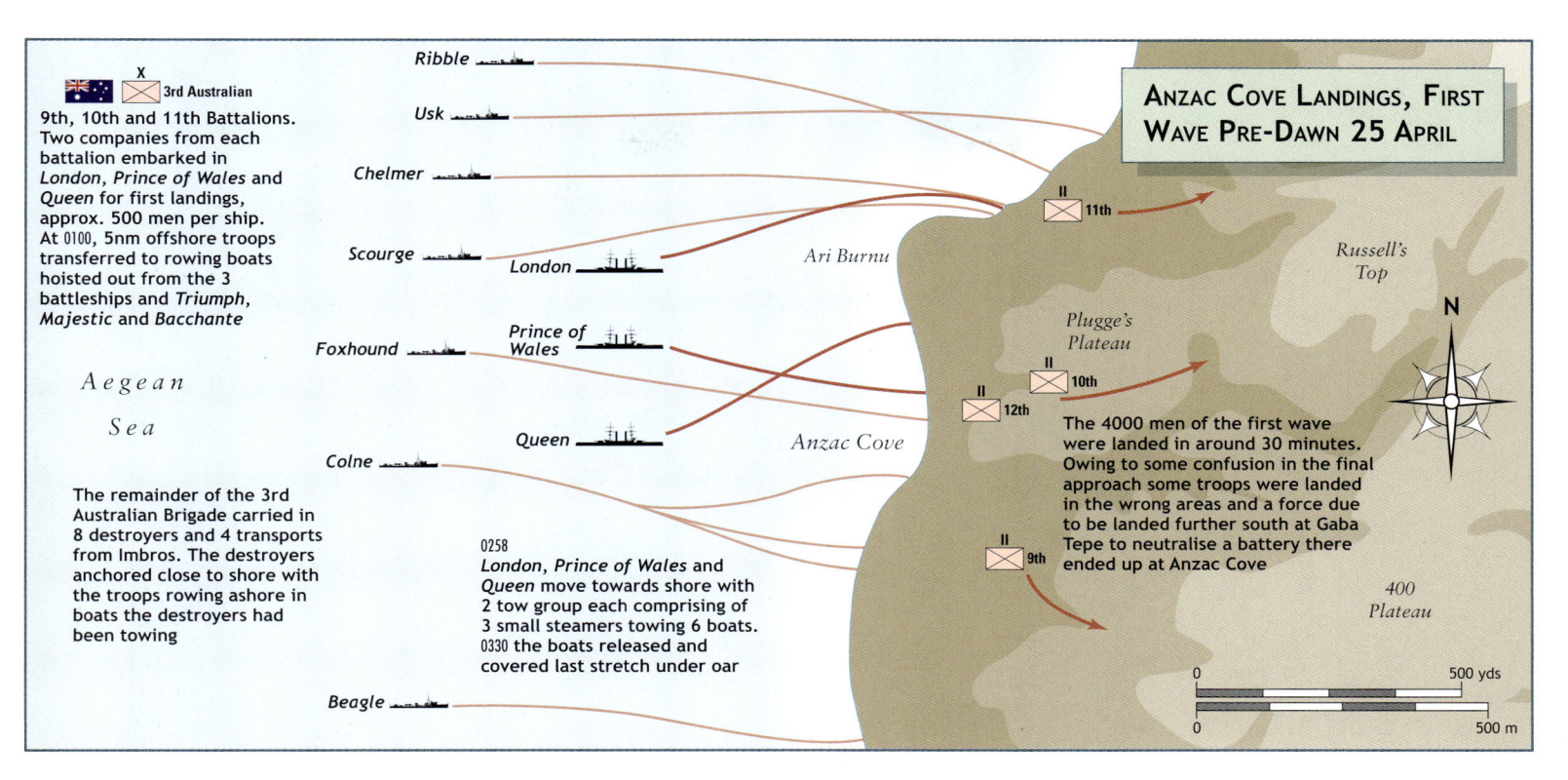

THE GREAT WAR AT SEA 1915

ANZAC COVE LANDINGS, FIRST WAVE PRE-DAWN 25 APRIL

3rd Australian
9th, 10th and 11th Battalions. Two companies from each battalion embarked in *London*, *Prince of Wales* and *Queen* for first landings, approx. 500 men per ship. At 0100, 5nm offshore troops transferred to rowing boats hoisted out from the 3 battleships and *Triumph*, *Majestic* and *Bacchante*

The remainder of the 3rd Australian Brigade carried in 8 destroyers and 4 transports from Imbros. The destroyers anchored close to shore with the troops rowing ashore in boats the destroyers had been towing

0258 *London*, *Prince of Wales* and *Queen* move towards shore with 2 tow group each comprising of 3 small steamers towing 6 boats. 0330 the boats released and covered last stretch under oar

The 4000 men of the first wave were landed in around 30 minutes. Owing to some confusion in the final approach some troops were landed in the wrong areas and a force due to be landed further south at Gaba Tepe to neutralise a battery there ended up at Anzac Cove

---

THE FAILURE TO force the straits by naval means alone on 18 March set in motion the process that led to the major landings and then to the Gallipoli campaign itself. Although the naval losses were quickly replaced and measures taken to improve allied capabilities, such as introducing destroyers to assist with minesweeping, and providing better aerial reconnaissance, no further attempt was made. By the end of March Rear-Admiral de Roebeck had decided that any naval assault would be too costly and although it might succeed, the presence of an allied fleet alone in the Sea of Marmara was not likely to induce the Turks to seek peace, and allied troops would be required.

The objective of the allied landings was to secure the high ground at the lower end of the Gallipoli peninsula that covered the fortifications on the European shore and could also be used to dominate the forts on the Asiatic shore. The terrain, the lack of suitable landing beaches and the Turkish positions made any operation difficult. The main landing would be at the tip of the peninsula in order to capture Achi Baba as quickly as possible. To distract and draw away Turkish troops a number of feints would be undertaken. The most important of these, the major Anzac landing north of Gaba Tepe, would, it was hoped, develop into a significant advance. No contested amphibious assault on this scale had ever been undertaken and the troops were not trained for such operations. There were no landing craft or other specialist equipment to assist in the landings and significant casualties were taken as a result.

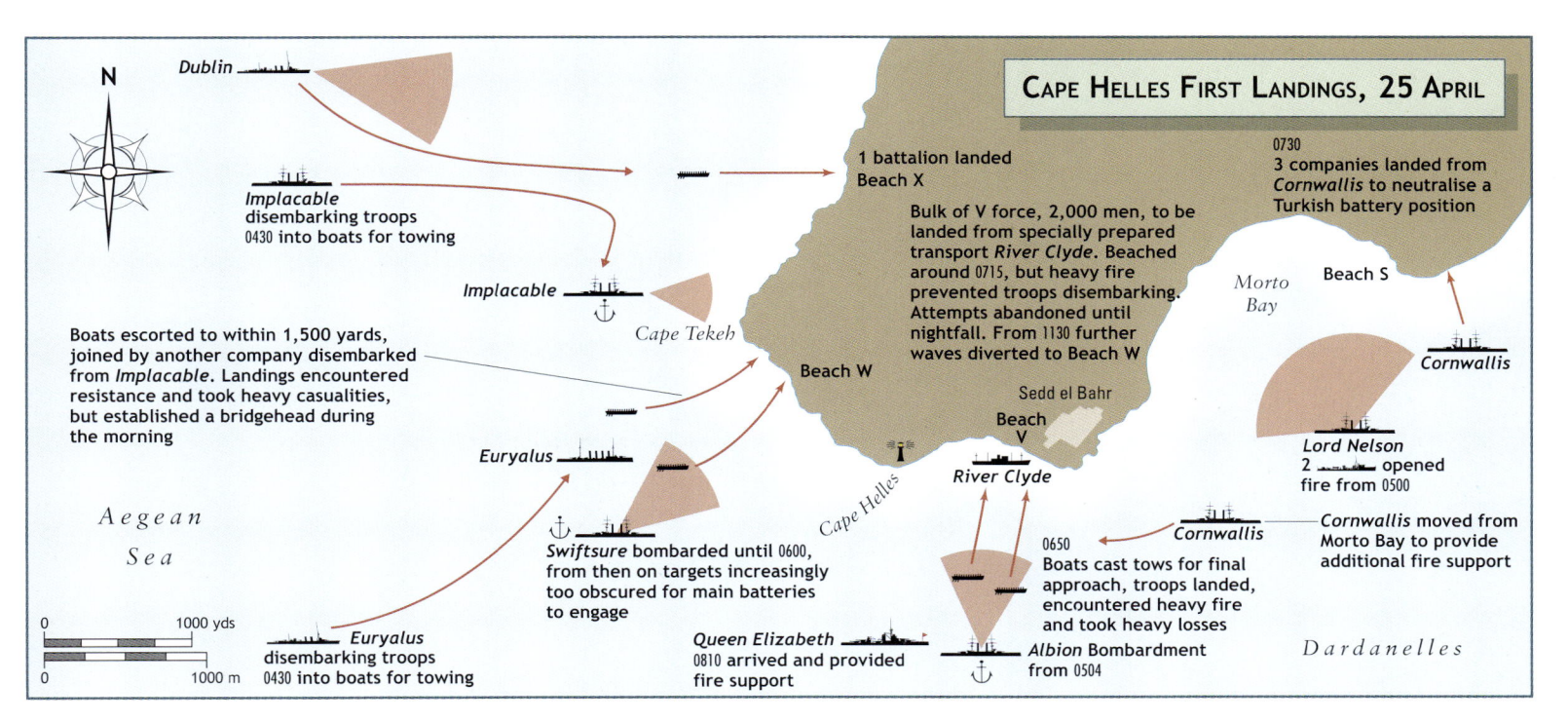

CAPE HELLES FIRST LANDINGS, 25 APRIL

Implacable disembarking troops 0430 into boats for towing

Boats escorted to within 1,500 yards, joined by another company disembarked from *Implacable*. Landings encountered resistance and took heavy casualties, but established a bridgehead during the morning

Euryalus disembarking troops 0430 into boats for towing

Swiftsure bombarded until 0600, from then on targets increasingly too obscured for main batteries to engage

Queen Elizabeth 0810 arrived and provided fire support

1 battalion landed Beach X

Bulk of V force, 2,000 men, to be landed from specially prepared transport *River Clyde*. Beached around 0715, but heavy fire prevented troops disembarking. Attempts abandoned until nightfall. From 1130 further waves diverted to Beach W

0730 3 companies landed from *Cornwallis* to neutralise a Turkish battery position

Lord Nelson 2 opened fire from 0500

Cornwallis moved from Morto Bay to provide additional fire support

0650 Boats cast tows for final approach, troops landed, encountered heavy fire and took heavy losses

Albion Bombardment from 0504

THE GERMAN U-BOAT CAMPAIGN, 1915–18

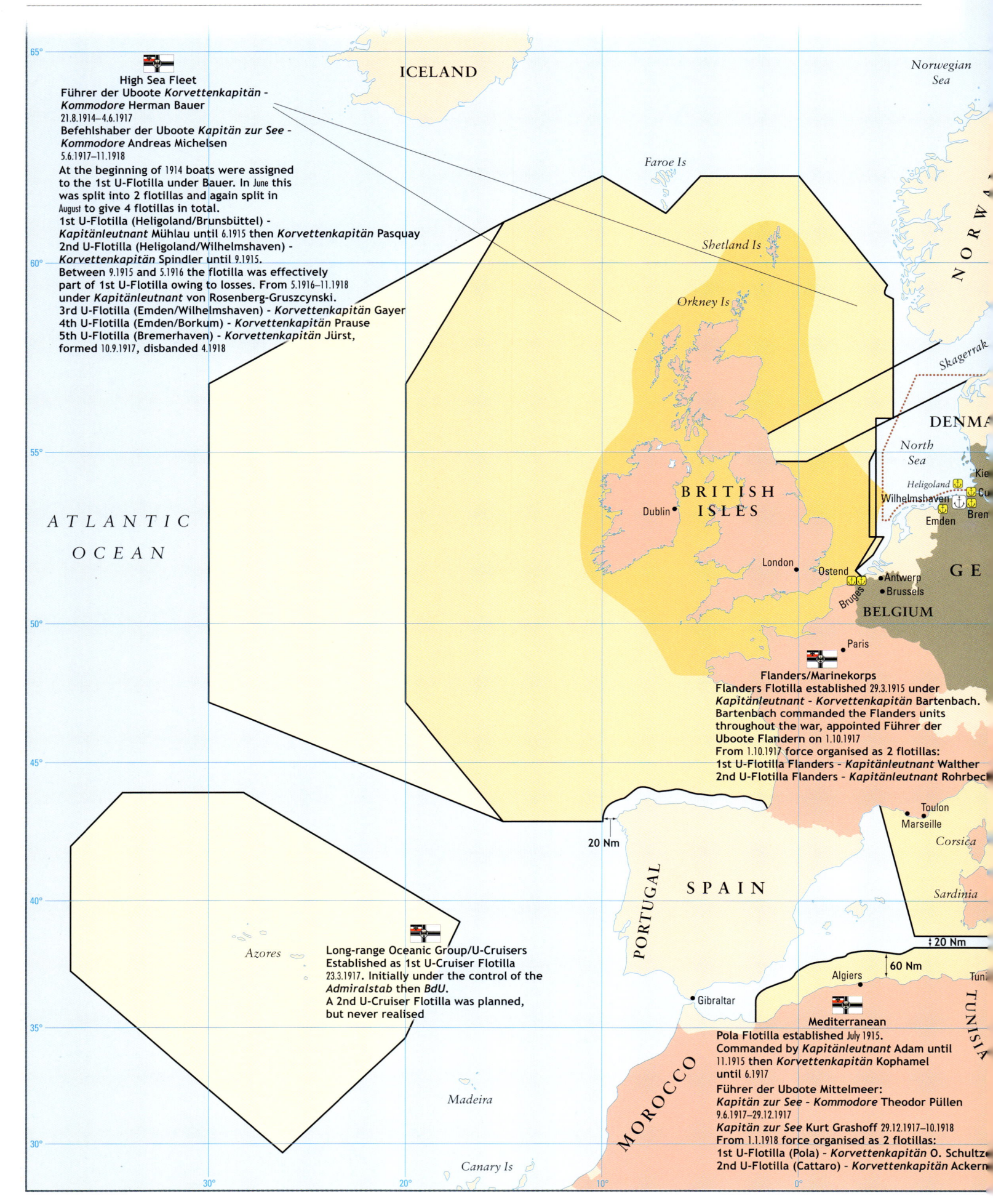

High Sea Fleet
Führer der Uboote *Korvettenkapitän* - *Kommodore* Herman Bauer
21.8.1914–4.6.1917
Befehlshaber der Uboote *Kapitän zur See* - *Kommodore* Andreas Michelsen
5.6.1917–11.1918
At the beginning of 1914 boats were assigned to the 1st U-Flotilla under Bauer. In June this was split into 2 flotillas and again split in August to give 4 flotillas in total.
1st U-Flotilla (Heligoland/Brunsbüttel) - *Kapitänleutnant* Mühlau until 6.1915 then *Korvettenkapitän* Pasquay
2nd U-Flotilla (Heligoland/Wilhelmshaven) - *Korvettenkapitän* Spindler until 9.1915.
Between 9.1915 and 5.1916 the flotilla was effectively part of 1st U-Flotilla owing to losses. From 5.1916–11.1918 under *Kapitänleutnant* von Rosenberg-Gruszcynski.
3rd U-Flotilla (Emden/Wilhelmshaven) - *Korvettenkapitän* Gayer
4th U-Flotilla (Emden/Borkum) - *Korvettenkapitän* Prause
5th U-Flotilla (Bremerhaven) - *Korvettenkapitän* Jürst, formed 10.9.1917, disbanded 4.1918

Flanders/Marinekorps
Flanders Flotilla established 29.3.1915 under *Kapitänleutnant* - *Korvettenkapitän* Bartenbach. Bartenbach commanded the Flanders units throughout the war, appointed Führer der Uboote Flandern on 1.10.1917
From 1.10.1917 force organised as 2 flotillas:
1st U-Flotilla Flanders - *Kapitänleutnant* Walther
2nd U-Flotilla Flanders - *Kapitänleutnant* Rohrbeck

Long-range Oceanic Group/U-Cruisers
Established as 1st U-Cruiser Flotilla 23.3.1917. Initially under the control of the *Admiralstab* then *BdU*.
A 2nd U-Cruiser Flotilla was planned, but never realised

Mediterranean
Pola Flotilla established July 1915. Commanded by *Kapitänleutnant* Adam until 11.1915 then *Korvettenkapitän* Kophamel until 6.1917
Führer der Uboote Mittelmeer:
Kapitän zur See - *Kommodore* Theodor Püllen 9.6.1917–29.12.1917
Kapitän zur See Kurt Grashoff 29.12.1917–10.1918
From 1.1.1918 force organised as 2 flotillas:
1st U-Flotilla (Pola) - *Korvettenkapitän* O. Schultze
2nd U-Flotilla (Cattaro) - *Korvettenkapitän* Ackerm

The Great War at Sea 1915

Throughout the conflict German U-boats sank 6,349 merchant ships, liners and military transports, amounting to around 11.9 million tons. This represented an unprecedented degree of destruction and one that had not been foreseen by either side. Two-thirds of the shipping sunk was British. Around 30,000 perished as a result of the submarine war, including around 5,000 U-boat crew, which represented about half the of Imperial Navy's submarine personnel.

Although the submarine changed commerce warfare it was an incremental process set against the changing nature of the war itself. This is underlined by the fact that 50 per cent of the shipping lost was sunk in 1917, a pivotal moment in the war and one when the U-boat constituted a great danger to the allied war effort. The U-boat campaign evolved gradually, and continuously, and was dependent on a host of political, technical, strategic and operational factors. Rather than being a single campaign, it was more a series of different ones both in chronological terms and in the theatres of operation. There was also very little coordination between these until mid-1916 and even then it was only quite tenuous as the operating conditions in each were very different.

As neither commerce warfare nor the submarine had received much pre-war interest the German navy simply did not have an adequate number of boats at the start of the conflict. It was not until 1916 that significant new construction entered operation and even then the boats were of small, limited design. As the submarine was a new weapon many of its technologies took time to develop and only from mid-war onwards were significant numbers of reliable boats able to operate west of Britain.

With the German navy's emphasis on surface action in the North Sea against the Grand Fleet there was always a tension between using U-boats to support the fleet and employing them in commerce warfare. Owing to their fragility and limitations, using submarines in commerce warfare while adhering to Prize Rules was very difficult. Stopping to search ships for contraband exposed boat and crew to danger. The most effective method was to wage unrestricted warfare, sinking shipping on sight and from a distance using torpedoes. Identifying the nationality of ships in this scenario was difficult, resulting in neutral vessels and cargoes being attacked and presenting the German government with diplomatic incidents.

The declaration of a war zone around Britain and the first phase of restricted U-boat warfare between February and September 1915 floundered through a lack of frontline boats and a number of disastrous diplomatic incidents, notably the sinking of RMS *Lusitania* in May, which necessitated the withdrawal of U-boats from commerce warfare. With, on average, less than six frontline boats British trade could hardly be choked off, while the political repercussions of war against neutral shipping were damaging. A second phase of restricted warfare between February and April 1916 was equally ineffective.

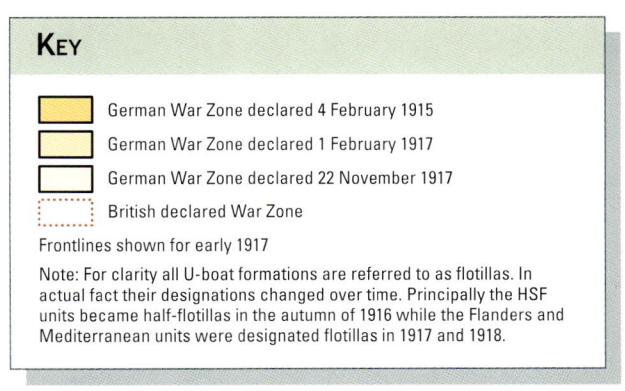

Development of the German U-boat Force 1914-1918

Month	1914 Additions	1914 Losses	1915 Additions	1915 Losses	1916 Additions	1916 Losses	1917 Additions	1917 Losses	1918 Additions	1918 Losses
January	–	–	2	3	3	–	6	2	3	10
February	–	–	4	–	5	–	4	6	6	3
March	–	–	7	3	9	2	4	5	8	7
April	–	–	6	1	8	3	5	1	8	7
May	–	–	8	1	9	3	5	8	11	17
June	–	–	6	4	8	1	8	3	12	3
July	–	–	5	3	9	3	11	9	9	6
August	3	2	2	2	10	2	12	4	8	7
September	3	–	2	3	10	–	8	13	9	10
October	1	–	2	1	10	1	13	7	12	20
November	2	1	2	2	13	5	5	8	2	12
December	2	2	6	–	14	3	6	9	–	–
Totals	11	5	52	23	108	23	87	75	88	102

At the start of the war the German navy possessed 28 U-boats. New construction throughout the war encompassed 346 U-boats - 115 fleet boats, 136 UB boats (coastal) and 95 UC boats (coastal minelayers). In total 229 U-boats were lost during war, 178 through enemy action and 50 through other causes like accidents or internment. Of the boats lost to enemy action the vast majority, 152 boats, were lost around the British Isles - 15 boats were lost in the Mediterranean.

Baltic

th U-Flotilla, replaced by
-Flotilla Kurland -
apitänleutnant Adam 8.1914–3.1915,
apitänleutnant Schött 7.1915–10.12.1917
his unit reported to the CinC Baltic.
t the end of 1917 the flotilla was
ssolved and its boats redistributed
 the other flotillas

Constantinople/Mittelmeerdivision
Detached boats from Pola assigned
to the Mittelmeerdivision

Key

- German War Zone declared 4 February 1915
- German War Zone declared 1 February 1917
- German War Zone declared 22 November 1917
- British declared War Zone

Frontlines shown for early 1917

Note: For clarity all U-boat formations are referred to as flotillas. In actual fact their designations changed over time. Principally the HSF units became half-flotillas in the autumn of 1916 while the Flanders and Mediterranean units were designated flotillas in 1917 and 1918.

THE ADRIATIC THEATRE, 1915–16

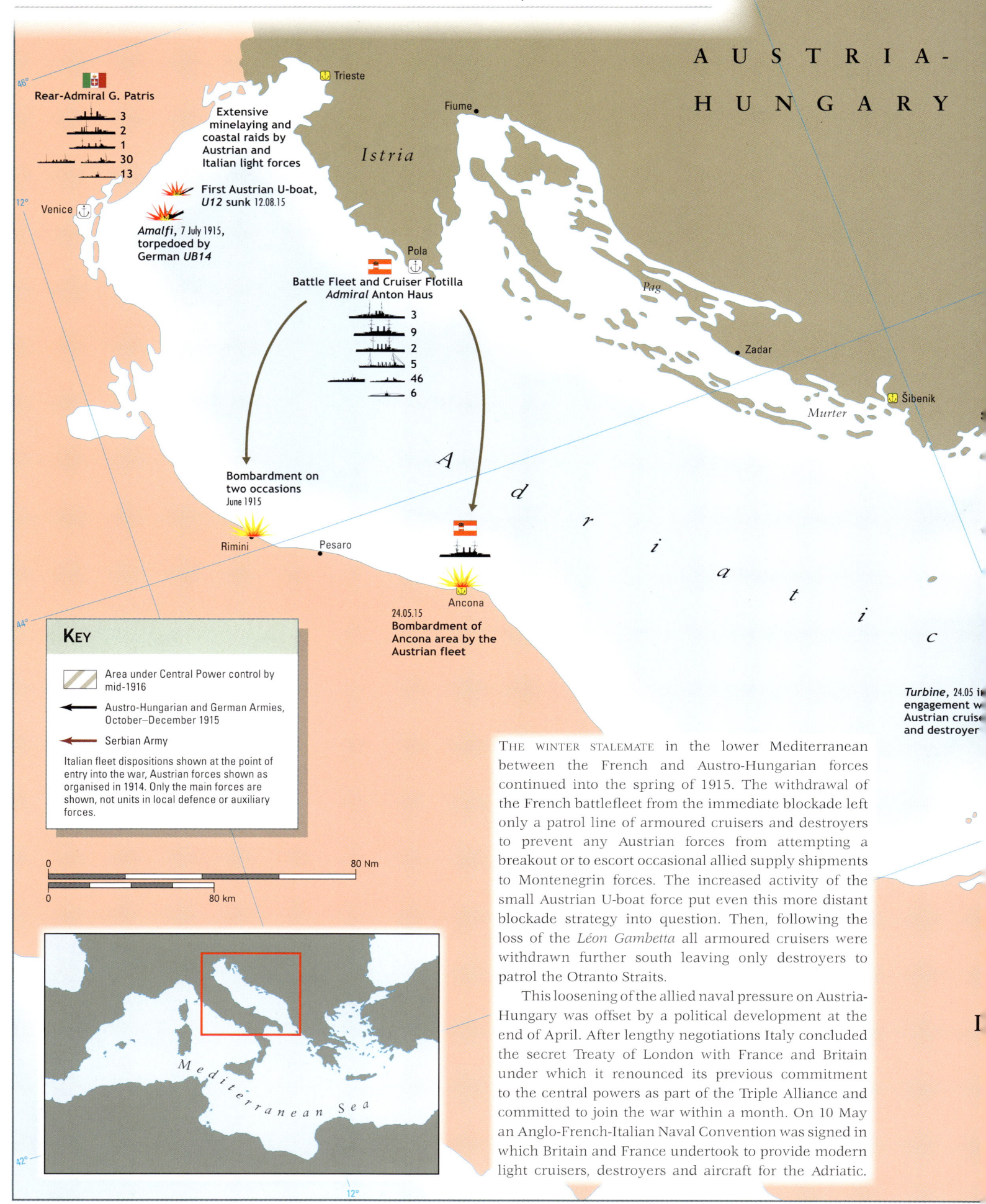

Rear-Admiral G. Patris
- 3
- 2
- 1
- 30
- 13

Trieste

Extensive minelaying and coastal raids by Austrian and Italian light forces

First Austrian U-boat, *U12* sunk 12.08.15

Amalfi, 7 July 1915, torpedoed by German *UB14*

Venice

Fiume

Istria

Pola

Battle Fleet and Cruiser Flotilla
Admiral Anton Haus
- 3
- 9
- 2
- 5
- 46
- 6

Pag

Zadar

Šibenik

Murter

Bombardment on two occasions June 1915

Rimini

Pesaro

Ancona

24.05.15 Bombardment of Ancona area by the Austrian fleet

AUSTRIA-HUNGARY

Adriatic

Turbine, 24.05 in engagement with Austrian cruiser and destroyer

KEY

- Area under Central Power control by mid-1916
- Austro-Hungarian and German Armies, October–December 1915
- Serbian Army

Italian fleet dispositions shown at the point of entry into the war, Austrian forces shown as organised in 1914. Only the main forces are shown, not units in local defence or auxiliary forces.

0 — 80 Nm
0 — 80 km

Mediterranean Sea

THE WINTER STALEMATE in the lower Mediterranean between the French and Austro-Hungarian forces continued into the spring of 1915. The withdrawal of the French battlefleet from the immediate blockade left only a patrol line of armoured cruisers and destroyers to prevent any Austrian forces from attempting a breakout or to escort occasional allied supply shipments to Montenegrin forces. The increased activity of the small Austrian U-boat force put even this more distant blockade strategy into question. Then, following the loss of the *Léon Gambetta* all armoured cruisers were withdrawn further south leaving only destroyers to patrol the Otranto Straits.

This loosening of the allied naval pressure on Austria-Hungary was offset by a political development at the end of April. After lengthy negotiations Italy concluded the secret Treaty of London with France and Britain under which it renounced its previous commitment to the central powers as part of the Triple Alliance and committed to join the war within a month. On 10 May an Anglo-French-Italian Naval Convention was signed in which Britain and France undertook to provide modern light cruisers, destroyers and aircraft for the Adriatic.

THE GREAT WAR AT SEA 1915

Italian entry into the war would also provide important bases for operations against Austria-Hungary.

The Italian battlefleet was based at its main base at Taranto while the majority of its cruisers, destroyers and torpedo boats were based at Brindisi. A far smaller force was based at the northern end of the Adriatic to protect Venice and its surrounding area. Forcing a naval battle on the Austrians based at Pola would be difficult and there were divisions within the navy as to what action to undertake in the event of a war and how assertive operations on the Dalmatian coastline would be.

The Austrians reacted immediately to the Italian declaration of war on 23 May and sent the battlefleet across the Adriatic to bombard Ancona. The long Italian coastline and the proximity of Pola meant that throughout the war it was easier for the Austrians to undertake such operations than for the *Regia Marina* to protect against them. The heavy units kept at Venice had little utility beyond protecting the city itself.

The Italian response was to conduct sweeps along lower Dalmatia to catch any detached Austrian warships and by means of bombardments lure the battlefleet south. This did not happen and losses to submarines eventually led to less assertive operations. The plan to capture outlying islands like Lagosta was abandoned although the threat of a potential Italian amphibious operation eventually led to nearly two divisions worth of Austro-Hungarian troops guarding the Dalmatian coast.

By the autumn a stalemate again descended upon the Adriatic that continued into 1916. The focus of allied naval operations was on the early development of the Otranto barrage in an effort to curtail German U-boat operations that were beginning to have a serious impact in the Mediterranean. Conversely, the Austrians increasingly brought down cruisers and destroyers to interfere with these efforts and to disrupt the evacuation of the Serbian army. The allied effort was also beset by politics and rivalry. The combined Franco-Italian battlefleet enjoyed a huge margin of superiority over the Austrians yet this had little impact on the situation in the Adriatic.

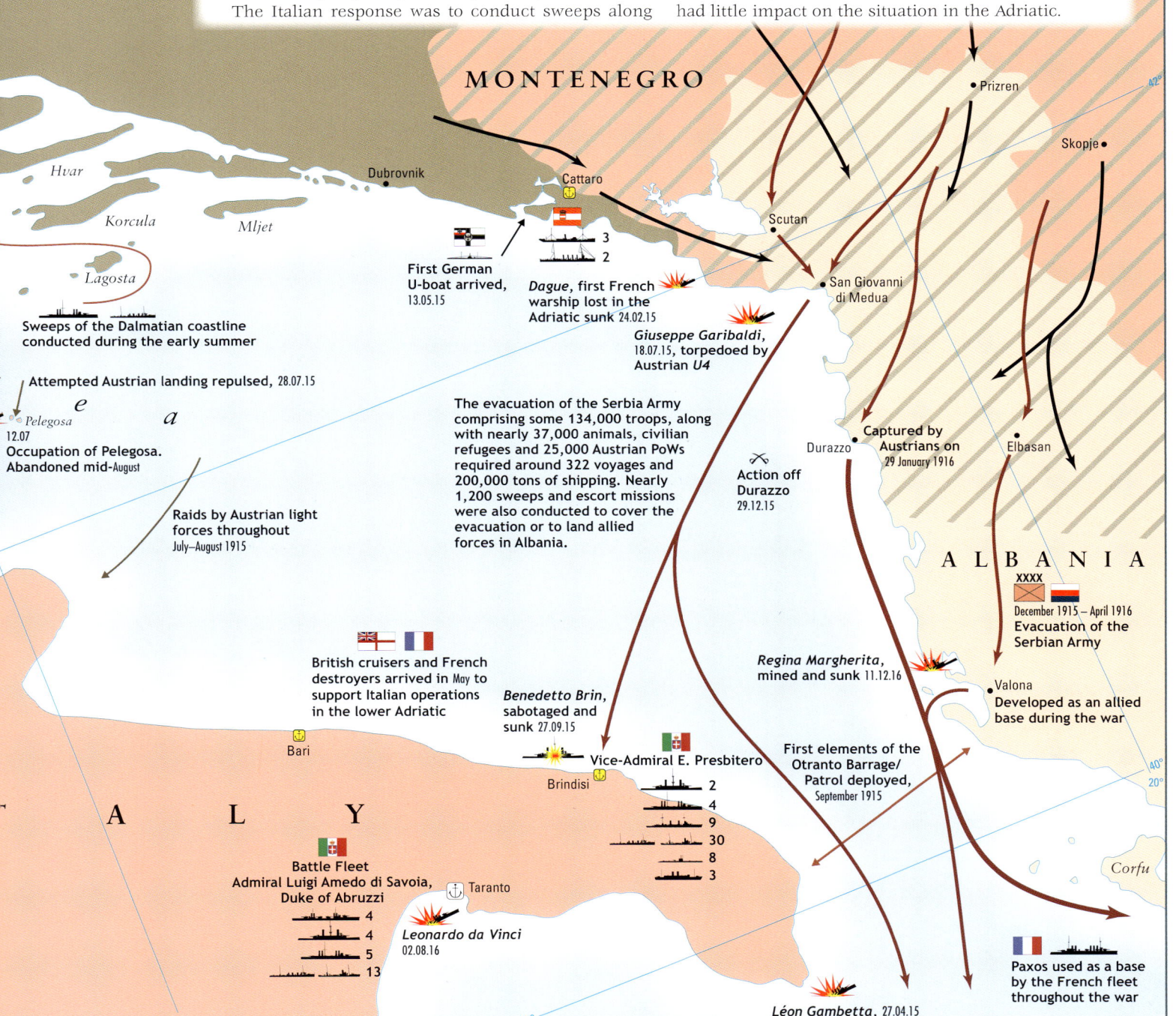

Strategic Communications

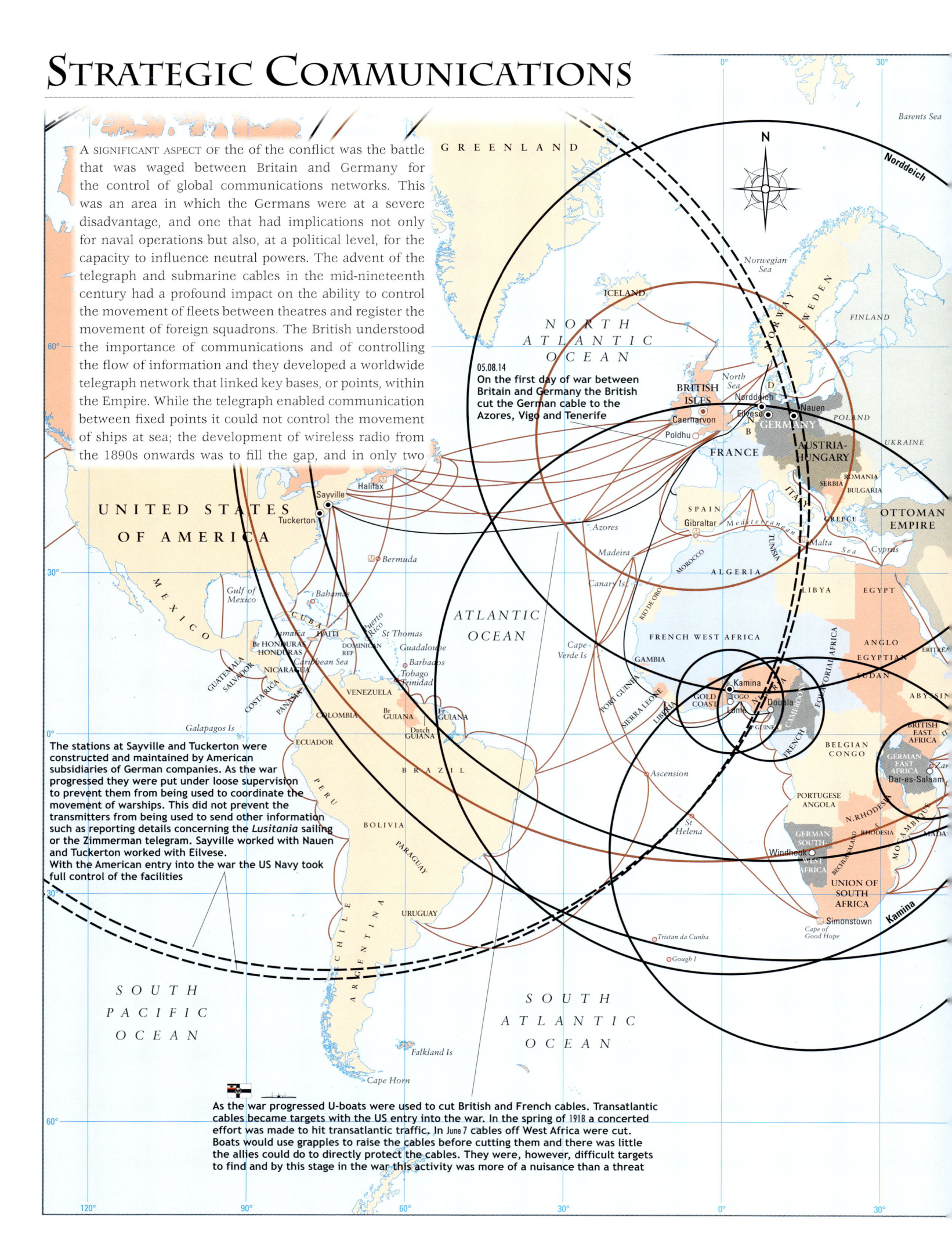

A significant aspect of the of the conflict was the battle that was waged between Britain and Germany for the control of global communications networks. This was an area in which the Germans were at a severe disadvantage, and one that had implications not only for naval operations but also, at a political level, for the capacity to influence neutral powers. The advent of the telegraph and submarine cables in the mid-nineteenth century had a profound impact on the ability to control the movement of fleets between theatres and register the movement of foreign squadrons. The British understood the importance of communications and of controlling the flow of information and they developed a worldwide telegraph network that linked key bases, or points, within the Empire. While the telegraph enabled communication between fixed points it could not control the movement of ships at sea; the development of wireless radio from the 1890s onwards was to fill the gap, and in only two

05.08.14
On the first day of war between Britain and Germany the British cut the German cable to the Azores, Vigo and Tenerife

The stations at Sayville and Tuckerton were constructed and maintained by American subsidiaries of German companies. As the war progressed they were put under loose supervision to prevent them from being used to coordinate the movement of warships. This did not prevent the transmitters from being used to send other information such as reporting details concerning the *Lusitania* sailing or the Zimmerman telegram. Sayville worked with Nauen and Tuckerton worked with Eilvese.
With the American entry into the war the US Navy took full control of the facilities

As the war progressed U-boats were used to cut British and French cables. Transatlantic cables became targets with the US entry into the war. In the spring of 1918 a concerted effort was made to hit transatlantic traffic. In June 7 cables off West Africa were cut. Boats would use grapples to raise the cables before cutting them and there was little the allies could do to directly protect the cables. They were, however, difficult targets to find and by this stage in the war this activity was more of a nuisance than a threat

THE GREAT WAR AT SEA 1915

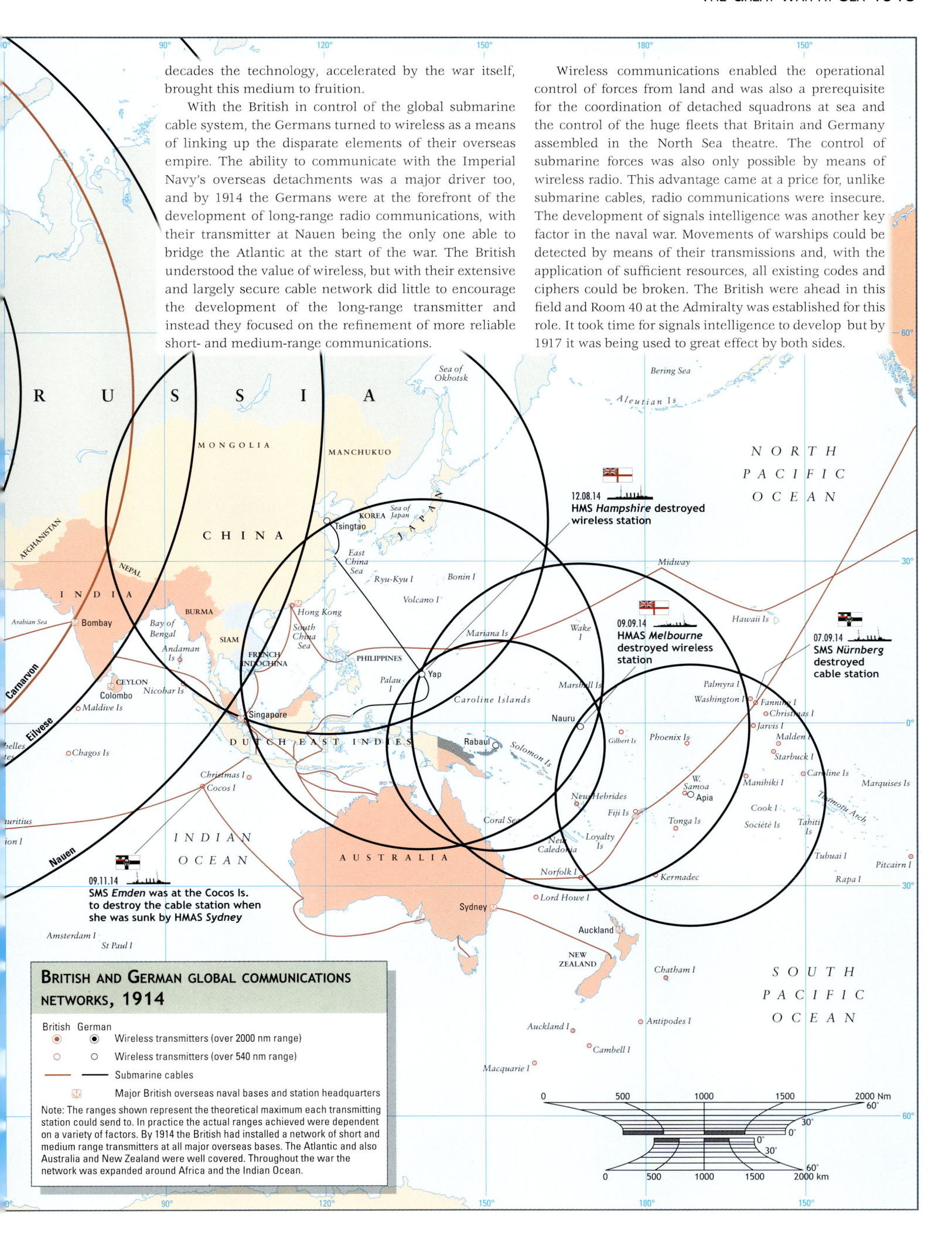

decades the technology, accelerated by the war itself, brought this medium to fruition.

With the British in control of the global submarine cable system, the Germans turned to wireless as a means of linking up the disparate elements of their overseas empire. The ability to communicate with the Imperial Navy's overseas detachments was a major driver too, and by 1914 the Germans were at the forefront of the development of long-range radio communications, with their transmitter at Nauen being the only one able to bridge the Atlantic at the start of the war. The British understood the value of wireless, but with their extensive and largely secure cable network did little to encourage the development of the long-range transmitter and instead they focused on the refinement of more reliable short- and medium-range communications.

Wireless communications enabled the operational control of forces from land and was also a prerequisite for the coordination of detached squadrons at sea and the control of the huge fleets that Britain and Germany assembled in the North Sea theatre. The control of submarine forces was also only possible by means of wireless radio. This advantage came at a price for, unlike submarine cables, radio communications were insecure. The development of signals intelligence was another key factor in the naval war. Movements of warships could be detected by means of their transmissions and, with the application of sufficient resources, all existing codes and ciphers could be broken. The British were ahead in this field and Room 40 at the Admiralty was established for this role. It took time for signals intelligence to develop but by 1917 it was being used to great effect by both sides.

12.08.14 HMS *Hampshire* destroyed wireless station

09.09.14 HMAS *Melbourne* destroyed wireless station

07.09.14 SMS *Nürnberg* destroyed cable station

09.11.14 SMS *Emden* was at the Cocos Is. to destroy the cable station when she was sunk by HMAS *Sydney*

BRITISH AND GERMAN GLOBAL COMMUNICATIONS NETWORKS, 1914

British German
- ● Wireless transmitters (over 2000 nm range)
- ○ Wireless transmitters (over 540 nm range)
- — Submarine cables
- Major British overseas naval bases and station headquarters

Note: The ranges shown represent the theoretical maximum each transmitting station could send to. In practice the actual ranges achieved were dependent on a variety of factors. By 1914 the British had installed a network of short and medium range transmitters at all major overseas bases. The Atlantic and also Australia and New Zealand were well covered. Throughout the war the network was expanded around Africa and the Indian Ocean.

THE AUXILIARY PATROL, 1914–15

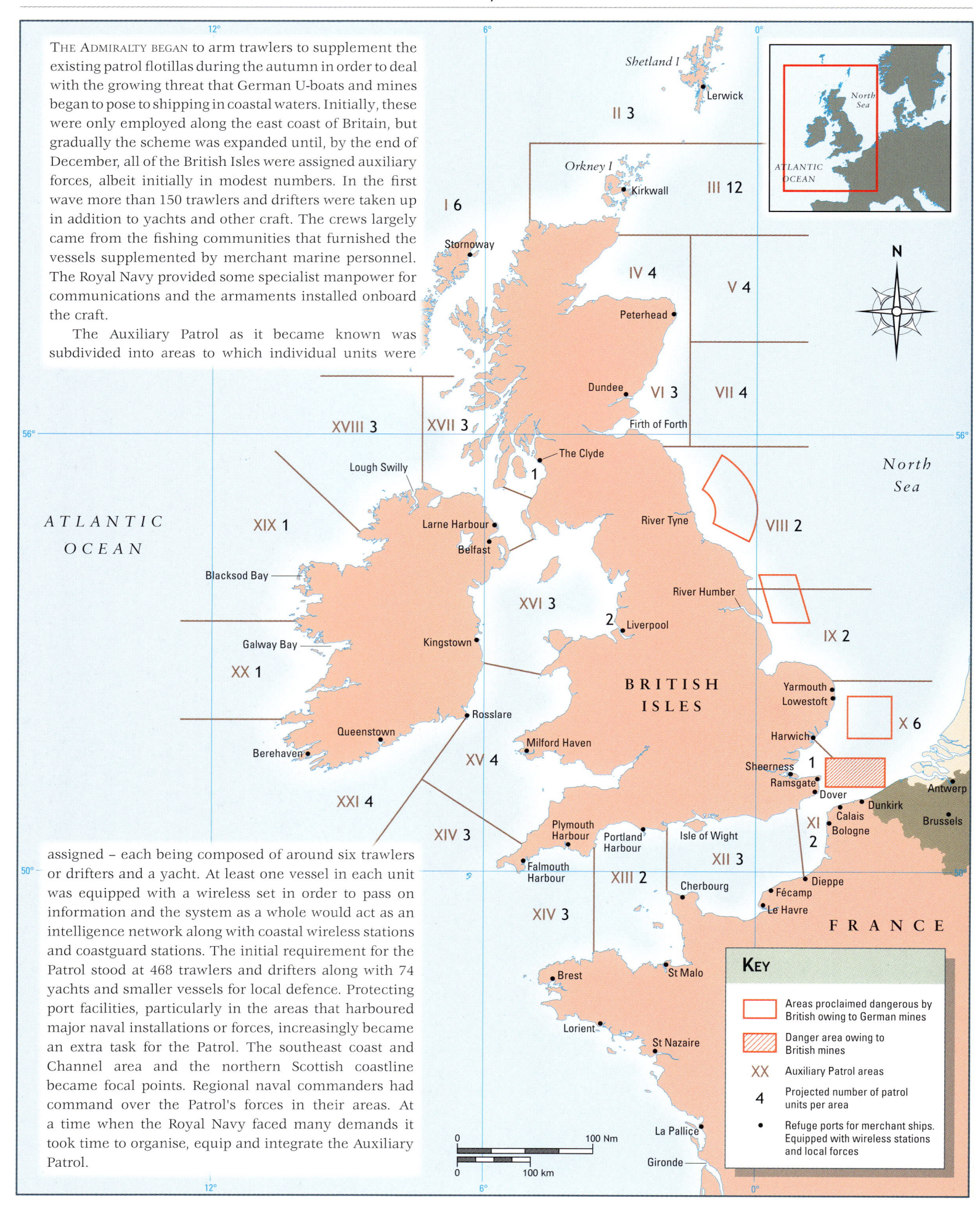

THE ADMIRALTY BEGAN to arm trawlers to supplement the existing patrol flotillas during the autumn in order to deal with the growing threat that German U-boats and mines began to pose to shipping in coastal waters. Initially, these were only employed along the east coast of Britain, but gradually the scheme was expanded until, by the end of December, all of the British Isles were assigned auxiliary forces, albeit initially in modest numbers. In the first wave more than 150 trawlers and drifters were taken up in addition to yachts and other craft. The crews largely came from the fishing communities that furnished the vessels supplemented by merchant marine personnel. The Royal Navy provided some specialist manpower for communications and the armaments installed onboard the craft.

The Auxiliary Patrol as it became known was subdivided into areas to which individual units were assigned – each being composed of around six trawlers or drifters and a yacht. At least one vessel in each unit was equipped with a wireless set in order to pass on information and the system as a whole would act as an intelligence network along with coastal wireless stations and coastguard stations. The initial requirement for the Patrol stood at 468 trawlers and drifters along with 74 yachts and smaller vessels for local defence. Protecting port facilities, particularly in the areas that harboured major naval installations or forces, increasingly became an extra task for the Patrol. The southeast coast and Channel area and the northern Scottish coastline became focal points. Regional naval commanders had command over the Patrol's forces in their areas. At a time when the Royal Navy faced many demands it took time to organise, equip and integrate the Auxiliary Patrol.

KEY

- Areas proclaimed dangerous by British owing to German mines
- Danger area owing to British mines
- XX Auxiliary Patrol areas
- 4 Projected number of patrol units per area
- • Refuge ports for merchant ships. Equipped with wireless stations and local forces

66

THE GREAT WAR AT SEA 1915

THE VOYAGE OF SMS METEOR, MAY–JUNE 1915

IN MARCH 1915 the General Staff asked the *Admiralstab* whether the flow of allied supplies to Russia could be interdicted. With German control of the main seaborne routes via the Baltic and the Dardanelles, the Arctic route became the main one for allied *materiel* shipments to Russia. Disruption of these shipments would have an impact on the fighting on the Eastern front as it was known the Russian army was suffering from a lack of supplies. Owing to the distances involved and the local ice conditions neither the available cruisers nor U-boats would be able to seriously disrupt the shipments. Instead, an auxiliary cruiser would be employed to lay mines to coincide with the thawing of the ice that in turn would see an increase in the shipping to and from Archangel.

For this purpose SMS *Meteor*, formerly the British freighter *Vienna* that had been in Hamburg at the outbreak of the war and seized by German authorities, was selected. She was an ideal vessel to employ as her appearance resembled many other vessels operating in British and northern waters. The operation was prepared with great secrecy and, under the cover of a fleet movement, *Meteor* put to sea late on 29 May and made her way to the Arctic Sea. The deployment area was reached and minefields sown in the shipping lanes without any major incidents. Allied naval forces in the area were very limited – a small number of British minesweepers only arrived at the beginning of June – thus surprise was achieved and for a short period the flow of supplies was affected. At the end of the return voyage *Meteor* sank three merchant ships in the Skagerrak.

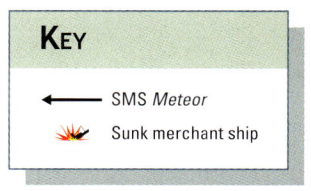

KEY

← SMS *Meteor*

💥 Sunk merchant ship

The Dardanelles: Allied Supply Routes

The Gallipoli campaign was waged at the end of long and increasingly vulnerable allied supply lines. During the early stages of the allied presence off the Dardanelles, the threat to British and French warships and their supporting vessels from submarine attack was negligible, while the transports carrying the forces destined for the April 1915 landings were also able to proceed in relative safety. The distant threat of submarine attacks prompted the French navy to conduct a blockade of the Adriatic, but Austrian U-boats seldom ventured further south or engaged in commerce warfare. However, the situation was transformed with the arrival of German U-boats from May onwards.

The first operational boat to arrive was *U21*; she had left Germany on 25 April, bound for the Austrian base at Cattaro. The British were aware of *U21*'s movements and her arrival was one factor that hastened the withdrawal of the battleship *Queen Elizabeth*. U-boats posed a serious threat to the older battleships, with their limited escorts and defences, operating off the Dardanelles in support of allied troops, and Germany now deployed them as a means of supporting the Turks against the allied assault. The build-up of the initial U-boat force in the Mediterranean occurred in two waves. From March onwards, smaller minelaying boats were sent in sections by rail and assembled at Pola. Most of these were sent on to operate in the Aegean and were based at Constantinople. In the late summer four larger fleet boats were sent via the Atlantic. These were to operate in the central Mediterranean.

The loss of *Majestic* and *Triumph* (see pages 58 and 81) to *U21* showed that the threat was real and led to some minor route adjustments to protect the movement of troop transports that were by now carrying large numbers of reinforcements. It was the loss of the French transport *Carthage*, however, that brought about a significant change in the way that troop transports sailed and supply shipments were despatched along defined routes that could be patrolled, but a lack of co-ordination and limited resources meant that these allied measures were never fully effective. With only a relatively small U-boat force the Germans inflicted heavy loses from the autumn onwards.

German U-boats deployed to the Mediterranean, 1915

By Sea	Arrived Cattaro	Commenced Operations
U21	13 May	20 May
U33	16 September	End of September
U34	23 August	1 September
U35	23 August	31 August
U39	15 September	End of September

Overland – By rail and assembled at Pola	Commissioned/Operational	
UB1	29 January	To Austrian Navy
UB3	14 March / 1 May	Lost 23 May
UB7	6 May / 11 May	To Constantinople
UB8	23 April / 2 May	To Constantinople
UB14	23 March / 1 July	To Constantinople
UB15	11 April / June	To Austrian Navy
UC12	2 May / 27 June	
UC13	15 May / 15 July	To Constantinople
UC14	5 June / 5 June	
UC15	28 June / 28 June	To Constantinople

First elements Otranto Barrage Patrol deployed September 1915

Vice-Admiral Augustin Boué de Lapeyrère
Malta acted as the main base for the French fleet

From 1 June all troop transports and supply ships were sent to Alexandria where troops and cargoes could be reorganised

From the end of August all troop transports from Britain sailed directly to Mudros, store and supply vessels continued to be sent to Alexandira first to have their cargoes reorganised

Key

- Routes planned to come into use mid-August 1915
- Routes ordered 29 August
- Routes issued mid-September
- Routes issued early October
- Areas of responsibility

The Great War at Sea 1915

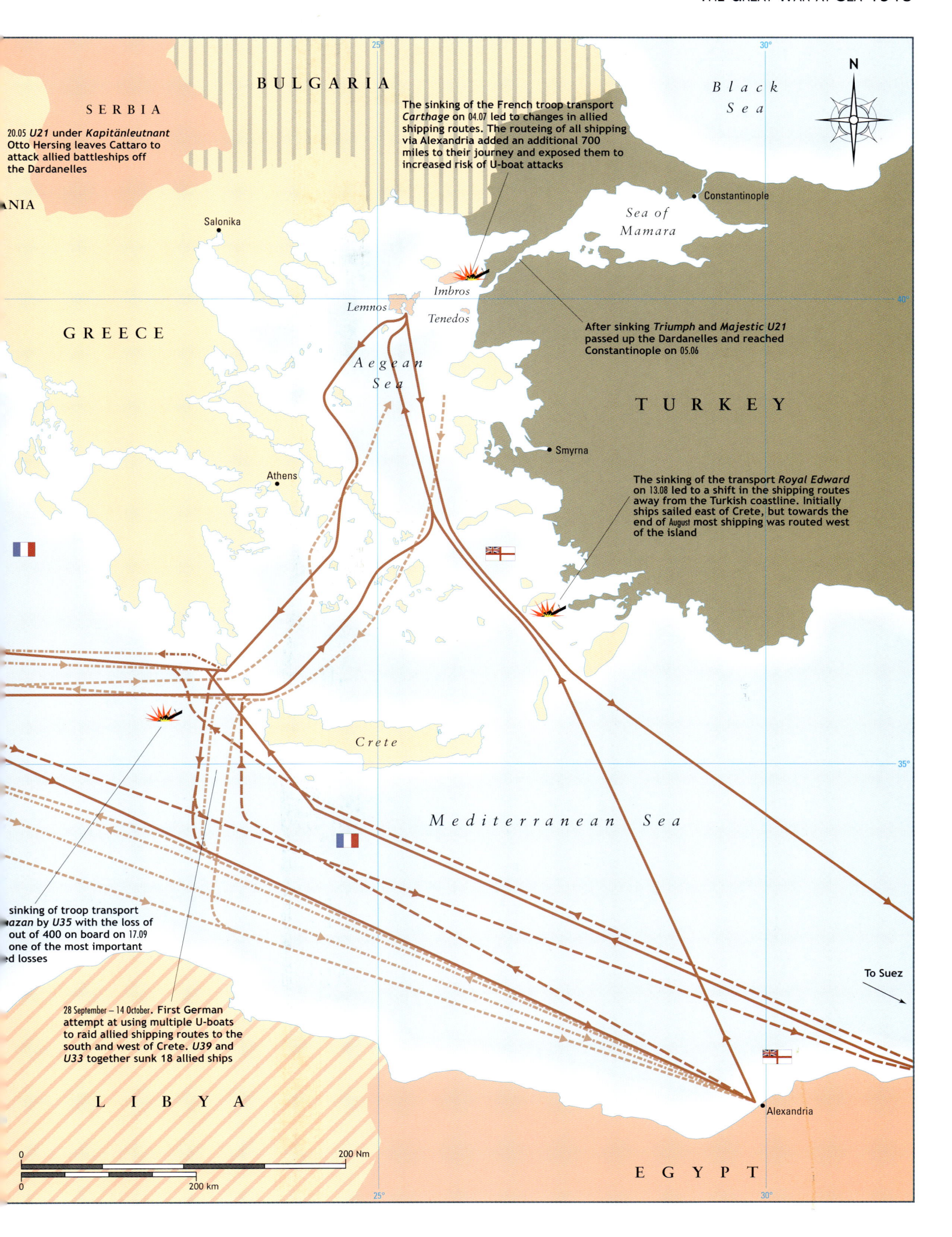

20.05 *U21* under *Kapitänleutnant* Otto Hersing leaves Cattaro to attack allied battleships off the Dardanelles

The sinking of the French troop transport *Carthage* on 04.07 led to changes in allied shipping routes. The routeing of all shipping via Alexandria added an additional 700 miles to their journey and exposed them to increased risk of U-boat attacks

After sinking *Triumph* and *Majestic* *U21* passed up the Dardanelles and reached Constantinople on 05.06

The sinking of the transport *Royal Edward* on 13.08 led to a shift in the shipping routes away from the Turkish coastline. Initially ships sailed east of Crete, but towards the end of August most shipping was routed west of the island

sinking of troop transport *azan* by *U35* with the loss of out of 400 on board on 17.09 one of the most important d losses

28 September – 14 October. First German attempt at using multiple U-boats to raid allied shipping routes to the south and west of Crete. *U39* and *U33* together sunk 18 allied ships

BATTLE OF THE ÅLAND ISLANDS, 2 JULY 1915

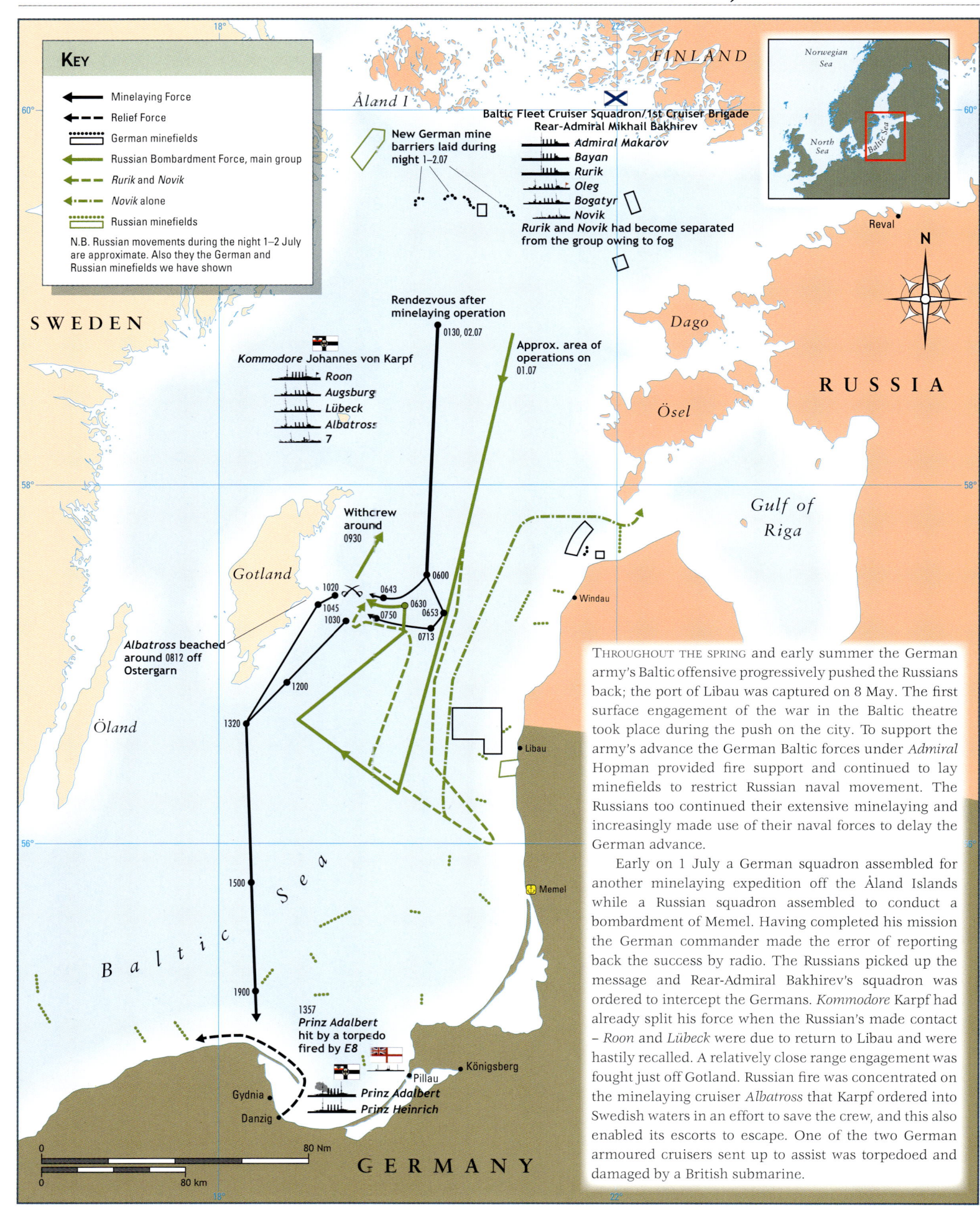

KEY
- ← Minelaying Force
- ←- - Relief Force
- •••••• German minefields
- ← Russian Bombardment Force, main group
- ←- - *Rurik* and *Novik*
- ←-·- *Novik* alone
- ▭▭▭ Russian minefields

N.B. Russian movements during the night 1–2 July are approximate. Also they the German and Russian minefields we have shown

Baltic Fleet Cruiser Squadron/1st Cruiser Brigade Rear-Admiral Mikhail Bakhirev
- Admiral Makarov
- Bayan
- Rurik
- Oleg
- Bogatyr
- Novik

Rurik and *Novik* had become separated from the group owing to fog

New German mine barriers laid during night 1–2.07

Rendezvous after minelaying operation 0130, 02.07

Approx. area of operations on 01.07

Kommodore Johannes von Karpf
- Roon
- Augsburg
- Lübeck
- Albatross
- 7

Withcrew around 0930

Albatross beached around 0812 off Ostergarn

1357 *Prinz Adalbert* hit by a torpedo fired by *E8*

Prinz Adalbert
Prinz Heinrich

THROUGHOUT THE SPRING and early summer the German army's Baltic offensive progressively pushed the Russians back; the port of Libau was captured on 8 May. The first surface engagement of the war in the Baltic theatre took place during the push on the city. To support the army's advance the German Baltic forces under *Admiral Hopman* provided fire support and continued to lay minefields to restrict Russian naval movement. The Russians too continued their extensive minelaying and increasingly made use of their naval forces to delay the German advance.

Early on 1 July a German squadron assembled for another minelaying expedition off the Åland Islands while a Russian squadron assembled to conduct a bombardment of Memel. Having completed his mission the German commander made the error of reporting back the success by radio. The Russians picked up the message and Rear-Admiral Bakhirev's squadron was ordered to intercept the Germans. *Kommodore* Karpf had already split his force when the Russian's made contact – *Roon* and *Lübeck* were due to return to Libau and were hastily recalled. A relatively close range engagement was fought just off Gotland. Russian fire was concentrated on the minelaying cruiser *Albatross* that Karpf ordered into Swedish waters in an effort to save the crew, and this also enabled its escorts to escape. One of the two German armoured cruisers sent up to assist was torpedoed and damaged by a British submarine.

THE GREAT WAR AT SEA 1915

DESTRUCTION OF SMS KÖNIGSBERG, JULY 1915

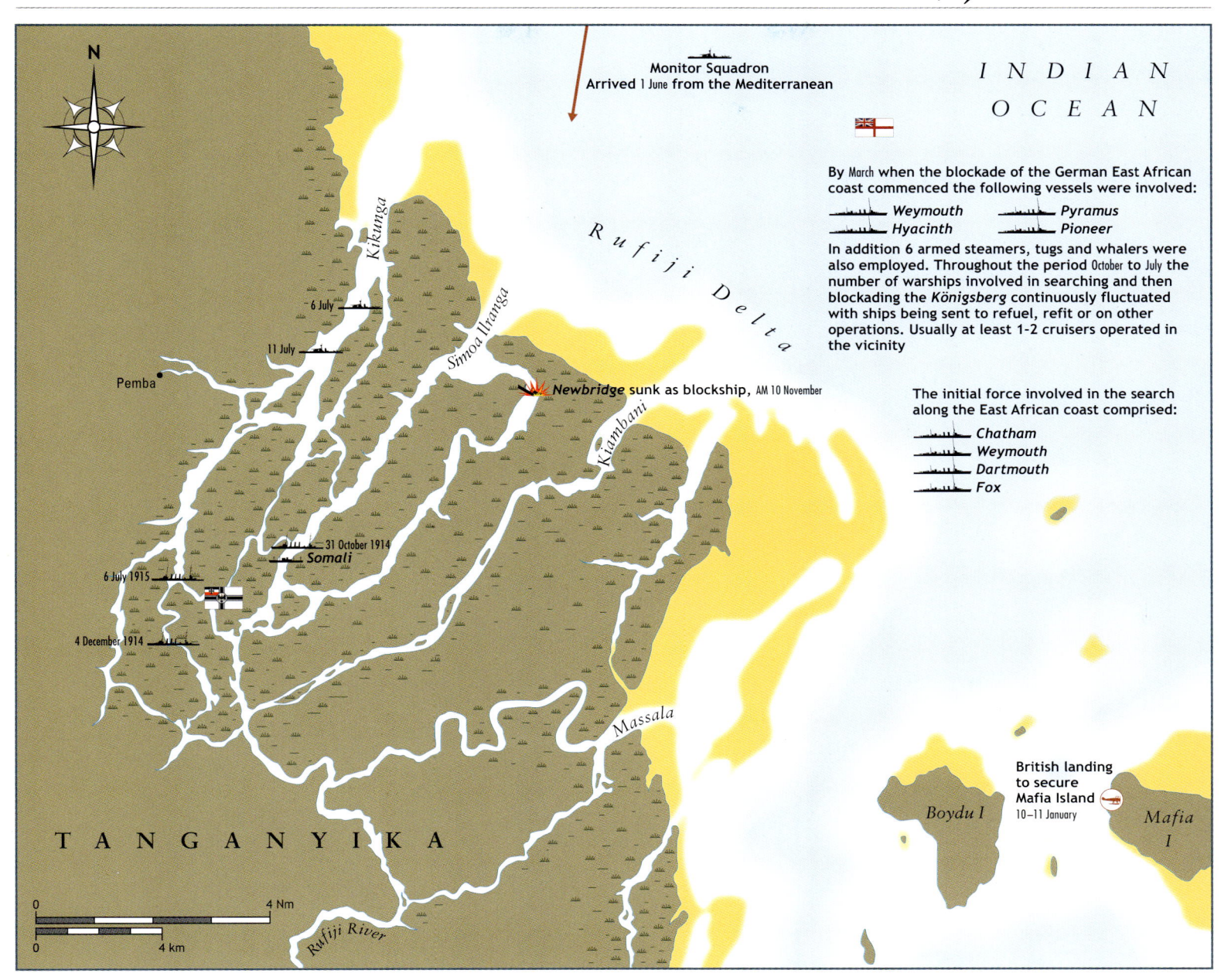

WITH KÖNIGSBERG'S ENGINES badly in need of maintenance and having exhausted her coal supply, *Fregattenkapitän* Looff had little choice but to remain in the Rufiji Delta. Although the attack on Zanzibar on 20 September had achieved the objective of sinking the small protected cruiser *Pegasus* and damaged shore installations, *Königsberg* was in no position to engage with the larger British warships off East Africa. She was also unable to undertake the necessary repairs in Dar-es-Salaam as the capital of German East Africa would inevitably become the target of a British attack. Instead, *Königsberg* would remain heavily camouflaged in the Rufiji while the parts that needed repair were taken over land to Dar-es-Salaam.

The British had no idea of *Königsberg*'s whereabouts and the prospect of a German cruiser on the loose in the Indian Ocean was hardly encouraging. It was not until 30 October that the light cruiser *Dartmouth* located *Königsberg* and then, along with the *Chatham* and *Weymouth*, began a blockade of the Delta.

On 3 November the cruisers bombarded *Königsberg*'s position in an attempt to destroy her, but the thick mangrove swamps offered ample protection from the indirect fire. A blockship was sunk to prevent escape and the pre-dreadnought *Goliath* brought in to provide heavier fire. This only induced the Germans to move out of range further upstream and while the crew was suffering from disease and shortages the British could not neutralise the threat. Nor could the British invest more into the operation as a concurrently-run expedition against Dar-es-Salaam ended in a defeat.

Only when shallow draught monitors were diverted from the Dardanelles campaign and aircraft brought in to spot the gunfire could *Königsberg* be neutralised. On the second attempt, on 11 July, she was mortally hit and scuttled by her crew. However, her value to the German war effort in Africa did not end. Her guns were salvaged, manned by the crew and provided artillery support to *Oberstleutnant* von Lettow-Verbeck's forces in East Africa. Her wireless set was also salvaged and put into use in establishing a radio link to Germany.

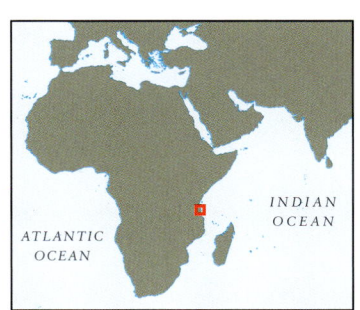

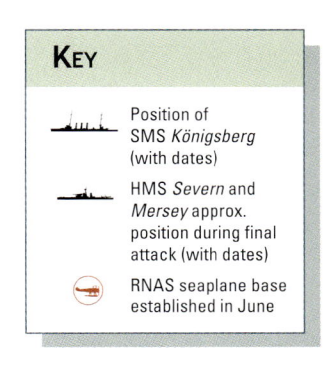

The Loss of SMS Meteor, 6–9 August 1915

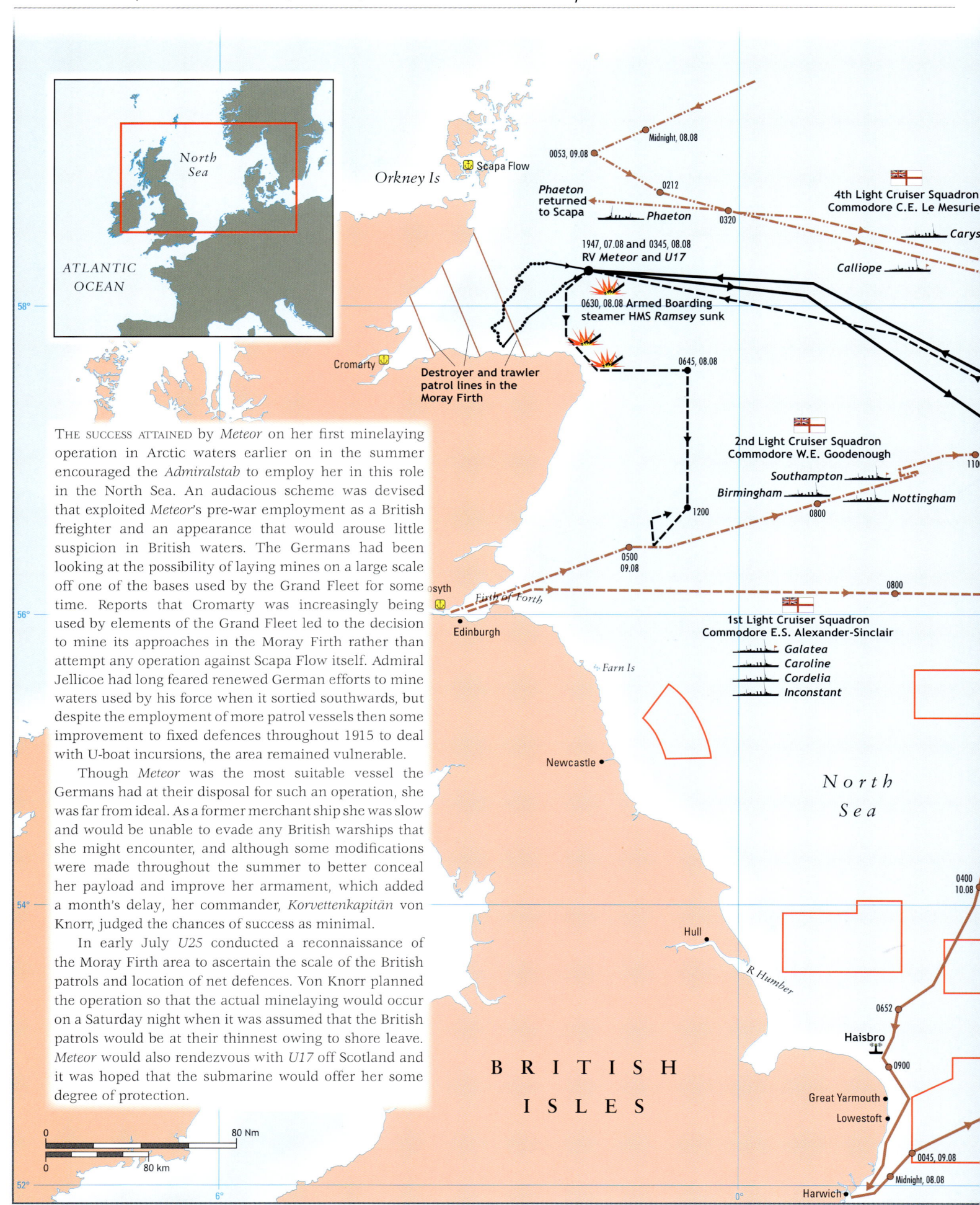

The success attained by *Meteor* on her first minelaying operation in Arctic waters earlier on in the summer encouraged the *Admiralstab* to employ her in this role in the North Sea. An audacious scheme was devised that exploited *Meteor*'s pre-war employment as a British freighter and an appearance that would arouse little suspicion in British waters. The Germans had been looking at the possibility of laying mines on a large scale off one of the bases used by the Grand Fleet for some time. Reports that Cromarty was increasingly being used by elements of the Grand Fleet led to the decision to mine its approaches in the Moray Firth rather than attempt any operation against Scapa Flow itself. Admiral Jellicoe had long feared renewed German efforts to mine waters used by his force when it sortied southwards, but despite the employment of more patrol vessels then some improvement to fixed defences throughout 1915 to deal with U-boat incursions, the area remained vulnerable.

Though *Meteor* was the most suitable vessel the Germans had at their disposal for such an operation, she was far from ideal. As a former merchant ship she was slow and would be unable to evade any British warships that she might encounter, and although some modifications were made throughout the summer to better conceal her payload and improve her armament, which added a month's delay, her commander, *Korvettenkapitän* von Knorr, judged the chances of success as minimal.

In early July *U25* conducted a reconnaissance of the Moray Firth area to ascertain the scale of the British patrols and location of net defences. Von Knorr planned the operation so that the actual minelaying would occur on a Saturday night when it was assumed that the British patrols would be at their thinnest owing to shore leave. *Meteor* would also rendezvous with *U17* off Scotland and it was hoped that the submarine would offer her some degree of protection.

THE GREAT WAR AT SEA 1915

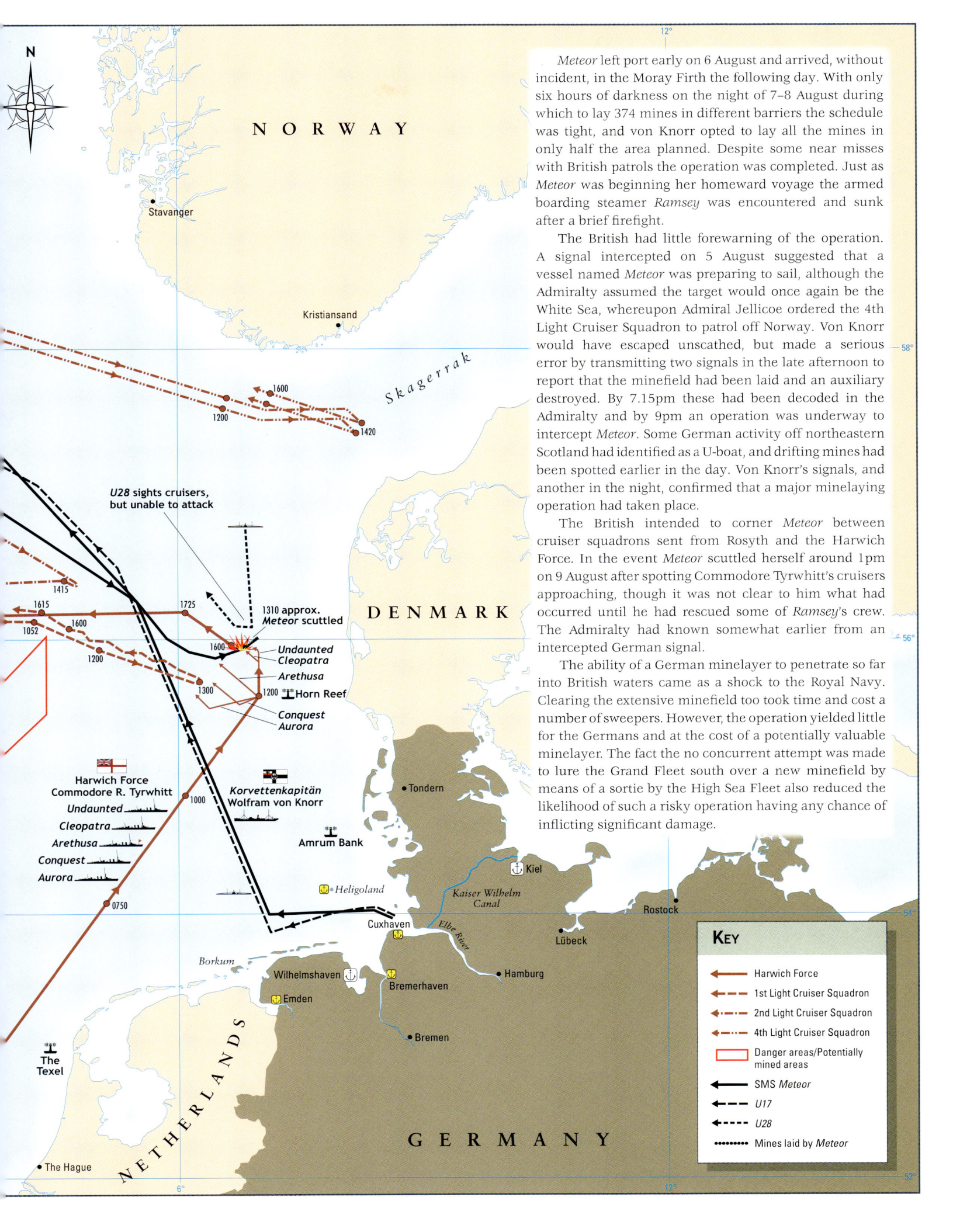

Meteor left port early on 6 August and arrived, without incident, in the Moray Firth the following day. With only six hours of darkness on the night of 7–8 August during which to lay 374 mines in different barriers the schedule was tight, and von Knorr opted to lay all the mines in only half the area planned. Despite some near misses with British patrols the operation was completed. Just as *Meteor* was beginning her homeward voyage the armed boarding steamer *Ramsey* was encountered and sunk after a brief firefight.

The British had little forewarning of the operation. A signal intercepted on 5 August suggested that a vessel named *Meteor* was preparing to sail, although the Admiralty assumed the target would once again be the White Sea, whereupon Admiral Jellicoe ordered the 4th Light Cruiser Squadron to patrol off Norway. Von Knorr would have escaped unscathed, but made a serious error by transmitting two signals in the late afternoon to report that the minefield had been laid and an auxiliary destroyed. By 7.15pm these had been decoded in the Admiralty and by 9pm an operation was underway to intercept *Meteor*. Some German activity off northeastern Scotland had identified as a U-boat, and drifting mines had been spotted earlier in the day. Von Knorr's signals, and another in the night, confirmed that a major minelaying operation had taken place.

The British intended to corner *Meteor* between cruiser squadrons sent from Rosyth and the Harwich Force. In the event *Meteor* scuttled herself around 1pm on 9 August after spotting Commodore Tyrwhitt's cruisers approaching, though it was not clear to him what had occurred until he had rescued some of *Ramsey*'s crew. The Admiralty had known somewhat earlier from an intercepted German signal.

The ability of a German minelayer to penetrate so far into British waters came as a shock to the Royal Navy. Clearing the extensive minefield too took time and cost a number of sweepers. However, the operation yielded little for the Germans and at the cost of a potentially valuable minelayer. The fact the no concurrent attempt was made to lure the Grand Fleet south over a new minefield by means of a sortie by the High Sea Fleet also reduced the likelihood of such a risky operation having any chance of inflicting significant damage.

Key

- Harwich Force
- 1st Light Cruiser Squadron
- 2nd Light Cruiser Squadron
- 4th Light Cruiser Squadron
- Danger areas/Potentially mined areas
- SMS *Meteor*
- U17
- U28
- Mines laid by *Meteor*

Gulf of Riga Operations, August 1915

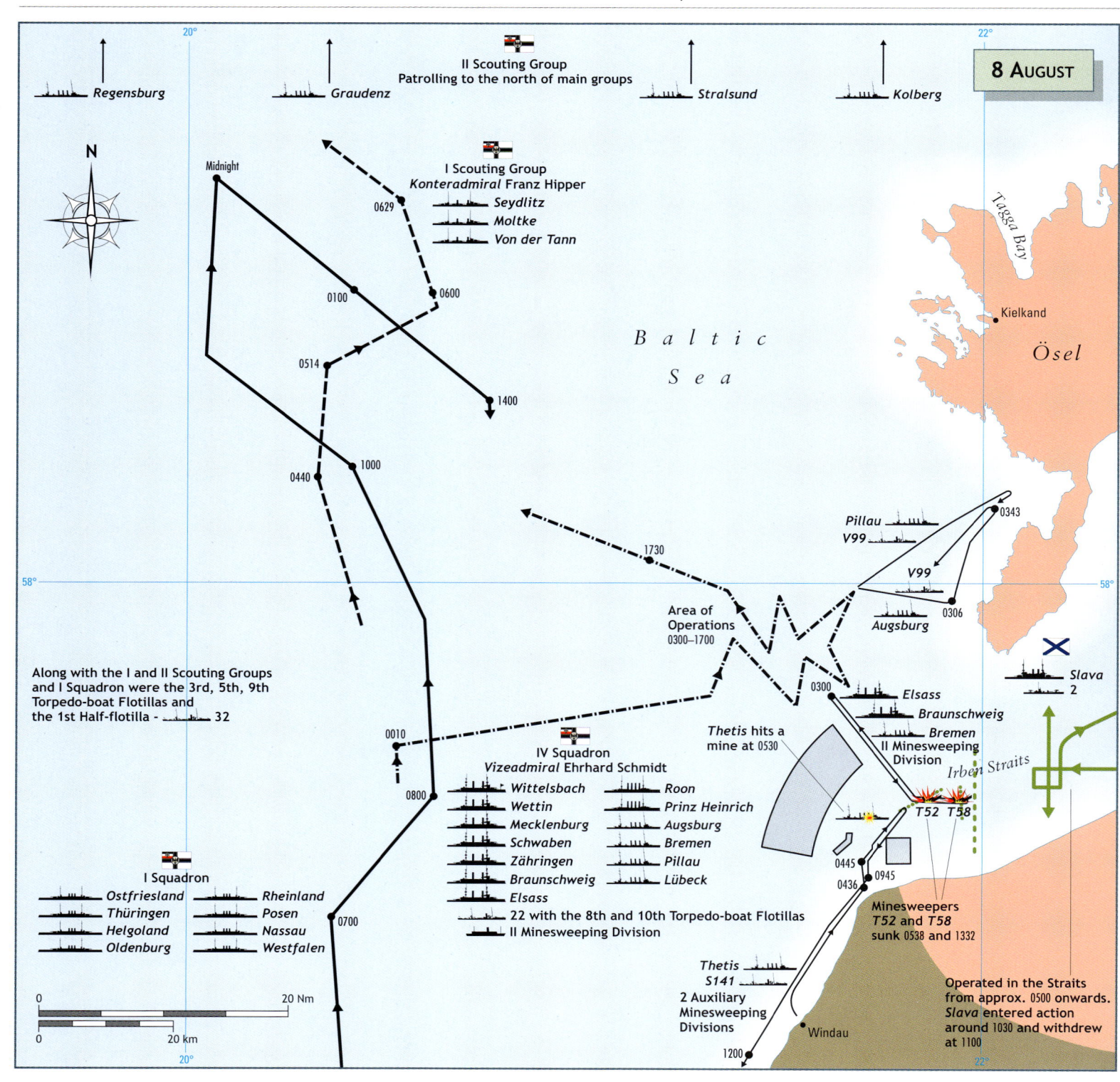

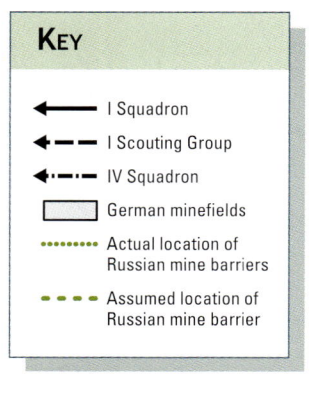

As the summer progressed naval support of the army's offensive on the Kurland peninsula continued to expand. After the engagement on 2 July had shown that the Russians could potentially corner the smaller German Baltic squadron and British submarines had inflicted significant damage to German warships, a redistribution of forces occurred. Vizeadmiral Schmidt's IV Squadron with torpedo boats was moved in from the North Sea resulting in a shift in the balance in the Baltic and soon German light cruisers were back operating on the fringes of the Gulf of Finland. The port of Windau fell to German forces on 18 July and a foothold on the Gulf of Riga was established.

The goal was the capture of Riga itself, but as the land front moved onto the shore of the Gulf of Riga the Russian navy increasingly provided support on the army's seaward flank. To assist the German army's advance, Vizeadmiral Schmidt planned an operation to break into the Gulf of Riga, destroy the local Russian naval forces and block the entrances of the ports it used. An extensive minefield would be laid in the Mood Sound to prevent it from being used as a Russian anchorage. To support the operation another eleven battleships and battlecruisers were brought in from the North Sea. The first attempt on 8 August was abandoned after the minesweeping proved too costly and time consuming in the face of Russian opposition.

The Great War at Sea 1915

19 August

Map annotations:
- 1747 Russian destroyers appear on the horizon and turn back after taken under fire by *Pillau*
- 1730 *Pillau*, minelayer *Deutschland*, 3 torpedoboats carrying mines sent ahead to lay mines in the Moon Sound
- 10th Torpedo-boat Flotilla left to guard the exit over night
- I Minesweeping Division
- *Feodora* sunk by *V153*
- *Koreets* burnt out and sunk 20.08
- II Minesweeping Division
- *Posen*, *Nassau*
- Bremen briefly caught in a net barrier
- At anchor 2255–0520 19–20.08
- *Sivuch* sunk by *Posen* and *Nassau*
- Sunk by *V29*
- *Augsburg*, *Graudenz*, 5 torpedoboats, 3 [...], Morning 20.09 approaches to *Pillau* mined and the blockships scuttled
- The 8th, 9th and 10th Torpedo-boat Flotillas were distributed to escort the battleships, cruisers and minesweeping force
- 3 blockships brought into the Gulf of Riga late on 19.08
- *S31* hits a mine at 2300 and sinks

Places: Moon, Kuiwast, Orissar, Ösel, Arensburg, Pernau, Testama, Kynö, Runö, Gulf of Riga

Key:
- Task force – main group
- Detached cruiser sweeps
- Actual location of Russian mine barriers
- Assumed location of Russian mine barrier

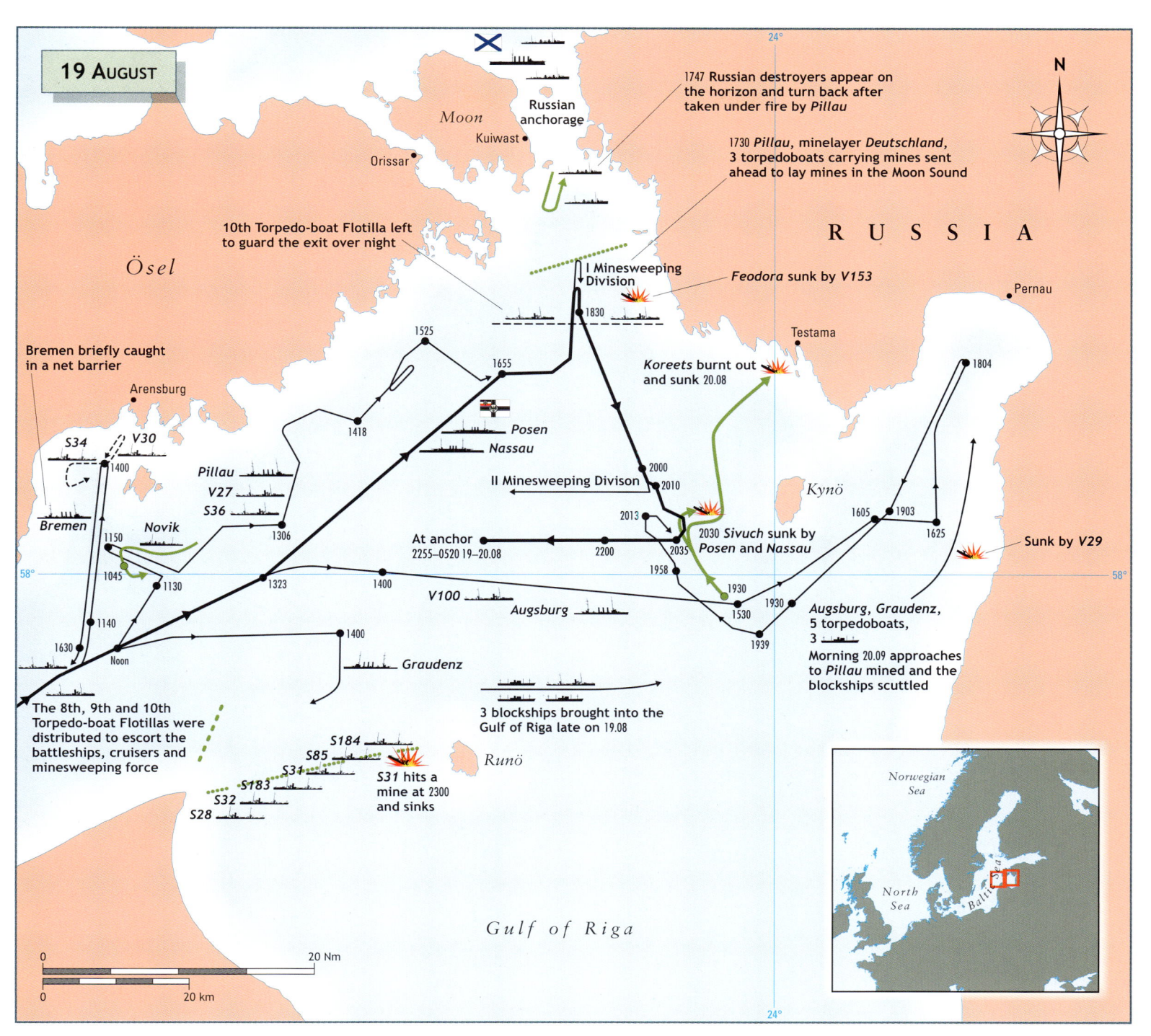

Despite having overwhelming firepower at his disposal, Vizeadmiral Schmidt realised that a more protracted operation would be necessary to sweep the Irben Straits sufficiently to allow German naval forces to enter the Gulf of Riga. The Russian position was strong, with shore batteries covering the northern part of the straits, and in addition they immediately began laying new mines in the areas swept by the Germans on 8 August. A day later the gaps had been filled with 350 new mines.

The second attempt began on 16 August and rather than taking a day it was calculated that five days would be needed to methodically neutralise the Russian defences and clear a pathway. Schmidt also sent most of his pre-dreadnoughts back to Libau as they were more of a liability than of assistance in view of the Russian mine threat. Instead, he selected two modern battleships to provide fire support as they had far superior underwater protection. Soon after the operation began a minesweeper hit a mine and sank and again the Russian pre-dreadnought *Slava* soon appeared and fired on the minesweepers. Each time *Posen* and *Nassau* attempted to engage her she pulled back and an attempted torpedo attack then led to the loss of a German destroyer.

It would take until evening on 18 August before a path was cleared into the Gulf and a German task force could enter, but another minesweeper was lost at the outset when it left one of the cleared paths. The main objective was to lay minefields in the Moon Sound to block Russian entry into the Gulf, but after progress was delayed as a result of false alarms over minefields, and a limited Russian counter attack, Schmidt chose to anchor overnight. The next day bad weather prevented the operation from being completed, though blockships were sunk in the approaches to Pernau. The Germans then withdrew from the Gulf and although some smaller Russian warships were sunk given the amount of resources expanded the long-term benefits were limited.

Naval Bombardments of the Belgian Coast, 1914–17

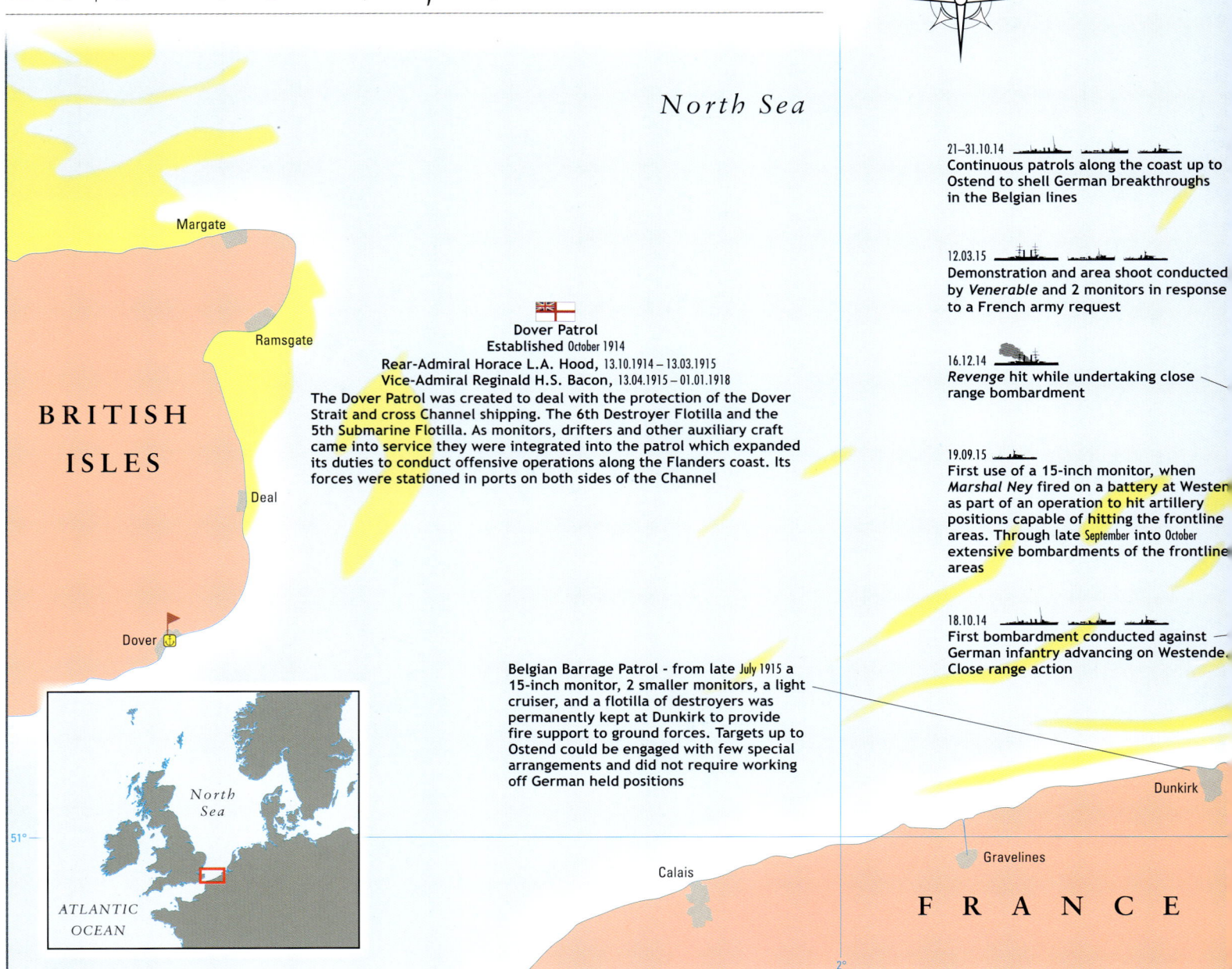

Dover Patrol
Established October 1914
Rear-Admiral Horace L.A. Hood, 13.10.1914 – 13.03.1915
Vice-Admiral Reginald H.S. Bacon, 13.04.1915 – 01.01.1918

The Dover Patrol was created to deal with the protection of the Dover Strait and cross Channel shipping. The 6th Destroyer Flotilla and the 5th Submarine Flotilla. As monitors, drifters and other auxiliary craft came into service they were integrated into the patrol which expanded its duties to conduct offensive operations along the Flanders coast. Its forces were stationed in ports on both sides of the Channel

Belgian Barrage Patrol - from late July 1915 a 15-inch monitor, 2 smaller monitors, a light cruiser, and a flotilla of destroyers was permanently kept at Dunkirk to provide fire support to ground forces. Targets up to Ostend could be engaged with few special arrangements and did not require working off German held positions

21–31.10.14 Continuous patrols along the coast up to Ostend to shell German breakthroughs in the Belgian lines

12.03.15 Demonstration and area shoot conducted by *Venerable* and 2 monitors in response to a French army request

16.12.14 *Revenge* hit while undertaking close range bombardment

19.09.15 First use of a 15-inch monitor, when *Marshal Ney* fired on a battery at Westen as part of an operation to hit artillery positions capable of hitting the frontline areas. Through late September into October extensive bombardments of the frontline areas

18.10.14 First bombardment conducted against German infantry advancing on Westende. Close range action

Key
- Anchorage for vessels conducting shoots of the frontline area or when deployed overnight
- Observation station, small portable island, dropped off intended targets to observe and correct bombardments
- Canal
- Sand banks/shallows

Note: The frontline in this sector remained generally static through the war

---

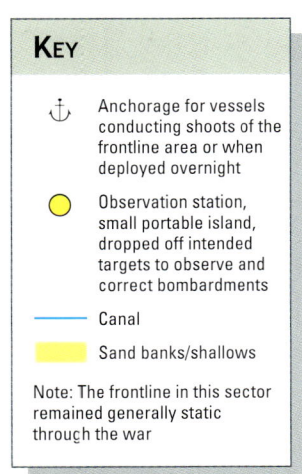

THE GERMAN OFFENSIVE against France stalled with a defeat at the First Battle of the Marne (5–12 September 1914) and a more static frontline developed as both sides dug in. In the northeast French and German forces engaged in a race towards the sea as each side tried to outflank the other in a drive to occupy the territory not previously involved in the fighting. By 19 October the first units reached coastal areas and at the same time the remainder of the Belgian army had been withdrawn westwards after Antwerp was abandoned and capitulated on 10 October. To cover the Belgian retreat a force of light cruisers, destroyers and monitors was sent over from Dover on 17 October to prevent German forces from using the coastal roads in their advance from Ostend towards Nieuwport. Meanwhile, the Germans quickly established artillery positions on the coast and started to lay defensive minefields.

The first British battleship, the pre-dreadnought *Venerable*, conducted bombardments of the frontline area at the end of the month when the Germans made another attempt to push on to Nieuwport as part of the wider Battle of the Yser. In December the French army looked increasingly to the Royal Navy, and the pre-dreadnoughts of the 5th Battle Squadron, as a source for heavy fire support in the coastal area, but though a few bombardments were conducted, the old battleships were unsuited to the role and as yet there was no way of observing indirect fire. From 1915 monitors, as more came into service, took over the role.

The bombardments, as they developed in 1915, had two main purposes. First, at the western end, they were carried out against inland targets in the area Westende to Middelkerke to support allied forces in the frontline and draw in German forces from other parts of the western front. The targets were predominantly German artillery positions or supply dumps. From the summer of 1915 a bombardment force was kept permanently at Dunkirk

THE GREAT WAR AT SEA 1915

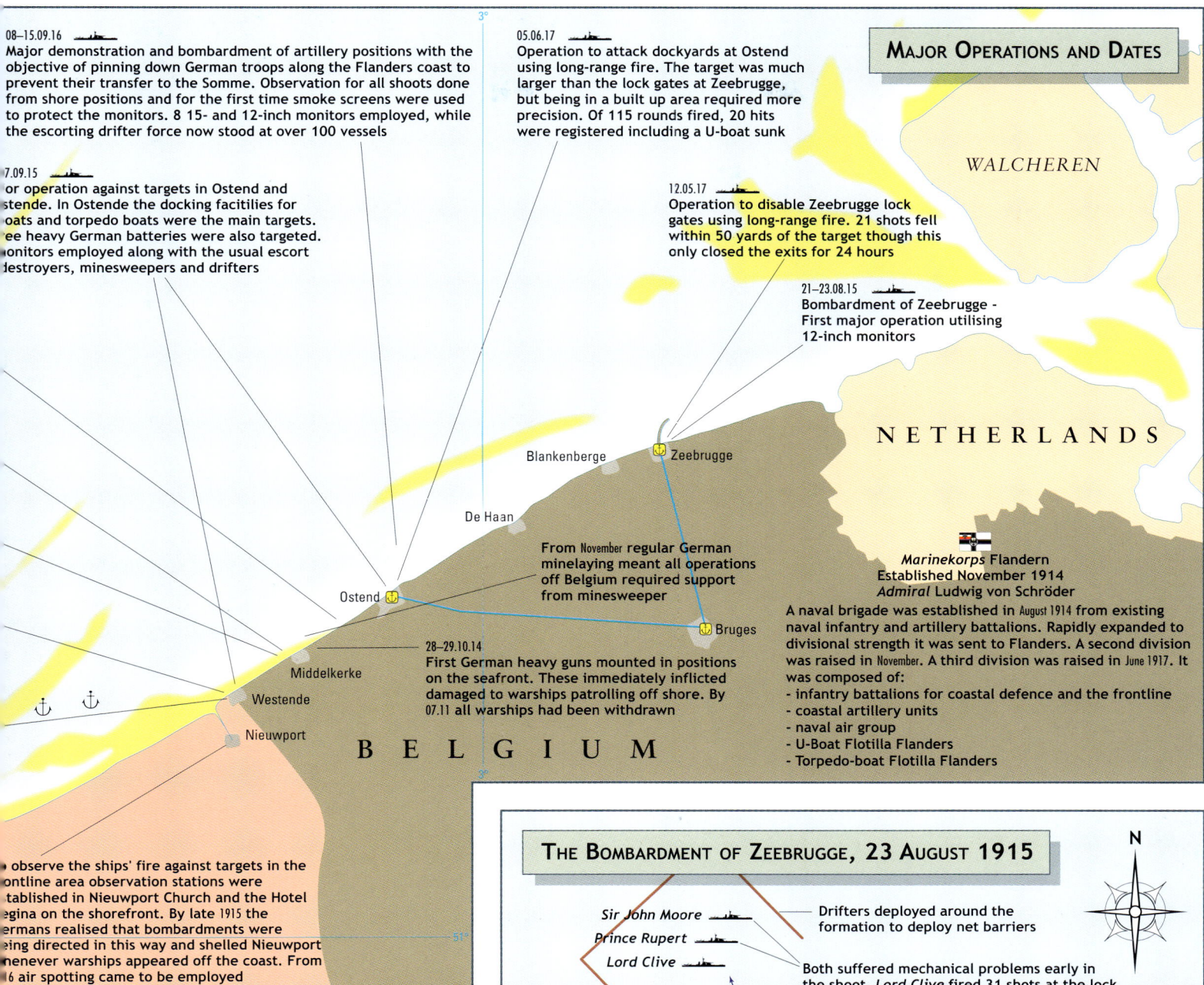

MAJOR OPERATIONS AND DATES

08–15.09.16
Major demonstration and bombardment of artillery positions with the objective of pinning down German troops along the Flanders coast to prevent their transfer to the Somme. Observation for all shoots done from shore positions and for the first time smoke screens were used to protect the monitors. 8 15- and 12-inch monitors employed, while the escorting drifter force now stood at over 100 vessels

7.09.15
or operation against targets in Ostend and stende. In Ostende the docking facilities for oats and torpedo boats were the main targets. ee heavy German batteries were also targeted. onitors employed along with the usual escort destroyers, minesweepers and drifters

05.06.17
Operation to attack dockyards at Ostend using long-range fire. The target was much larger than the lock gates at Zeebrugge, but being in a built up area required more precision. Of 115 rounds fired, 20 hits were registered including a U-boat sunk

12.05.17
Operation to disable Zeebrugge lock gates using long-range fire. 21 shots fell within 50 yards of the target though this only closed the exits for 24 hours

21–23.08.15
Bombardment of Zeebrugge - First major operation utilising 12-inch monitors

From November regular German minelaying meant all operations off Belgium required support from minesweeper

28–29.10.14
First German heavy guns mounted in positions on the seafront. These immediately inflicted damaged to warships patrolling off shore. By 07.11 all warships had been withdrawn

WALCHEREN

NETHERLANDS

Blankenberge Zeebrugge
De Haan
Ostend
Bruges
Middelkerke
Westende
Nieuwport

BELGIUM

Marinekorps Flandern
Established November 1914
Admiral Ludwig von Schröder
A naval brigade was established in August 1914 from existing naval infantry and artillery battalions. Rapidly expanded to divisional strength it was sent to Flanders. A second division was raised in November. A third division was raised in June 1917. It was composed of:
- infantry battalions for coastal defence and the frontline
- coastal artillery units
- naval air group
- U-Boat Flotilla Flanders
- Torpedo-boat Flotilla Flanders

observe the ships' fire against targets in the ontline area observation stations were tablished in Nieuwport Church and the Hotel egina on the shorefront. By late 1915 the ermans realised that bombardments were eing directed in this way and shelled Nieuwport enever warships appeared off the coast. From 6 air spotting came to be employed

or at the forward anchorage to provide fire support and vessels were rotated from bases in England.

The second role was to degrade the naval infrastructure supporting the Flanders-based U-boats. Beginning with the August 1915 attack on Zeebrugge, these were complex, large-scale operations that consumed considerable resources. As the Germans began fortifying the coastline with larger and more modern batteries, the British responded by commissioning monitors mounting ever bigger guns. Attacking small targets at very long ranges required new techniques and equipment, and only with the introduction of air spotting could long-range bombardments be undertaken with any reasonable degree of accuracy. Smoke screens were laid on an enormous scale to shield attacking flotillas from German fire.

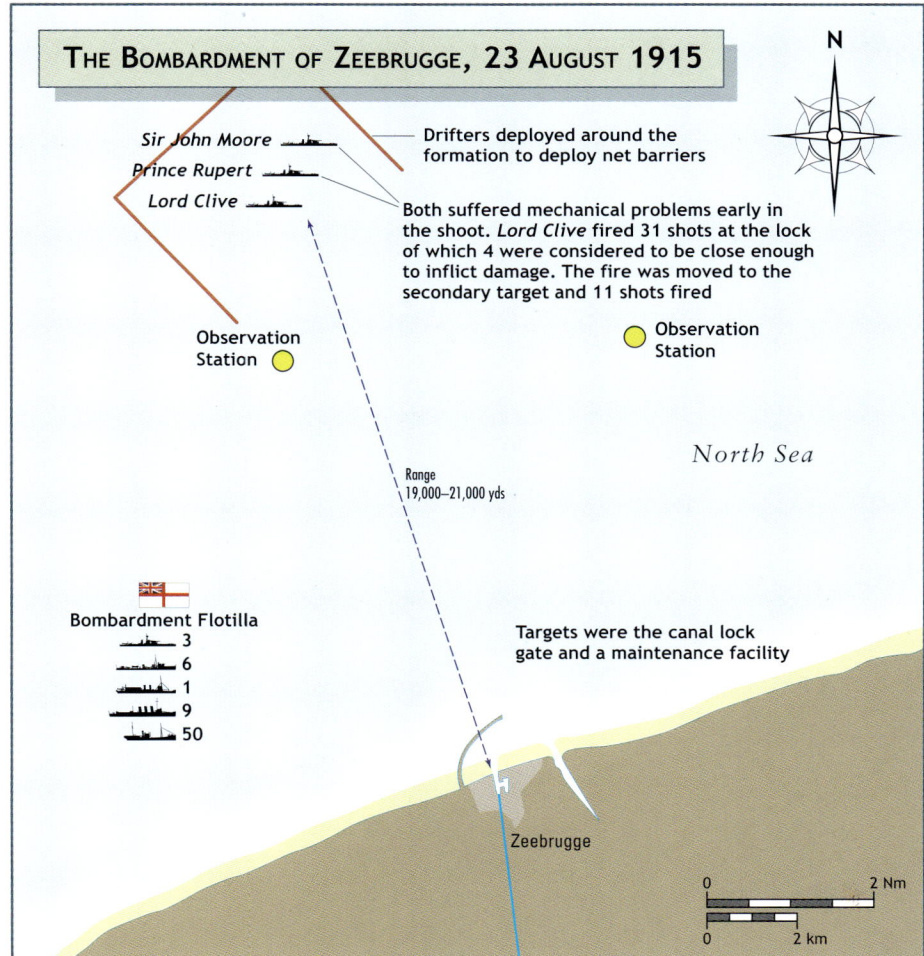

THE BOMBARDMENT OF ZEEBRUGGE, 23 AUGUST 1915

Sir John Moore
Prince Rupert
Lord Clive

Drifters deployed around the formation to deploy net barriers

Both suffered mechanical problems early in the shoot. *Lord Clive* fired 31 shots at the lock of which 4 were considered to be close enough to inflict damage. The fire was moved to the secondary target and 11 shots fired

Observation Station
Observation Station

Range 19,000–21,000 yds

North Sea

Bombardment Flotilla
3
6
1
9
50

Targets were the canal lock gate and a maintenance facility

Zeebrugge

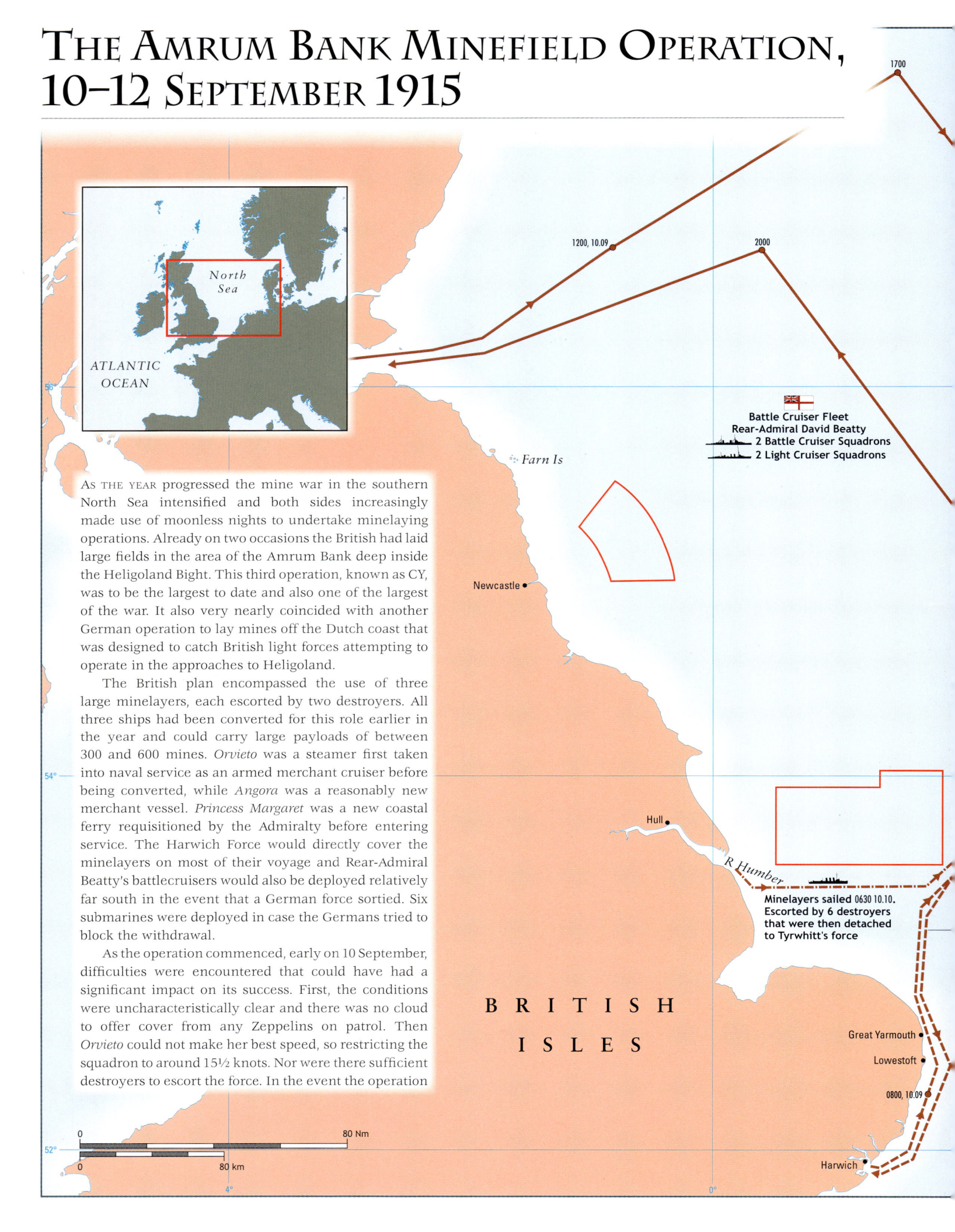

The Amrum Bank Minefield Operation, 10–12 September 1915

As the year progressed the mine war in the southern North Sea intensified and both sides increasingly made use of moonless nights to undertake minelaying operations. Already on two occasions the British had laid large fields in the area of the Amrum Bank deep inside the Heligoland Bight. This third operation, known as CY, was to be the largest to date and also one of the largest of the war. It also very nearly coincided with another German operation to lay mines off the Dutch coast that was designed to catch British light forces attempting to operate in the approaches to Heligoland.

The British plan encompassed the use of three large minelayers, each escorted by two destroyers. All three ships had been converted for this role earlier in the year and could carry large payloads of between 300 and 600 mines. *Orvieto* was a steamer first taken into naval service as an armed merchant cruiser before being converted, while *Angora* was a reasonably new merchant vessel. *Princess Margaret* was a new coastal ferry requisitioned by the Admiralty before entering service. The Harwich Force would directly cover the minelayers on most of their voyage and Rear-Admiral Beatty's battlecruisers would also be deployed relatively far south in the event that a German force sortied. Six submarines were deployed in case the Germans tried to block the withdrawal.

As the operation commenced, early on 10 September, difficulties were encountered that could have had a significant impact on its success. First, the conditions were uncharacteristically clear and there was no cloud to offer cover from any Zeppelins on patrol. Then *Orvieto* could not make her best speed, so restricting the squadron to around 15½ knots. Nor were there sufficient destroyers to escort the force. In the event the operation

Battle Cruiser Fleet
Rear-Admiral David Beatty
2 Battle Cruiser Squadrons
2 Light Cruiser Squadrons

Minelayers sailed 0630 10.10. Escorted by 6 destroyers that were then detached to Tyrwhitt's force

THE GREAT WAR AT SEA 1915

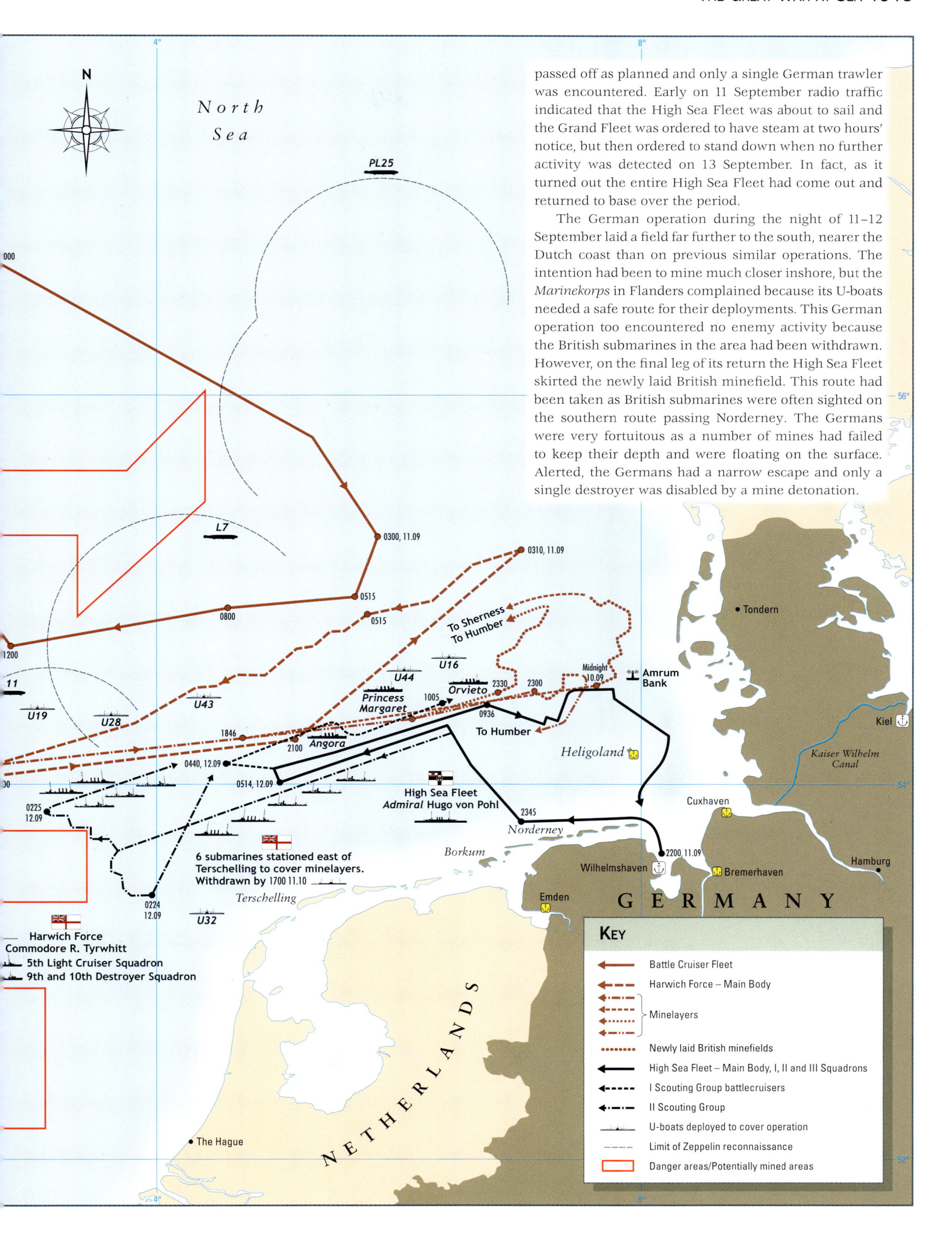

passed off as planned and only a single German trawler was encountered. Early on 11 September radio traffic indicated that the High Sea Fleet was about to sail and the Grand Fleet was ordered to have steam at two hours' notice, but then ordered to stand down when no further activity was detected on 13 September. In fact, as it turned out the entire High Sea Fleet had come out and returned to base over the period.

The German operation during the night of 11–12 September laid a field far further to the south, nearer the Dutch coast than on previous similar operations. The intention had been to mine much closer inshore, but the *Marinekorps* in Flanders complained because its U-boats needed a safe route for their deployments. This German operation too encountered no enemy activity because the British submarines in the area had been withdrawn. However, on the final leg of its return the High Sea Fleet skirted the newly laid British minefield. This route had been taken as British submarines were often sighted on the southern route passing Norderney. The Germans were very fortuitous as a number of mines had failed to keep their depth and were floating on the surface. Alerted, the Germans had a narrow escape and only a single destroyer was disabled by a mine detonation.

Key

- Battle Cruiser Fleet
- Harwich Force – Main Body
- Minelayers
- Newly laid British minefields
- High Sea Fleet – Main Body, I, II and III Squadrons
- I Scouting Group battlecruisers
- II Scouting Group
- U-boats deployed to cover operation
- Limit of Zeppelin reconnaissance
- Danger areas/Potentially mined areas

- Harwich Force Commodore R. Tyrwhitt
- 5th Light Cruiser Squadron
- 9th and 10th Destroyer Squadron

6 submarines stationed east of Terschelling to cover minelayers. Withdrawn by 1700 11.10

High Sea Fleet Admiral Hugo von Pohl

British Submarine Operations in the Baltic, 1915

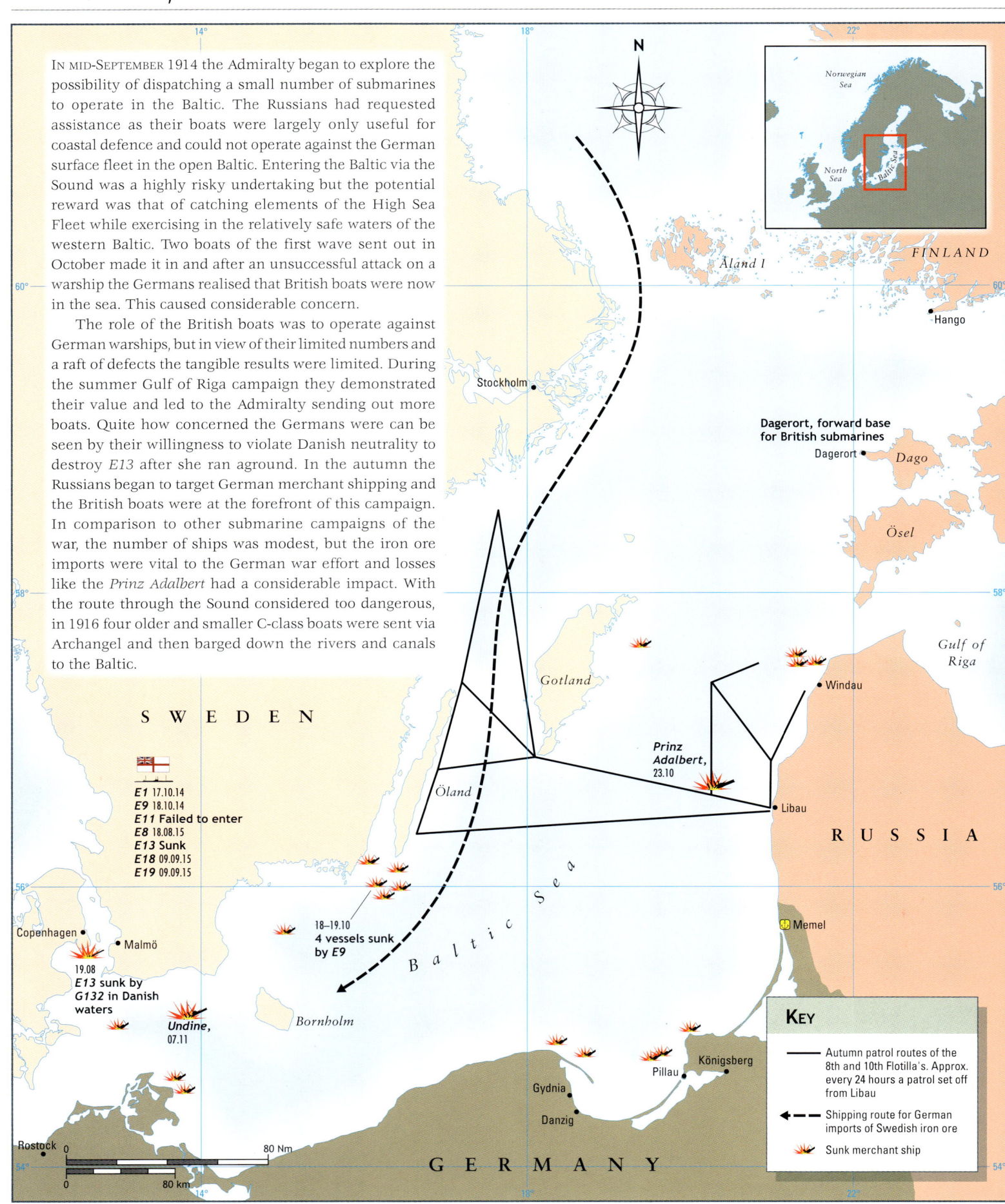

In mid-September 1914 the Admiralty began to explore the possibility of dispatching a small number of submarines to operate in the Baltic. The Russians had requested assistance as their boats were largely only useful for coastal defence and could not operate against the German surface fleet in the open Baltic. Entering the Baltic via the Sound was a highly risky undertaking but the potential reward was that of catching elements of the High Sea Fleet while exercising in the relatively safe waters of the western Baltic. Two boats of the first wave sent out in October made it in and after an unsuccessful attack on a warship the Germans realised that British boats were now in the sea. This caused considerable concern.

The role of the British boats was to operate against German warships, but in view of their limited numbers and a raft of defects the tangible results were limited. During the summer Gulf of Riga campaign they demonstrated their value and led to the Admiralty sending out more boats. Quite how concerned the Germans were can be seen by their willingness to violate Danish neutrality to destroy *E13* after she ran aground. In the autumn the Russians began to target German merchant shipping and the British boats were at the forefront of this campaign. In comparison to other submarine campaigns of the war, the number of ships was modest, but the iron ore imports were vital to the German war effort and losses like the *Prinz Adalbert* had a considerable impact. With the route through the Sound considered too dangerous, in 1916 four older and smaller C-class boats were sent via Archangel and then barged down the rivers and canals to the Baltic.

E1 17.10.14
E9 18.10.14
E11 Failed to enter
E8 18.08.15
E13 Sunk
E18 09.09.15
E19 09.09.15

Key
— Autumn patrol routes of the 8th and 10th Flotilla's. Approx. every 24 hours a patrol set off from Libau
◂--- Shipping route for German imports of Swedish iron ore
💥 Sunk merchant ship

NAVAL LOSSES IN THE DARDANELLES, 1915

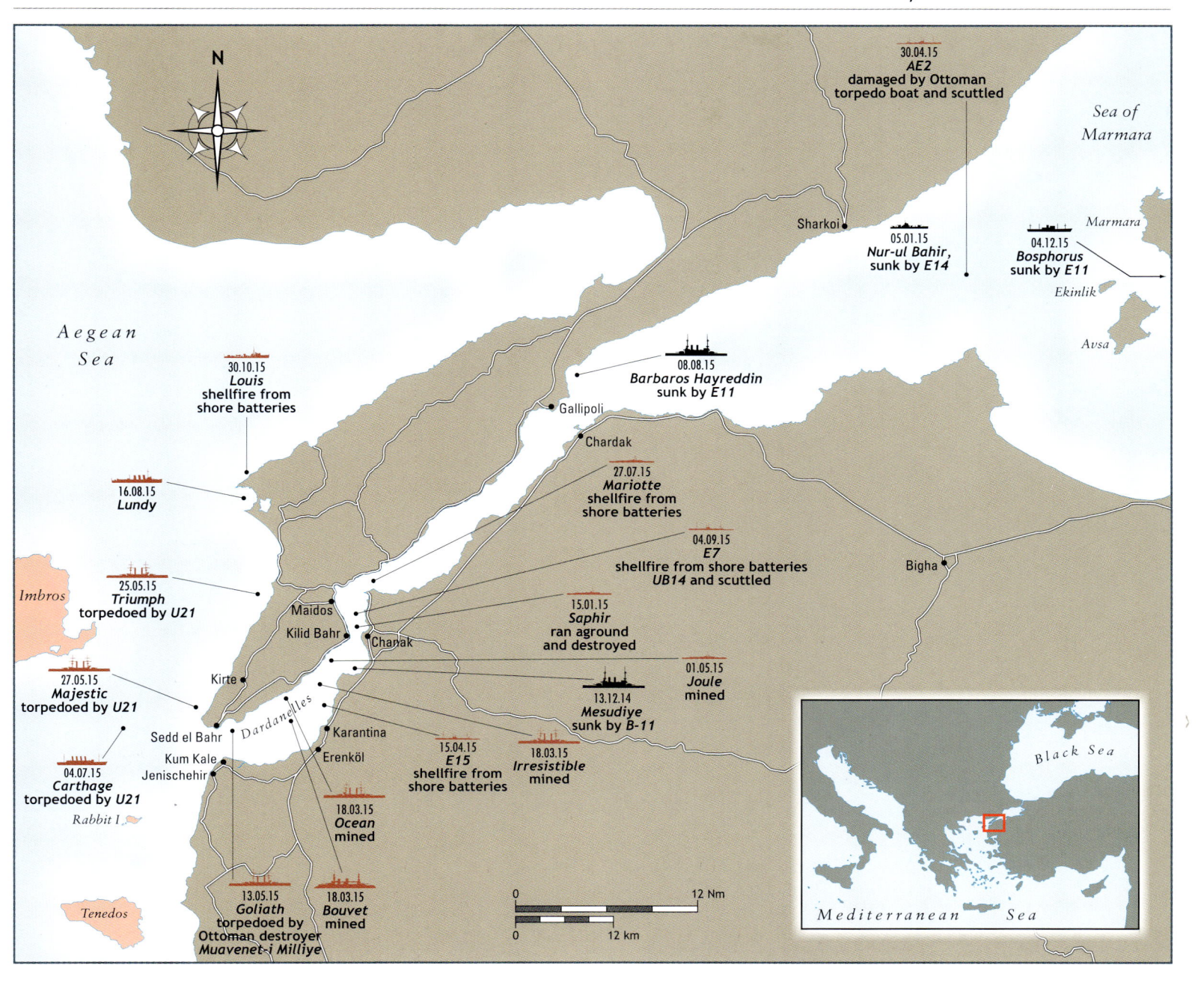

THE NEARLY YEAR-long campaign in and around the Dardanelles resulted in considerable losses of men and material on both sides. Of the more than half million allied troops deployed, around 132,000 were killed or wounded in action and a similar number became casualties from other causes such as disease. On the Ottoman side around 300,000 troops took part in the campaign and although estimates of casualties vary considerable it is likely that these were in similar proportion to allied losses.

In the naval sphere the Turks lost two old and largely obsolete battleships, three destroyers, one torpedo boat and a gunboat. In addition to a large number of small coast craft, fourteen larger merchant ships totalling around 15,000 tons were sunk. Most of these were as a result of allied submarines operating in the Sea of Marmara. The principal allied naval losses were battleships and submarines. Just like the Turks, the Allies too lost or had a large number of small craft damaged beyond repair. Through to the end of the war nine allied submarines were lost in the Dardanelles: four French, four British and an Australian boat. Six pre-dreadnought type battleships were lost in a two-month period during the spring of 1915. This was a substantial number, but the material loss was hardly significant given the huge margin of superiority the Allies had in this largely obsolete type of warship. They could be expended, but their crews were valuable and their loss mattered.

During the attack on 18 March *Bouvet* lost nearly her entire complement with around 660 sailors killed. As *Irresistible* and *Ocean* sank in more controlled circumstances most of their crews were rescued with around 150 being lost between the two. In addition to the problems involved in subduing coastal defences, the Dardanelles campaign demonstrated the vulnerability of a fleet if it operated off an enemy shoreline for any length of time with only limited escorts or fixed defences. A daring Turkish destroyer raid sank *Goliath* – pre-dreadnoughts were vulnerable to torpedo attacks – with heavy loss of life. *U21* under *Kapitänleutnant* Otto Hersing sunk *Triumph* and *Majestic* with single torpedo attacks.

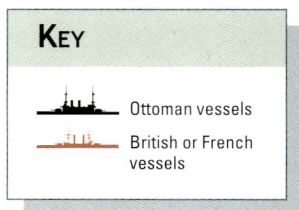

KEY

- Ottoman vessels
- British or French vessels

THE MESOPOTAMIAN CAMPAIGN, 1914–16

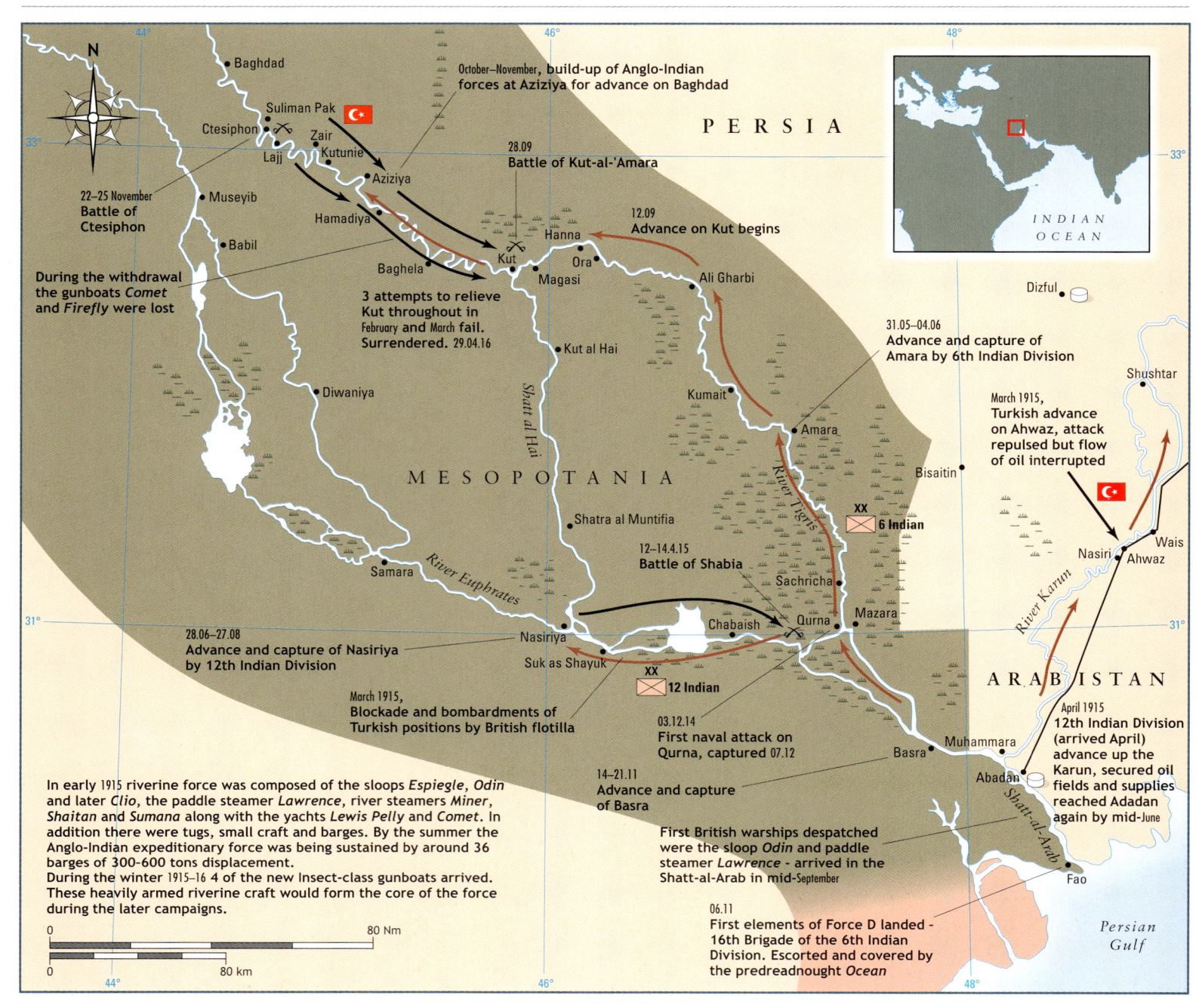

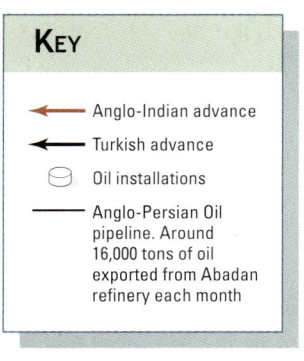

Map annotations

- **October–November**, build-up of Anglo-Indian forces at Aziziya for advance on Baghdad
- **28.09** Battle of Kut-al-'Amara
- **12.09** Advance on Kut begins
- **22–25 November** Battle of Ctesiphon
- During the withdrawal the gunboats *Comet* and *Firefly* were lost
- 3 attempts to relieve Kut throughout in February and March fail. Surrendered. 29.04.16
- **31.05–04.06** Advance and capture of Amara by 6th Indian Division
- **March 1915**, Turkish advance on Ahwaz, attack repulsed but flow of oil interrupted
- **12–14.4.15** Battle of Shabia
- **28.06–27.08** Advance and capture of Nasiriya by 12th Indian Division
- **March 1915**, Blockade and bombardments of Turkish positions by British flotilla
- **03.12.14** First naval attack on Qurna, captured 07.12
- **14–21.11** Advance and capture of Basra
- **April 1915** 12th Indian Division (arrived April) advance up the Karun, secured oil fields and supplies reached Adadan again by mid-June
- First British warships despatched were the sloop *Odin* and paddle steamer *Lawrence* - arrived in the Shatt-al-Arab in mid-September
- **06.11** First elements of Force D landed - 16th Brigade of the 6th Indian Division. Escorted and covered by the predreadnought *Ocean*

In early 1915 riverine force was composed of the sloops *Espiegle*, *Odin* and later *Clio*, the paddle steamer *Lawrence*, river steamers *Miner*, *Shaitan* and *Sumana* along with the yachts *Lewis Pelly* and *Comet*. In addition there were tugs, small craft and barges. By the summer the Anglo-Indian expeditionary force was being sustained by around 36 barges of 300-600 tons displacement.
During the winter 1915–16 4 of the new Insect-class gunboats arrived. These heavily armed riverine craft would form the core of the force during the later campaigns.

Key

- Anglo-Indian advance
- Turkish advance
- Oil installations
- Anglo-Persian Oil pipeline. Around 16,000 tons of oil exported from Abadan refinery each month

---

THE DECISION, TAKEN only a few years before the outbreak of the war, to begin the transition from coal to oil as the fuel for the battlefleet meant that security of the northern end of the Persian Gulf was no longer merely a commercial concern for the British. Oil was not just a more efficient source of fuel but it did not require the considerable amount of manpower necessary to fill the bunkers of a battleship with coal. While an oil-fired fleet, or parts thereof, would provide the Royal Navy with a tactical and strategic advantage, it also created a dependency on foreign fuel supplies. Persian oil fields were a primary source for British oil and their proximity to the Ottoman empire became an increasing source of concern in the late summer.

To protect the oil fields the Indian Army raised a fourth expeditionary force, Force D, which arrived in the Gulf in mid-October, and landed on the Al-Fao peninsula once war broke out. Initial British aims were limited to securing the Persian oil fields and the approaches from Mesopotamia. Basra was occupied and a few probing operations northwards along the river systems undertaken. In early 1915 a Turkish attack into Arabistan, combined with a local insurrection that resulted in a cut in the flow of oil, led to another Indian division being dispatched.

Having secured lower Mesopotamia and defeated local Turkish counterattacks, the British expanded their bridgehead. In view of the limited resistance and the reverses in other theatres, the possibility of moving up the Tigris to take Baghdad became an increasingly attractive option. In September the key town of Kut-al-'Amara was taken and the route north seemed open. The entire campaign was dependent on naval forces that provided mobile heavy firepower and the necessary logistical support. The further north the Anglo-Indian forces advanced the more strained the supply lines became. The Ottoman forces were also stronger than estimated and a defeat at Ctesiphon led to 6th Indian Division being pushed back and encircled at Kut.

THE GERMAN SWEEP OF THE SKAGERRAK 16–18 DECEMBER 1915

THE MARITIME TRAFFIC between Britain and Scandinavia presented an increasingly tempting target for the Germans in the second half of 1915. Leaving aside the political ramifications of interfering with the trade of neutral powers, it was far easier to interdict this traffic than elsewhere. The terminus in the Kattegat and Skagerrak was well within the striking distance of surface forces. The Germans harboured longstanding concerns that British forces would enter the Baltic via this route; submarines had already done so and intercepting further reinforcements was a German priority.

The increase in shipping throughout October and reports of British warships in the Skagerrak at the beginning of November led to more assertive German action. A first cautious sweep of the Kattegat was undertaken in mid-November by torpedo boats operating from Baltic ports. This was done to avoid any British force potentially cutting off the line of retreat. Although the actual results were limited, the operation showed potential and further use of the Belts led to no Danish protests. Thus the stage was set for a much larger operation in mid-December.

A large force of cruisers and destroyers would sortie from Wilhelmshaven, sweep up along the Danish coast at night to arrive in the Kattegat by early next morning, and conduct a thorough search of the waters and approaches to Swedish and Danish ports. A U-boat was also positioned to cover approaches. In the event that the British might attempt to intercept the force, the remainder of the Scouting Groups, foremost the battlecruisers, were kept at heightened readiness in Wilhelmshaven. The operation unfolded as planned. In total fifty-two vessels were searched during the operation, but only a single one was found to be carrying goods that the Germans considered to be contraband.

ACTION OFF DURAZZO, 29 DECEMBER 1915

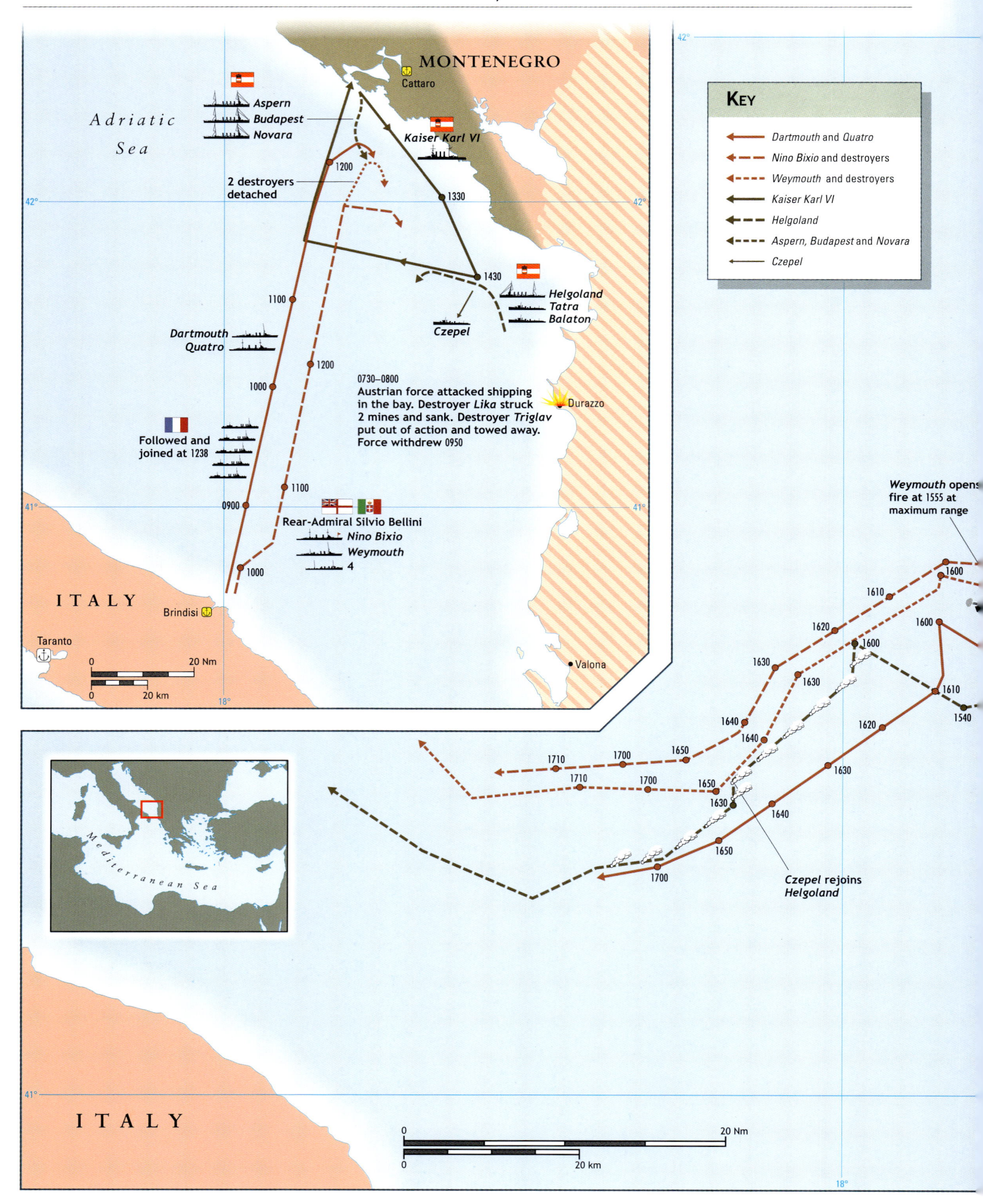

Key
- Dartmouth and Quatro
- Nino Bixio and destroyers
- Weymouth and destroyers
- Kaiser Karl VI
- Helgoland
- Aspern, Budapest and Novara
- Czepel

Aspern
Budapest
Novara

Kaiser Karl VI

2 destroyers detached

Helgoland
Tatra
Balaton

Czepel

Dartmouth
Quatro

0730–0800 Austrian force attacked shipping in the bay. Destroyer *Lika* struck 2 mines and sank. Destroyer *Triglav* put out of action and towed away. Force withdrew 0950

Durazzo

Followed and joined at 1238

Rear-Admiral Silvio Bellini
Nino Bixio
Weymouth
4

ITALY
Brindisi
Taranto

Valona

Weymouth opens fire at 1555 at maximum range

Czepel rejoins *Helgoland*

Adriatic Sea

MONTENEGRO
Cattaro

Mediterranean Sea

ITALY

84

THE GREAT WAR AT SEA 1915

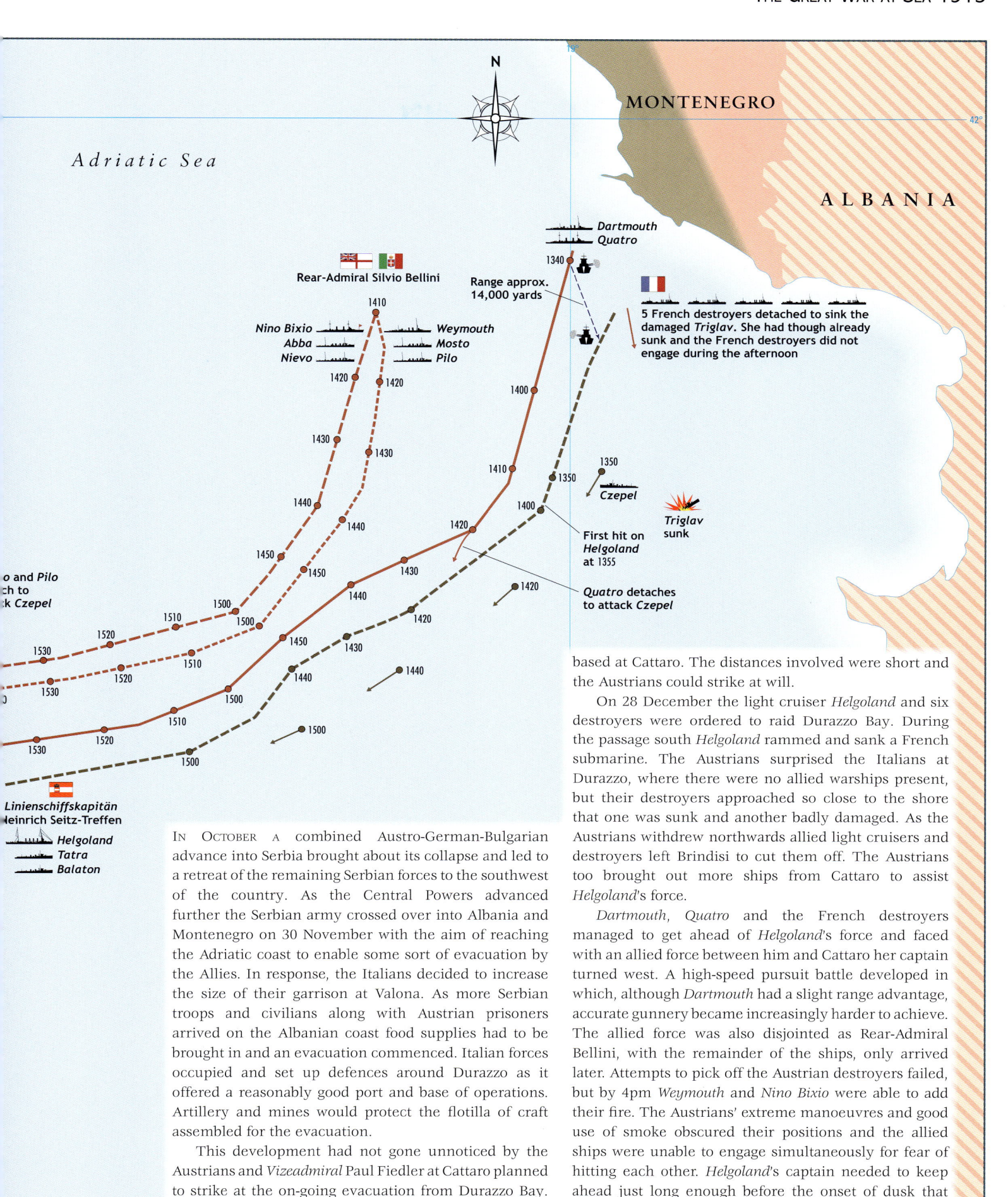

IN OCTOBER a combined Austro-German-Bulgarian advance into Serbia brought about its collapse and led to a retreat of the remaining Serbian forces to the southwest of the country. As the Central Powers advanced further the Serbian army crossed over into Albania and Montenegro on 30 November with the aim of reaching the Adriatic coast to enable some sort of evacuation by the Allies. In response, the Italians decided to increase the size of their garrison at Valona. As more Serbian troops and civilians along with Austrian prisoners arrived on the Albanian coast food supplies had to be brought in and an evacuation commenced. Italian forces occupied and set up defences around Durazzo as it offered a reasonably good port and base of operations. Artillery and mines would protect the flotilla of craft assembled for the evacuation.

This development had not gone unnoticed by the Austrians and *Vizeadmiral* Paul Fiedler at Cattaro planned to strike at the on-going evacuation from Durazzo Bay. Austrian raids against traffic in the straits had increased throughout December and although the allied naval forces in the area were more numerous the Austrians had a sizeable force of light cruisers and destroyers based at Cattaro. The distances involved were short and the Austrians could strike at will.

On 28 December the light cruiser *Helgoland* and six destroyers were ordered to raid Durazzo Bay. During the passage south *Helgoland* rammed and sank a French submarine. The Austrians surprised the Italians at Durazzo, where there were no allied warships present, but their destroyers approached so close to the shore that one was sunk and another badly damaged. As the Austrians withdrew northwards allied light cruisers and destroyers left Brindisi to cut them off. The Austrians too brought out more ships from Cattaro to assist *Helgoland*'s force.

Dartmouth, *Quatro* and the French destroyers managed to get ahead of *Helgoland*'s force and faced with an allied force between him and Cattaro her captain turned west. A high-speed pursuit battle developed in which, although *Dartmouth* had a slight range advantage, accurate gunnery became increasingly harder to achieve. The allied force was also disjointed as Rear-Admiral Bellini, with the remainder of the ships, only arrived later. Attempts to pick off the Austrian destroyers failed, but by 4pm *Weymouth* and *Nino Bixio* were able to add their fire. The Austrians' extreme manoeuvres and good use of smoke obscured their positions and the allied ships were unable to engage simultaneously for fear of hitting each other. *Helgoland*'s captain needed to keep ahead just long enough before the onset of dusk that would make it hard for the allied warships to keep touch. This was achieved and by around 6pm the engagement had run its course and the Austrians turned north under the cover of darkness.

Naval Operations 1916

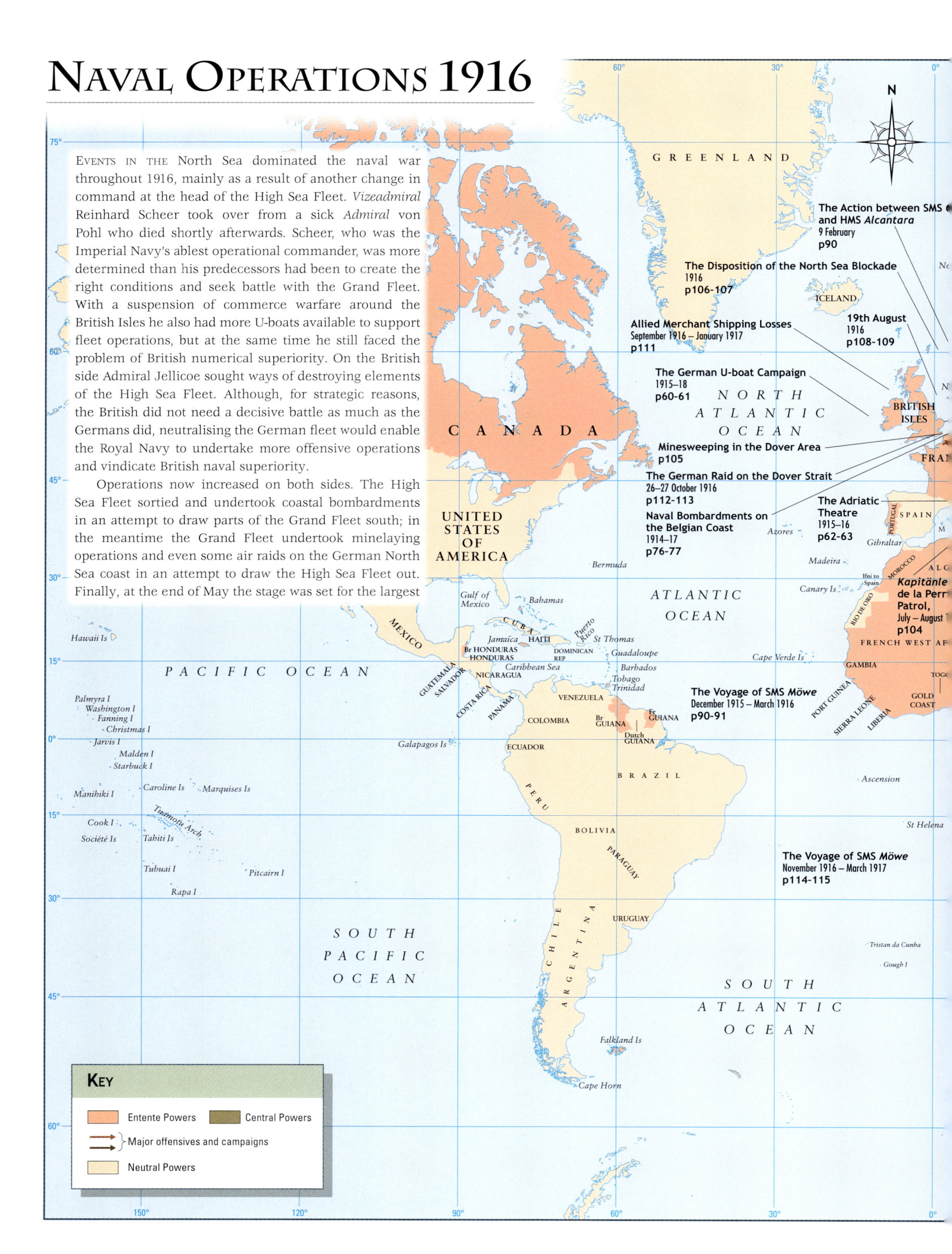

Events in the North Sea dominated the naval war throughout 1916, mainly as a result of another change in command at the head of the High Sea Fleet. *Vizeadmiral* Reinhard Scheer took over from a sick *Admiral* von Pohl who died shortly afterwards. Scheer, who was the Imperial Navy's ablest operational commander, was more determined than his predecessors had been to create the right conditions and seek battle with the Grand Fleet. With a suspension of commerce warfare around the British Isles he also had more U-boats available to support fleet operations, but at the same time he still faced the problem of British numerical superiority. On the British side Admiral Jellicoe sought ways of destroying elements of the High Sea Fleet. Although, for strategic reasons, the British did not need a decisive battle as much as the Germans did, neutralising the German fleet would enable the Royal Navy to undertake more offensive operations and vindicate British naval superiority.

Operations now increased on both sides. The High Sea Fleet sortied and undertook coastal bombardments in an attempt to draw parts of the Grand Fleet south; in the meantime the Grand Fleet undertook minelaying operations and even some air raids on the German North Sea coast in an attempt to draw the High Sea Fleet out. Finally, at the end of May the stage was set for the largest

The Action between SMS and HMS *Alcantara*
9 February
p90

The Disposition of the North Sea Blockade
1916
p106-107

Allied Merchant Shipping Losses
September 1916 – January 1917
p111

19th August
1916
p108-109

The German U-boat Campaign
1915–18
p60-61

Minesweeping in the Dover Area
p105

The German Raid on the Dover Strait
26–27 October 1916
p112-113

Naval Bombardments on the Belgian Coast
1914–17
p76-77

The Adriatic Theatre
1915–16
p62-63

Kapitänleutnant de la Perrière Patrol
July – August
p104

The Voyage of SMS *Möwe*
December 1915 – March 1916
p90-91

The Voyage of SMS *Möwe*
November 1916 – March 1917
p114-115

Key

- Entente Powers
- Central Powers
- Major offensives and campaigns
- Neutral Powers

THE GREAT WAR AT SEA 1916

The Battle of Jutland
31 May – 1 June
p96-102

Operation XX
2–5 May 1916
p94-95

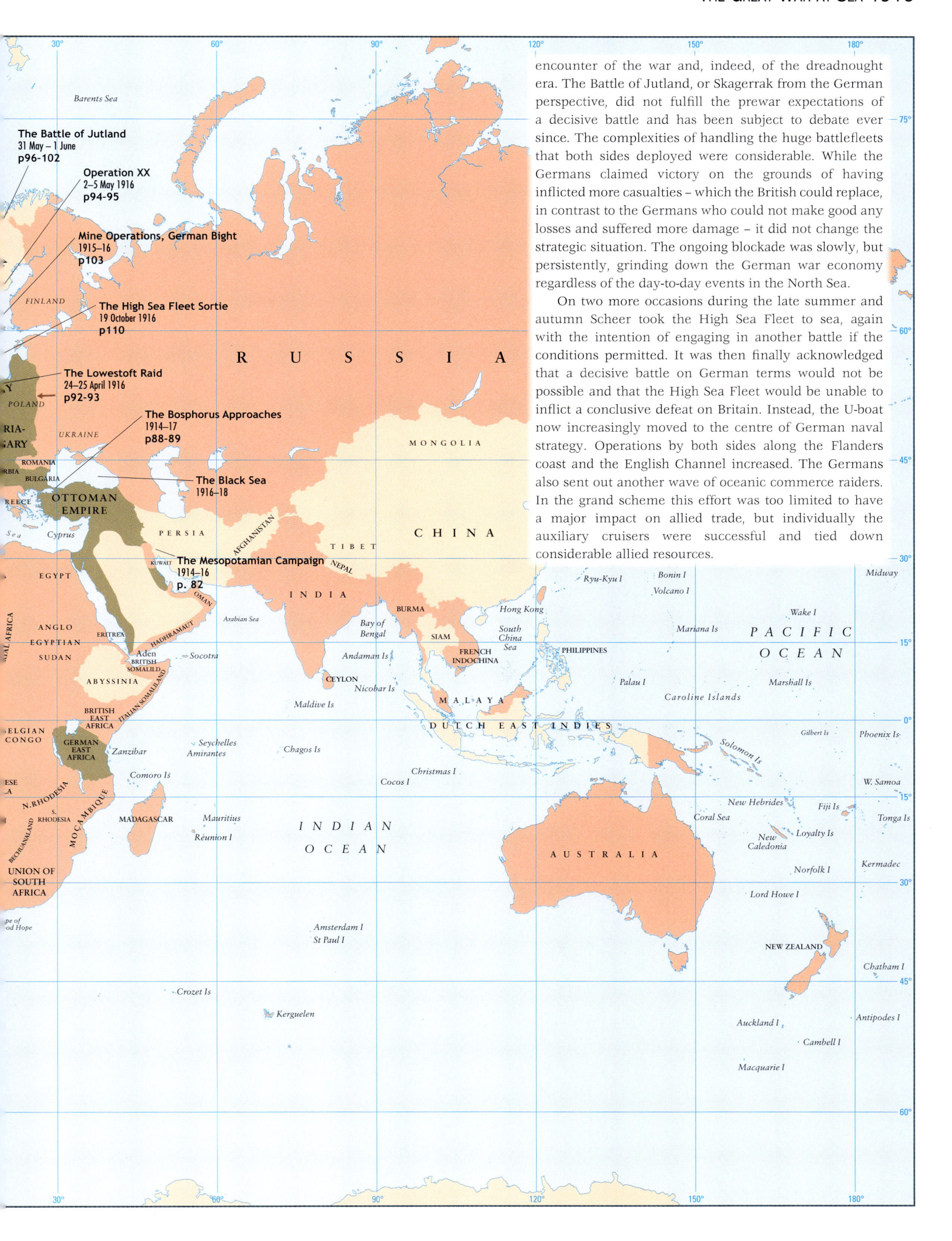

Mine Operations, German Bight
1915–16
p103

The High Sea Fleet Sortie
19 October 1916
p110

The Lowestoft Raid
24–25 April 1916
p92-93

The Bosphorus Approaches
1914–17
p88-89

The Black Sea
1916–18

The Mesopotamian Campaign
1914–16
p. 82

encounter of the war and, indeed, of the dreadnought era. The Battle of Jutland, or Skagerrak from the German perspective, did not fulfill the prewar expectations of a decisive battle and has been subject to debate ever since. The complexities of handling the huge battlefleets that both sides deployed were considerable. While the Germans claimed victory on the grounds of having inflicted more casualties – which the British could replace, in contrast to the Germans who could not make good any losses and suffered more damage – it did not change the strategic situation. The ongoing blockade was slowly, but persistently, grinding down the German war economy regardless of the day-to-day events in the North Sea.

On two more occasions during the late summer and autumn Scheer took the High Sea Fleet to sea, again with the intention of engaging in another battle if the conditions permitted. It was then finally acknowledged that a decisive battle on German terms would not be possible and that the High Sea Fleet would be unable to inflict a conclusive defeat on Britain. Instead, the U-boat now increasingly moved to the centre of German naval strategy. Operations by both sides along the Flanders coast and the English Channel increased. The Germans also sent out another wave of oceanic commerce raiders. In the grand scheme this effort was too limited to have a major impact on allied trade, but individually the auxiliary cruisers were successful and tied down considerable allied resources.

The Bosporus Approaches, 1914–17

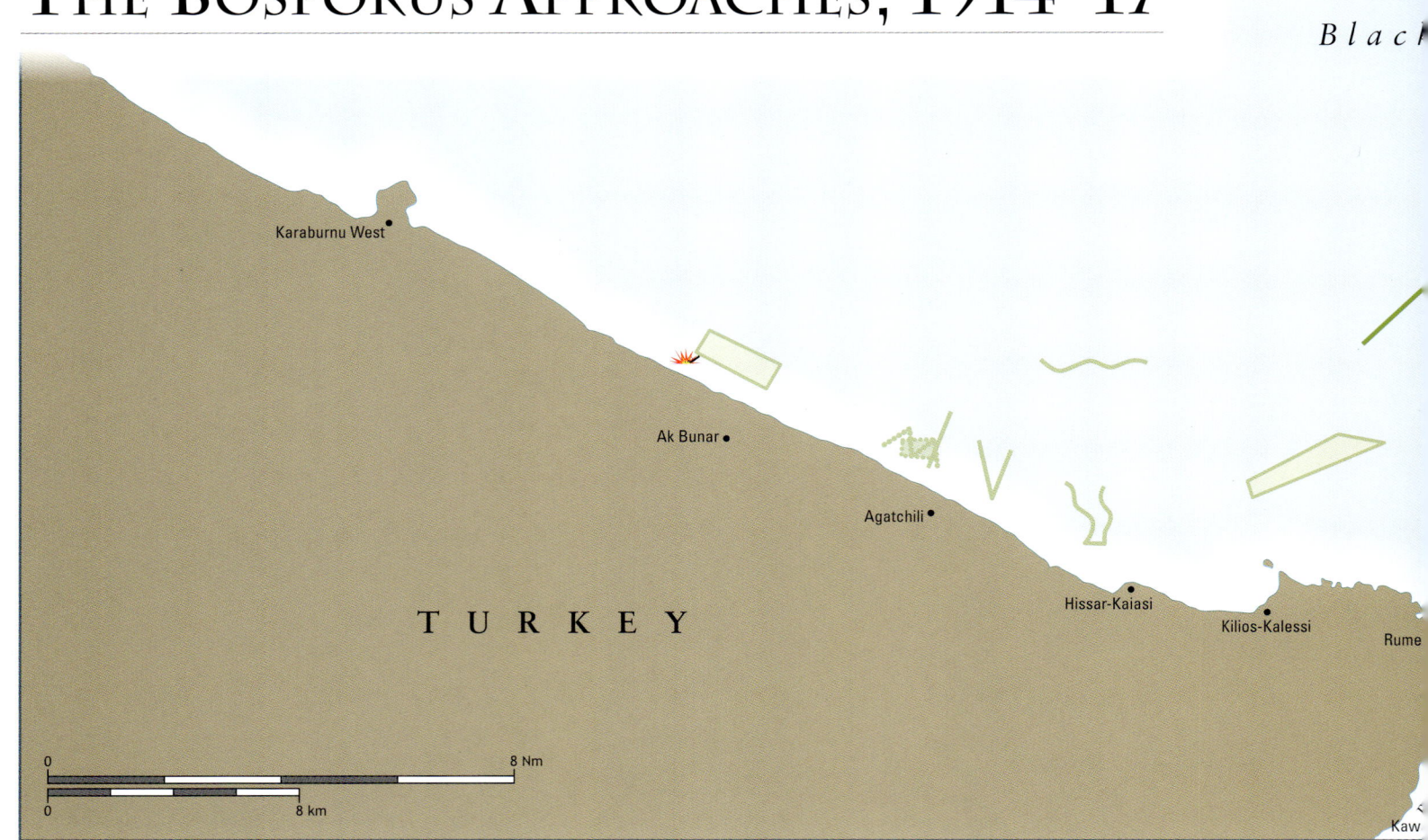

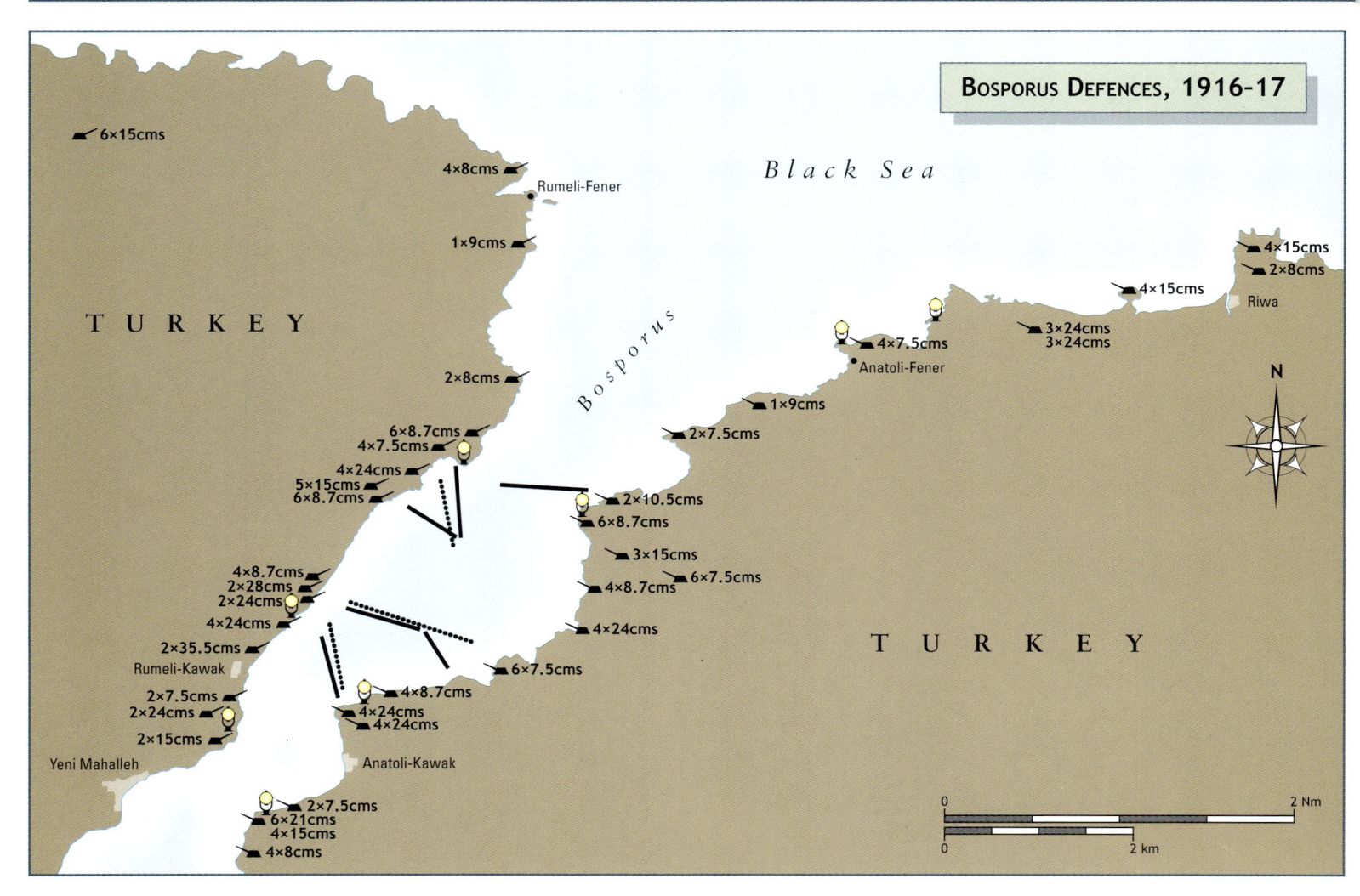

Bosporus Defences, 1916–17

THE GREAT WAR AT SEA 1916

RUSSIAN MINELAYING, 1914-17

Key
- Russian mines laid 1914
- Russian mines laid 1915
- Russian mines laid 1916
- Russian mines laid 1917
- Mined Turkish vessel
- *Goeben* – *Yavûz Sultân Selîm* in Ottoman service
- *Breslau* – *Midilli* in Ottoman Service

Key
- Ottoman/German minefields laid 1916
- Ottoman/German minefields laid 1917
- Coastal gun battery
- Searchlights

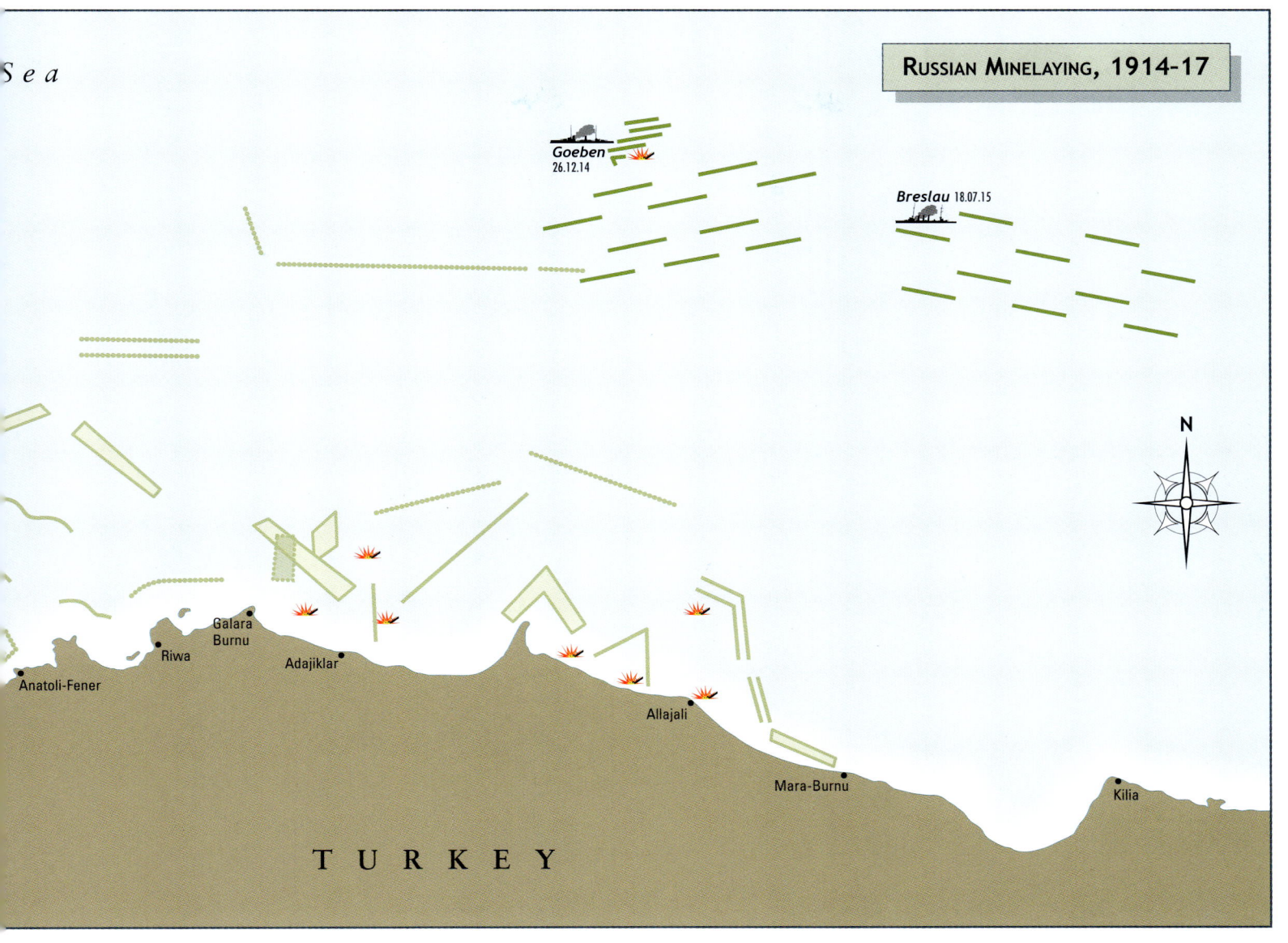

OFFENSIVE AND DEFENSIVE minelaying along with hit-and-run raids against coastal targets and shipping were a key feature of Russian naval strategic thinking. In line with the historic Russian aim of securing control of Constantinople and a route to the Mediterranean the Bosporus had featured heavily in pre-war planning. From the outset it was a target for the Black Sea Fleet and the first major operation was a sortie to cover four destroyers laying mines in its approaches. The next minelaying effort took place on 21 December 1914 and these set a pattern for numerous similar operations over the subsequent years.

Mines from these early fields damaged both *Goeben* and *Breslau* and, while the Russians never succeeded in permanently blockading the Bosporus, the effort complicated the passage of warships and at times restricted the coastal trade that was a key feature of the Ottoman economy. A comparatively small number of mines were laid in 1915, although in July the first purpose-built minelaying submarine, *Krab*, laid a barrier in the Bosporus.

The first coastal bombardment took place on 18 March 1915 when elements of the Black Sea Fleet bombarded the coastal defences in support of allied efforts at the Dardanelles. Further bombardments were conducted in April and May and while they had little military value they demonstrated the vulnerability of the Turkish coastline so close to the Ottoman capital. The Russians were not able to capitalize further from their ability to raid the coast as they lacked a transport capability to embark an amphibious force.

In July 1916 Russian minelaying was stepped up. *Krab* laid another barrier in the Bosporus, and this was followed by destroyer-laid fields further out but near enough to the shoreline to enable surface units to conduct close-range bombardments. Around 880 mines were laid within a week and the effect was to briefly lock in the Turkish-German surface force.

The Romanian entry into the war caused the Turks to withdraw many of their coastal defence units for service further north, but the Russians were unable to profit from this development as their two army corps designated for operations against the Bosporus were sent to the Romanian front. In order to support U-boat operations the Germans took charge of minesweeping and, in May 1917, a German minesweeping flotilla was established.

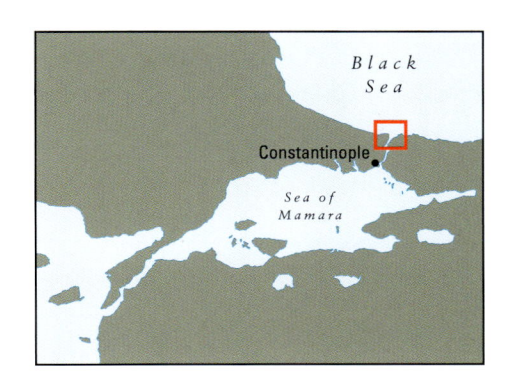

The Voyage of SMS Möwe, December 1915–March 1916

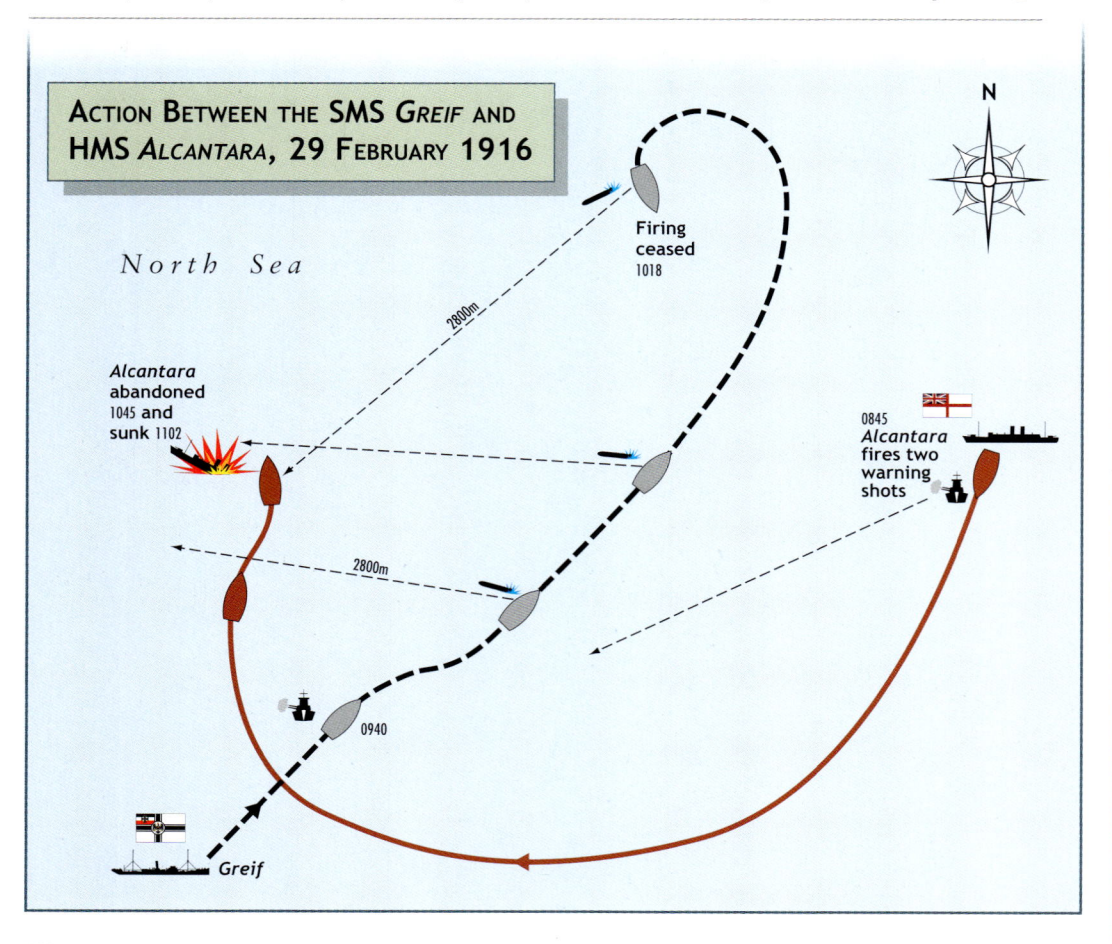

Action Between the SMS *Greif* and HMS *Alcantara*, 29 February 1916

The first wave of German commerce warfare against allied oceanic shipping came to an end in the spring of 1915 as, by then, all the warships and auxiliary cruisers that were overseas upon the outbreak of war had been either sunk or interned in neutral ports. Thus it was left to U-boats to attack allied shipping and, while individual boats were successful, operational and political limitations restricted the overall impact of German efforts. Crucially, with U-boat operations confined to the waters around the British Isles and the Mediterranean, global allied trade and military movements could be undertaken with little German interference. The *Admiralstab* was keen to increase the pressure on allied maritime communications and to this end prepared a second group of auxiliary cruisers for service in late 1915. Following on from the experience gathered with *Meteor*, these auxiliary cruisers were converted merchant ships that had far greater endurance and were less conspicuous than liners and could combine minelaying with commerce warfare.

The first to sea at the end of 1915 was the *Möwe*, a relatively new and large freighter that had been built for the banana trade with West Africa. Sailing in the middle of the winter she could take advantage of the long hours of darkness and generally poor conditions in northern latitudes to avoid detection. First, she was to lay mines off the Scottish and French coasts and for this carried a large payload of some 500 mines. Then she was to the proceed to the central Atlantic to conduct commerce warfare in the waters between Africa and South America, and area that had been a profitable hunting ground in 1914.

German minelaying had become a serious issue for the Grand Fleet and when the pre-dreadnought *King Edward VII* was sunk by one of *Möwe*'s mines (the British did not know the source of the minelaying at the time) the repercussions were considerable with Admiral Jellicoe requesting that more trawlers be sent north immediately to ensure he would be able to put to sea safely. At this point the allies lacked sufficient minesweeping vessels for all theatres. After laying her remaining mines in the Gironde estuary *Möwe* enjoyed a reasonably successful time in the eastern Atlantic. In total *Möwe* accounted for some 16 ships of just under 60,000ts sunk before she returned home in March. Her captain on two occasions sent prizes back to neutral ports to disembark passengers and crews from captured vessels.

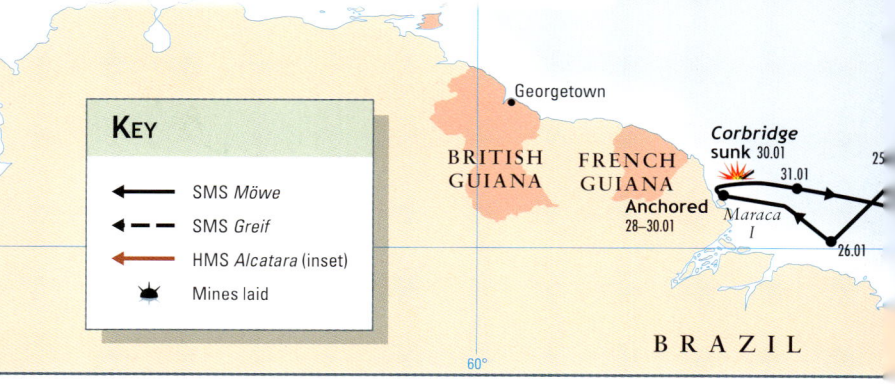

Key
- SMS *Möwe*
- SMS *Greif*
- HMS *Alcatara* (inset)
- Mines laid

THE GREAT WAR AT SEA 1916

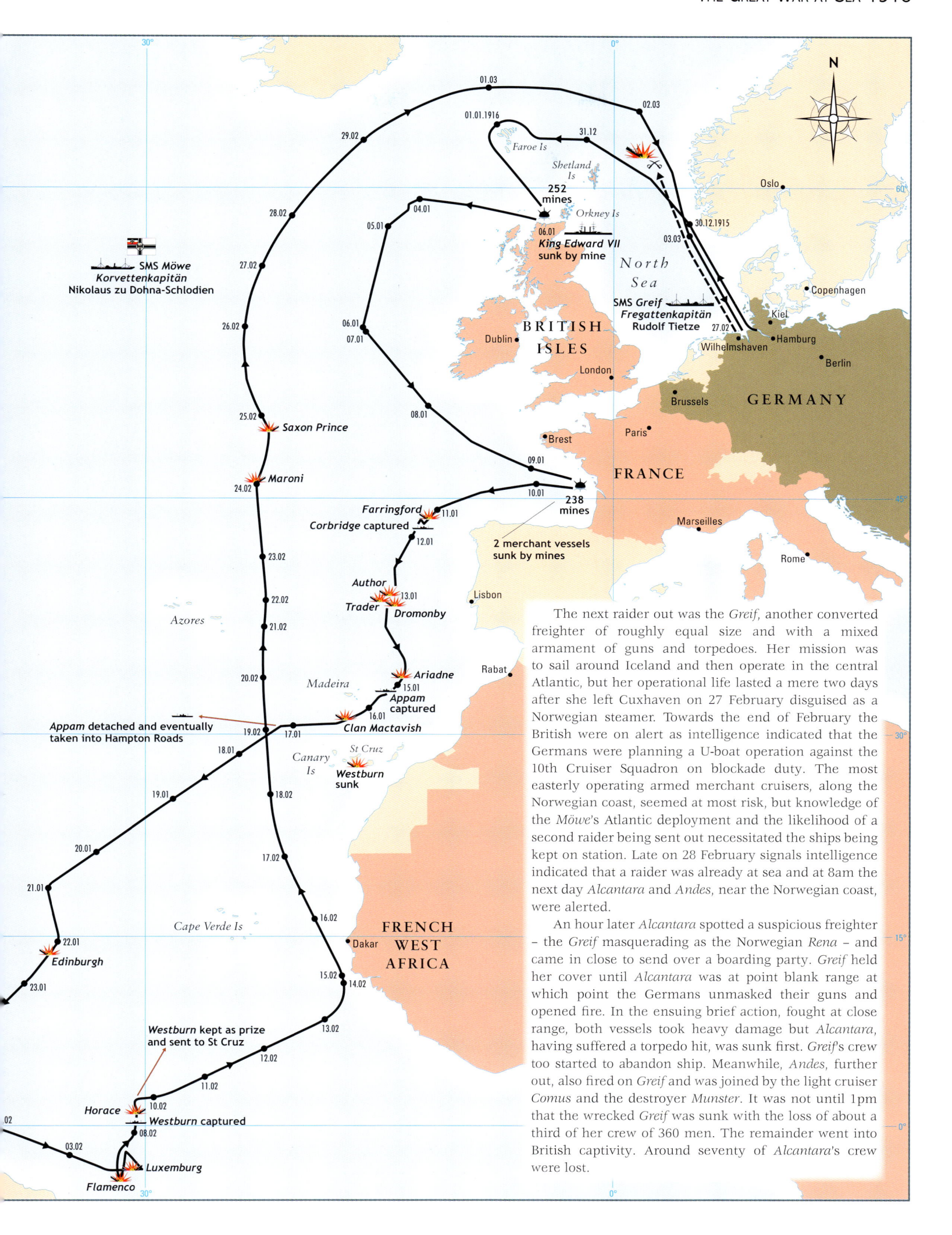

The next raider out was the *Greif*, another converted freighter of roughly equal size and with a mixed armament of guns and torpedoes. Her mission was to sail around Iceland and then operate in the central Atlantic, but her operational life lasted a mere two days after she left Cuxhaven on 27 February disguised as a Norwegian steamer. Towards the end of February the British were on alert as intelligence indicated that the Germans were planning a U-boat operation against the 10th Cruiser Squadron on blockade duty. The most easterly operating armed merchant cruisers, along the Norwegian coast, seemed at most risk, but knowledge of the *Möwe*'s Atlantic deployment and the likelihood of a second raider being sent out necessitated the ships being kept on station. Late on 28 February signals intelligence indicated that a raider was already at sea and at 8am the next day *Alcantara* and *Andes*, near the Norwegian coast, were alerted.

An hour later *Alcantara* spotted a suspicious freighter – the *Greif* masquerading as the Norwegian *Rena* – and came in close to send over a boarding party. *Greif* held her cover until *Alcantara* was at point blank range at which point the Germans unmasked their guns and opened fire. In the ensuing brief action, fought at close range, both vessels took heavy damage but *Alcantara*, having suffered a torpedo hit, was sunk first. *Greif*'s crew too started to abandon ship. Meanwhile, *Andes*, further out, also fired on *Greif* and was joined by the light cruiser *Comus* and the destroyer *Munster*. It was not until 1pm that the wrecked *Greif* was sunk with the loss of about a third of her crew of 360 men. The remainder went into British captivity. Around seventy of *Alcantara*'s crew were lost.

THE LOWESTOFT RAID, 24–25 APRIL 1916

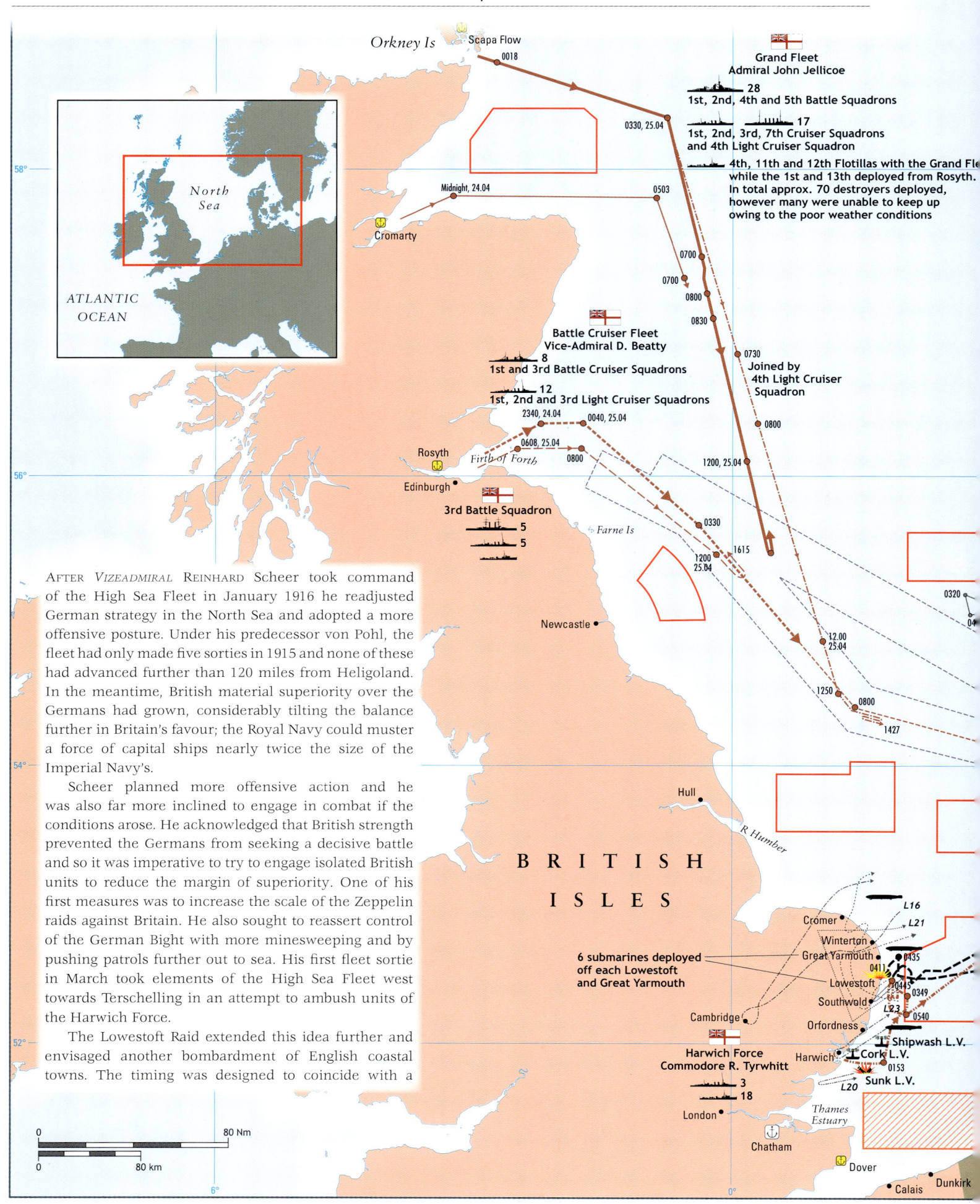

After *Vizeadmiral* Reinhard Scheer took command of the High Sea Fleet in January 1916 he readjusted German strategy in the North Sea and adopted a more offensive posture. Under his predecessor von Pohl, the fleet had only made five sorties in 1915 and none of these had advanced further than 120 miles from Heligoland. In the meantime, British material superiority over the Germans had grown, considerably tilting the balance further in Britain's favour; the Royal Navy could muster a force of capital ships nearly twice the size of the Imperial Navy's.

Scheer planned more offensive action and he was also far more inclined to engage in combat if the conditions arose. He acknowledged that British strength prevented the Germans from seeking a decisive battle and so it was imperative to try to engage isolated British units to reduce the margin of superiority. One of his first measures was to increase the scale of the Zeppelin raids against Britain. He also sought to reassert control of the German Bight with more minesweeping and by pushing patrols further out to sea. His first fleet sortie in March took elements of the High Sea Fleet west towards Terschelling in an attempt to ambush units of the Harwich Force.

The Lowestoft Raid extended this idea further and envisaged another bombardment of English coastal towns. The timing was designed to coincide with a

THE GREAT WAR AT SEA 1916

nationalist uprising in Ireland and the Germans sent a shipment of weapons to Ireland to support this effort though in the event the merchant ship carrying the weapons had to scuttle itself to avoid capture. Heavy Zeppelin raids were to take place at the time of the raid. A planned British sweep of the Skagerrak and Royal Navy submarine activity in the Bight delayed the Germans, but by the afternoon of 24 April the operation was underway.

Shortly after commencement the battlecruiser *Seydlitz* struck a mine and abandoned the operation, but Scheer was undeterred and ordered the fleet to proceed. German radio traffic alerted the British that a sortie was underway and by the evening it was reasonably clear what the target was. The Grand Fleet and Battle Cruiser Fleet had been at heightened readiness since the afternoon and the first units started to sail around 8pm. Heavy seas made it hard for the accompanying destroyers to keep up and not only was progress constrained, but also cohesion of the forces disrupted. In the south the Harwich Force was reduced in strength as around half of its destroyers had been detailed off to another operation.

At around 3.50am on the 25th the screen of the I and II Scouting Groups was sighted by the Harwich Force but, despite Commodore Tyrwhitt's effort, *Konteradmiral* Boedicker, who was standing in for the sick *Konteradmiral* Hipper, could not be enticed away from bombarding, first, Lowestoft at 4.10am, and then Yarmouth at around 4.42am. Tyrwhitt could do little more than shadow the superior German force and in the process his flagship, the light cruiser *Conquest*, was heavily damaged by battlecruiser fire. Boedicker, however, made no attempt to overwhelm the British light forces and around 4.55am turned east. Soon Scheer also turned for home.

Tyrwhitt continued the pursuit until called off by the Admiralty at 8.30am. With the Germans withdrawing, the main British forces stood little chance of catching them. The closest ships, Vice-Admiral Beatty's battlecruisers, were too far north to have any impact, and his support, the fast battleships of the 5th Battle Squadron, even further off; so shortly after noon the British units were ordered back to port. For all their efforts the Germans had achieved little and had let an opportunity to inflict heavy damage on the British pass. In addition to *Seydlitz*'s damage, two of the eleven U-boats employed were lost while the British lost a submarine and had two cruisers damaged.

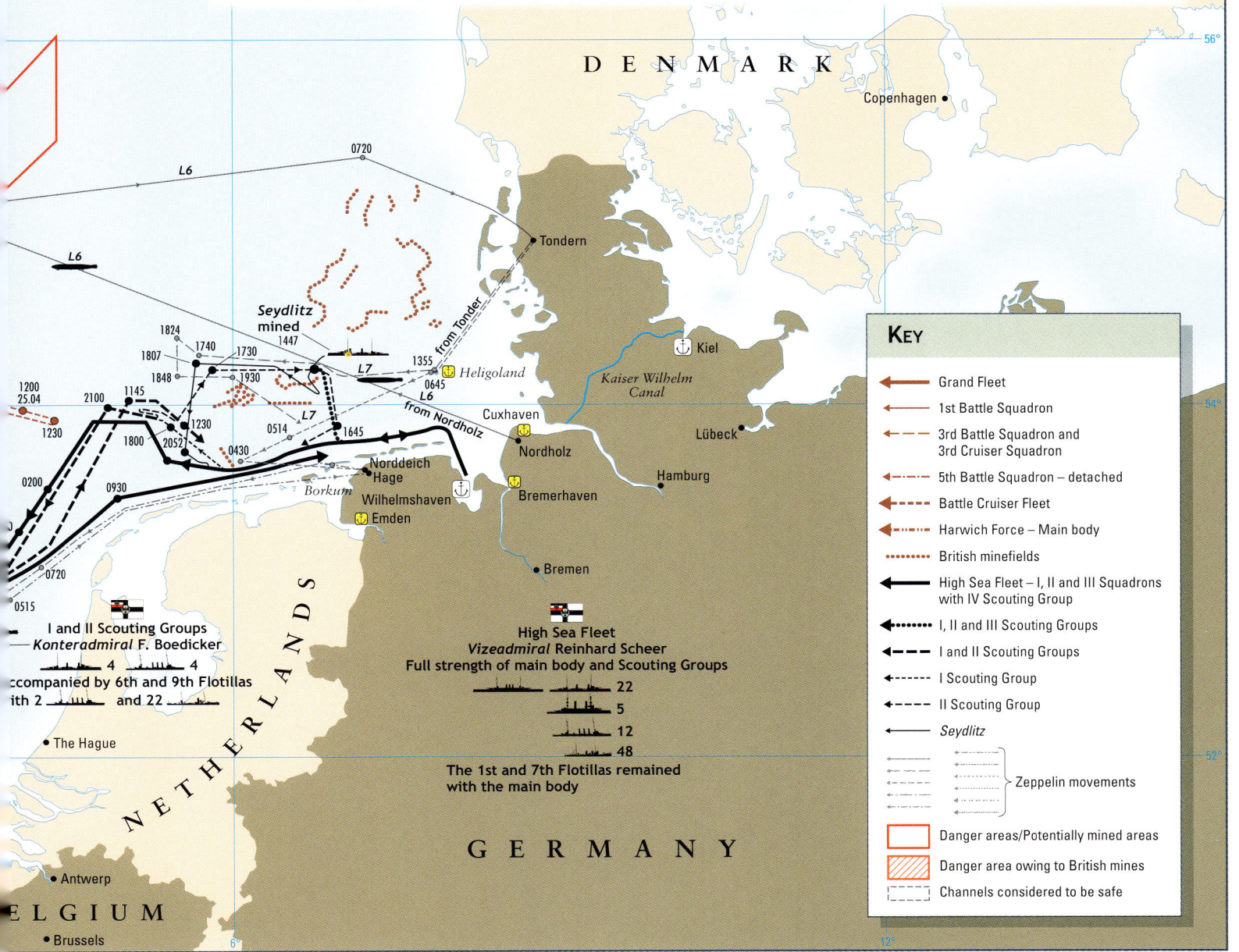

Operation XX, 2–5 May 1916

During the spring of 1916 the British conducted a number of operations deep within the German Bight in an effort to degrade the Imperial Navy's maritime aviation by attacking its bases. A plan to attack the air base at Hoyer on the Schleswig coast had been under consideration since June 1915, and in the intervening time the threat from German aircraft and Zeppelins, not only to fleet operations in the North Sea, but also against the British Isles themselves had only increased. In March a raid against Hoyer by seaplanes launched from the *Vindex*, and covered by the Harwich Force and the Battle Cruiser Fleet, had nearly resulted in an engagement with the High Sea Fleet. Drawing from this experience, the British devised a more complex operation designed to draw out the High Sea Fleet and force it into battle. It was calculated that if British forces appeared within close proximity of the German coast the Imperial Navy would be compelled to sortie.

What became known as Operation XX was designed as a combined air and minelaying operation in the Bight. Two minefields would be laid, one in the northern exit route of the Bight via the Amrum Channel, and another on the southern exit route that the High Sea Fleet took near the Borkum Riff. Concurrently, an air raid against the Zeppelin sheds at Tondern would act as bait for the High Sea Fleet in an attempt to lure it out and draw it over the newly laid mines. In addition, submarines would be deployed to ambush the Germans, and the largest number of boats yet brought together for a single operation was deployed for the operation. In order to achieve surprise both the Battle Cruiser Fleet and main body of the Grand Fleet would maintain strict radio silence. It was thus hoped that the High Sea Fleet would come out to defeat the light forces covering the air raid and find themselves facing nearly the entire British battlefleet. Apart from destroyers detached to escort *Princess Margaret*, the Harwich Force played no

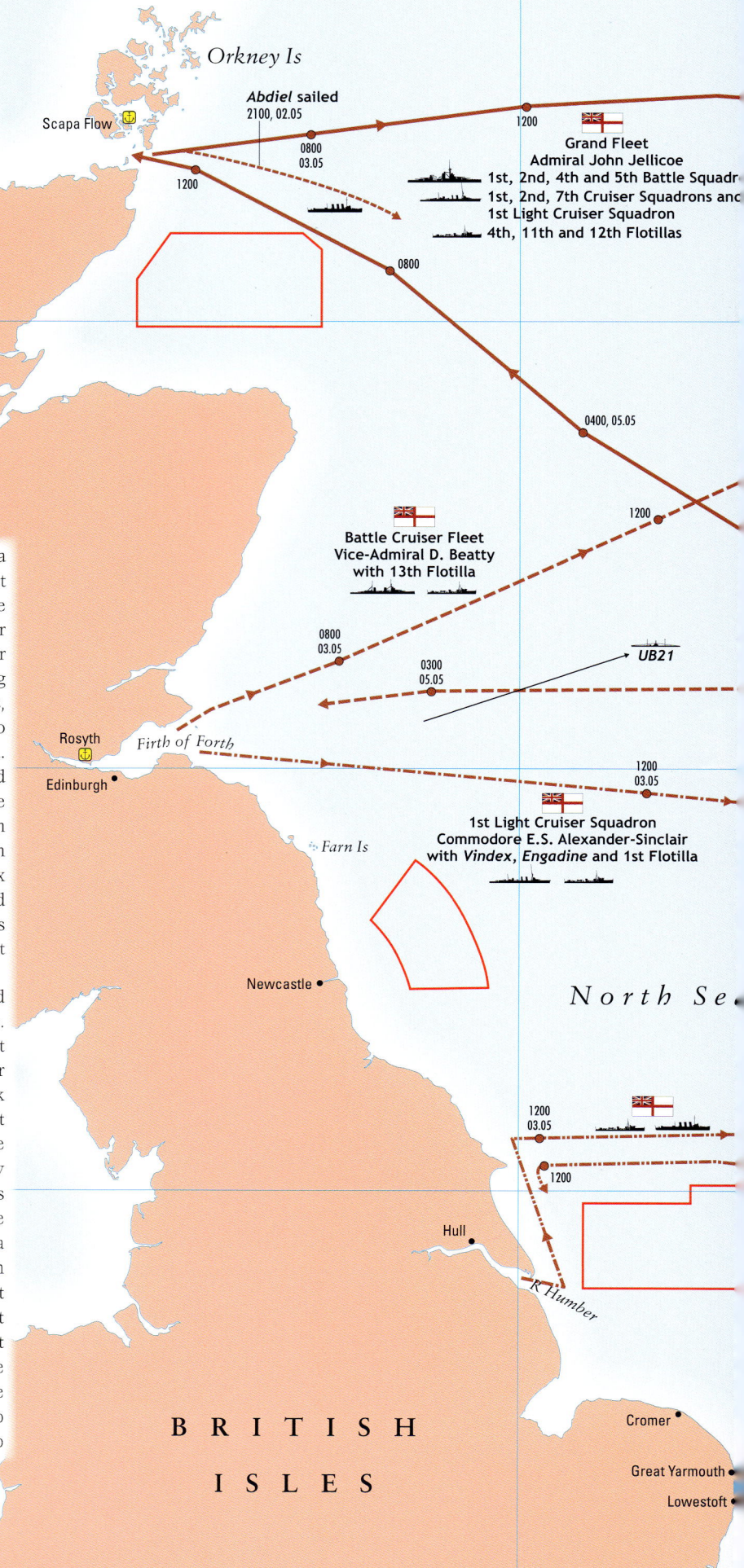

The Great War at Sea 1916

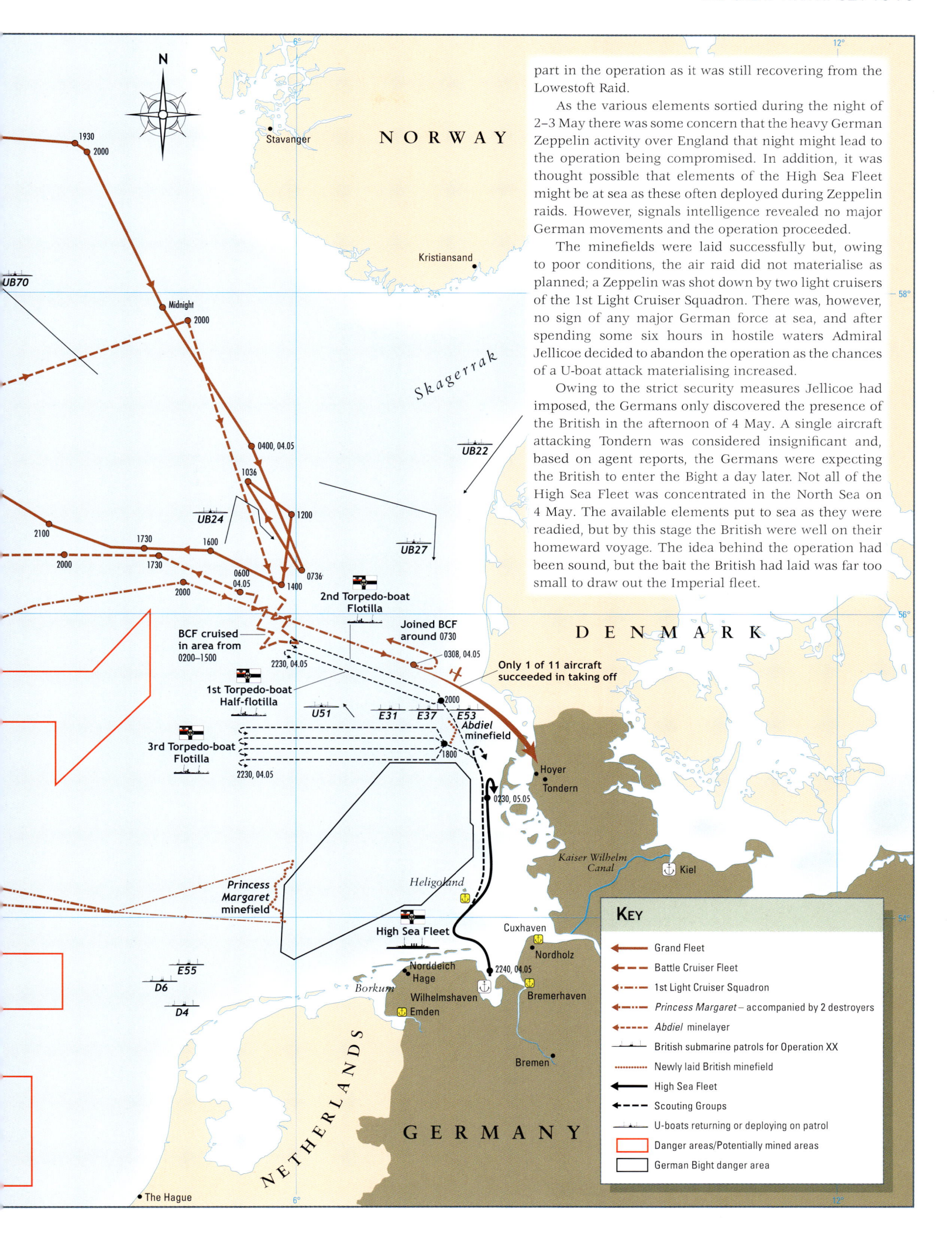

part in the operation as it was still recovering from the Lowestoft Raid.

As the various elements sortied during the night of 2–3 May there was some concern that the heavy German Zeppelin activity over England that night might lead to the operation being compromised. In addition, it was thought possible that elements of the High Sea Fleet might be at sea as these often deployed during Zeppelin raids. However, signals intelligence revealed no major German movements and the operation proceeded.

The minefields were laid successfully but, owing to poor conditions, the air raid did not materialise as planned; a Zeppelin was shot down by two light cruisers of the 1st Light Cruiser Squadron. There was, however, no sign of any major German force at sea, and after spending some six hours in hostile waters Admiral Jellicoe decided to abandon the operation as the chances of a U-boat attack materialising increased.

Owing to the strict security measures Jellicoe had imposed, the Germans only discovered the presence of the British in the afternoon of 4 May. A single aircraft attacking Tondern was considered insignificant and, based on agent reports, the Germans were expecting the British to enter the Bight a day later. Not all of the High Sea Fleet was concentrated in the North Sea on 4 May. The available elements put to sea as they were readied, but by this stage the British were well on their homeward voyage. The idea behind the operation had been sound, but the bait the British had laid was far too small to draw out the Imperial fleet.

THE BATTLE OF JUTLAND, 31 MAY – 1 JUNE 1916

By late spring 1916 both the British and Germans were seeking ways of forcing the other into a major engagement on favourable terms. *Admiral* Scheer's first two sorties earlier in the year had been more aggressive, but attacks against the southeast coast of England, aimed at drawing the Grand Fleet south for an engagement somewhere north of the Dutch coast, could never bring about the desired effect; the distance the British needed to cover was too great for the High Sea Fleet to wait in the southern North Sea for an engagement owing to British submarines and dwindling fuel supplies.

The withdrawal of the U-boats from commerce warfare around Britain gave Scheer the option of integrating these into the next fleet operation. A large number would be deployed off the British bases to degrade the Grand Fleet's superiority, and a raid by Hipper's battlecruisers against Sunderland would be the catalyst to draw the British out. However, being in a numerically inferior position Scheer was dependent on every ship and his timetable was thrown into disarray when repairs to the battlecruiser *Seydlitz* took longer than planned, postponing the operation until late May. Having already deployed the U-boats Scheer now opted for a sortie into the Skagerrak approaches to draw the British out.

Concurrently, Admiral Jellicoe was looking for a way to lure the High Sea Fleet out of the relative safety of the German Bight. To do this he intended to use a sweep by two light cruiser squadrons as bait to lure the Germans into submarine ambushes and mines placed at the exits of the Bight. The operation was to take place at the beginning of June. After detecting the large-scale deployment of U-boats in mid-May the British were increasingly vigilant, sure that a major German operation was underway. When on 30 May signals intelligence suggested that the High Sea Fleet was assembling in the Jade Jellicoe ordered the Grand Fleet out and was at sea before Scheer had even sortied.

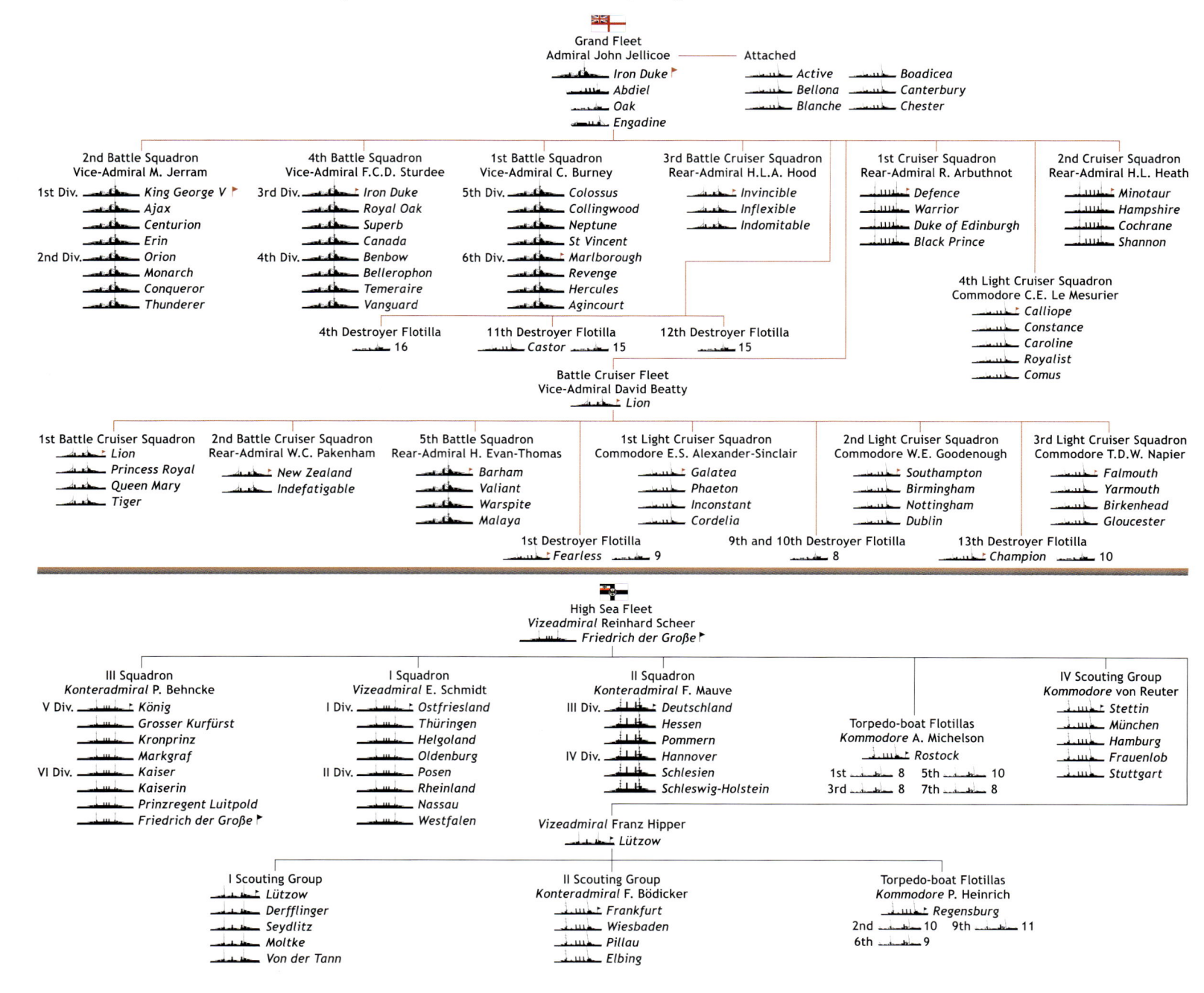

Grand Fleet
Admiral John Jellicoe

- Iron Duke
- Abdiel
- Oak
- Engadine

Attached
- Active
- Bellona
- Blanche
- Boadicea
- Canterbury
- Chester

2nd Battle Squadron
Vice-Admiral M. Jerram
- 1st Div.: King George V, Ajax, Centurion, Erin
- 2nd Div.: Orion, Monarch, Conqueror, Thunderer

4th Battle Squadron
Vice-Admiral F.C.D. Sturdee
- 3rd Div.: Iron Duke, Royal Oak, Superb, Canada
- 4th Div.: Benbow, Bellerophon, Temeraire, Vanguard

1st Battle Squadron
Vice-Admiral C. Burney
- 5th Div.: Colossus, Collingwood, Neptune, St Vincent
- 6th Div.: Marlborough, Revenge, Hercules, Agincourt

3rd Battle Cruiser Squadron
Rear-Admiral H.L.A. Hood
- Invincible
- Inflexible
- Indomitable

1st Cruiser Squadron
Rear-Admiral R. Arbuthnot
- Defence
- Warrior
- Duke of Edinburgh
- Black Prince

2nd Cruiser Squadron
Rear-Admiral H.L. Heath
- Minotaur
- Hampshire
- Cochrane
- Shannon

4th Light Cruiser Squadron
Commodore C.E. Le Mesurier
- Calliope
- Constance
- Caroline
- Royalist
- Comus

- 4th Destroyer Flotilla: 16
- 11th Destroyer Flotilla: Castor, 15
- 12th Destroyer Flotilla: 15

Battle Cruiser Fleet
Vice-Admiral David Beatty
- Lion

1st Battle Cruiser Squadron
- Lion
- Princess Royal
- Queen Mary
- Tiger

2nd Battle Cruiser Squadron
Rear-Admiral W.C. Pakenham
- New Zealand
- Indefatigable

5th Battle Squadron
Rear-Admiral H. Evan-Thomas
- Barham
- Valiant
- Warspite
- Malaya

1st Light Cruiser Squadron
Commodore E.S. Alexander-Sinclair
- Galatea
- Phaeton
- Inconstant
- Cordelia

2nd Light Cruiser Squadron
Commodore W.E. Goodenough
- Southampton
- Birmingham
- Nottingham
- Dublin

3rd Light Cruiser Squadron
Commodore T.D.W. Napier
- Falmouth
- Yarmouth
- Birkenhead
- Gloucester

- 1st Destroyer Flotilla: Fearless, 9
- 9th and 10th Destroyer Flotilla: 8
- 13th Destroyer Flotilla: Champion, 10

High Sea Fleet
Vizeadmiral Reinhard Scheer
- Friedrich der Große

III Squadron
Konteradmiral P. Behncke
- V Div.: König, Grosser Kurfürst, Kronprinz, Markgraf
- VI Div.: Kaiser, Kaiserin, Prinzregent Luitpold, Friedrich der Große

I Squadron
Vizeadmiral E. Schmidt
- I Div.: Ostfriesland, Thüringen, Helgoland, Oldenburg
- II Div.: Posen, Rheinland, Nassau, Westfalen

II Squadron
Konteradmiral F. Mauve
- III Div.: Deutschland, Hessen, Pommern
- IV Div.: Hannover, Schlesien, Schleswig-Holstein

Torpedo-boat Flotillas
Kommodore A. Michelson
- Rostock
- 1st: 8, 5th: 10
- 3rd: 8, 7th: 8

IV Scouting Group
Kommodore von Reuter
- Stettin
- München
- Hamburg
- Frauenlob
- Stuttgart

Vizeadmiral Franz Hipper
- Lützow

I Scouting Group
- Lützow
- Derfflinger
- Seydlitz
- Moltke
- Von der Tann

II Scouting Group
Konteradmiral F. Bödicker
- Frankfurt
- Wiesbaden
- Pillau
- Elbing

Torpedo-boat Flotillas
Kommodore P. Heinrich
- Regensburg
- 2nd: 10, 9th: 11
- 6th: 9

THE GREAT WAR AT SEA 1916

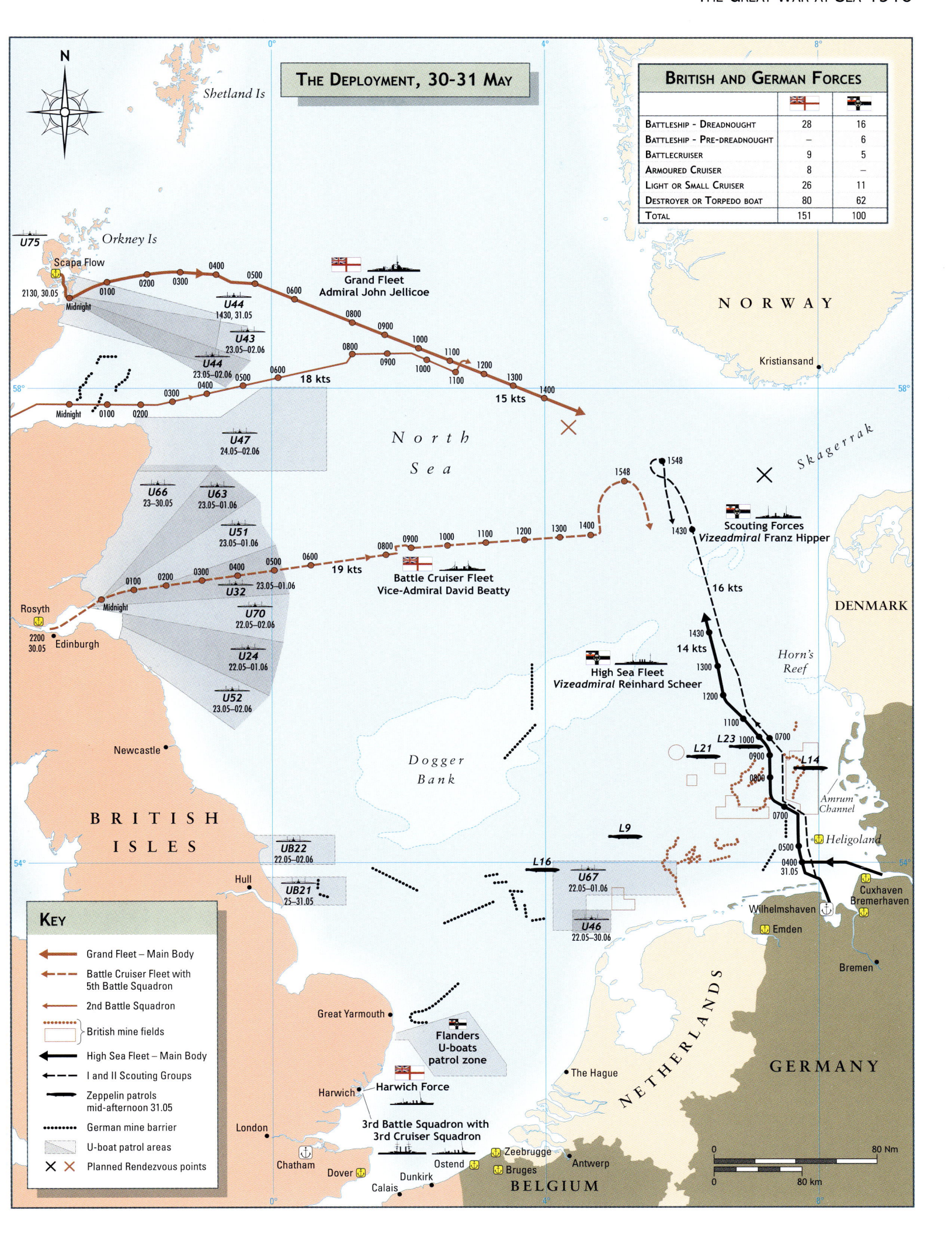

THE DEPLOYMENT, 30–31 MAY

BRITISH AND GERMAN FORCES

	🇬🇧	🇩🇪
BATTLESHIP – DREADNOUGHT	28	16
BATTLESHIP – PRE-DREADNOUGHT	–	6
BATTLECRUISER	9	5
ARMOURED CRUISER	8	–
LIGHT OR SMALL CRUISER	26	11
DESTROYER OR TORPEDO BOAT	80	62
TOTAL	151	100

KEY

- Grand Fleet – Main Body
- Battle Cruiser Fleet with 5th Battle Squadron
- 2nd Battle Squadron
- British mine fields
- High Sea Fleet – Main Body
- I and II Scouting Groups
- Zeppelin patrols mid-afternoon 31.05
- German mine barrier
- U-boat patrol areas
- × × Planned Rendezvous points

Phase 1 1548-1648 - The Run to the South

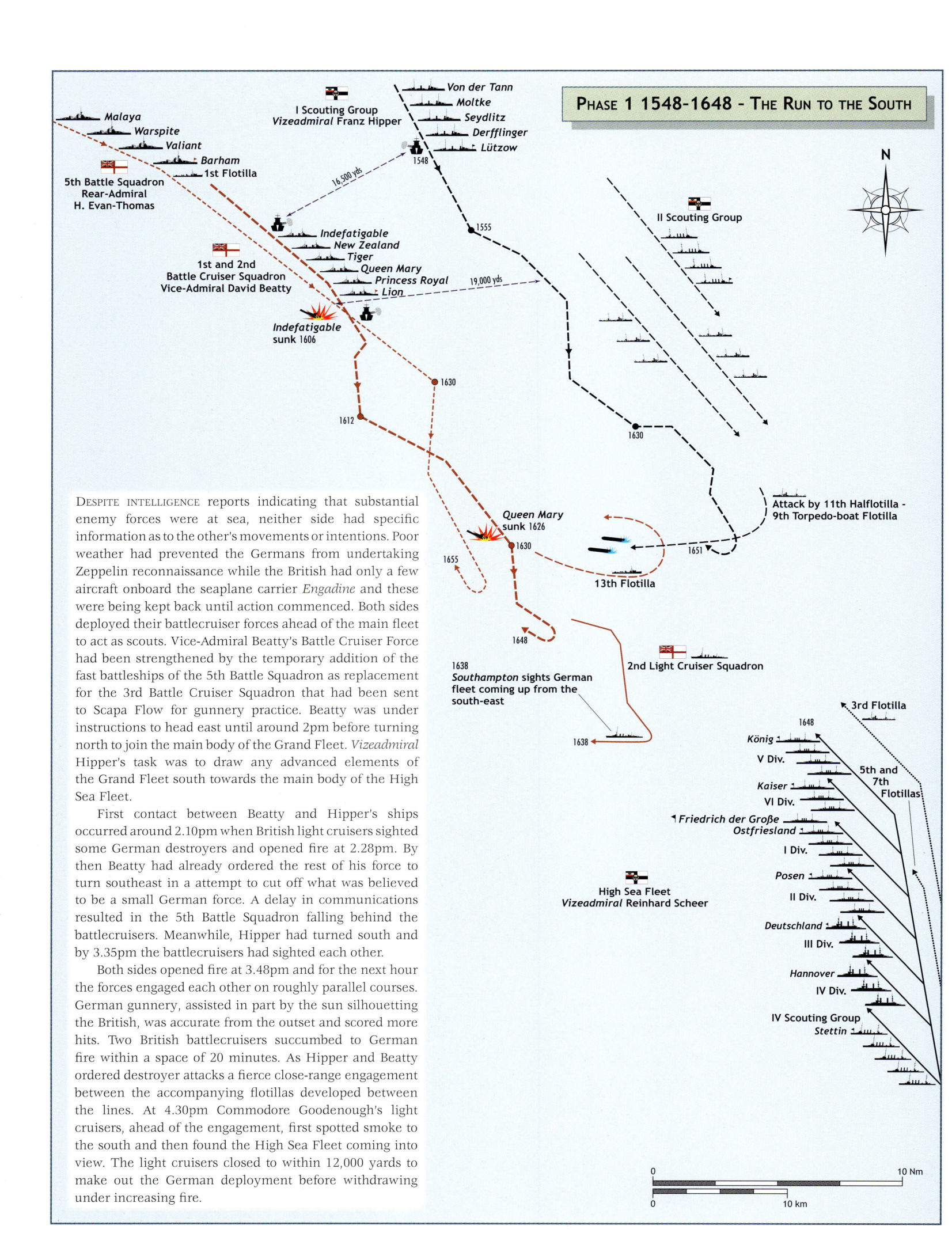

Despite intelligence reports indicating that substantial enemy forces were at sea, neither side had specific information as to the other's movements or intentions. Poor weather had prevented the Germans from undertaking Zeppelin reconnaissance while the British had only a few aircraft onboard the seaplane carrier *Engadine* and these were being kept back until action commenced. Both sides deployed their battlecruiser forces ahead of the main fleet to act as scouts. Vice-Admiral Beatty's Battle Cruiser Force had been strengthened by the temporary addition of the fast battleships of the 5th Battle Squadron as replacement for the 3rd Battle Cruiser Squadron that had been sent to Scapa Flow for gunnery practice. Beatty was under instructions to head east until around 2pm before turning north to join the main body of the Grand Fleet. *Vizeadmiral* Hipper's task was to draw any advanced elements of the Grand Fleet south towards the main body of the High Sea Fleet.

First contact between Beatty and Hipper's ships occurred around 2.10pm when British light cruisers sighted some German destroyers and opened fire at 2.28pm. By then Beatty had already ordered the rest of his force to turn southeast in a attempt to cut off what was believed to be a small German force. A delay in communications resulted in the 5th Battle Squadron falling behind the battlecruisers. Meanwhile, Hipper had turned south and by 3.35pm the battlecruisers had sighted each other.

Both sides opened fire at 3.48pm and for the next hour the forces engaged each other on roughly parallel courses. German gunnery, assisted in part by the sun silhouetting the British, was accurate from the outset and scored more hits. Two British battlecruisers succumbed to German fire within a space of 20 minutes. As Hipper and Beatty ordered destroyer attacks a fierce close-range engagement between the accompanying flotillas developed between the lines. At 4.30pm Commodore Goodenough's light cruisers, ahead of the engagement, first spotted smoke to the south and then found the High Sea Fleet coming into view. The light cruisers closed to within 12,000 yards to make out the German deployment before withdrawing under increasing fire.

The Great War at Sea 1916

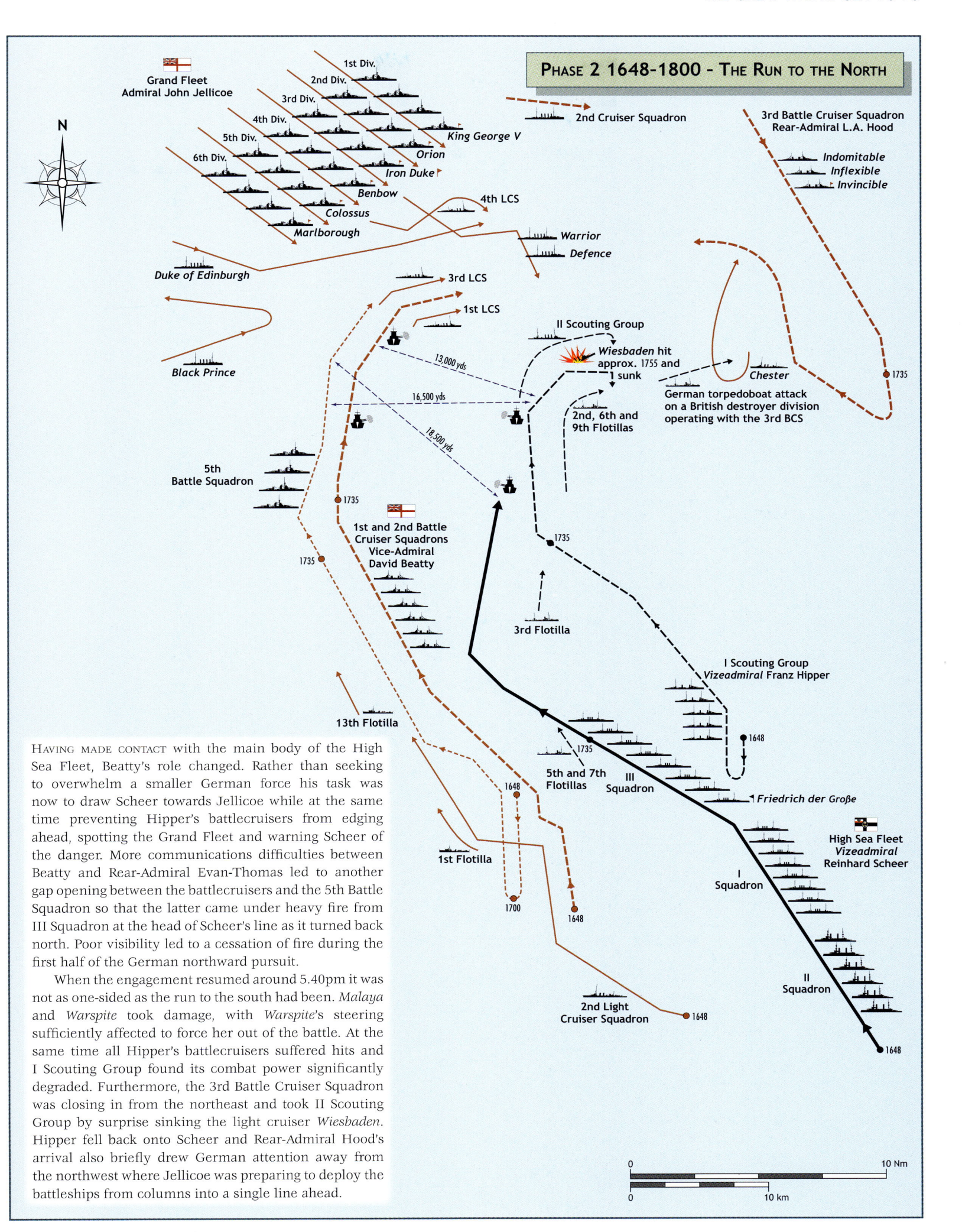

Phase 2 1648-1800 – The Run to the North

Having made contact with the main body of the High Sea Fleet, Beatty's role changed. Rather than seeking to overwhelm a smaller German force his task was now to draw Scheer towards Jellicoe while at the same time preventing Hipper's battlecruisers from edging ahead, spotting the Grand Fleet and warning Scheer of the danger. More communications difficulties between Beatty and Rear-Admiral Evan-Thomas led to another gap opening between the battlecruisers and the 5th Battle Squadron so that the latter came under heavy fire from III Squadron at the head of Scheer's line as it turned back north. Poor visibility led to a cessation of fire during the first half of the German northward pursuit.

When the engagement resumed around 5.40pm it was not as one-sided as the run to the south had been. *Malaya* and *Warspite* took damage, with *Warspite*'s steering sufficiently affected to force her out of the battle. At the same time all Hipper's battlecruisers suffered hits and I Scouting Group found its combat power significantly degraded. Furthermore, the 3rd Battle Cruiser Squadron was closing in from the northeast and took II Scouting Group by surprise sinking the light cruiser *Wiesbaden*. Hipper fell back onto Scheer and Rear-Admiral Hood's arrival also briefly drew German attention away from the northwest where Jellicoe was preparing to deploy the battleships from columns into a single line ahead.

Phase 3 The Main Engagement 1800-2100

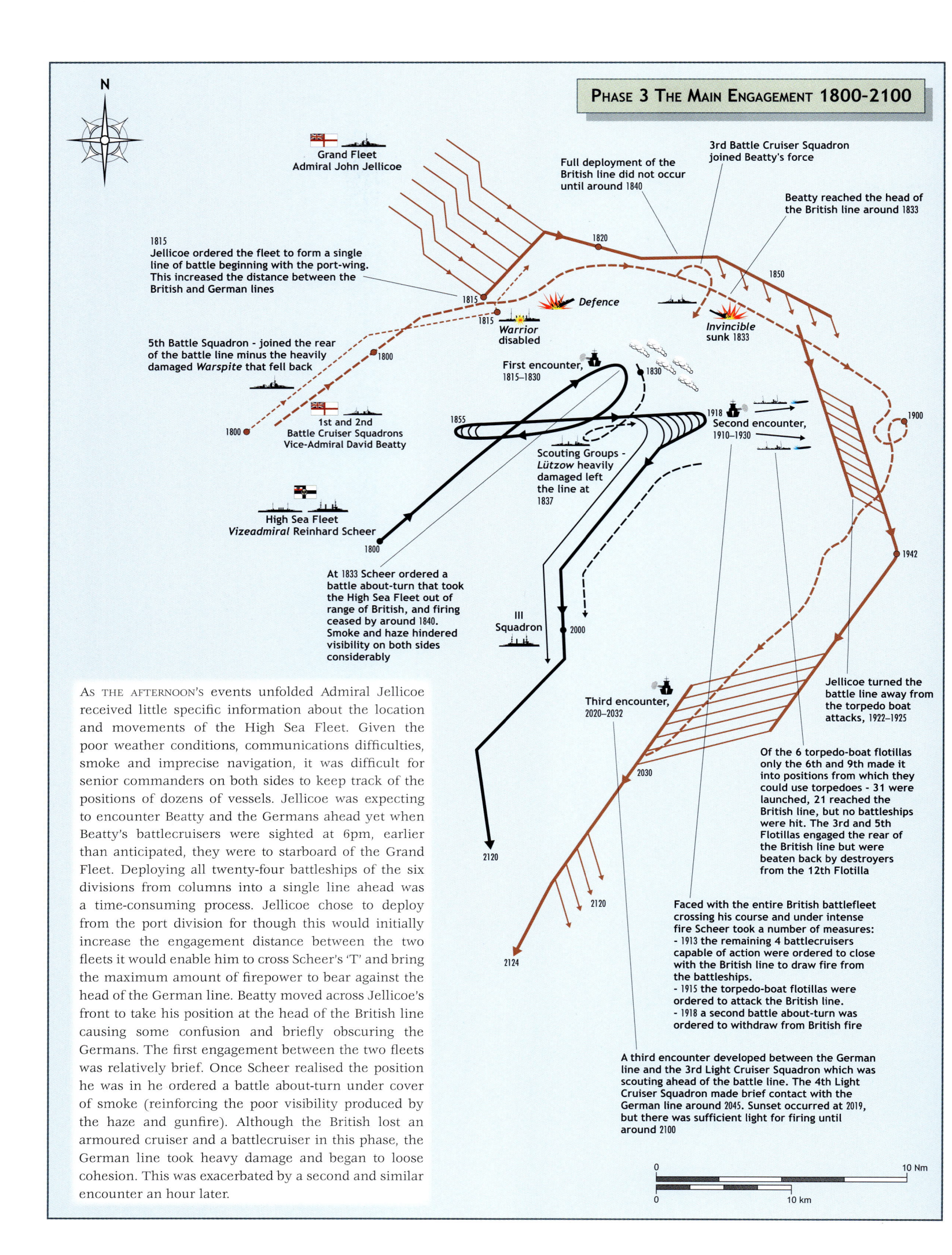

Grand Fleet Admiral John Jellicoe

3rd Battle Cruiser Squadron joined Beatty's force

Full deployment of the British line did not occur until around 1840

Beatty reached the head of the British line around 1833

1815 Jellicoe ordered the fleet to form a single line of battle beginning with the port-wing. This increased the distance between the British and German lines

Defence

Warrior disabled

Invincible sunk 1833

5th Battle Squadron – joined the rear of the battle line minus the heavily damaged *Warspite* that fell back

First encounter, 1815–1830

1st and 2nd Battle Cruiser Squadrons Vice-Admiral David Beatty

Second encounter, 1910–1930

Scouting Groups – *Lützow* heavily damaged left the line at 1837

High Sea Fleet Vizeadmiral Reinhard Scheer

At 1833 Scheer ordered a battle about-turn that took the High Sea Fleet out of range of British, and firing ceased by around 1840. Smoke and haze hindered visibility on both sides considerably

III Squadron

Third encounter, 2020–2032

Jellicoe turned the battle line away from the torpedo boat attacks, 1922–1925

Of the 6 torpedo-boat flotillas only the 6th and 9th made it into positions from which they could use torpedoes – 31 were launched, 21 reached the British line, but no battleships were hit. The 3rd and 5th Flotillas engaged the rear of the British line but were beaten back by destroyers from the 12th Flotilla

Faced with the entire British battlefleet crossing his course and under intense fire Scheer took a number of measures:
- 1913 the remaining 4 battlecruisers capable of action were ordered to close with the British line to draw fire from the battleships.
- 1915 the torpedo-boat flotillas were ordered to attack the British line.
- 1918 a second battle about-turn was ordered to withdraw from British fire

A third encounter developed between the German line and the 3rd Light Cruiser Squadron which was scouting ahead of the battle line. The 4th Light Cruiser Squadron made brief contact with the German line around 2045. Sunset occurred at 2019, but there was sufficient light for firing until around 2100

As the afternoon's events unfolded Admiral Jellicoe received little specific information about the location and movements of the High Sea Fleet. Given the poor weather conditions, communications difficulties, smoke and imprecise navigation, it was difficult for senior commanders on both sides to keep track of the positions of dozens of vessels. Jellicoe was expecting to encounter Beatty and the Germans ahead yet when Beatty's battlecruisers were sighted at 6pm, earlier than anticipated, they were to starboard of the Grand Fleet. Deploying all twenty-four battleships of the six divisions from columns into a single line ahead was a time-consuming process. Jellicoe chose to deploy from the port division for though this would initially increase the engagement distance between the two fleets it would enable him to cross Scheer's 'T' and bring the maximum amount of firepower to bear against the head of the German line. Beatty moved across Jellicoe's front to take his position at the head of the British line causing some confusion and briefly obscuring the Germans. The first engagement between the two fleets was relatively brief. Once Scheer realised the position he was in he ordered a battle about-turn under cover of smoke (reinforcing the poor visibility produced by the haze and gunfire). Although the British lost an armoured cruiser and a battlecruiser in this phase, the German line took heavy damage and began to loose cohesion. This was exacerbated by a second and similar encounter an hour later.

# THE GREAT WAR AT SEA 1916

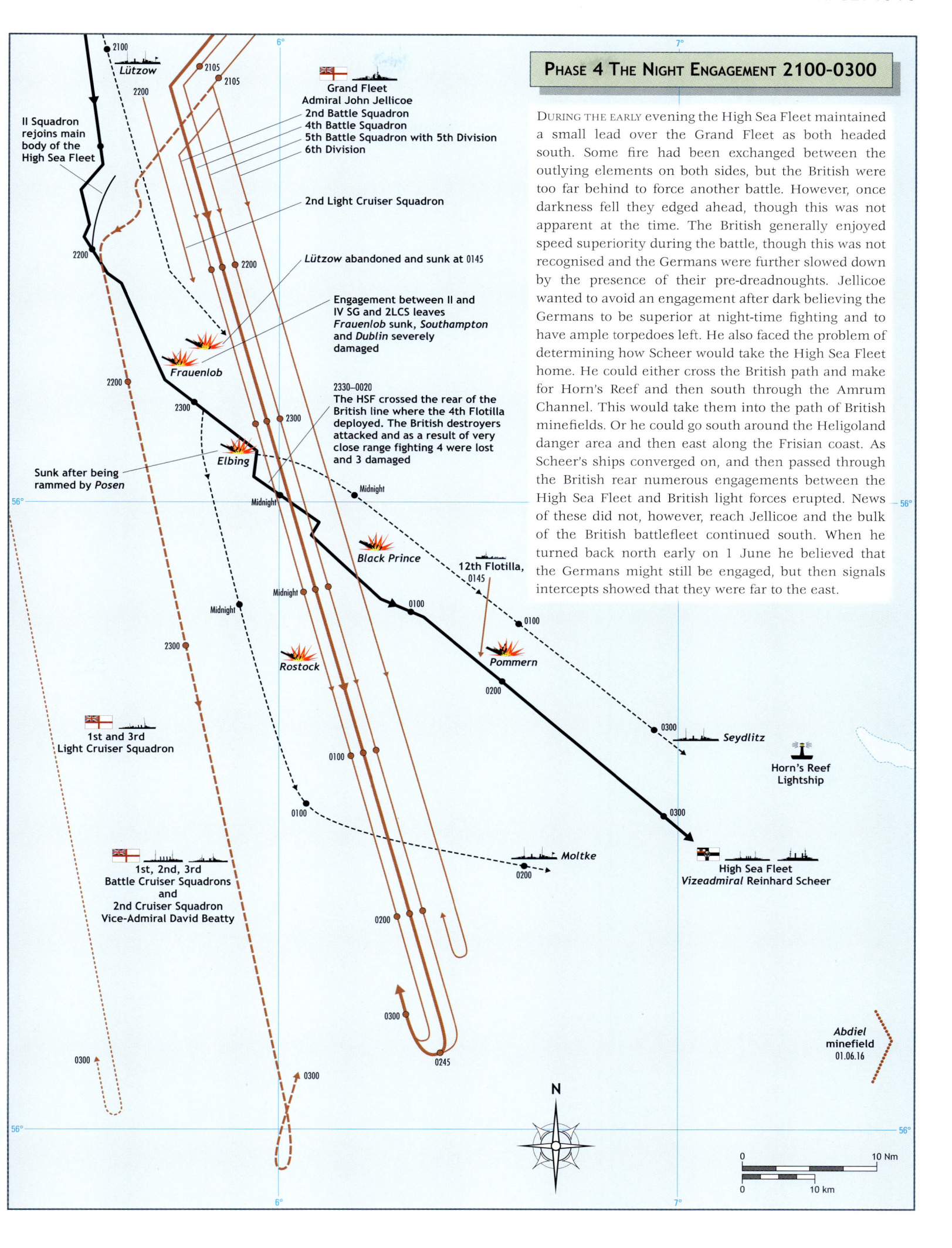

PHASE 4 THE NIGHT ENGAGEMENT 2100-0300

DURING THE EARLY evening the High Sea Fleet maintained a small lead over the Grand Fleet as both headed south. Some fire had been exchanged between the outlying elements on both sides, but the British were too far behind to force another battle. However, once darkness fell they edged ahead, though this was not apparent at the time. The British generally enjoyed speed superiority during the battle, though this was not recognised and the Germans were further slowed down by the presence of their pre-dreadnoughts. Jellicoe wanted to avoid an engagement after dark believing the Germans to be superior at night-time fighting and to have ample torpedoes left. He also faced the problem of determining how Scheer would take the High Sea Fleet home. He could either cross the British path and make for Horn's Reef and then south through the Amrum Channel. This would take them into the path of British minefields. Or he could go south around the Heligoland danger area and then east along the Frisian coast. As Scheer's ships converged on, and then passed through the British rear numerous engagements between the High Sea Fleet and British light forces erupted. News of these did not, however, reach Jellicoe and the bulk of the British battlefleet continued south. When he turned back north early on 1 June he believed that the Germans might still be engaged, but then signals intercepts showed that they were far to the east.

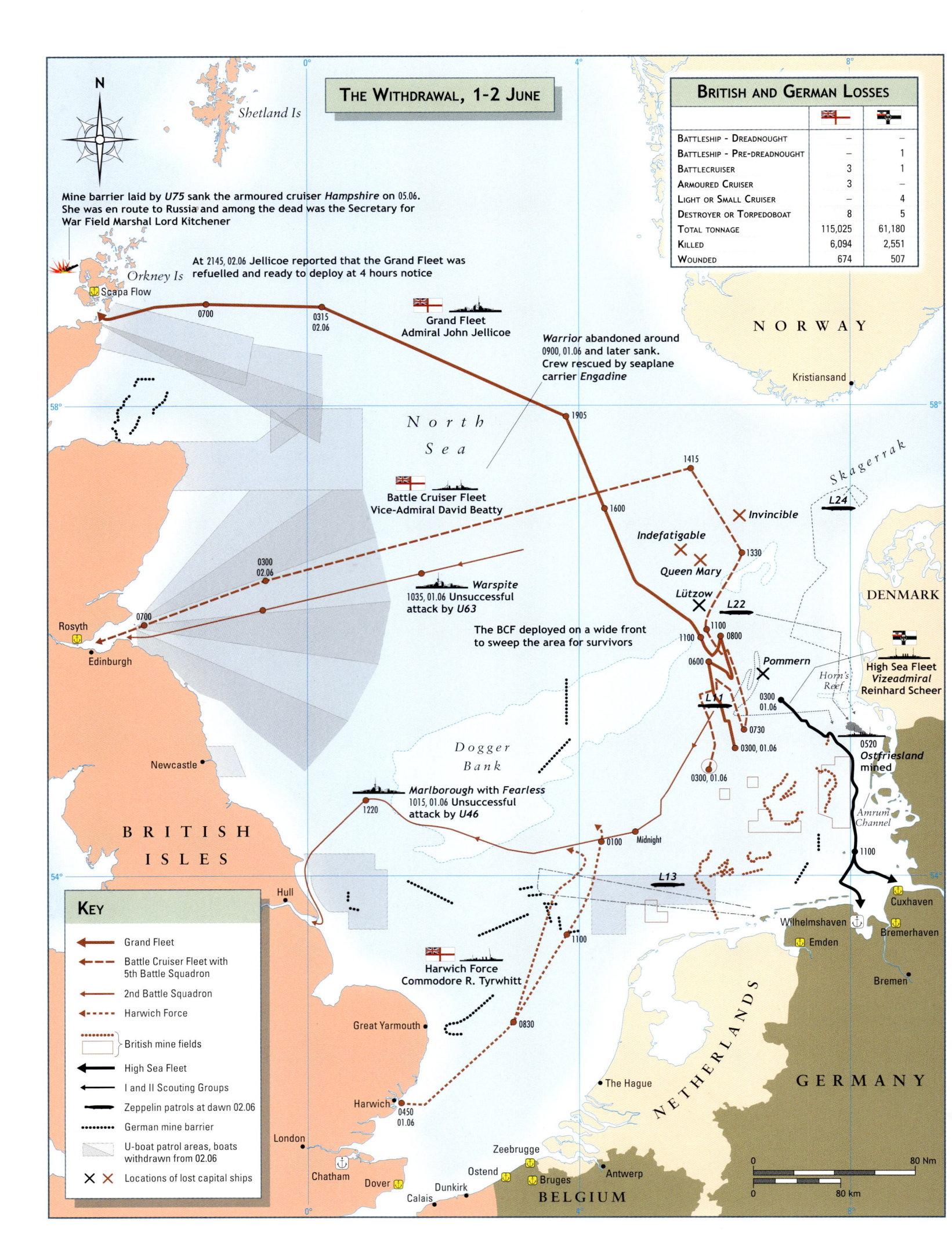

The Withdrawal, 1–2 June

British and German Losses

	British	German
Battleship – Dreadnought	–	–
Battleship – Pre-dreadnought	–	1
Battlecruiser	3	1
Armoured Cruiser	3	–
Light or Small Cruiser	–	4
Destroyer or Torpedoboat	8	5
Total tonnage	115,025	61,180
Killed	6,094	2,551
Wounded	674	507

Mine barrier laid by *U75* sank the armoured cruiser *Hampshire* on 05.06. She was en route to Russia and among the dead was the Secretary for War Field Marshal Lord Kitchener

At 2145, 02.06 Jellicoe reported that the Grand Fleet was refuelled and ready to deploy at 4 hours notice

Warrior abandoned around 0900, 01.06 and later sank. Crew rescued by seaplane carrier *Engadine*

Grand Fleet — Admiral John Jellicoe

Battle Cruiser Fleet — Vice-Admiral David Beatty

Warspite 1035, 01.06 Unsuccessful attack by *U63*

The BCF deployed on a wide front to sweep the area for survivors

Marlborough with *Fearless* 1015, 01.06 Unsuccessful attack by *U46*

Harwich Force — Commodore R. Tyrwhitt

High Sea Fleet — Vizeadmiral Reinhard Scheer

Ostfriesland mined

Key

- Grand Fleet
- Battle Cruiser Fleet with 5th Battle Squadron
- 2nd Battle Squadron
- Harwich Force
- British mine fields
- High Sea Fleet
- I and II Scouting Groups
- Zeppelin patrols at dawn 02.06
- German mine barrier
- U-boat patrol areas, boats withdrawn from 02.06
- X Locations of lost capital ships

MINE OPERATIONS, GERMAN BIGHT 1915–16

THE GERMANS WERE quick to claim victory on the basis of the larger number of British ships sunk, and by any measure British casualties had been higher (*opposite page*). The failure to inflict a decisive defeat on an inferior High Sea Fleet, and the initial lack of information from the Royal Navy about the battle, seemed to reinforce this claim. The British certainly had experienced problems with their gunnery, with the quality of their shells, and in other areas, particularly communications. Some of Vice-Admiral Beatty's decisions were questionable and the ammunition handling procedures within the Battle Cruiser Fleet had contributed to the loss of three ships. Admiral Jellicoe's cautious handling of the battle, though much criticised later on, was however sound; the British did not need to defeat the Germans at all costs, and strategically, at the end of the battle, nothing had changed.

ALTHOUGH THE BRITISH had given mine warfare attention in pre-war planning, its implementation in 1914 floundered on the shortage and inadequate quality of mines and minelayers. Admiral Jellicoe had briefly considered mining half the Heligoland Bight and using submarines to patrol the other half. However, it was felt that the effort involved was not worth the risk and that submarines could be used more effectively countering the High Sea Fleet in the German Bight. Furthermore, German U-boat penetration into the English Channel and raids along the East Coast necessitated British mines being employed in defensive minefields. Jellicoe also needed fast minelayers that could be used to lay mine barriers in those areas that returning German warships might pass through. In 1915 the British began to lay a small number of large minefields in an effort to restrict German movements in and out of the Bight

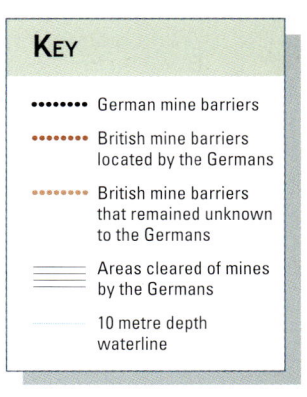

KEY

- German mine barriers
- British mine barriers located by the Germans
- British mine barriers that remained unknown to the Germans
- Areas cleared of mines by the Germans
- 10 metre depth waterline

Kapitänleutnant de la Perière's Patrol, July–August 1916

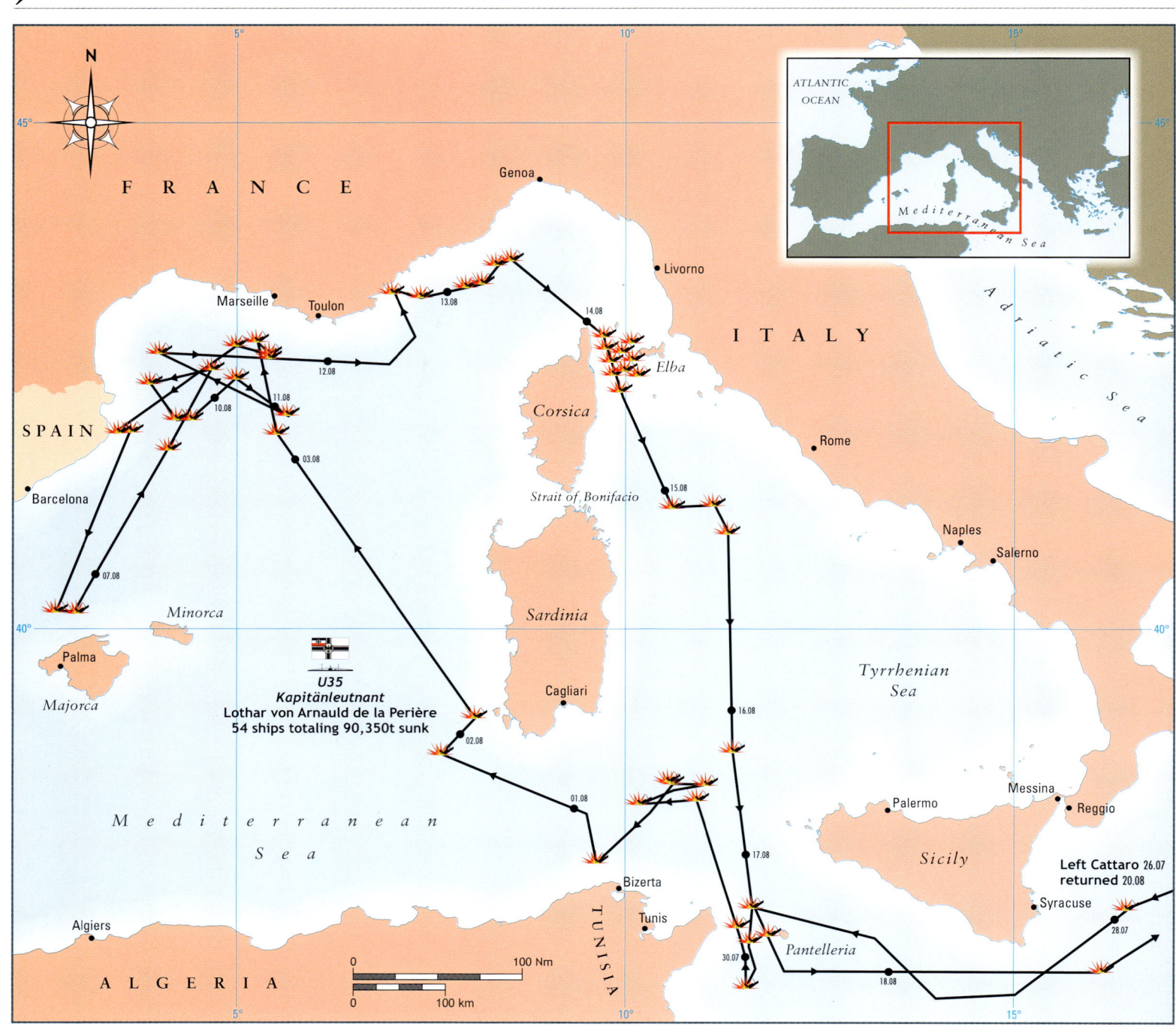

THE MEDITERRANEAN SEA proved to be a very profitable hunting ground for German and Austrian U-boats during the war. Three of the five top U-boat commanders and five of the most successful boats served in the Mediterranean. In a war that surpassed all previous conflicts, the U-boat emerged as one of the symbols of modern warfare and their captains as heroes or modern pirates to friend and foe respectively. Like the fighter pilot aces on land a small number were supremely successful in their operations. The character of U-boat captains varied considerably; some sought to wage lawful commerce warfare while others had little compassion for their victims.

Lothar von Arnauld de la Perière was the most successful U-boat commander of the war and, indeed, in terms of merchant shipping ever sunk by an individual. He started the war as a staff officer, but wanting a frontline command first applied to become an aviator and then a submariner. In April 1915 he commenced his training and in November took command of U35 based at Pola in the Adriatic. His patrol in July and August of 1916 was the single most destructive patrol of the war and throughout the conflict he undertook fifteen patrols while in command of U35 and then U139. He sank 194 merchant ships totalling 453,716 tons as well as two small warships and took care to avoid casualties where possible. His record was all the more remarkable considering that the second most successful U-boat captain, Walther Forstmann, sank just over 384,000 tons of merchant shipping, but took nearly three times as many patrols to do so.

MINESWEEPING IN THE DOVER AREA, 1916–17

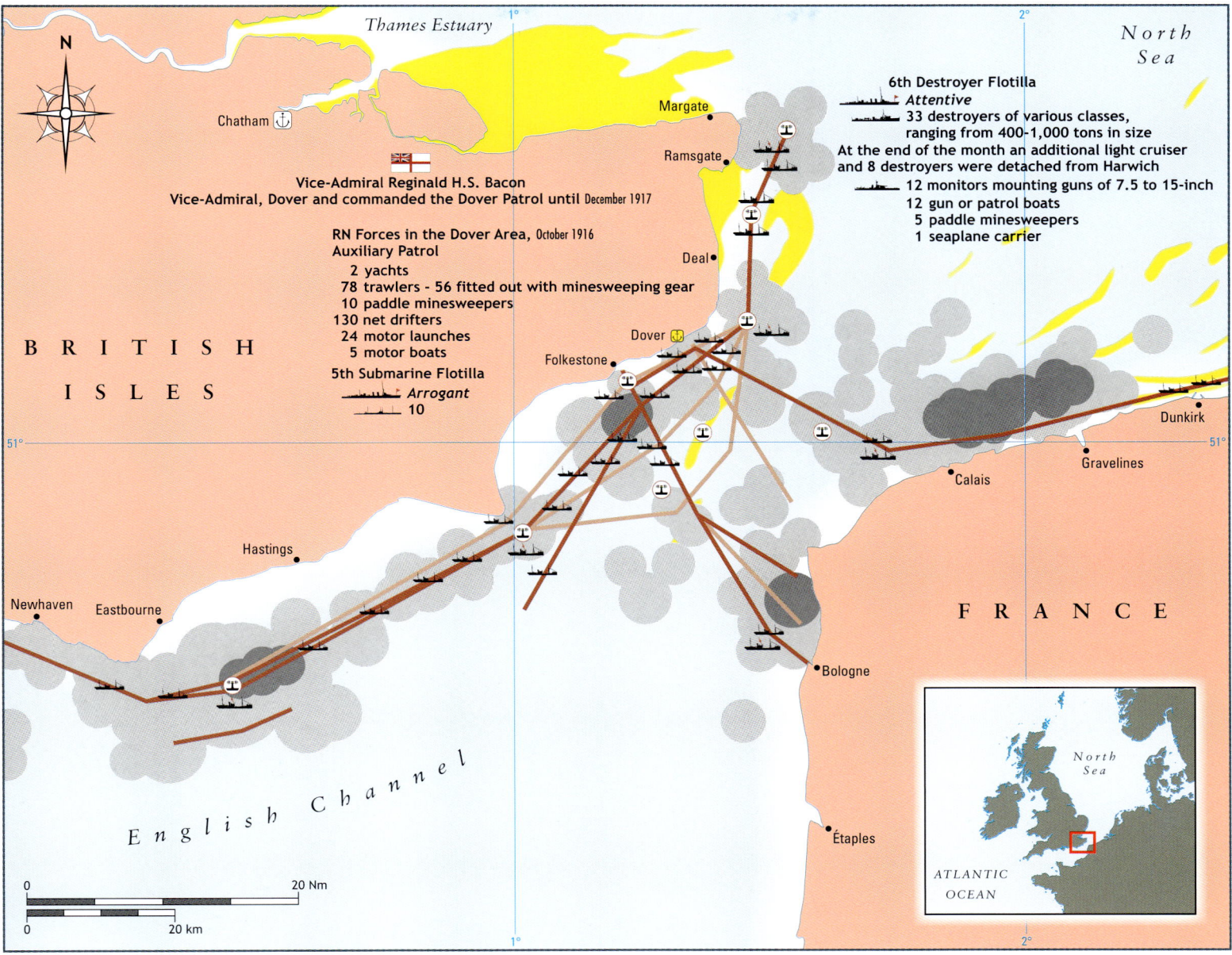

THE GREAT WAR AT SEA 1916

Vice-Admiral Reginald H.S. Bacon
Vice-Admiral, Dover and commanded the Dover Patrol until December 1917

RN Forces in the Dover Area, October 1916
Auxiliary Patrol
2 yachts
78 trawlers - 56 fitted out with minesweeping gear
10 paddle minesweepers
130 net drifters
24 motor launches
5 motor boats
5th Submarine Flotilla
Arrogant
10

6th Destroyer Flotilla
Attentive
33 destroyers of various classes, ranging from 400-1,000 tons in size
At the end of the month an additional light cruiser and 8 destroyers were detached from Harwich
12 monitors mounting guns of 7.5 to 15-inch
12 gun or patrol boats
5 paddle minesweepers
1 seaplane carrier

KEY
- Main routes swept daily
- Alternative routes swept as required
- Spiral sweeps around buoys
- Mine sweeping, non-wireless trawlers on patrol
- Mine sweeping, trawlers on patrol
- Areas of German mines
- Concentrated areas of German mines
- Sand banks/shallows

THE ENGLISH CHANNEL and specifically its eastern end at Dover, was one of the busiest allied shipping routes of the war. Not only was this the direct route by which the British Expeditionary Force in France was supplied, but it was the main access to London which was then the most important British port. Coastal shipping carrying bulk products was vital to the economy and, in addition to the military traffic to France, British coal shipments to the continent increased dramatically during the war. These replaced the French coal supplies from areas now occupied by the German army, and Boulogne, Calais and Le Havre were all major recipient ports. Between 1915 and 1917 over 100,000 merchant vessels passed through the Dover area equating to roughly 80–100 a day.

The German use of mine warfare evolved during the war and increasingly the U-boat rather than warships became the primary means of delivery in British waters. In the winter of 1914–15 the construction of minelaying U-boats commenced and once in operation they proved very successful. These boats proved difficult to counter as they changed their tactics, improved their mines and adapted to British countermeasures. Initially, boats laid all their mines in small areas. Then groups of six or so were laid and then even smaller numbers were scattered, hugely complicating the task the British faced.

Even the fairly constricted waters of the English Channel encompassed a huge area and one that was impossible to clear completely. In the Dover area itself only around ten per cent of the actual sea space was regularly swept. The trawlers taken up as minesweepers were spread out to cover these routes, with each one responsible for a small section and alternating between four days at sea and a similar number in port.

The most heavily mined area was just to the north in the Thames estuary, extending up to Harwich and Lowestoft. The relative proximity of the U-boat base at Zeebrugge explains this, but the Dover area itself also saw substantial minelaying activity. In the second half of 1916 the average number of merchant ships sunk or damaged by mines in British waters was just under six per month and then increased to ten in the first half of 1917 before dropping down to four in the second. During 1916 the average number of mines swept was 178 per month; by 1917 this rose to 355 with April seeing a record 515 destroyed.

THE DISPOSITION OF THE NORTH SEA BLOCKADE, 1916

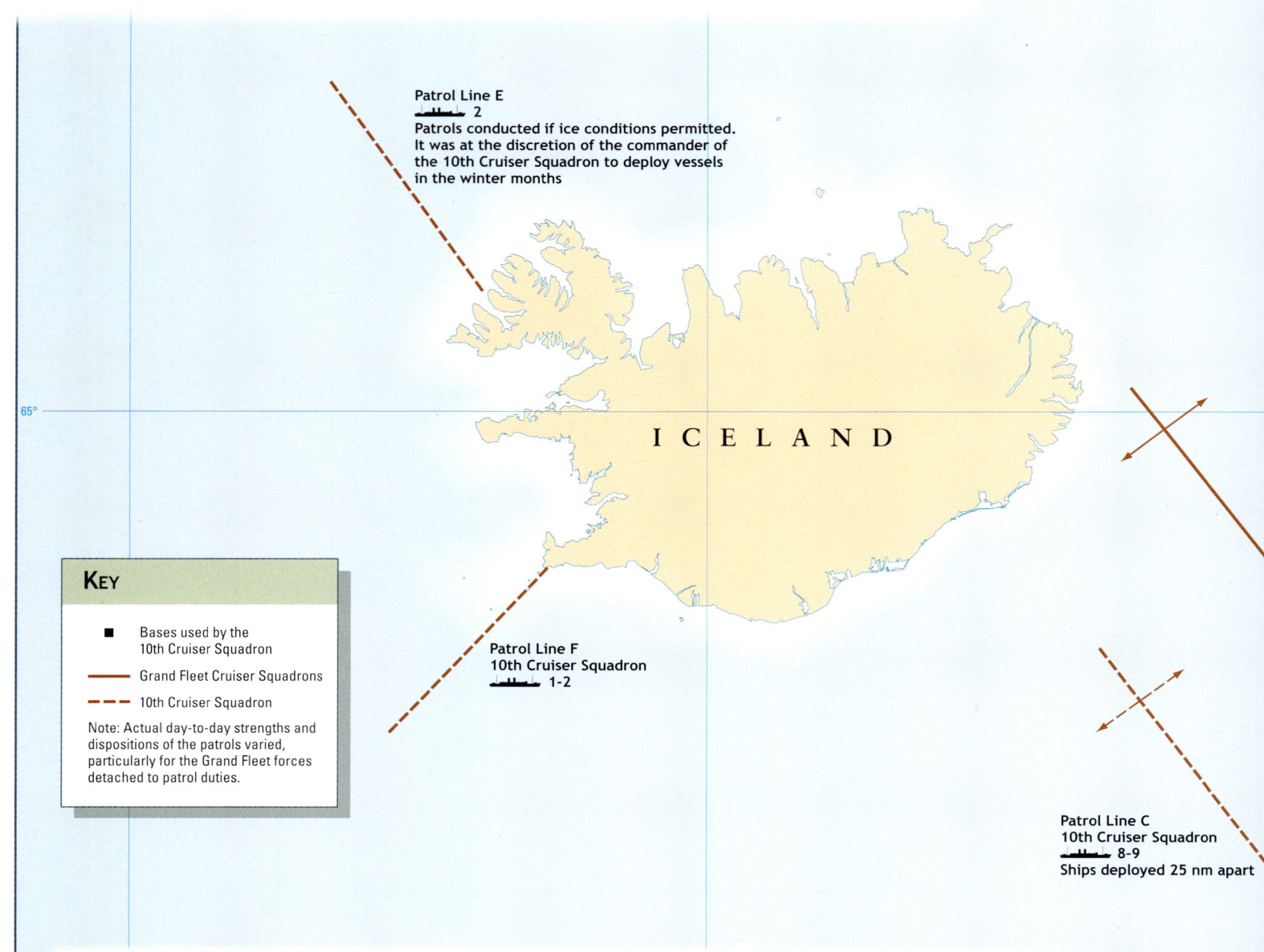

Patrol Line E
2
Patrols conducted if ice conditions permitted. It was at the discretion of the commander of the 10th Cruiser Squadron to deploy vessels in the winter months

ICELAND

Key
- Bases used by the 10th Cruiser Squadron
- Grand Fleet Cruiser Squadrons
- 10th Cruiser Squadron

Note: Actual day-to-day strengths and dispositions of the patrols varied, particularly for the Grand Fleet forces detached to patrol duties.

Patrol Line F
10th Cruiser Squadron
1-2

Patrol Line C
10th Cruiser Squadron
8-9
Ships deployed 25 nm apart

Rockall

Throughout 1915 3,098 ships were intercepted and examined with 743 of these being sent into British ports for further searches. What complicated the blockade was the trade undertaken by the neutral north European states and the concerns the British had that goods imported by them might be re-exported to Germany. Between 1915 and 1916 agreements were reached on the level of such imports with most governments, Sweden being somewhat of an exception.

In a number of ways 1916 marked a turning point in the conduct of the blockade and its effect on Germany. The deployment of the Northern Patrol reached its maximum size and scope. Most of the patrol was conducted by the 10th Cruiser Squadron, concentrated into two main patrol lines with some ships also off Iceland and the Norwegian coast. The individual ships patrolled back and forth perpendicularly to the patrol line they were assigned to. This was an arduous and costly operation as the ships spent most of the year at sea. Throughout the war a total of forty-two vessels served on the patrol. Cruisers from the Grand Fleet occasionally took part in patrols, particularly when German breakouts were expected, and also covered the gap to the Norwegian coast.

The overall organisation of the blockade was tightened with the creation of the Ministry of Blockade in February 1916, which coordinated British efforts globally. Over time the utility of the patrols declined as ships were inspected prior to sailing, even in neutral ports, and information on their cargoes sent on by telegraph to London. Increasingly too, neutral shipping voluntarily came into British ports for inspection. American entry into the war made such measures all the more effective and soon the Northern Patrol was abandoned with most of its ships being used for convoy duties. Although the blockade was an important element in the defeat of Germany it took some three years before it was tight enough to have a serious effect.

THE GREAT WAR AT SEA 1916

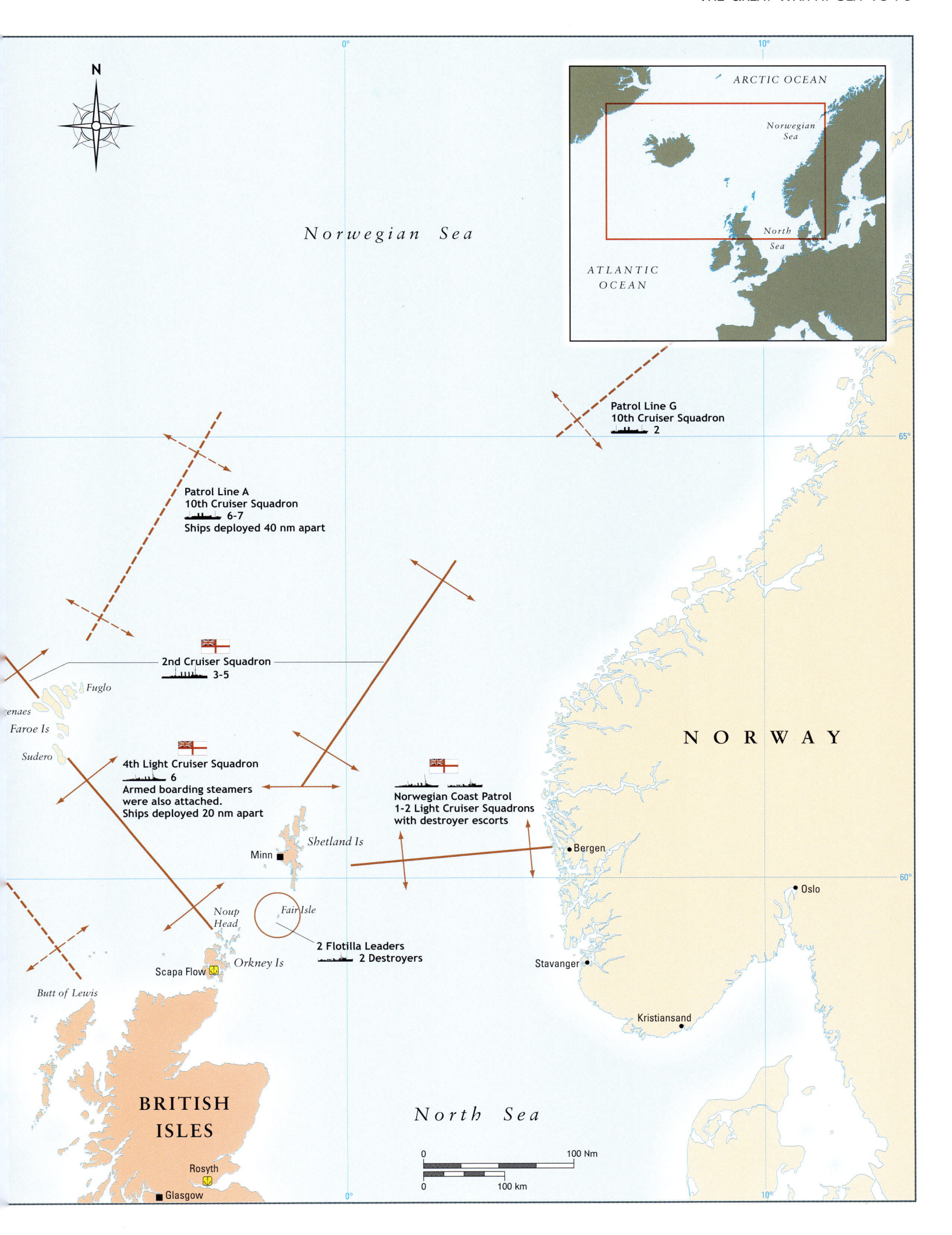

Patrol Line G
10th Cruiser Squadron
2

Patrol Line A
10th Cruiser Squadron
6-7
Ships deployed 40 nm apart

2nd Cruiser Squadron
3-5

Fuglo
Faroe Is
Sudero

4th Light Cruiser Squadron
6
Armed boarding steamers
were also attached.
Ships deployed 20 nm apart

Norwegian Coast Patrol
1-2 Light Cruiser Squadrons
with destroyer escorts

Norwegian Sea

NORWAY

• Bergen

Shetland Is
Minn

• Oslo

Noup Head
Fair Isle
Orkney Is
Scapa Flow

2 Flotilla Leaders
2 Destroyers

Stavanger •

Butt of Lewis

Kristiansand •

BRITISH
ISLES

North Sea

Rosyth
■ Glasgow

0   100 Nm
0   100 km

19th August 1916

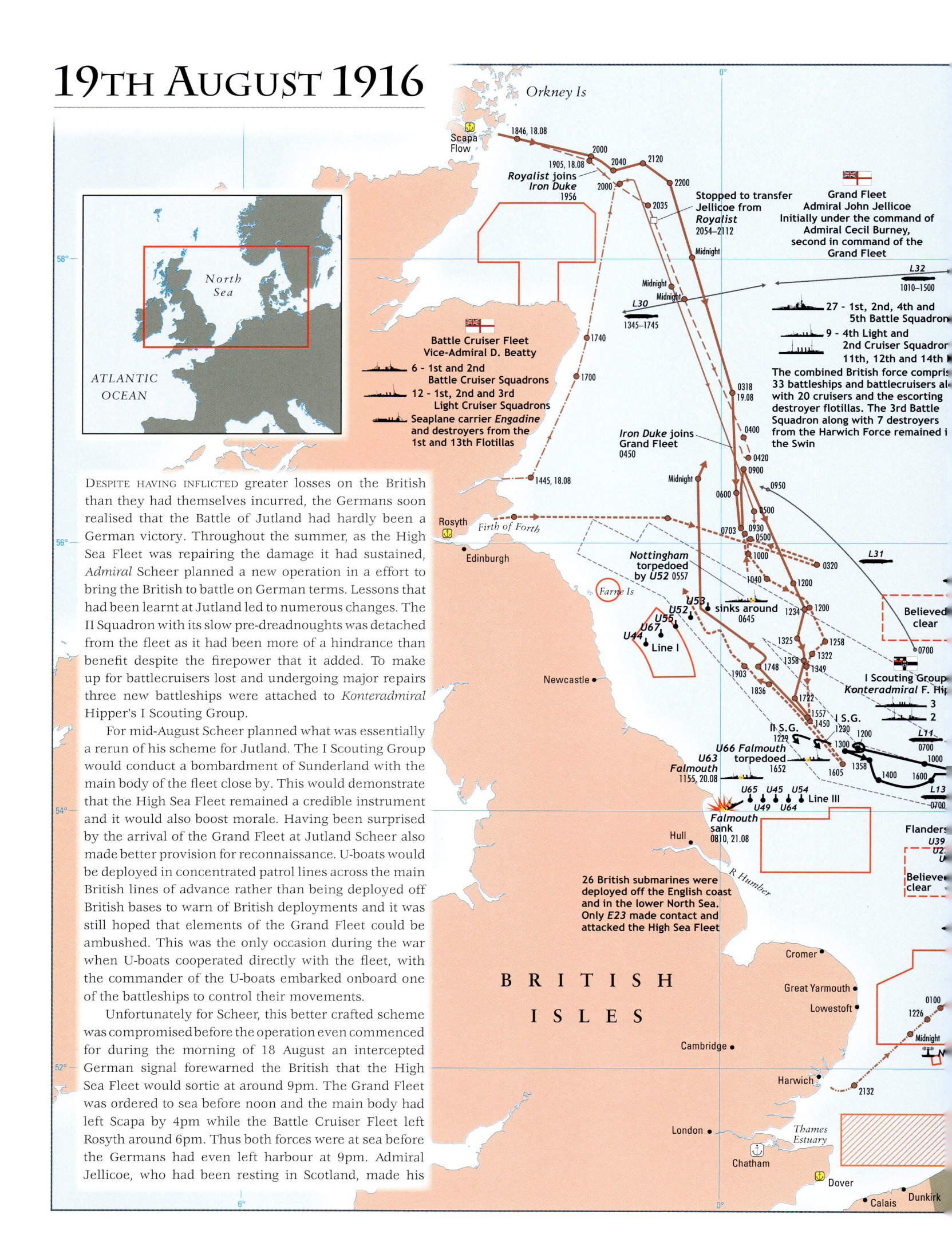

Despite having inflicted greater losses on the British than they had themselves incurred, the Germans soon realised that the Battle of Jutland had hardly been a German victory. Throughout the summer, as the High Sea Fleet was repairing the damage it had sustained, *Admiral* Scheer planned a new operation in a effort to bring the British to battle on German terms. Lessons that had been learnt at Jutland led to numerous changes. The II Squadron with its slow pre-dreadnoughts was detached from the fleet as it had been more of a hindrance than benefit despite the firepower that it added. To make up for battlecruisers lost and undergoing major repairs three new battleships were attached to *Konteradmiral* Hipper's I Scouting Group.

For mid-August Scheer planned what was essentially a rerun of his scheme for Jutland. The I Scouting Group would conduct a bombardment of Sunderland with the main body of the fleet close by. This would demonstrate that the High Sea Fleet remained a credible instrument and it would also boost morale. Having been surprised by the arrival of the Grand Fleet at Jutland Scheer also made better provision for reconnaissance. U-boats would be deployed in concentrated patrol lines across the main British lines of advance rather than being deployed off British bases to warn of British deployments and it was still hoped that elements of the Grand Fleet could be ambushed. This was the only occasion during the war when U-boats cooperated directly with the fleet, with the commander of the U-boats embarked onboard one of the battleships to control their movements.

Unfortunately for Scheer, this better crafted scheme was compromised before the operation even commenced for during the morning of 18 August an intercepted German signal forewarned the British that the High Sea Fleet would sortie at around 9pm. The Grand Fleet was ordered to sea before noon and the main body had left Scapa by 4pm while the Battle Cruiser Fleet left Rosyth around 6pm. Thus both forces were at sea before the Germans had even left harbour at 9pm. Admiral Jellicoe, who had been resting in Scotland, made his

THE GREAT WAR AT SEA 1916

way north on a light cruiser kept at Dundee for such an event and joined his flagship so being back in command of the Grand Fleet by 5am on 19 August. Harwich Force had been ordered to be in the Hoofden by dawn and put to sea at 10.30pm.

Scheer's passage was uneventful until the battleship *Westfalen* was torpedoed by *E23*. Although not heavily damaged she was sent back, but once again the ensuing radio traffic gave the British a fix on the German fleet. Meanwhile, *U52* torpedoed the light cruiser *Nottingham* and Jellicoe, concerned that the Grand Fleet might be running into a newly-laid minefield, turned north for four hours. Only at around 9am, once it had been established that *Nottingham* had been torpedoed and news of *E23*'s attack reached Jellicoe, did he turn south again. Around noon he then decided to take the more southerly of the two channels considered to be safe of mines to avoid a concentration of U-boats reported to the east.

The available information suggested that an engagement was imminent and this time the weather conditions were near perfect; the entire Grand Fleet was concentrated and ready. However, by this time Scheer had turned southeast after a report from *L13*, shortly after noon, erroneously reported a force of British battleships to the south; this was, in fact, the Harwich Force. Scheer believed he had the opportunity to annihilate a detached element of the Grand Fleet, but the error soon became clear and he turned home. This was fortuitous for otherwise the High Sea Fleet would have run into a fully deployed and readied Grand Fleet and would most likely have been decimated. Shortly before 4pm Jellicoe ordered the fleet back to harbour.

Although the fleets did not engage, 19 August was a crucial turning point in the war. It was the last time that the High Sea Fleet attempted an operation on the English coast. For the British, the large number of reported U-boat sightings, the heavy Zeppelin presence and the loss of two cruisers proved unsettling. The Grand Fleet had only seventy of its eighty-six destroyers available and Jellicoe believed that in the future the fleet could not risk sortieing unless it had more escorts. More destroyers were under construction, but the increased allocation for the Grand Fleet would then have consequences when unrestricted U-boat warfare commenced in 1917.

KEY

- Grand Fleet
- *Iron Duke* – Grand Fleet flagship, escorted by 2 destroyers
- 5th Battle Squadron
- Admiral Jellicoe in *Royalist*
- Battle Cruiser Fleet
- Harwich Force
- High Sea Fleet
- U-boat patrol lines at the outset of the operation
- Zeppelin patrols with times on station
- Danger areas/Potentially mined areas
- Danger area owing to British mines
- Channels considered to be safe

109

The High Sea Fleet Sortie, 19 October 1916

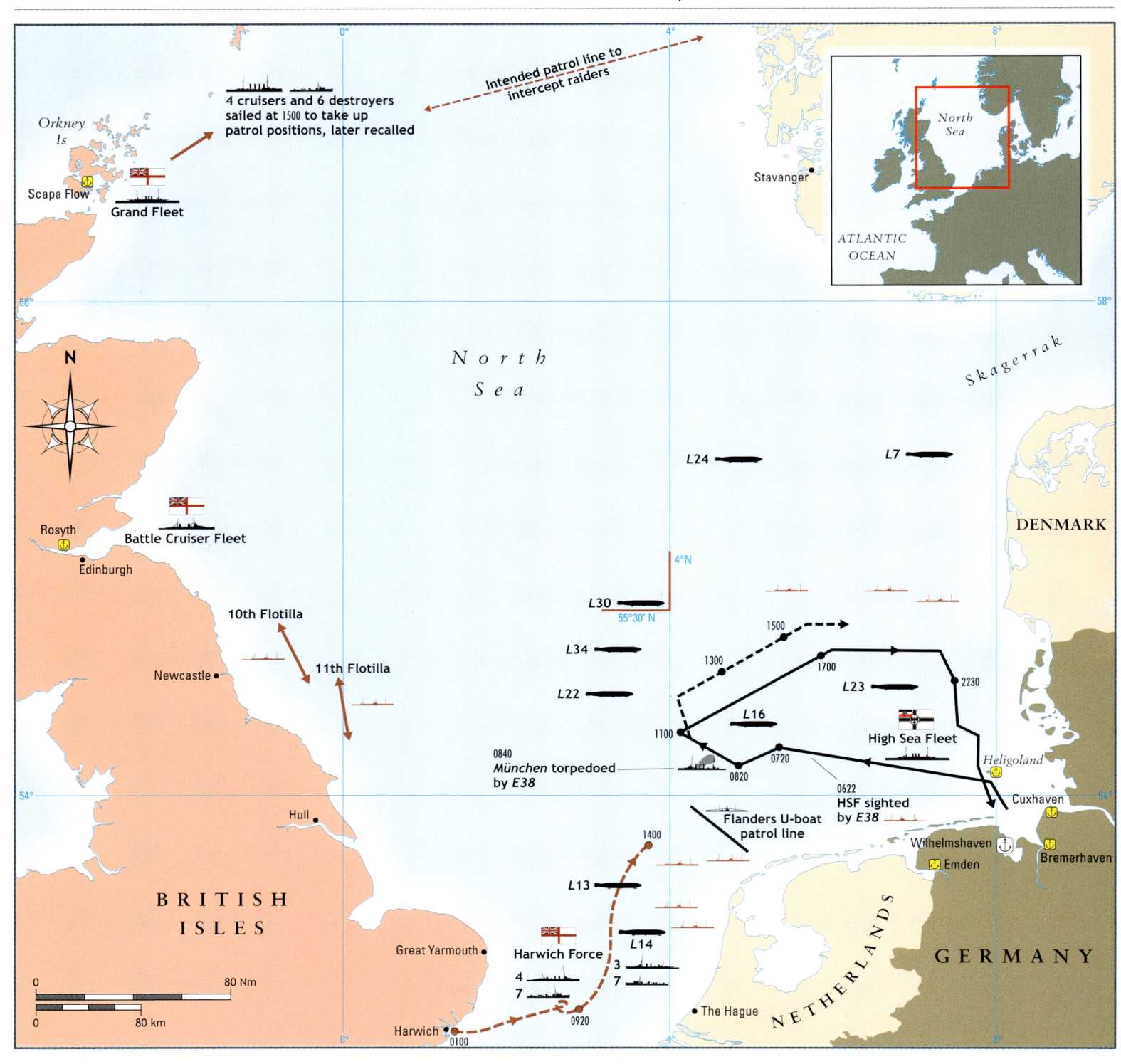

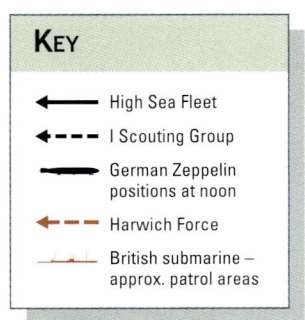

The engagement on 19 August brought about changes in how both sides operated in the North Sea. Owing to the lack of destroyers to escort the entire Grand Fleet, Admiral Jellicoe proposed it would not normally operate south of 55°30' N or east of 4° as in this area the Germans might prepare ambushes by U-boats or minefields. Until more destroyers reached the fleet the burden would rest on submarines operating in the German Bight and local forces would initially deal with German raids. Although this put the British more on the defensive it did not offer the Germans any tangible advantage. The High Sea Fleet's options too were limited as Admiral Scheer increasingly lost the U-boats he depended on for reconnaissance to the commerce war against Britain.

Scheer planned another fleet operation aimed at sweeping up British shipping rather than a coastal raid; without U-boats the Zeppelins provided reconnaissance. Late on 18 October signals intelligence suggested a German sortie and the Admiralty moved light forces into position and the Grand Fleet was ordered to short notice. Next morning *E38* made contact with the Germans and torpedoed a light cruiser. This, the poor weather forcing back the escorting destroyers and signals intelligence reporting that the British had cleared the sea of shipping, led Scheer to abandon the operation. The withdrawal was observed by the British and so no attempt was made by their capital ships to force battle on the Germans.

THE GREAT WAR AT SEA 1916

ALLIED MERCHANT SHIPPING LOSSES, 1916–17

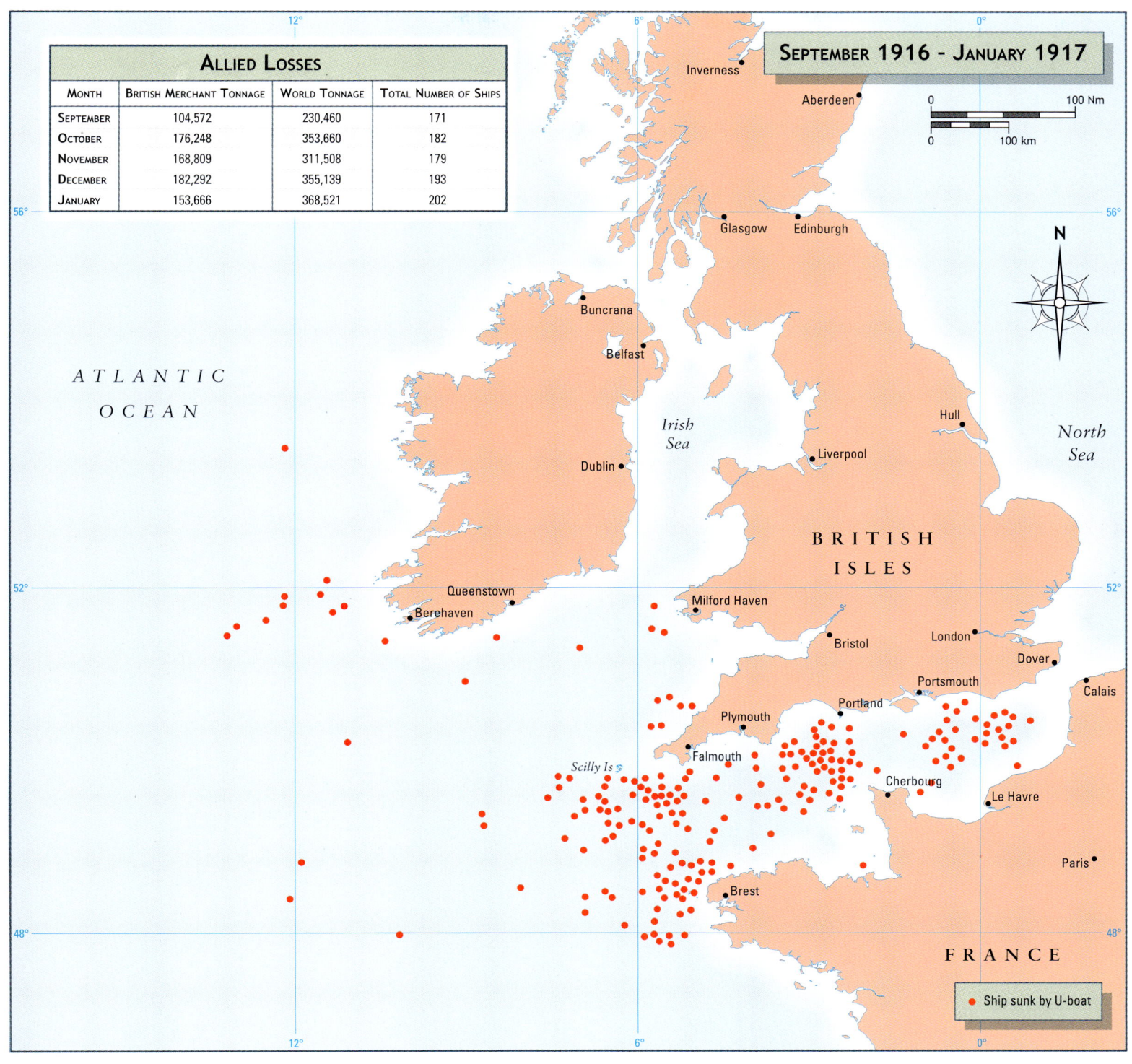

SEPTEMBER 1916 - JANUARY 1917

ALLIED LOSSES

MONTH	BRITISH MERCHANT TONNAGE	WORLD TONNAGE	TOTAL NUMBER OF SHIPS
SEPTEMBER	104,572	230,460	171
OCTOBER	176,248	353,660	182
NOVEMBER	168,809	311,508	179
DECEMBER	182,292	355,139	193
JANUARY	153,666	368,521	202

• Ship sunk by U-boat

IN THE LATE summer of 1916 German strategy shifted, and the submarine arm rather than the fleet increasingly took centre stage in the war against Britain. Jutland had demonstrated that after nearly two years of war the High Sea Fleet was no nearer to creating favourable conditions to decisively defeat the Grand Fleet. This was only reinforced by the outcome of the August and October fleet operations. At the same time the need to weaken the British war effort took on greater importance as ever increasing quantities of men and material were drafted in to compensate for French losses on the Western Front. The attritional battles at Verdun and on the Somme were exhausting German resources and pressure was put on the navy to undertake some action against Britain.

Since May the U-boats of the High Sea Fleet and the Flanders Flotillas had been withdrawn from commerce raiding and thus allied shipping in the Channel and North Atlantic remained largely unscathed. By October a third phase of restricted submarine warfare was in full swing around Britain. The effect was immediately felt as shipping losses rose to the highest level of the war so far. The increased number of U-boats ensured successes even while largely adhering to Prize Rules. By December 1916 around 3.3 million tons of allied shipping had been sunk during the war, but while this was a sizable figure its impact was minimal as over 90 per cent of allied pre-war equivalent tonnage remained intact.

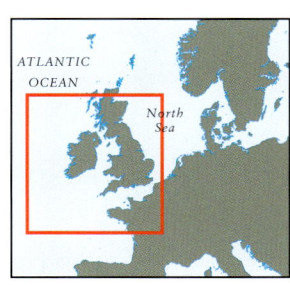

The German Raid on the Dover Strait, 26–27 October 1916

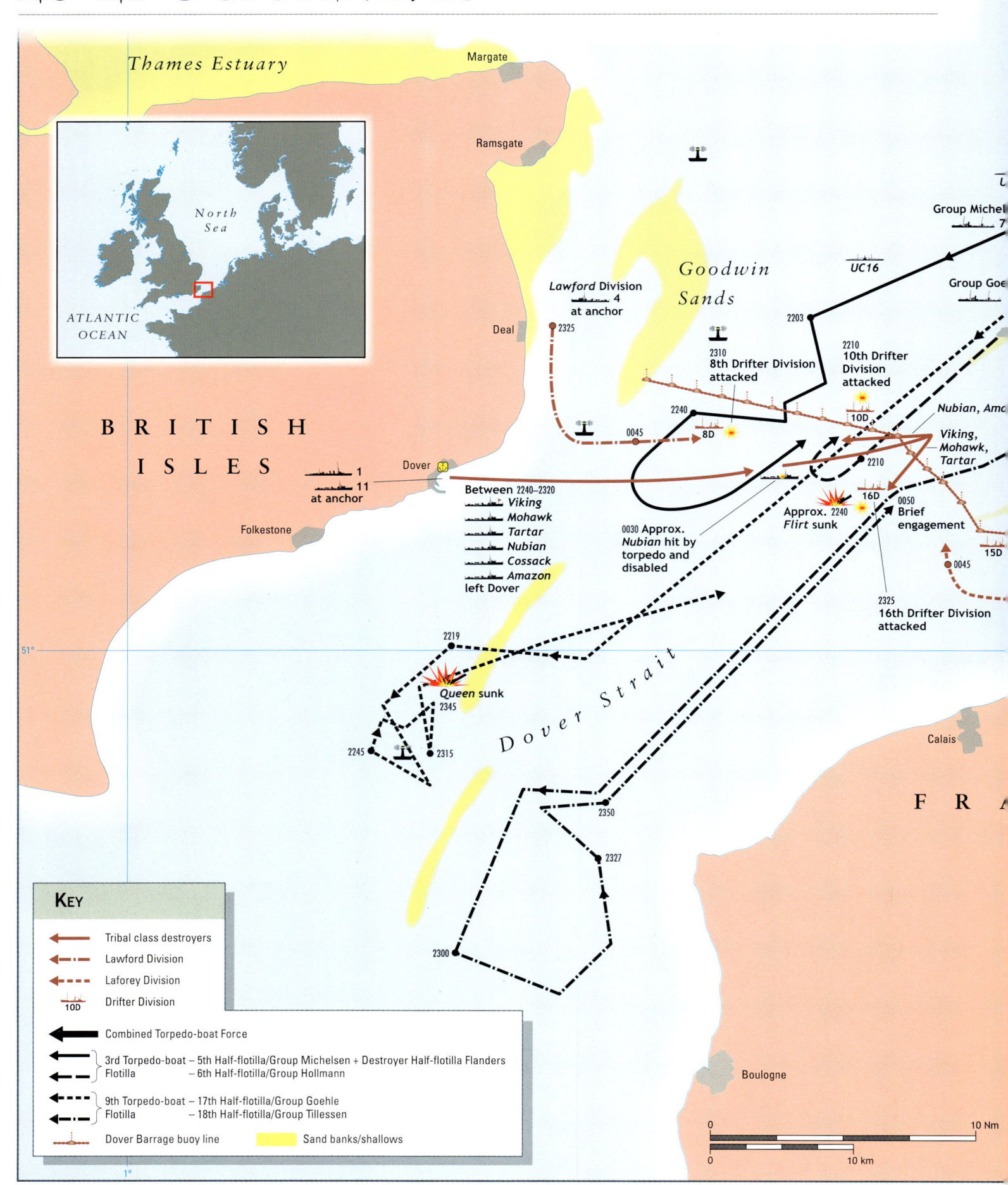

THE GREAT WAR AT SEA 1916

North Sea

U-boats deployed to assist in navigation
UB10 UB17 UB16

3rd and 9th Torpedo-boat Flotillas
Kommodore Andreas Michelsen
V71
Total Force comprised
24 Torpedo-boats

up Hollmann 6
Group Tillessen 5
2048

Ostend

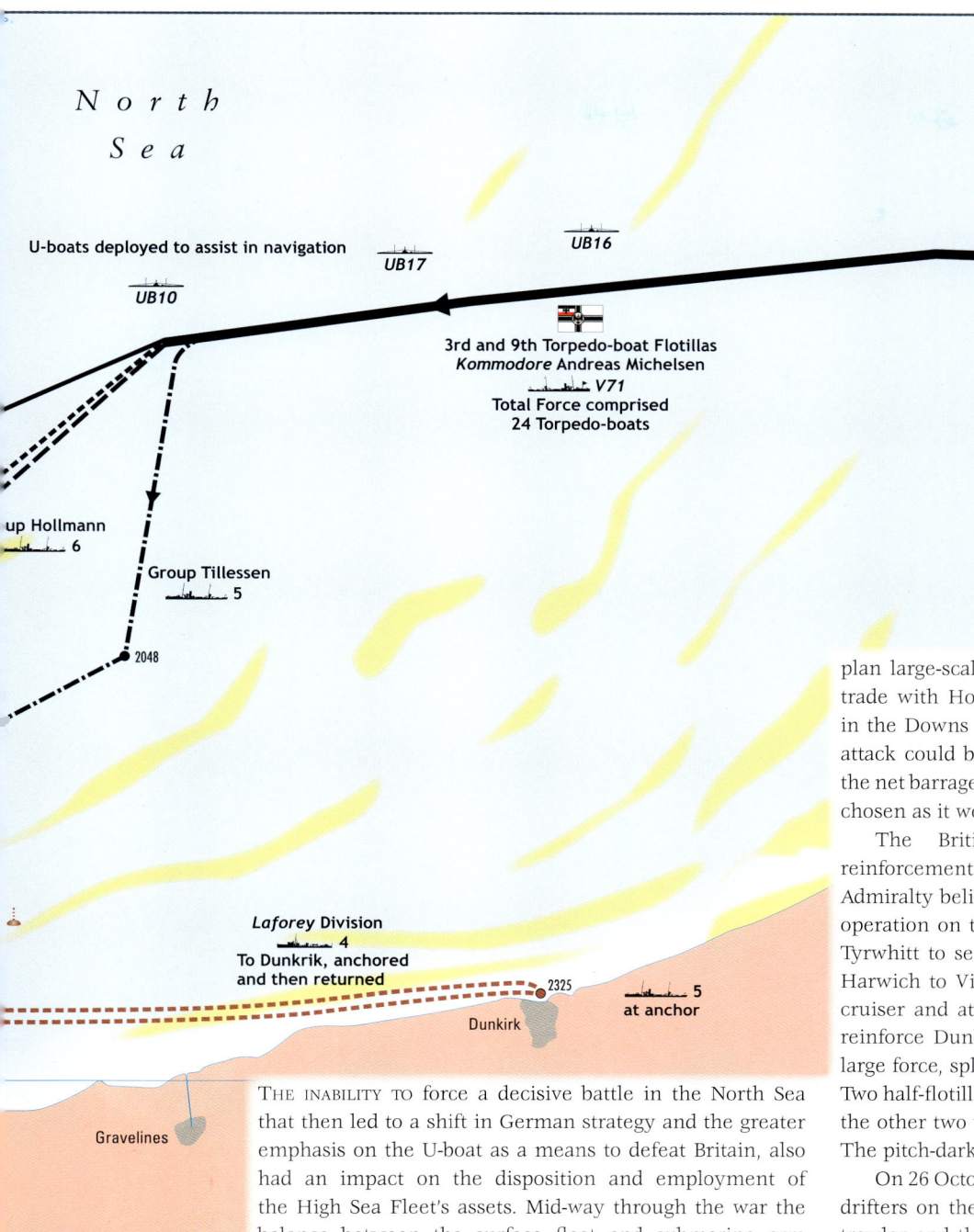

Laforey Division 4
To Dunkrik, anchored and then returned
2325   5 at anchor
Dunkirk

Gravelines

THE INABILITY TO force a decisive battle in the North Sea that then led to a shift in German strategy and the greater emphasis on the U-boat as a means to defeat Britain, also had an impact on the disposition and employment of the High Sea Fleet's assets. Mid-way through the war the balance between the surface fleet and submarine arm altered and rather than the latter supporting the former in its operations, the High Sea Fleet's activity now served to support the U-boats. Particularly in the heavily defended waters of the English Channel, U-boat operations were difficult. By interfering with the flow of British troops and resources to France the navy would also be assisting the army directly at a time when the two major campaigns on the Western Front were proving to be exhausting.

A small number of German torpedo boats had been deployed in Flanders for some time and during the summer of 1916 these were augmented by additional boats from Germany that enabled some offensive operations. When these were subsequently withdrawn the Flanders-based forces alone were inadequate for any major actions. However, in the immediate aftermath of the 19 October High Sea Fleet operation two well-equipped torpedo-boat flotillas, the 3rd and 9th, were sent to Flanders, arriving on 24 October. *Kommodore* Michelsen, commander of the torpedo boats, was also sent out and *Admiral* von Schröder, commander of the *Marinekorps Flandern*, allowed him to plan large-scale operations. Three options existed. British trade with Holland could be interdicted, British shipping in the Downs and Thames Estuary could be raided, or an attack could be launched against the Channel defences – the net barrages and patrolling auxiliary forces. The last was chosen as it would directly support the Flanders U-boats.

The British detected the arrival of German reinforcements, but underestimated the size of the force. The Admiralty believed the Germans were intending a landing operation on the Flanders coast and ordered Commodore Tyrwhitt to send a light cruiser and four destroyers from Harwich to Vice-Admiral Bacon at Dover. Bacon kept the cruiser and at 8pm on 26 October sent the destroyers to reinforce Dunkirk. The German plan was to send a very large force, split into four groups, to the Channel entrance. Two half-flotillas would attack transports in the straits while the other two would attack the drifters on the net barrage. The pitch-dark conditions suited the German attack.

On 26 October there were twenty-eight largely unarmed drifters on the net barrage along with a yacht, an armed trawler and the old destroyer *Flirt*. These would bear the brunt of the attack and with the element of surprise the Germans sank six drifters and *Flirt*. In the darkness the rest were able to disperse and escape. Although there were fifty-seven merchant ships crossing the Channel that night the Germans only found and sank one vessel. News of the first attack on the barrage reached Dover at 10.20pm. Bacon ordered six Tribal class destroyers to put to sea from Dover, but their departure was piecemeal and the force lost its cohesion. Brief engagements were fought with the two German groups coming up the Strait, but the Germans escaped unharmed. The two other destroyer divisions arrived too late to have any impact.

Although surprise and the prevailing conditions favoured the Germans they achieved comparatively little. The situation that Bacon faced defending the Straits was complex, and the separation of the Dover-based destroyers as well as the communications problems that delayed the other divisions from coming into action enabled the German escape. The raid brought about a rapid reinforcement and reorganisation of British forces in the area.

The Voyage of SMS Möwe, November 1916–March 1917

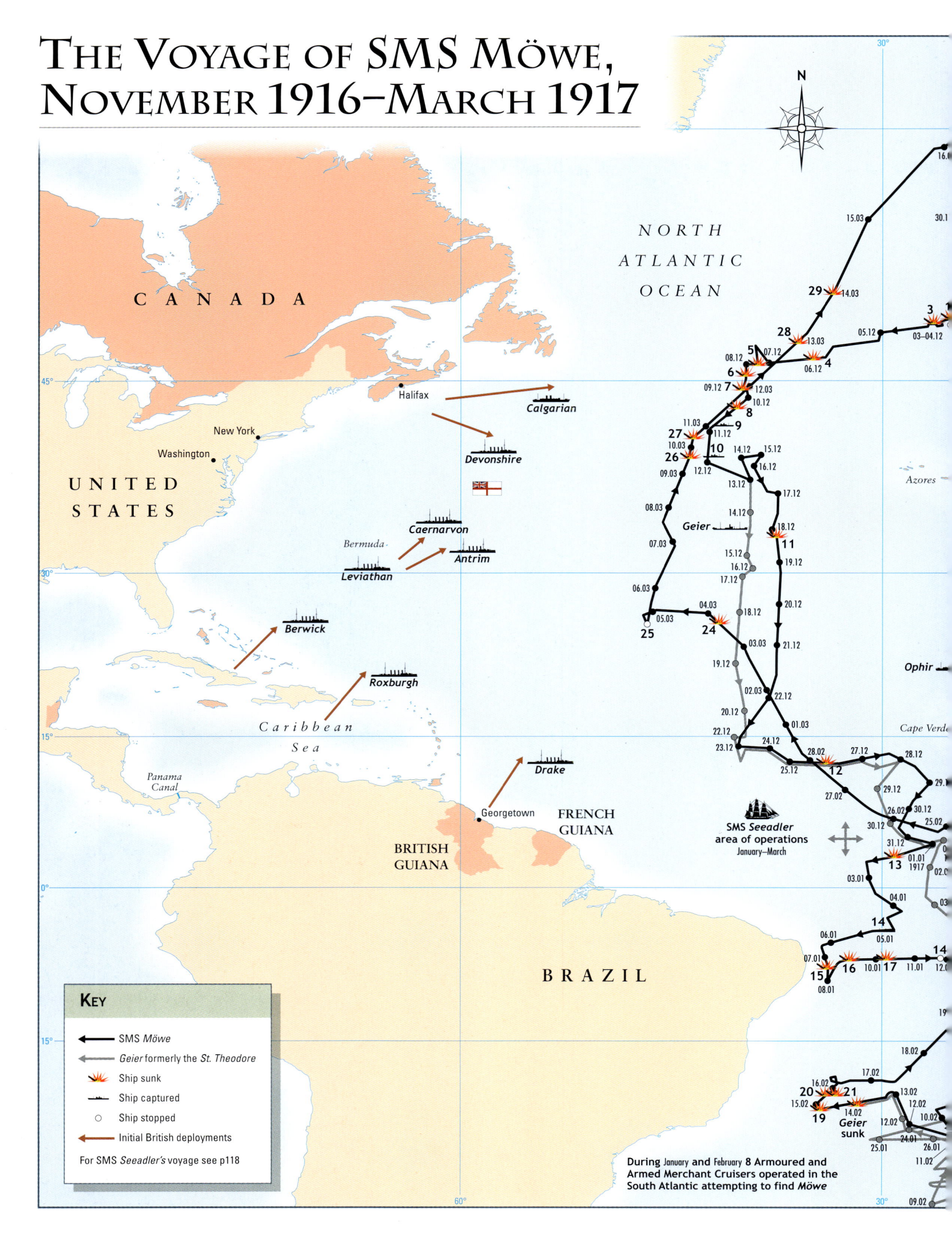

Key
- SMS *Möwe*
- *Geier* formerly the *St. Theodore*
- Ship sunk
- Ship captured
- Ship stopped
- Initial British deployments

For SMS *Seeadler's* voyage see p118

During January and February 8 Armoured and Armed Merchant Cruisers operated in the South Atlantic attempting to find *Möwe*

THE GREAT WAR AT SEA 1916

Following her first Atlantic voyage *Möwe* went into refit and then undertook three short operations in the Baltic during the spring and summer. In the autumn she was prepared for another Atlantic voyage and departed Kiel on 22 November. Having evaded the British patrols in the Faroe-Iceland gap, *Möwe* reached the main North Atlantic shipping routes and soon began to achieve successes. The second vessel encountered, the *Samland*, was a Belgian relief vessel that had been guaranteed safe passage by the German government. Although *Samland*'s wireless was disabled to prevent her from sending a distress call; when she arrived in Falmouth a few days later the British became aware that a German surface raider was at large.

The Admiralty reacted by ordering all the cruisers in the Atlantic to concentrate in the areas where a German raider might operate: the central Atlantic and gap between Africa and South America. The French too redeployed forces in an effort to hunt down the raider. Provisionally, troop transports along the West African coast down to the Cape were ordered to remain in port. *Möwe*'s success continued into mid-December. The British steamer *Yarrowdale* was given a prize crew and used to transfer around 400 prisoners, captured thus far, back to Germany. She would later be fitted out as the auxiliary cruiser *Leopard*. The next ship encountered, the *St. Theodore*, was also kept as a prize owing to the large consignment of coal she was carrying from which *Möwe* could replenish her stocks. *St. Theodore* was also renamed *Geier* and given a light armament to operate as an auxiliary cruiser.

Both ships moved south and evaded the British search. The closest encounter came on 9 January when the *Minieh* – a collier to the British forces off South America – was sunk. Knowing that British ships were in the area, Dohna-Schlodien moved eastwards and sent a batch of prisoners to Pernambuco in the *Hudson Maru*. *Geier* kept reasonably close to *Möwe* to enable the latter to replenish her coal stocks. *Geier*'s independent operations yielded just two sailing ships sunk. Simultaneously another German raider, the *Seeadler*, also operated in the same area. In mid-February *Geier*, in need of repair and her coal stocks exhausted, was scuttled.

Möwe moved back into the central Atlantic in March en route for Germany. The area was relatively free of allied warships as most were engaged in covering convoys. The four-month voyage was the most successful of the war and resulted in twenty-two steamers sunk or captured along with three sailing ships sunk, totalling 123,265 tons.

Allied Ships Sunk, Captured or Stopped

1	Voltaire	Sunk	16	Minieh	Sunk
2	Samland	Stopped	17	Metherby Hall	Sunk
3	Halibjörg	Sunk	18	Tysla	Stopped
4	Mount Temple	Sunk	19	Brecknockshire	Sunk
5	Dutchess of Cornwall	Sunk	20	French Prince	Sunk
6	King George	Sunk	21	Eddie	Sunk
7	Cambrian Range	Sunk	22	Dagny	Stopped
8	Georgic	Sunk	23	Katherine	Sunk
9	Yarrowdale	Captured	24	Rhodanthe	Sunk
10	St. Theodore (Geier)	Captured	25	Edderside	Stopped
11	Dramatist	Sunk	26	Esmeraldas	Sunk
12	Nantes	Sunk	27	Otaki	Sunk
13	Asnières	Sunk	28	Demeterton	Sunk
14	Hudson Maru	Stopped	29	Governor	Sunk
15	Radnorshire	Sunk			

Naval Operations 1917

The U-boat campaign dominated the war at sea throughout 1917. Although merchant ship losses had been on the increase since the early autumn of 1916 the German adoption of unrestricted submarine warfare in February fundamentally changed the nature of commerce warfare. Within a short time allied maritime communications in the eastern Atlantic, the Mediterranean and around the British Isles came under serious threat. The increased number of U-boats, their ability to evade detection and attack unsuspecting merchant vessels from a distance using torpedoes, sent losses to an level never seen before. By the late spring allied losses had become unsustainable and Britain, with its dependency on imports of food and raw materials, was particularly hard hit.

The success of the U-boat campaign meant that other naval operations became increasingly tied to supporting U-boat warfare or, in the case of the allies, attempting to curtail its effects. The High Sea Fleet now played a supporting role, rather than receiving the support of U-boats for its own operations. It now provided manpower for the U-boats, and torpedo boats were detached to Flanders to raid those British defences in the English Channel area that constituted a threat to transiting U-boats. As the Heligoland Bight became increasingly subjected to British minelaying,

Action off Lerwick/Norwegian Convoy Attack
17 October 1917
p137

Allied Merchant Shipping Losses
February – April 1917
p121

Allied Merchant Shipping Losses
May – July 1917
p130

Allied Merchant Shipping Losses
August – October 1917
p136

Allied Merchant Shipping Losses
November 1917 – January 1918
p140

The German U-boat Campaign
1915–18
p60-61

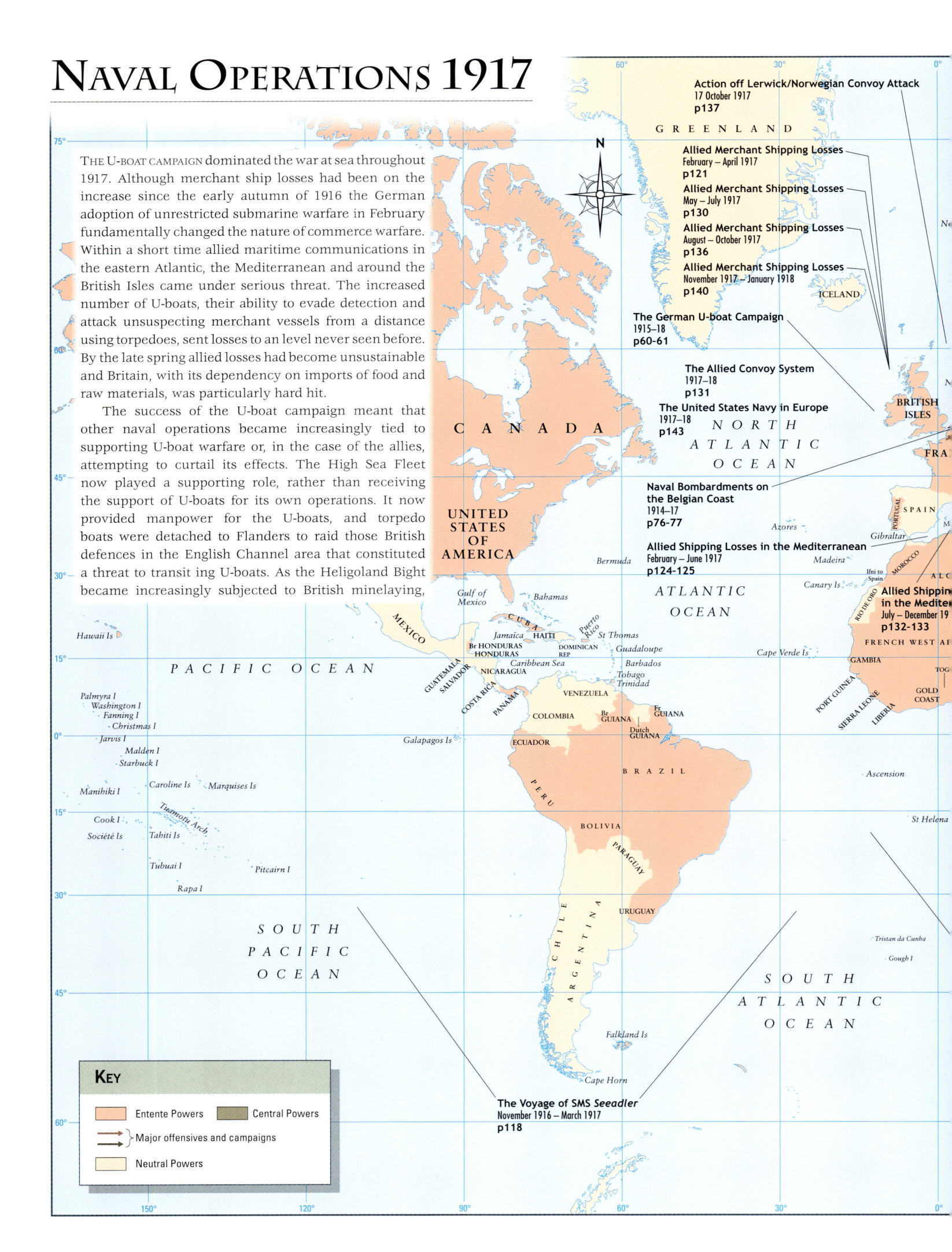

The Allied Convoy System
1917–18
p131

The United States Navy in Europe
1917–18
p143

Naval Bombardments on the Belgian Coast
1914–17
p76-77

Allied Shipping Losses in the Mediterranean
February – June 1917
p124-125

Allied Shipping in the Mediterranean
July – December 1917
p132-133

The Voyage of SMS *Seeadler*
November 1916 – March 1917
p118

Key

- Entente Powers
- Central Powers
- Major offensives and campaigns
- Neutral Powers

THE GREAT WAR AT SEA 1917

so the High Seas Fleet cruisers and torpedo boats were required as escorts for the minesweeping forces that kept lanes open for U-boats. The battlefleet remained largely at anchor, although it did enjoy a final successful operation in undertaking an amphibious assault on the outlying islands in the Gulf of Riga in the Baltic.

For the British, the scale of the losses required fundamental changes too. After long deliberation convoy was finally adopted in the late summer as a means of reducing the losses. A key issue was the desperate lack of escorts to cover the movement of merchant ships and counter the U-boat threat. Having received new ships, better equipment and training, the Grand Fleet was now more powerful than ever, but this degree of superiority counted for little if the High Sea Fleet was not willing to engage in battle. Offensive minelaying, both in the German Bight and off Flanders, was conducted on a greater scale than ever before. An amphibious operation against the U-boat bases in Flanders was considered, but was then dropped, and, finally, the persistent intensity of the U-boat threat and the failure to counter it led to the dismissal of Admiral Jellicoe as First Sea Lord in December.

The situation in the Mediterranean was equally critical and also the result of the divided nature of the allied command structure. Attempts to block the passage of German U-boats in and out of the Adriatic had so far had little effect. At the eastern end of the sea the Royal Navy supported the advance into Palestine. In the Black Sea the Russians were the dominant force, but events on land meant that the naval success had little strategic value. Meanwhile, one of the first repercussions of the American entry into the war was the arrival of the United States Navy in European waters.

117

THE VOYAGE OF SMS SEADLER, 1916–17

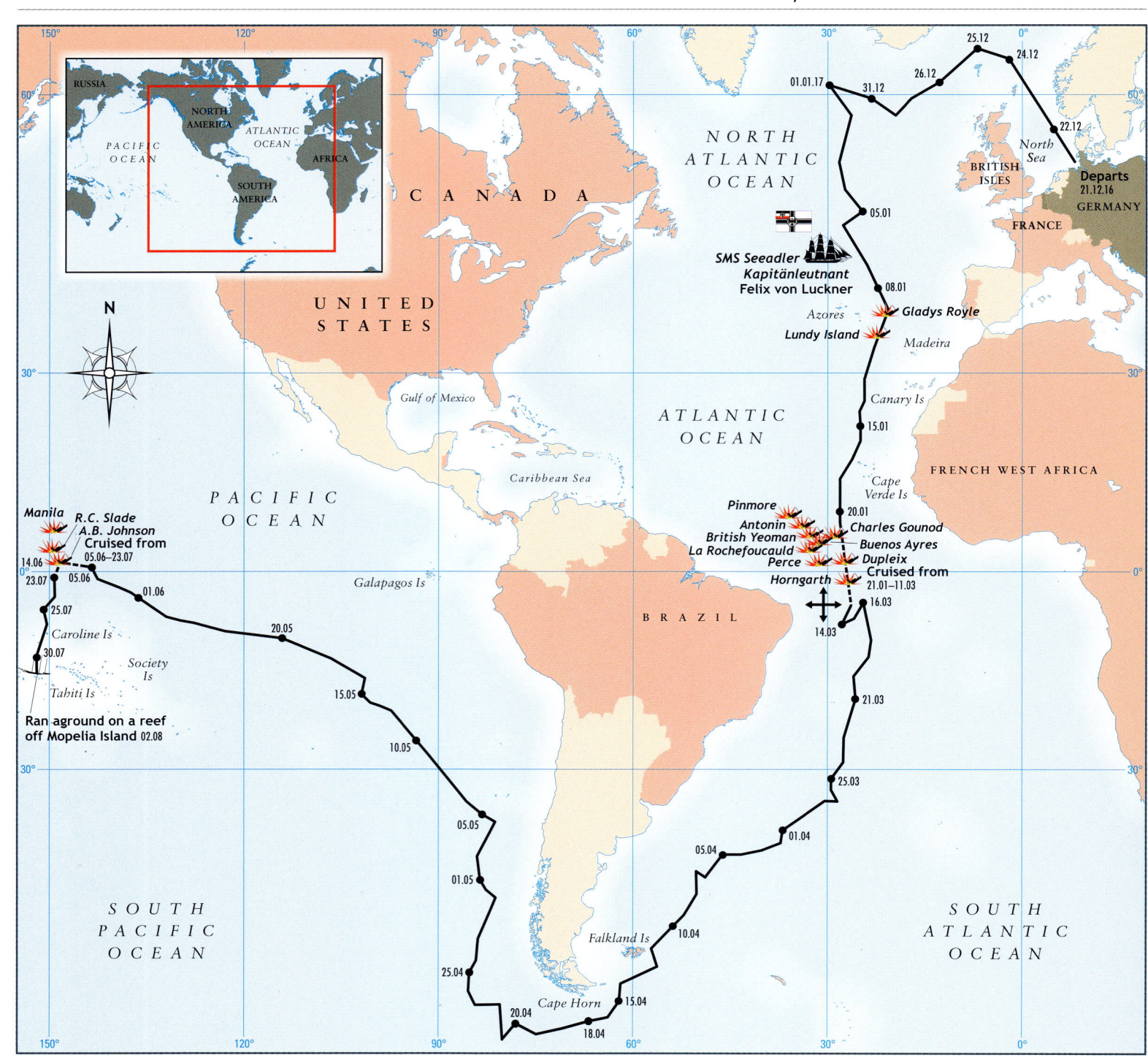

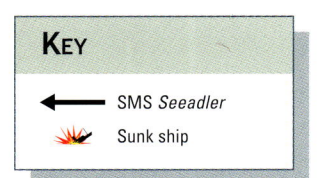

SEEADLER WAS THE last auxiliary cruiser to leave Germany in late 1916 and was unique in that she was a three-masted windjammer and the last sailing vessel to be used in this way. Formerly, she had been the American-owned and -flagged *Pass of Balmaha* which had been captured by *U36* in the North Sea and taken into German service. As a sailing vessel she would not be dependent on capturing coal supplies, but she was fitted with an auxiliary engine. The preparations for the operation were extensive as there would be little chance of escaping from any inspection by British cruisers. She was disguised as a Norwegian timber transport and around a third of the crew were able to speak Norwegian to keep the camouflage. In the event this allowed her to pass inspection by a British armed merchant cruiser between the Faroes and Iceland.

By the end of March *Seeadler* had captured so many prisoners that von Luckner decided to send them to Brazil onboard a captured vessel. As this would inevitably alert the British to his presence he moved his area of operations into the Pacific. There, *Seeadler* was wrecked on a reef in the Society Islands. Some of the crew made for Fiji where they became French prisoners, while others captured a French schooner and made for Easter Island where they were interned by the Chilean authorities. *Seeadler* had captured or sunk sixteen vessels, three freighters and thirteen sailing ships totalling 30,100 tons destroyed, a small yield in comparison with the other auxiliary cruisers fitted out.

THE BLACK SEA THEATRE, 1916-18

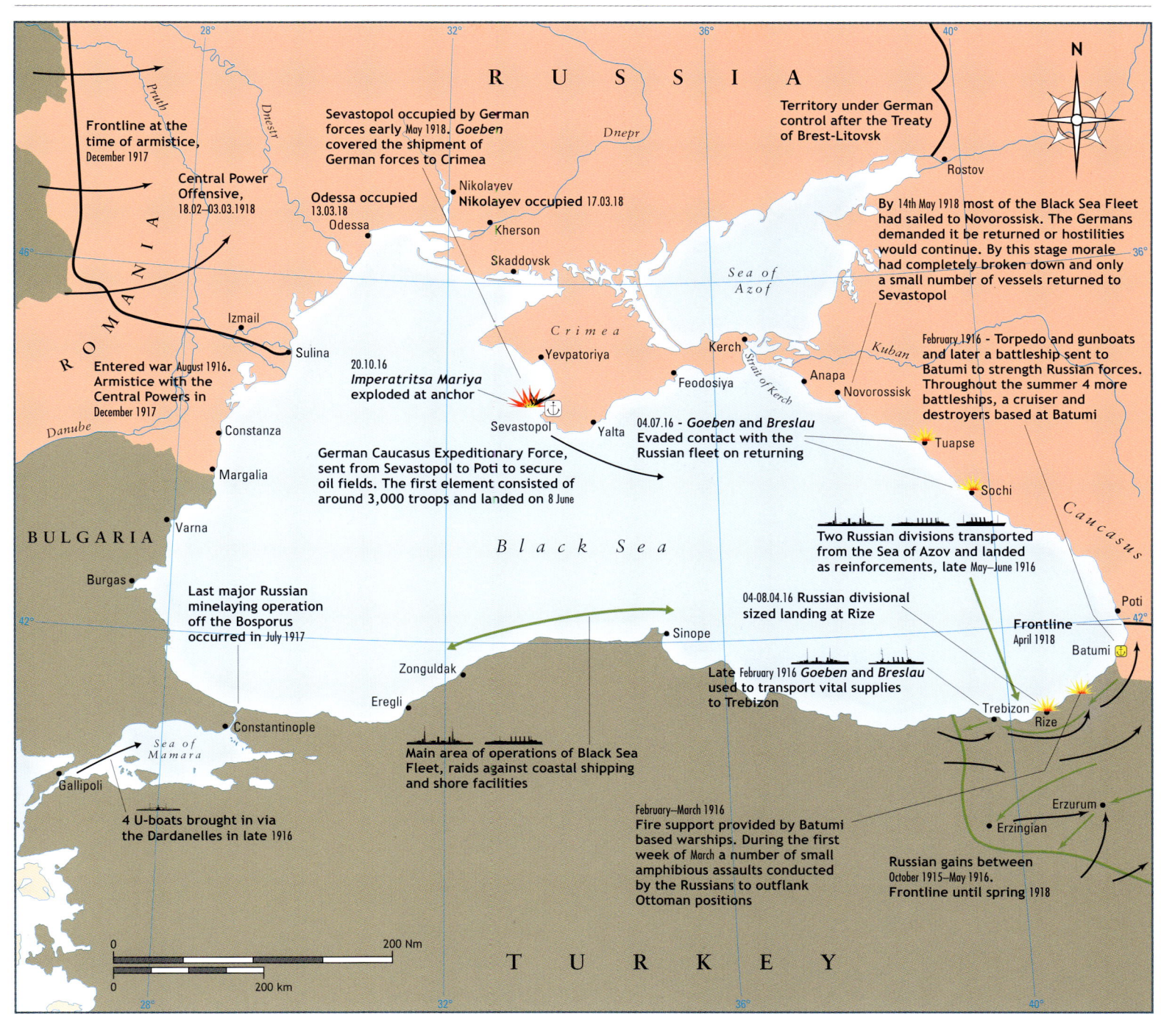

Map annotations

- **Frontline at the time of armistice,** December 1917
- **Central Power Offensive,** 18.02–03.03.1918
- **Sevastopol occupied by German forces early May 1918.** *Goeben* covered the shipment of German forces to Crimea
- **Odessa occupied** 13.03.18
- **Nikolayev occupied** 17.03.18
- **Territory under German control after the Treaty of Brest-Litovsk**
- **Entered war** August 1916. **Armistice with the Central Powers in** December 1917
- **20.10.16** *Imperatritsa Mariya* exploded at anchor
- **By 14th May 1918** most of the Black Sea Fleet had sailed to Novorossisk. The Germans demanded it be returned or hostilities would continue. By this stage morale had completely broken down and only a small number of vessels returned to Sevastopol
- **February 1916** - Torpedo and gunboats and later a battleship sent to Batumi to strength Russian forces. Throughout the summer 4 more battleships, a cruiser and destroyers based at Batumi
- **04.07.16** - *Goeben* and *Breslau* Evaded contact with the Russian fleet on returning
- **German Caucasus Expeditionary Force,** sent from Sevastopol to Poti to secure oil fields. The first element consisted of around 3,000 troops and landed on 8 June
- **Two Russian divisions transported from the Sea of Azov and landed as reinforcements,** late May–June 1916
- **Last major Russian minelaying operation off the Bosporus occurred in** July 1917
- **04-08.04.16 Russian divisional sized landing at Rize**
- **Late February 1916** *Goeben* and *Breslau* used to transport vital supplies to Trebizon
- **Frontline** April 1918
- **Main area of operations of Black Sea Fleet, raids against coastal shipping and shore facilities**
- **4 U-boats brought in via the Dardanelles in late 1916**
- **February–March 1916** Fire support provided by Batumi based warships. During the first week of March a number of small amphibious assaults conducted by the Russians to outflank Ottoman positions
- **Russian gains between** October 1915–May 1916. **Frontline until spring 1918**

Throughout 1916 the Russian navy extended its control over the Black Sea. By the spring Russian raids against Zonguldak and coastal shipping in the southern area had a significant impact on the amount of coal reaching Constantinople. Germany had to step in and make up the shortfall with shipments by rail through Bulgaria; at times these accounted for nearly half of Turkish monthly consumption. Russian naval operations not only grew in scale, but also in complexity. Seaplane carriers were added to the fleet and occasionally air raids were conducted against Turkish positions. As Russian incursions increased, *Goeben* and *Breslau* were drawn more into defensive escort operations, and only the former was really powerful enough to deal with groups of Russian warships.

The second area in which the Russians were active was the development of an amphibious capability. Initially, a small number of old warships were sent to support the army on the coast in its advance into Turkey. A flotilla of small transport craft were constructed and brought down the Black Sea to assist in landing forces and keeping them sustained. By 1917 the Russians had a reasonable capacity to transport sizeable forces and land them on a foreign shoreline.

By 1917 the Black Sea Fleet was clearly in control of the whole sea and continued to be until 1918. The political instability, a result of the revolutions in Russia, inevitably had an impact on morale within the fleet and its operations. The conclusion of an armistice between the Central Powers and the Bolshevik government brought about a brief cessation of hostilities. When these resumed the German army occupied the Ukraine and although most of the Black Sea Fleet escaped it was no longer an operational force.

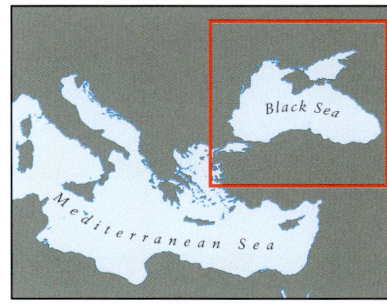

The Voyage of SMS Wolf, December 1916–February 1918

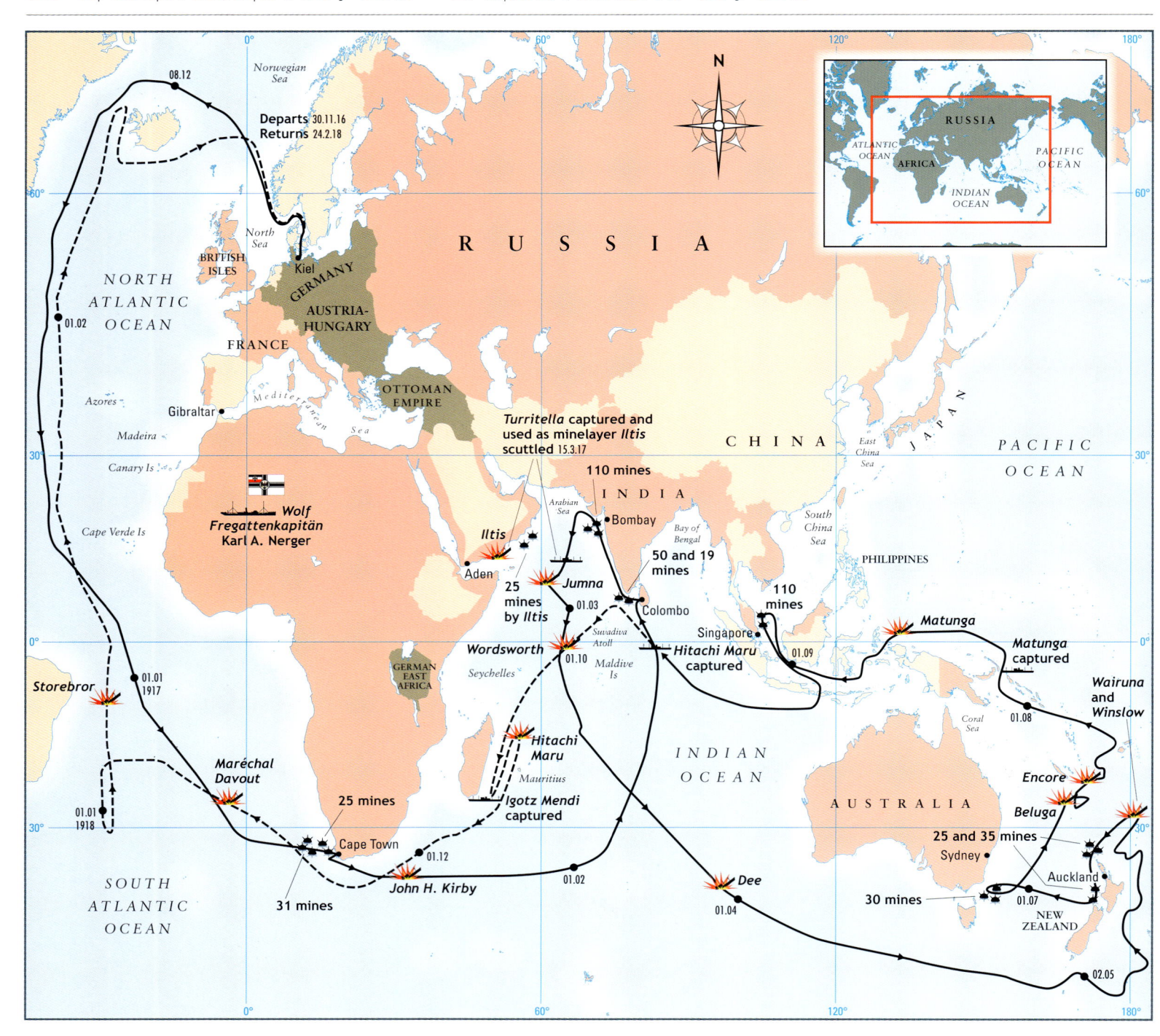

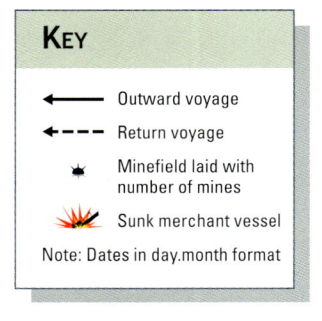

Key
- Outward voyage
- Return voyage
- Minefield laid with number of mines
- Sunk merchant vessel

Note: Dates in day.month format

In early 1916 the *Admiralstab* sought to extend the activity of German auxiliary cruisers and again subject allied communications in the Indian Ocean to attack. The objective was to disrupt the vital grain trade between Australia and Europe by mining the approaches to key ports, capitalising on surprise to inflict damage, and then waging commerce warfare on the trade routes. The first ship fitted out for operations ran aground in the Lower Elbe in February 1916 before undertaking her voyage. In April *Fregattenkapitän* Karl Nerger was ordered to prepare another ship and for this he chose the relatively new freighter *Wachtfels* that was renamed *Wolf*. Although slow she was innocuous and very economical, enabling an unsupported return voyage to the Indian Ocean.

After six months of preparations *Wolf* left Germany in December and embarked on what would become the longest unsupported voyage of the war. A six-month operation to Indian waters was planned, but Nerger proposed staying out for more than a year drawing supplies from captured ships. He was largely successful, even managing to use a captured British freighter as an auxiliary minesweeper and undertaking an extensive overhaul in the Kermadecs during the summer. Only in March 1917 did the Allies become aware of a raider operating in the Indian Ocean and around fifty allied warships, including a substantial Japanese force, were engaged in a year-long hunt. The *Wolf* captured and sank fourteen merchant ships totalling 38,391 tons while her mines accounted for another thirteen ships totalling 75,888 tons.

The Great War at Sea 1917

Allied Merchant Shipping Losses, 1917

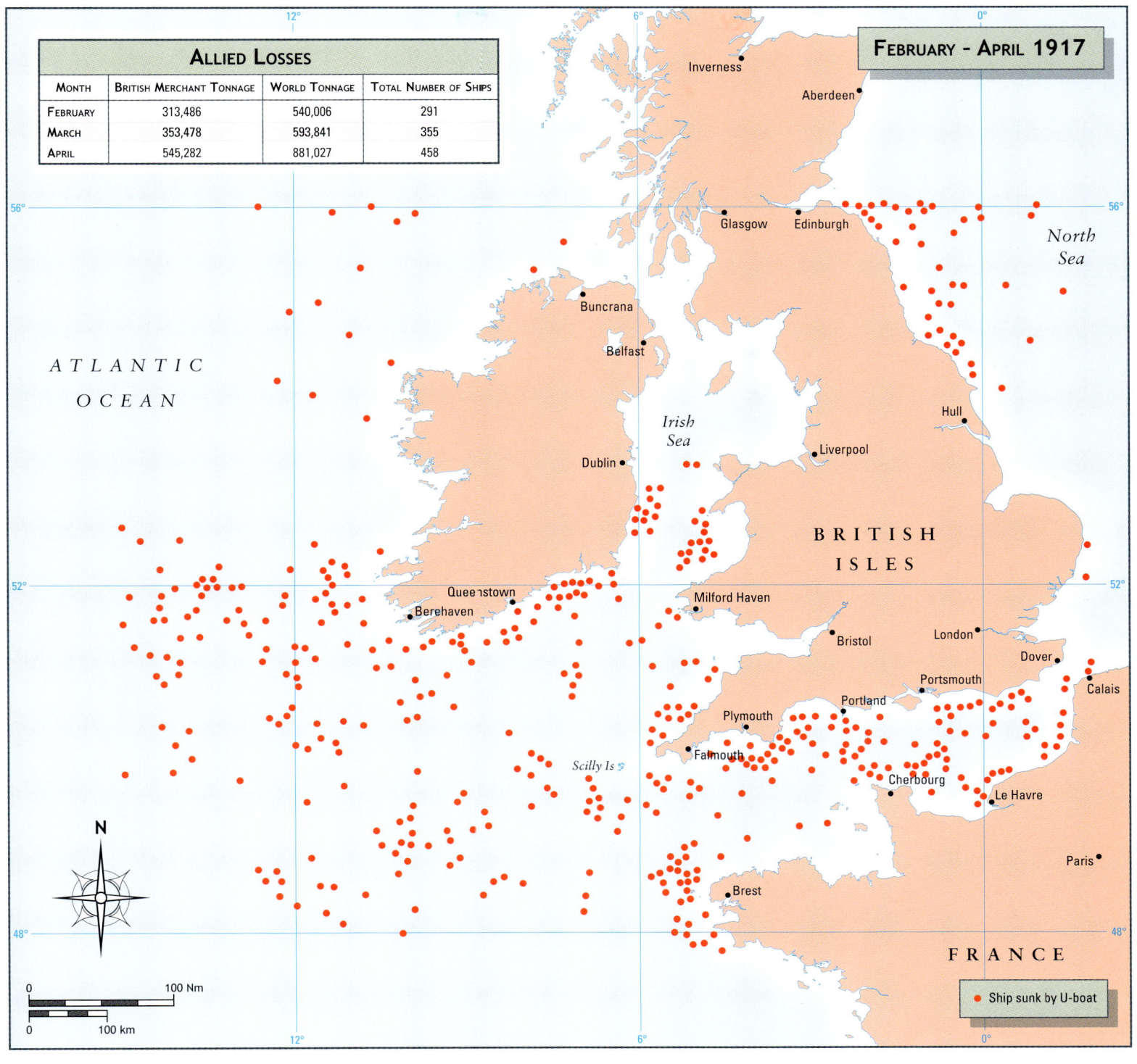

February – April 1917

Allied Losses			
Month	British Merchant Tonnage	World Tonnage	Total Number of Ships
February	313,486	540,006	291
March	353,478	593,841	355
April	545,282	881,027	458

• Ship sunk by U-boat

The process that led to unrestricted submarine warfare was set in motion in December 1916 and driven by the relative success of the autumn U-boat campaign and the realisation that the allied war effort needed to be substantially weakened by the autumn of 1917. Admiral von Holtzendorff, chief of the *Admiralstab*, argued that if 600,000 tons of shipping a month could be sunk – around double of what was currently being achieved – Britain could be defeated within six months. In addition, neutral shipping would be scared off from supplying Britain.

The army and naval high commands supported the proposal and on 9 January the Kaiser formally approved waging unrestricted submarine warfare. The Chancellor Bethmann-Hollweg opposed the move fearing that the Americans would join the Allies, but the military believed that Britain would be defeated long before this happened.

The focus of the campaign would be in the Western Approaches. The U-boat force numbered 105 boats in February and increased to 117 and 120 in March and April respectively. Of these around a third were at the front at any time, the highest number being 58 during a spell in April. Freed from the need to adhere to Prize Rules, or be concerned about neutral shipping, U-boats could sink merchant vessels on sight. Against light allied defences the results were devastating; losses soared, reaching an unprecedented record in April. The American declaration of war came on 6 April.

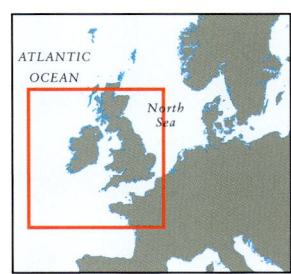

The German Raid on the Dover Strait, 25 February 1917

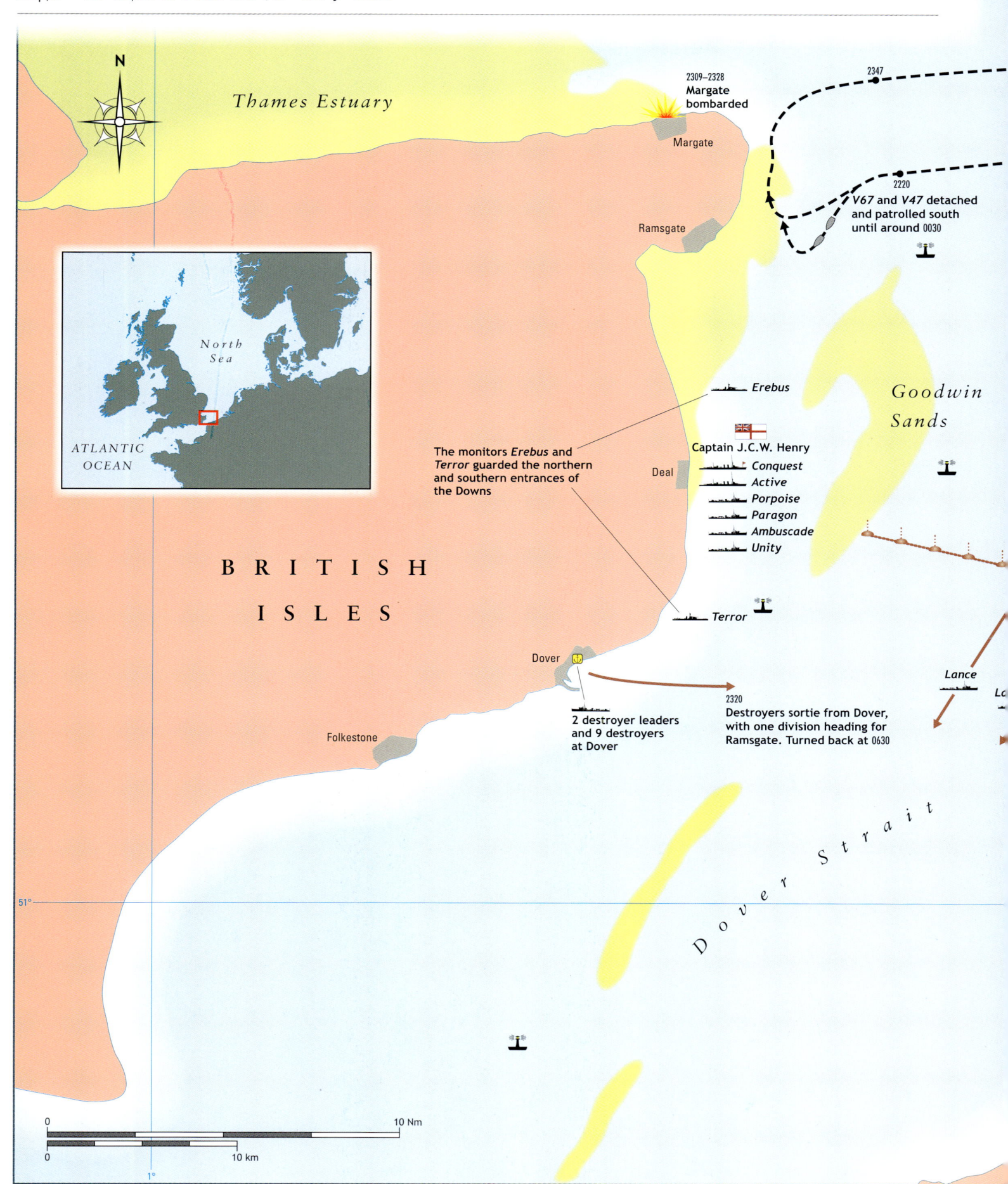

Margate bombarded 2309–2328

2347

2220 V67 and V47 detached and patrolled south until around 0030

Thames Estuary

Ramsgate

North Sea

ATLANTIC OCEAN

Erebus

Captain J.C.W. Henry
Conquest
Active
Porpoise
Paragon
Ambuscade
Unity

The monitors *Erebus* and *Terror* guarded the northern and southern entrances of the Downs

Deal

Goodwin Sands

BRITISH ISLES

Terror

Dover

2 destroyer leaders and 9 destroyers at Dover

2320 Destroyers sortie from Dover, with one division heading for Ramsgate. Turned back at 0630

Lance

Folkestone

Dover Strait

THE GREAT WAR AT SEA 1917

North Sea

1st Zeebrugge Half-flotilla
Korvettenkapitän K. Albrecht
- G95
- G96
- V67
- V68
- V47

6th Torpedo-boat Flotilla
Korvettenkapitän W. Tillessen
- V44
- G37
- V45
- V46
- S49

t destroyer patrols
he barrage buoys

Laverock
nvar
2230
2235

**2230–2241
Engagement between
Laverock and
German flotilla**

Calais

Gravelines

Dunkirk

FRANCE

KEY
- British destroyers on patrol
- 6th Torpedo-boat Flotilla
- 1st Zeebrugge Half-flotilla (approximate movement)
- Dover Barrage buoy line
- Sand banks/shallows

AS A CONSEQUENCE of the October raid on the Dover Strait the British implemented a number of measures to improve their defences. Materially, the Germans had inflicted relatively little damage considering the size of the force employed, but as the Channel was the most important allied waterway its protection was of paramount concern. More destroyers, supported by light cruisers, were stationed in the Dover area. The nightly guard force in the Downs was augmented and monitors were used to patrol its exits. The vulnerable drifters were pulled back from the net barrage at night and replaced by destroyer patrols.

From the German perspective the Dover area equally continued to be of importance as U-boats passed through to attack shipping in the Channel and it was well within range of Flanders-based torpedo boats. Throughout January and early February a number of attempts were made to raid British shipping, but bad weather generally frustrated the Germans. For the end of February a large-scale operation was prepared, including a sweep along the Dutch coast and a sortie by light forces from the High Sea Fleet (this part was then cancelled). Two forces would be employed off the British coast: one to break through the net barrage and attack transiting shipping, the other to conduct a bombardment of Margate and sink any shipping coming out of the Downs.

The German forces left Zeebrugge between 6 and 7pm. At 10.30pm the southern group made contact with the destroyer *Laverock* and after a very brief engagement turned for home. Numerous torpedoes were fired at the British destroyer and one hit, though it failed to explore. As the northern group closed on the English shoreline, it was sighted by an armed British drifter that immediately sent off a signal. Captain Henry's force from Deal, and Captain Wither's destroyers from Dover put to sea soon after the alarm was raised, but were in no position to catch the retreating Germans. The actual bombardment of Margate was brief and ineffectual, and neither did two detached torpedo boats find any shipping to attack further south.

The third German force, operating off the Maas also failed to encounter any shipping. As Admiral Bacon pointed out, there was little that could be done against such high-speed raids by torpedo boats, but their actual impact was minimal even if this did not deter further such raids.

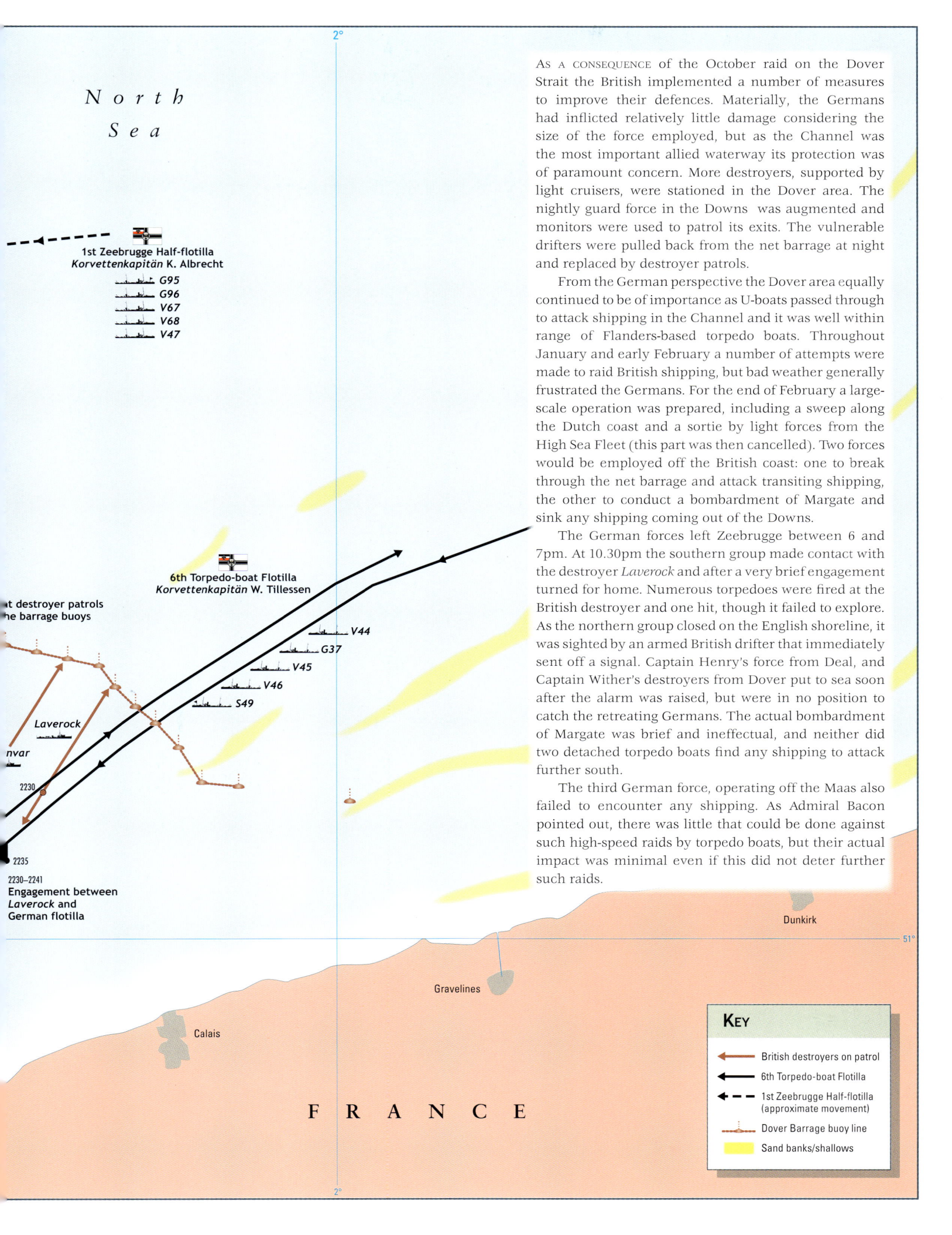

Allied Shipping Losses in the Mediterranean, February–June 1917

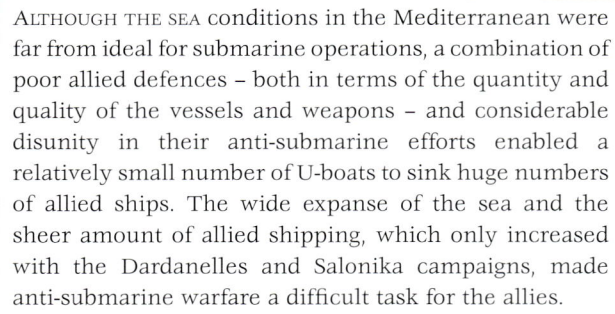

Although the sea conditions in the Mediterranean were far from ideal for submarine operations, a combination of poor allied defences – both in terms of the quantity and quality of the vessels and weapons – and considerable disunity in their anti-submarine efforts enabled a relatively small number of U-boats to sink huge numbers of allied ships. The wide expanse of the sea and the sheer amount of allied shipping, which only increased with the Dardanelles and Salonika campaigns, made anti-submarine warfare a difficult task for the allies.

In a first step to co-ordinate efforts in December 1915, the Mediterranean was divided up between the British, French and Italians into eighteen patrol areas to facilitate the hunt for U-boats. This was streamlined down to eleven areas in March 1916, but different national approaches meant cooperation was never easy or effective. It was also not until August 1916 that Italy and Germany were actually at war. From the allied perspective the U-boat problem was not solved in 1916 and only mitigated by the small, though growing, U-boat force and the fact that some boats were diverted to the Black Sea. Austrian U-boats played almost no part and hardly ever left the Adriatic.

With the adoption of unrestricted submarine warfare in February 1917 most of the Mediterranean was declared a war zone. The German Mediterranean U-boat force was expanded and it was found that smaller boats were ideally suited to the theatre. Weather conditions were better than around Britain and the distances to the main hunting grounds from Pola and Cattaro in the Adriatic were relatively short.

In February ten U-boats were at sea and by April there were fourteen on patrol. A year previously the numbers at sea were in the region of two or three. The result was a substantial increase in allied shipping losses. By June the number of U-boats on patrol increased to eighteen, nearly all of them operating in the central and western Mediterranean.

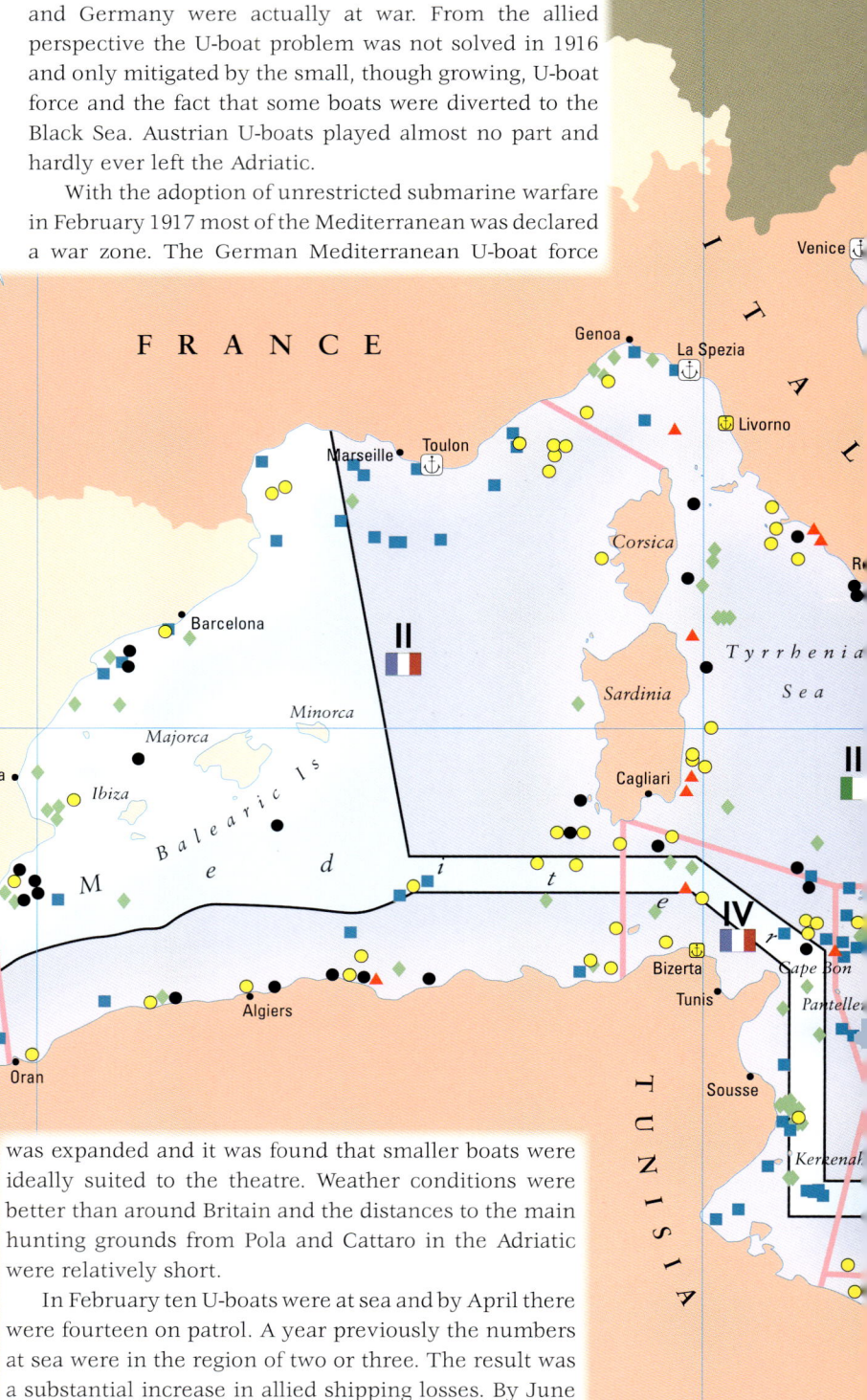

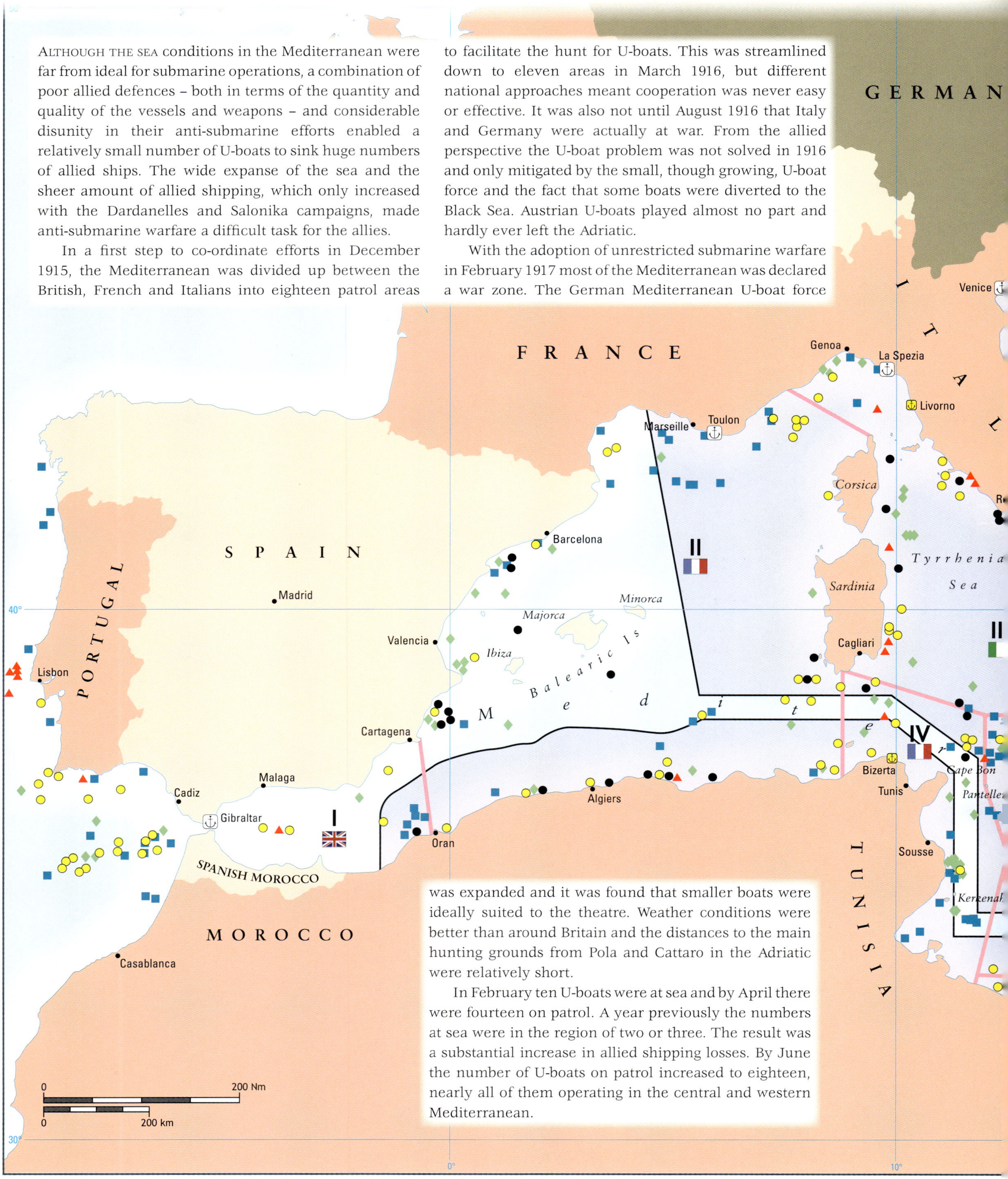

THE GREAT WAR AT SEA 1917

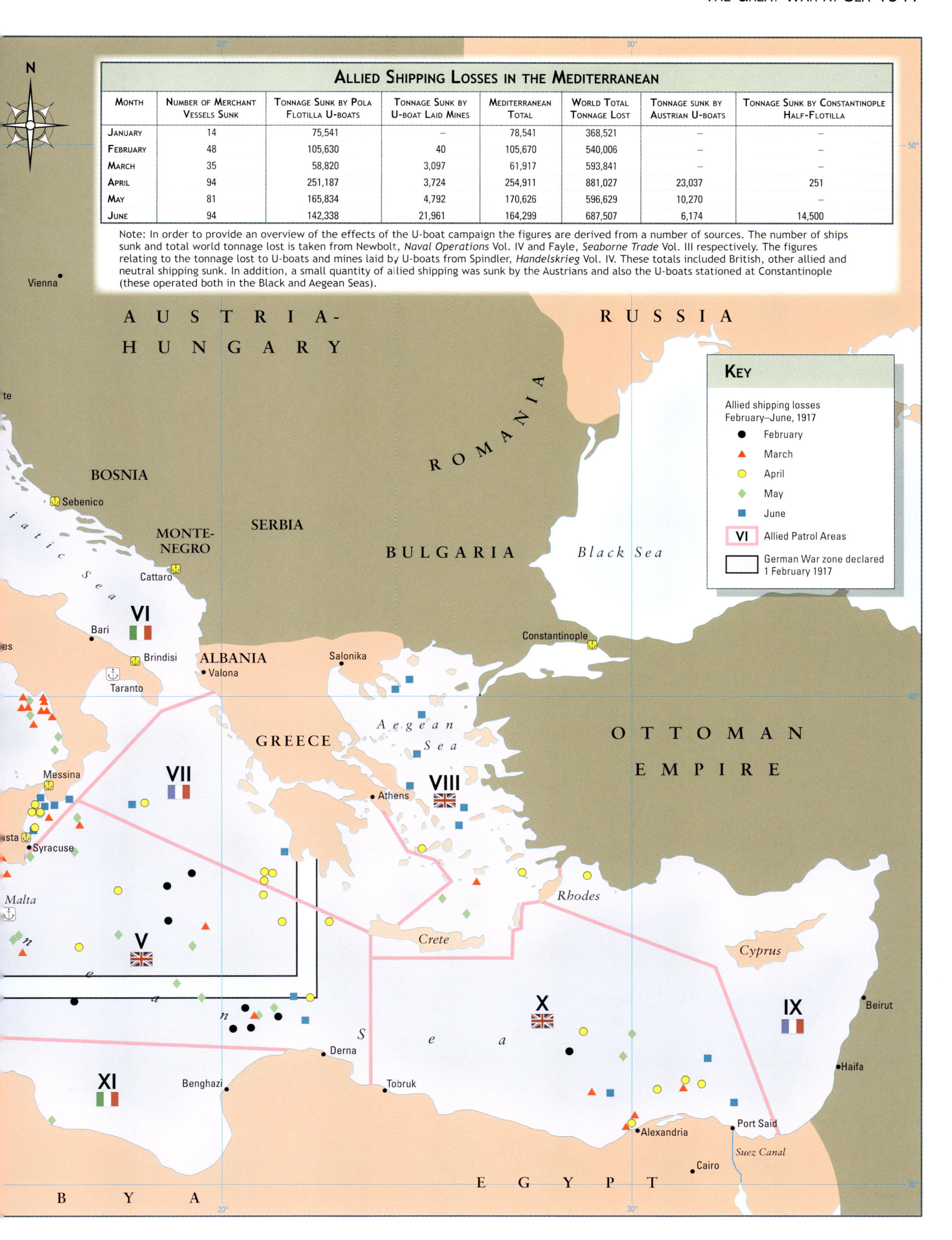

ALLIED SHIPPING LOSSES IN THE MEDITERRANEAN

Month	Number of Merchant Vessels Sunk	Tonnage Sunk by Pola Flotilla U-boats	Tonnage Sunk by U-boat Laid Mines	Mediterranean Total	World Total Tonnage Lost	Tonnage sunk by Austrian U-boats	Tonnage Sunk by Constantinople Half-Flotilla
January	14	75,541	—	78,541	368,521	—	—
February	48	105,630	40	105,670	540,006	—	—
March	35	58,820	3,097	61,917	593,841	—	—
April	94	251,187	3,724	254,911	881,027	23,037	251
May	81	165,834	4,792	170,626	596,629	10,270	—
June	94	142,338	21,961	164,299	687,507	6,174	14,500

Note: In order to provide an overview of the effects of the U-boat campaign the figures are derived from a number of sources. The number of ships sunk and total world tonnage lost is taken from Newbolt, *Naval Operations* Vol. IV and Fayle, *Seaborne Trade* Vol. III respectively. The figures relating to the tonnage lost to U-boats and mines laid by U-boats from Spindler, *Handelskrieg* Vol. IV. These totals included British, other allied and neutral shipping sunk. In addition, a small quantity of allied shipping was sunk by the Austrians and also the U-boats stationed at Constantinople (these operated both in the Black and Aegean Seas).

Key

Allied shipping losses February–June, 1917
- ● February
- ▲ March
- ● April (yellow)
- ♦ May
- ■ June
- VI Allied Patrol Areas
- German War zone declared 1 February 1917

The German Raid on the Dover Strait, 20–21 April 1917

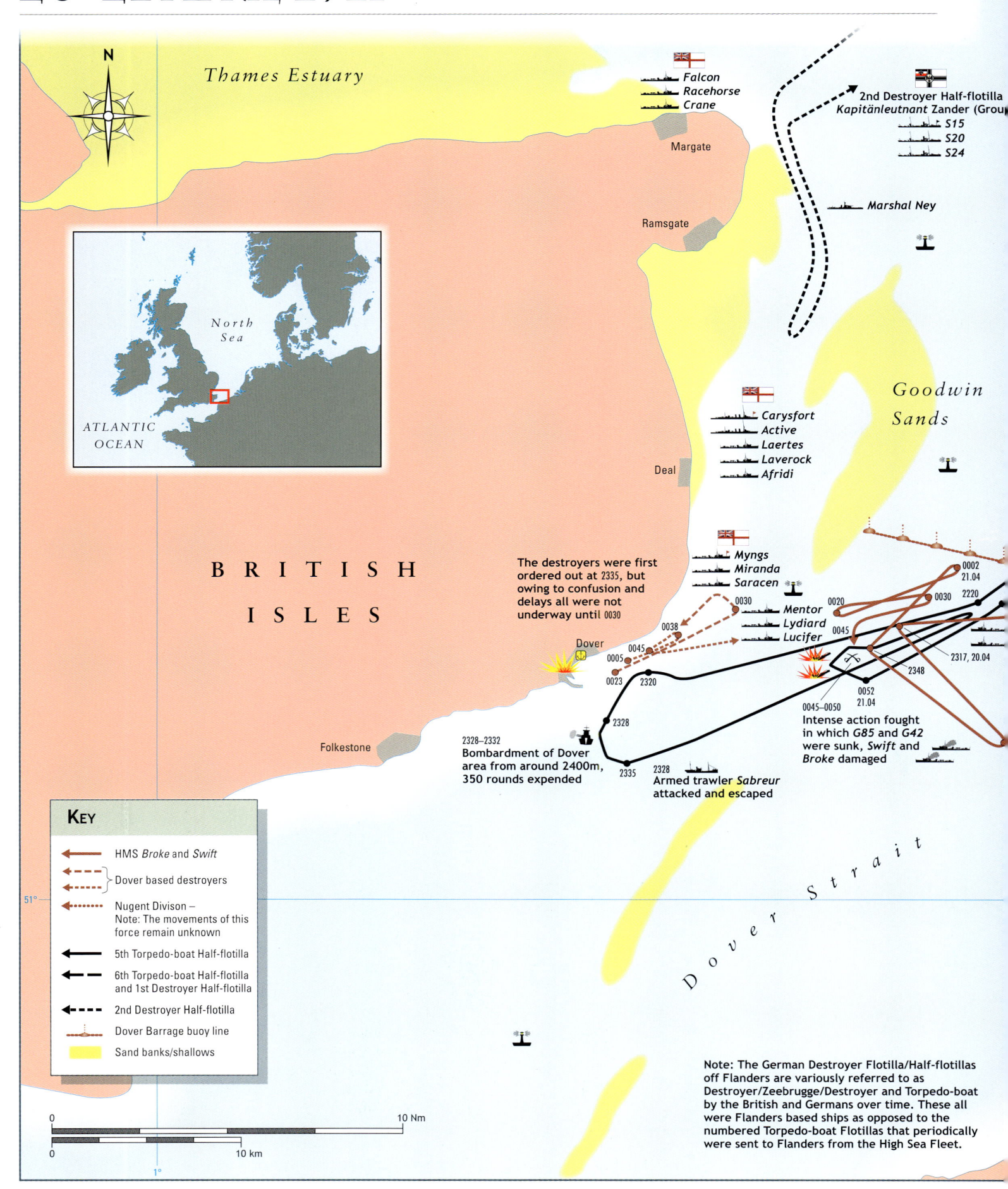

Key

- HMS *Broke* and *Swift*
- Dover based destroyers
- Nugent Division – Note: The movements of this force remain unknown
- 5th Torpedo-boat Half-flotilla
- 6th Torpedo-boat Half-flotilla and 1st Destroyer Half-flotilla
- 2nd Destroyer Half-flotilla
- Dover Barrage buoy line
- Sand banks/shallows

Thames Estuary

Falcon
Racehorse
Crane

Margate

2nd Destroyer Half-flotilla Kapitänleutnant Zander (Group)
- S15
- S20
- S24

Marshal Ney

Ramsgate

Goodwin Sands

Carysfort
Active
Laertes
Laverock
Afridi

Deal

British Isles

The destroyers were first ordered out at 2335, but owing to confusion and delays all were not underway until 0030

Myngs
Miranda
Saracen

Mentor
Lydiard
Lucifer

Dover

0005
0023
2320
2328
2335

0038
0045

0030
0045
0020
0002 21.04
0030
2220
2317, 20.04
2348
0052 21.04
0045–0050

Intense action fought in which G85 and G42 were sunk, *Swift* and *Broke* damaged

Folkestone

2328–2332 Bombardment of Dover area from around 2400m, 350 rounds expended

2328 Armed trawler *Sabreur* attacked and escaped

Dover Strait

North Sea

Atlantic Ocean

Note: The German Destroyer Flotilla/Half-flotillas off Flanders are variously referred to as Destroyer/Zeebrugge/Destroyer and Torpedo-boat by the British and Germans over time. These all were Flanders based ships as opposed to the numbered Torpedo-boat Flotillas that periodically were sent to Flanders from the High Sea Fleet.

THE GREAT WAR AT SEA 1917

Map labels

North Sea

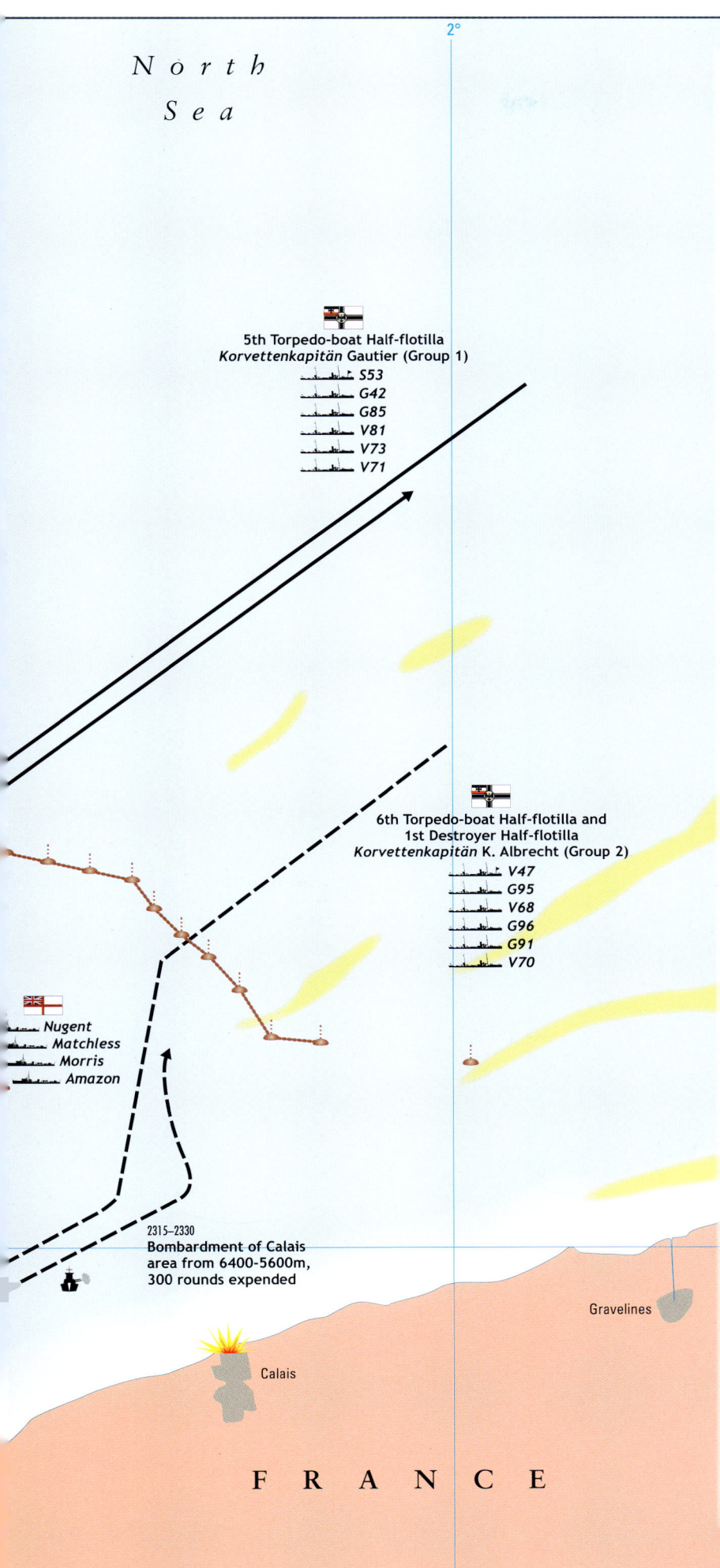

5th Torpedo-boat Half-flotilla
Korvettenkapitän Gautier (Group 1)
- S53
- G42
- G85
- V81
- V73
- V71

6th Torpedo-boat Half-flotilla and 1st Destroyer Half-flotilla
Korvettenkapitän K. Albrecht (Group 2)
- V47
- G95
- V68
- G96
- G91
- V70

- Nugent
- Matchless
- Morris
- Amazon

2315–2330
Bombardment of Calais area from 6400–5600m, 300 rounds expended

Calais
Gravelines

FRANCE

Text

THROUGHOUT THE SPRING the situation off Flanders and in the lower North Sea remained volatile as the Germans intensified U-boats operations and the British sought to strengthen the Dover defences. In mid-March another German attack in the Dover area was undertaken. Numerous skirmishes between light forces were fought off the Flanders coast and the Germans also periodically raided the shipping routes between Britain and Holland. The next major German operation was planned for the night of 20–21 April using the 3rd Torpedo-boat Flotilla and the Flanders-based boats. It had also been envisaged to employ U-boats off the French coast, but there were insufficient boats available.

The German force was split into three separate groups. The half-flotillas of the 3rd Torpedo-boat Flotilla would attack the net barrage with the objective of sinking any patrolling vessels. As a secondary objective, bombardments of Calais and Dover would be undertaken. The third group would operate north of the Downs and surprise any British forces sent south to deal with the incursion. The forces put to sea just after 6pm on 20 April and remained undetected by the British so that, once again, the Germans enjoyed the element of surprise.

That night the British had two forces at sea off the barrage. The routine night patrol on the barrage consisted of one division of destroyers (Nugent's Division) and additionally two flotilla leaders, *Broke* and *Swift*, patrolled along the northern end of the barrage. The division off the Downs consisted off two cruisers and three destroyers, while the monitor *Marshal Ney* was the guard ship at the northern exits and three old destroyers patrolled off Margate. Six destroyers were at reserve in Dover.

The German group in the south encountered no resistance and proceeded straight to Calais to conduct its bombardment and made for home. Attracted by this gunfire, *Broke* and *Swift* turned south to investigate. Once it became clear that Nugent's division was not yet engaged the two turned north. At this point the northern German group arrived off Dover, had a brief skirmish with the armed trawler *Sabreur* and then undertook its bombardment before turning east.

Once the German bombardment had ceased the British destroyers prepared to leave port. This was briefly delayed when some of the British coastal artillery opened fire in an attempt to hit the retreating Germans. In the confusion the destroyers were split into two groups. By the time all ships were at sea *Broke* and *Swift* were already engaged with the German force.

The conditions that night were calm and very dark so the British and German ships came into very close proximity before registering the presence of each other. A very intense short action was fought in which torpedoes and gunfire was employed and both sides took hits. Two German boats were sunk before the rest made off eastwards. Three days later the Germans conducted a night-time attack on Dunkirk but it was not until February 1918 that German torpedo boats again attempted to venture into the Dover Strait.

Battle of the Strait of Otranto, 14–15 May 1917

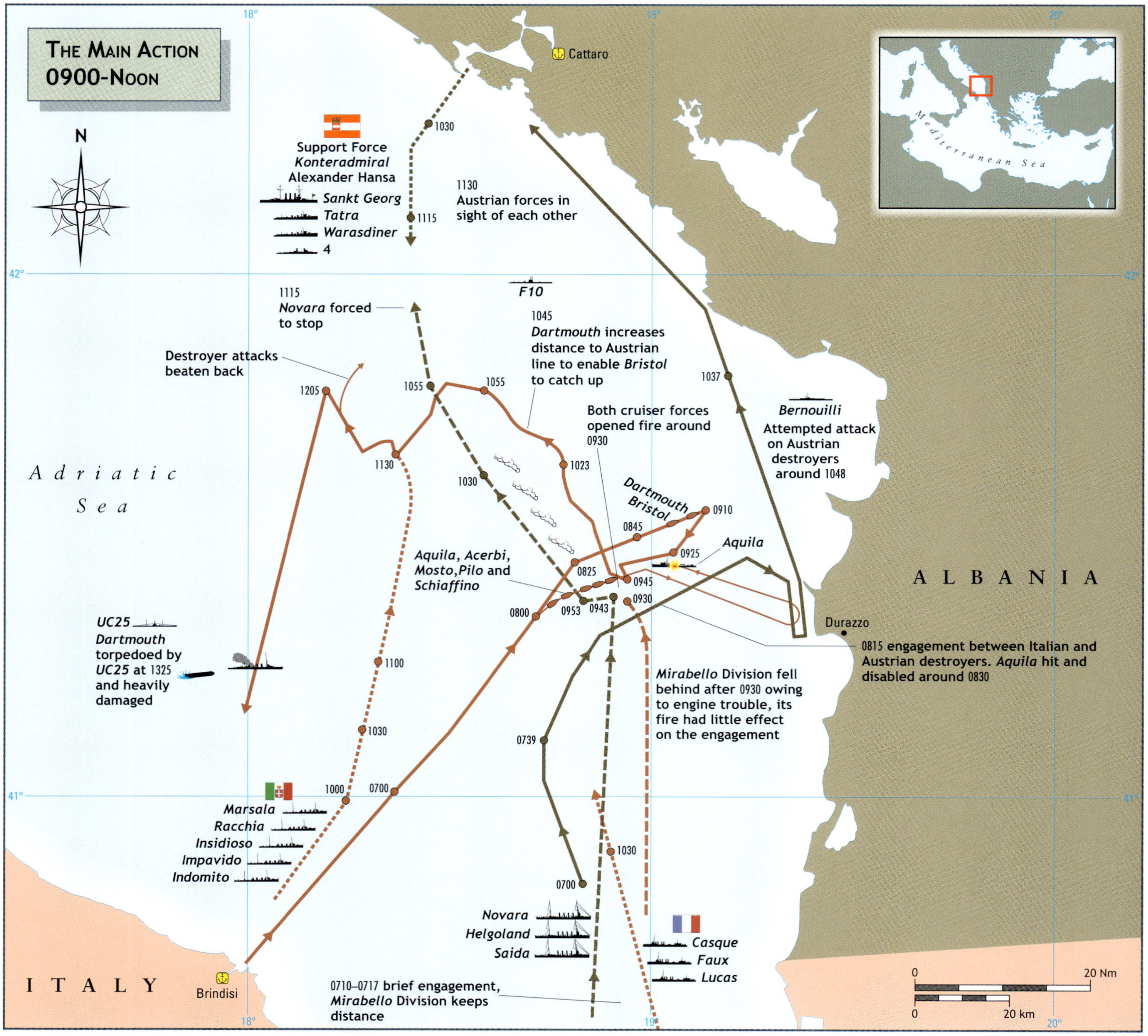
The Main Action
0900-Noon
N
18°
19°
20°
42°
41°
Cattaro
1030
Support Force
Konteradmiral
Alexander Hansa
Sankt Georg
Tatra
Warasdiner
4
1115
1130
Austrian forces in
sight of each other
Mediterranean Sea
F10
1115
Novara forced
to stop
1045
Dartmouth increases
distance to Austrian
line to enable Bristol
to catch up
1037
Destroyer attacks
beaten back
1205
1055
1055
Both cruiser forces
opened fire around
0930
Bernouilli
Attempted attack
on Austrian
destroyers
around 1048
Adriatic
Sea
1130
1023
1030
Dartmouth
Bristol
0910
0845
0925
Aquila
Aquila, Acerbi,
Mosto, Pilo and
Schiaffino
0825
0945
0930
0943
0953
0800
ALBANIA
Durazzo
0815 engagement between Italian and
Austrian destroyers. Aquila hit and
disabled around 0830
UC25
Dartmouth
torpedoed by
UC25 at 1325
and heavily
damaged
1100
Mirabello Division fell
behind after 0930 owing
to engine trouble, its
fire had little effect
on the engagement
1030
0739
1000
0700
Marsala
Racchia
Insidioso
Impavido
Indomito
1030
0700
Novara
Helgoland
Saida
Casque
Faux
Lucas
ITALY
Brindisi
0710–0717 brief engagement,
Mirabello Division keeps
distance
0
20 Nm
0
20 km

Key

Austro-Hungarian Forces
- Diversionary Force
- Raid Force
- Support Force

Allied Forces
- Acton's Force
- Mirabello's Division
- Additional forces
- Allied submarine patrol areas

N.B. approximate movement of forces

Although the allied anti-submarine measures in the Straits of Otranto were more of a nuisance than an impediment to German U-boats, in May the Austrians planned a major raid on the drifter line. The aim was as much with giving the surface fleet something to do as it was about inflicting damage on the Allies. Throughout April a number of destroyer operations were launched to probe allied defences in the Straits and on 13 May three fast light cruisers arrived from Pola to undertake the actual raid. The plan was to attack the drifter line while two destroyers conducted a diversionary sweep along the Albanian coast. Additional forces were kept ready at Cattaro.

The raid caught the Allies by surprise and although they had more forces in the area they were widely dispersed, at varying states of readiness and afflicted by convoluted command structures. A force set sail from Brindisi to intercept the withdrawing Austrians, but in an exchange of fire with the diversionary force the *Aquila* was hit and disabled. In the main engagement between the cruisers the British slowly gained the upper hand and inflicted heavy damage on the Austrians, but were unable to press home their advantage as their accompanying destroyers were out of action. To regroup his force Rear-Admiral Acton briefly turned away from the engagement which allowed the Austrians to pull ahead and join with the support force coming south from Cattaro.

The Great War at Sea 1917

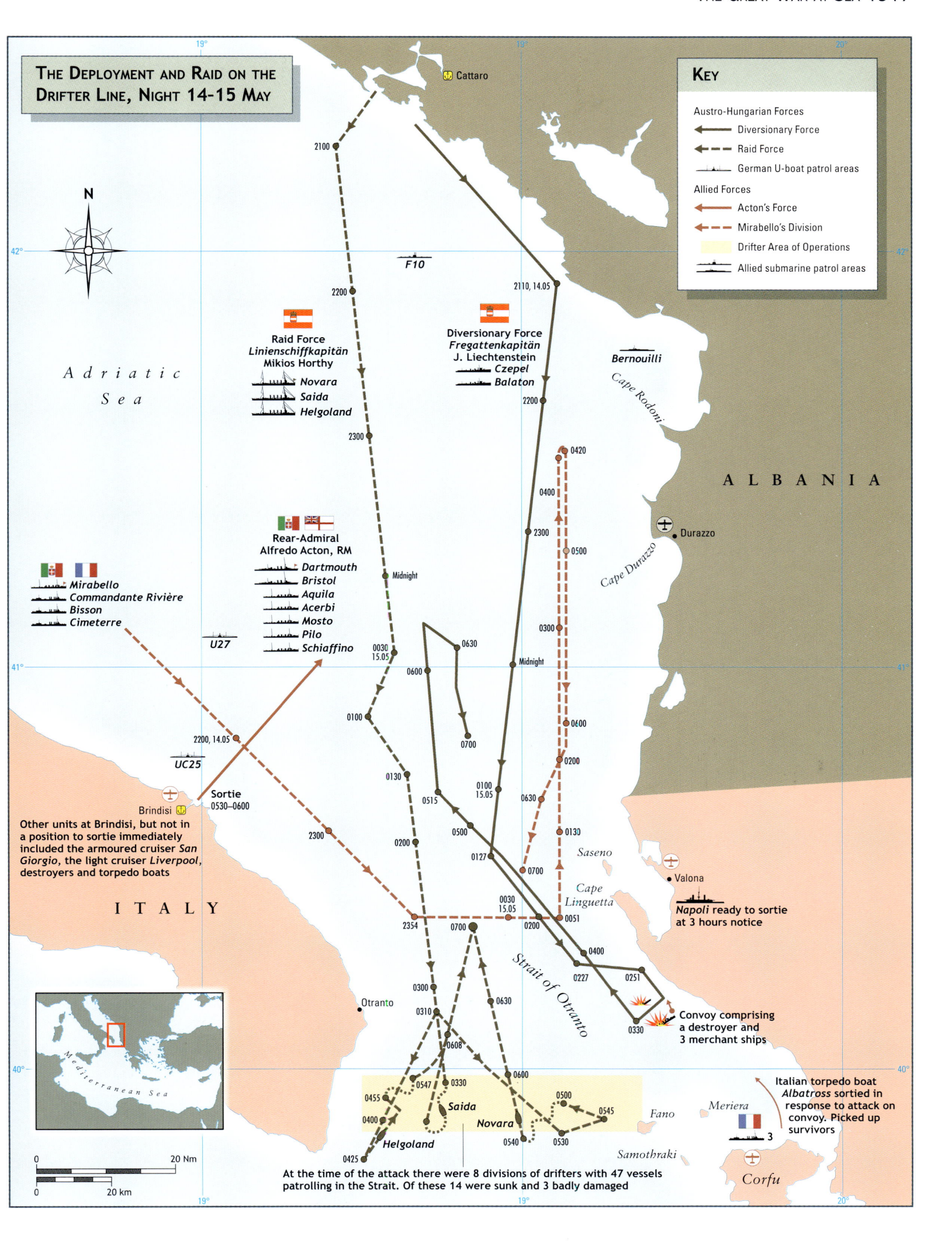

The Deployment and Raid on the Drifter Line, Night 14-15 May

Key

Austro-Hungarian Forces
- Diversionary Force
- Raid Force
- German U-boat patrol areas

Allied Forces
- Acton's Force
- Mirabello's Division
- Drifter Area of Operations
- Allied submarine patrol areas

Raid Force Linienschiffkapitän Miklos Horthy
- Novara
- Saida
- Helgoland

Diversionary Force Fregattenkapitän J. Liechtenstein
- Czepel
- Balaton

Rear-Admiral Alfredo Acton, RM
- Dartmouth
- Bristol
- Aquila
- Acerbi
- Mosto
- Pilo
- Schiaffino

- Mirabello
- Commandante Rivière
- Bisson
- Cimeterre

Other units at Brindisi, but not in a position to sortie immediately included the armoured cruiser *San Giorgio*, the light cruiser *Liverpool*, destroyers and torpedo boats

Napoli ready to sortie at 3 hours notice

Convoy comprising a destroyer and 3 merchant ships

Italian torpedo boat *Albatross* sortied in response to attack on convoy. Picked up survivors

At the time of the attack there were 8 divisions of drifters with 47 vessels patrolling in the Strait. Of these 14 were sunk and 3 badly damaged

Allied Merchant Shipping Losses, 1917

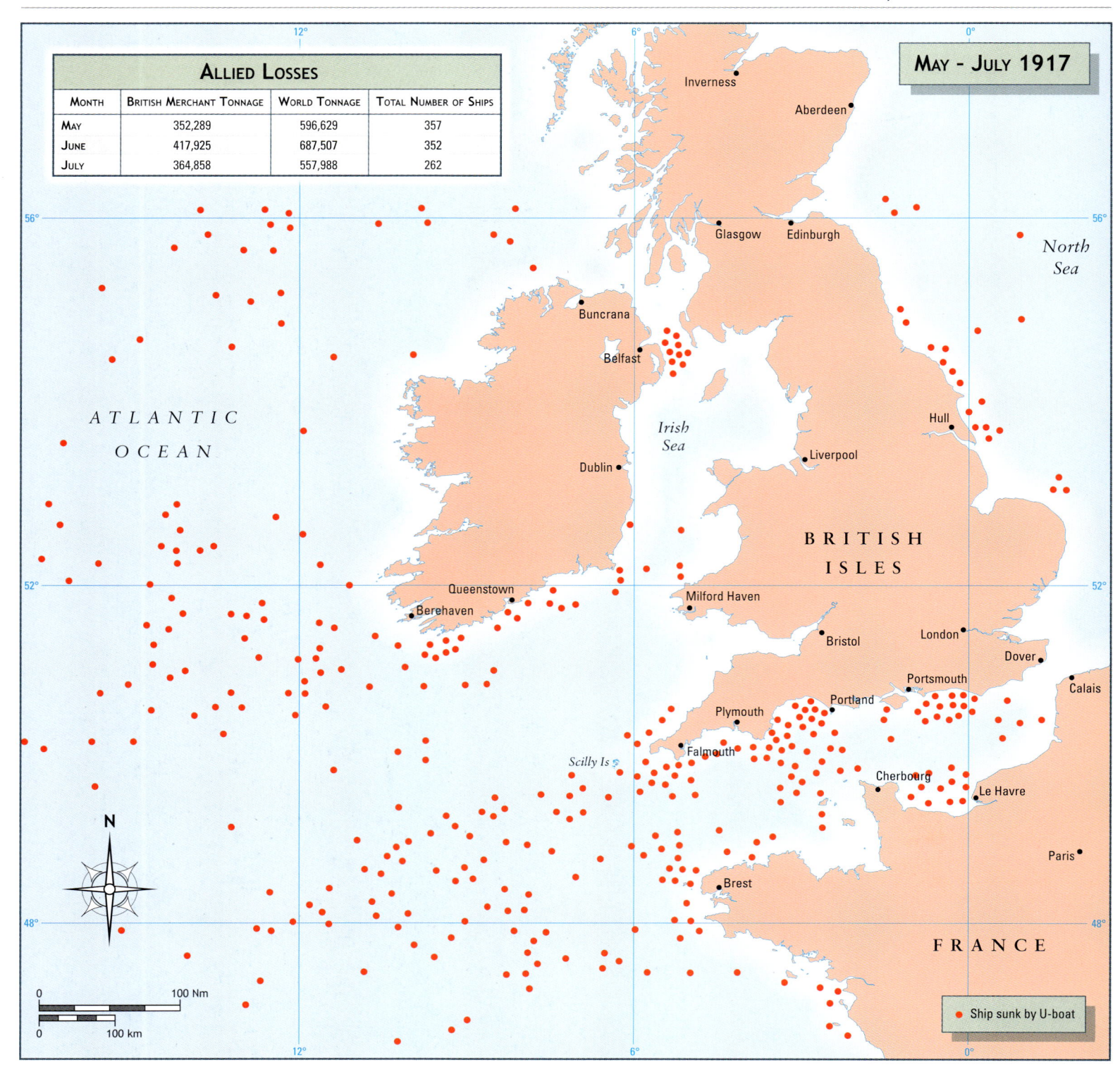

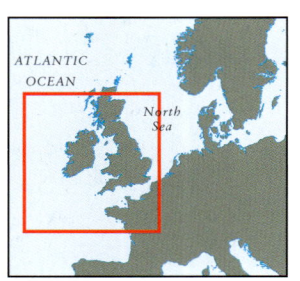

May - July 1917

Allied Losses

Month	British Merchant Tonnage	World Tonnage	Total Number of Ships
May	352,289	596,629	357
June	417,925	687,507	352
July	364,858	557,988	262

● Ship sunk by U-boat

THE SCALE OF the German success in the first months of unrestricted submarine warfare profoundly shocked the British government and it was a problem for which the Admiralty seemingly had no solution. Although the high losses in April were never again repeated, sinkings remained above what could be weathered. In the first five months of unrestricted submarine warfare the Allies lost as much shipping as in the entire war to date. If losses were not curbed the ability to sustain overseas military campaigns would be jeopardised, and by the end of the year Britain would face starvation.

U-boats of the High Sea Fleet accounted for around half of the sinkings and the Western Approaches remained the focus. By June operations were slowly extended out into the Atlantic and Mediterranean boats increasingly operated west of Gibraltar. U-boat losses did increase, but as they were less than new construction the overall size of the force continued to grow. The exchange rate between U-boats and merchant ships was firmly in Germany's favour with over fifty merchant ships being sunk for every U-boat lost.

Increased sinkings were not only the product of greater U-boat numbers; the use of torpedo attacks was also on the increase and, in the first quarter, around 60 per cent of ships were sunk by torpedo.

THE GREAT WAR AT SEA 1917

THE ALLIED CONVOY SYSTEM 1917–18

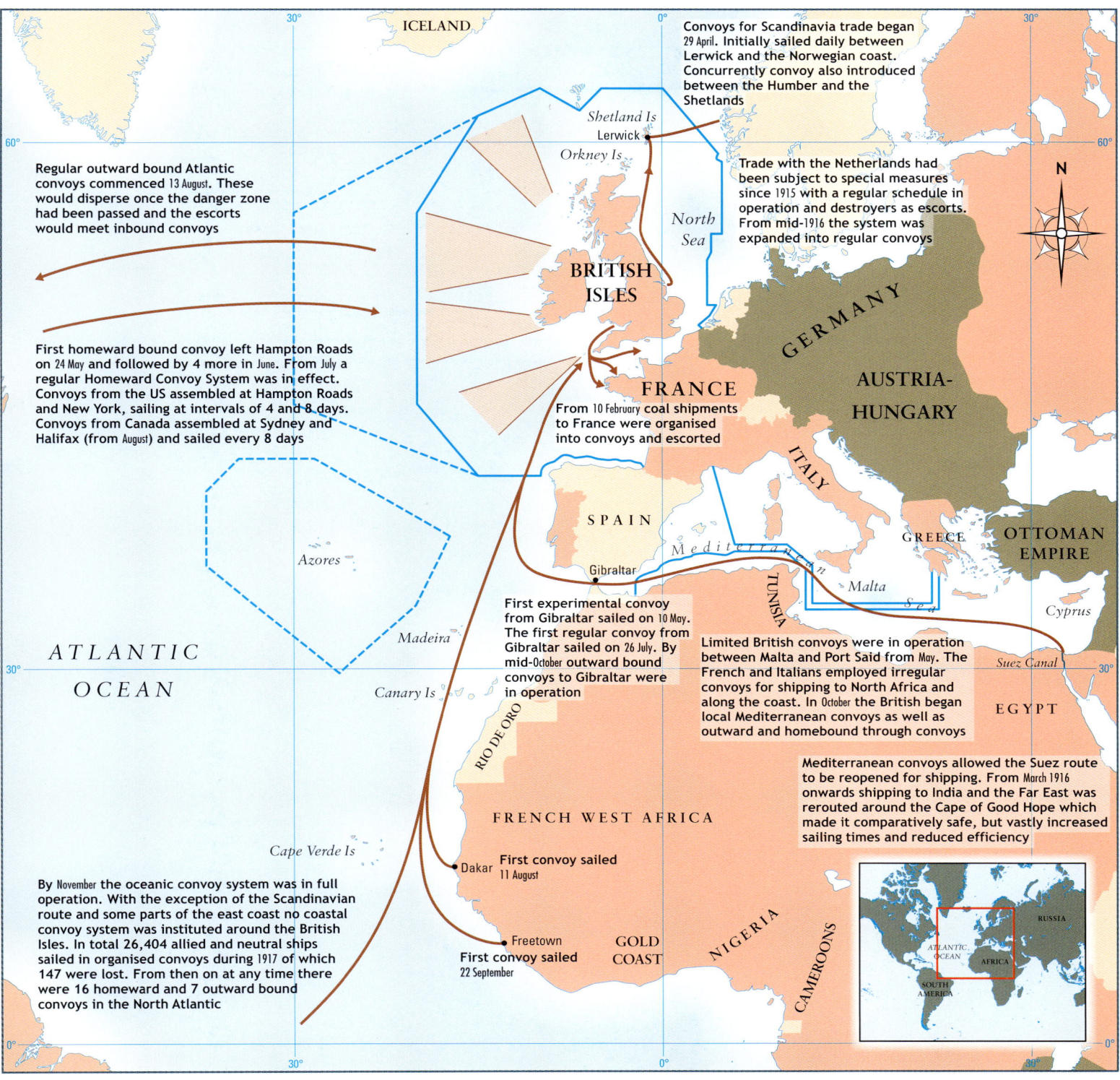

Convoys for Scandinavia trade began 29 April. Initially sailed daily between Lerwick and the Norwegian coast. Concurrently convoy also introduced between the Humber and the Shetlands

Regular outward bound Atlantic convoys commenced 13 August. These would disperse once the danger zone had been passed and the escorts would meet inbound convoys

Trade with the Netherlands had been subject to special measures since 1915 with a regular schedule in operation and destroyers as escorts. From mid-1916 the system was expanded into regular convoys

First homeward bound convoy left Hampton Roads on 24 May and followed by 4 more in June. From July a regular Homeward Convoy System was in effect. Convoys from the US assembled at Hampton Roads and New York, sailing at intervals of 4 and 8 days. Convoys from Canada assembled at Sydney and Halifax (from August) and sailed every 8 days

From 10 February coal shipments to France were organised into convoys and escorted

First experimental convoy from Gibraltar sailed on 10 May. The first regular convoy from Gibraltar sailed on 26 July. By mid-October outward bound convoys to Gibraltar were in operation

Limited British convoys were in operation between Malta and Port Said from May. The French and Italians employed irregular convoys for shipping to North Africa and along the coast. In October the British began local Mediterranean convoys as well as outward and homebound through convoys

Mediterranean convoys allowed the Suez route to be reopened for shipping. From March 1916 onwards shipping to India and the Far East was rerouted around the Cape of Good Hope which made it comparatively safe, but vastly increased sailing times and reduced efficiency

First convoy sailed 11 August

First convoy sailed 22 September

By November the oceanic convoy system was in full operation. With the exception of the Scandinavian route and some parts of the east coast no coastal convoy system was instituted around the British Isles. In total 26,404 allied and neutral ships sailed in organised convoys during 1917 of which 147 were lost. From then on at any time there were 16 homeward and 7 outward bound convoys in the North Atlantic

---

THE ADOPTION OF convoy was historically the most effective way of protecting maritime trade. By concentrating shipping the oceans were swept clear of easy targets for raiders to sink. In the vastness of the ocean a convoy's footprint was only marginally larger than that of a single ship. With shipping organised into groups escorting forces could be used more efficiently. Set against these advantages though were issues that made convoy unappealing to both shipowners and the military planners. They were complex to organise and they disrupted the global shipping system and created bottlenecks in ports. Furthermore, a convoy could only sail as fast as the slowest vessel. Navies generally also preferred to actively hunt raiders rather than engage in the passive defence of trade.

Prior to 1914 the Royal Navy had given little thought to convoy as the threat to trade would come, it was believed, primarily from a small number of German warships. Only troop transports and other very high value cargoes were organised in convoys. The vast increase in U-boat operations by 1917 fundamentally altered the trade defence problem. The Admiralty was reluctant to introduce convoy owing to the scale of the task and a lack of escorts, but the huge spring losses required some action. The first convoys demonstrated their potential for defending shipping as losses incurred during the summer were negligible.

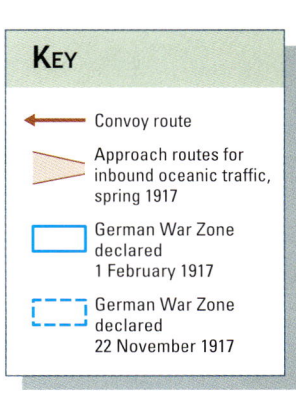

KEY

→ Convoy route

Approach routes for inbound oceanic traffic, spring 1917

German War Zone declared 1 February 1917

German War Zone declared 22 November 1917

Allied Shipping Losses in the Mediterranean, July–December 1917

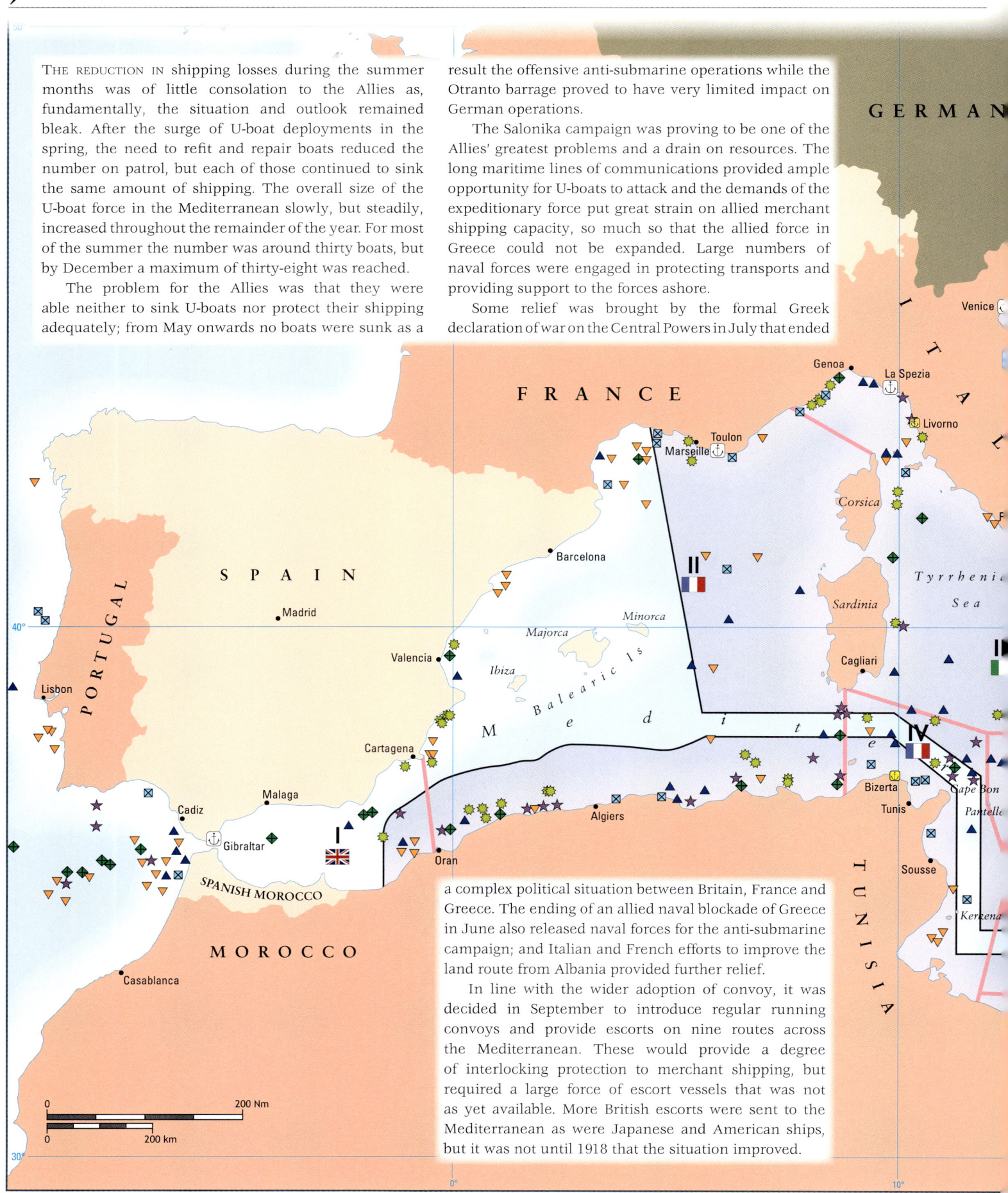

The reduction in shipping losses during the summer months was of little consolation to the Allies as, fundamentally, the situation and outlook remained bleak. After the surge of U-boat deployments in the spring, the need to refit and repair boats reduced the number on patrol, but each of those continued to sink the same amount of shipping. The overall size of the U-boat force in the Mediterranean slowly, but steadily, increased throughout the remainder of the year. For most of the summer the number was around thirty boats, but by December a maximum of thirty-eight was reached.

The problem for the Allies was that they were able neither to sink U-boats nor protect their shipping adequately; from May onwards no boats were sunk as a result the offensive anti-submarine operations while the Otranto barrage proved to have very limited impact on German operations.

The Salonika campaign was proving to be one of the Allies' greatest problems and a drain on resources. The long maritime lines of communications provided ample opportunity for U-boats to attack and the demands of the expeditionary force put great strain on allied merchant shipping capacity, so much so that the allied force in Greece could not be expanded. Large numbers of naval forces were engaged in protecting transports and providing support to the forces ashore.

Some relief was brought by the formal Greek declaration of war on the Central Powers in July that ended a complex political situation between Britain, France and Greece. The ending of an allied naval blockade of Greece in June also released naval forces for the anti-submarine campaign; and Italian and French efforts to improve the land route from Albania provided further relief.

In line with the wider adoption of convoy, it was decided in September to introduce regular running convoys and provide escorts on nine routes across the Mediterranean. These would provide a degree of interlocking protection to merchant shipping, but required a large force of escort vessels that was not as yet available. More British escorts were sent to the Mediterranean as were Japanese and American ships, but it was not until 1918 that the situation improved.

THE GREAT WAR AT SEA 1917

Allied Shipping Losses in the Mediterranean

Month	Tonnage Sunk by Pola Flotilla U-boats	Tonnage Sunk by U-boat Laid Mines	Mediterranean Total	World Total Tonnage Lost	Tonnage Sunk by Austrian U-boats	Tonnage Sunk by Constantinople Half-Flotilla
July	84,319	6,015	90,334	557,988	16,969	–
August	73,403	6,146	79,549	511,730	38,823	–
September	111,241	–	111,241	351,748	–	445
October	143,793	810	144,603	458,558	12,663	2,175
November	94,329	10,150	104,479	289,212	4,016	1,201
December	144,290	4,041	148,331	399,111	–	–

Note: In order to provide an overview of the effects of the U-boat campaign the figures are derived from a number of sources. The total world tonnage lost is taken from Fayle, *Seaborne Trade* Vol. III. The figures relating to the tonnage lost to U-boats and mines laid by U-boats from Spindler, *Handelskrieg* Vol. IV. These totals included British, other allied and neutral shipping sunk. In addition a small quantity of allied shipping was sunk by the Austrians and also the U-boats stationed at Constantinople (these operated both in the Black Sea and the Aegean Sea).

Key

Allied shipping losses July–December, 1917
- ▲ July
- ⊠ August
- ▽ September
- ◆ October
- ★ November
- ✺ December
- VI Allied Patrol Areas
- German War zone declared 1 February 1917

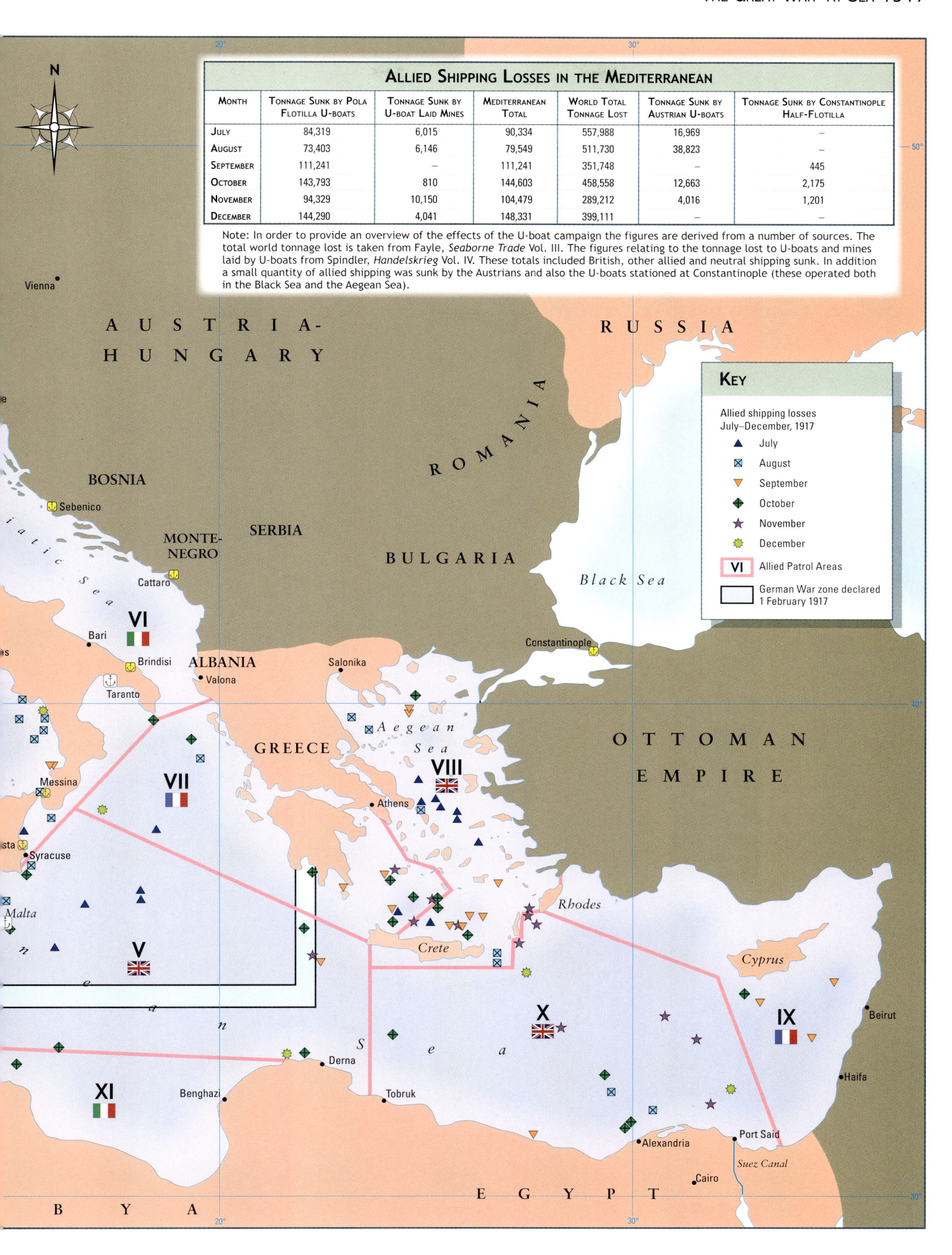

133

Operation Albion, 10–20 October 1917

Dislodging the Russian forces from around the Gulf of Riga area was one of the main German objectives on the eastern front during the summer of 1917. Although Russia was suffering increasingly from internal unrest it remained in the war and tied down a significant number of German troops that were needed in the west. At the beginning of September the German Eighth Army captured Riga and pushed back the defending Russian Twelfth Army. The Germans could not though secure the Baltic coastline from the landward side alone in view of Russian naval superiority in the Gulf of Riga that both facilitated bombardments and reduced the flow of German supplies to the front. Securing Ösel and the surrounding islands was key to securing the region, but since 1915 the Russians had increased the defences, gun emplacements and minefields. The Moon Sound had been dredged to allow warships, battleships excepted, to enter the Gulf without having to use the Baltic itself.

In mid-September the German army and navy agreed to conduct an amphibious operation to capture the Ösel. The High Sea Fleet consented, providing as it did an opportunity for the fleet to undertake some offensive action. The plan was to land a divisional sized force at Tagga Bay on Ösel with some smaller and diversionary landings elsewhere. The troops with substantial fire support from the fleet would clear out the Russian positions and cross over to Moon Island.

Poor weather conditions on the day of the landings gave the Germans the element of surprise over the Russian defenders. However, shallow waters and mines caused problems from the outset. German light forces and minesweepers found it hard to operate in the Soela Sound in the face of heavier Russian firepower while German battleships could not be brought in from the west owing to shallow water and new Russian mine barriers.

Instead, *Vizeadmiral* Behncke took a task force into the Gulf of Riga on 16 October to attack from the south and help isolate Moon Island for an assault. By this stage all available Russian warships had left the Gulf and only three British submarines remained. On the morning of 17 October the Battle of the Moon Sound was fought in which *Slava* was sunk. Over the next days the Russian naval forces retreated back into the Gulf of Finland.

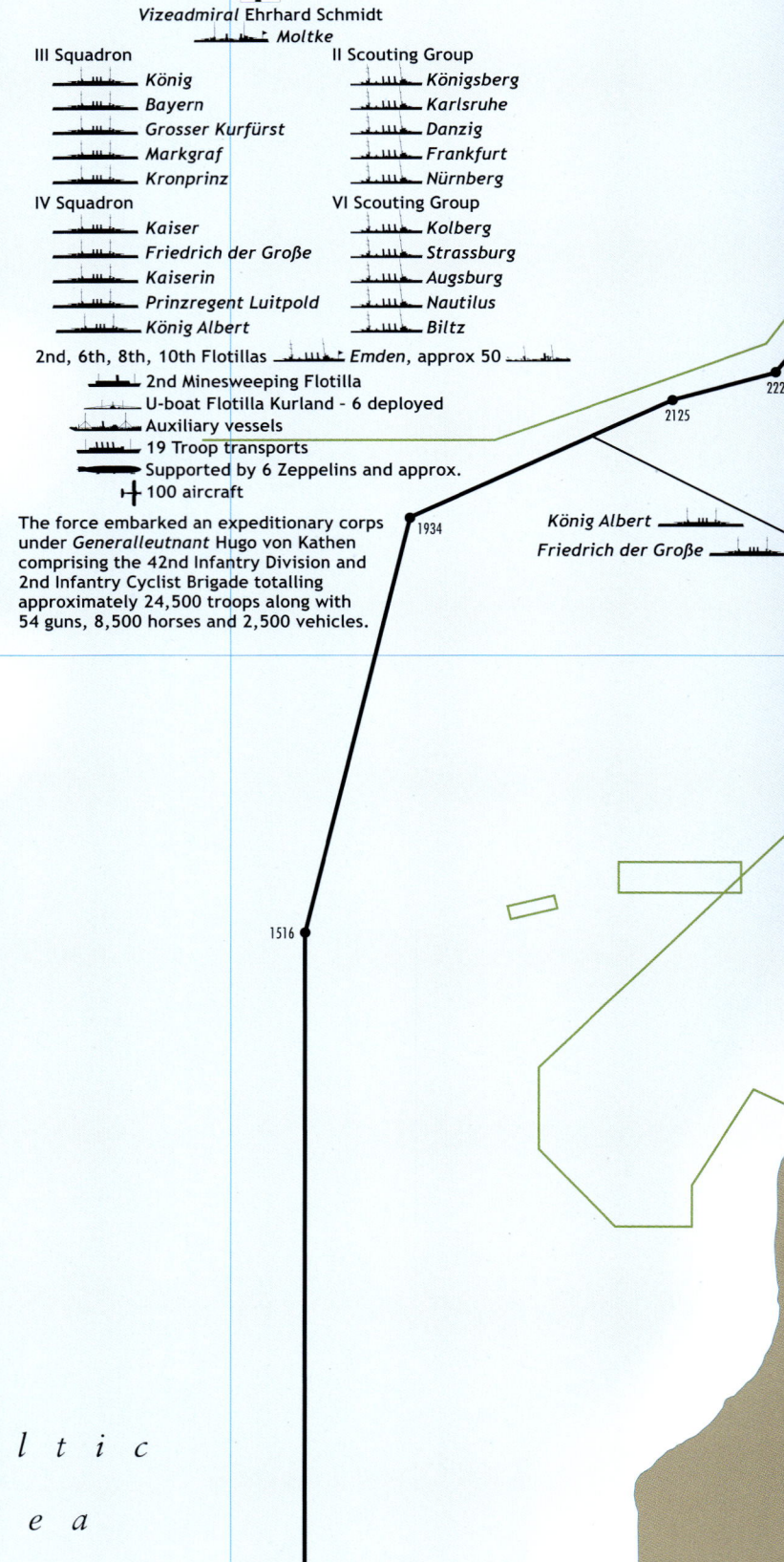

Vizeadmiral Ehrhard Schmidt
Moltke

III Squadron
- König
- Bayern
- Grosser Kurfürst
- Markgraf
- Kronprinz

IV Squadron
- Kaiser
- Friedrich der Große
- Kaiserin
- Prinzregent Luitpold
- König Albert

II Scouting Group
- Königsberg
- Karlsruhe
- Danzig
- Frankfurt
- Nürnberg

VI Scouting Group
- Kolberg
- Strassburg
- Augsburg
- Nautilus
- Biltz

2nd, 6th, 8th, 10th Flotillas — Emden, approx 50
2nd Minesweeping Flotilla
U-boat Flotilla Kurland – 6 deployed
Auxiliary vessels
19 Troop transports
Supported by 6 Zeppelins and approx. 100 aircraft

The force embarked an expeditionary corps under *Generalleutnant* Hugo von Kathen comprising the 42nd Infantry Division and 2nd Infantry Cyclist Brigade totalling approximately 24,500 troops along with 54 guns, 8,500 horses and 2,500 vehicles.

König Albert
Friedrich der Große

THE GREAT WAR AT SEA 1917

Key

- Landing Force, 11–12 October
- Detached bombarding force
- Movements by Gruppe Behncke, accompanied by destroyers and minesweeper, 16–17 October
- German naval bombardments
- Russian movements 17.10
- Russian minefields/areas considered dangerous by the Germans
- Russian defensive positions

h mined while taking bombardment position

Dago Garrison surrendered 20 October

Attempts by German light forces to break out of the Soela Sound and conduct minesweeping defeated by Russian destroyers and heavy gunfire

Dago

Hapsal

Anchorage 0300–0443

Bayern

12 Oct.

Soela Sound

Grosser Kurfürst

Moon Sound

Admiral Makarov
Grazhdanin
Slava

Moon Is. fell 18 October

Moltke

Tagga Bay

Ösel

Moon

Slava sunk

XX 107 Surrendered 15 October

12 Oct.

14 Oct.

Arensburg

12 Oct.

17.10

Anchorage

• Pernau

König
Kronprinz
Kolberg
Strassburg

R U S S I A

16.10

19.10
Kolberg and *Strassburg* along with torpedo boats break into Moon Sound. *König* towed in to provide fire support on 20.10

C26 grounded while attempting attack on German task force

Rear-Admiral Mikhail Bakhirev
Based in the main Russian anchorage in the Kuwast Roads between Moon Island and the mainland. Elements operating all around the Gulf of Riga

- *Grazhdanin*
- *Slava*
- *Bayan*
- *Admiral Makaroff*
- 26
- Gunboats
- minesweepers
- auxiliary craft

Irben Strait

British submarines *C27* and *C32* attempted attacks on the force on 16.10

• Salas

G u l f
o f
R i g a

XXXX Twelfth
General Vladislav Klembovski

• Riga

German assault 1–5th September

XXXX Eighth
Generalleutnant Oskar von Hutier

C O U R L A N D

0 ———— 40 Nm
0 ———— 40 km

Allied Merchant Shipping Losses, 1917

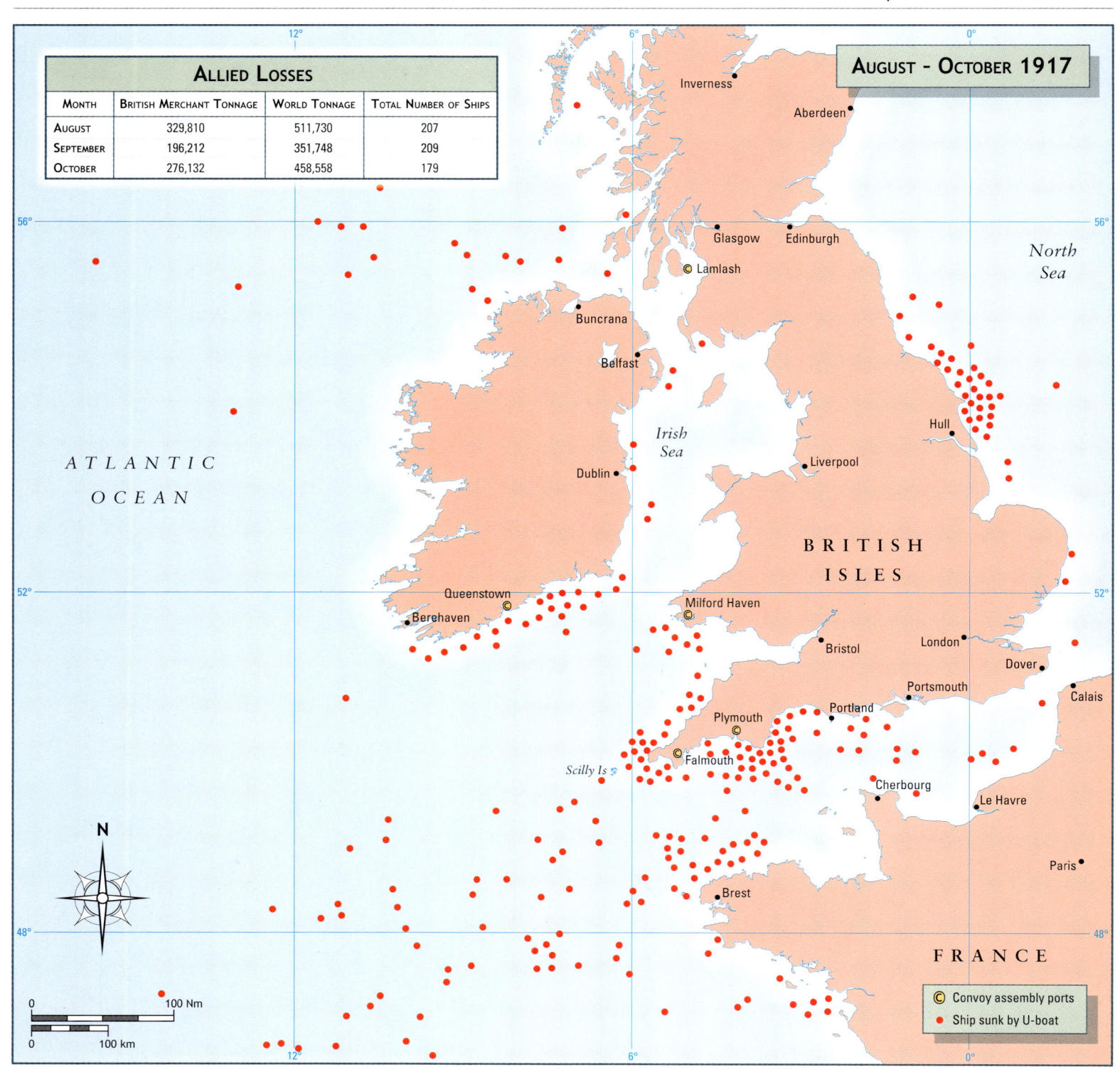

Allied Losses

Month	British Merchant Tonnage	World Tonnage	Total Number of Ships
August	329,810	511,730	207
September	196,212	351,748	209
October	276,132	458,558	179

August – October 1917

- Convoy assembly ports
- Ship sunk by U-boat

Six months into the campaign Britain was neither on the verge of surrendering and nor could the Germans detect any sign that a political settlement might be forthcoming. In most months U-boats had come close to, or exceeded, the 600,000-ton figure deemed necessary to defeat Britain, and in August again more than half a million tons of shipping was sunk. From that point though the losses began to drop off.

Global shipping and British domestic requirements consisted of so many varied strands that they were difficult to damage. Overall, allied losses were high, but the campaign had not been focused enough to deliver a decisive blow against any single aspect of British trade.

By the autumn U-boat operations around the British Isles began to change and move inshore as western coastal shipping as yet remained largely unconvoyed.

There was no single solution from the British perspective. Convoy played an important role and new construction of merchant ships was prioritised at the expense of warships. Throughout 1917 about 1.1 million tons were built and while insufficient as replacement this helped bridge the gap until American construction came online. Domestic food production was also increased. Allied expansion of minelaying in the German Bight and off the Flanders coast was also undertaken.

Action off Lerwick/Norwegian Convoy Attack, 17 October 1917

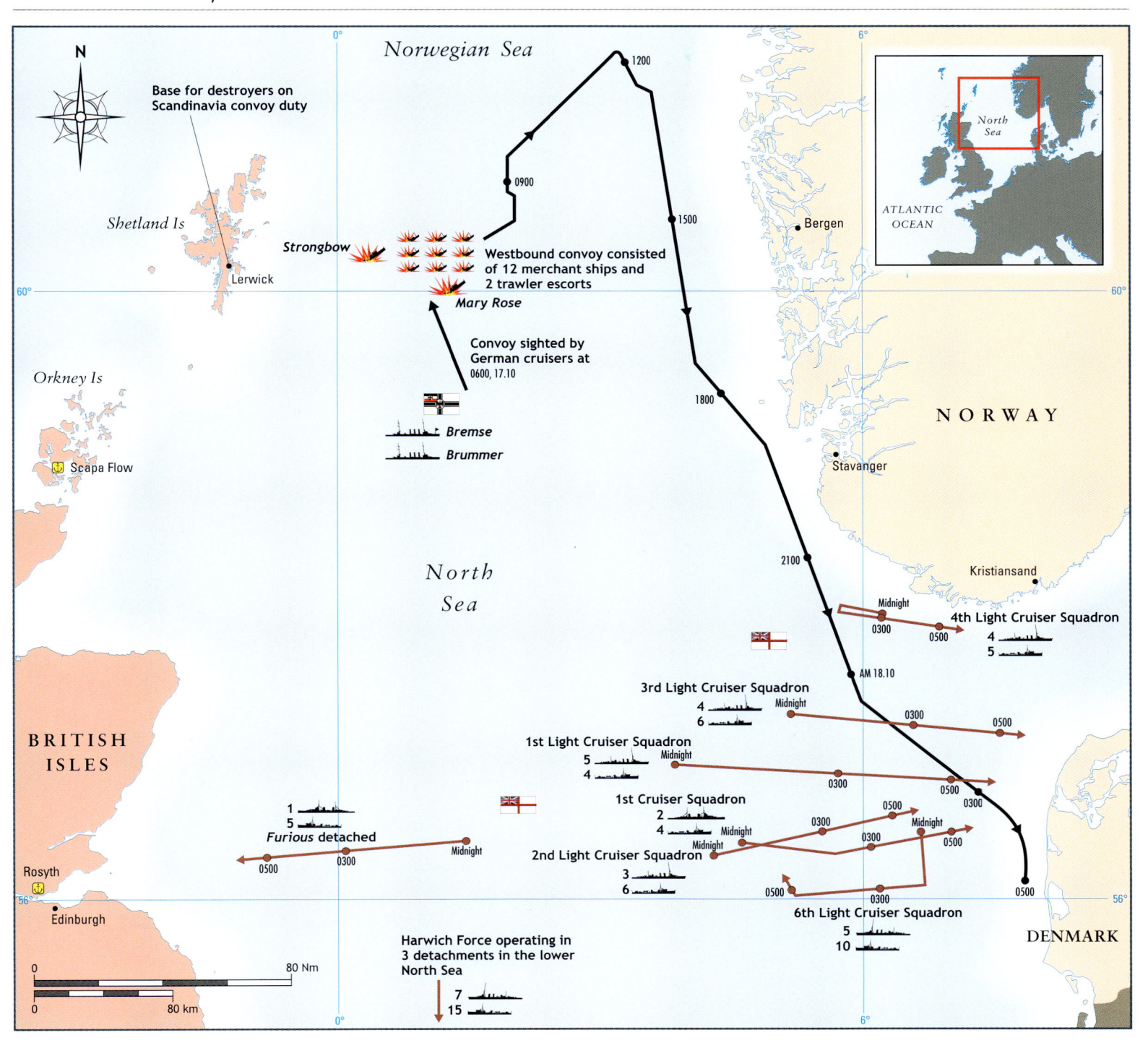

WHILE THE BULK of the High Sea Fleet was in the Baltic or refitting after Operation Albion, the Germans decided to undertake a new type of operation in the North Sea and raid the route between Lerwick and Bergen with cruisers. It was the only trade route that could realistically be attacked by surface raiders. The cruisers *Brummer* and *Bremse* had originally been designed as fast minelayers for the Russian navy and possessed a relatively large radius of action. The objective was to interrupt this traffic and force the British to redirect forces from the anti-U-boat campaign. Recently, the British had engaged in very aggressive minelaying and had claimed a number of boats in the North Sea.

The British were alerted to a potential threat, but it was assumed to be a minelaying operation. Admiral Beatty and Commodore Tyrwhitt deployed three battlecruisers, *Furious* now refitted for carrying aircraft, twenty-seven light cruisers and fifty-four destroyers in numerous patrol lines in the central and eastern areas. However, the German cruisers managed to evade detection and in the early morning of 17 October found and destroyed a convoy. Having previously been only threatened by U-boats these had light escorts. News of the attack only reached Beatty around 5pm and although forces were moved to cover a gap in the original deployment, the returning German cruisers escaped unchallenged.

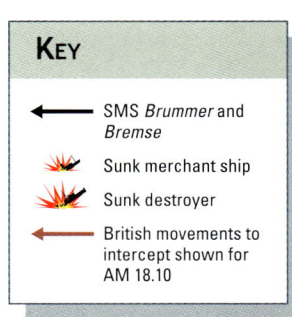

Key
- SMS *Brummer* and *Bremse*
- Sunk merchant ship
- Sunk destroyer
- British movements to intercept shown for AM 18.10

The Second Battle of Heligoland Bight, 17 November 1917

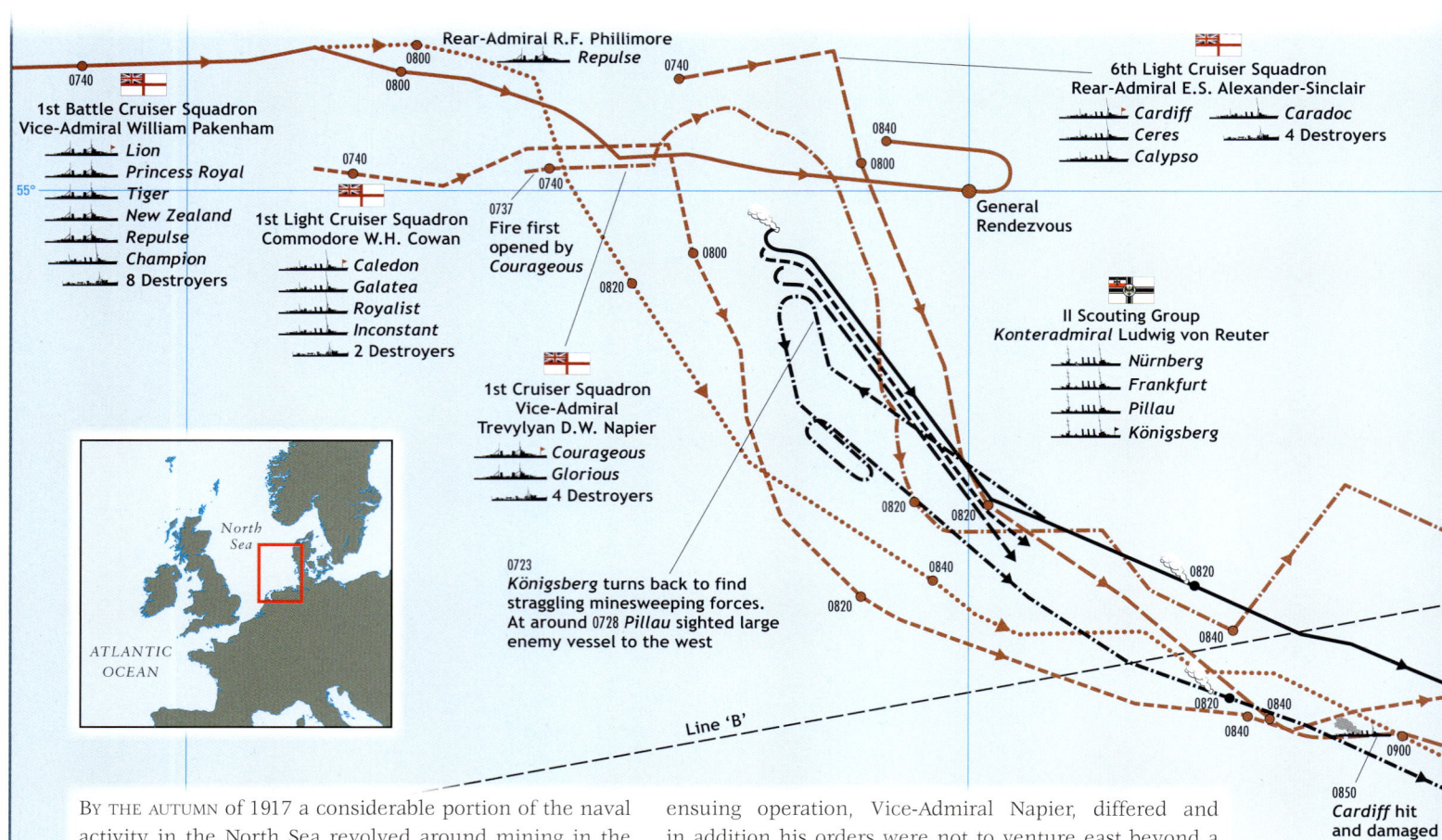

By the autumn of 1917 a considerable portion of the naval activity in the North Sea revolved around mining in the Heligoland Bight area. The British had massively increased their minelaying operations in an attempt to impede U-boat movements. The Germans conversely increased their sweeping activities to ensure U-boats could reach open waters safely. Large numbers of auxiliary warships were employed and sweeps right up to the edge of the mine barrier were conducted. The minesweepers were supported by cruisers and torpedo boats, while at times battleships too would loiter in the vicinity of Heligoland to provide distant cover.

On 31 October a British cruiser-destroyer force succeeded in destroying a German auxiliary force in the Kattegat and by this stage the British had very good intelligence on German operations. The Admiralty decided to undertake a much larger sweep in mid-November supported by the 1st Battle Cruiser Squadron with the 1st Battle Squadron providing distant cover. The object was to move across the North Sea up to the German minefields and then turn northwards towards the battleships, sweeping up any German forces on the outer edge of the barrier.

The problem the British faced was that any attempt at catching German forces would entail British warships coming close to, or even entering, the dangerous areas in any pursuit. Although the Admiralty possessed very accurate charts of British and German minefields in the Bight, this information was only given to Vice-Admiral Beatty and the commander of the Battle Cruiser Force, Vice-Admiral Pakenham. The chart of his deputy in the ensuing operation, Vice-Admiral Napier, differed and in addition his orders were not to venture east beyond a certain limit. His subordinates, Rear-Admiral Alexander-Sinclair and Commodore Cowan, had even less accurate information and assumed they could operate further to the east.

Just at the time the British launched their operation, *Konteradmiral* von Reuter was covering a minesweeping operation to the edge of the barrier and then northwards on 17 November. Both forces sighted each other around 7.30am. The German cruisers and torpedo boats made for the British forces and laid a huge smoke screen to enable the auxiliaries to escape, and only a single armed trawler was lost. A pursuit battle developed in which the various British forces attempted to catch and destroy the retreating German warships.

The Germans made good use of smoke, which forced the British formations to evade the screens, slowing them down and increasing the engagement ranges. Shortly before 9am, Pakenham ordered the pursuit to be abandoned but control of the situation was difficult. Napier withdrew 9.32am as he had reached the boundary of the danger area but the light cruiser squadrons continued. At 9.40am *Calypso* took a hit that killed nearly her entire bridge crew and then the British light cruisers came into range of the two German battleships, prompting a retreat. The arrival of the battlecruiser *Repulse* added some heavy British fire, but the appearance of fog brought the battle to an end. Although the British had enjoyed overwhelming superiority little material damage was inflicted on the Germans.

THE GREAT WAR AT SEA 1917

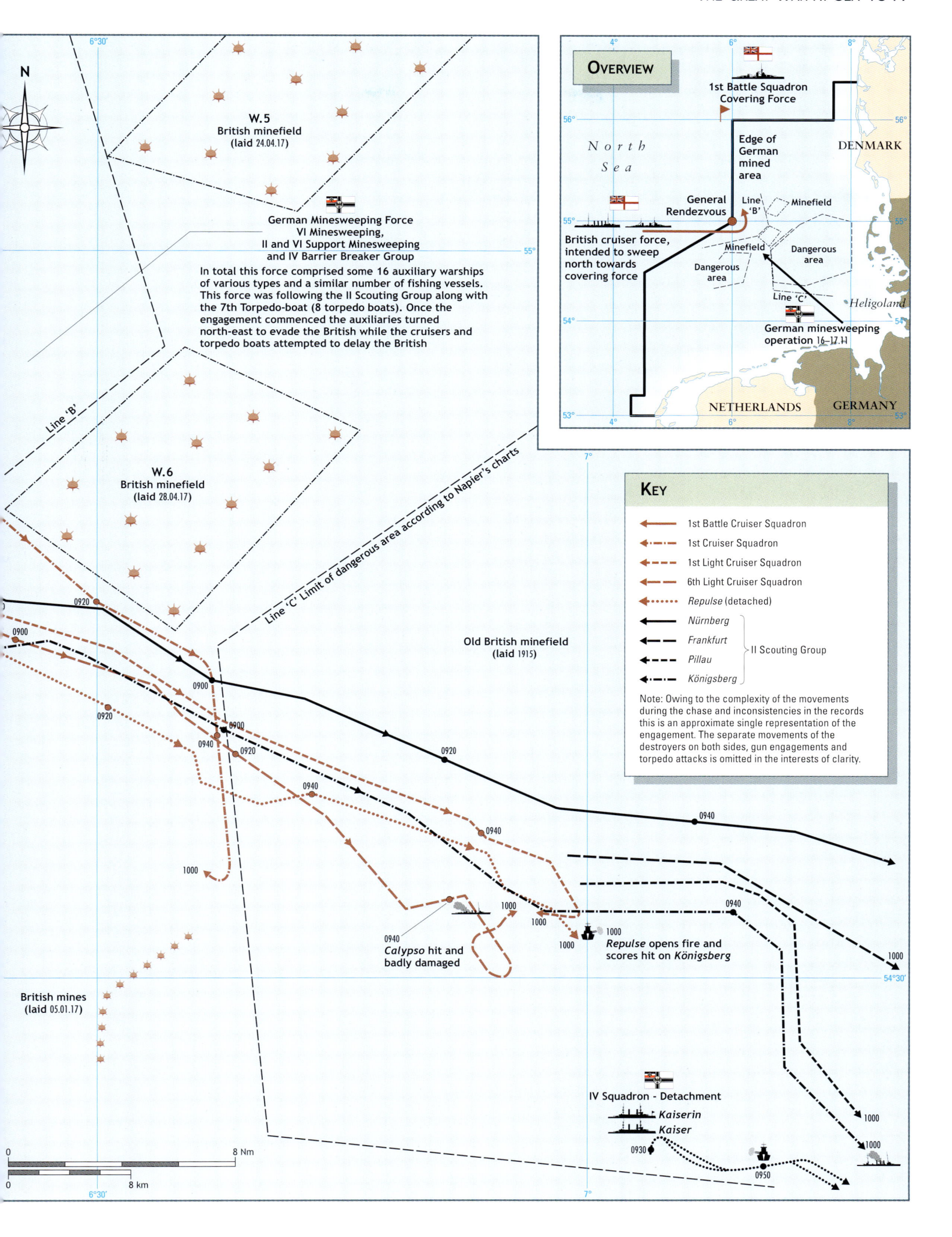

Overview

- 1st Battle Squadron Covering Force
- Edge of German mined area
- North Sea
- DENMARK
- General Rendezvous
- Line 'B'
- Minefield
- British cruiser force, intended to sweep north towards covering force
- Dangerous area
- Minefield
- Dangerous area
- Line 'C'
- Heligoland
- German minesweeping operation 16–17.11
- NETHERLANDS
- GERMANY

W.5 British minefield (laid 24.04.17)

German Minesweeping Force
VI Minesweeping, II and VI Support Minesweeping and IV Barrier Breaker Group

In total this force comprised some 16 auxiliary warships of various types and a similar number of fishing vessels. This force was following the II Scouting Group along with the 7th Torpedo-boat (8 torpedo boats). Once the engagement commenced the auxiliaries turned north-east to evade the British while the cruisers and torpedo boats attempted to delay the British

Line 'B'

W.6 British minefield (laid 28.04.17)

Line 'C' Limit of dangerous area according to Napier's charts

Old British minefield (laid 1915)

Key

- 1st Battle Cruiser Squadron
- 1st Cruiser Squadron
- 1st Light Cruiser Squadron
- 6th Light Cruiser Squadron
- *Repulse* (detached)
- *Nürnberg*
- *Frankfurt*
- *Pillau*
- *Königsberg*

II Scouting Group

Note: Owing to the complexity of the movements during the chase and inconsistencies in the records this is an approximate single representation of the engagement. The separate movements of the destroyers on both sides, gun engagements and torpedo attacks is omitted in the interests of clarity.

Calypso hit and badly damaged

Repulse opens fire and scores hit on *Königsberg*

British mines (laid 05.01.17)

IV Squadron – Detachment
- *Kaiserin*
- *Kaiser*

139

Allied Merchant Ship Losses, 1917–1918

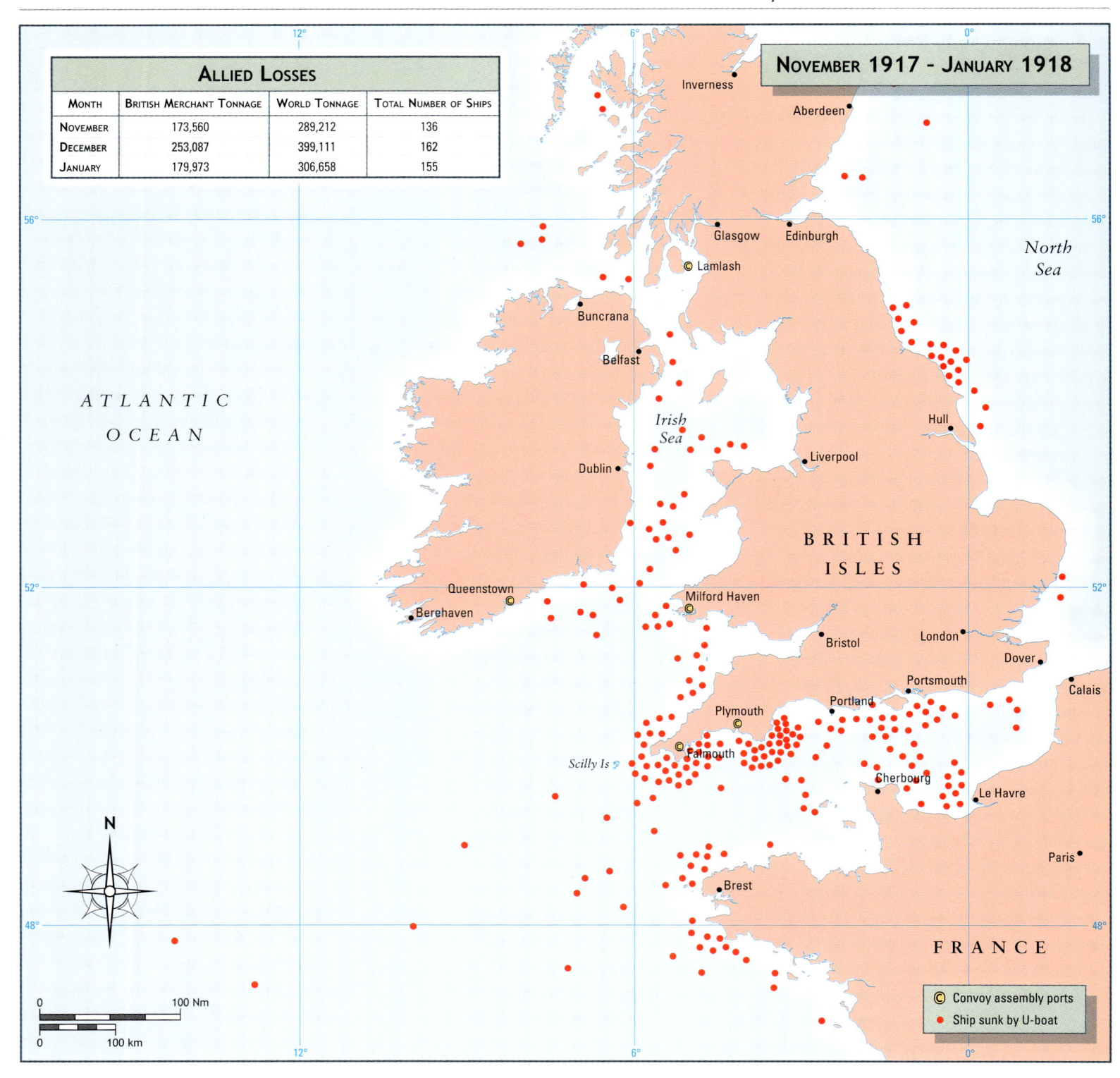

November 1917 - January 1918

Allied Losses

Month	British Merchant Tonnage	World Tonnage	Total Number of Ships
November	173,560	289,212	136
December	253,087	399,111	162
January	179,973	306,658	155

- Ⓒ Convoy assembly ports
- • Ship sunk by U-boat

By the end of 1917 the losses incurred throughout the year were beginning to a have serious effect on British imports and allied maritime traffic. Around half of all allied shipping lost during the war was sunk in 1917, around six million tons. From the British perspective, around three times as much shipping was sunk than replaced through new construction. The margin between the tonnage deemed necessary to ensure Britain remained supplied and that actually available decreased to around 600,000 tons. One consequence was the introduction of rationing during the winter, although the British never came close to experiencing food shortages as the Germans did.

Britain had not been defeated, but neither had the U-boat threat been negated. More U-boats became available, but the overall efficiency of the force dropped off. This was the result of experienced crews being lost and the increased maintenance requirements that resulted from the surge in operations. November was the least productive month for the Germans. Improved allied defences were beginning to have an effect and the ratio between merchant ships to U-boats lost decreased considerably – around twenty-one ships were sunk per U-boat lost, down from more than eighty-five in the first quarter. The widespread use of convoy shifted U-boat operations inshore where proportionally more single merchant ships could be found.

THE GREAT WAR AT SEA 1917

NORWEGIAN CONVOY ATTACK, 12 DECEMBER 1917

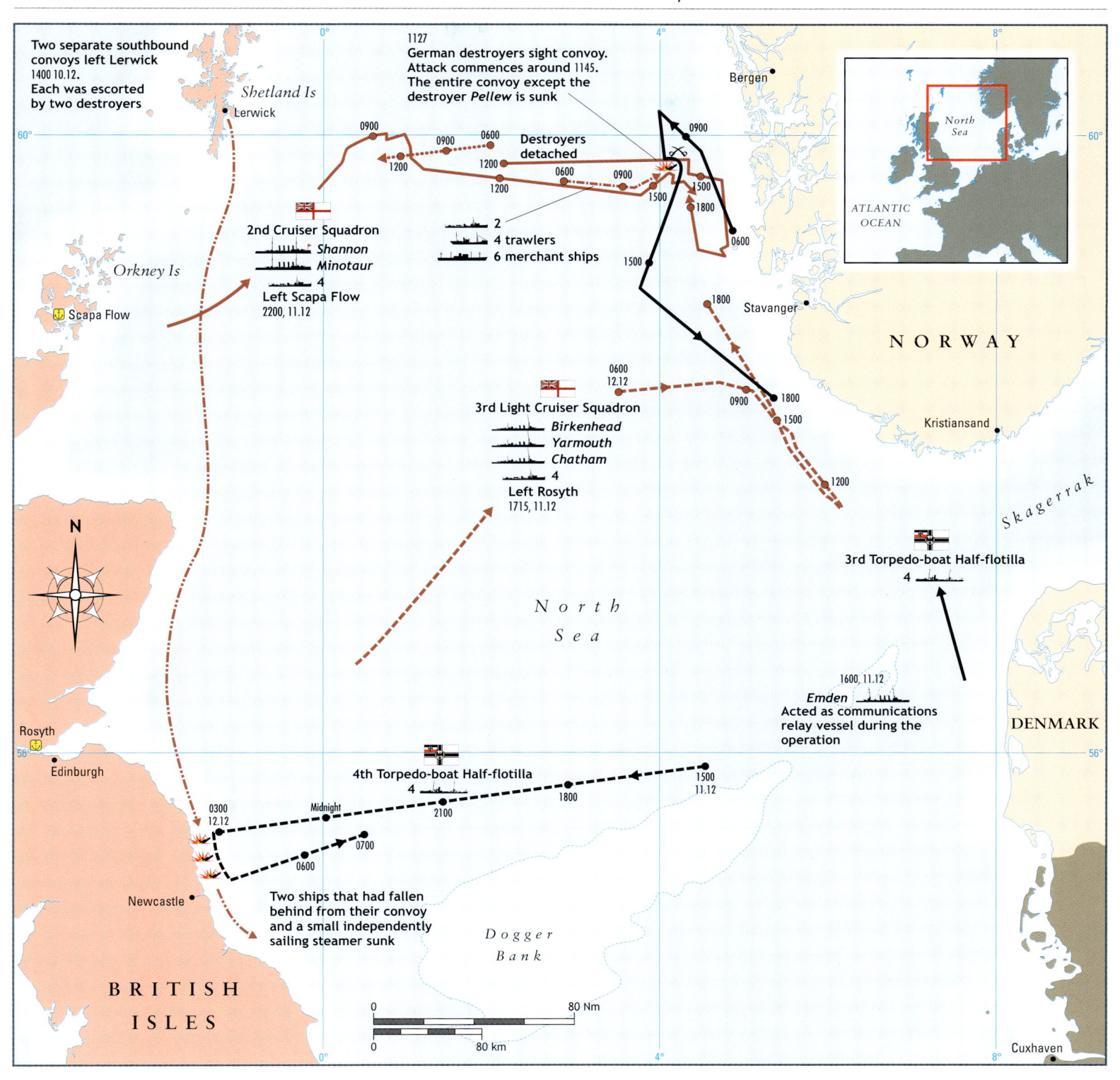

Buoyed by the success of the October raid against the Scandinavian convoy the Germans planned a second, more expansive, operation for mid-December. Instead of cruisers destroyers would be employed and for this purpose the 2nd Torpedo-Boat Flotilla was selected as it was equipped with the largest, most capable destroyers the Germans possessed. Rather than one, two simultaneous attacks would be conducted - one on the northern route and the other on the coastal convoy route along the east coast. Early on 11 December the force set out and at 4pm off the northeastern tip of Dogger Bank split into its two subdivisions while the flotilla's command vessel, the light cruiser *Emden*, remained behind.

On this occasion the British had no forewarning. Two cruiser squadrons were at sea in line with the practice of making periodic sweeps up to Bergen and exits to the German Bight. Based on wireless intercepts the German destroyers in the south erroneously expected to find a convoy from Rosyth, but in fact picked off stragglers from an east coast convoy. Because the British ships had become separated early on no German attack was registered and thus no warning was sent out. Thus the eastbound Scandinavia convoy was taken by complete surprise at noon on 12 December and annihilated. Although the 3rd Light Cruiser Squadron crossed the course of the retreating Germans bad weather saved the latter from being spotted.

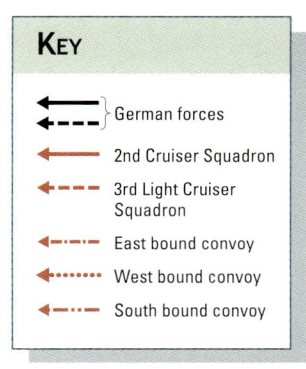

141

Naval Operations 1918

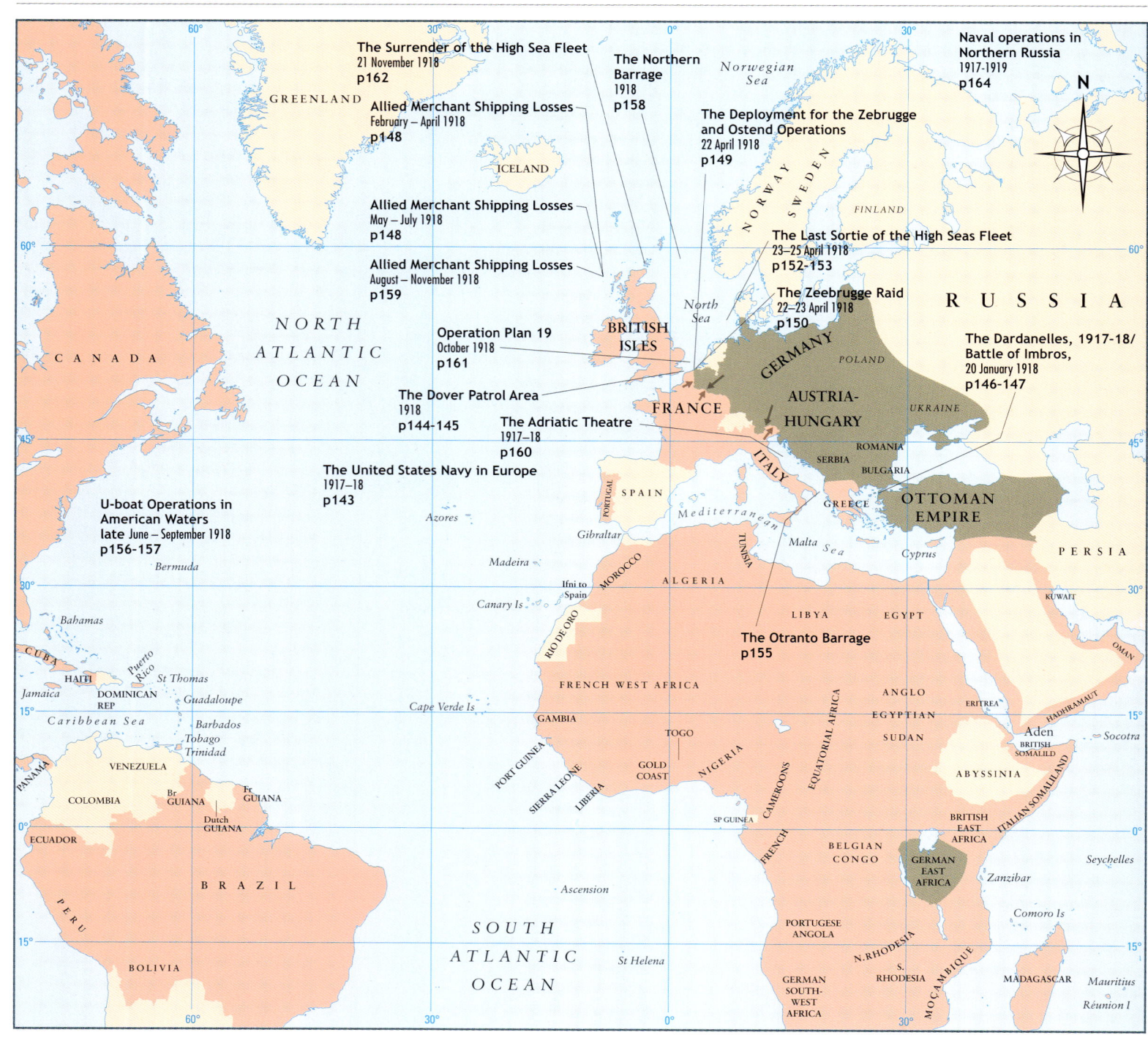

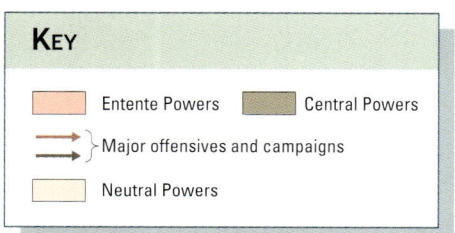

Although Allied losses to U-boats had been reduced to more manageable levels in late 1917, the threat to shipping in the Atlantic and Mediterranean still remained high, and a number of large-scale schemes were undertaken in 1918 to deal with this threat. Three defensive barrier systems were constructed across the North Sea, English Channel and Strait of Otranto to prevent the movements of U-boats between their bases and operational areas. The British also raided Ostend and Zeebrugge in an attempt to immobilise German forces in Flanders. None of these projects themselves would have a decisive effect on the U-boat campaign, but the sum total of allied activity and the strengthening of the convoy system were slowly grinding down the German effort.

The Germans attempted to counteract allied measures by means of pushing the U-boat campaign further out into the Atlantic, off West Africa and along the east coast of the United States. Although some local successes were achieved the numbers of sinkings of 1917 were never repeated and the threat to the British Isles receded. Crucially, the U-boat campaign never seriously threatened the build-up of American troops in France as had been promised by the *Admiralstab*. Now, inactivity became a root cause of unrest and a major issue for a number of the navies. Sailors of the Russian navy had played a significant part in the Russian revolutions of 1917 and, similarly, in the dying days of the war, the German and Austro-Hungarian fleets mutinied.

THE GREAT WAR AT SEA 1918

THE UNITED STATES NAVY IN EUROPE, 1917–18

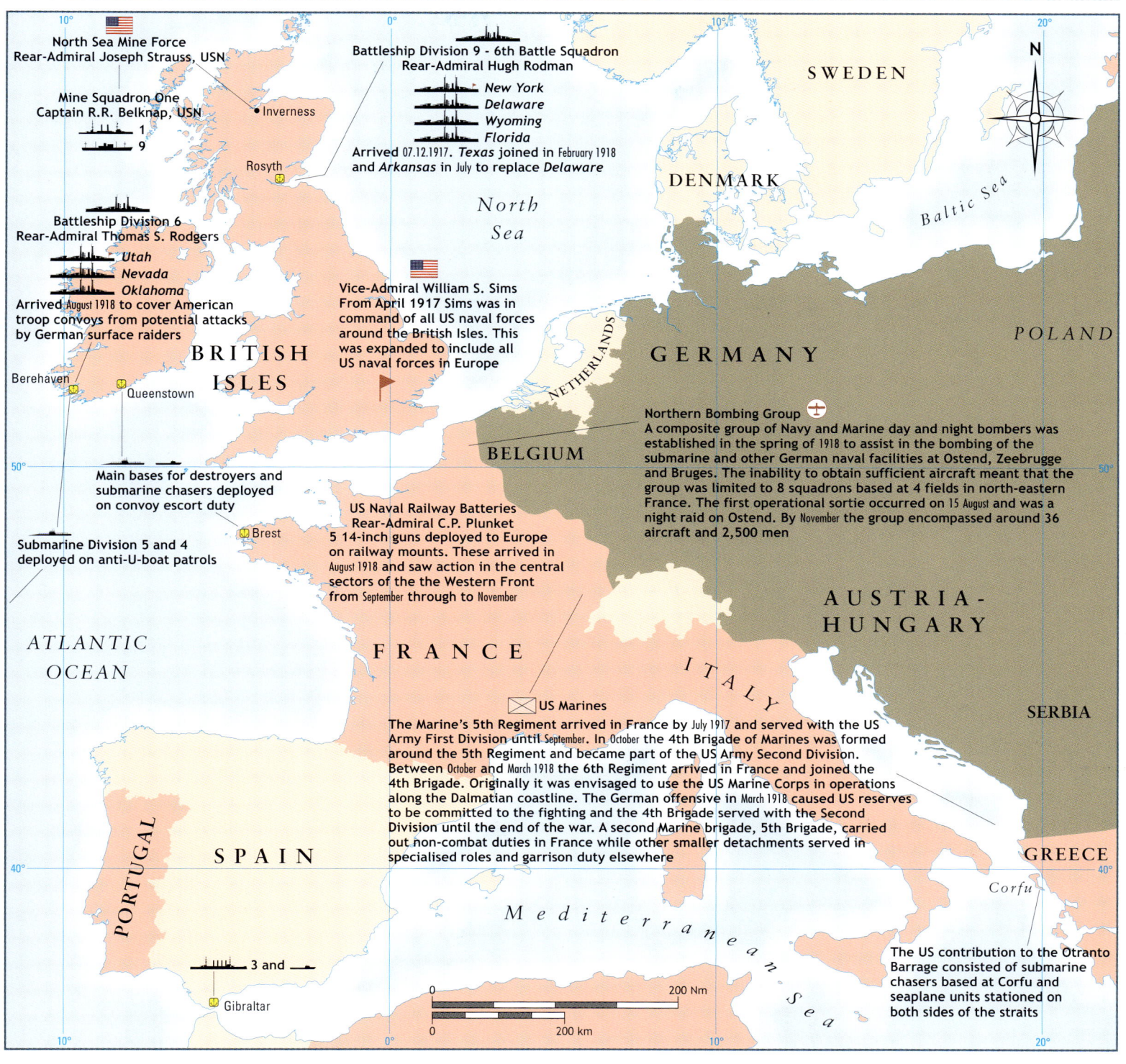

North Sea Mine Force
Rear-Admiral Joseph Strauss, USN

Mine Squadron One
Captain R.R. Belknap, USN

Battleship Division 9 - 6th Battle Squadron
Rear-Admiral Hugh Rodman
- New York
- Delaware
- Wyoming
- Florida

Arrived 07.12.1917. *Texas* joined in February 1918 and *Arkansas* in July to replace *Delaware*

Battleship Division 6
Rear-Admiral Thomas S. Rodgers
- Utah
- Nevada
- Oklahoma

Arrived August 1918 to cover American troop convoys from potential attacks by German surface raiders

Vice-Admiral William S. Sims
From April 1917 Sims was in command of all US naval forces around the British Isles. This was expanded to include all US naval forces in Europe

Main bases for destroyers and submarine chasers deployed on convoy escort duty

Submarine Division 5 and 4 deployed on anti-U-boat patrols

Northern Bombing Group
A composite group of Navy and Marine day and night bombers was established in the spring of 1918 to assist in the bombing of the submarine and other German naval facilities at Ostend, Zeebrugge and Bruges. The inability to obtain sufficient aircraft meant that the group was limited to 8 squadrons based at 4 fields in north-eastern France. The first operational sortie occurred on 15 August and was a night raid on Ostend. By November the group encompassed around 36 aircraft and 2,500 men

US Naval Railway Batteries
Rear-Admiral C.P. Plunket
5 14-inch guns deployed to Europe on railway mounts. These arrived in August 1918 and saw action in the central sectors of the the Western Front from September through to November

US Marines
The Marine's 5th Regiment arrived in France by July 1917 and served with the US Army First Division until September. In October the 4th Brigade of Marines was formed around the 5th Regiment and became part of the US Army Second Division. Between October and March 1918 the 6th Regiment arrived in France and joined the 4th Brigade. Originally it was envisaged to use the US Marine Corps in operations along the Dalmatian coastline. The German offensive in March 1918 caused US reserves to be committed to the fighting and the 4th Brigade served with the Second Division until the end of the war. A second Marine brigade, 5th Brigade, carried out non-combat duties in France while other smaller detachments served in specialised roles and garrison duty elsewhere

The US contribution to the Otranto Barrage consisted of submarine chasers based at Corfu and seaplane units stationed on both sides of the straits

---

AT THE OUTBREAK of war in Europe the United States possessed one of the largest fleets in the world. The United States Navy (USN) had built up a powerful force of battleships and was also at the forefront of replacing its pre-dreadnoughts with more modern dreadnought designs and adopting oil fuel. In other areas, however, the fleet was less developed and lacked sufficient numbers of modern cruisers and destroyers. Although the USN was divided into Atlantic, Pacific and Asiatic fleets, the majority of its forces were concentrated in the Atlantic. The principal role of the navy was the defence of the United States and over the previous decade Imperial Germany had been perceived as the most likely enemy. The USN was thus a relatively short-legged navy that had focused on operations in the western Atlantic and Caribbean.

As the war in Europe escalated and American interests were increasingly threatened, massive expansion of the USN was instigated. In 1916 a new Naval Act was passed that envisaged creating the world's largest navy, but before any significant progress had been made the US found itself at war. The most important American maritime contribution to the war effort lay in the huge shipbuilding programme, designed to replace the ever-increasing losses that the Allies suffered as a result of the U-boat campaign. The USN also provided large numbers of escorts for convoy protection and by the end of the war more than 300 American warships were operating in European waters.

THE DOVER PATROL AREA, 1918

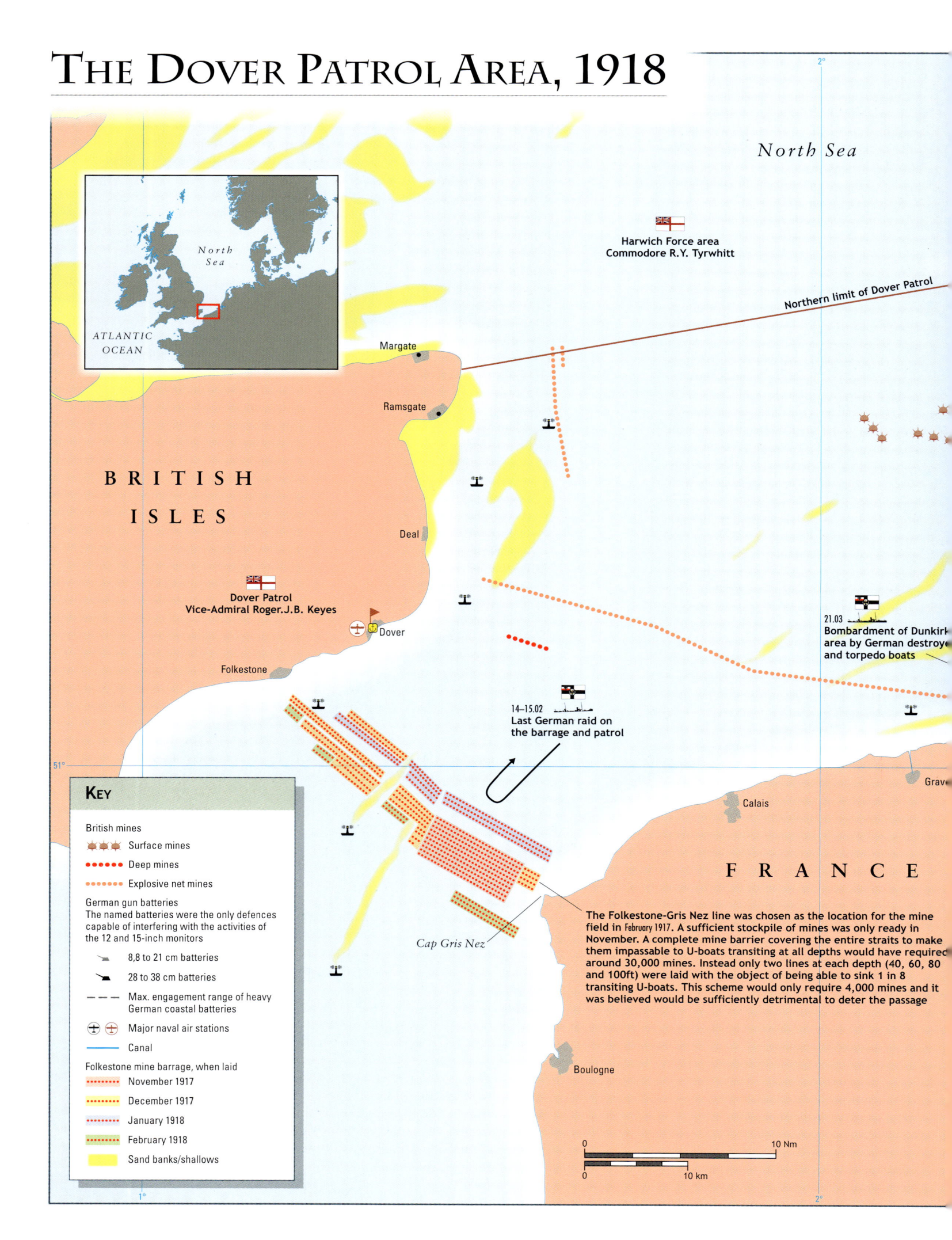

North Sea

Harwich Force area
Commodore R.Y. Tyrwhitt

Northern limit of Dover Patrol

Margate

Ramsgate

BRITISH ISLES

Deal

Dover Patrol
Vice-Admiral Roger.J.B. Keyes

Dover

Folkestone

21.03
Bombardment of Dunkirk area by German destroyers and torpedo boats

14–15.02
Last German raid on the barrage and patrol

Calais

Grav[elines]

FRANCE

Cap Gris Nez

The Folkestone-Gris Nez line was chosen as the location for the mine field in February 1917. A sufficient stockpile of mines was only ready in November. A complete mine barrier covering the entire straits to make them impassable to U-boats transiting at all depths would have required around 30,000 mines. Instead only two lines at each depth (40, 60, 80 and 100ft) were laid with the object of being able to sink 1 in 8 transiting U-boats. This scheme would only require 4,000 mines and it was believed would be sufficiently detrimental to deter the passage

Boulogne

KEY

British mines
- Surface mines
- Deep mines
- Explosive net mines

German gun batteries
The named batteries were the only defences capable of interfering with the activities of the 12 and 15-inch monitors
- 8,8 to 21 cm batteries
- 28 to 38 cm batteries
- Max. engagement range of heavy German coastal batteries
- Major naval air stations
- Canal

Folkestone mine barrage, when laid
- November 1917
- December 1917
- January 1918
- February 1918
- Sand banks/shallows

THE GREAT WAR AT SEA 1918

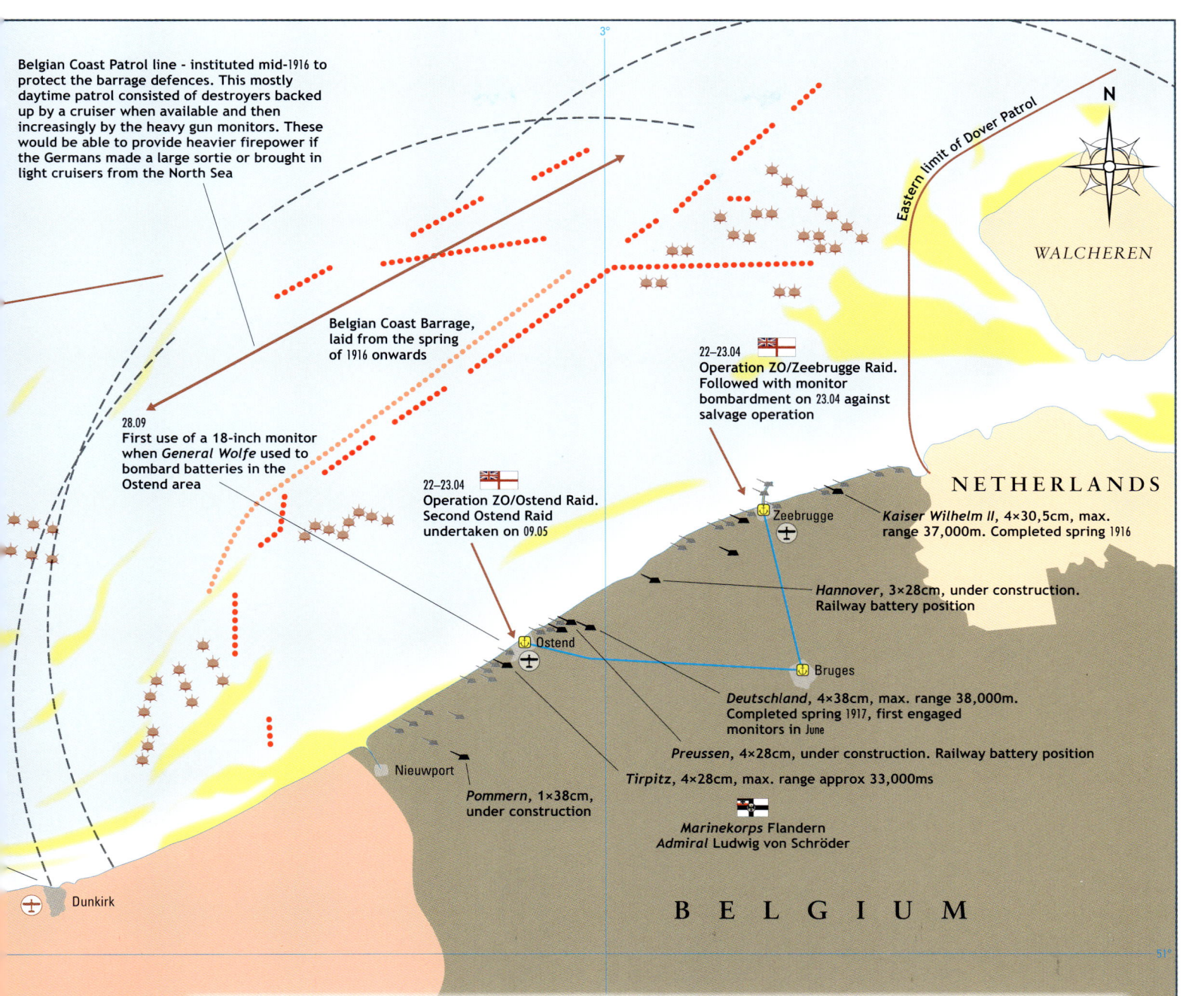

Belgian Coast Patrol line - instituted mid-1916 to protect the barrage defences. This mostly daytime patrol consisted of destroyers backed up by a cruiser when available and then increasingly by the heavy gun monitors. These would be able to provide heavier firepower if the Germans made a large sortie or brought in light cruisers from the North Sea

Belgian Coast Barrage, laid from the spring of 1916 onwards

28.09 First use of a 18-inch monitor when *General Wolfe* used to bombard batteries in the Ostend area

22–23.04 Operation ZO/Ostend Raid. Second Ostend Raid undertaken on 09.05

22–23.04 Operation ZO/Zeebrugge Raid. Followed with monitor bombardment on 23.04 against salvage operation

Eastern limit of Dover Patrol

WALCHEREN

NETHERLANDS

Kaiser Wilhelm II, 4×30,5cm, max. range 37,000m. Completed spring 1916

Hannover, 3×28cm, under construction. Railway battery position

Deutschland, 4×38cm, max. range 38,000m. Completed spring 1917, first engaged monitors in June

Preussen, 4×28cm, under construction. Railway battery position

Tirpitz, 4×28cm, max. range approx 33,000ms

Pommern, 1×38cm, under construction

Marinekorps Flandern *Admiral* Ludwig von Schröder

Zeebrugge

Ostend

Bruges

Nieuwport

Dunkirk

BELGIUM

By 1918, the sea area between the Dover Strait and the Flanders coast resembled something akin to a maritime extension of the western front, the years of war having generated a complex system of fixed defences supplementing the large number of light, coastal and auxiliary naval forces that both sides had amassed. Increasingly too aviation played an important role, and both sides waged a protracted campaign to secure air superiority over the southern North Sea. At this stage all British and German efforts focused on U-boat operations. After the huge shipping losses sustained in the Channel and off the east coast in 1917, the British strove to prevent U-boats from operating in these waters and, even, stop them from putting to sea at all. For the Germans it was essential to keep open those seaways used by the U-boats and to raid allied fixed defences.

A plan for a large, divisional-sized amphibious landing on the Flanders coast with the objective of capturing and destroying the U-boat bases had received considerable attention in 1917, but it was ultimately abandoned; the British did not have sufficient amphibious craft and German defences were formidable. Along the Belgian coast the *Marinekorps* Flanders had established fifty-six batteries mounting heavy, medium and anti-aircraft guns. Over half of these were of 6in to 15in calibre and, while only the new heavy guns could hit the monitors out to sea, the older emplacements were more than sufficient to inflict heavy casualties on any landing forces. Instead, the British tried to take the bases from the landward side and one of the objectives of the Passchendaele offensive in late 1917 was to drive the Germans from the coast.

The existing nets and moored mines in the Dover Strait never had the intended impact on U-boat transits and so in early 1917 it was decided to expand these by means of extensive mine barriers. However, the resources needed did not become available until the winter of 1917–18. Although a number of U-boats were lost in the Strait, British efforts never succeeded in negating the German threat, their fixed defences, bombardments, and even the raids on Zeebrugge and Ostend having only a marginal impact on the Flanders boats.

The Dardanelles, 1917–18

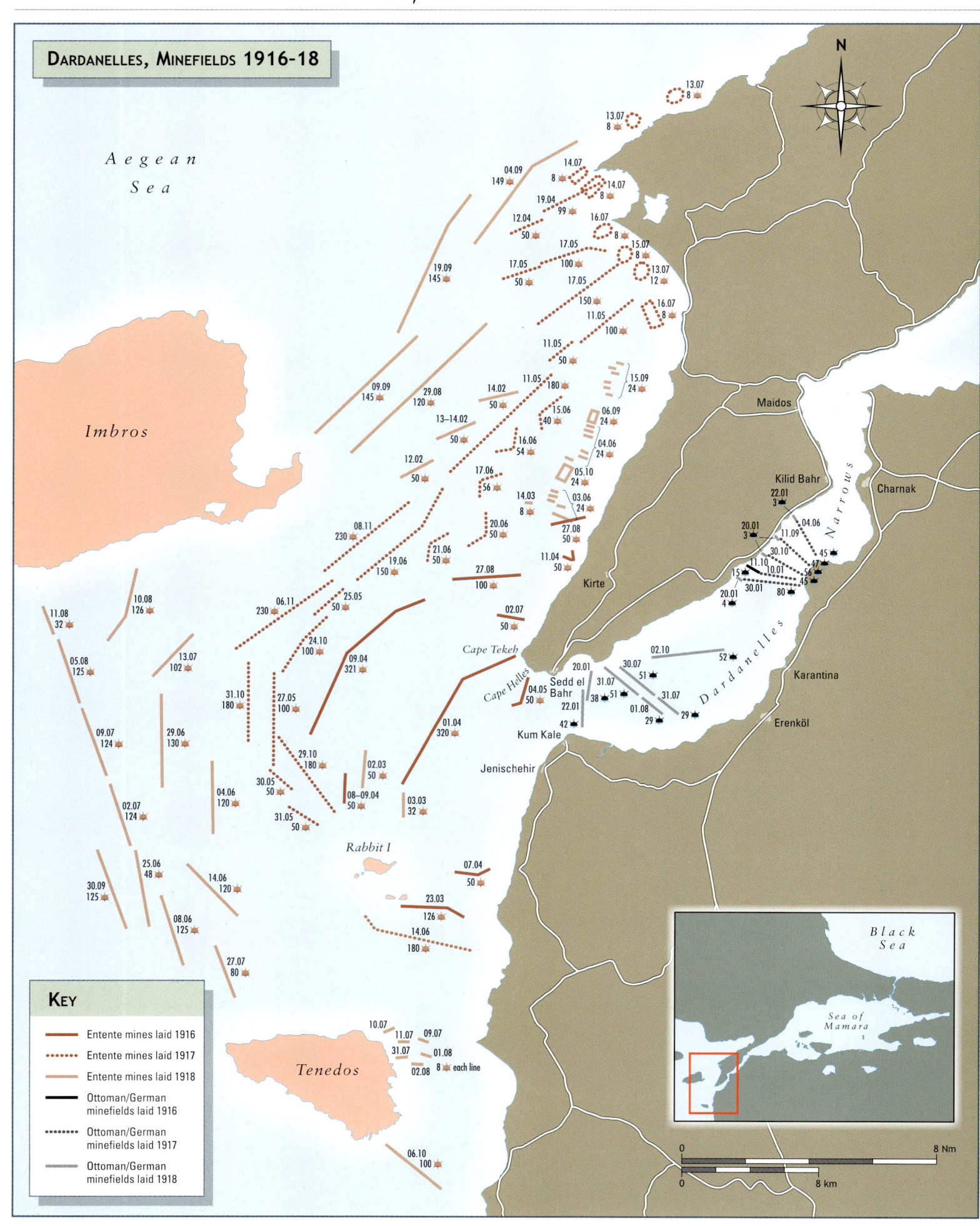

THE GREAT WAR AT SEA 1918

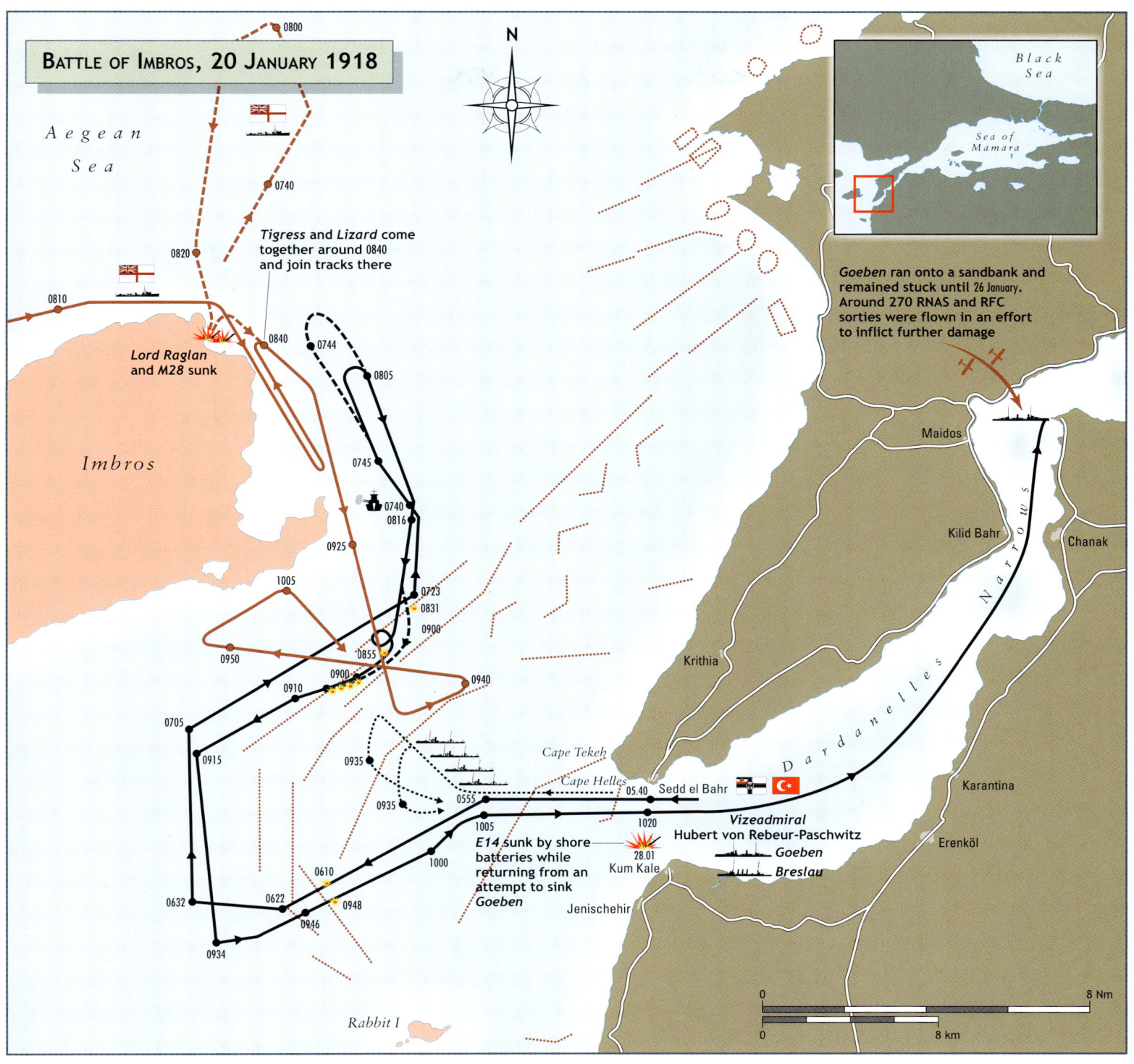

Battle of Imbros, 20 January 1918

The importance of the Dardanelles to allied strategy decreased after the evacuation of the expeditionary force in January 1916. It could not, however, be neglected as the opening of the Salonika front in the autumn of 1915 and the presence of an allied force in Northern Greece meant that the security of the maritime communications through the Aegean needed to be safeguarded. The *Goeben* and *Breslau* remained powerful units and while they spent much of their time in the Black Sea there was always the potential for them to break out from the Dardanelles and wreak havoc in the Aegean. The British Aegean squadron was hardly powerful and its heavy units, usually a small number of pre-dreadnought battleships, were slower than the German ships, and maintaining a stronger force in the area was not an option given the multitude of demands elsewhere. Instead, the Dardanelles was to be blockaded by extensive minefields backed up by destroyers. Monitors provided some heavier firepower and occasionally harassed Turkish positions.

In September 1917 *Vizeadmiral* Rebeur-Paschwitz took command of the Ottoman-German naval forces, and with the cessation of hostilities on the eastern front in December the Black Sea passed under Central Power control. Consequently, he envisaged a raid into the Aegean against the various allied island bases, primarily to boost Turkish morale after setbacks in Palestine. Based on observations, he reckoned that the allied minefields could be avoided, but in fact not all allied minelaying had been recorded. The breakout on 21 January caught the British by surprise – Aegean Squadron battleships were distributed across the theatre – and a number of vessels were sunk. However, after Imbros had been attacked *Breslau* took a number of mine hits and foundered, while *Goeben* too was damaged, forcing Rebeur-Paschwitz to abandon the rest of the operation.

Key

- ← *Goeben* – Yavûz Sultân Selîm in Ottoman service
- ←--- *Breslau* – Midilli in Ottoman Service
- ←···· Ottoman destroyers
- ← *Tigress*
- ←--- *Lizard*
- ✦ Mine explosions
- ······ Allied minefields laid 1916–17

Allied Merchant Shipping Losses, 1918

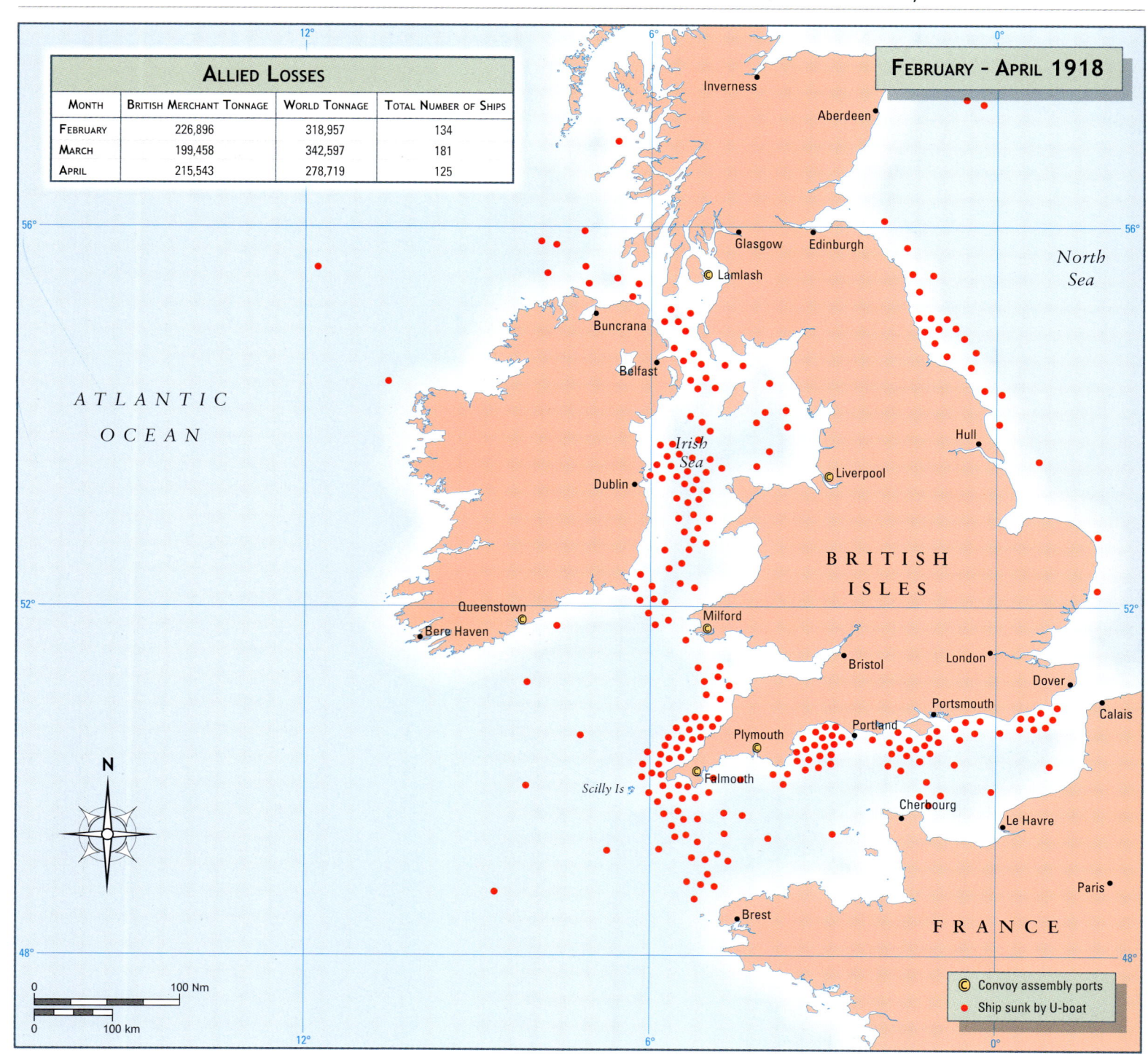

February – April 1918

Allied Losses			
Month	British Merchant Tonnage	World Tonnage	Total Number of Ships
February	226,896	318,957	134
March	199,458	342,597	181
April	215,543	278,719	125

- Ⓒ Convoy assembly ports
- ● Ship sunk by U-boat

BOTH SIDES UNDERSTOOD that the success or otherwise of the U-boat campaign would be crucial to determining the events on the Western Front and in the war in 1918. As a result more resources were poured into the campaign by both sides. The Imperial Navy at last did what it should have done far earlier in the war and prioritised U-boat construction, but Germany now lacked the resources to undertake a programme of mass submarine construction, and there was a shortage of manpower for the shipyards. Throughout early 1918 the army was reluctant to transfer manpower from military to naval production, and with German hopes focused on the Ludendorff Offensive in March the army had little interest in transferring resources for longer-term aims.

As the German offensive stalled, the emphasis of the U-boat campaign gradually shifted rom starving Britain into submission towards preventing a build up of American military power in France. With more long-range boats becoming available the war zone off West Africa was increased.

By 1918 around 90 per cent of transatlantic shipping and around half of all British maritime trade sailed in convoy, and the vast majority of allied ships lost to U-boat attacks were solitary unescorted vessels. Convoy was still seen as primarily a defensive tool, and more active measures were needed to defeat the U-boat menace in the North Sea and Mediterranean; consequently, the Allies now invested heavily in new mine barriers and minelaying in enemy waters.

The Deployment for the Zeebrugge and Ostend Operations, 22 April 1918

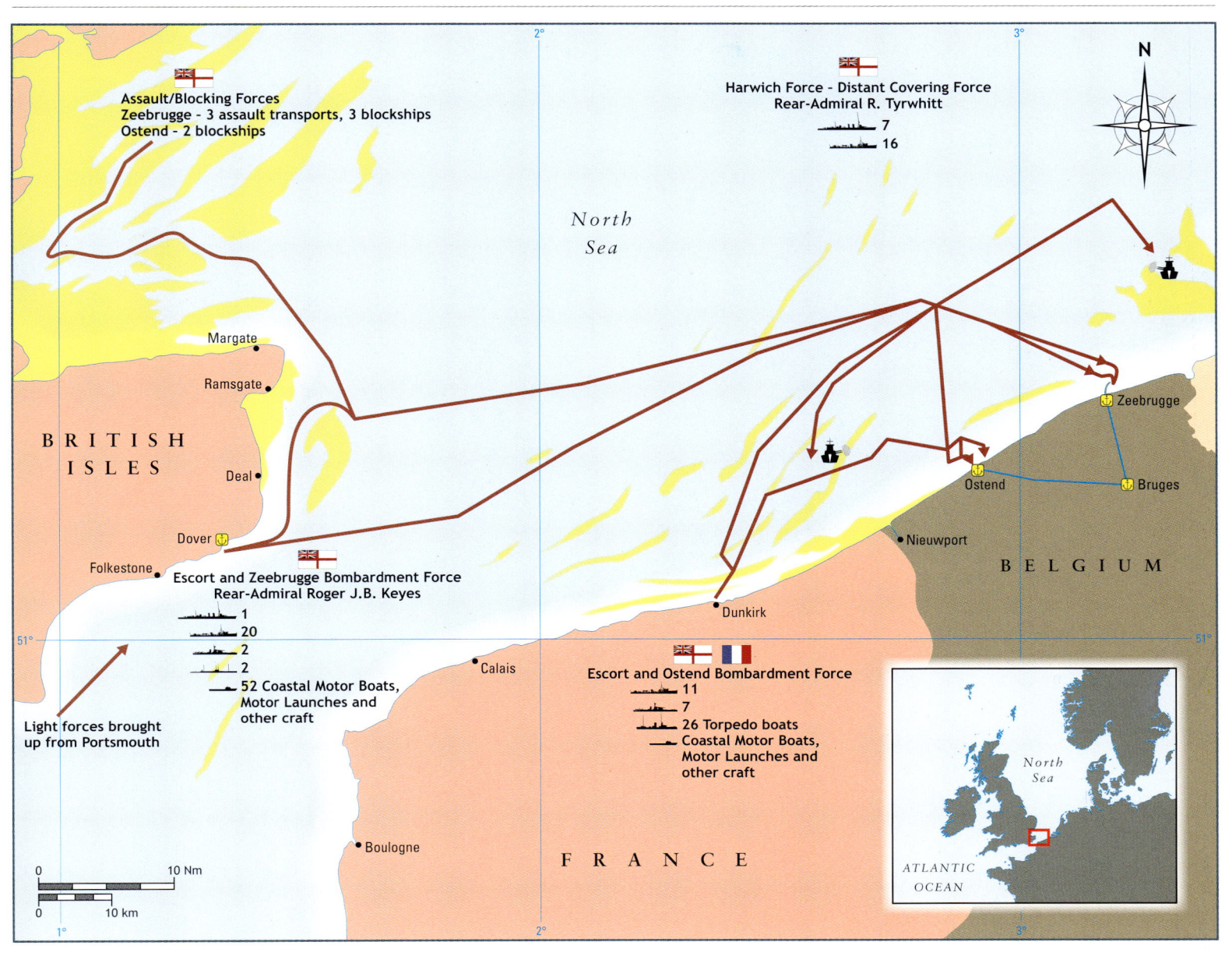

Schemes to immobilise the Flanders-based U-boats by means of destroying or blocking their exits into the North Sea dated back to the end of 1915. The main German base was at Bruges where massive concrete pens were constructed to protect U-boats from air attacks and the location that far inland also made bombardments by British monitors impractical. The principal route taken by the U-boats was via the canal to Zeebrugge, but Ostend was also connected by means of a number of smaller canals and served as a smaller base. When the High Sea Fleet began to send sizeable parts of its torpedo boat force to Flanders in the autumn of 1916 these were based at Bruges alongside the small surface force attached to the *Marinekorps*.

Over the years the issue of undertaking operations to block the ports caused considerable debate between the Admiralty and the commands at Dover and Harwich. Although the canal exit at Zeebrugge was susceptible to being blocked, the complexity and risk of any operation would be considerable. It was also far from clear that such an operation would have any lasting effect. In addition, until 1917 the British had little interest in wrecking the ports that would be vital to supporting the army if a breakthrough on the Western Front was attained.

The failure of the Third Ypres offensive in late 1917 reignited the interest in a naval operation for though anti-U-boat measures were beginning to show results the threat remained considerable. Rear-Admiral Keyes undertook the detailed planning, first as Director of Plans at the Admiralty and then when in command of the Dover Patrol from January 1918. His scheme envisaged attacking Ostend and Zeebrugge simultaneously with the objective of sinking old cruisers filled with cement as blockships in the canal exits.

Approval for the scheme was given in late February, but given the extensive preparations that were necessary it was April before the assault force was ready. A first attempt was undertaken on the night of 11–12 April but abandoned when the wind turned unfavourable. Rather than waiting another month for a moonless night Keyes selected 22 April for the attack.

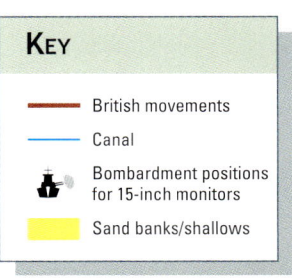

The Zeebrugge Raid, 22–23 April 1918

Zeebrugge was a formidable target to assault. While there were more heavy gun batteries in the Ostend area, Zeebrugge itself was more heavily defended and, crucially, a mole covered the direct access to the lock and canal system. Gun batteries on its tip could easily defeat any attempt to sink blockships in the approach to the lock and so taking out the defences on the mole was of fundamental importance

Rear-Admiral Keyes's plan emphasised surprise and speed. First, an assault force of around 900 marines and sailors would be landed on the mole to destroy the German guns. Most of this force would be carried in *Vindictive*, an obsolete protected cruiser, with two ferries assisting her into position and keeping her against the mole. The force needed to be landed as close to the guns as possible otherwise it might incur heavy casualties while attempting to fight its way through the German positions. *Vindictive* was far from an ideal assault ship, but Keyes did not want to use more specialised landing vessels which would be much slower.

To prevent reinforcements reaching the garrison on the mole, two old submarines were fitted with huge explosive charges that were to be detonated under the railway viaduct. The heavy German batteries would be neutralised by preliminary monitor bombardments, and similar bombardments would be conducted in the weeks prior to the operation to make them seem routine. To maintain surprise for as long as possible, and cause confusion, smoke screens were to be spread across the target.

On the night of the attack the plan very nearly succeeded. At around 11pm mist and rain, combined with smoke, covered *Vindictive*'s approach. However, just before midnight, and just short of the target, the wind went round and revealed the force to the Germans who promptly opened fire. *Vindictive* increased speed and avoided being destroyed but as a result landed the assault force beyond the guns on the end of the mole and was poorly positioned to provide covering fire for the assault force as it fought its way back east.

With the German guns remaining operational, the blockships came under heavy fire and *Thetis* ran aground short of the canal lock. The two others succeeded in reaching the canal entrance, but were not sunk in the allocated positions. By 1am the operation was over and *Vindictive* was towed away by *Daffodil*. A destroyer and two motor launches were sunk while well over 500 marines and sailors were killed or wounded. German casualties were negligible.

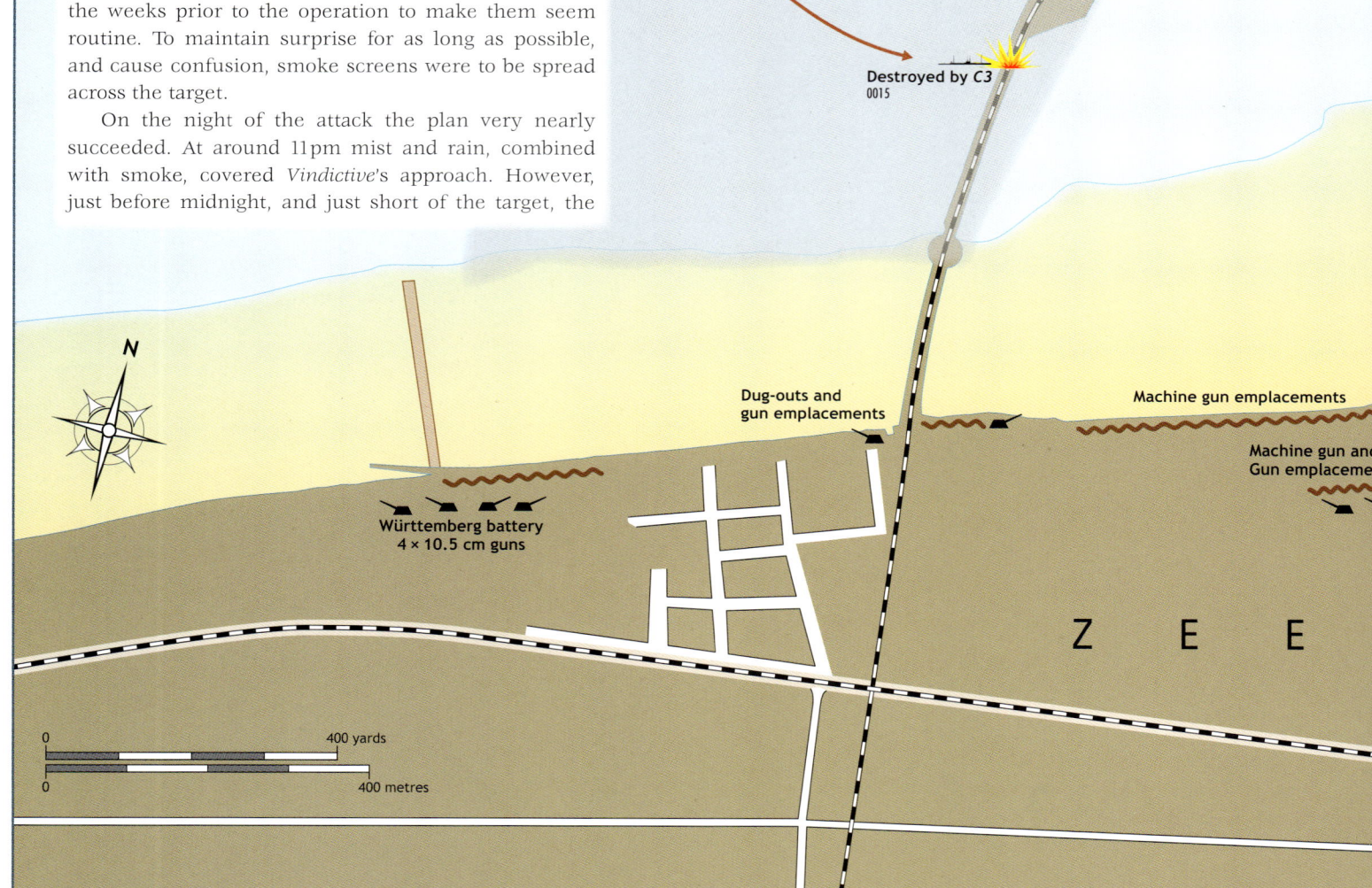

THE GREAT WAR AT SEA 1918

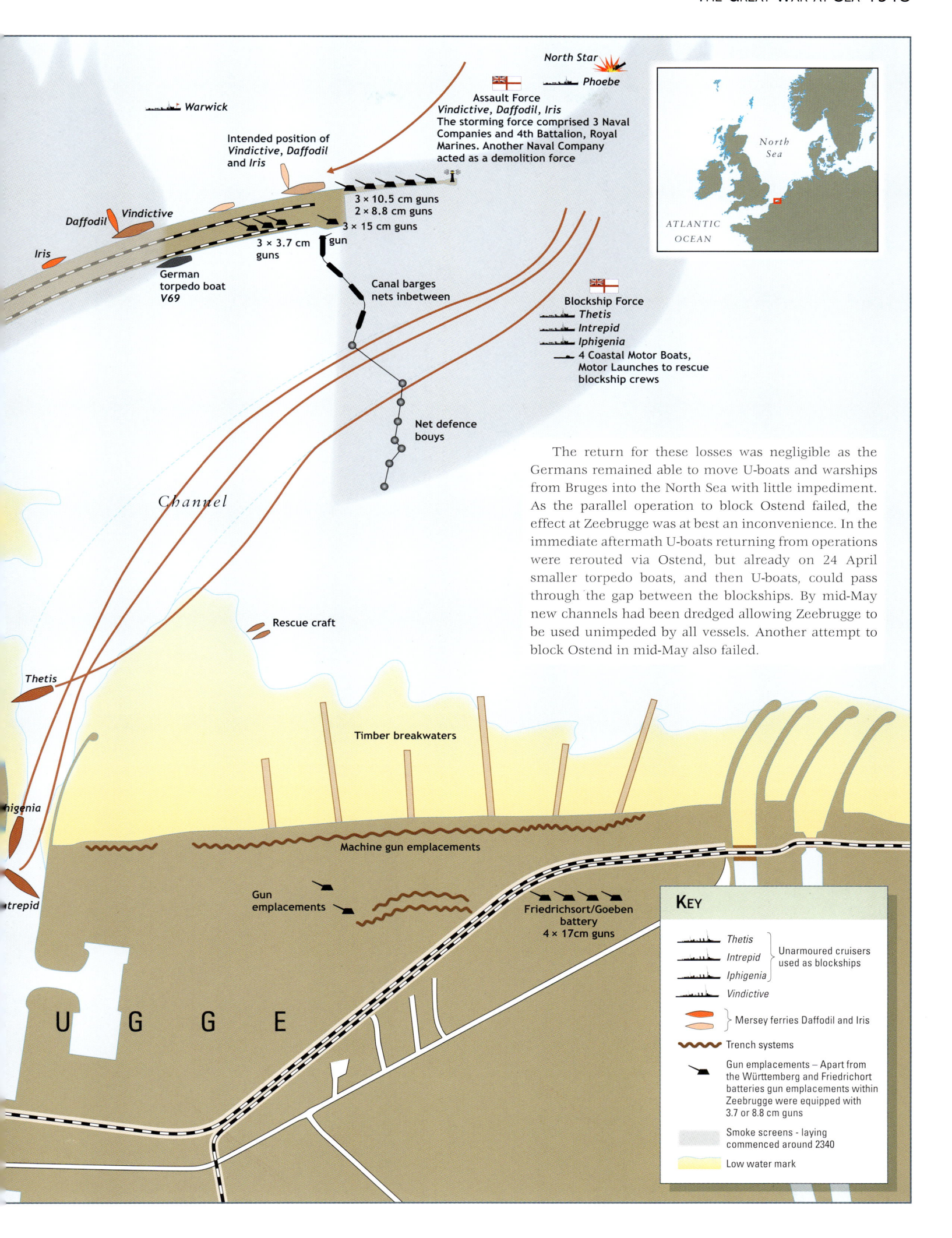

North Star
Phoebe

Warwick

Assault Force
Vindictive, Daffodil, Iris
The storming force comprised 3 Naval
Companies and 4th Battalion, Royal
Marines. Another Naval Company
acted as a demolition force

Intended position of
Vindictive, Daffodil
and Iris

3 × 10.5 cm guns
2 × 8.8 cm guns
3 × 15 cm guns

Daffodil Vindictive

Iris

3 × 3.7 cm
guns
gun

German
torpedo boat
V69

Canal barges
nets inbetween

Blockship Force
Thetis
Intrepid
Iphigenia
4 Coastal Motor Boats,
Motor Launches to rescue
blockship crews

Net defence
bouys

North Sea

ATLANTIC OCEAN

Channel

The return for these losses was negligible as the Germans remained able to move U-boats and warships from Bruges into the North Sea with little impediment. As the parallel operation to block Ostend failed, the effect at Zeebrugge was at best an inconvenience. In the immediate aftermath U-boats returning from operations were rerouted via Ostend, but already on 24 April smaller torpedo boats, and then U-boats, could pass through the gap between the blockships. By mid-May new channels had been dredged allowing Zeebrugge to be used unimpeded by all vessels. Another attempt to block Ostend in mid-May also failed.

Rescue craft

Thetis

Timber breakwaters

Iphigenia

Machine gun emplacements

Intrepid

Gun
emplacements

Friedrichsort/Goeben
battery
4 × 17cm guns

UGGE

KEY

Thetis
Intrepid   Unarmoured cruisers
Iphigenia   used as blockships
Vindictive

Mersey ferries Daffodil and Iris

Trench systems

Gun emplacements – Apart from
the Württemberg and Friedrichort
batteries gun emplacements within
Zeebrugge were equipped with
3.7 or 8.8 cm guns

Smoke screens - laying
commenced around 2340

Low water mark

151

The Last Sortie of the High Sea Fleet, 23–25 April 1918

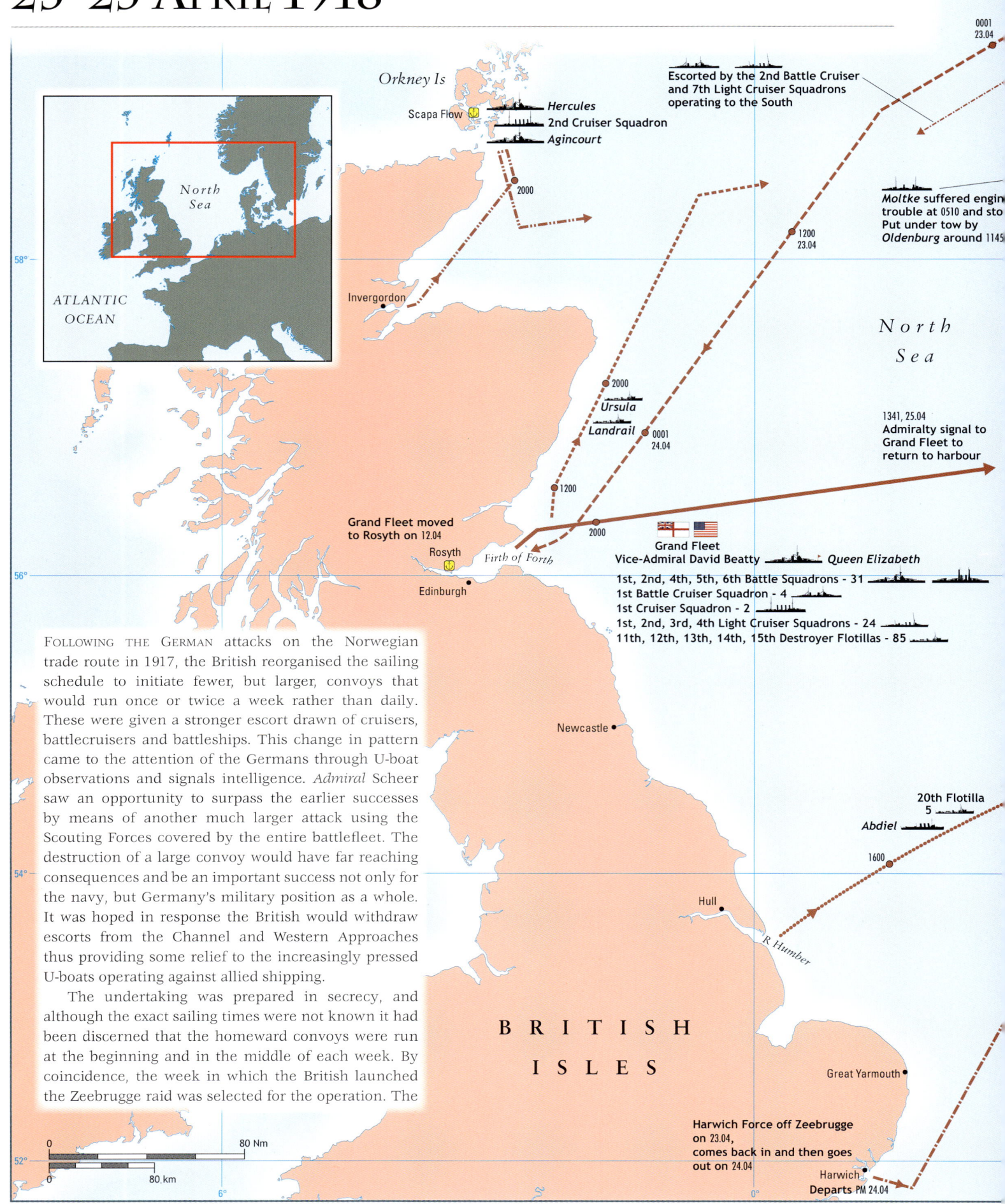

Escorted by the 2nd Battle Cruiser and 7th Light Cruiser Squadrons operating to the South

0001 23.04

Moltke suffered engine trouble at 0510 and sto Put under tow by *Oldenburg* around 1145

Orkney Is
Scapa Flow — *Hercules* / 2nd Cruiser Squadron / *Agincourt*
2000

1200 23.04

North Sea

Invergordon

2000
Ursula
Landrail 0001 24.04

1341, 25.04 Admiralty signal to Grand Fleet to return to harbour

1200

Grand Fleet moved to Rosyth on 12.04
Rosyth
Firth of Forth
Edinburgh

2000
Grand Fleet
Vice-Admiral David Beatty — *Queen Elizabeth*
1st, 2nd, 4th, 5th, 6th Battle Squadrons - 31
1st Battle Cruiser Squadron - 4
1st Cruiser Squadron - 2
1st, 2nd, 3rd, 4th Light Cruiser Squadrons - 24
11th, 12th, 13th, 14th, 15th Destroyer Flotillas - 85

Newcastle

20th Flotilla 5
Abdiel
1600

Hull
R Humber

BRITISH ISLES

Great Yarmouth

Harwich Force off Zeebrugge on 23.04, comes back in and then goes out on 24.04
Harwich Departs PM 24.04

Following the German attacks on the Norwegian trade route in 1917, the British reorganised the sailing schedule to initiate fewer, but larger, convoys that would run once or twice a week rather than daily. These were given a stronger escort drawn of cruisers, battlecruisers and battleships. This change in pattern came to the attention of the Germans through U-boat observations and signals intelligence. *Admiral* Scheer saw an opportunity to surpass the earlier successes by means of another much larger attack using the Scouting Forces covered by the entire battlefleet. The destruction of a large convoy would have far reaching consequences and be an important success not only for the navy, but Germany's military position as a whole. It was hoped in response the British would withdraw escorts from the Channel and Western Approaches thus providing some relief to the increasingly pressed U-boats operating against allied shipping.

The undertaking was prepared in secrecy, and although the exact sailing times were not known it had been discerned that the homeward convoys were run at the beginning and in the middle of each week. By coincidence, the week in which the British launched the Zeebrugge raid was selected for the operation. The

The Great War at Sea 1918

German force was assembled on 22 April under the guise of a training exercise and left port around 7am the next day, but progress across the heavily mined Heligoland Bight was slowed owing to fog. By the evening the boundary of the mined area was passed and the escorting minesweepers returned to port. As the Germans increasingly resorted to radio silence the British had no forewarning of the sortie. The submarine *J6* did spot some elements of the German force, but assumed these were British ships undertaking a mining operation.

Early on 24 April the Admiralty suspected a German operation was taking place and assumed it would be a raid against the southeast coast and in anticipation the Harwich Force was sent back to sea. Little threat to the Norwegian route was suspected so the outward convoy was not delayed. Meanwhile, the battlecruiser *Moltke* had suffered serious engine damage and fell back from Hipper's force before coming to a stop. This forced Hipper to turn back before Scheer ordered the battleship *Oldenburg* to take the *Moltke* under tow and turn back. Transmissions throughout the morning alerted the British that the High Sea Fleet was far further north than anticipated. A small force put to sea to cover the Orkneys while the 2nd Battle Cruiser Squadron now covered the outward convoy. Beatty took the Grand Fleet out in the afternoon to intercept the Germans.

Hipper's second foray northwards also found no traffic so he too turned south to catch up with Scheer. During the afternoon intelligence confirmed the British convoy had passed a day earlier. Scheer's passage was limited by the speed at which *Moltke* could be towed safely and by dawn on 25 April the whole German force had reunited and prepared to pass through the minefield with the assistance of minesweepers. A minesweeper struck a mine and sank and in the evening *Moltke*, now able to operate on her own, was attacked and damaged by the British submarine *E42*. This would be the last sortie the High Sea Fleet undertook and it was one of its longest both in terms of duration and reach.

Key

- Grand Fleet
- Homeward convoy
- Outward convoy
- Harwich Force
- 2nd Battle Cruiser and 7th Light Cruiser Squadrons
- 2nd Cruiser Squadron
- 20th Destroyer Flotilla
- Initial position of British submarine patrol
- High Sea Fleet
- Scouting Forces

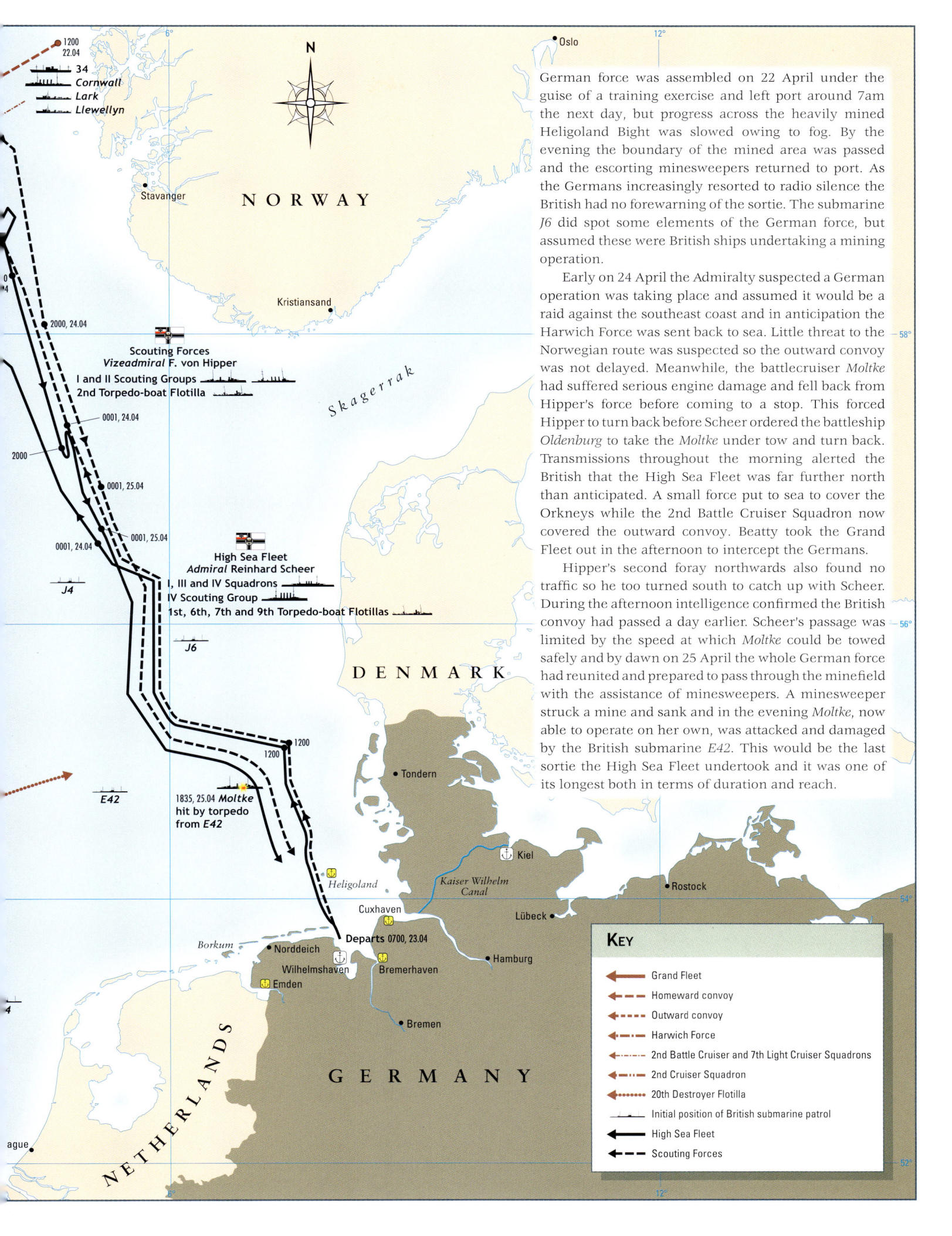

Allied Merchant Shipping Losses, 1918

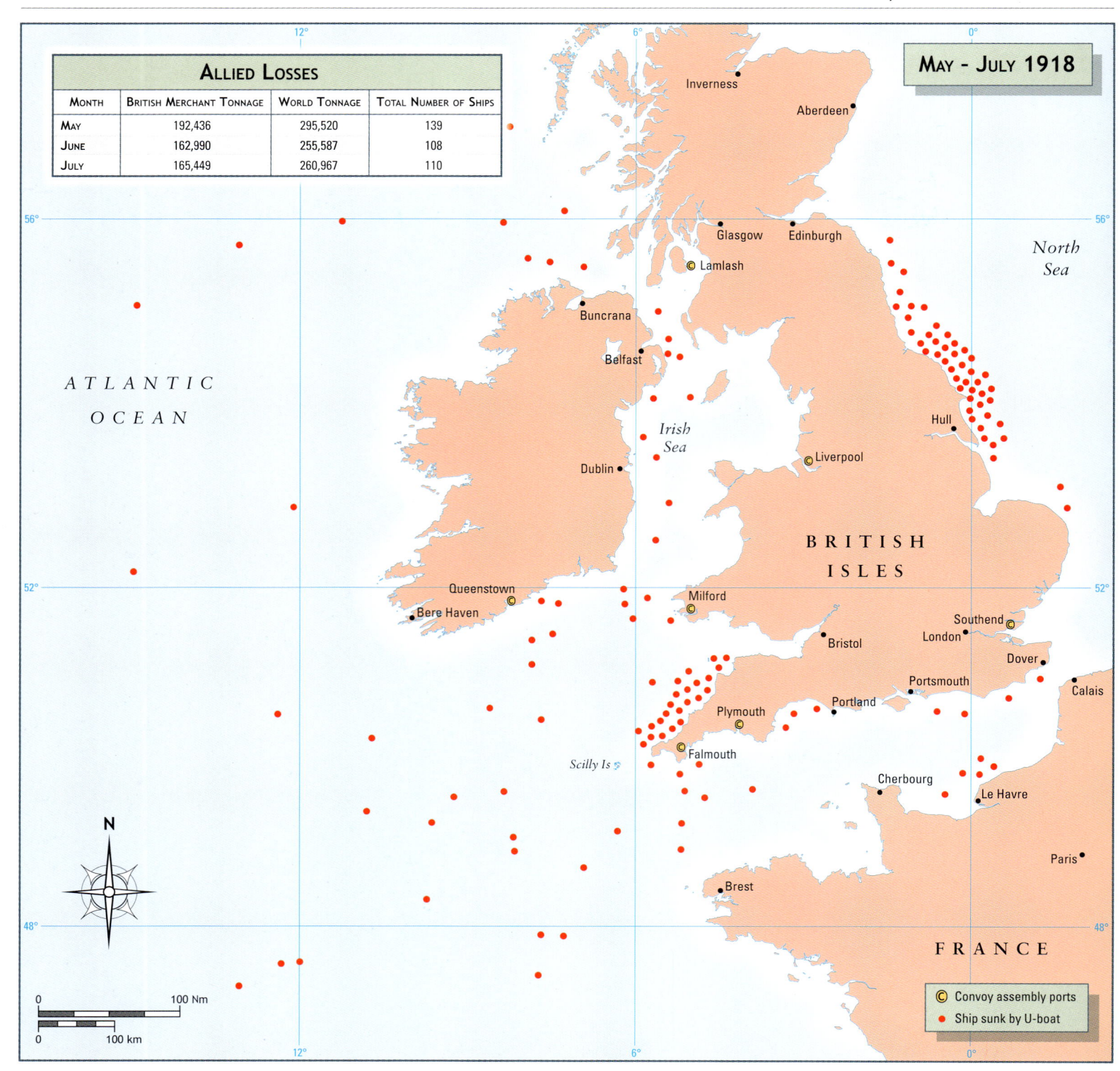

Allied Losses

Month	British Merchant Tonnage	World Tonnage	Total Number of Ships
May	192,436	295,520	139
June	162,990	255,587	108
July	165,449	260,967	110

May - July 1918

- Convoy assembly ports
- Ship sunk by U-boat

Throughout the first half of 1918 allied shipping losses remained constant at around 300,000 tons per month. Though they were far from insignificant, the U-boat threat was being contained; it was not, however, being defeated. In the late spring British domestic construction once again exceeded monthly sinkings, but the overall losses could not be replaced and American yards were key to replacing lost allied tonnage.

The size of the U-boat force, too, remained constant with new boats cancelling out the losses. However, the downward trend in U-boat productivity continued. The number of U-boats at sea each day declined and though losses might be replaced, both crews and boats were becoming increasingly exhausted and there was little likelihood inflicting a decisive blow to allied shipping. The U-boat campaign had become another attritional campaign.

The Germans had found no way of countering the oceanic convoys, and so the focus moved to coastal waters. Here the British could make greater use of smaller escort craft so that the U-boats had to rely on long-range torpedo attacks – reducing the number of targets that could be sunk per patrol. Despite increases to the auxiliary patrol, more escort construction and the transfer of escorts from the Grand Fleet, there were never enough to fulfil all requirements. Coastal convoys were brought into widespread use in June.

THE GREAT WAR AT SEA 1918

THE OTRANTO BARRAGE, 1918

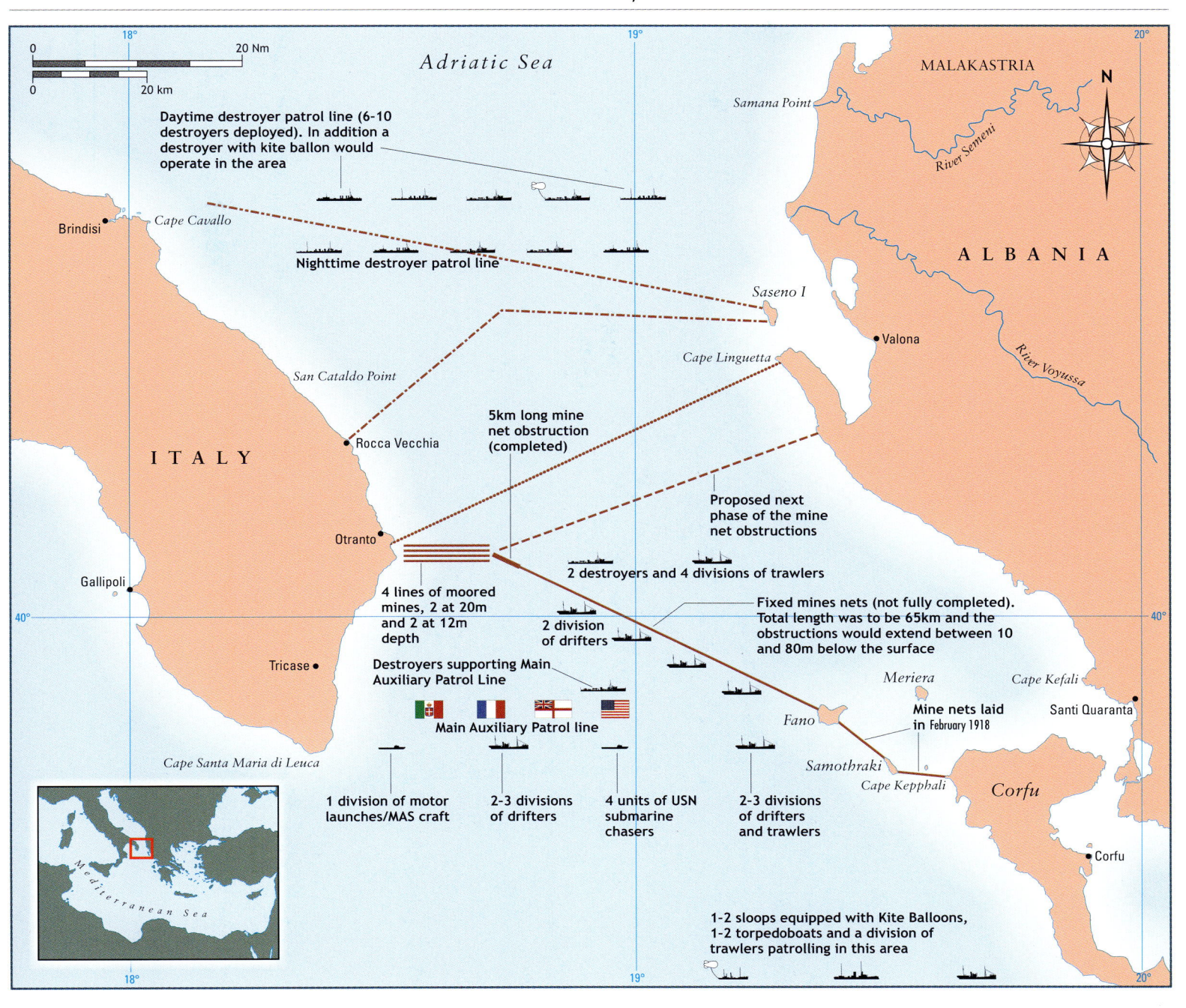

Map annotations

- Daytime destroyer patrol line (6-10 destroyers deployed). In addition a destroyer with kite ballon would operate in the area
- Nighttime destroyer patrol line
- 5km long mine net obstruction (completed)
- Proposed next phase of the mine net obstructions
- 2 destroyers and 4 divisions of trawlers
- 4 lines of moored mines, 2 at 20m and 2 at 12m depth
- 2 division of drifters
- Fixed mines nets (not fully completed). Total length was to be 65km and the obstructions would extend between 10 and 80m below the surface
- Destroyers supporting Main Auxiliary Patrol Line
- Main Auxiliary Patrol line
- Mine nets laid in February 1918
- 1 division of motor launches/MAS craft
- 2-3 divisions of drifters
- 4 units of USN submarine chasers
- 2-3 divisions of drifters and trawlers
- 1-2 sloops equipped with Kite Balloons, 1-2 torpedoboats and a division of trawlers patrolling in this area

Key
- Barrage defences
- Alternative lines for mine barriers

Since 1915 allied forces had attempted to restrict the movement of German, and to far lesser extent Austrian, U-boats from the Adriatic. What began as an operation by the Royal Navy with a couple of divisions of drifters operating from Brindisi, had gradually expanded with Italian and French contributions. A lack of resources, the low quality of *materiel* sent out for the task and inter-allied squabbling meant that these efforts had little impact on U-boat operations while the drifter units that patrolled the Otranto Strait became targets of attack.

Until October 1917 only naval patrols were employed, and there was never a full line of drifters and other craft covering the straits. The British then experimented with a small fixed-net barrage which fell foul of the weather and was abandoned. However, the Italians and French wanted to create a large-scale defensive system and asked for British resources. The British were initially reluctant, but the year's merchant ship losses and Italy's precarious position in the war required action.

In January 1918 Vice-Admiral Calthorpe, British Commander-in-Chief in the Mediterranean, succeeded in getting Italian and French support for a British-led effort to reorganise and substantially expand the barrage. New minefields would be laid, more submarine patrols off Cattaro conducted, and the auxiliary forces would receive better equipment. The United States Navy would also become involved. By the summer around 30 destroyers and more than 200 auxiliary craft were operating on maintaining the barrage.

Ultimately, the barrage proved ineffective and only two U-boats were confirmed destroyed with perhaps two more succumbing while transiting the area. Had the war continued into 1919 the barrage might have become sufficiently developed to present a major obstacle to the U-boats. The Americans were planning to make use of their minelaying forces currently still employed on the Northern Barrage between Scotland and Norway to lay more extensive mine barriers across the straits.

U-Boat Operations in American Waters, late June–September 1918

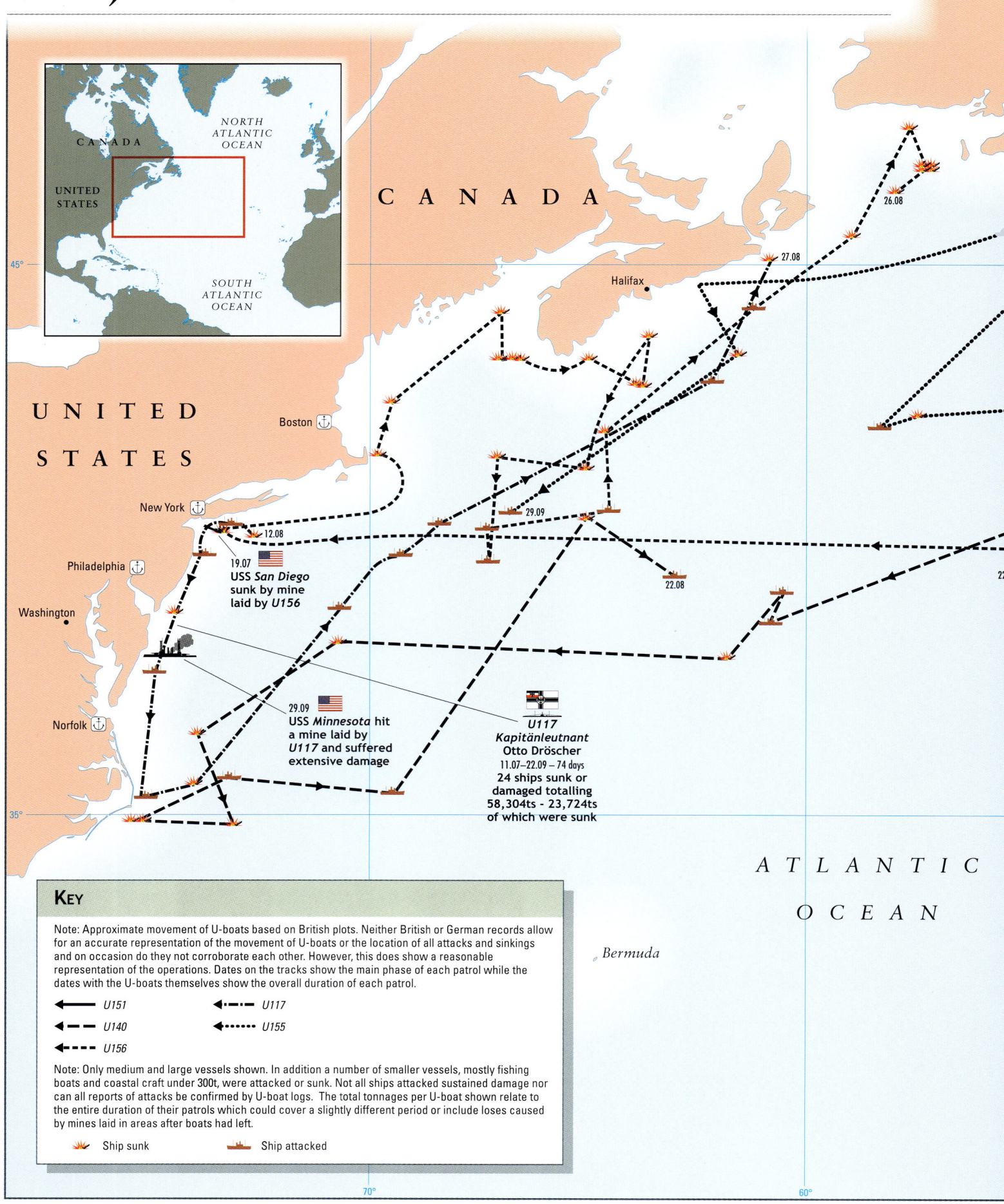

Key

Note: Approximate movement of U-boats based on British plots. Neither British or German records allow for an accurate representation of the movement of U-boats or the location of all attacks and sinkings and on occasion do they not corroborate each other. However, this does show a reasonable representation of the operations. Dates on the tracks show the main phase of each patrol while the dates with the U-boats themselves show the overall duration of each patrol.

- ⬅ U151
- ⬅ U140
- ⬅ U156
- ⬅ U117
- ⬅ U155

Note: Only medium and large vessels shown. In addition a number of smaller vessels, mostly fishing boats and coastal craft under 300t, were attacked or sunk. Not all ships attacked sustained damage nor can all reports of attacks be confirmed by U-boat logs. The total tonnages per U-boat shown relate to the entire duration of their patrols which could cover a slightly different period or include loses caused by mines laid in areas after boats had left.

- Ship sunk
- Ship attacked

Map annotations

- 19.07 USS *San Diego* sunk by mine laid by *U156*
- 29.09 USS *Minnesota* hit a mine laid by *U117* and suffered extensive damage
- *U117* Kapitänleutnant Otto Dröscher 11.07–22.09 – 74 days 24 ships sunk or damaged totalling 58,304ts - 23,724ts of which were sunk

THE GREAT WAR AT SEA 1918

U140
Korvettenkapitän
Waldemar Kophamel
02.07–20.09 – 81 days
28 ships sunk totalling
around 30,500ts

U155
Korvettenkapitän
Ferdinand Studt
11.08–14.11 – 96 days
9 ships sunk or
damaged totalling
24,934ts - 15,812ts
of which were sunk

U156
Kapitänleutnant Richard Feldt
16.06 - Sunk 25.09 by a
mine, probably in the
Northern Barrage Area A.
At least 30 ships, mostly
trawlers, sunk or
damaged totalling
around 42,000ts

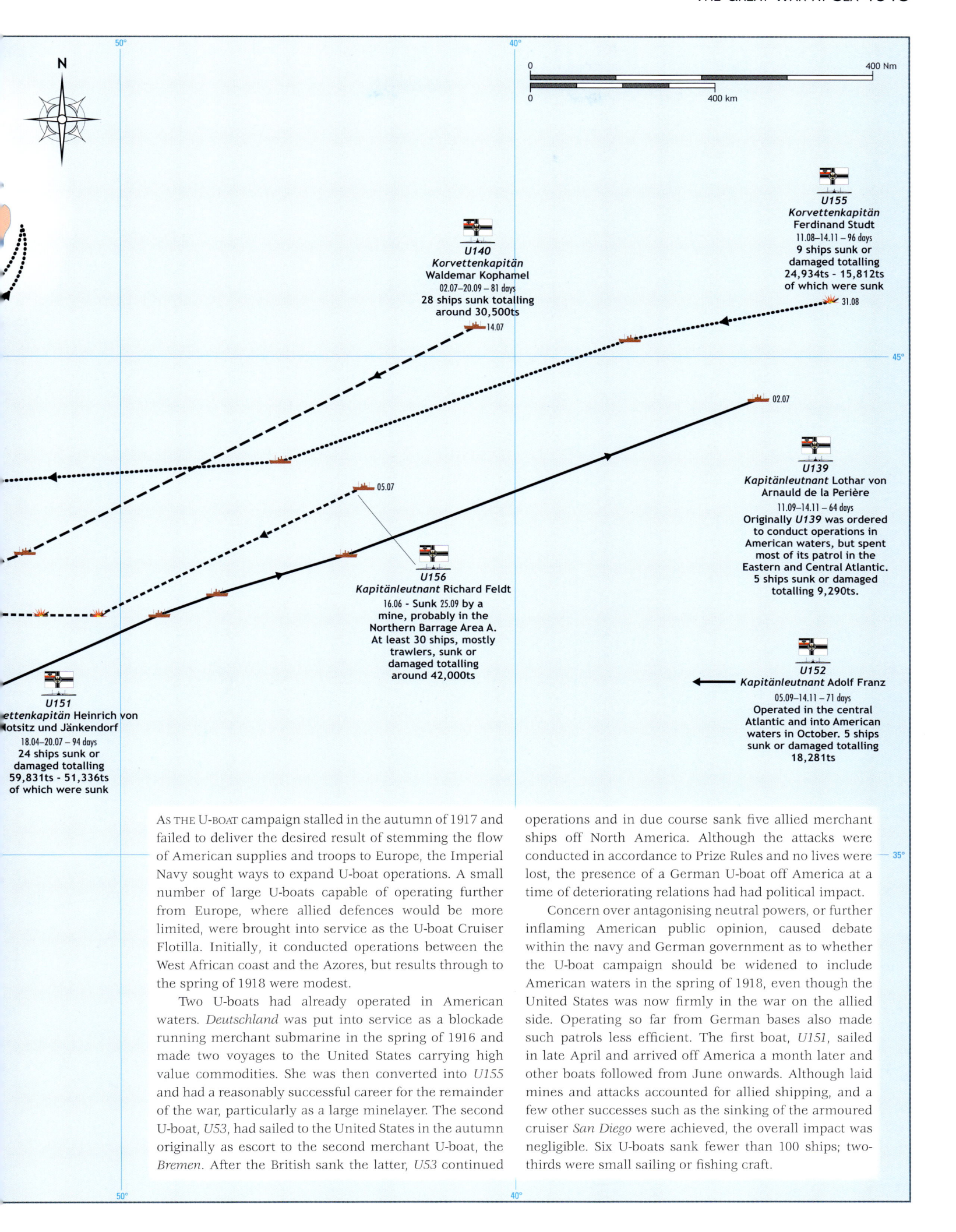

U139
Kapitänleutnant Lothar von
Arnauld de la Perière
11.09–14.11 – 64 days
Originally U139 was ordered
to conduct operations in
American waters, but spent
most of its patrol in the
Eastern and Central Atlantic.
5 ships sunk or damaged
totalling 9,290ts.

U152
Kapitänleutnant Adolf Franz
05.09–14.11 – 71 days
Operated in the central
Atlantic and into American
waters in October. 5 ships
sunk or damaged totalling
18,281ts

U151
Korvettenkapitän Heinrich von
Nostitz und Jänkendorf
18.04–20.07 – 94 days
24 ships sunk or
damaged totalling
59,831ts - 51,336ts
of which were sunk

As the U-boat campaign stalled in the autumn of 1917 and failed to deliver the desired result of stemming the flow of American supplies and troops to Europe, the Imperial Navy sought ways to expand U-boat operations. A small number of large U-boats capable of operating further from Europe, where allied defences would be more limited, were brought into service as the U-boat Cruiser Flotilla. Initially, it conducted operations between the West African coast and the Azores, but results through to the spring of 1918 were modest.

Two U-boats had already operated in American waters. *Deutschland* was put into service as a blockade running merchant submarine in the spring of 1916 and made two voyages to the United States carrying high value commodities. She was then converted into *U155* and had a reasonably successful career for the remainder of the war, particularly as a large minelayer. The second U-boat, *U53*, had sailed to the United States in the autumn originally as escort to the second merchant U-boat, the *Bremen*. After the British sank the latter, *U53* continued operations and in due course sank five allied merchant ships off North America. Although the attacks were conducted in accordance to Prize Rules and no lives were lost, the presence of a German U-boat off America at a time of deteriorating relations had had political impact.

Concern over antagonising neutral powers, or further inflaming American public opinion, caused debate within the navy and German government as to whether the U-boat campaign should be widened to include American waters in the spring of 1918, even though the United States was now firmly in the war on the allied side. Operating so far from German bases also made such patrols less efficient. The first boat, *U151*, sailed in late April and arrived off America a month later and other boats followed from June onwards. Although laid mines and attacks accounted for allied shipping, and a few other successes such as the sinking of the armoured cruiser *San Diego* were achieved, the overall impact was negligible. Six U-boats sank fewer than 100 ships; two-thirds were small sailing or fishing craft.

THE NORTHERN BARRAGE, 1918

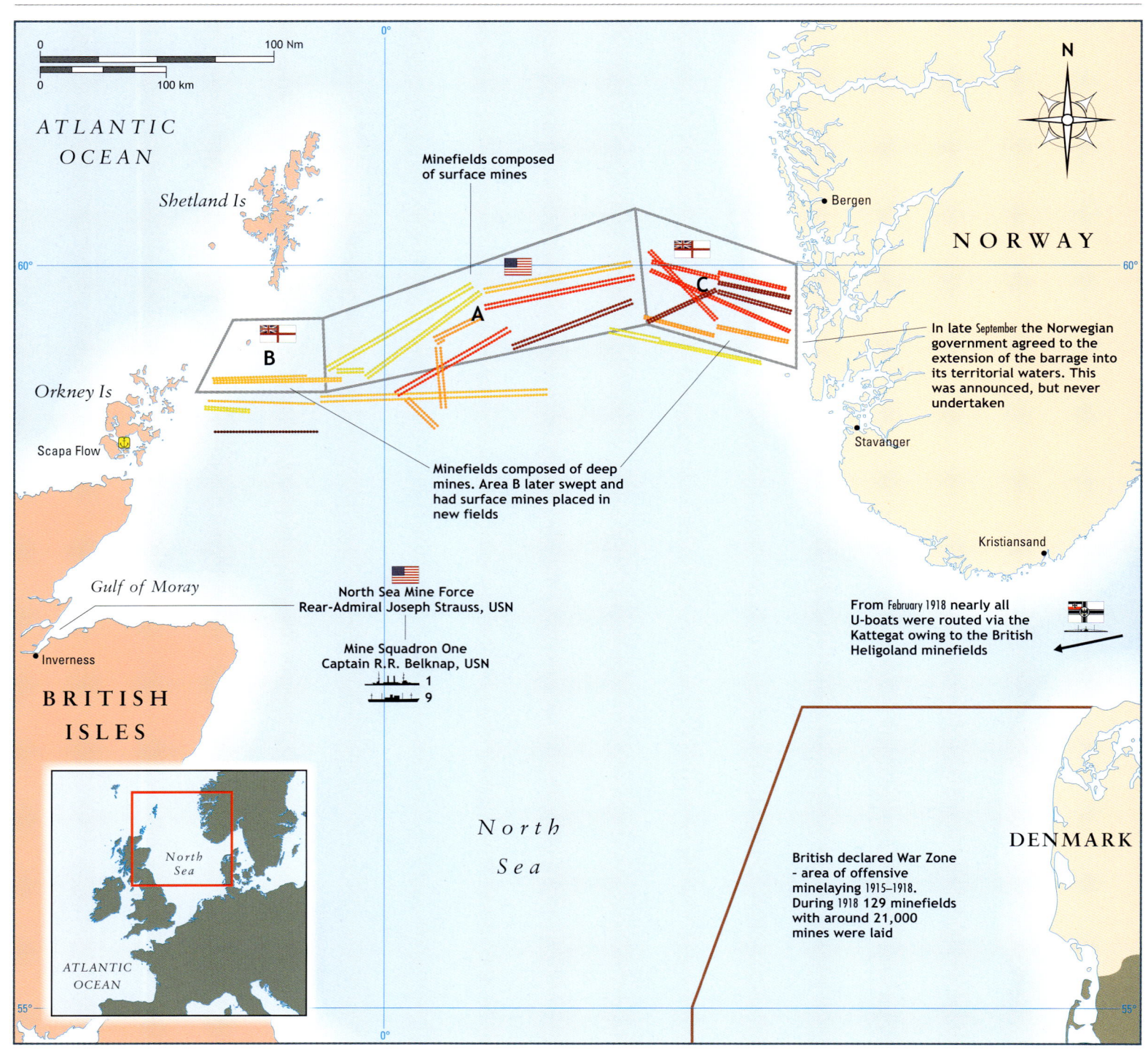

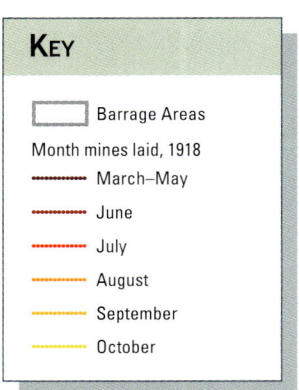

Minefields composed of surface mines

In late September the Norwegian government agreed to the extension of the barrage into its territorial waters. This was announced, but never undertaken

Minefields composed of deep mines. Area B later swept and had surface mines placed in new fields

North Sea Mine Force
Rear-Admiral Joseph Strauss, USN

Mine Squadron One
Captain R.R. Belknap, USN

From February 1918 nearly all U-boats were routed via the Kattegat owing to the British Heligoland minefields

British declared War Zone – area of offensive minelaying 1915–1918. During 1918 129 minefields with around 21,000 mines were laid

Key

- Barrage Areas

Month mines laid, 1918
- March–May
- June
- July
- August
- September
- October

Of the three allied fixed naval defence systems created during the war, the Northern Barrage between the Orkneys and Norway was the largest and most complex. Not only was the whole sea area covered and the number of mines required far greater than in the Dover or Otranto Straits, but the conditions in which the barrage would be laid also posed far greater challenges. First consideration to laying a minefield in the North Sea was given as early as 1916 and rejected on the grounds of the scale, depth of water and lack of suitable mines. There was, however, strong support for the idea in America and its entry into the war, coupled with the impact the U-boats were having on allied shipping, meant the scheme was seriously considered in the summer of 1917.

Formerly agreed upon in September 1917, the barrage was primarily an American undertaking and dependent on its industrial capacity. Although the first mines were sown by the British in March off the Orkneys, the majority were laid by the US Navy's minelaying force in fifteen operations between June and October – in total 15,093 British and 56,033 American mines were employed. The cost of the mines alone was estimated at around $40 million. The barrage's success was limited in view of its scale and cost. Technical problems with mines, the lack of auxiliary craft to patrol adjacent areas and the ability of German U-boats to bypass the eastern end using Norwegian waters all reduced its impact. The barrage sank six U-boats and a similar number were also damaged.

THE GREAT WAR AT SEA 1918

ALLIED MERCHANT SHIPPING LOSSES, 1918

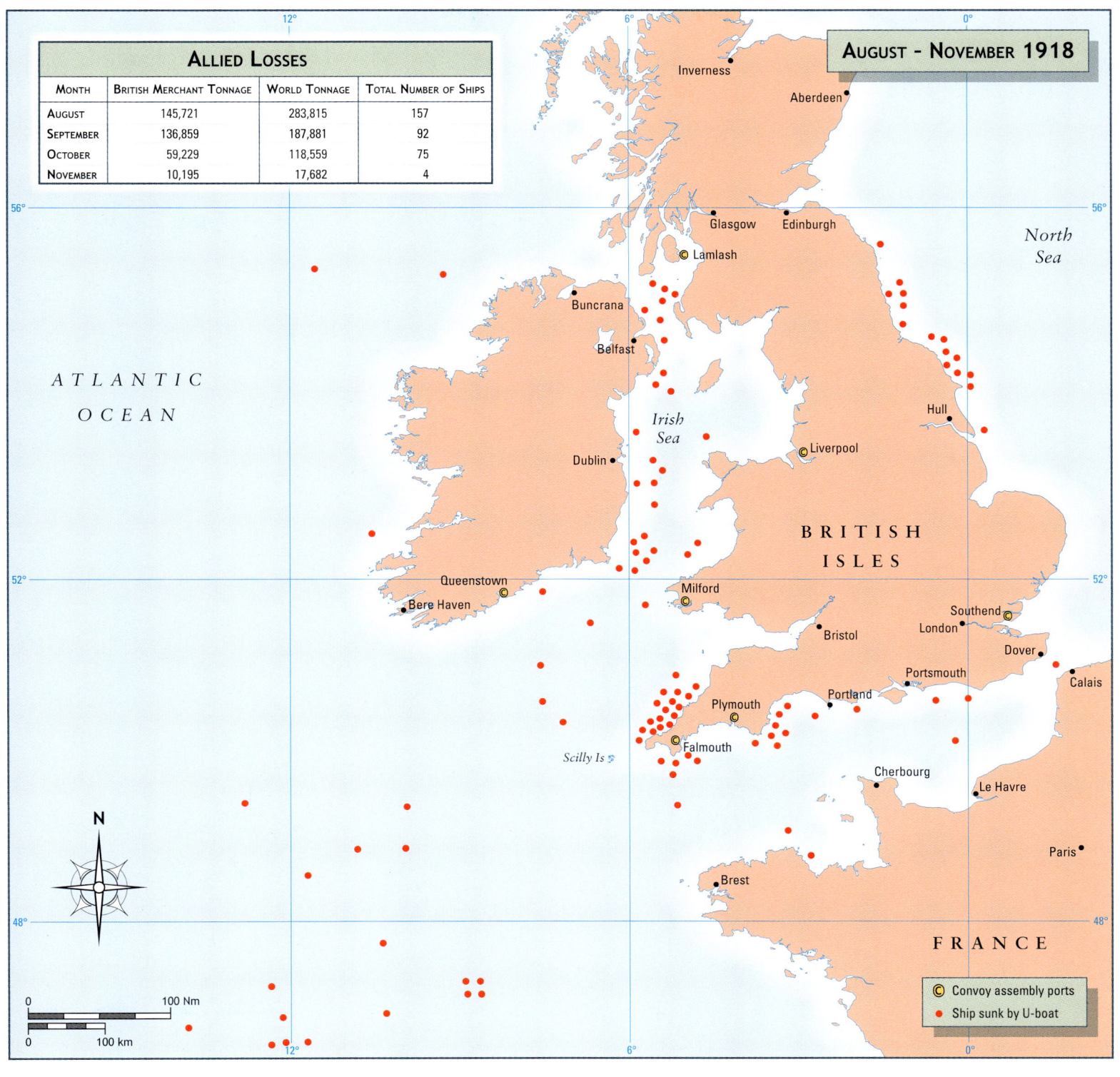

AUGUST – NOVEMBER 1918

ALLIED LOSSES			
MONTH	BRITISH MERCHANT TONNAGE	WORLD TONNAGE	TOTAL NUMBER OF SHIPS
AUGUST	145,721	283,815	157
SEPTEMBER	136,859	187,881	92
OCTOBER	59,229	118,559	75
NOVEMBER	10,195	17,682	4

Ⓒ Convoy assembly ports
• Ship sunk by U-boat

By January 1918 over 200,000 US troops had arrived in Europe and throughout the year the number increased dramatically, with the largest movement in single month occurring in July when 300,000 troops were brought across. By November 1918 just over two million had crossed the Atlantic and by the time of the second battle of the Marne, which commenced in July, the US Army was a determinant factor on the Western Front. U-boats only managed to sink three troop transports and most of the troops were rescued. Around 300 US soldiers were lost as a result of direct U-boat action, a figure far removed from *Admiral* von Holtzendorff's assurance that no US troops would reach Europe.

The U-boat campaign stalled in the late summer. Allied anti-submarine measures were having an effect on operations in both main theatres and much of the U-boat force was in need of repair and crews were exhausted. The Scheer Programme authorised in August envisaged massive new U-boat construction to force a decision in 1919, but this was beyond German resources. As the German government began to explore an end to the war in October, the American government demanded an end to the U-boat campaign. With their bases threatened, the Mediterranean and Flanders boats were recalled to Germany and on 21 October all U-boats were ordered to cease commerce warfare.

The Adriatic Theatre, 1917–18

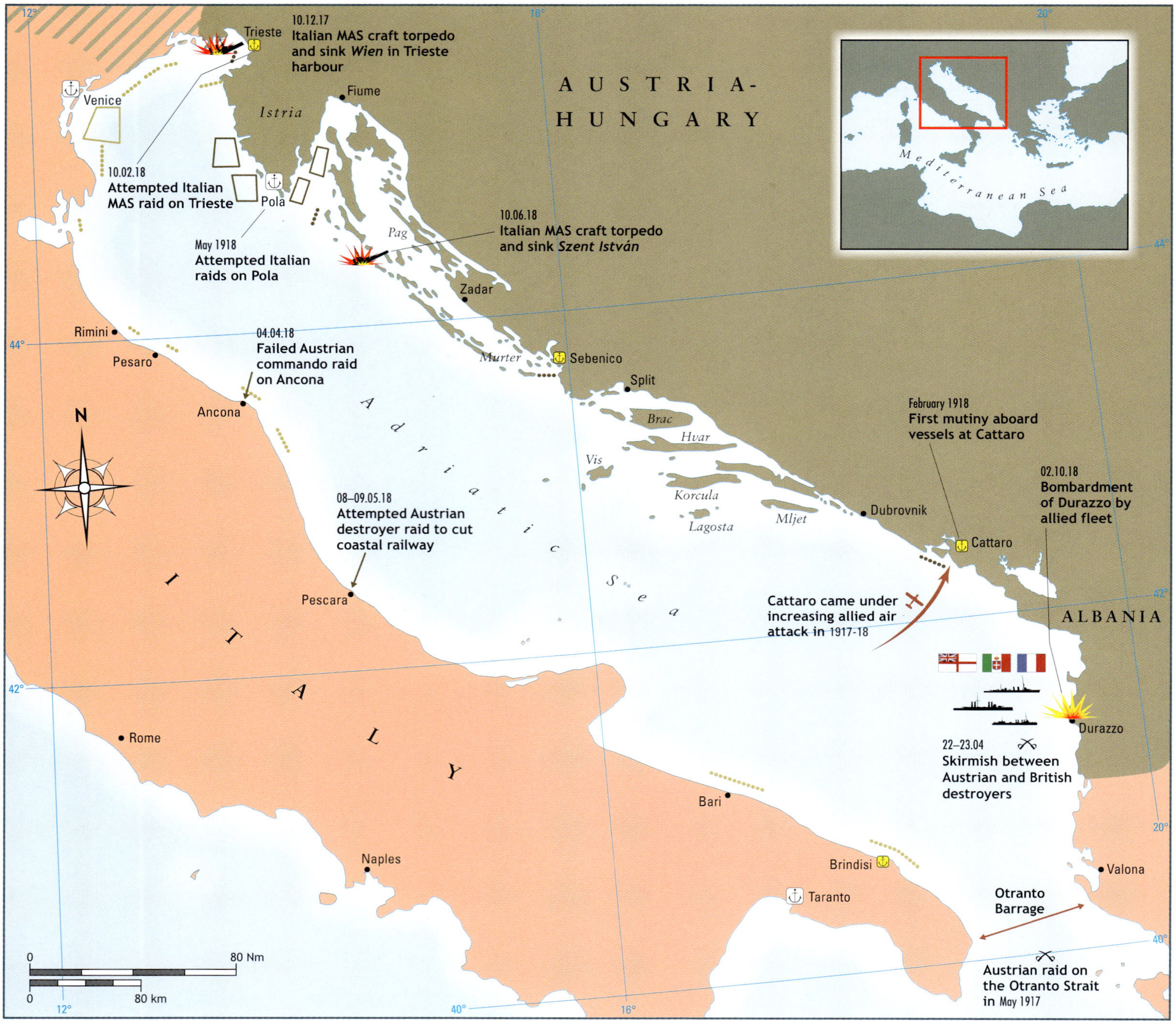

10.12.17
Italian MAS craft torpedo and sink *Wien* in Trieste harbour
Trieste
Venice
Fiume
Istria
AUSTRIA-HUNGARY
10.02.18
Attempted Italian MAS raid on Trieste
Pola
May 1918
Attempted Italian raids on Pola
Pag
10.06.18
Italian MAS craft torpedo and sink *Szent István*
Zadar
Rimini
Pesaro
04.04.18
Failed Austrian commando raid on Ancona
Ancona
Murter
Sebenico
Split
Brac
Hvar
Vis
Korcula
Lagosta
Mljet
Dubrovnik
Cattaro
February 1918
First mutiny aboard vessels at Cattaro
02.10.18
Bombardment of Durazzo by allied fleet
N
Adriatic Sea
08–09.05.18
Attempted Austrian destroyer raid to cut coastal railway
Pescara
Cattaro came under increasing allied air attack in 1917-18
ALBANIA
ITALY
Rome
Durazzo
22–23.04
Skirmish between Austrian and British destroyers
Bari
Naples
Brindisi
Taranto
Valona
Otranto Barrage
Austrian raid on the Otranto Strait in May 1917
0
80 Nm
0
80 km
12°
16°
20°
40°
42°
44°
Mediterranean Sea

Key

- Area occupied by Austro-Hungarian forces by 1918
- Main defensive minefields
  - Austrian
  - Italian

Major surface operations in the Adriatic became progressively infrequent during the last two years of the war. The increased use of mines and the larger number of submarines operating in the sea made it an inhospitable environment for capital ships. Minefields restricted the Austrians' ability not only to deploy the battlefleet but also to undertake training. Dwindling resources and the death of the fleet commander *Admiral* Haus in February 1917 only compounded this. During the war the Austrians laid around 6,000 mines. Two thirds were in defensive fields, mostly covering the approaches to the main base at Pola. The remainder were laid off the Albanian coast and Venice. The Italians laid around 12,000 mines in defensive fields off the major ports, among the Dalmatian Islands and off Istria.

The loss of a significant number of battleships, the inability to inflict a decisive defeat on the fleet and the problems in protecting the Italian coastline led many in Italy to question the utility of the navy. However, in the north the forces based at Venice were crucial in protecting the seaward flank during the Austro-Hungarian offensive in the autumn of 1917.

The focus of naval operations rotated around the allied defences in the Strait of Otranto. Austrian light forces repeatedly tried to interfere with these and achieved the greatest success of the war with the surprise raid on 14–15 May 1917. A few minor skirmishes between destroyers occurred throughout the spring of 1918, then a large raid involving the four modern battleships was planned for June 1918. However, as forces were assembling *Szent István* was torpedoed by an Italian MAS motor torpedo boat. The final allied operation of the war was a massive naval bombardment of Durazzo by a force of more than fifty warships.

OPERATION PLAN 19, OCTOBER 1918

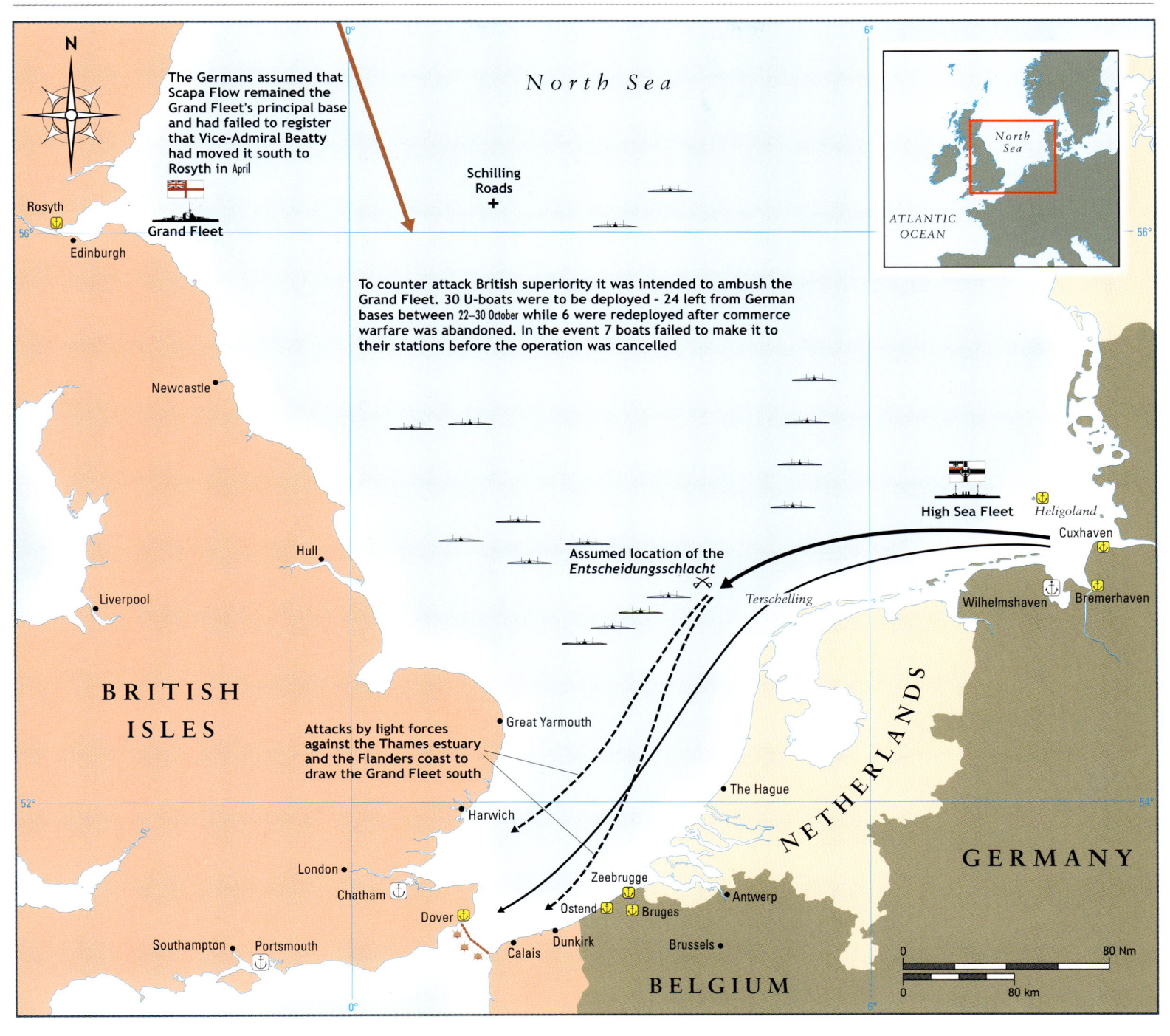

The Germans assumed that Scapa Flow remained the Grand Fleet's principal base and had failed to register that Vice-Admiral Beatty had moved it south to Rosyth in April

To counter attack British superiority it was intended to ambush the Grand Fleet. 30 U-boats were to be deployed – 24 left from German bases between 22–30 October while 6 were redeployed after commerce warfare was abandoned. In the event 7 boats failed to make it to their stations before the operation was cancelled

Attacks by light forces against the Thames estuary and the Flanders coast to draw the Grand Fleet south

KEY
- Assumed approach route of the Grand Fleet
- Original plan
- Modified plan
- Planned U-boat patrol lines
- Dover Barrage

THE INABILITY, SINCE the early days of the war, to force a decisive battle upon the Royal Navy on German terms caused deep frustration within the officer corps. Smaller tactical or operational successes against the British at sea had not translated into any strategic advantage and the abandonment of a surface warfare strategy in favour of commerce warfare in the autumn of 1916 put into question Germany's huge pre-war investment in its navy. The High Sea Fleet, the second largest fleet in the world, henceforth existed to support the U-boats and even they failed in the long-term to live up to expectations.

In contrast the army had been engaged in combat since the outset, fought in multiple theatres and even during the retreat on the Western Front in 1918 still controlled considerable territories outside Germany. Languishing at anchor morale in the fleet plummeted and disturbances had occurred as early as the summer of 1917. For the officers who had dreamed of an *Entscheidungsschlacht* – a decisive battle – against the Royal Navy somewhere between Heligoland and the Thames it was intolerable that the navy might have to surrender without a fight.

Throughout October plans were drawn up for final engagement, a 'deathride' against the British. The very secret Operation Plan 19 of 24 October envisaged using light forces in attacks against the Thames and Flanders coastline to lure the Grand Fleet south towards the High Sea Fleet. U-boats and minefields would whittle down British superiority. It was a very questionable plan. The fleet assembled in the Schilling Roads during 29 October with a view to sailing the next day. However, unrest amongst the sailors spread quickly as rumours of the undertaking circulated. *Admiral* Hipper had little choice but to cancel the operation and return the fleet to base.

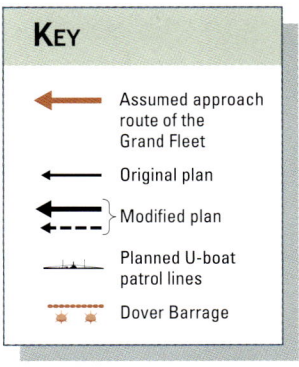

The Surrender of the High Sea Fleet, 21 November 1918

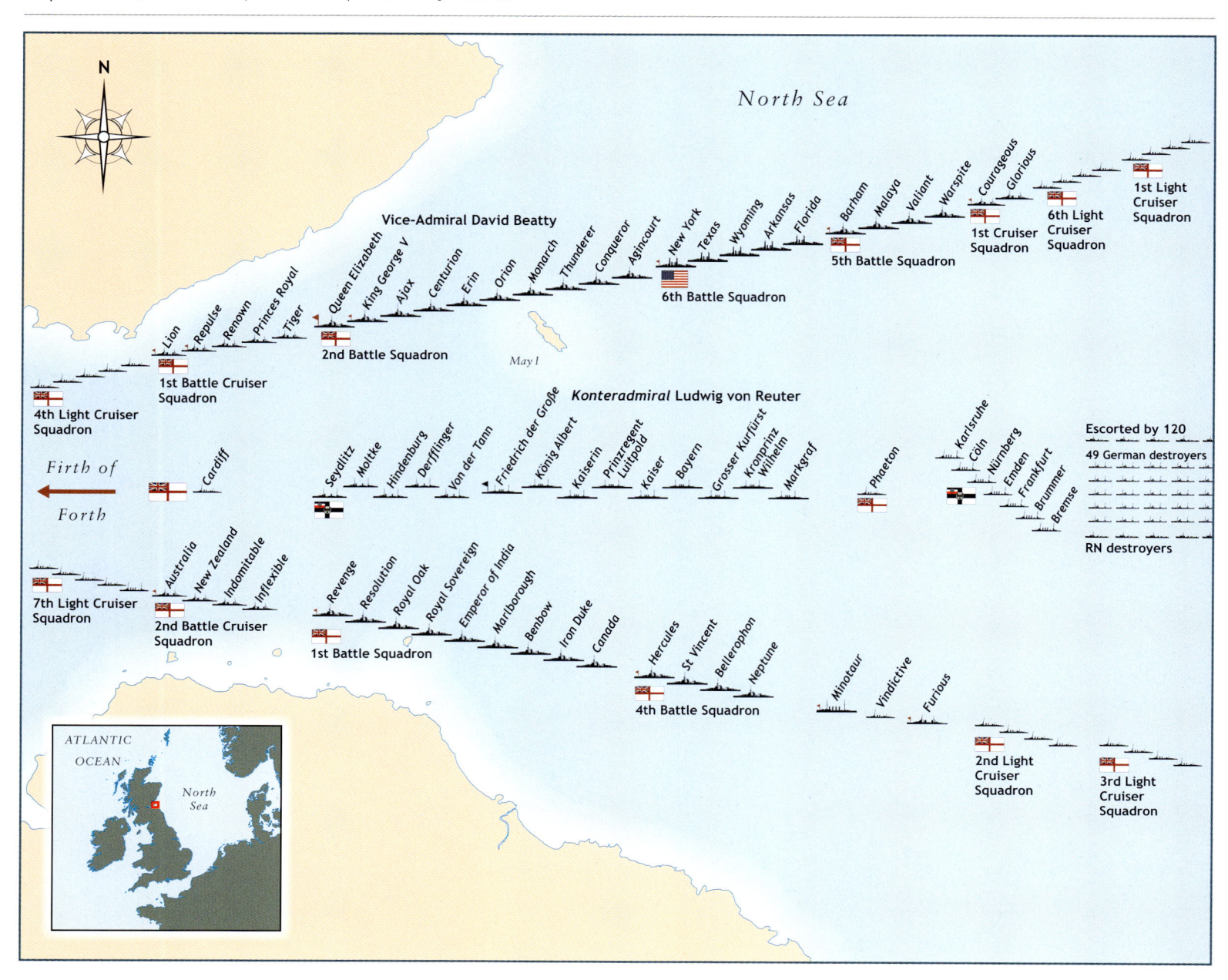

Key

◁ ◀ Fleet flagships
◁ Squadron flagships

Note: The deployment order and relative positions is illustrative rather than an accurate representation. There are discrepancies in the position of a small number of vessels in the existing British and German records. For clarity the attendant destroyers and other small escorts to the British squadrons are not shown and for similar reasons the names of the light cruisers too are omitted. To the North and South a large number of auxiliary vessels were also deployed.

For the Imperial Navy the war ended in a state of chaos. The unrest amongst the sailors, that had led Admiral Hipper to cancel his plan for a last engagement in the North Sea, increased. In an effort to prevent an open revolt by the crews Hipper decided to split the fleet up and distribute it between all the major naval bases; this only led to an acceleration of the process of disintegration. By 5 November at the latest the fleet had ceased to function as an organised force. Many of the port towns were in the hands of rebellious sailors and throughout Germany there was a progressive breakdown of law and order. The exceptions in the naval sphere included most of the U-boat crews and elements of the *Marinekorps* that remained loyal.

Throughout the autumn the fate of the German fleet had become a fiercely debated issue in allied naval circles. The British preferred it either destroyed in battle or surrendered as internment would not assure a decisive victory and it would become a bargaining chip during the ensuing peace negotiations. Others did not want Great Britain to acquire the bulk of a fleet that would only assure their naval superiority.

Under the naval terms of the Armistice of 11 November all U-boats were to be surrendered, the vast majority of the fleet interned in neutral ports with reduced crews, and equipment or naval infrastructure permitted to be destroyed pending a final peace settlement. No neutral power wanted to take charge of the fleet and so it was to come to Britain; no senior German admiral wished to take the fleet into internment, an act perceived as a surrender. Thus *Konteradmiral* von Reuter, commander of the Scouting Forces, undertook the task. Vice-Admiral Beatty carefully orchestrated the handover, termed Operation ZZ, and the High Sea Fleet sailed into internment flanked by some 370 predominantly British warships. At sunset on 21 November the German flags were hauled down for the last time.

NAVAL OPERATIONS 1919

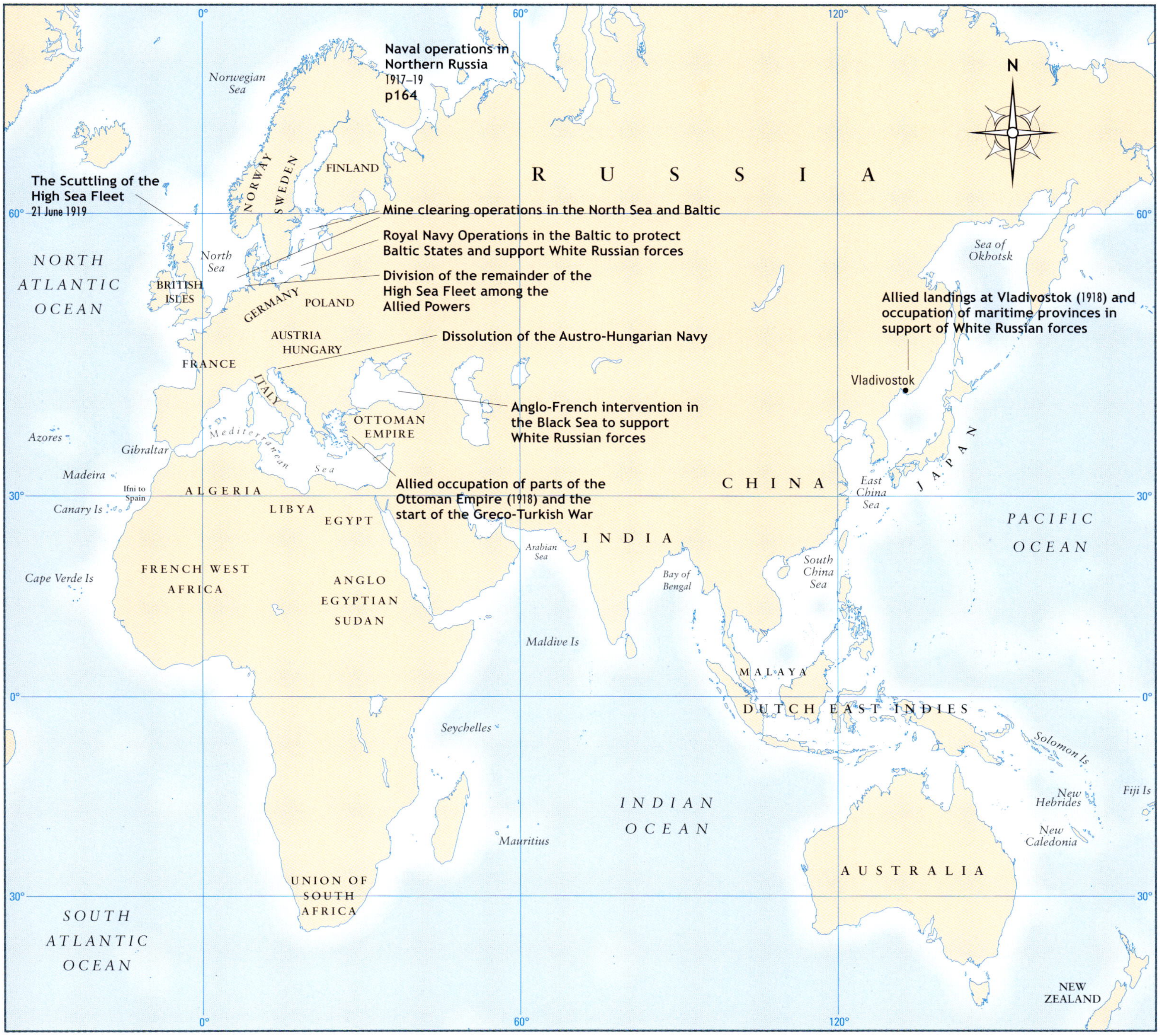
Naval operations in Northern Russia 1917–19 p164
The Scuttling of the High Sea Fleet 21 June 1919
Mine clearing operations in the North Sea and Baltic
Royal Navy Operations in the Baltic to protect Baltic States and support White Russian forces
Division of the remainder of the High Sea Fleet among the Allied Powers
Dissolution of the Austro-Hungarian Navy
Anglo-French intervention in the Black Sea to support White Russian forces
Allied occupation of parts of the Ottoman Empire (1918) and the start of the Greco-Turkish War
Allied landings at Vladivostok (1918) and occupation of maritime provinces in support of White Russian forces
Vladivostok
N
0°
60°
120°
30°
Norwegian Sea
North Sea
NORWAY
SWEDEN
FINLAND
R U S S I A
NORTH ATLANTIC OCEAN
BRITISH ISLES
GERMANY
POLAND
AUSTRIA HUNGARY
FRANCE
ITALY
Mediterranean Sea
OTTOMAN EMPIRE
Azores
Gibraltar
Madeira
Ifni to Spain
Canary Is
ALGERIA
LIBYA
EGYPT
CHINA
East China Sea
JAPAN
Sea of Okhotsk
PACIFIC OCEAN
INDIA
Arabian Sea
Bay of Bengal
South China Sea
Cape Verde Is
FRENCH WEST AFRICA
ANGLO EGYPTIAN SUDAN
Maldive Is
MALAYA
DUTCH EAST INDIES
Seychelles
Solomon Is
New Hebrides
Fiji Is
New Caledonia
INDIAN OCEAN
Mauritius
AUSTRALIA
UNION OF SOUTH AFRICA
SOUTH ATLANTIC OCEAN
NEW ZEALAND

THE ARMISTICE ON 11 November 1918 brought the war to an end in the principal theatres of operation, but it did not halt all the fighting, and new conflicts erupted as a result of political and social upheaval. The First World War brought about the immediate demise of three empires - the German, Austro-Hungarian and Russian - and another shortly thereafter, the Ottoman. New states were created and the British and French experienced internal unrest in parts of their colonial empires and newly acquired territories.

From a political perspective, the fate of the High Sea Fleet, and to a lesser extent that of the Austro-Hungarian navy, was one of the issues that had a significant impact on the allied negotiations and it caused friction throughout the winter. From the naval perspective, the clearing of the waters from the Baltic, the North Sea and Adriatic became the prime objective. Just as the largely static front lines in France, Italy and elsewhere had transformed landscapes beyond recognition, the years of fighting at sea had left a legacy of minefields, wrecks and other barriers that needed clearing in order to allow free navigation and the resumption of trade.

The progressive expansion of fighting in Russia as a result of the Bolshevik revolution had already drawn allied forces into the conflict in 1918. Initially, allied troops had been sent to Northern Russia and to Vladivostok in the Far East to secure the vast stockpiles of *materiel* that had been sent to Russia during the war and never used. The objective then shifted to supporting anti-Bolshevik forces in the civil war and in 1919 the British sent a naval expedition to the Baltic while a joint Anglo-French force was sent into the Black Sea.

OPERATIONS IN NORTHERN RUSSIA, 1917–19

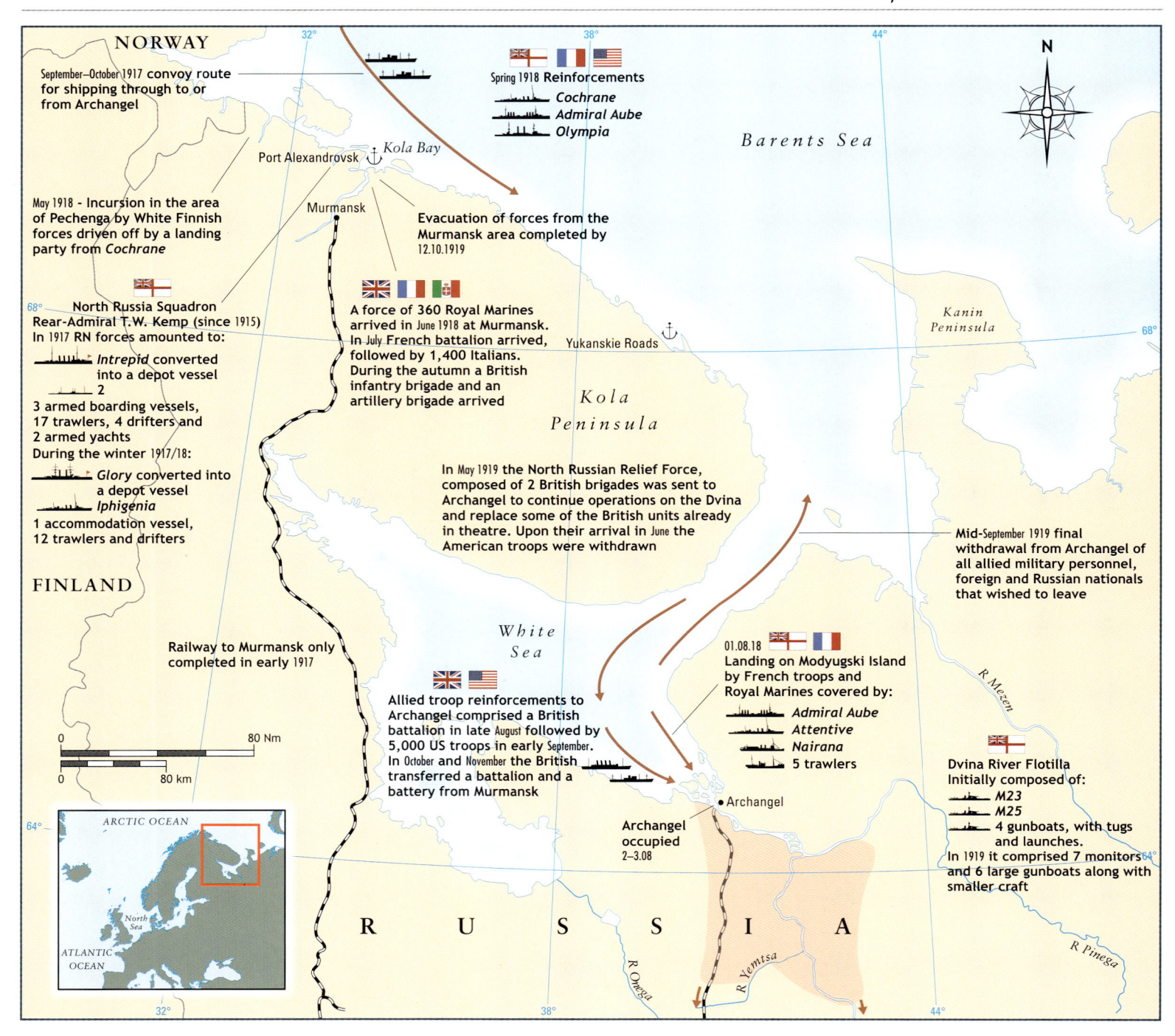

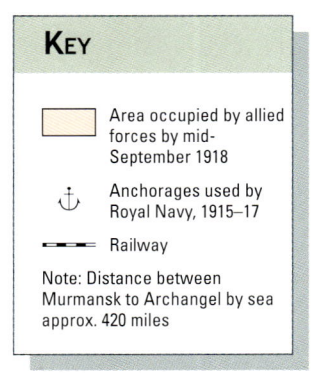

September–October 1917 convoy route for shipping through to or from Archangel

Spring 1918 Reinforcements
- Cochrane
- Admiral Aube
- Olympia

May 1918 – Incursion in the area of Pechenga by White Finnish forces driven off by a landing party from *Cochrane*

Evacuation of forces from the Murmansk area completed by 12.10.1919

North Russia Squadron
Rear-Admiral T.W. Kemp (since 1915)
In 1917 RN forces amounted to:
- *Intrepid* converted into a depot vessel
- 2
- 3 armed boarding vessels, 17 trawlers, 4 drifters and 2 armed yachts

During the winter 1917/18:
- *Glory* converted into a depot vessel
- *Iphigenia*
- 1 accommodation vessel, 12 trawlers and drifters

A force of 360 Royal Marines arrived in June 1918 at Murmansk. In July French battalion arrived, followed by 1,400 Italians. During the autumn a British infantry brigade and an artillery brigade arrived

In May 1919 the North Russian Relief Force, composed of 2 British brigades was sent to Archangel to continue operations on the Dvina and replace some of the British units already in theatre. Upon their arrival in June the American troops were withdrawn

Mid-September 1919 final withdrawal from Archangel of all allied military personnel, foreign and Russian nationals that wished to leave

Railway to Murmansk only completed in early 1917

Allied troop reinforcements to Archangel comprised a British battalion in late August followed by 5,000 US troops in early September. In October and November the British transferred a battalion and a battery from Murmansk

01.08.18 Landing on Modyugski Island by French troops and Royal Marines covered by:
- Admiral Aube
- Attentive
- Nairana
- 5 trawlers

Dvina River Flotilla Initially composed of:
- M23
- M25
- 4 gunboats, with tugs and launches.

In 1919 it comprised 7 monitors and 6 large gunboats along with smaller craft

Archangel occupied 2–3.08

KEY

- Area occupied by allied forces by mid-September 1918
- Anchorages used by Royal Navy, 1915–17
- Railway

Note: Distance between Murmansk to Archangel by sea approx. 420 miles

With the Turkish entry into the war in the autumn of 1914 the only route for British and French supplies to Russia was through Russia's Arctic ports. As the war progressed and Russian need for war materiel, food and coal increased so the shipments grew. Arctic Russia was one of the least developed parts in the west of the country and during the winter months weather conditions were extreme. Archangel, the main port, had reasonable facilities and a railway connection, but was closed by ice from December to May; Murmansk was ice-free all year round, but considerably smaller and had no railway connection until 1917. Both were completely overwhelmed by the quantities of supplies shipped in.

Until 1917, apart from the occasional U-boat patrol or minelaying operation, the region was free of German activity. A small British naval force was based at Murmansk from 1915 onwards. The expansion of the U-boat war in 1917 had minimal impact, but the political turmoil in Russia, that also led to the independence of Finland, did. A force of marines arrived in June 1918 to secure Murmansk followed by other allied troops. In August another force was sent on to Archangel to secure the vast stockpiles of supplies. By then the Allies had decided to restore the former Russian government and forces were sent south along the railway and rivers with the object of linking up with other anti-Bolshevik and anti-German forces. Throughout the winter the campaign stalled and a Bolshevik offensive in early 1919 forced the Allies back towards Archangel. This led to a larger expedition being sent out in the summer, though by then the political appetite for intervention in Russia had waned and it was withdrawn.

The Great War at Sea 1919

The Scuttling of the High Sea Fleet, 21 June 1919

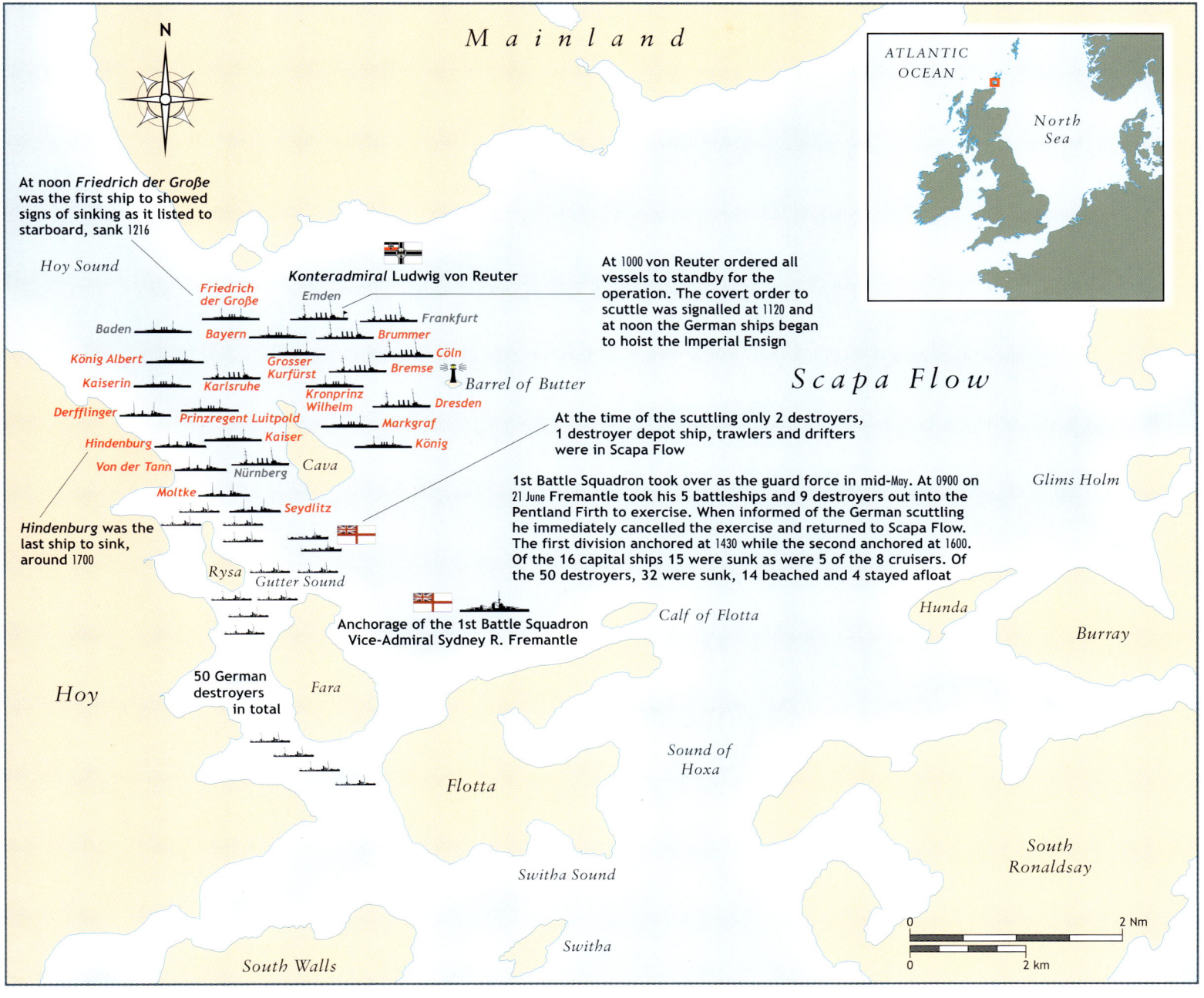

At noon *Friedrich der Große* was the first ship to showed signs of sinking as it listed to starboard, sank 1216

Konteradmiral Ludwig von Reuter

At 1000 von Reuter ordered all vessels to standby for the operation. The covert order to scuttle was signalled at 1120 and at noon the German ships began to hoist the Imperial Ensign

At the time of the scuttling only 2 destroyers, 1 destroyer depot ship, trawlers and drifters were in Scapa Flow

1st Battle Squadron took over as the guard force in mid-May. At 0900 on 21 June Fremantle took his 5 battleships and 9 destroyers out into the Pentland Firth to exercise. When informed of the German scuttling he immediately cancelled the exercise and returned to Scapa Flow. The first division anchored at 1430 while the second anchored at 1600. Of the 16 capital ships 15 were sunk as were 5 of the 8 cruisers. Of the 50 destroyers, 32 were sunk, 14 beached and 4 stayed afloat

Hindenburg was the last ship to sink, around 1700

Anchorage of the 1st Battle Squadron Vice-Admiral Sydney R. Fremantle

50 German destroyers in total

Key

Bayern Sunk ships
Emden Beached ships

A DAY AFTER the High Sea Fleet had sailed into the Firth of Forth and been interned the process of inspecting and then relocating it up to Scapa Flow began. At Scapa Flow the warships had their wireless gear removed while guns were immobilised by the removal of the breechblocks. The vessels had sailed to Britain with reduced crews and during the subsequent months more were sent home; by June only some 1,800 remained with the ships. The U-boat force, totalling some 176 boats, had been interned at Harwich.

Conditions for the German sailors in internment were difficult. Communication with the outside world was limited, daily duties became increasingly monotonous owing to the lack of recreation, and while sufficient food was sent out from Germany it was generally of poor quality. In addition, the breakdown of discipline that had occurred in the navy had continued in the interned vessels; *Konteradmiral* von Reuter was forced to transfer his flag as a result.

Meanwhile, the fate of the High Sea Fleet was being negotiated by the Allies at the Paris Peace Conference. The British wanted it sunk; German naval power would be crushed and the marked British naval superiority maintained. The French and Italians wanted it divided up to augment their navies. Vice-Admiral Fremantle prepared a plan to board the vessels at midnight on 21–22 June when the Armistice came to an end to be replaced by the Treaty of Versailles. In the event, confusion over a delay in the signing of the treaty led Fremantle to take his squadron out to exercise on 21 June, leaving von Reuter unobserved to set in motion a carefully prepared plan to scuttle the fleet to prevent it from falling into the hands of Germany's erstwhile opponents.

BIBLIOGRAPHY

Note on Sources

Both the British and Germans began to prepare accounts of their naval operations and the events at sea early on in the conflict for the purposes of analysing their conduct and ultimately feeding material into the process of writing official accounts. As the principal navies in the war the British and German accounts have come to dominate the historiography of the war at sea between 1914 and 1918. The resources both navies put into the process were considerable and in many ways the quality and quantity of the output was superior to that produced during and after the Second World War.

From the start, lavish general perspective maps, charts and operational/tactical overviews of engagements supported the official accounts. The introduction of gunnery and flag plots before 1914 meant that the representation of what occurred in engagements could be far more accurately reproduced than before. The 'battle' map, full of ship tracks, times and other detailed information, henceforth became a fundamental part of naval historic writing for both professional and popular audiences. The very first autobiographical accounts to appear after the war ended, by Admirals John Jellicoe and Reinhard Scheer and published in 1919 and 1920 respectively, contained fairly detailed maps to help convey to readers the nature of the North Sea theatre and the operations conducted there.

The British official accounts may be divided into two parts. First are the official histories by Julian Corbett (on naval operations) and Ernest Fayle (on seaborne trade), produced under the aegis of the Committee of Imperial Defence and work on which began during the war. Corbett's history was designed as a strategic overview of maritime operations rather than a detailed narrative of all events. The second group consists of the Naval Staff Monographs produced by the Admiralty for naval use only. These were quality products, very well researched, and to a large extent forgotten today. Some were started early on in the war, but all were redrafted and expanded after the war to incorporate some of Corbett's views, new materials and, in particular, early German accounts.

From 1919 onwards the Germans opted to produce an extensive twenty-five-volume account of their naval efforts supervised by the *Marine Archive*. Most of the publications, as part of the *Der Krieg zur See 1914-1918* project, were completed by the early 1930s, although two were only finished long after the Second World War had ended. The British and German official records combined encompass nearly a thousand maps and charts.

The analysis of the Battle of Jutland marks the highpoint of the cartographic process with both sides preparing in excess of thirty maps each to help understand the battle. The British even expended considerable resources in translating the German maps into English once these became available in the mid-1920s. The British also mapped out aspects of the Dardanelles campaign in great detail for the benefit of the wartime Dardanelles Commission, set up to establish the cause of its failure, and the post-war Dardanelles Committee, which was established to conduct first-hand analysis of the campaign, terrain and Turkish defences.

It is this body of material which forms the basis of nearly all the maps that have been produced until now. For example, Arthur Marder's magisterial account of the naval war made direct use of British material. Some maps of key events in this atlas, like the Battle of the Falklands or Dogger Bank, will thus be familiar: many though will not. It is important to note that despite the quantity and general quality of the British and German sources they are neither complete nor flawless. Often the different accounts are not reconciled so that times, units or even movements are sometimes inaccurate or simply wrong.

The quality of the accounts decline as the war progresses. After Corbett died in 1922 his colleague and friend Henry Newbolt took on the project, but the quality of Newbolt's work is significantly poorer. The last two volumes of *Naval Operations* are riddled with factual mistakes or ambiguities that significantly alter the account of certain operations. The Admiralty produced no naval staff monograph covering the end of the war and the German official histories decline in scope and detail, most noticeably for the U-boat war volumes. Establishing which ships were at sea on a given day for an operation often constitutes a considerable challenge for the years 1917–1918.

As many of the engagements or operations were conducted over the course of a day or longer there was a tendency to split up the depiction of events into numerous maps. While this allows for a more detailed understanding it often makes it hard to follow the general course of an action. Often there is far too much detail in tactical overviews to be of real use. For example, the Battle of Heligoland Bight, early on in the war, was an incredibly complex and confusing affair. No single map was produced by either the British or Germans and as a result it remains a very difficult battle to understand. The map employed in this atlas is an attempt to draw both accounts together and provide a concise but detailed overview of the action. Other examples would be the action off Durazzo or the Battle of the Strait of Otranto that have similarly been depicted in compartmentalised form.

The sheer scale of the Battle of Jutland poses problems in itself and a careful balance between detail and understanding must be struck. Its representation here of the main phases offers this balance. Another problematic area exists in relation to merchant ship losses as no single authoritative set of figures or charts depicting the position of losses exists. German figures are more detailed but tend to overestimate losses while British figures tend to ignore other allied or neutral shipping and also fail to account for the cause of a loss. Throughout the atlas the best effort has been made to reconcile the differing accounts and each map has been compiled by drawing upon at least three sources where this is possible. The official maps have needed to be carefully checked and also reinterpreted in the light of more recent scholarship.

Primary Sources

The National Archives, Kew, Surrey, United Kingdom

Admiralty: Historical Section: Records used for Official History, First World War
ADM 137/552 Heligoland Bight, Maps
ADM 137/1445 Charts from Papers: Foreign, Volume I
Admiralty Publications
ADM 186/589 The German Squadron in the Pacific, 1914
ADM 186/590 Operations leading up to the Battle of Coronel, Nov 1914
ADM 186/591 Operation leading up to the Battle of the Falkland Islands, Nov 1914
ADM 186/593 Operations in the Mediterranean 4-10 Aug 1914
ADM 186/600 Dardanelles Committee Report, 1919
ADM 186/601 Dardanelles Committee Report, Plates, 1919
ADM 186/602 Dardanelles Committee Report, Maps, 1919
ADM 186/603 The Economic Blockade 1914–1919
ADM 186/605 Naval Staff Monographs: CORONEL, German cruiser squadron in the Pacific, Falklands and GOEBEN and BRESLAU, 1920
ADM 186/606 Organisation of the Archangel River Flotilla 1919
ADM 186/607 Naval Staff Monographs: East Africa to July 1915 and Cameroons 1914
ADM 186/608 Naval Staff Monographs: Naval operations in Mesopotamia and the Persian Gulf
ADM 186/609 The Tenth Cruiser Squadron during the command of Admiral de Chair
ADM 186/610 Naval Staff Monographs: The Action of Dogger Bank, 24 Jan 1915
ADM 186/611 History of the White Sea Station 1914–1919
ADM 186/612 Naval Staff Monographs: The Eastern Squadrons 1914
ADM 186/613 Naval Staff Monographs: The Dover Command
ADM 186/614 Naval Staff Monographs: Tenth Cruiser Squadron I and The Baltic 1914
ADM 186/617 Naval Staff Monographs: The Atlantic Ocean 1914–1915
ADM 186/618 Naval Staff Monographs: The Mediterranean 1914–1915
ADM 186/619 Naval Staff Monographs: Home Waters from the outbreak of War to 27 Aug 1914
ADM 186/620 Naval Staff Monographs: Home Waters Sept–Oct 1914
ADM 186/621 Naval Staff Monographs: Home Waters Nov 1914–Jan 1915
ADM 186/622 Naval Staff Monographs: Feb–July (Home Water 1915)
ADM 186/623 Naval Staff Monographs: Home Waters July–Oct 1915
ADM 186/624 Naval Staff Monographs: Home Waters Oct 1915–May 1915
ADM 186/626 The Battle of Jutland: Official German Account (contains translated German maps)
ADM 186/627 Naval Staff Monographs: Lowestoft Raid 24–25 (April 1916)
ADM 186/628 Naval Staff Monographs: Home Waters June–Nov 1916
ADM 186/629 Mining operations by German submarines around the British Isles 1915–1918

Admiralty: Navy Reference Books (OU Series)
ADM 275/22 OU 6337(40) Review of German Cruiser Warfare 1914–1918 (1940)

National Maritime Museum, Greenwich, London

Naval Staff Monographs: Home Waters – Part VIII December 1916–April 1917

Official Histories

Kurt Aßmann, *Die Kämpfe der Kaiserlichen Marine in den deutschen Kolonien* (Berlin: Verlag E.S. Mittler, 1937)
Julian Corbett & Henry Newbolt, *Naval Operations* 5 Vols. (revised edition London: Longmans, 1931)
Ernest C. Fayle, *Seaborne Trade* 3 Vols. (London: John Murray, 1920–24)
Rudolph Firle & Ernst Freiherr von Gagern, *Der Krieg in der Ostsee* 3 Vols. (Berlin: Verlag E.S. Mittler, 1921–1964)
Otto Groos & Walter Gladisch, *Der Krieg in der Nordsee* 7 Vols. (Berlin: Verlag E.S. Mittler, 1920–2006)
Arthur W. Jose, *The Royal Australian Navy, 1914–1918* (*Official History of Australia in the War of 1914–1918*) 9th ed. (Sydney: Angus and Robertson, 1941)
Herman Lorey, *Der Krieg in den türkischen Gewässern* 2 Vols. (Berlin: Verlag E.S. Mittler, 1927-38)
Erich Raeder & Eberhard von Mantey, *Der Kreuzerkrieg in den ausländischen Gewässern* 3 Vols. (Berlin: Verlag E.S. Mittler, 1922–1937)
Arno Spindler, *Der Handelskrieg mit U-Booten* 5 Vols. (Berlin: Verlag E.S. Mittler, 1932–1966)

Books, Chapters and Articles

'The Operations at Tsingtau and the Work of the Triumph. Part I', *The Naval Review* 3/2 (1915) pp. 322–40
John J. Abbatiello, *Anti-Submarine Warfare in World War I: British naval aviation and the defeat of the U-Boats* (London: Routledge, 2006)
Reginald Bacon, *The Dover Patrol, 1915–1917* 2 Vols. (London: Hutchinson & Co, 1919)
Michael B. Barrett, *Operation Albion: The German Conquest of the Baltic Islands* (Bloomington, IN: Indiana University Press, 2008)
Lutz Bengelsdorf, *Der Seekrieg in der Ostsee, 1914–1918* (Bremen: H.M. Haushild, 2008)
Michael Epkenhans, Jörg Hillmann & Frank Nägler, *Skagerrakschlacht: Vorgeschichte – Ereignis – Verarbeitung* (München: Oldenbourg, 2009)
Charles E.J. Fryer, *The Royal Navy on the Danube* (New York: Columbia university Press, 1988)

James Goldrick, *The King's Ships Were at Sea: The War in the North Sea, August 1914–February 1915* (Annapolis, MD: Naval Institute Press, 1984)

Andrew Gordon, *The Rules of the Game: Jutland and British Naval Command* (London: John Murray, 2005)

John D. Grainger (ed.), *The Maritime Blockade of Germany in the Great War: The Northern Patrol, 1914–1918* (Aldershot: Ashgate, 2003)

Richard Guilliatt & Peter Hohnen, *The Wolf: The mystery raider that terrorized the seas during World War I* (New York: Free Press, 2010)

Paul G. Halpern, *The Naval War in the Mediterranean 1914–1918* (London: Allen & Unwin, 1987)

———, *A Naval History of World War I* (Abingdon: Routledge, 2003)

———, *The Battle of the Otranto Straits: Controlling the Gateway to the Adriatic in WW1* (Bloomington, IN: Indiana University Press, 2004)

Holger K. Herwig, *"Luxury" Fleet: The Imperial German Navy 1888–1918* (London: Ashfield Press, 1987)

Bodo Herzog, *Deutsche U-Boote 1906-1966* (Erlangen: Karl Müller, 1993)

Arthur Hezlet, *The Submarine & Sea Power* (London: Peter Davies, 1967)

Mark D. Karau, *The Naval Flank of the Western Front: The German MarineKorps Flandern 1914–1918* (Barnsely: Seaforth, 2014)

Paul Kemp, *U-boats Destroyed: German Submarine Losses in the Two World Wars* (Annapolis, MD: Naval Institute Press, 1997)

R.D. Layman, *The Cuxhaven Raid: The World's First Carrier Air Strike* (London: Conway, 1985)

John Jellicoe, *The Grand Fleet, 1914–1916: Its creation, development and work* (London: Cassell, 1919)

———, *The Crisis of the Naval War* (London: Cassell, 1920)

Roger Keyes, *The Naval Memoirs of Admiral of the Fleet Sir Roger Keyes* 2 Vols. (London: Butterworth, 1934–35)

Selcuk Kolay et. al, *Echoes From the Deep: Wrecks of the Dardanelles Campaign* (Istanbul: Vwhbi Koc Foundation & Ayhan Sahenk Foundation, 2013)

Arthur Marder, *From the Dreadnought to Scapa Flow: The Royal Navy in the Fischer Era, 1904–1919* 5 Vols. (Barnsley: Seaforth, 2013–14)

Dwight R. Messimer, *Verschollen: World War I U-boat Losses* (Annapolis, MD: Naval Institute Press, 2002)

George Nekrasov, *North of Gallipoli: The Black Sea Fleet at War 1914–1917* (New York: Columbia University Press, 1992)

Wilfred Nunn, *Tigris Gunboats: The Forgotten War in Iraq 1914–1917* (London: Chatham, 2007)

Eric W. Osborne, *The Battle of Heligoland Bight* (Bloomington, IN: Indiana University Press, 2006)

Vincent O'Hara, David Dickson & Richard Worth, *To Crown the Waves: The Great Navies of the First World War* (Annapolis, MD: Naval Institute Press, 2013)

Phillip G. Pattee, *At War in Distant Waters: British Colonial Defense in the Great War* (Annapolis, MD: Naval Institute Press, 2013)

Tobias R. Philbin, *Battle of Dogger Bank: The First Dreadnought Engagement, January 1915* (Bloomington, IN: Indiana University Press, 2006)

Timothy D. Saxon, 'Anglo-Japanese Naval Cooperation, 1914–1918', Naval War College Review LIII/1 (2000)

Reinhard Scheer, *Germany's High Sea Fleet in the World War* (London: Cassell, 1920)

Joachim Schröder, *Die U-Boote des Kaisers: Die Geschicht des deutschen U-Boot-Kriegs gegen Großbritannien im Ersten Weltkrieg* (Bonn: Bernard & Graefe, 2003)

William S. Sims, *The Victory at Sea* (New York: Doubleday, Page and Co 1920)

Lawrence Sondhaus, *The Great War at Sea: A Naval History of the First World War* (Cambridge: Cambridge University Press, 2014)

David Stevenson, *1914–1918: The History of the First World War* (London: Penguin, 2005)

———, *With Our Backs To The Wall: Victory and Defeat in 1918* (London: Allen Lane, 2011)

William N. Still Jr., *Crisis at Sea: The United States Navy in European Waters in World War I* (Gainesville, FL: University Press of Florida, 2006)

Hew Strachan, *The First World War. Volume I: To Arms* (Oxford: Oxford university Press, 2001)

V.E. Tarrant, *Jutland: The German Perspective – A New View of the Great Battle, 31 May 1916* (London: Arms & Armour, 1997)

———, *Kurs West: Die deutschen U-Boot-Offensiven 1914–1945* (Stuttgart: Motorbuch Verlag, 1996)

Tim Travers, *Gallipoli 1915* (Stroud: Tempus, 2001)

Andrew W. Weist, *Passchendale and the Royal Navy* (Westport, CT: Greenwood Press, 1995)

Jonathan Reed Winkler, *Nexus: Strategic Communication and American Security in World War I* (London: Harvard University Press, 2008)

Klaus Wolf, *Gallipoli 1915: Das deutsch-türkische Militärbündnis im Ersten Weltkrieg* (Bonn: Report Verlag, 2008)

Nicolas Wolz, *From Imperial Splendour to Internment: The German Navy in the First World War* (Barnsley: Seaforth, 2015)

Keith Yates, *Graf Spee's Raiders: Challenge to the Royal Navy, 1914–1915* (London: Leo Cooper, 1995)

Websites

The following websites are of great use when researching the naval war between 1914–1918 and deserve particular mention.

Naval History Homepage – http://www.naval-history.net – has a wealth of memoirs, chronologies, contemporary accounts and other primary sources relating to the Great War.

The Dreadnought Project – http://www.dreadnoughtproject.org – focuses on the development of naval technology in the period 1880–1920. However, the website also contains an ever expanding amount of material on naval personalities, ships and units that is invaluable for the purposes of cross referencing with other sources.

Uboat.net – http://www.uboat.net – deals with all manner of materials relating to the German U-boat arm in both wars. One of the best contemporary sources for merchant ship losses.

Index

For individual German submarines, see under 'U-boats'.
For individual German airships, see under 'Zeppelins'.

Abbreviations Used
A-H = Austro-Hungarian
Fr = French
HMAS = His Majesty's Australian Ship
HMS = His Majesty's Ship
HMSm = His Majesty's Submarine
It = Italian
Jpn = Japanese
RMS = Royal Mail Ship
Rus = Russian
sm = submarine
SMS = *Seiner Majestät Schiff* (Imperial German warship)
Tur = Turkish
USS = United States Ship

Abba (It) 84–5
Abdiel, HMS 94–5, 96, 152–3
Aboukir, HMS 4–5, 12, 13, 16–17, 23
Acerbi (It) 128–9
Active, HMS 96, 122–3, 126–7
Admiral Aube (Fr) 164
Admiral Makarov (Rus) 70, 134–5
Afridi, HMS 126–7
Agamemnon, HMS 44, 52, 53, 54–5, 58
Agincourt, HMS 96, 152–3, 162
Ajax, HMS 96, 162
Akashi (Jpn) 29
Akitsushima (Jpn) 29
Åland Islands, battle of the 26–7, 42–3, 70
Albatross (It) 128–9
Albatross, SMS 26–7, 70
Albion, HMS 53, 54–5, 58, 59
Albion, Operation 116–17, 134–5
Alcantara, HMS 86–7, 90–1
Almanzora, HMS 114–15
Amalfi (It) 62–3
Amazon, HMS 126–7
Ambuscade, HMS 122–3
Amethyst, HMS 58
Amphion, HMS 25
Andes, HMS 90–1
Angora, HMS 78–9
Antrim, HMS 114–15
Aquila (It) 128–9
Arethusa, HMS 13, 14–15, 32–3, 40–1, 72–3
Ariadne, SMS 14–15
Ark Royal, HMS 58
Arkansas, USS 162
Asama (Jpn) 20–1
Askold (Rus) 58
Aspern (A-H) 84–5
Astraea, HMS 11
Attentive, HMS 105, 164
Audacious, HMS 25
Augsburg, SMS 26–7, 70, 74, 75, 134–5
Aurora, HMS 72–3
Australia, HMAS 20–1, 48–9, 162

Bacchante, HMS 13, 58
Balaton (A-H) 84–5, 128–9
Barbaros Hayreddin (Tur) 36–7, 81
Barham, HMS 96, 98, 162
Bayan (Rus) 70, 134–5
Bayern, SMS 134–5, 162, 165
Beagle, HMS 59
Belgian coast, bombardments of 4–5, 76–7, 86–7
Bellerophon, HMS 96, 162
Bellona, HMS 96
Benbow, HMS 96, 99, 162
Benedetto Brin (It) 62–3
Berlin, SMS 25
Bernouilli (It sm) 128–9
Berwick, HMS 10, 114–15
Birkenhead, HMS 96, 141
Birmingham, HMS 12, 13, 14–15, 46–7, 72–3, 96
Bisson (Fr) 128–9
Black Prince, HMS 8–9, 96, 99, 101
Blanche, HMS 96
Blitz, SMS 134–5
Blücher, SMS 12, 14–15, 32–3, 38–9, 46–7
Boadicea, HMS 96
Bogatyr (Rus) 70
Bouvet (Fr) 52, 54–5, 81
Braunschweig, SMS 74
Bremen, SMS 74, 75

Bremse, SMS 137, 162, 165
Breslau, SMS/(Tur) 4–5, 8–9, 34, 36–7, 89, 119, 147
Bristol, HMS 10, 31, 48–9, 128–9
Broke, HMS 126–7
Brummer, SMS 137, 162, 165
Budapest (A-H) 84–5

C26, HMSm 134–5
C27, HMSm 134–5
C32, HMSm 134–5
Caledon, HMS 138–9
Calegarian, HMS 114–15
Calliope, HMS 72–3, 96
Calypso, HMS 138–9
Canada, HMS 96, 162
Canopus, HMS 31, 54–5
Canterbury, HMS 96
Cap Trafalgar, SMS 18–19
Caradoc, HMS 138–9
Cardiff, HMS 138–9, 162
Carmania, HMS 18–19
Carnarvon, HMS 31, 48–9, 114–15
Caroline, HMS 72–3, 96
Carthage, HMS 81
Carysfort, HMS 72–3, 126–7
Casque (Fr) 128–9
Castor, HMS 96
Centurion, HMS 96, 162
Ceres, HMS 138–9
Champion, HMS 96, 138–9
Charlemagne (Fr) 53, 54–5, 58
Chatham, HMS 8–9, 11, 71, 141
Chelmer, HMS 59
Chester, HMS 96, 99
Chitose (Jpn) 29
Chiyoda (Jpn) 29
Cimeterre (Fr) 128–9
Cleopatra, HMS 72–3
Cochrane, HMS 96, 164
Collingwood, HMS 96
Cöln, SMS 14–15, 162, 165
Colne, HMS 59
Colossus, HMS 96, 99
Comet, HMS 82
Commandante Rivierè (Fr) 128–9
Comus, HMS 90–1, 96
Conqueror, HMS 96, 162
Conquest, HMS 72–3, 92–3, 122–3
Constance, HMS 96
Cormoran, SMS 20–1, 29
Cornwall, HMS 31, 48–9
Cornwallis, HMS 52, 53, 54–5, 58, 59
Coronel, battle of 4–5, 20–1, 30
Cossack, HMS 112–13
Courageous, HMS 138–9, 162
Crane, HMS 126–7
Cressy, HMS 4–5, 12, 13, 16–17, 23
Curie (Fr sm) 28
Cuxhaven Raid, the 4–5, 12, 40–1
Czepel (A-H) 84–5, 128–9

D2, HMSm 12, 13
D5, HMSm 12
D4, HMSm 94–5
D6, HMSm 40–1, 94–5
D8, HMSm 13
Daffodil, HMS 150–1
Dague (Fr) 62–3
Danzig, SMS 14–15, 134–5
Dardanelles, the bombardments:
  3 November 1914 4–5, 34, 51
  19 February 1915 42–3, 51, 52
  25 February 1915 42–3, 51, 53
  18 March 1915 42–3, 51, 54–5
  landing operations 42–3, 51, 58, 59
Dartmouth, HMS 11, 71, 84–5, 128–9
Defence, HMS 8–9, 28, 96, 99, 100
Delaware, USS 143
D'Entrecasteux (Fr) 50
Derfflinger, SMS 38–9, 46–7, 96, 98, 162, 165
Deutschland, SMS 96, 98
Devonshire, HMS 114–15
Diamond, HMS 44
Dogger Bank, battle of 12, 42–3, 45–7
Donegal, HMS 114–15
Dover Strait, German raids on:
  26–27 October 1916 86–7, 112–13
  25 February 1917 116–17, 122–3
  20–21 April 1917 116–17, 126–7
Drake, HMS 114–15

Dresden (1907), SMS 4–5, 10, 20–1, 30, 31, 48–9
Dresden (1916), SMS 165
Dublin, HMS 8–9, 42–3, 53, 58, 59, 96
Duke of Cornwall, HMS 152–3
Duke of Edinburgh, HMS 8–9, 96, 99
Durazzo, action off 62–3, 84–5

E1, HMSm 80
E3, HMSm 12
E4, HMSm 13, 14–15
E5, HMSm 13
E6, HMSm 13, 14–15
E7, HMSm 13, 14–15, 81
E8, HMSm 13, 14–15, 70
E9, HMSm 12, 13, 80
E10, HMSm 12
E11, HMSm 40–1, 80, 81
E13, HMSm 80
E14, HMSm 81, 147
E15, HMSm 81
E18, HMSm 80
E19, HMSm 80
E31, HMSm 94–5
E37, HMSm 94–5
E38, HMSm 110
E42, HMSm 152–3
E53, HMSm 94–5
E55, HMSm 94–5
Eber, SMS 18–19
Elbing, SMS 96, 101
Elsass, SMS 74
Emden (1908), SMS 4–5, 13, 20–1, 35
Emden (1916), SMS 141, 162
Emperor of India, HMS 162
Empress, HMS 40–1
Engadine, HMS 40–1, 94–5, 96, 102
Erebus, HMS 122–3
Erin, HMS 96, 162
Espiegle, HMS 82
Essex, HMS 10, 19
Euryalus, HMS 13, 58, 59

F10 (It sm) 128–9
Falcon, HMS 126–7
Falklands, battle of the 4–5, 20–1, 31
Falmouth, HMS 13, 14–15, 96, 108–9
Faux (Fr) 128–9
Fearless, HMS 13, 14–15, 40–1, 96, 102
Flirt, HMS 112–13
Florida, USS 143, 162
Formidable, HMS 12, 42–3, 44
Fox, HMS 71
Foxhound, HMS 59
Frankfurt, SMS 83, 96, 134–5, 138–9, 162
Frauenlob, SMS 13, 14–15, 96, 101
Friedrich der Große, SMS 6–732–3, 38–9, 96, 98, 99, 134–5, 162, 165
Friedrich Karl, SMS 26–7
Furious, HMS 162

G37, SMS 122–3
G42, SMS 126–7
G85, SMS 126–7
G91, SMS 126–7
G95, SMS 122–3, 126–7
G96, SMS 122–3, 126–7
G132, SMS 80
G194, SMS 14–15
Galatea, HMS 72–3, 96, 138–9
Gaulois (Fr) 52, 53, 54–5
Gazelle, SMS 26–7
General Wolfe, HMS 143
Giuseppe Garibaldi (It) 62–3
Glasgow, HMS 30, 31, 48–9
Glorious, HMS 138–9, 162
Glory, HMS 164
Gloucester, HMS 8–9, 96
Gloucestershire, HMS 114–15
Gneisenau, SMS 20–1, 30, 31
Goeben, SMS/(Tur) 4–5, 8–9, 34, 36–7, 89, 119, 147
Goliath, HMS 71, 81
Good Hope, HMS 30
Graudenz, SMS 32–3, 46–7, 74, 75
Grazhdanin (Rus) 134–5
Greif, SMS 86–7, 90–1
Grosser Kurfürst, SMS 96, 134–5, 162

Halcyon, HMS 32–3
Hamburg, SMS 96
Hamidiye (Tur) 36–7
Hampshire, HMS 13, 20–1, 96, 102
Hannover, SMS 96, 98

Hardinge, HMS 50
Hartlepool, raid on 4–5, 12, 38–9
Hawke, HMS 12, 22
Hela, SMS 12
Helgoland (A-H) 84–5, 128–9
Helgoland, SMS 74, 96
Heligoland Bight:
  First battle of 4–5, 12, 13, 14–15
  Second battle of 116–17, 138–9
Henry IV (Fr) 58
Hercules, HMS 96, 152–3, 162
Hermes, HMS 12
Hessen, SMS 96
Highflyer, HMS 19, 114–15
Himalaya, HMS 50
Hindenburg, SMS 162, 165
Hizen (Jpn) 20–1
Hogue, HMS 4–5, 12, 13, 16–17, 23
Hyacinth, HMS 11, 71

Ibuki (Jpn) 20–1, 35
Idzumo (Jpn) 20–1
Imbros, battle of 142, 147
Impavido (It) 128–9
Imperatritsa Maria (Rus) 119
Implacable, HMS 44, 58, 59
Inconstant, HMS 72–3, 96, 138–9
Indefatigable, HMS 8–9, 34, 96, 98, 102
Indomitable, HMS 8–9, 34, 46–7, 96, 99, 162
Indomito (It) 128–9
Inflexible, HMS 8–9, 20–1, 31, 48–9, 52, 53, 54–5, 96, 99, 162
Insidioso (It) 128–9
Intrepid, HMS 150–1, 164
Invincible, HMS 13, 14–15, 20–1, 31, 96, 99, 100, 102
Iphigenia, HMS 150–1, 164
Iris, HMS 150–1
Irresistible, HMS 53, 54–5, 81
Iron Duke, HMS 96, 99, 108–9, 162
Iwami (Jpn) 29
Iwate (Jpn) 29

J4, HMSm 152–3
J6, HMSm 152–3
Jauréguiberry (Fr) 58
Jean Bart (Fr) 28
Joule (Fr sm) 81
Jutland, battle of 86–7, 96–102

Kaiser, SMS 96, 98, 134–5, 138–9, 162, 165
Kaiser Karl VI (A-H) 84–5
Kaiser Wilhelm der Große, SMS 4–5, 18–19
Kaiserin, SMS 96, 134–5, 138–9, 162, 165
Kaiserin Elizabeth, SMS 29
Karlsruhe (1912), SMS 4–5, 10, 18–19
Karlsruhe (1916), SMS 134–5, 162, 165
Kent, HMS 31, 48–9
King Alfred, HMS 114–15
King Edward VII, HMS 90–1
King George V, HMS 96, 99, 162
Kolberg, SMS 14–15, 25, 38–9, 46–7, 74, 134–5
König, SMS 96, 98, 134–5, 165
König Albert, SMS 134–5, 162, 165
Königin Luise, SMS 24, 25
Königsberg (1905), SMS 4–5, 11, 42–3, 71
Königsberg (1916), SMS 134–5, 138–9
Korietz (Rus) 75
Kronprinz, SMS 96, 134–5, 162
Kronprinz Wilhelm (1901), SMS 10, 18–19
Kronprinz Wilhelm (1914), SMS, see *Kronprinz*

Laertes, HMS 126–7
Laforey, HMS 112–13
Lancaster, HMS 10
Lance, HMS 122–3
Landrail, HMS 122–3, 152–3
Lark, HMS 152–3
Laverock, HMS 122–3, 126–7
Lawford, HMS 40–1, 112–13
Lawrence, HMS 82
Leipzig, SMS 20–1, 30, 31
Lennox, HMS 40–1
Léon Gambetta (Fr) 62–3
Leonardo da Vinci (It) 62–3
Leonidas, HMS 40–1
Leviathan, HMS 114–15
Lewis Pelly, HMS 82
Lika (A-H) 84–5
Lion, HMS 13, 14–15, 46–7, 96, 98, 138–9, 162
Liverpool, HMS 13, 14–15
Lizard, HMS 147
Llewellyn, HMS 152–3

169

Lochinvar, HMS 122–3
London, HMS 44, 58, 59
Lookout, HMS 40–1
Lord Clive, HMS 76–7
Lord Nelson, HMS 44, 54–5, 58, v
Lord Raglan, HMS 147
Louis (Fr) 81
Lowestoft, HMS 13, 14–15, 46–7
Lowestoft, raid on 86–7, 92–3
Lübeck, SMS 70, 74
Lucas (Fr) 128–9
Lucifer, HMS 126–7
Lundy, HMS 81
Lurcher, HMS 40–1
Lusitania, RMS 42–3, 61
Lützow, SMS 96, 98, 101, 102
Lydiard, HMS 40–1, 126–7

M23, HMS 164
M24, HMS 164
M28, HMS 147
Magdeburg, SMS 26–7
Mainz, SMS 14–15
Majestic, HMS 54–5, 58, 68–9, 81
Malaya, HMS 96, 98, 162
Mariotte (Fr sm) 81
Markgraf, SMS 96, 134–5, 162, 165
Marlborough, HMS 96, 99, 102, 162
Marsala (It) 128–9
Marshal Ney, HMS 76–7
Mary Rose, HMS 137
Matchless, HMS 126–7
Mecidiye (Tur) 36–7
Mecklenburg, SMS 74
Melbourne, HMAS 13, 20–1, 35
Mentor, HMS 126–7
Mersey, HMS 71
Mesudiye (Tur) 36–7, 81
Meteor, SMS 42–3, 67, 72–3
Miner, HMS 82
Minerva, HMS 50, 58
Minnesota, USS 156–7
Minos, HMS 40–1
Minotaur, HMS 20–1, ¬35, 96, 141, 162
Mirabello (It) 128–9
Miranda, HMS 40–1, 126–7
Mishima (Jpn) 29
Mogami (Jpn) 29
Mohawk, HMS 112–13
Moltke, SMS 14–15, 32–3, 38–9, 46–7, 74, 96, 98, 101, 152–3, 162, 165
Monarch, HMS 96, 162
Monmouth, HMS 30
Montcalm (Fr) 20–1
Morris, HMS 126–7
Mosta (It) 84–5, 128–9
Mousquet (Fr) 35
Möwe, SMS 86–7, 90–1, 114–15
München, SMS 96, 110
Munster, HMS 90–1
Myngs, HMS 126–7

Nairana, HMS 164
Napoli (It) 128–9
Nassau, SMS 74, 96
Nautilus, SMS 25, 134–5
Neptune, HMS 96, 162
Nevada, USS 143
New York, USS 143, 162
New Zealand, HMS 13, 14–15, 46–7, 96, 98, 138–9, 162
Newcastle, HMS 20–1
Nievo (It) 84–5
Nino Bixio (It) 84–5
Norwegian convoy attack 116–17, 141
Nottingham, HMS 13, 14–15, 46–7, 72–3, 96, 108–9
Novara (A-H) 84–5, 128–9
Novik (Rus) 70, 75
Nubian, HMS 112–13
Nugent, HMS 126–7
Nürnberg (1906), SMS 13, 20–1, 30, 31
Nürnberg (1916), SMS 134–5, 138–9, 162

Oak, HMS 96
Ocean, HMS 50, 54–5, 81
Odin, HMS 82
Okinoshima (Jpn) 29
Oldenburg, SMS 74, 96, 152–3
Oleg (Rus) 70
Oklahoma, USS 143
Olympia, USS 164
Ophir, HMS 114–15
Orama, HMS 48–9
Orcoma, HMS 114–15
Orion, HMS 96, 99, 162
Orvieto, HMS 78–9
Ostfriesland, SMS 74, 96, 98, 102

Otranto, HMS 30
Otranto, battle of the Straits of 116–17, 128–9, 160
Pallada (Rus) 26–7
Paragon, HMS 122–3
Pathfinder, HMS 12, 23
Pegasus, HMS 11, 71
Phaeton, HMS 72–3, 96, 162
Philomel, HMS 20–1
Pillau, SMS 74, 75, 83, 96, 138–9
Pilo (It) 84–5, 128–9
Pioneer, HMS 71
Pommern, SMS 96, 101, 102
Porpoise, HMS 122–3
Posen, SMS 74, 96, 98
Prince Adalbert, SMS 26–7, 70, 80
Prince George, HMS 54–5, 58
Prince of Wales, HMS 44, 58, 59
Prince Rupert, HMS 76–7
Princess Margaret, HMS 78–9, 94–5
Princess Royal, HMS 13, 14–15, 46–7, 96, 98, 138–9, 162
Prinz Adalbert, SMS 26–7, 70, 80
Prinz Eitel Friedrich, SMS 20–1, 29, 48–9
Prinz Heinrich, SMS 70, 74
Prinzregent Luitpold, SMS 96, 134–5, 162, 165
Psyche, HMS 20–1
Pyramus, HMS 20–1, 71

Quatro (It) 84–5
Queen, HMS 44, 58, 59
Queen Elizabeth, HMS 53, 54–5, 59, 152–3, 162
Queen Mary, HMS 13, 14–15, 96, 98, 102

Racchia (It) 128–9
Racehorse, HMS 126–7
Radetzky (A-H) 28
Rainbow, HMS 20–1
Ramsey, HMS 72–3
Regensburg, SMS 74, 83, 96
Regina Margherita (It) 62–3
Renown, HMS 162
Repulse, HMS 138–9, 162
Resolution, HMS 162
Revenge (1892), HMS 76–7
Revenge (1915), HMS 96, 162
Rhineland, SMS 74, 96
Ribble, HMS 59
Riga, attacks on the Gulf of 26–7, 42–3
 8 August 1915 74
 19 August 1915 75
Riviera, HMS 40–1
Roon, SMS 70, 74
Rostock, SMS 46–7, 83, 96, 101
Roxburgh, HMS 114–15
Royal Oak, HMS 96, 162
Royal Sovereign, HMS 162
Royalist, HMS 96, 138–9
Rurik (Rus) 70

S15, SMS 126–7
S20, SMS 126–7
S24, SMS 126–7
S28, SMS 75
S31, SMS 75
S32, SMS 75
S36, SMS 75
S49, SMS 122–3
S53, SMS 126–7
S85, SMS 75
S90, SMS 29
S141, SMS 74
S183, SMS 75
S184, SMS 75
Sabreur, HMS 126–7
Saida (A-H) 128–9
San Diego, USS 156–7
Sankt Georg (A-H) 128–9
Saphir (Fr sm) 81
Saracen, HMS 126–7
Scarborough, raid on 4–5, 12, 38–9
Scharnhorst, SMS 20–1, 30, 31
Schiaffino (It) 128–9
Schleswig-Holstein, SMS 96
Schliesen, SMS 96
Schwaben, SMS 74
Scourge, HMS 59
Seeadler, SMS 86–7, 114–15, 116–17, 118
Severn, HMS 71
Seydlitz, SMS 14–15, 32–3, 38–9, 46–7, 74, 92–3, 96, 98, 101, 162, 165
Shaitan, HMS 82
Shannon, HMS 96, 141
Shirotae (Jpn) 29
Sir John Moore, HMS 76–7
Sivuch (Rus) 75
Slava (Rus) 74, 134–5
Southampton, HMS 13, 14–15, 46–7, 72–3, 96, 98
St Vincent, HMS 96, 162

Stettin, SMS 13, 14–15, 96, 98
Stralsund, SMS 14–15, 25, 32–3, 46–7, 56–7, 74, 83
Strassburg, SMS 14–15, 32–3, 56–7, 83, 134–5
Strongbow, HMS 137
Stuttgart, SMS 96
Suffolk, HMS 10
Suffren (Fr) 34, 52, 53, 54–5
Sumana, HMS 82
Superb, HMS 96
Sutlej, HMS 114–15
Suwo (Jpn) 29
Swiftsure, HMS 50, 54–5, 58, 59, 114–15
Sydney, HMAS 20–1, 35

T47, SMS 26–7
T49, SMS 26–7
T51, SMS 26–7
T52, SMS 74
T54, SMS 26–7
T58, SMS 74
Takachiho (Jpn) 29
Takiwa (Jpn) 29
Tango (Jpn) 29
Tartar, HMS 112–13
Tatra (A-H) 84–5, 128–9
Temeraire, HMS 96
Terror, HMS 122–3
Texas, USS 162
Thetis, HMS 150–1
Thetis, SMS 74
Thunderer, HMS 96, 162
Thüringen, SMS 74, 96
Tiger, HMS 46–7, 96, 138–9, 162
Tigress, HMS 147
Tone (Jpn) 29
Topaze, HMS 44
Triglav (A-H) 84–5
Triumph, HMS 29, 52, 53, 54–5, 58, 68–9, 81
Tsingtao, siege of 4–5, 29
Turbine (It) 62–3
Turgut Reis (Tur) 36–7

U4 (A-H sm) 62–3
U12 (A-H sm) 28, 62–3
U-boats:
  Deutschland, see *U155*
  U5 12
  U6 40–1, 56–7, 108–9
  U7 12
  U8 12
  U9 12, 22, 23
  U11 12
  U12 12, 108–9
  U13 12
  U14 12
  U15 12
  U16 14–15, 78–9, 108–9
  U18 12, 16–17, 108–9
  U19 78–9, 108–9
  U20 40–1, 42–3
  U21 51, 68–9, 23
  U22 40–1, 56–7
  U23 108–9
  U24 44, 97
  U25 14–15, 72–3
  U27 12
  U28 38–9, 72–3, 78–9
  U29 12, 108–9
  U30 38–9, 40–1
  U32 40–1, 78–9, 97
  U33 68–9
  U35 68–9, 104, 108–9
  U37 12, 108–9
  U39 68–9, 108–9
  U40 12
  U43 78–9, 97
  U44 78–9, 97, 108–9
  U45 108–9
  U46 97, 102
  U47 97
  U48 108–9
  U49 108–9
  U51 94–5, 97
  U52 97, 108–9
  U53 108–9
  U54 97
  U55 108–9
  U56 108–9
  U63 97, 102
  U64 108–9
  U65 108–9
  U66 97
  U67 97, 108–9
  U69 108–9
  U70 97
  U75 97, 102
  U117 156–7

U139 156–7
U140 156–7
U151 156–7
U152 156–7
U155 156–7
U156 156–7
UB7 36–7
UB8 36–7
UB10 112–13
UB14 36–7, 62–3
UB16 112–13
UB17 112–13
UB21 97
UB22 94–5, 97
UB24 94–5
UB27 94–5
UB38 112–13
UB70 94–5
UC13 36–7
UC25 (A-H sm) 128–9
UC56 134–5
Undaunted, HMS 40–1, 72–3
Undine, SMS 26–7, 80
Unity, HMS 122–3
Ursula, HMS 152–3
Usk, HMS 29, 59
Utah, USS 143

V4, HMSm 152–3
V27, SMS 75
V44, SMS 123
V45, SMS 122–3
V46, SMS 122–3
V47, SMS 122–3, 126–7
V67, SMS 122–3
V68, SMS 122–3, 126–7
V69, SMS 150–1
V70, SMS 126–7
V71, SMS 112–13, 126–7
V73, SMS 126–7
V81, SMS 126–7
V99, SMS 74
V100, SMS 75
V187, SMS 14–15
Valiant, HMS 96, 98, 162
Vanguard, HMS 96
Venerable, HMS 76–7, 44
Vengeance, HMS 52, 53, 54–5, 58
Vérité (Fr), 34
Viking, HMS 112–13
Vindex, HMS 94–5
Vindictive, HMS 150–1, 162
Von der Tann, SMS 14–15, 32–3, 38–9, 74, 96, 98, 162, 165

Wakamiya (Jpn) 29
Warasdiner (A-H) 128–9
Warrior, HMS 8–9, 28, 96, 99, 100, 102
Warspite, HMS 96, 98, 102, 162
Westfalen, SMS 74, 96, 108–9
Wettin, SMS 74
Weymouth, HMS 8–9, 11, 71, 84–5
Whitby, raid on 4–5, 12, 38–9
Wiesbaden, SMS 83, 96, 99
Wittelsbach, SMS 74
Wolf, SMS 116–17, 120
Wyoming, USS 143, 162

XX, Operation 86–7, 94–5

Yakuma (Jpn) 29
Yarmouth, HMS 20–1, 35, 96, 141
Yarmouth raid on 4–5, 12, 32–3
Yodo (Jpn) 29

Zähringen, SMS 74
Zeebrugge and Ostend operations, 142, 149–51
Zenta (A-H) 28
Zeppelins:
  L5 40–1
  L6 40–1, 92–3
  L7 56–7, 78–9, 110
  L9 56–7, 92–3, 97
  L11 78–9, 108–9
  L13 102, 108–9, 110
  L14 92–3, 97, 110
  L16 97, 110
  L21 92–3, 97
  L22 102, 108–9, 110
  L23 92–3, 97, 110
  L24 102, 108–9, 110
  L30 108–9, 110
  L31 97
  L32 108–9
  L34 110

Zhemchug (Rus) 35

170